COMMUNICATION ACTIVISM

Volume 1
Communication for Social Change

Edited by

Lawrence R. Frey
University of Colorado at Boulder

Kevin M. Carragee
Suffolk University

HAMPTON PRESS, INC.
CRESSKILL, NEW JERSEY

Printed in the United States of America

Library of Congress Cataloging-in-Publication Data

Communication activism/edited by Lawrence R. Frey, Kevin M. Carragee.
   v. cm.
  Includes bibliograhpical references and index.
  Contents: V. 1. Communication for social change.
  ISBN 1-57273-696-8 (casebound) -- ISBN 1-57273-697-6 (paperbound)
  1. Communication in social action. 2. Communication--Social aspects. 3.
  Communication--Political aspects. I. Frey, Lawrence R. II. Carragee,
  Kevin M.
   HM1206.C6475 2007
   361.201`4--dc22
                  2006035764

Hampton Press, Inc.
23 Broadway
Cresskill, NJ 07626

CONTENTS

II. COMMUNICATION CONSULTING
FOR SOCIAL CHANGE

Introduction

COMMUNICATION ACTIVISM AS ENGAGED SCHOLARSHIP

Lawrence R. Frey

University of Colorado at Boulder

Kevin M. Carragee

Suffolk University

There certainly is no shortage of controversial issues confronting contemporary U.S. society. Consider, for instance, the highly contested Iraq War, with, as of October 3, 2006, 2,721 U.S. soldiers dead and 19,910 wounded (Iraq Coalition Casualty Count, 2006); the concerns raised about the continued use of capital punishment, with, since 1973, 123 people from 25 states released from death row because of evidence of factual innocence (Death Penalty Information Center, 2006); the arguments raging across the country in courtrooms, state legislatures, and at ballot boxes over same-sex marriage, with nearly half the states having outlawed or poised to ban such marriages in their constitution (Peterson, 2006); or the controversy surrounding immigration, with hundreds of thousands of immigrants and advocates taking to U.S. city streets on May 1, 2006, to protest proposed immigration laws ("Thousands March," 2006), as U.S. President George W. Bush tries to balance sending the National Guard to help patrol the U.S. border with Mexico with offering a temporary guest worker program and paths to citizenship for long-term illegal immigrants.

One might think that the members of the academy would be at the forefront of confronting these and other important social issues. After all, as Crabtree and Ford point out in their chapter in Volume 1 of these texts, many U.S. colleges and universities were established, as part of their mission, to generate knowledge to better their communities (see, e.g., C. W. Anderson, 1993; Barber, 1992; Checkoway, 2001; Kennedy, 1997). Unfortunately, however, over the years, higher educational institutions tended to abandon this civic mission (see, e.g., Boyer, 1987; Butler, 2000; Sandmann & Lewis, 1991; Sirianni & Friedland, 1997) in favor of research directed toward a relatively small, insular group of fellow scholars, with the number of scholarly journals now estimated to be between 80,000-100,000 (Tenopir & King, 2000). This focus on research directed toward other scholars rather than toward helping communities to solve societal problems probably was related to the privileging of "theory" over "application" in the academy, for if one follows the etymology of the word *theory*, derived from the Greek words *theoria* ("contemplation, speculation, a looking at, things looked at"), *theorein* ("to consider, speculate, look at"), *theoros* ("spectator"), and *thea* ("a view") (Online Etymology Dictionary, 2006), scholars are supposed to be spectators whose work is best done by looking at and contemplating what occurs without trying to affect it.

One might think that communication scholars, in particular, would be confronting societal issues. After all, communication inherently is a "practical discipline" (Craig, 1989, 1995; Craig & Tracy, 1995) concerned with cultivating communicative *praxis* that yields useful knowledge. The historical roots of the formal discipline of communication (with the study of communication dating back at least to antiquity) certainly were grounded in producing useful knowledge, such as teaching people to become better speakers in their everyday interactions and in the public sphere (e.g., W. H. Davis, 1915, on debating as related to nonacademic life) and engage in effective communicative practices (e.g., Dewey's, 1910, reflective thinking process) for democratic group decision making (see, e.g., A. C. Baird, 1927; Elliott, 1927; McBurney & Hance, 1939; Sheffield, 1926; for a review, see Frey, 1996), as well as mass communication research directed toward understanding and, hopefully, improving media practices and people's ability to process mediated messages (such as not being easily persuaded by propaganda; for historical overviews of such research, see, e.g., Delia, 1987; Rogers, 1994;

Schramm, 1997). Unfortunately, however, communication scholars, like their counterparts in the other social sciences and humanities, and perhaps, in part, because of their desire to obtain disciplinary legitimacy in the eyes of those colleagues, all too frequently, over the course of time, shied away from addressing important societal issues to focus, instead, on disciplinary theoretical concerns, such as the great metatheoretical debates, starting during the 1970s and continuing for quite some time, about what theories should be employed in communication research (see, e.g., Benson & Pearce, 1977) and what criteria should be used to judge the admissibility of evidence to support theoretical propositions in communication scholarship (see, e.g., Cronkhite & Liska, 1977).

This failure to confront salient social issues is unfortunate, for given the sheer volume and significance of these issues and the potential contributions that communication knowledge can make to managing them, the exigency for communication scholars to engage in direct vigorous action in support of needed social change has never been more apparent and important. In short, communication scholars need to engage in "communication activism."

COMMUNICATION ACTIVISM

Ac·tiv·ism: A doctrine or practice that emphasizes direct vigorous action especially in support of or opposition to one side of a controversial issue

　　　　　　　　　　　　　　　　—Merriam-Webster Online (2006)

"Activism" has a long and distinguished history (see, e.g., Downs & Manion, 2004; Eno, 1920; Reed, 2005; Santiago, 1972; Wigginton, 1991). Literally thousands of books have been written about activism theory and practice (e.g., W. Clark, 2000; Falconer, 2001; Schragge, 2003; Weissberg, 2005), activism art and performance (e.g., Bass, 1999; Gómez-Peña, 2005), and activist individuals (e.g., Avakian, 2000; DeLeon, 1994) and networks (e.g., Ferree & Tripp, 2006; Keck & Sikkink, 1999), as well as particular contexts/forms of activism—including abortion (e.g., Seaton, 1996; Staggenborg, 1991), AIDS (e.g., R. A. Smith & Siplon, 2006; Stockdill, 2003), animal rights (e.g., Beers, 2006; Guither, 1998), antinuclear (e.g., Dawson, 1996; Holsworth, 1989), corporate (e.g., Eisenhofer & Barry, 2006; Monks, 1999); environmental (e.g., DeLuca, 1999; Mauch, Stolzfus, & Weiner, 2006), gay and lesbian (e.g., Leyland, 2002; Stevenson & Cogan, 2003), legal (e.g., Fisher, 1997; Wolfe, 1997), Native American (e.g., T. R. Johnson, 1996; T. Johnson, Nagel, & Champagne, 1997), race (Alleyne, 2002; Jennings, 1997), religious/spiritual (e.g., Lampert, 2005; Weiss, 2002), student/youth (e.g., Ginwright, Noguera, & Cammarota, 2006; Rhoads, 1998), women/feminism (e.g., Baumgadner & Richards, 2005; Hawkesworth, 2006b), and worker activism (e.g., de Witte, 2005; Markowitz, 2000)—and specific countries and regions of the world, in addition to the United States, where activism has been documented—such as China (Chan, 1985), Eastern Europe (e.g., Bugajski & Pollack, 1989), Guatemala (e.g., Warren, 1998), India (Bharucha, 1998), and Yemen (Carapico, 1998).

To this literature, we add the concept of communication activism, which has a number of historical roots and related branches. Rhetoricians, for instance, especially during the turbulent decade of the 1960s, examined the communicative practices of social protest by activist individuals, groups, organizations, and movements (see, e.g., Andrews, 1969; J. E. Baird, 1970; Benson & Johnson, 1968; Bowen, 1963a, 1963b, 1967; Fernandez, 1968; Gregg, 1971; Haiman, 1967; Kerr, 1959; Kosokoff & Carlmichael, 1970; Lawton, 1968; Lomas, 1960, 1963; Martin, 1966; McEdwards, 1968; Rude, 1969; Scott & Smith, 1969; D. H. Smith, 1967; Toch, Deutsch, & Wilkins, 1960; Yoder, 1969).

Historical and contemporary analyses of activist communicative practices are alive and well today (recent examples include Chvasta, 2006; DeLuca & Peeples, 2002; Grano, 2002; Hasian, 2001; Hung, 2003; Knight & Greenberg, 2002; Kowal, 2000; McChesney, 2004a; McGee, 2003; Peeples, 2003; Pezzullo, 2001, 2003; Reber & Berger, 2005; Sanchez & Stuckey, 2000; Sender, 2001; Shi, 2005; Sowards & Renegar, 2004; Theodore, 2002; West & Gastil, 2004). Many contemporary studies focus on media activism, such as activists' use of media (especially the internet) and efforts by social movement organizations to influence news media coverage of societal issues (recent examples include Atkinson & Dougherty, 2006; Bennett, 2003; Bullert, 2000; Carroll & Hackett, 2006; Coopman, 2000; de Jong, Shaw, & Stammers, 2005; Diani, 2000; Dichter, 2004; Garrett, 2006; Gibson, 2003; Gillett, 2003; Greenberg & Knight, 2004; Harold, 2004; Kahn & Kellner, 2004; McCaughey & Ayers, 2003; Meikle, 2002; Palczewski, 2001; Palmeri, 2006; Pickerill, 2003; Pini, Brown, & Previte, 2004; Ryan, 1991; Ryan, Carragee, & Meinhofer, 2001; Ryan, Carragee, & Schwerner, 1998; Stengrim, 2005; Van de Donk, Loader, Nixon, & Rucht 2004).

These studies of activists' communicative practices are part of the larger grounding of communication activism in *applied communication scholarship*. As Cissna (1982) explained:

> *Applied* research sets out to contribute to knowledge by answering a real, pragmatic, social question or by solving a real pragmatic, social problem. Applied *communication* research involves such a question or problem of human communication or examines human communication

in order to provide an answer or solution to the question or problem. The intent or goal of the inquiry (as manifest in the research report itself) is the hallmark of applied communication research. Applied communication research involves the development of knowledge regarding a real human communication problem or question. (p. ii)

This applied view of communication scholarship grew out of the 1968 New Orleans Conference on Research and Instructional Development, which encouraged research on the communication dimensions of current social problems (see Kibler & Barker, 1969, especially the essay in that text by Cronkhite, 1969). (The concept of "applied research" in the social sciences dates back to Lazarsfeld's sociological research during the 1940s and his creation in 1944 of the Bureau of Applied Social Research at Columbia University; see, e.g., Delia, 1987; Rogers, 1994; Schramm, 1997.) Five years later, in 1973, the *Journal of Applied Communications Research* was created (see Hickson, 1973), which subsequently became the *Journal of Applied Communication Research*, which now is sponsored (along with an Applied Communication Division) by the National Communication Association (NCA; for a historical overview of applied communication scholarship, see Cissna, Eadie, & Hickson, in press). Although applied communication research, as compared with *basic communication research* (designed to test communication theory), certainly was a hotly contested issue for many years (see, e.g., Eadie, 1982; Ellis, 1982, 1991; Kreps, Frey, & O'Hair, 1991; Miller, 1995; Miller & Sunnafrank, 1984; O'Hair, Kreps, & Frey, 1990; Seibold, 1995; Wood, 1995), today, applied scholarship is an integral part of the communication discipline and its focal areas (see, e.g., Frey & Cissna, in press).

Applied communication scholars have contributed substantially to understanding the communicative practices of activist individuals, groups, and organizations. One of the best examples is the communication research on *health activism*, which Zoller (2005) defined as "a challenge to the existing order and power relationships that are perceived to influence some aspects of health negatively or to impede health promotion" (p. 344; see also Geist-Martin, Ray, & Sharf, 2003). Brashers, Haas, and Neidig (1999), for instance, created the Patient Self-Advocacy Scale to measure people's involvement in their healthcare decision-making interactions with physicians. Brashers, Haas, Klingle, and Neidig (2000) later showed that those engaged in AIDS activism at the collective level (by participating in the AIDS activist organization ACT UP) exhibited a number of self-advocacy behaviors that affected their interactions with physicians, including increased education about illness and treatment options, which allowed activist patients to challenge physicians' expertise; assertiveness toward their healthcare, which led them to confront physicians who communicated using a paternalistic or authoritarian style; and a willingness to be mindfully non-adherent, which resulted in them sometimes rejecting treatments recommended by physicians and articulating reasons for doing so. Brashers, Haas, Neidig, and Rintamaki (2002) also found important differences in the healthcare practices of activist and nonactivist individuals with HIV or AIDS, with activists employing more problem-focused and less emotion-focused coping, possessing greater knowledge of HIV-treatment information sources, and having greater HIV social network integration. (Regarding the communication tactics of ACT UP and other AIDS activist individuals, groups, and organizations, see Brashers & Jackson, 1991; Brouwer, 1998, 2001; Christiansen & Hanson, 1996; Dow, 1994; Fabj & Sobnowsky, 1993, 1995; McGee, 2003; Melcher, 1995; Meyers & Brashers, 2002; Sobnowsky & Hauser, 1998.)

Although the scholarship cited here has contributed substantially to understanding activist communication, most of it constitutes *third-person-perspective studies* in which researchers study individuals, groups, and organizations engaging in communication activism. Third-person-perspective researchers, thus, stand outside the stream of human events and observe, describe, interpret, explain, and (in rhetorical criticism) critique what occurs, as well as (in applied communication scholarship) offer suggestions for what could or should occur. These studies stand in sharp contrast to *first-person-perspective studies* in which researchers want to get in the stream and affect it in some significant ways (e.g., build a dam or change its flow).

The call for first-person-perspective communication research directed toward solving significant social issues (what we call *communication activism scholarship*) emanated from a number of directions in the communication discipline. One source was communication scholars, especially in rhetoric and organizational communication, who employed critical theory to not just understand or explain society but to critique and change it (in communication scholarship, see, e.g., Carey, 1982; Farrell & Aune, 1979; Hardt, 1986, 1992, 1993; Held, 1982; Real, 1984; Strine, 1991), and/or engaged in cultural studies to analyze cultural practices in relation to social and political issues such as power, ideology, race, social class, and gender (in communication scholarship, see, e.g., Artz & Murphy, 2000; Carey, 1983, 1989; Carragee, 1990; Carragee & Roefs, 2004; Grossberg, 1993a, 1993b, 1997; Grossberg, Nelson, & Treichler, 1992). Rhetoricians working from these perspectives argued for "ideological criticism" (see, e.g., Rushing & Frentz, 1991; Wander, 1983, 1984; Wander & Jenkins, 1972), "critical rhetoric" (see, e.g., N. Clark, 1996; McGuire & Slembeck, 1987; McKerrow, 1989, 1991, 1993; Ono & Sloop, 1992) and, most recently, "partisan criticism" (Swartz, 2004, 2005)—forms of rhetorical theory and criticism that certainly represent an "activist" turn (see Andersen, 1993; for critical responses to this rhetorical turn, see, e.g., Charland, 1991; Condit, 1993; Hariman, 1991;

Hill, 1983; Kuypers, 2000; Rosenfield, 1983). Organizational communication scholars who advocated these perspectives questioned the traditional privileging of management's interests and argued that research should root out normative systems of control to represent all stakeholders' voices and, thereby, promote democracy in the workplace (see, e.g., Carlone & Taylor, 1998; Cheney, 1995; Deetz, 1982, 1988, 1992; Deetz & Mumby, 1990; Mumby, 1993).

Another impetus for communication activism scholarship (albeit one that stressed the need for first-person-perspective activism research rather than demonstrated activism per se) came from applied communication scholars. Frey (2000), for instance, argued that given the common dictionary definition of the term *applied* as meaning "to put into practice," the most pressing question facing applied communication scholars was not whether to put communication into practice (which is what is done in a "practical discipline" like communication) or what to put into practice (communication knowledge and skills), but *who* should put communication into practice. As Frey (2000) argued:

> We should start from the premise that in research, "to put into practice" applies to *researchers*, as opposed to simply anyone who puts communication into practice (e.g., the research participants studied). Accordingly *applied communication scholarship* might be defined as "the study of researchers putting their communication knowledge and skills into practice." (p. 179; for a critique of this position, see Seibold, 2000)

Although all this work certainly helped to set the stage for communication activism scholarship, it constituted calls for such research, not activism research per se. The work done from critical theory and cultural studies perspectives remained, for the most part, theoretical and abstract, with scholars staying in the realm of discourse rather than intervening into discourses (see, e.g., Cloud, 1994; Frey, 2006a; Rakow, 2005), and much of the applied communication research that did adopt a first-person perspective was directed toward serving the interests of the powerful and well resourced (such as communication consulting work with for-profit organizations that serves corporate interests; see, e.g., Eadie, 1994; Phillips, 1992; C. K. Stewart, 1991), often at the expense of marginalized and underresourced populations (see, e.g., Frey, Pearce, Pollock, Artz, & Murphy, 1996).

One perspective that both articulated and resulted in some communication activism research was the "communication and social justice approach" advanced by Frey et al. (1996; see also W. B. Pearce, 1998; Pollock, Artz, Frey, Pearce, & Murphy, 1996; Swan, 2002; the essays in Swartz, 2006; for critiques of this perspective, see Makau, 1996; Olson & Olson, 2003; Wood,

1996). Frey et al. described *social justice* as "the engagement with and advocacy for those in our society who are economically, socially, politically,
and/or culturally underresourced" (p. 110), and called on communication
scholars to conduct research that "identifies and foregrounds the grammars
that oppress or underwrite relationships of domination and then recon-
structs those grammars" (p. 112). Frey et al. maintained that this "social justice sensibility" meant adopting, among other things, an activist orientation,
claiming:

> It is not enough merely to demonstrate or bemoan the fact that some
> people lack the minimal necessities of life, that others are used regularly
> against their will and against their interest by others for their pleasure or
> profit, and that some are defined as "outside" the economic, political, or
> social system because of race, creed, lifestyle, or medical condition, or
> simply because they are in the way of someone else's project. A social
> justice sensibility entails a moral imperative to *act* as effectively as we
> can to do something about structurally sustained inequalities. To con-
> tinue to pursue justice, it is perhaps necessary that we who act be per-
> sonally ethical, but that is not sufficient. Our actions must engage and
> transform social structures. (p. 111)

Frey (1998a) subsequently edited a special issue of the *Journal of
Applied Communication Research* on "Communication and Social Justice
Research" that featured "original, empirically grounded case studies that
demonstrated ways in which applied communication researchers have made
a difference in the lives of those who are disadvantaged by prevalent social
structures" (Frey, 1998b, p. 158). Ryan et al. (1998) showed how their work
as members of the Media Research and Action Project (MRAP), an organization that assists marginalized groups in employing news as a social
resource, had a significant impact on Boston-area newspaper coverage of
workplace reproductive rights stemming from a U.S. Supreme Court case
alleging discrimination against a battery-producing company because it
excluded fertile women from working in high-lead areas, and how the
Court's finding of discrimination against that company stressed media
frames that MRAP highlighted. Crabtree (1998) documented two case studies in El Salvador and Nicaragua of a mutual empowerment approach to
cross-cultural participatory development communication projects that
employed service learning with her university students and was directed
toward social change and social justice. Artz (1998) examined a campaign by
his undergraduate rhetoric students to increase the number of African
American students at the university where he taught. Hartnett (1998)
explained a project from one of his communication classes taught in a prison
that combined progressive pedagogical practices with traditional public

speaking skills—with students/prisoners restaging the 1858 Lincoln/ Douglas debates as a 3-way debate that included the Black abolitionist, David Walker—to create a "heuristic social space" in which these marginalized individuals could engage in serious and thoughtful political debate about the complicated political, economic, and cultural systems that supported and contested slavery, many of which still exist today in the fight for racial equality and social justice. Varallo, Ray, and Ellis (1998) reported on follow-up interviews conducted with adult survivors of incest whom they had interviewed in previous research to reveal how those survivors had benefited from participating in that research. Subsequent communication studies by T. S. Jones and Bodtker (1998), Novek (2005), and Palmeri (2006) adopted this social justice perspective as well.

The study by Varallo et al. (1998) points to another important influence driving communication activism scholarship: the articulation of various research methods that promote "research as an empowering act, as a way of uniting people working for social change, disrupting restrictive ways of thinking, and transforming the social world" (Ristock & Pennell, 1996, p. 113; see also M. Fine, 2006; Sanford & Angel-Ajani, 2006; Swartz, 1997). Such methods include, among others, (a) (social/participatory) action research (see, e.g., the journal *Action Research*; Costello, 2003; Greenwood & Levin, 2000; Kemmis & McTaggart, 2005; McNiff & Whitehead, 2002, 2006; Reason & Bradbury, 2001; Stringer, 1999; in communication scholarship, see Anyaegbunam, Karnell, Cheah, & Youngblood, 2005; Clift & Freimuth, 1997; Gatenby & Humphries, 1996; Jensen, 1990; Pilotta et al., 2001; Quigley, Sanchez, Handy, Goble, & George, 2000; Schoening & Anderson, 1995); (b) critical ethnography (see, e.g., Foley & Valenzula, 2005; Madison, 2005a, 2005b; Thomas, 1993; in communication, see Artz, 2001; Carbaugh, 1989/1990; Carragee, 1996; Conquergood, 1991b; Cushman, 1989/1990; Gibson, 2000); (c) feminist methods (see, e.g., Gaternby & Humphries, 1996; Hawkesworth, 2006a; Hesse-Biber, 2006; Nielsen, 1990; Oleson, 2005; Reinharz, 1992; Sprague, 2005; in communication, see Carter & Spitzack, 1989; Condit, 1988; M. G. Fine, 1990; Lemish, 2002; Lengel, 1998); and (d) performance ethnography (see, e.g., Denzin, 2003; McCall, 2000; Mienczakowski, 1995; Turner & Turner, 1982, 1988; in communication, see Alexander, 2005; Conquergood, 1985, 1991b, 2002b; J. L. Jones, 2002a; Olomo, 2006).

One of the best examples in the communication discipline of employing such methods to promote social change and social justice are the critical ethnographic studies of gang communication by Conquergood (1991a, 1992a, 1994; see also the communication studies of the Hmong by Conquergood, 1988, 1992b; Conquergood & Siegel, 1985). To understand gang communication, Conquergood lived for 20 months in Big Red, a dilapidated tenement building located in northwest Chicago's "Little

Beirut" area, a territory controlled by Latin King gang members. He slowly developed a relationship with these gang members and was allowed to observe and interview them and participate in their activities. Conquergood showed in his published work how gang communication (e.g., graffiti and reppin' practices) is a complex system of signification that creates a sense of place and security for these marginalized members of U.S. society. By offering a compassionate, alternative reading of gangs and their communication, his work contests dominant descriptions (e.g., by the media and government officials) of gang members as vicious animals, descriptions that, Conquergood (1994) contended, "help redirect material resources away from educational and employment programs that could help these youngsters and toward the much more costly buildup of a state apparatus of surveillance, control, and punishment—gang squads, jails, and prisons" (pp. 54-55). Conquergood, however, did not just describe, interpret, and explain gang communication or critique dominant rhetoric about gangs; he spent countless hours teaching these youth to read and write, and taught them marketable skills as camera operators in the making of his award-winning documentary about gang communication (Conquergood & Siegel, 1990). He also raised bail money for gang members who had been arrested, and he testified on their behalf in court trials. Conquergood's studies, therefore, demonstrated some of the promises, possibilities, and practices of communication activism scholarship.

Communication activism scholarship, thus, emerges from this confluence of scholarly streams. Such scholarship is grounded in communication scholars immersing themselves in the stream of human life, taking direct vigorous action in support of or opposition to a controversial issue for the purpose of promoting social change and justice. The purpose of this 2-volume text, therefore, is to showcase communication scholars who have engaged in activism and, thereby, promote activism as a significant form of communication scholarship.

OVERVIEW OF THE TEXTS

To select the chapters for these texts, an open call was issued through various print and online sources seeking proposals for original research studies that documented communication activism. All domains of communication scholarship (e.g., interpersonal, group, organizational, and media studies), theoretical perspectives, and methodological approaches (e.g., qualitative, quantitative, and rhetorical) were welcome, as long as the proposed chapter focused on an intervention conducted by the *researcher* (as opposed to someone else) that was designed to assist groups and communities to secure social reform. We, thus, sought to showcase original studies of how communication scholars have employed their resources (e.g., theories, methods, and other practices) to promote social change. We were especially interested in studies that assisted marginalized groups and communities to secure political and social reform in the quest for social justice. Chapter proposals explained the nature of the communication activism, including the groups and communities involved, the interventions designed to secure needed change/reform, the theories and methods that informed the projects, and what lessons might be learned from the study about engaging in communication activism scholarship.

This call resulted in more than 70 chapter proposals being submitted, a large number considering that only about 15 manuscripts were submitted for the special issue of the *Journal of Applied Communication Research* on "Communication and Social Justice Research" that Frey (1998a) edited about 10 years earlier, which suggests that such scholarship has substantially increased over that time period. We were so impressed with the number and high quality of the proposals that we asked Barbara Bernstein of Hampton Press, who had contracted with us for this text, whether it might be possible to produce a 2-volume set, and she immediately saw the advantages of doing so. We thank Barbara for her enthusiastic support of this project (and for the other texts that Frey, 1995, 2006b, has published with Hampton Press). We also thank the contributors to these texts for their excellent chapters (and for their receptivity to our editing suggestions). In addition, we are grateful for a grant that was awarded by Dr. Michele Jackson, chair of the Department of Communication at the University of Colorado at Boulder, that helped to cover the cost of the subject indexes for these volumes, and we thank Jane Callahan and Fran Penner for their initial subject index of Volume 2.

In discussing the commissioned chapters, we let authors know that there was no one way to write them and that we were open to whatever worked best for each chapter. There were, however, some things that we asked authors to consider. First, we asked them to provide a thorough explanation of the situation, problem/issue, and activities that comprised their communication activism. Second, to the extent possible, we wanted them to situate the analysis of their communication activism within relevant theory, research, and practice. Third, we encouraged them to reflect on the dialectical tensions/paradoxes they experienced in performing their communication activism. Fourth, we suggested that they share salient lessons learned about communication activism that might benefit others who either are engaged in or wish to engage in this form of scholarship.

As explained next, Volume 1, subtitled *Communication for Social Change*, showcases original research studies on "Promoting Public Dialogue, Debate, and Discussion" and "Communication Consulting for

Social Change"; Volume 2, subtitled *Media and Performance Activism*, presents original studies on "Managing the Media" and "Performing Social
Change." Together, these texts provide needed empirical research on communication activism and offer important insights about engaging in such
scholarship.

Volume 1, Part I: Promoting Public Dialogue, Debate, and Discussion

Since at least the time of ancient Greece, rhetoricians have stressed the relationship between public communicative practices and civic processes and
outcomes—most notably, democracy. Today, communication (and other)
scholars talk about "deliberative democracy" (e.g., Asen, 2005; Gastil, 2006;
Gastil & Levine, 2005; Hauser & Benoit-Barne, 2002; Hicks, 2002;
Ishikawa, 2002; Ivie, 1998; Kim, Wyatt, & Katz, 1999; Kurpius &
Mendelson, 2002; Mattson, 2002; Murphy, 2004; Pingree, 2006; Ryfe, 2002,
2005; Salter, 2004; Welsh, 2002), "rhetorical democracy" (e.g., Hauser &
Grim, 2004; Whedbee, 2003, 2004), and a "discourse theory of democracy"
(e.g., Habermas, 1996) and "citizenship" (e.g., Asen, 2004). This communication approach to democracy, and its attendant commitments and practices
(e.g., the quest for justice) rests, of course, on people employing appropriate
and effective public communicative practices, from the everyday "vernacular rhetoric" that occurs between interactants on street corners and other
public places (see Hauser, 1998, 2002) to group deliberation and discussion
(see, e.g., Burkhalter, Gastil, & Kelshaw, 2002; Gastil, 2004; Gastil & Dillard,
1999; Gastil & Levine, 2005; Levine, Fung, & Gastil, 2005) to civic argumentation and debate (see, e.g., Auer, 1939; Fleming, 1998; Hicks, 1998; Hicks &
Greene, 2000; Hicks & Langsdorf, 1998; Hitchcock, 2002; Jørgensen, 1998;
Shotter, 1997; D. C. Williams, Ishiyama, Young, & Launer, 1997) to
public/community dialogue (see, e.g., R. Anderson, Cissna, & Arnett, 1994;
R. Anderson, Cissna, & Clune, 2003; Arnett, 2001; Barge, 2002; Hyde &
Bineham, 2000; K. A. Pearce & Pearce, 2001; W. B. Pearce & Pearce, 2000a,
2000b; K. A. Pearce, Spano, & Pearce, in press; Spano, 2001, 2006) to social
protest rhetoric (see previous citations). The chapters in this section document communication scholars' collaborations with individuals, groups,
organizations, and communities to develop their repertoire of public communicative practices that promote social change.

    In Chapter 1, Spoma Jovanovic, Carol Steger, Sarah Symonds, and
Donata Nelson document their efforts as communication scholars teaching
and learning at the University of North Carolina at Greensboro and as residents of the Greensboro community to assist the Greensboro Truth and
Community Reconciliation Project (GTCRP). The GTCRP's mission is to

help the citizens of that city engage in dialogue about what had been an "undiscussable" event for nearly 25 years: the killing of 5 people and the wounding of 10 others by members of the Klu Klux Klan (KKK) and neo-Nazis during a social protest on November 3, 1979, against the growing influence of the KKK. Jovanovic et al. first describe their involvement with the GTCRP, which arose from a graduate course on "Communication and Social Change" taught by Jovanovic, and their social action research plan for this project, which was grounded in a dialogic partnership with community members and included participating and observing, examining historical records and news media representations of the 1979 event, interviewing task force members and others, surveying community members, raising funds, designing a web site, and creating many documents to share the project's process with the community. They then explain two theoretical influences on their communication activism: Young's (2000) political theory of inclusion, community, and democracy; and Levinas's (1961/1969) philosophy of ethics. They subsequently describe how the GTCRP promoted dialogue about this critical incident, and analyze that social change effort through the lens of social justice communication scholarship and the conceptual connection between communication and community development, to show how new, more socially just community narratives were and can be constructed. They conclude the chapter by talking about some important challenges to their communication activism, including overcoming opposition to dialogue—in this case, in large measure because of norms of Southern U.S. civility—dialectical tensions they experienced in performing this community action—such as balancing being intimately involved and remaining outsiders to the social change process—and some lessons learned about communication activism—including, most importantly, how to help communities dialogue about difficult issues.

Following up on the importance of public dialogue about difficult issues, Chapter 2, by Carey Adams, Charlene Berquist, Randy Dillon, and Gloria Galanes, details three public dialogue projects with which these scholars have been involved as members of the Department of Communication at Missouri State University. They first explicate public dialogue as a form of "practical theory" designed to "improve the lives of people and have applicability for enhancing their capacity for action" (Barge, 2001, p. 6; see also Barge & Craig, in press), and their particular approach to dialogue, promoted by the Public Dialogue Consortium (PDC), which is based on the coordinated management of meaning (CMM) theory and action research principles. They then describe the three public dialogue projects, all based in the state of Missouri: (a) the Every Kid Counts Initiative, designed to confront disturbing trends about the quality of life for youth in Springfield, Missouri; (b) the Older Adults Project, to improve the life of older adults; and (c) the Raise Your Voice—Student

Action for Change Campaign, an initiative by Campus Compact (a national coalition of more than 950 college and university presidents dedicated to promoting community service, civic engagement, and service learning in higher education; see http://www.compact.org/) to promote students' participation in public life—in this case, by engaging them in conversations about civic engagement and social and political issues important to them. Adams et al. conclude the chapter by discussing some lessons learned about communication activism from these public dialogue projects—most importantly, the significance of talk for promoting social change.

Mark P. Orbe, in Chapter 3, confronts the important question of civil rights in U.S. communities. Offering leadership to a team of researchers from Western Michigan University, where he teaches, Orbe worked with the Michigan Department of Civil Rights and local communities across that state on the Civil Rights Health (CRH) Project to develop a community-based assessment instrument for systematically describing the state of civil rights health in communities, a first step in facilitating needed social change. After describing the history and goals of the CRH Project, Orbe explains how co-cultural theory, derived from the lived experiences of a variety of "nondominant" or "co-cultural" groups, served as the theoretical foundation for the civil rights health assessment, and how phenomenological inquiry—a 3-step methodology used to gather, thematize, and analyze descriptions of lived experiences—was employed in the project in three pilot communities. He explains how this research resulted in the creation of a CRH Resource Manual that serves as a guide for groups interested in facilitating a civil rights health assessment in their communities, and how that manual was used in Kalamazoo, Michigan. He concludes the chapter by exploring some important challenges confronted in this project, and lessons learned from those challenges, including (a) managing individual, oftentimes competing, agendas; (b) sustaining community participation; (c) negotiating tensions between processes and outcomes; (d) creating meaningful processes and outcomes with long-term impact; and (e) facilitating social change.

Chapter 4 explains the work of Donald C. Shields and C. Thomas Preston, Jr. with urban debate leagues (UDLs), which provide training in argumentation and debate for disadvantaged inner-city high school students and their faculty. Shields and Preston start by examining the inherent relationship between public policy debate and the promotion of democracy and democratic values, as well as empirical evidence showing the value of educational training in debate, but they point out that within most major U.S. cities, until the formation of the UDLs, such training had not been available to at-risk, underserved students attending public schools. As co-principal investigators on a 3-year grant (1998-2001), Shields and Preston formed the Urban Debate League–St. Louis (SLUDL), with Preston as the primary administrator of the project and Shields an unpaid advisor on project activities and research studies about the project. To explain the history and purpose of the UDLs across the nation and the SLUDL, in particular, Shields and Preston use symbolic convergence theory to articulate the UDL rhetorical vision (and accompanying plot lines) of sharing debate with traditionally underserved student populations and communities as an educational tool of empowerment (in line with the vision of Brazilian educator Paulo Freire, 1970, 1994, 1997, 1998) for changing inequitable conditions in U.S. society. They also document research studies and participants' narratives showing the benefits of and reactions to the UDL movement nationally. The authors then present their case study of the SLUDL, including its structure and student and teacher participation, and the extent to which its activities over that 3-year period, as assessed in multiple ways (including research studies conducted), promoted engagement and empowerment for the participants. Shields and Preston conclude the chapter by sharing important lessons learned from this communication activism about perpetuating rhetorical visions concerned with reducing gaps between the "haves" and "have-nots."

Chapter 5, by Stephen John Hartnett, concludes this section of Volume 1 by focusing on antiwar activism—specifically, the war on Iraq. Starting with, and grounding the chapter in Eugene Victor Debs's (1918) plea that "You are fit for something better than slavery and cannon fodder" (p. 26), said publicly in protest against the United States entering World War I and the passing of the Sedition Act and the Espionage Act, Hartnett documents (including visually) antiwar efforts by he and his colleagues in Champaign-Urbana, Illinois. He first politically situates the need for communication activism against the war on Iraq by explicating and showing how President George W. Bush's national security strategy is tied to globalizing capitalism and the quest for empire, and how, historically, the use of military force to champion "free markets" and build empire (such as by the British Empire) has failed. Hartnett then outlines four theses—(a) interweaving the local and the global, (b) defending democratic practices, (c) the mysterious logic of multiplier effects, and (d) the power of delayed impact—that have guided his antiwar activism, along with six thematically organized sets of communication strategies—(a) teach-ins, working groups, and pedagogical communication; (b) political art and startling communication; (c) marches, vigils, rallies, and the public communication of anger and hope; (d) postering, e-mailing, chance communication, and targeted networks; (e) media communication; and (f) picnics, parties, and interpersonal communication—he has employed to protest the war and reclaim democracy from empire. He concludes the chapter by talking, as undoubtedly Debs would, about communication activism as a way of being in the world with others and communicating hope in an age of terror, war, and empire. Following the chapter, Laura Stengrim and Hartnett offer an extensive appendix of 113 online and print resources, organized into 9 themes, that scholars and activists can use to inform and enrich their communication activism.

Volume 1, Part II: Communication Consulting for Social Change

The term *communication consulting* most likely brings to mind the image of an "expert" who is paid to help for-profit organizations (typically large ones, such as IBM) to communicate more effectively for the ultimate purpose of promoting management's bottom line—making money. Indeed, the scholarly communication literature invariably associates consulting with for-profit organizations (see, e.g., Browning, 1982; Browning & Hawes, 1991; B. D. Davis & Krapels, 1999; Gieselman & Philpott, 1969; Goodall, 1989; Hildebrandt, 1978; Kreps, 1989; Lange, 1984; March, 1991; Muir, 1996; Phillips, 1992; Plax, 1991; Poe, 2002; Sussman, 1982). Even scholars concerned with the ethical practice of communication consulting have viewed that activity primarily within the context of business organizations (e.g., Goldberg, 1983; Harrison, 1982; Montgomery, Wiseman, & DeCaro, 2001; J. Stewart, 1983), as have those who teach communication consulting within the educational context (see, e.g., Alderton, 1983; Cronin & Hall, 1990; Dallimore & Souza, 2002; Freeman, 1986; Jarboe, 1989; Redding, 1979).

There is, however, no reason why communication consulting should be tied to for-profit organizations per se, or engaged in for payment. Jarboe (1992), in arguing for a scholar-practitioner approach to communication consulting, asserted that "to have honesty and integrity, consulting should be done for scholarly knowledge and public service" (p. 232). Although some communication scholars have consulted for these purposes (e.g., some political communication consulting; see, e.g., Friedenberg, 1997; Johnson-Cartee & Copeland, 1997; Whillock, 1989), often as part of community service, there is a lack of scholarly literature about communication consulting with nonprofit groups and organizations (or underresourced for-profit organizations that promote social good). The lack of such scholarship is unfortunate, for there are many such groups and organizations in need of the consulting expertise that communication scholars can offer, providing rich sites for shedding light on and hopefully encouraging other scholars to engage in communication activism consulting. The chapters in this section document communication scholarship that has reclaimed consulting to promote social change.

In Chapter 6, Robbin D. Crabtree and Leigh Arden Ford discuss their experiences working with a sexual assault recovery center (SARC). After situating their work within the historical mission of, and contemporary need for, civic engagement by faculty and students at U.S. universities, they examine sexual assault as a social justice issue. They then illustrate how "activist consulting" can emerge organically from a scholar's life in a community by sharing personal narratives of their long-term involvement with SARC. Crabtree's narrative reveals how her work with SARC—which emerged from an MA service-learning course she taught on "Communication and Social Change" and included media relations, promotion, fund-raising, training, and special event planning—was part of her healing process from sexual assault victim to survivor to activist. Ford's narrative documents how her involvement with SARC—including serving first as a board member and later, after the executive director resigned and the agency experienced a financial crisis that threatened to close it, as a grant-writer and supervisor of SARC personnel—evolved from her feminist politics and desire to put her expertise in organizational theory into practice. Interpreting their experiences with SARC using feminist narrative analysis, Crabtree and Ford recast the traditional activist-consultant dichotomy as a dialectical relationship filled with tensions that need to be managed, including tensions that result from (a) participating and observing, (b) balancing dialogic with authoritarian communication, and (c) blending the professional and the personal (especially in situations in which someone has been as deeply affected by an issue as Crabtree was in this case). They conclude the chapter by talking about the benefits of communication activism for (a) groups, agencies, and communities served; (b) activist scholars; and (c) institutions of higher education, as well as some of the risks involved in the activist mode of communication consulting.

Chapter 7 focuses on how Sunwolf, a communication professor and lawyer, helps defense attorneys to create collaborative courtroom conversations with potential jurors to prevent their clients from receiving the death penalty. Sunwolf first examines the controversial topic of capital punishment, including evidence that has led to the release of numerous innocent people from death row but also shows that others have been put to death. She explains the enormous challenges that confront capital defense attorneys, including citizens' preconceived ideas about the jury deliberation task, the death-qualification selection process that dismisses those who are not willing to give the death penalty, the lack of resources available to these lawyers, and the dialectical challenges they confront when engaging in "death talk" with potential jurors. Drawing on her experiences as a capital defense lawyer and her communication scholarship on the dynamics of social influence during group decision making, Sunwolf describes an intervention that she created and uses in national workshops conducted with criminal defense attorneys who have been appointed by the court to represent an indigent client who faces the death penalty to help them dialogue with potential jurors about their views of the death penalty. She explains the workshops, focusing on specific communication challenges facing defense attorneys in talking about death with potential jurors and new communication tools she has created to cope with these challenges that employ an "empathic attunement" technique (see Sunwolf, 2006) to shift those interactions from interrogations to collaborative conversations that promote empathy. She ends the chapter by reflecting on lessons learned from these workshops about communication activism, including the challenges of coping with unsuccessful interventions (in this case, resulting in a person's death) and being an "itinerate" activist who often never knows the consequences of his or her activism.

Chapter 8 documents David L. Palmer's involvement as a member of Meta-, a progressive activist antiglobalization group, and how he collaborated with that group to engage more formally and effectively in consensus building, as the group planned for and took part in an international trade summit protest—the Free Trade Area of the Americas (FTAA) protest in Miami, in November 2003. After explaining the rise of globalization and the antiglobalization movement that has mobilized in the form of *affinity groups*, small progressive groups that act together to resist globalization, Palmer describes how affinity groups rely on consensus building as their primary means for making democratic decisions, but how those groups, including Meta-, do not always practice effective consensus building. He, thus, invited the members of Meta- to analyze and, if necessary, modify their discussion and decision-making practices as the group prepared for the FTAA protest. He reviews the methodology that he developed for this project—the emergent-consensus program—which relies on meta-discussion (discussion about the discussion process; hence, the pseudonym for this affinity group) and is grounded in the work on consensus models, group diagnostic models, and inductive models of inquiry. Palmer then walks through the emergent-consensus program in action, explaining, both in narrative and expository form, how the group analyzed its discussion and decision-making practices and the changes it did (and did not) make prior to the week of the protest, with the protest week, itself, captured vividly through photographic evidence. Palmer reflects on the lessons learned from this communication activism, including the need for scholar-activists to be involved in projects of popular resistance, helping social movement activists to build network infrastructures, and how such groups and movements provide rich sites for gaining insights into important communication concerns, such as group communication and consensus building.

Shelly Campo and M. Somjen Frazer, in Chapter 9, combine participatory action research (PAR) and communication activism to affect community health—in this case, to improve services for women who partner with women (WPW) at the college healthcare center where the authors taught and studied, respectively, at the time. They start by explaining the barriers to effective healthcare for WPW, in general, and the particular healthcare center and groups with which they partnered to conduct this research. Campo and Frazer then articulate their methodological and theoretical groundings—PAR, queer theory and feminism, and health communication theories (specifically, the health belief model, the theory of planned behavior, and fear appeals)—followed by an explanation of their research project, which included both qualitative and quantitative components. They describe the process of creating a PAR project (including obtaining financial support and establishing a trusting research relationship), the interviews conducted with and questionnaires completed by WPW students about the healthcare center, and the interviews conducted with key informants and clinicians at the center. Campo and Frazer present the results of the data analysis (which included creating a concept map of barriers to healthcare that WPW experienced at that center) and describe how they used those results as the basis for conducting workshops with students and clinicians. They explain the key institutional changes that were made in the center's practices and space to make healthcare more accessible and friendly to WPW as a result of sharing the research findings and conducting the workshops, the connections made between university units, and the general raising of awareness about the healthcare needs of WPW as a result of the project. They conclude the chapter by sharing lessons learned about communication activism, including the importance of establishing trust between oppositional groups and between those groups and researchers, conducting an effective PAR project, and conducting PAR in the university context.

In Chapter 10, Stuart L. Esrock, Joy L. Hart, and Greg Leichty, from the University of Louisville, report their most recent efforts with Kentucky Health Investment for Kids (KHIK), a coalition working to raise the cigarette excise tax in Kentucky for the first time in 30-plus years, in line with public health advocates' findings that a substantial state tax is the single-best means of reducing smoking. After discussing tobacco use, in general, they focus on the state of Kentucky (ranking second highest in tobacco production, second lowest in cigarette excise tax, and first in death rate from lung cancer) and KHIK's campaign, including their association with this activist group. They then explain how they employed rhetorical theory (on cultural topoi and defensive rhetoric) and the literature on media framing to conceptually understand the culture of tobacco in Kentucky and inform the strategic development of counterarguments that KHIK could use against opponents' arguments. They describe their research, which included rhetorical analysis of three television shows about the proposed tax increase to uncover successful and unsuccessful arguments on both sides, survey questionnaires completed by campaign leaders and interested state representatives about the arguments they used to support the tax increase, and focus groups conducted with KHIK leaders and lawmakers to further refine arguments in favor of and responses to arguments against the tax increase. The presentation of their findings and recommendations to KHIK resulted in the group changing some of its rhetorical strategies. Esrock et al. conclude the chapter by discussing some tensions and paradoxes that arose during their intervention research—including those related to working with savvy and relatively resourced activists and with colleagues who smoke—and some lessons learned about communication activism—including the need for patience when working on issues, such as this one, that have little chance of succeeding in the short run, as well as the effects of activism on scholars' research and their roles as academics and citizens.

Chapter 11 concludes this section and this volume, with Leah Ritchie's case study of being an organizational activist consultant with a nonprofit organization. She begins by pointing out how critical communication scholars have rightfully identified the need for more balanced systems of power that promote democracy in the workplace, but have done little to intervene on behalf of workers. To fill this gap between theory and practice, Ritchie employs Habermas's (1984) concept of the *ideal speech situation*—a discursive space that provides full and equal access to communication for all parties—and a functionalist perspective of social activism—people using persuasive discourse to create new perspectives on their situations—to explain her attempt as a pro bono consultant to decentralize power at the Massachusetts-based neighborhood center (MNC, a pseudonym), a nonprofit, faith-based organization that had recently fallen on hard times. Ritchie and her graduate students first conducted peer-only focus groups, followed by private interviews, with MNC employees to determine the root causes of communication problems in the organization. Their analysis of the interview data showed that the controlling and hierarchical culture at MNC—exercised through pressure for employees to silence themselves and interpersonal distance and lack of trust between organizational groups—had a significant negative effect on employees. Ritchie explains her use of a communication intervention process called "Organizational Fitness Profiling" (Beer & Eisenstat, 1996, 2000; Beer, Eisenstat, & Spector, 1990), which involves lower level employees in organizational strategic planning, to attempt to produce a "quasi-ideal" speech situation at MNC. She concludes the chapter by analyzing her activities at MNC, including her successes and failures, through a functionalist lens that draws parallels between activist strategies and consulting work, and by sharing lessons learned about engaging in communication activism within the constraints of organizational settings.

Volume II, Part I: Managing the Media

Scholars and activists have long viewed the media as crucial political and cultural arenas, shaping definitions of, and policies toward, issues, events, groups, and communities. Although mainstream social-scientific approaches to the media have been faulted for their failure to examine the media's ideological role, multiple perspectives—including the Frankfurt School, cultural studies, political economy approaches, and critical media sociology—have devoted extensive attention to the media's role in sustaining social systems characterized by significant economic and political inequalities. These perspectives have played an essential role in describing, explaining, and critiquing the media's political and cultural roles by exploring significant issues related to power, ideology, hegemony, cultural resistance, and the consequences of economic concentration (see, e.g., Alasuutari, 1999; Artz & Murphy, 2000; Bagdikian, 2004; Carragee, 1993, 1996; Dines & Humez, 2002; Dow, 1996; Durham & Kellner, 2005; Entman, 1989; Gamson, Croteau, Hoynes, & Sasson, 1992; Grossberg, Wartella, Whitney, & Wise, 2005; Hall, 1977, 1997; Hallin, 1987; Herman & Chomsky, 1988; Horkheimer & Adorno, 1972; Kellner, 1990, 1995; Lewis, 1999, 2001; McChesney, 1999, 2004b; Meehan & Riordan, 2001; Morley, 1980, 1992; Mosco, 1996; Schiller 1989, 1996; R. Williams, 1975).

Unfortunately, this longstanding critique of the media has not been accompanied by extensive efforts by scholar-activists to assist marginalized groups and communities in using or influencing the media to secure social and political reform. Thus, there is a striking imbalance between critiques of the media's role in contemporary societies and interventions designed to help disenfranchised groups use the media in their quest for social justice. This imbalance is particularly evident in studies exploring the relationship between social movements and the news media. Extensive scholarship exists on the interaction between news organizations and social movements, with much of this literature documenting the media's support of the status quo by disparaging and delegitimizing movements seeking meaningful social and political change (see, e.g., Ashley & Olson, 1998; Barker-Plummer, 1995; Carragee, 1991, 2003; Carragee & Roefs, 2004; Deluca & Peeples, 2002; Entman & Rojecki, 1993; Gamson, 1992; Gamson & Wolfsfeld, 1993; Gitlin, 1980; Hertog & McLeod, 1995; Kielbowicz & Scherer, 1986; McAdam, 1996; Noakes & Wilkins, 2002; Oliver & Myers, 1999; Rojecki, 1999, 2002; Shoemaker, 1984; J. Smith, McCarthy, McPhail, & Augustyn, 2001; Tuchman, 1978; Zald, 1996). However, only a few scholars have engaged in interventions designed to assist social movement organizations in securing their goals (e.g., Carragee, 2005; Hoynes, 2005; McHale, 2004; Ryan, 1991, 2005; Ryan et al., 1998, 2001). The chapters in this section address this imbalance by documenting the efforts of scholar-activists to help marginalized groups and communities use the media to achieve meaningful social and political change.

In Chapter 1, Eleanor Novek and Rebecca Sanford explore the multilayered paradoxes confronting their teaching of journalism classes and producing a newspaper at a state prison for women. After documenting the rise of prisons (including those for women) in the United States, they explain the specific context for their work, the Clara Barton Correctional Facility for Women (a pseudonym), and the difficulties they encounter there. Their theoretically informed activist research—relying on feminist perspectives (especially given the special impact of prisons on women), Foucault's (1979) work on prisons, and social justice research—and use of methodological triangulation—participant observation, interviewing, and textual analysis—creates a richly documented account of how journalistic writing helped these women to express their cultural understandings of prison life and, thereby, served as a path to empowerment for them. The authors also explore how these prison journalists confronted institutional constraints in researching and writing news stories about, for instance, the harshness of prison life and the incompetent medical care they receive. Novek and Sanford also carefully detail the complexities and challenges of the relationships formed between the women who contributed to the prison newspaper, as well as how they, as authors, try to treat the women fairly in their written and oral representations of them. They conclude the chapter by reflecting on the significant dilemmas confronting their intervention, including the tension between their desire to engage in activist research to improve the life of these women coupled with the simultaneous need to follow prison rules and regulations to have continued access to them.

Sue Ellen Christian, in Chapter 2, also discusses an intervention linked to the production of a newspaper—The Student Newspaper Diversity Project, a high school newspaper community project that Christian spearheads that focuses on issues related to diversity. Supported by the NCA's Communicating Common Ground initiative, the Southern Poverty Law Center, Campus Compact, and the American Association for Higher Education, this 15-week project involves the student newspaper staff of an economically and racially diverse urban public high school in southwest Michigan and journalism and communication students from Western Michigan University who serve as mentors and editors for the high school journalists, and results in the publication of a once-a-year special edition of the student newspaper that focuses on a community issue related to diversity. After describing the project, Christian explains how service-learning and civic journalism traditions shaped her communication activism, for despite their manifest differences and significant shortcomings (e.g., both frequently ignore structural inequalities in U.S. society), they share a common concern with promoting civic responsibility and engagement, activism, and social change. Christian then documents important outcomes of this project, including heightened sensitivity of issues related to diversity and increased journalistic skills among the high school newspaper staff, as well as the impact of the newspaper on readers. At the same time, she notes important limitations of the project, such as the lack of specific school reforms after exposing patterns of segregation and integration in the high school, with the tracking of students of color continuing and the school failing to hire additional minority faculty. Christian also addresses the thorny issue of the censorship of newspaper content by the high school administration and how that affects staff self-censorship to avoid administrative rejection of specific stories, ultimately concluding that the issue provided the student newspaper staff with valuable lessons regarding the limitations of journalism as an agent of social change.

Sharing Christian's commitment to service learning as a means for social change, Leda Cooks and Erica Scharrer, in Chapter 3, explain their media literacy service-learning project focused on violence and conflict resolution. An ongoing university-community collaboration, the Media Literacy and Violence Prevention Program (MLVPP) fosters learning, transformation, and advocacy about mediated and interpersonal violence and conflict resolution strategies for participating sixth graders, their teachers, and their families, as well as for the undergraduate students at the University of Massachusetts at Amherst engaged in service learning. Cooks and Scharrer first articulate their social constructionist perspective, making their intervention very different from traditional media literacy projects because of its focus on "learning-as-change," with learning and change viewed as grounded in the same social processes, such that as people learn, they change, and vice versa. At the same time, their intervention reflects the longstanding interest of media literacy projects in developing a critical understanding of the processes that shape both the production and reception of media texts. Cooks and Scharrer explain the MLVPP and assess, using a pre/postprogram design, the learning that occurs from exposure to it via questionnaires completed by the children, their written responses after viewing a media clip, and videotapes of classroom interactions, with the influence of the service-learning project assessed through university students' journals and response papers. Cooks and Scharrer document the project's multiple influences on the sixth graders, including their more sophisticated understanding of conflict resolution, media violence, and media decision-making processes, as well as how children resisted aspects of the project, such as discounting the influence of media violence on their life and displacing it onto their younger brothers and sisters. They also reveal that some of the undergraduate students redefined their social activism role from educating others to educating themselves. The authors conclude the chapter by examining the implications of the learning-as-change perspective for communication activism.

Van M. Cagle, in Chapter 4, documents his tenure as the first Director of Research & Analysis at the Center for the Study of Media & Society (CSMS) sponsored by the Gay & Lesbian Alliance Against Defamation (GLAAD), an advocacy organization that encourages fair and inclusive representation of gay, lesbian, bisexual, and transgendered (LGBT) people in news and entertainment media. The CSMS was established in 2000 to promote relationships between media scholarship and GLAAD's media activism. Cagle first explains GLAAD's research needs, the CSMS, and his role in commissioning, producing, and promoting multimethodological scholarship focusing on media representations of LGBT people and audience interpretations of these representations that could provide practical benefits for GLAAD's activists. He then focuses on four recurring struggles he experienced in forging connections between media scholarship and LGBT activism. First, he notes that GLAAD activists perceived a disconnect between their work and that of scholars, with activists preferring quantitative data to support their lobbying of media professionals and viewing qualitative studies, mainly driven by cultural studies and queer theory, as "academic theorizing" that was irrelevant to their work. Second, the pace of activist and scholarly work differs considerably, with GLAAD's activists facing pressing deadlines and needing to respond quickly to breaking news events related to LGBT issues, whereas research necessitates considerable time for data collection and reflection. Third, activists demand studies documenting clear causal relationships between, for instance, stereotypical media depictions of gays and lesbians and negative attitudes and behaviors toward those groups, but scholars question such simple causal relationships and believe there are diverse audience interpretations of the same media text. Fourth, Cagle contrasts the commitment of GLAAD's activists to a form of identity politics, which often assumes a gay/straight binary, with queer theorists' critique of this binary and fixed gay and lesbian identities. Cagle concludes the chapter by examining some lessons learned about communication activism from trying to navigate the different assumptions and practices of the academic world and the world of LGBT activism.

In Chapter 5, John P. McHale examines how his video documentary, *Unreasonable Doubt: The Joe Amrine Case* (McHale, Wylie, & Huck, 2002; available from Hampton Press) helped to free a man on death row in Missouri who had been falsely convicted of a murder. McHale first reviews scholarship on media, in general, and video and film documentary, in particular, as tools for social protest, but points out that little work has been done on the use of documentary video/film by activists engaged in social movements, such as those seeking to abolish the death penalty. He provides background on Amrine's case, including how he became involved with Amrine, and the strong relationship that existed between the video documentary and those involved in the antideath penalty movement. McHale describes the creation and distribution of the documentary, from preproduction, production, and postproduction, to its promotion and exhibition, a discussion informed by McHale's (2004) recent ethnographic, grounded theory of activists' use of media. He then addresses the documentary's multiple influences, including educating viewers on the miscarriage of justice in the Amrine case, shaping news media coverage of the case, mobilizing advocates in their campaign against capital punishment, and, most importantly, the significant role the documentary played in influencing the Missouri Supreme Court to release Amrine. McHale's conclusions include the important connection that activist-scholars need to make, when possible, between their communication activism and broader social movements working on an issue. In this case, the considerable connections between McHale's project and the movement against capital punishment in Missouri significantly enhanced the making and influence of the documentary. McHale argues, therefore, that the effectiveness of a film/video documentary as an agent of social reform is largely dependent on the amount of coordination between the producers of the documentary and the broader collective effort by activists to secure social justice.

Like McHale's communication activism, Ted M. Coopman's intervention, detailed in Chapter 6, involved extensive interaction with a social movement. As a scholar-activist in the micro radio movement, which stemmed from pursuing his master's degree in mass communication, Coopman played an essential role in bridging differences in this movement's effort to secure the legalization of low-power FM radio services. After providing a brief history of the micro radio movement, Coopman highlights important characteristics of new social movements such as this one, including their heterogeneity (in this case, anarchists, community groups, and libertarians of the political left and right who had very different visions for micro radio) and how they function as an emergent network (in this case, a *dissent network*, or *dissentwork*, terms Coopman coins to reference a network of individuals opposing entrenched hierarchical systems) that relies to a great extent on communication technology (e.g., the internet, e-mail, and listservs). Coopman narrates how these characteristics made it very difficult to craft a joint statement that could influence the Federal Communication Commission's (FCC) rule-making concerning low-power radio. Coopman, however, succeeded in drafting a document, the Joint Statement on Micro Radio (JSMR), which attracted widespread support within the micro radio movement and influenced the FCC's decision to legalize micro radio in 2000. He details how his scholarly knowledge of First Amendment law, federal regulation, and FCC culture shaped the drafting of the JSMR, and how activists' perceptions of him as an "honest broker" between diverse groups attracted support for the document. Coopman concludes the chapter with suggestions about negotiating the chasm that often exists between simultaneously being a communication scholar and activist.

Following up on Coopman's discussion of technology and social change, Andrew P. Herman and James S. Ettema, in Chapter 7, describe their efforts to reduce the digital divide among groups and organizations in a lower income African American community in Chicago. Their Neighborhood Communication Project, a partnership between Northwestern University (where Herman was a doctoral student at the time and Ettema is a professor) and a community-based organization (CBO) in need of technology expertise, involved creating a community technology coordinator to assist this CBO. Herman and Ettema first explain two theoretical perspectives informing their intervention: (a) the theory of asset-based community development, which recognizes that communities need external assistance but stresses understanding and mapping the resources and capacities that exist within all communities; and (b) the work on social capital highlighting the significance of social networks and relationships in enhancing community life. The authors describe mapping this community's assets and how, in response to the need, the community technology coordinator (an African American raised in Chicago whom Herman and Ettema mentored) brokered relationships between organizations to reduce the digital divide in the community by creating additional social capital (networks of useful relationships) and intellectual capital (problem-solving abilities and leadership). They document the benefits that accrued to the community, including creating a community web site, the dramatic increase in the number of community technology centers, and the sharing of technology information that eventually occurred among 50 community groups and small businesses. Organizational leaders also completed a quantitative questionnaire to assess the project's effectiveness, with the results showing how these groups engaged in communicative behaviors to increase their social capital, although the digital divide among participating organizations did not diminish because of the scarcity of technical expertise in the community and the tendency for assistance to flow to those best positioned to seek and use it. The authors conclude that communication activism addressing the digital divide may well result in one divide closing but other divides opening.

Volume 2, Part II: Performing Social Change

Art, although certainly used at times to maintain the status quo (see Cohen-Cruz, 2006; Glassberg, 1990), has long been employed as a form of activism to communicate community needs and promote social change (see, e.g., Barndt, 2006; Felshin, 1995; Kaplan, 2006; Korza & Bacon, 2005). As Cohen-Cruz (2006) explained, "Activist art is aesthetic production as part of a struggle for social change, such as seeking more rights for people who are being exploited, or resistance to changes that are deemed detrimental" (p. 427). Performance/theater activism, in particular, has a deep history in the United States (see, e.g., Dijkstra, 2003; Lubin, 1994) and elsewhere (see, e.g., Shepherd, 1998; van Erven, 1992), including the workers theater during the 1930s Great Depression (see, e.g., Friedman, 1985), the Black arts movement (see Neal, 1968; regarding Black performance studies, see, e.g., E. P. Johnson, 2006; Ugwu, 1995) and Chicano theater groups (such as El Teatro Campesino; see, e.g., Broyles-González, 1994) during the 1960s, and, later, the global movement of the "Theatre of the Oppressed" started by Brazilian director and Worker Party activist Augusto Boal (e.g., 1979, 1995) and based on the critical pedagogy articulated by Freire (e.g., 1970, 1994, 1998). Today, scholars in communication, literature, performance studies, theater, education, and many other disciplines study performance as a significant form of communication activism (see, e.g., Billingham, 2005; Capo, 1983; Caster, 2004; Cohen-Cruz, 1998, 2006; Conquergood, 1988, 1998, 2002a, 2002b; Denzin, 2003; Dolan, 2001a, 2001b; Elam, 2003; Fuoss, 1997; Gómez-Peña, 2005; Haedicke & Nellhaus, 2001; Inomata & Cohen, 2006; J. L. Jones, 2002b; Kershaw, 1992; Klope, 1994; Madison, 2006; Park-Fuller, 2003; Strine, 1992; Stucky, 2006; Taylor, 2003; Toc, 1971). However, only a few scholars, such as Hartnett's (1998) work on performance in a prison setting (see also Conquergood, 1988), have employed and documented performance as a form of communication activism. The chapters in this section report three such efforts by communication scholars to use performance to promote social change.

In Chapter 8, Lynn Harter, Devendra Sharma, Saumya Pant, Arvind Singhal, and Yogita Sharma discuss their complex integration of an entertainment-education (E-E) project with participatory theater workshops and performances in India's Bihar State. After surveying the social landscape of India and Bihar, Harter et al. historically situate the workshops and performances conducted within a broader E-E project—the Indian radio soap opera, *Taru*, which promoted the values of gender equality, small family size, reproductive health, and communal and caste harmony. The authors' dialogic interventions are informed by the work of Freire and Boal (cited previously), whose vision of social activism is rooted in the lived experience of groups and communities suffering oppression and disenfranchisement coupled with the recognition that marginalized people are active subjects rather than objects. Boal's Theatre of the Oppressed, a participatory form of theater used to challenge and change repressive social practices, directly shaped the design of the workshops and performances facilitated by Harter et al. They explain how 50 members of *Taru* listening groups in four Bihar villages first participated in theater workshops, developing script-writing and performance skills, and then put those skills into practice to produce three plays, with all aspects of the plays and performances created by the participants. Interviews with participants and audience members, along with photographic evidence, document the multiple influences of their interventions. They show, for example, how the content of the plays provided striking counter-narratives to dominant cultural practices in Bihar by criticizing both the caste and dowry systems. The workshops and performances also created enduring social networks among the participants, increasing their social capital and likely setting the stage for future grassroots initiatives for social change. They end the chapter by examining how communication activism is enabled and constrained by structural and cultural forces, noting, for example, the lack of caste diversity among participants, which resulted in their communication activism more effectively challenging gender (by bringing men and women together to perform, a unique occurrence in India) than caste inequalities.

Chapter 9, by Marc D. Rich and José I. Rodríguez, provides a unique and insightful analysis of a participatory theater project focusing on sexual assault. After documenting the pervasiveness of sexual assault and date rape on college campuses and criticizing traditional sexual assault intervention programs for being didactic, they explain a university-based performance troupe, interACT (headed by Rich since 2000), that employs techniques and strategies associated with participatory theater to educate college students about sexual assault. Rich and Rodríguez, like Harter et al., use Boal's Theatre of the Oppressed as the theoretical grounding for their facilitation of social change through participatory theatre. They discuss the interACT performance, which combines two scripted scenes of a potential sexual assault episode with four proactive scenes created by audience members. Their study is methodologically unique and innovative because they employed a quasi-experimental design involving 458 undergraduate students to assess the effects of the performance. Multiple social-scientific models—the elaboration likelihood model, the affective learning model, and the altruistic and egoistic models—shape their research questions and the variables assessed for students in the experimental group (the interACT performance) and those in a control group (a lecture/demonstration on a web-based instructional program related to course content). In comparison to the control group, students exposed to the interACT performance reported higher levels of affective and cognitive learning, value-relevant involvement, and issue-relevant thinking. Rich and Rodríguez's findings, thus, support participatory theater as an influential form of communication activism, and they offer guidelines for engaging in this type of activism, although they are quick to note limitations of their study and the need for additional research that directly compares performance-based projects with more didactic forms of communication activism. They also argue persuasively for how quantitative studies can complement what has heretofore been qualitative evidence (because of performance studies scholars' suspicion of quantitative research) for the effects of performance activism.

In the final chapter in this volume, Deborah Cunningham Walker and Elizabeth A. Curry reflect on their participation (as graduate students) in the

University Community Initiative (UCI) Project, a collaboration between Community Action Stops Abuse (CASA), a nonprofit organization devoted to preventing domestic violence, and the communication and sociology departments of the University of South Florida. They first provide an overview of CASA's range of services for survivors of domestic violence, which include emergency assistance and long-term support, and they explain the UCI Project, a long-term, comprehensive participatory ethnography employing interactive interviews to collect narratives from CASA staff, which has resulted in numerous products, including a booklet of stories that CASA uses as a lobbying, recruiting, and fundraising tool. Walker and Curry then explicate their theoretical and methodological frameworks: social action research, feminist perspectives, and Gergen's (2000) narrative concept of "poetic activism," in which scholar-activists approach social change with an emphasis on both the process of developing research relationships and the products of those relationships. They illustrate this unique form of activism by providing a detailed autoethnographic narrative of a university colloquium that involved them and two CASA staff members sharing the evolution of their research as a process of forging trusting relationships, with the colloquium becoming an enactment of their relationship. Walker and Curry reflect on both the successes and the challenges of their communication activism, paying particular attention to the need to cultivate a dialogic relationship between researchers and activists characterized by trust, empathy, mutual respect, active listening, metacommunication, and collaborative learning.

LESSONS LEARNED
ABOUT COMMUNICATION ACTIVISM

The chapters in these two volumes, as a set, shed significant light on the nature and practice of communication activism scholarship. Here, we share some broad lessons learned from these studies about engaging in communication activism (citing relevant sample chapters in the order they appear in the volumes).

First, communication activism research, like all scholarship, reflects a choice that scholars make about what communication phenomena they will study, how they will study those phenomena, and to what ends they will put the findings from their research. The scholars who contributed to these texts consciously chose to engage in research that potentially could make an important difference in the world. Of course, all communication scholars undoubtedly are interested in making a difference, but the question that needs to be asked is whose interests are being served by their research. As Becker (1995) pointed out, "The major question most of us face in our lives as scholars is not whether our research should be useful; it is, rather, what it should be useful for and for whom it should be useful" (p. 102).

These scholars chose to conduct research that potentially could make an important difference for marginalized and underresourced individuals, groups, organizations, and communities attempting to promote social change and social justice. In that sense, there is a significant difference between, for instance, serving as a pro bono consultant to a struggling non-profit organization (e.g., as Ritchie did) and being a paid consultant to the management of IBM. Although we certainly respect scholars' right to choose how to devote their resources, scholars also need to realize that they are embedded within economic, political, social, and cultural systems, meaning that their research has important implications for maintaining or challenging those systems; consequently, their research choices must be open to being called into question. Conquergood (1995) forcefully explained the choice confronting researchers:

> The choice is no longer between pure and applied research. Instead, we must choose between research that is "engaged" or "complicit." By engaged I mean a clear-eyed, self-critical awareness that research does not proceed in epistemological purity or moral innocence. There is no immaculate perception. Engaged individuals take responsibility for how the knowledge that they produce is used instead of hiding behind pretenses and protestations of innocence. In a post-colonial, late capitalistic world, marked by sexism, racism, homophobia, and class bias, we understand, with Said (1989), that "Innocence is now out of the question of course" (p. 213). As communication scholars who traffic in symbols, images, representations, rhetorical strategies, signifying practices, the media, and the social work of talk, we should understand better than anyone else that our disciplinary practice is *in* the world. As engaged intellectuals we understand that we are entangled within world systems of oppression and exploitation. . . . Our choice is to stand alongside or against domination, but not outside, above, or beyond it. (p. 85)

The communication scholars in these volumes chose to stand against domination, oppression, and other social injustices by using their resources to fight against capital punishment (Sunwolf; McHale), domestic violence (Walker & Curry), globalization (Palmer), homophobia (Campo & Frazer; Cagle), racism (Jovanovic et al.; Orbe), sexism (Harter et al.), sexual assault (Crabtree & Ford; Rich & Rodríguez), and war (Hartnett), among many other things. Their reasons for choosing these particular issues undoubtedly differ, with some scholars, for instance, readily admitting in their chapter that they have experienced the issue personally, such as Crabtree being a victim of sexual assault, or are associated with the group being studied, such as Campo and Frazer's promotion of better healthcare for lesbians, with both of them being women who partner with other women. In other cases, they became involved because the opportunity presented itself. Jovanovic, for example, recently moved to Greensboro, North Carolina, and discovered the grassroots movement there for truth, justice, and reconciliation; Hartnett responded to the exigency of the moment created by the war on Iraq; and McHale, as he reported, found out serendipitously from one of his former students about Joe Amrine, well after Amrine had been on death row but, fortunately, before he had been executed. In these and the other cases, these scholars were particularly well suited and positioned to take advantage of the opportunity presented to them (e.g., because of Jovanovic's deep concern with ethics; Hartnett's scholarly focus on war and empire, as well as his involvement in other protest movements; and McHale's immersion in the antideath penalty movement). In fact, in some of these cases, the activism came first, followed by the documenting of it for research purposes. Ultimately, then, their choice to work for social change and social justice on behalf of those who have been marginalized springs from who they are as people and what they value, showing, as Adelman and Frey (2001) contended in an autoethnographic account of their longitudinal communication activism program on communication and community in a AIDS residential facility (see, e.g., Adelman & Frey, 1997), "that the most meaningful research (to researchers and participants alike) is that which resonates with researchers' personal values and characteristics" (pp. 208-209). Other scholars, of course, will make their own choices based on their personal values and characteristics, but they also must be willing to own those choices and the values those choices represent.

Second, communication activism, as "engaged" scholarship (see also Applegate, 2001, 2002; Cheney, Wilhelmsson, & Zorn, 2002), transforms researchers into citizen-scholars (see, e.g., Grund, Cherwitz, & Darwin, 2001; Pestello, Saxton, Miller, & Donnelly, 1996; Rakow, 2005) connected with their communities and the significant issues that confront them. Most of the projects featured in these volumes involve scholars promoting social change and social justice with/in their local communities. Rakow (2005), in talking about the need for community research in the communication discipline, asserted, in both a joking and serious manner:

> According to the timeworn joke, the chicken crossed the road to get to the other side. So why did the scholar cross the road? To do research on the other side, presumably. Why do scholars go elsewhere to do research, like the proverbial wandering chicken, instead of staying right where we are? Is there nothing of significance in our own communities that is worthy of study? Is there no role for our research in the daily struggles of local citizens to create healthy and just communities? Is a scholar also a citizen? (p. 6)

The scholars spotlighted in these volumes did not, for the most part, cross the road but, instead, stayed in their communities. They engaged in communication activism with/for students in their classes and/or the universities where they taught or went to school (Jovanovic et al.; Crabtree & Ford; Campo & Frazer; Christian; Cooks & Scharrer; Rich & Rodríguez; Walker & Curry); the local organizations and institutions where their fellow citizens worked, went to school, or, in the case of prison, were kept (Crabtree & Ford; Ritchie; Novek & Sanford; Christian; Cooks & Scharrer; Walker & Curry); the neighborhoods, towns, and states where they lived (Jovanovic et al.; Adams et al.; Orbe; Shields & Preston; Esrock et al.; McHale; Herman & Ettema); or, in the case of Harter et al., the home country of some of the authors (India). In some cases, they sought policy changes at the national level (Hartnett campaigning against the war on Iraq in his hometown with local groups; Palmer protesting globalization with a local affinity group where he lives; Coopman promoting the legalization of low-power FM radio, and Cagle seeking fair media coverage of GLBT people), in large measure because those policy changes would have significant effects at the local community level (e.g., preventing men and women from Hartnett's town and state from being killed and wounded, keeping workers' jobs in Palmer's town, allowing "mom and pop" radio stations where Coopman lived, and promoting fair local media coverage of GLBT people in Cagle's city). Sunwolf's case may be the most unique in that she worked with capital defense attorneys who came from afar to attend her workshops, but the goal still was to have substantial effects at the local level (the prevention of state execution).

These studies, thus, reveal that even as broader (e.g., national or global) communication activism needs to be expressed via local activism, the efficacy of local activism is linked to and animated by its engagement with broader social movements seeking to secure social and political change. For example, Jovanovic et al.'s local activism with the citizens of Greensboro to seek truth and reconciliation regarding a racial incident that occurred more than 30 years ago assumes significance given its connection to the civil rights movement and the problems that the U.S. South, in particular, has experienced with civil rights; Palmer showed how his local affinity group's activism could not have happened were it not for the group's connection to and coordination with other affinity groups fighting globalization; Hartnett illustrated how the local actions of peace groups in Champaign-Urbana, Illinois connected to the actions of an international peace movement protesting the war on Iraq, noting how seemingly local actions can have "multiplier effects" that spread through space to reach audiences never imagined by "local" activists; and McHale increased the influence of his video documentary that helped to save an innocent person on death row through his close association and interactions with activists in the antideath penalty movement in Missouri. The chapters, thus, show that communication activism truly is both local and global.

Third, communication activism necessitates citizen-scholars intervening in some way, for this type of scholarship, as explained earlier, involves first-person- rather than third-person-perspective research. The interventions may differ slightly with respect to the degree to which scholars are positioned and participate in the group, organization, or community with which they are connected (e.g., Ford serving as an actual organizational member of a sexual assault recovery services center versus Ritchie consulting for a non-profit neighborhood organization), but all the interventions that communication scholars employ revolve, of course, around some form of communication practice that they facilitate. Hence, the interventions documented in these chapters include, among many others: (a) facilitating public dialogues (Jovanovic et al.; Adams et al.); (b) crafting reports and other documents (Jovanovic et al.; Orbe; Cagle; Coopman; Walker & Curry); (c) providing training in debate and argumentation skills (Shields & Preston; Esrock et al.); (d) leading marches, vigils, protests, and rallies (Hartnett; Palmer); (e) offering workshops (Sunwolf; Campo & Frazer); (f) helping groups to meta-communicate (Palmer); (g) producing newspapers (Novek & Sanford; Christian) and video documentaries (McHale); and (h) performing (Harter et al.; Rich & Rodríguez; Walker & Curry). These interventions and the issues they address span the communication discipline from, for instance, interpersonal and group communication to organizational communication to media studies, demonstrating that all communication scholars can engage in communication activism if they choose to do so.

Fourth, these interventions are informed by and, in turn, inform theory. Wood (1996) cautioned communication scholars interested in pursuing social justice to:

> Bear in mind that passion alone is no guarantee of positive results, nor does the intent to empower oppressed peoples necessarily cohabit with genuine understanding of and respect for others and their interpretations of their lives. Such passion and intents are most effective when they are infused by theoretical understandings. (p. 165)

The chapters in these texts demonstrate how theoretical understandings infuse communication activism. Not surprisingly, given their focus on describing and explaining systems of domination and subordination and their interest in forms/practices of cultural and political resistance, critical theories shaped many of the interventions (especially those directed toward managing the media and performing social change). For example, Ritchie's organizational study relied on Habermas's critical theory, especially his concept of the "ideal speech situation" (Habermas, 1984); Novek and Sanford consulted Foucault's (1979) work on prisons; Campo and Frazer, along with Cagle, employed queer theory; and Harter et al. and Rich and Rodríguez grounded their performance-based interventions in Freire's (1970, 1994, 1997, 1998) critical pedagogy theory and Boal's (1979) application of that theory in the Theatre of the Oppressed. Many of these scholars also based their interventions on feminist theories and perspectives (Crabtree & Ford; Novek & Sanford; Campo & Frazer; Walker & Curry). These chapters extend the scholarship on critical and feminist theory in a significant manner by using these theories to inform practical interventions designed to assist marginalized individuals, groups, organizations, and communities achieve social change and social justice.

Interpretive theories also inform many of these communication activism studies. For example, Jovanovic et al. used ethics theory, Orbe linked his civil rights project to co-cultural theory, Adams et al. and Cooks and Scharrer located their studies firmly within social constructionism, Shields and Preston relied on symbolic convergence theory, Sunwolf employed dialectical theory, Esrock et al. applied rhetorical theory (on cultural topoi and defensive rhetoric) and media framing theory, and Harter et al. and Walker and Curry used narrative theory. These chapters highlight the need for communication activism research to examine the complex processes of meaning making by individuals, groups, organizations, and communities. Together with the chapters employing critical perspectives, these studies underscore that people live in both a symbolic and material world and that they are purposive social actors who define, interpret, critique, and can attempt to change oppressive structures and practices. Indeed, many, if not most, of the chapters stress the tension or clash between the construction and expression of meaning by those who are marginalized and broader hegemonic meanings produced, disseminated, and enforced by elite actors and institutions.

Mainstream social-scientific theories also inform these interventions and research projects, such as Sunwolf's use of group decision-making theory; Palmer's adoption of group consensus and group diagnostic models; the grounding of Campo and Scharrer's study in the health belief model, theory of planned behavior, and fear appeals; the incorporation of media effects theory by Cooks and Scharrer and by McHale; Coopman's review of computer-mediated communication theory and research; Herman and Ettema's application of asset-based community development theory, and Rich and Rodríguez's testing of the elaboration likelihood, affective learning, altruistic, and egoistic models. Importantly, all the studies just mentioned consciously combined critical/interpretive and social-scientific perspectives, such as Cooks and Scharrer's bridging of the gap between the two main camps in media literacy scholarship—the intervention-oriented, media effects-based approach and the cultural studies-based perspective.

Using theory to inform and make sense of communication interventions has the important consequence of contributing to those theories by testing and fleshing them out in practice. Consequently, communication activism research, as Wood (1995) contended about applied communication research, "is practicing theory and theorizing practice" (p. 157). Moreover, an important lesson learned from the theoretical pluralism and integration demonstrated within and across this set of studies is that the distinctions often drawn between the three major social-scientific paradigms—the critical, interpretive, and mainstream social-scientific paradigms—are facile when it comes to communication activism scholarship, for these paradigms can be employed individually or in combination to promote social change and social justice.

Fifth, leading directly from this last point, these studies demonstrate that virtually any research method and technique can be used to guide and document communication activism. Frey, Botan, and Kreps (2000) identified four major methods employed by communication scholars: experimental, survey, textual analysis (e.g., rhetorical criticism, content analysis, and performance studies), and naturalistic inquiry (e.g., ethnography, critical ethnography, and autoethnography). All these studies, given that they are, in one sense, case studies that employ (because they are first-person-perspective research) participant observation at the very least, could be labeled naturalistic inquiry, but some of the studies also use the other three methods, either as part of their communication interventions or to document the nature and effects of their activism: (a) experimental (Cooks & Scharrer; Rich & Rodríguez); (b) survey (Jovanovic et al.; Campo & Frazer; Christian; Cagle); and (c) textual analysis–rhetorical criticism (Jovanovic et al.; Hartnett; Esrock et al.), content analysis (Orbe; Cagle), and performance studies (Harter et al.; Rich & Rodríguez; Walker & Curry). Besides participant observation, these studies also employ numerous research techniques, including: (a) interviews, both individual (Jovanovic et al.; Orbe; Ritchie; Novek & Sanford; Christian; Cooks & Scharrer; McHale; Herman & Ettema; Harter et al.; Walker & Curry) and group (Adams et al.; Orbe; Campo & Frazer; Ritchie; McHale; Harter et al.; Walker and Curry); (b) questionnaires (Shields & Preston; Campo & Frazer; Cooks & Scharrer; Herman & Ettema; Rich & Rodríguez); and (c) document analysis (Jovanovic et al.; Orbe; Hartnett; Esrock et al.; Novek & Sanford; Cooks & Scharrer; Cagle; McHale). Three of the authors also document their intervention efforts via photography (Hartnett; Palmer; Harter et al.). Most of these studies, in fact, enlist multiple research methods and techniques as part of their communication interventions and/or to enrich the insights derived from analyzing those interventions.

The methodological pluralism demonstrated in these studies as a set, like the theoretical pluralism, deeply questions the traditional divide drawn between quantitative, rhetorical, and qualitative research by demonstrating that all the various methods and techniques available can be employed in communication activism scholarship. Moreover, by grounding interventions in and contributing back to theoretical perspectives and using research methods as part of those interventions and/or to document intervention efforts, the chapters realize the elusive goal of *praxis*—no small accomplishment.

Sixth, the *praxis* of communication activism is based, in large measure, on the creation of a trusting, collaborative partnership that produces a reflexive research process shaped by both researchers and the social actors seeking social change. Novek and Sanford, for instance, talked about how they work with the women inmates to produce the prison newspaper, negotiating the content of the paper with these women and learning from them the explicit and implicit constraints of prison life, with the collaborative character of this project extending, as it does in many of the chapters, to inmates' review of drafts of Novek and Sanford's scholarship. Harter et al. explained how the plays and performances that characterized their intervention were the result of collaboration with the participants and their families, and in Walker and Curry's case, they and their collaborators performed the colloquium together and cogenerated the knowledge derived from their interventions. By recognizing that marginalized individuals and groups are purposive social actors and involving them in the research process, these projects democratize research (Greenwood & Levin, 2000) and, thereby, deconstruct the traditional divide drawn between researchers and the impoverished and patronizing view of people as "research subjects." Communication activism scholarship, as Frey (1998b) noted about social justice scholarship, is grounded in "researchers' involvement in the life of 'another,' as opposed to studying 'an other'" (p. 162).

Seventh, we would be remiss if we did not point out that attempting to enact these and other principles of communication activism scholarship presents significant challenges. Some of these challenges are experienced in other forms of communication scholarship (e.g., gaining access to community groups, obtaining informed consent, and collecting data), but many of them spring from the unique nature of communication activism scholarship. Cagle and Coopman, for instance, talked about conflicts that can exist between activists and scholars because of their different backgrounds, needs, interests, and agendas, and Crabtree and Ford, as well as Ritchie, noted significant tensions associated with being both an activist and a consultant. Novek and Sanford discussed how they must negotiate the fine balance between challenging prison authorities and working with them to have continued access to the prison. Esrock et al. stressed tensions that exist between researchers assisting people and, at the same time, critically evaluating their actions, with Harter et al. underscoring the difficulty in deciding when to accept and when to challenge local customs and practices. As "outsiders-within" (Collins, 2000; see Crabtree & Ford), scholar-activists need to identify and engage with those with whom they seek meaningful social and political reforms, but identification and engagement should not blind scholar-activists to weaknesses that hinder people from securing those goals. Moreover, as Jovanovic et al. pointed out, communication activism, if it is to be successful in the long run, demands wide involvement, even by those who are against a social change project, although obtaining and maintaining their involvement is no easy matter. These and the many other challenges discussed in the chapters appear inevitable in communication activism.

Challenges also result from conducting communication activism research within the university context and academia, as well as within the communication discipline. All the scholars here are embedded within and subject to the constraints of the university context, and many of them talked about how they and others who conduct such research are affected by that context. For instance, communication activism scholarship can take a much longer period of time than some other forms of scholarship (e.g., handing out questionnaires in a large lecture class and analyzing the data), making such scholarship vulnerable to the "quantity" argument that often surfaces in tenure and promotion considerations. However, scholars also pointed out that universities can provide enormous resources for communication activism (such as the video equipment and facilities that McHale used), and, in some cases, communication activism resonates with the mission of a university and can bring much prestige to that university and those who conduct such research (such as at the Jesuit university where Crabtree teaches).

There are, unfortunately, those in the academy who argue against the engaged scholarship reflected in communication activism. Fish (2004), for example, on leaving his position as Dean of the College of Liberal Arts and Sciences at the University of Illinois at Chicago, offered the following advice to academics in an op-ed piece titled, "Why We Built the Ivory Tower," published in *The New York Times*:

> Don't confuse your academic obligations with the obligation to save the world; that's not your job as an academic. . . . In short, don't cross the boundary between academic work and partisan advocacy, whether the advocacy is yours or someone else's.
>
> Marx famously said that our job is not to interpret the world, but to change it. In the academy, however, it is exactly the reverse: our job is not to change the world, but to interpret it. (p. A23)

Although the communication discipline probably is one of the better disciplines with respect to supporting communication activism scholarship (having long ago dismissed the "debate" about quantitative versus qualitative research and recognizing the centrality of applied communication scholarship, including the articulation of a social justice communication approach), some members of the discipline do share the anti-activism position preached by Fish (2004). Kuypers (2000), for instance, asked the question, "Must we all be political activists?" and then answered it by arguing that "the leaders of our discipline have gone too far in their attempt to foster social change, both within the discipline and society" and suggesting that "if critics in our discipline wish to engage in such [political partisanship] they should leave the academy. . . . We should be professors, not social activists" ("Conclusion," ¶ 1, 16).

We certainly are not suggesting that all communication scholars should engage in communication activism. We do, however, advocate creating a space for activism in communication scholarship, contest the notion that communication scholars can remain politically neutral in what they study (and how they study and report it), and call on communication scholars to own their choices and be explicit about whose interests they privilege.

Finally, despite the pragmatic and systemic challenges involved, this scholarship can have tremendously important effects. Among the many effects documented in the chapters, communities talked, many for the first time, about the significant problems they faced (Jovanovic et al.; Adams et al.), and they now have an instrument to assess the state of their civil rights health (Orbe); inner-city youth who participated in the urban debate leagues went on to college (Shield & Preston); nonprofit organizations dealing with sexual assault and domestic violence and a neighborhood center now are more stable (Crabtree & Ford; Ritchie; Walker & Curry); women who partner with women have a healthcare center that is more receptive to their needs (Campo & Frazer); women prisoners (Novek & Sanford) and high school students (Christian) learned journalistic skills and practices; 6th-grade children became more critical viewers of the daily mediated violence to which they are exposed (Cooks & Scharrer); fairer media coverage of gay, lesbian, bisexual, and transgendered people was obtained (Cagle); low-power FM radio now is legal (Coopman); needed social capital was created in a lower income community (Herman & Ettema); women were able to perform with men in India to express their outrage with dowry (Harter et al.); college students learned how to respond more appropriately to women who have been sexually assaulted (Rich & Rodríguez); and, in perhaps the most dramatic example of all, an innocent man was saved from being executed because of McHale's documentary and, hopefully, other people will be spared that fate as a result of Sunwolf's workshops.

Communication activism also has important implications for a person's scholarship and teaching. Many of the authors talked about how their activism deepened their understanding of the research topic studied, the theories on which they relied, and the research methods they employed, and how their research inspired them to continue wanting to engage in scholarship that promotes social change and social justice. In six of the cases (Jovanovic; Crabtree; Ritchie; Christian; Cooks & Scharrer; Herman & Ettema), the research projects stemmed from teaching a service-learning course (with Jovanovic and Crabtree each teaching a course titled "Communication and Social Change") and/or working with graduate students (including involving them as coauthors in Jovanovic's case), and the activism by Coopman and by Walker and Curry resulted from being communication graduate students. Although scholars have raised important questions and critiques of service learning, they also agree that service learning can be an important vehicle for promoting social change and social justice (see, e.g., Artz, 2001; Christian, this volume; Crabtree, 1998; Novek, 1999). Most importantly, many of the scholars talked about how their communication activism influenced their teaching, providing them, for instance, with real-life examples to use in their classes and ultimately making them better teachers.

Communication activism, however, is not done simply to achieve the end products, for in many cases, the particular changes being advocated may take a long time to occur (the "power of delayed impact," as Hartnett called it) or they may never occur at all. Hartnett has not stopped the war on Iraq; Palmer has not prevented globalization; Esrock et al. have not been successful getting the Kentucky legislature to discuss an increase in the cigarette excise tax, let alone approve one; and Sunwolf, as an itinerate activist, typically does not know the results of her activism. Scholars engaging in communication activism, thus, have to manage the tensions between processes and outcomes, learning, among many other things, to be patient, sustain passion in the face of significant opposition, tolerate imperfect planning and execution, operate within contextual constraints, develop contingency plans, and cope with unsuccessful interventions. Hopefully, the expertise of communication scholar-activists in being able to talk about such issues will help to manage the inevitable tensions and challenges they will experience.

CONCLUSION

Communication activism is a significant form of communication scholarship that can be engaged in by scholars from across the communication discipline using a wide range of interventions, theories, and methods to promote social change and social justice for marginalized and underresourced individuals, groups, organizations, and communities. In the final analysis, although there are many potential rewards, scholars engage in communication activism because they are engaged citizens, using their knowledge and expertise to promote social change and social justice. They do it because, on so many levels, communication activism is the right thing to do.

REFERENCES

Adelman, M. B., & Frey, L. R. (1997). *The fragile community: Living together with AIDS*. Mahwah, NJ: Erlbaum.

Adelman, M. B., & Frey, L. R. (2001). Untold tales from the field: Living the autoethnographic life in an AIDS residence. In S. L. Herndon & G. L. Kreps (Eds.), *Qualitative research: Applications in organizational life* (2nd ed., pp. 205-226). Cresskill, NJ: Hampton Press.

Alasuutari, P. (Ed.). (1999). *Rethinking the media audience: The new agenda*. Thousand Oaks, CA: Sage.

Alderton, S. M. (1983). Survey course in organizational communication consulting: A processual model. *Communication Education, 32*, 413-420.

Alexander, B. (2005). Performance ethnography: The reenacting and inciting of culture. In N. K. Denzin & Y. S. Lincoln (Eds.), *Handbook of qualitative research* (3rd ed., pp. 411-442). Thousand Oaks, CA: Sage.

Alleyne, B. W. (2002). *Radicals against race: Black activism and cultural politics*. New York: Berg.

Andersen, P. A. (1993). Beyond criticism: The activist turn in the ideological debate. *Western Journal of Communication, 57*, 247-256.

Anderson, C. W. (1993). *Prescribing the life of the mind: An essay on the purpose of the university, the aims of liberal education, the competence of citizens, and the cultivation of practical reason*. Madison: University of Wisconsin Press.

Anderson, R., Cissna, K. N., & Arnett, R. A. (Eds.). (1994). *The reach of dialogue: Confirmation, voice, and community*. Cresskill, NJ: Hampton Press.

Anderson, R., Cissna, K. N., & Clune, M. K. (2003). The rhetoric of public dialogue. *Communication Research Trends, 22*, 1-34.

Andrews, J. R. (1969). Confrontation at Columbia: A case study in coercive rhetoric. *Quarterly Journal of Speech, 55*, 9-16.

Anyaegbunam, C., Karnell, A. P., Cheah, W. H., & Youngblood, J. D. (2005). Designing communication research for empowering marginalized populations: A participatory method. In S. H. Priest (Ed.), *Communication impact: Designing research that matters* (pp. 49-65). Lanham, MD: Rowman & Littefield.

Applegate, J. L. (2001, September). Engaged graduate education: Skating to where the puck will be. *Spectra*, pp. 2-5.

Applegate, J. L. (2002). Skating to where the puck will be: Engaged research as a funding activity. *Journal of Applied Communication Research, 30*, 402-410.

Arnett, R. C. (2001). Dialogic civility as pragmatic ethical praxis: An interpersonal metaphor for the public domain. *Communication Theory, 11*, 315-338.

Artz, L. (1998). African-Americans and higher education: An exigence in need of applied communication. *Journal of Applied Communication Research, 26*, 210-231.

Artz, L. (2001). Critical ethnography for communication studies: Dialogue and social justice in service-learning. *Southern Communication Journal, 66*, 239-250.

Artz, L., & Murphy, B. O. (2000). *Cultural hegemony in the United States*. Thousand Oaks, CA: Sage.

Asen, R. (2004). A discourse theory of citizenship. *Quarterly Journal of Speech, 90,* 189-211.

Asen, R. (2005). Why deliberative democracy? *Argumentation & Advocacy, 42,* 48-49.

Ashley, L., & Olson, B. (1998). Constructing reality: Print media's framing of the women's movement. *Journalism & Mass Communication Quarterly, 75,* 263-277.

Atkinson, J., & Dougherty, D. S. (2006). Alternative media and social justice movements: The development of a resistance performance paradigm of audience analysis. *Western Journal of Communication, 70,* 64-88.

Auer, J. J. (1939). Tools of social inquiry: Argumentation, discussion and debate. *Quarterly Journal of Speech, 25,* 533-539.

Avakian, M. (2000). *Reformers: Activists, educators, religious leaders.* Austin, TX: Raintree Steck-Vaughn.

Bagdikian, B. H. (2004). *The new media monopoly.* Boston: Beacon Press.

Baird, A. C. (1927). *Public discussion and debate.* Boston: Guinn.

Baird, J. E. (1970). The rhetoric of youth in controversy against the religious establishment. *Western Speech, 34,* 53-61.

Barber, B. R. (1992). *An aristocracy of everyone: The politics of education and the future of America.* New York: Ballantine Books.

Barge, J. K. (2001). Practical theory as mapping, engaged reflection, and transformative practice. *Communication Theory, 11,* 5-13.

Barge, J. K. (2002). Enlarging the meaning of group deliberation: From discussion to dialogue. In L. R. Frey (Ed.), *New directions in group communication* (pp. 159-177). Thousand Oaks, CA: Sage.

Barge, J. K., & Craig, R. T. (in press). Practical theory. In L. R. Frey & K. N. Cissna (Eds.), *Handbook of applied communication.* Mahwah, NJ: Erlbaum.

Barker-Plummer, B. (1995). News as a political resource: Media strategies and political identity in the U.S. women's movement, 1966-1975. *Critical Studies in Mass Communication, 12,* 306-324.

Barndt, D. (Ed.). (2006). *Wild fire: Art as activism.* Toronto, Canada: Sumach Press.

Bass, R. (1999). *Brown dog of the Yaak: Essays on art and activism.* Minneapolis, MN: Milkweed.

Baumgadner, J., & Richards, A. (2005). *Grassroots: A field guide for feminist activism.* New York: Farrar, Strauss and Giroux.

Becker, S. L. (1995). Response to Conquergood: Don Quixotes in the academy — Are we tilting at windmills? In K. N. Cissna (Ed.), *Applied communication in the 21st century* (pp. 1-19). Mahwah, NJ: Erlbaum.

Beer, M., & Eisenstat, R. A. (1996). Developing an organization capable of strategy implementation and learning. *Human Relations, 49,* 597-619.

Beer, M., & Eisenstat, R. A. (2000). The silent killers of strategy implementation and learning. *Sloan Management Review, 41,* 29-40.

Beer, M., Eisenstat, R. A., & Spector, B. (1990). *The critical path to corporate renewal.* Boston: Harvard Business School Press.

Beers, D. L. (2006). *For the prevention of cruelty: The history and legacy of animal rights activism in the United States.* Athens: Swallow Press/Ohio University Press.

Bennett, W. L. (2003). Communicating global activism: Strengths and vulnerabilities of networked politics. *Information, Communication & Society, 6*, 143-168.

Benson, T. W., & Johnson, B. (1968). The rhetoric of resistance: Confrontation with the warmakers, Washington, D.C., October, 1967. *Today's Speech, 16*(3), 35-42.

Benson, T. W., & Pearce, W. B. (Eds.). (1977). Alternative theoretical bases for the study of human communication: A symposium [Special issue]. *Communication Quarterly, 25*(1).

Bharucha, R. (1998). *In the name of the secular: Contemporary cultural activism in India.* New York: Oxford University Press.

Billingham, P. (Ed.). (2005). *Radical initiatives in interventionist and community drama.* Portland, OR: Intellect.

Boal, A. (1979). *Theatre of the oppressed* (A. Charles & M. O. Leal-McBride, Trans.). New York: Urizen Books.

Boal, A. (1995). *Rainbow of desire: The Boal method of theater and therapy* (A. Jackson, Trans.). New York: Routledge.

Bowen, H. W. (1963a). Does non-violence persuade? *Today's Speech, 11*(1), 10-11.

Bowen, H. W. (1963b). The future of non-violence. *Today's Speech, 11*(3), 3-4.

Bowen, H. W. (1967). A realistic view of non-violent assumptions. *Today's Speech, 15*(3), 9-10.

Boyer, E. L. (1987). *Scholarship reconsidered: Priorities of the professorate.* Princeton, NJ: Carnegie Foundation for the Advancement of Teaching.

Brashers, D. E., Haas, S.M., Klingle, R.S., & Neidig, J.L. (2000). Collective AIDS activism and individuals' perceived self-advocacy in physician-patient communication. *Human Communication Research, 26*, 372-402.

Brashers, D. E., Haas, S. M., & Neidig, J. L. (1999). The patient self-advocacy scale: Measuring patient involvement in health care decision-making interactions. *Health Communication, 11*, 97-121.

Brashers, D. E., Haas, S. M., Neidig, J. L., & Rintamaki, L. S. (2002). Social activism, self-advocacy, and coping with HIV illness. *Journal of Social and Personal Relationships, 19*, 113-133.

Brashers, D. E., & Jackson, S. (1991). "Politically-savvy sick people": Public penetration of the technical sphere. In D. W. Parson (Ed.), *Argument in controversy: Proceedings of the Seventh Speech Communication Association/American Forensics Association Conference on Argumentation* (pp. 284-288). Annandale, VA: Speech Communication Association.

Brouwer, D. (1998). The precarious visibility politics of self-stigmatization: The case of HIV/AIDS tattoos. *Text and Performance Quarterly, 18*, 114-137.

Brouwer, D. (2001). ACT-ing UP in Congressional hearings. In R. Asen & D. C. Brouwer (Eds.), *Counterpublics and the state* (pp. 87-109). Albany: State University of New York Press.

Browning, L. D. (1982). The ethics of intervention: A communication consultant's apology. *Journal of Applied Communication Research, 10*, 101-116.

Browning, L. D., & Hawes, L. C. (1991). Style, process, surface, context: Consulting as postmodern art. *Journal of Applied Communication Research, 19*, 32-54.

Broyles-González, Y. (1994). *El teatro campesino: Theater in the Chicano movement.* Austin: University of Texas Press.

Bugajski, J., & Pollack, M. (1989). *East European fault lines: Dissent, opposition, and social activism.* Boulder, CO: Westview Press.

Bullert, B. J. (2000). Progressive public relations, sweatshops, and the net. *Political Communication, 17*, 403-407.

Burkhalter, S., Gastil, J., & Kelshaw, T. (2002). A conceptual definition and theoretical model of public deliberation in small face-to-face groups. *Communication Theory, 12*, 398-422.

Butler, J. E. (2000). Democracy, diversity, and civic engagement. *Academe, 86*(4), 52-55.

Capo, K. E. (1983). From academic to social-political uses of performance. In D. W. Thompson (Ed.), *Performance of literature in historical perspectives* (pp. 437-457). Lanham, MD: University Press of America.

Carapico, S. (1998). *Civil society in Yemen: The political economy of activism in modern Arabia*. New York: Cambridge University Press.

Carbaugh, D. (1989/1990). The critical voice in ethnography of communication research. *Research on Language and Social Interaction, 23*, 261-282.

Carey, J. W. (1982). The mass media and critical theory: An American view. In M. Burgoon (Ed.), *Communication yearbook* (Vol. 6, pp. 18-33). Beverly Hills, CA: Sage.

Carey, J. W. (1983). The origins of the radical discourse on cultural studies in the United States. *Journal of Communication, 33*(3), 311-313.

Carey, J. W. (1989). *Communication as culture: Essays on media and society*. Boston: Unwin Hyman.

Carlone, D., & Taylor, B. (1998). Organizational communication and cultural studies: A review essay. *Communication Theory, 8*, 337-367.

Carragee, K. M. (1990). Interpretive media study and interpretive social science. *Critical Studies in Mass Communication, 7*, 81-96.

Carragee, K. M. (1991). News and ideology: An analysis of coverage of the West German Green Party by the *New York Times*. *Journalism Monographs, 128*, 1-30.

Carragee, K. M. (1993). A critical evaluation of the media hegemony thesis. *Western Journal of Communication, 57*, 330-348.

Carragee, K. M. (1996). Critical ethnographies and the concept of resistance. In M. Morgan & S. Leggett (Eds.), *Mainstream(s) and margins: Cultural politics in the 90s* (pp. 126-142). Westport, CT: Greenwood Press.

Carragee, K. M. (2003). Evaluating polysemy: An analysis of *The New York Times'* coverage of the end of the Cold War. *Political Communication, 20*, 287-308.

Carragee, K. M. (2005). Housing crisis: Gaining standing in a community coalition. In D. Croteau, W. Hoynes, & C. Ryan (Eds.), *Rhyming hope and history: Activists, academics, and social movement scholarship* (pp. 79-96). Minneapolis: University of Minnesota Press.

Carragee, K. M., & Roefs, W. (2004). The neglect of power in recent framing research. *Journal of Communication, 54*, 214-233.

Carroll, W. K., & Hackett, R. A. (2006). Democratic media activism through the lens of social movement theory. *Media, Culture & Society, 28*, 83-104.

Carter, K., & Spitzack, C. (Eds.). (1989). *Doing research on women's communication: Perspectives on theory and method*. Norwood, NJ: Ablex.

Caster, P. (2004). Staging prisons: Performance, activism, and social bodies. *TDR: The Drama Review, 48*, 107-116.

Chan, A. (1985). *Children of Mao: Personality development and political activism in the Red Guard generation.* Seattle: University of Washington Press.

Charland, M. (1991). Finding a horizon and telos: The challenge to critical rhetoric. *Quarterly Journal of Speech, 77,* 71-74.

Checkoway, B. (2001). Renewing the civic mission of the American research university. *Journal of Higher Education, 72,* 125-147.

Cheney, G. (1995). Democracy in the workplace: Theory and practice from the perspective of communication. *Journal of Applied Communication Research, 23,* 167-200.

Cheney, G., Wilhelmsson, M., & Zorn, T., Jr. (2002). 10 strategies for engaged scholarship. *Management Communication Quarterly, 16,* 92-100.

Christiansen, A. E., & Hanson, J. J. (1996). Comedy as cure for tragedy: ACT UP and the rhetoric of AIDS. *Quarterly Journal of Speech, 82,* 157-170.

Chvasta, M. (2006). Anger, irony, and protest: Confronting the issues of efficacy, again. *Text and Performance Quarterly, 26,* 5-16.

Cissna, K. N. (1982). Editor's note: What is applied communication research? *Journal of Applied Communication Research, 10,* i-iii.

Cissna, K. N., Eadie, W. F., & Hickson, M., III. (in press). The development of applied communication research. In L. R. Frey & K. N. Cissna (Eds.), *Handbook of applied communication.* Mahwah, NJ: Erlbaum.

Clark, N. (1996). The critical servant: An Isocratean contribution to critical rhetoric. *Quarterly Journal of Speech, 82,* 111-124.

Clark, W. (2000). *Activism in the public sphere: Exploring the discourse of political participation.* Burlington, VT: Ashgate.

Clift, E., & Freimuth, V. (1997). Changing women's lives: A communication perspective on participatory qualitative research techniques for gender equality. *Journal of Gender Studies, 6,* 289-296.

Cloud, D. L. (1994). The materiality of discourse as oxymoron: A challenge to critical rhetoric. *Western Journal of Communication, 58,* 141-163.

Cohen-Cruz, J. (Ed.). (1998). *Radical street performance: An international anthology.* New York: Routledge.

Cohen-Cruz, J. (2006). The problem democracy is supposed to solve: The politics of community-based performance. In D. S. Madison & J. Hamera (Eds.), *The Sage handbook of performance studies* (pp. 427-445). Thousand Oaks, CA: Sage.

Collins, P. H. (2000). *Black feminist thought: Knowledge, consciousness, and the politics of empowerment* (rev. ed.). New York: Routledge.

Condit, C. M. (1988). What makes our scholarship feminist? A radical/liberal view. *Women's Studies in Communication, 11*(1), 6-8.

Condit, C. M. (1993). The critic as empath: Moving away from totalizing theory. *Western Journal of Communication, 57,* 178-190.

Conquergood, D. (1985). Performing as a moral act: Ethical dimensions of the ethnography of performance. *Literature in Performance, 5*(2), 1-13.

Conquergood, D. (1988). Health theatre in a Hmong refugee camp: Performance, communication, and culture. *TDR: The Drama Review, 32,* 174-208.

Conquergood, D. (1991a). "For the nation!": How street gangs problematize patriotism. In R. Troester (Ed.), *Peacemaking through communication* (pp. 8-21). Annandale, VA: Speech Communication Association.

Conquergood, D. (1991b). Rethinking ethnography: Towards a critical cultural politics. *Communication Monographs, 58,* 179-194.

Conquergood, D. (1992a). Life in Big Red: Struggles and accommodations in a Chicago polyethnic tenement. In L. Lamphere (Ed.), *Structuring diversity: Ethnographic perspectives on the new immigration* (pp. 95-144). Chicago: University of Chicago Press.

Conquergood, D. (1992b). Performance theory, Hmong shamans, and cultural politics. In J. G. Reinelt & J. R. Roach (Eds.), *Critical theory and performance* (pp. 41-64). Ann Arbor: University of Michigan Press.

Conquergood, D. (1994). Homeboys and hoods: Gang communication and cultural space. In L. R. Frey (Ed.), *Group communication in context: Studies of natural groups* (pp. 23-55). Hillsdale, NJ: Erlbaum.

Conquergood, D. (1995). Between rigor and relevance: Rethinking applied communication. In K. N. Cissna (Ed.), *Applied communication for the 21st century* (pp. 79-96). Mahwah, NJ: Erlbaum.

Conquergood, D. (1998). Beyond the text: Toward a performative cultural politics. In S. Dailey (Ed.), *The future of performance studies: Visions and revisions* (pp. 25-36). Annandale, VA: National Communication Association.

Conquergood, D. (2002a). Lethal theatre: Performance, punishment, and the death penalty. *Theatre Journal, 54,* 339-367.

Conquergood, D. (2002b). Performance studies: Interventions and radical research. *TDR: The Drama Review, 46,* 145-156.

Conquergood, D. (Producer), & Siegel, T. (Producer & Director). (1985). *Between two worlds: The Hmong shaman in America* [Videotape]. (Available from Filmmakers Library, 124 E. 40th Street, New York, NY 10016)

Conquergood, D. (Producer), & Siegel, T. (Producer & Director). (1990). *The heart broken in half* [Videotape]. (Available from Filmmakers Library, 124 East 40th Street, New York, NY 10016)

Coopman, T. M. (2000). High speed access: Micro radio, action, and activism on the internet. *American Communication Journal, 3*(3). Retrieved May 15, 2006, from http://www.acjournal.org/holdings/vol3/Iss3/rogue4/highspeed.html

Costello, P. J. M. (2003). *Action research.* New York: Continuum.

Crabtree, R. D. (1998). Mutual empowerment in cross-cultural participatory development and service learning: Lessons in communication and social justice from projects in El Salvador and Nicaragua. *Journal of Applied Communication Research, 26,* 182-209.

Craig, R. T. (1989). Communication as a practical discipline. In B. Dervin, L. Grossberg, B. J. O'Keefe, & E. Wartella (Eds.), *Rethinking communication: Vol. 1. Paradigm issues* (pp. 97-122). Newbury Park, CA: Sage.

Craig, R. T. (1995). Applied communication research in a practical discipline. In K. N. Cissna (Ed.), *Applied communication in the 21st century* (pp. 147-155). Mahwah, NJ: Erlbaum.

Craig, R. T., & Tracy, K. (1995). Grounded practical theory: The case of intellectual discussion. *Communication Theory, 5,* 248-272.

Cronin, M., & Hall, P. (1990). A survey of employment opportunities for graduates with a master's in corporate and professional communication: A case study. *Journal of the Association for Communication Administration, 73,* 23-28.

Cronkhite, G. L. (1969). Out of the ivory tower: A proposal for useful research in communication and decision. In R. J. Kibler & L. L. Barker (Eds.), *Conceptual frontiers in speech-communication: Report of the New Orleans Conference on Research and Instructional Development* (pp. 113-135). New York: Speech Association of America.

Cronkhite, G., & Liska, J. (Eds.). (1977). Symposium: What criteria should be used to judge the admissibility of evidence to support theoretical propositions in communication research? [Special issue]. *Western Journal of Speech Communication, 41*(1).

Cushman, D. P. (1989/1990). The role of critique in the ethnographic study of human communication practices. *Research on Language and Social Interaction, 23*, 243-250.

Dallimore, E. J., & Souza, T. J. (2002). Consulting course design: Theoretical framework and pedagogical strategies. *Business Communication Quarterly, 65*(4), 86-113.

Davis, B. D., & Krapels, R. H. (1999). Applied communication consulting. *Business Communication Quarterly, 62*(3), 96-100.

Davis, W. H. (1915). Debating as related to non-academic life. *Quarterly Journal of Public Speaking, 1*, 105-113.

Dawson, J. I. (1996). *Eco-nationalism: Anti-nuclear activism and national identity in Russia, Lithuania, and Ukraine.* Durham, NC: Duke University Press.

Death Penalty Information Center. (2006). *Innocence: List of those freed from death row.* Retrieved May 15, 2006, from http://www.deathpenaltyinfo.org/article.php?scid=6&did=412

Debs, E. V. (1918). Debs's Canton speech. In E. V. Debs, *The Debs white book* (pp. 3-36). Girard, KS: Appeal to Reason.

Deetz, S. (1982). Critical-interpretive research in organizational communication. *Western Journal of Speech Communication, 46*, 131-149.

Deetz, S. (1988). Cultural studies: Studying meaning and action in organizations. In J. A. Anderson (Ed.), *Communication yearbook* (Vol. 11, pp. 335-345). Thousand Oaks, CA: Sage.

Deetz, S. A. (1992). *Democracy in an age of corporate colonization: Developments in communication and the politics of everyday life.* Albany: State University of New York Press.

Deetz, S., & Mumby, D. (1990). Power, discourse, and the workplace: Reclaiming the critical tradition in communication studies in organizations. In J. A. Anderson (Ed.), *Communication yearbook* (Vol. 13, pp. 18-47). Thousand Oaks, CA: Sage.

de Jong, W., Shaw, M., & Stammers, N. (2005). *Global activism, global media.* Ann Arbor, MI: Pluto Press.

DeLeon, D. (Ed.). (1994). *Leaders from the 1960s: A biographic sourcebook of American activism.* Westport, CT: Greenwood Press.

Delia, J. G. (1987). Communication research: A history. In C. R. Berger & S. H. Chaffee (Eds.), *Handbook of communication science* (pp. 20-98). Newbury Park, CA: Sage.

DeLuca, K. M. (1999). *Image politics: The new rhetoric of environmental activism.* New York: Guilford Press.

DeLuca, K. M., & Peeples, J. (2002). From public sphere to public screen: Democracy, activism, and the "violence" of Seattle. *Critical Studies in Media Communication, 19*, 125-151.

Denzin, N. (2003). *Performance ethnography: Critical pedagogy and the politics of culture.* Thousand Oaks, CA: Sage.

Dewey, J. (1910). *How we think.* Boston: D. C. Heath.

de Witte, H. (Ed.). (2005). *Job insecurity, union involvement, and union activism.* Burlington, VT: Ashgate.

Diani, M. (2000). Social movement networks virtual and real. *Information, Communication & Society, 3*, 386-401.

Dichter, D. (2004). U.S. media activism and the search for constituency. *Media Development, 51*, 8-13.

Dijkstra, B. (2003). *American expressionism: Art and social change, 1920-1950.* New York: H. N. Abrams.

Dines, G., & Humez, J. M. (Eds.). (2002). *Gender, race, and class in media: A text-reader* (2nd ed.). Thousand Oaks, CA: Sage.

Dolan, J. (2001a). *Geographies of learning: Theatre and practice, activism and performance.* Middletown, CT: Wesleyan University Press.

Dolan, J. (2001b). Rehearsing democracy: Advocacy, public intellectuals, and civic engagement in theatre and performance studies. *Theatre Topics, 11*, 1-17.

Dow, B. J. (1994). AIDS, perspective by incongruity, and gay identity in Larry Kramer's "1,112 and Counting." *Communication Studies, 45*, 225-240.

Dow, B. J. (1996). *Prime-time feminism: Television, media culture, and the women's movement since 1970.* Philadelphia: University of Pennsylvania Press.

Downs, J., & Manion, J. (Eds.). (2004). *Taking back the academy!: History of activism, history as activism.* New York: Routledge.

Durham, M. G., & Kellner, D. M. (2005). *Media and cultural studies: Keyworks* (rev. ed.). Malden, MA: Blackwell.

Eadie, W. F. (1982, November). The case for applied communication research. *Spectra*, pp. 1-2.

Eadie, W. F. (1994). On having an agenda. *Journal of Applied Communication Research, 22*, 81-85.

Eisenhofer, J. W., & Barry, M. J. (2006). *Shareholder activism handbook.* New York: Aspen.

Elam, H. J. (Ed.). (2003). Theatre and activism [Special issue]. *Theatre Journal, 55*(4).

Elliott, H. S. (1927). *The why and how of group discussion.* New York: Association Press.

Ellis, D. G. (1982, March). The shame of speech communication. *Spectra*, pp. 1-2.

Ellis, D. G. (1991). The oneness of opposites: Applied communication and theory. *Journal of Applied Communication Research, 19*, 116-122.

Eno, H. L. (1920). *Activism.* Princeton: NJ: Princeton University Press.

Entman, R. M. (1989). *Democracy without citizens: Media and the decay of American politics.* New York: Oxford University Press.

Entman, R. M., & Rojecki, A. (1993). Freezing out the public: Elite and media framing of the US anti-nuclear movement. *Political Communication, 10*, 155-173.

Fabj, V., & Sobnowsky, M. J. (1993). Responses from the street: ACT UP and community organizing against AIDS. In S. C. Ratzan (Ed.), *AIDS: Effective health communication for the 90s* (pp. 91-109). Washington, DC: Taylor & Francis.

Fabj, V., & Sobnowsky, M. J. (1995). AIDS activism and the rejuvenation of the public sphere. *Argumentation and Advocacy, 31,* 163-184.

Falconer, T. (2001). *Watchdogs and gadflies: Activism from marginal to mainstream.* Toronto, Canada: Penguin Books.

Farrell, T. B., & Aune, J. A. (1979). Critical theory and communication: A selective literature review. *Quarterly Journal of Speech, 65,* 93-107.

Felshin, N. (1995). *But is it art?: The spirit of art as activism.* Seattle, WA: Bay Press.

Fernandez, T. L. (1968). Jonathan Baldwin Turner at Illinois College: Era of protest. *Today's Speech, 16*(3), 9-14.

Ferree, M. M., & Tripp, A. M. (Eds.). (2006). *Global feminism: Transnational women's activism, organizing, and human rights.* New York: New York University Press.

Fine, M. (2006). Bearing witness: Methods for researching oppression and resistance—A textbook for critical research. *Social Justice Research, 19,* 83-108.

Fine, M. G. (1990). Epistemological and methodological commitments of a feminist perspective. *Women & Language, 13*(2), 35-36.

Fish, S. (2004, May 21). Why we built the ivory tower. *The New York Times,* p. A23.

Fisher, R. E. (1997). *The concept of judicial activism: Its nature and function in United States constitutional law.* Sherman Oaks, CA: Banner Books International.

Fleming, D. (1998). The space of argumentation: Urban design, civic discourse, and the dream of the good city. *Argumentation, 12,* 147-166.

Foley, D., & Valenzula, A. (2005). Critical ethnography: The politics of collaboration. In N. K. Denzin & Y. S. Lincoln (Eds.), *The Sage handbook of qualitative methods* (3rd ed., pp. 217-234). Thousand Oaks, CA: Sage.

Foucault, M. (1979). *Discipline and punish: The birth of the prison* (A. Sheridan, Trans.). New York: Vintage Books.

Freeman, D. E. (1986). A student communication consulting firm: An experiential education option. *Journal of the Association for Communication Administration, 48,* 72-73.

Freire, P. (1970). *Pedagogy of the oppressed* (M. B. Ramos, Trans.). New York: Herder and Herder.

Freire, P. (1994). *Pedagogy of hope: Reliving pedagogy of the oppressed* (R. R. Barr, Trans.). New York: Continuum.

Freire, P. (1997). *Pedagogy of the heart* (D. Macedo & A. Oliveira, Trans.). New York: Continuum.

Freire, P. (1998). *Pedagogy of freedom: Ethics, democracy, and civic courage* (P. Clarke, Trans). New York: Rowman & Littlefield.

Frey, L. R. (Ed.). (1995). *Innovations in group facilitation: Applications in natural settings.* Cresskill, NJ: Hampton Press.

Frey, L. R. (1996). Remembering and "re-membering": A history of theory and research on communication and group decision making. In R. Y. Hirokawa & M. S. Poole (Eds.), *Communication and group decision making* (2nd ed., pp. 19-51). Thousand Oaks, CA: Sage.

Frey, L. R. (Ed.). (1998a). Communication and social justice research [Special issue]. *Journal of Applied Communication Research, 26*(2).

Frey, L. R. (1998b). Communication and social justice research: Truth, justice, and the applied communication way. *Journal of Applied Communication Research, 26,* 155-164.

Frey, L. R. (2000). To be applied or not to be applied, that isn't even the question; but wherefore art thou, applied communication researcher? Reclaiming applied communication research and redefining the role of the researcher. *Journal of Applied Communication Research, 28,* 178-182.

Frey, L. R. (2006a). Across the great divides: From nonpartisan criticism to partisan criticism to applied communication activism for promoting social change and social justice. In O. Swartz (Ed.), *Social justice and communication scholarship* (pp. 35-51). Mahwah, NJ: Erlbaum.

Frey, L. R. (Ed.). (2006b). *Facilitating group communication in context: Innovations and applications with natural groups* (2 vols.). Cresskill, NJ: Hampton Press.

Frey, L. R., Botan, C. H., & Kreps, G. L. (2000). *Investigating communication: An introduction to research methods* (2nd ed.). Boston: Allyn and Bacon.

Frey, L. R., & Cissna, K. N. (Eds.). (in press). *Handbook of applied communication.* Mahwah, NJ: Erlbaum.

Frey, L. R., Pearce, W. B., Pollock, M. A., Artz, L., & Murphy, B. A. O. (1996). Looking for justice in all the wrong places: On a communication approach to social justice. *Communication Studies, 47,* 110-127.

Friedenberg, R. V. (1997). *Communication consultants in political campaigns: Ballot box warriors.* Westport, CT: Praeger.

Friedman, D. (1985). Workers theatre of the 1930s. In B. McConachie & D. Friedman (Eds.), *Theatre for working-class audiences: 1830-1980* (pp. 111-120). Westport, CT: Greenwood Press.

Fuoss, K. (1997). *Striking performances/performing strikes.* Jackson: University of Mississippi Press.

Gamson, W. A. (1992). *Talking politics.* New York: Cambridge University Press.

Gamson, W. A., Croteau, D., Hoynes, W., & Sasson, T. (1992). Media images and the social construction of reality. *Annual Review of Sociology, 18,* 373-393.

Gamson, W. A., & Wolfsfeld, G. (1993). Media and movements as interacting systems: *Annals of the American Academy of Political and Social Science, 528,* 114-125.

Garrett, K. R. (2006). Protest in an information society: A review of literature on social movements and new ICTs. *Information, Communication & Society, 9,* 202-224.

Gastil, J. (2004). Adult civic education through the National Issues Forums: Developing democratic habits and dispositions through public deliberation. *Adult Education Quarterly, 54,* 308-328.

Gastil, J. (2006). Communication as deliberation. In G. J. Shepherd, J. St. John, & T. Striphas (Eds.), *Communication as . . . : Perspectives on theory* (pp. 164-173). Thousand Oaks, CA: Sage.

Gastil, J., & Dillard, J. (1999). Increasing political sophistication through public deliberation. *Political Communication, 16,* 3-23.

Gastil, J., & Levine, P. (Eds.). (2005). *The deliberative democracy handbook: Strategies for effective civic engagement in the twenty-first century.* San Francisco: Jossey-Bass.

Gatenby, B., & Humphries, M. (1996). Feminist commitments in organizational communication: Participatory action research as feminist praxis. *Australian Journal of Communication, 23*(2), 73-88.

Geist-Martin, P., Ray, E. B., & Sharf, B. F. (2003). *Communicating health: Personal, cultural, and political complexities.* Belmont, CA: Thomson/Wadsworth.

Gergen, K. J. (2000). *Invitation to social construction*. Thousand Oaks, CA: Sage.

Gibson, D. (2003). Use of the staged event in successful community activism. *Public Relations Quarterly, 48*(1), 35-40.

Gibson, T. A. (2000). Beyond cultural populism: Notes toward the critical ethnography of media audiences. *Journal of Communication Inquiry, 24,* 253-274.

Gieselman, R. D., & Philpott, J. (1969). Business communication consulting: A survey of faculty practices. *Journal of Business Communication, 7*(1), 15-22.

Gillett, J. (2003). The challenges of institutionalization for AIDS media activism. *Media, Culture & Society, 25,* 607-624.

Ginwright, S., Noguera, P., & Cammarota, J. (Eds.). (2006). *Beyond resistance! Youth activism and community change: New democratic possibilities for practice and policy for America's youth*. New York: Routledge.

Gitlin, T. (1980). *The whole world is watching: Mass media in the making and unmaking of the New Left*. Berkeley: University of California Press.

Glassberg, D. (1990). *American historical pageantry: The uses of tradition in the early twentieth century*. Chapel Hill: University of North Carolina Press.

Goldberg, A. (1983). Resolved: That paid consulting is contrary to the best interests of academia: The affirmative. *Journal of the Association for Communication Administration, 44,* 14-16.

Gómez-Peña, G. (2005). *Ethno-techno: Writing on performance, activism, and pedagogy* (E. Peña, Ed.). New York: Routledge.

Goodall, H. L., Jr. (1989). On becoming an organizational detective: The role of context sensitivity and intuitive logics in communication consulting. *Southern Communication Journal, 55,* 42-54.

Grano, D. A. (2002). Spiritual-material identification in the deep ecology movement. *Southern Communication Journal, 68,* 27-39.

Greenberg, J., & Knight, G. (2004). Framing sweatshops: Nike, global production, and the American news media. *Communication & Critical/Cultural Studies, 1,* 151-175.

Greenwood, D. J., & Levin, M. (2000). Introduction to action research: Social research for social change. In N. K. Denzin & Y. S. Lincoln (Eds.), *Handbook of qualitative research* (2nd ed., pp. 85-106). Thousand Oaks, CA: Sage.

Gregg, R. B. (1971). The ego-function of the rhetoric of protest. *Philosophy and Rhetoric, 4,* 71-91.

Grossberg, L. (1993a). Can cultural studies find true happiness in communication? *Journal of Communication, 43,* 89-97.

Grossberg, L. (1993b). Cultural studies and/in new worlds. *Critical Studies in Mass Communication, 10,* 1-22.

Grossberg, L. (1997). *Bringing it all back home: Essays on cultural studies*. Durham, NC: Duke University Press.

Grossberg, L., Nelson, C., & Treichler, P. A. (Eds.). (1992). *Cultural studies*. New York: Routledge.

Grossberg, L., Wartella, E. A., Whitney, D. C., & Wise, J. M. (2005). *Mediamaking: Mass media in popular culture*. Thousand Oaks, CA: Sage.

Grund, L., Cherwitz, R., & Darwin, T. (2001, December 3). Learning to be a citizen-scholar. *Chronicle of Higher Education*. Retrieved July 6, 2006, from http://chronicle.com/jobs/news/2001/12/2001120302c/careers.html

Guither, H. D. (1998). *Animal rights: History and scope of a radical social movement*. Carbondale: Southern Illinois University Press.

Habermas, J. (1984). *The theory of communicative action: Vol. 1. Reason and the rationalization of society* (T. McCarthy, Trans.). Boston: Beacon Press.

Habermas, J. (1996). *Between facts and norms: Contributions to a discourse theory of law and democracy* (W. Rehg, Trans). Cambridge, MA: MIT Press.

Haedicke, S. C., & Nellhaus, T. (Eds.). (2001). *Performing democracy: Interactional perspectives on urban community-based performance.* Ann Arbor: University of Michigan Press.

Haiman, F. S. (1967). The rhetoric of the streets: Some legal and ethical considerations. *Quarterly Journal of Speech, 53,* 99-114.

Hall, S. (1977). Culture, media and the "ideological effect." In J. Curran, M. Gurevitch, & J. Woollacot (Eds.), *Mass communication and society* (pp. 315-348). London: Edward Arnold/Open University Press.

Hall, S. (Ed.). (1997). *Representation: Cultural representations and signifying practices.* Thousand Oaks, CA: Sage/Open University Press.

Hallin, D. (1987). Hegemony: The American news media from Vietnam to El Salvador, a study of ideological change and its limits. In D. L. Paletz (Ed.), *Political communication research: Approaches, studies, assessments* (pp. 3-25). Norwood, NJ: Ablex.

Hardt, H. (1986). Critical theory in historical perspective. *Journal of Communication, 36*(3), 144-154.

Hardt, H. (1992). *Critical communication studies: Communication, history and theory in America.* New York: Routledge.

Hardt, H. (1993). Authenticity, communication, and critical theory. *Critical Studies in Mass Communication, 10,* 49-69.

Hariman, R. (1991). Critical rhetoric and postmodern theory. *Quarterly Journal of Speech, 77,* 67-70.

Harold, C. (2004). Pranking rhetoric: "Culture jamming" as media activism. *Critical Studies in Media Communication, 21,* 189-211.

Harrison, T. M. (1982). Toward an ethical framework for communication consulting. *Journal of Applied Communication Research, 10,* 87-100.

Hartnett, S. (1998). Lincoln and Douglas meet the abolitionist David Walker as prisoners debate slavery: Empowering education, applied communication, and social justice. *Journal of Applied Communication Research, 26,* 232-253.

Hasian, M., Jr. (2001). Vernacular legal discourse: Revisiting the public acceptance of the "right to privacy" in the 1960s. *Political Communication, 18,* 89-105.

Hauser, G. A. (1998). Vernacular dialogue and the rhetoricality of public opinion. *Communication Monographs, 65,* 83-107.

Hauser, G. A. (2002). *Vernacular voices: The rhetorics of publics and public spheres.* Columbia: University of South Carolina Press.

Hauser, G. A., & Benoit-Barne, C. (2002). Reflections on rhetoric, deliberative democracy, civil society, and trust. *Rhetoric & Public Affairs, 5,* 261-275.

Hauser, G. A., & Grim, A. (Eds.). (2004). *Rhetorical democracy: Discursive practices of civic engagement.* Mahwah, NJ: Erlbaum.

Hawkesworth, M. E. (2006a). *Feminist inquiry: From political conviction to methodological innovation.* New Brunswick, NJ: Rutgers University Press.

Hawkesworth, M. E. (2006b). *Globalization and feminist activism.* Lanham, MD: Rowman & Littlefield.

Held, D. (1982). Critical theory and political transformation. *Media, Culture & Society, 4*, 153-160.

Herman, E. S., & Chomsky, N. (1988). *Manufacturing consent: The political economy of the mass media.* New York: Pantheon Books.

Hertog, J. K., & McLeod, D. M. (1995). Anarchists wreak havoc in downtown Minneapolis: A multi-level study of media coverage of radical protest. *Journalism Monographs, 151*, 1-48.

Hesse-Biber, S. N. (Ed.). (2006). *Handbook of feminist research: Theory and praxis.* Thousand Oaks, CA: Sage.

Hicks, D. (1998). Public debate and the ideal of public reason. *Southern Journal of Forensics, 2*, 350-362.

Hicks, D. (2002). The promise(s) of deliberative democracy. *Rhetoric & Public Affairs, 5*, 224-229.

Hicks, D., & Greene, R. (2000). Debating both sides: Argument pedagogy and the production of the deliberative citizen. In M. Hollihan (Ed.), *Argument at century's end: Reflecting on the past and envisioning the future* (pp. 300-308). Annandale, VA: National Communication Association.

Hicks, D., & Langsdorf, L. (1998). Proceduralist theories of public deliberation: Implications for the production of citizens. In J. Klumpp (Ed.), *Argument in a time of change: Definitions, frameworks, and critiques* (pp. 150-156). Annandale, VA: National Communication Association.

Hickson, M., III. (1973). Applied communications research: A beginning point for social relevance. *Journal of Applied Communications Research, 1*, 1-5.

Hildebrandt, H. W. (1978). Business communication consulting and research in multinational companies. *Journal of Business Communication, 15*(3), 19-26.

Hill, F. (1983). A turn against ideology: Reply to Professor Wander. *Central States Speech Journal, 34*, 121-126.

Hitchcock, D. (2002). The practice of argumentative discussion. *Argumentation, 16*, 287-299.

Holsworth, R. D. (1989). *Let your life speak: A study of politics, religion, and antinuclear weapons activism.* Madison: University of Wisconsin Press.

Horkheimer, M., & Adorno, T. W. (1972). *Dialectics of enlightenment* (J. Cumming, Trans.). New York: Herder and Herder.

Hoynes, W. (2005). Media research and media activism. In D. Croteau, W. Hoynes, & C. Ryan (Eds.), *Rhyming hope and history: Activists, academics, and social movement scholarship* (pp. 97-114). Minneapolis: University of Minnesota Press.

Hung, C-j. F. (2003). Relationship building, activism, and conflict resolution. *Asian Journal of Communication, 13*, 21-49.

Hyde, B., & Bineham, J. L. (2000). From debate to dialogue: Toward a pedagogy of nonpolarized public discourse. *Southern Communication Journal, 65*, 208-223.

Inomata, T., & Cohen, L. S. (Eds.). (2006). *Archaeology of performance: Theaters of power, community, and politics.* Lanham, MD: Altamira Press.

Iraq Coalition Casualty Count. (2006, October 3). Retrieved October 4, 2006, from http://www.icasualties.org/oif/

Ishikawa, Y. (2002). Calls for deliberative democracy in Japan. *Rhetoric & Public Affairs, 5*, 331-345.

Ivie, R. L. (1998). Democratic deliberation in a rhetorical republic. *Quarterly Journal of Speech, 84,* 491-505.

Jarboe, S. (1989). Teaching communication consulting and training (or, reminisces of a trainer). *Southern Communication Journal, 55,* 22-41.

Jarboe, S. (1992). They do it for the money (?): A response to G. M. Phillips. *Journal of Applied Communication Research, 20,* 225-233.

Jennings, J. (Ed.). (1997). *Race and politics: New challenges and responses for Black activism.* New York: Verso.

Jensen, K. B. (1990). Television futures: A social action methodology for studying interpretive communities. *Critical Studies in Mass Communication, 7,* 129-146.

Johnson, E. P. (2006). Black performance studies. In D. S. Madison & J. Hamera (Eds.), *The Sage handbook of performance studies* (pp. 446-463). Thousand Oaks, CA: Sage.

Johnson, T., Nagel, J., & Champagne, D. (Eds.). (1997). *American Indian activism: Alcatraz to the Longest Walk.* Urbana: University of Illinois Press.

Johnson, T. R. (1996). *The occupation of Alcatraz Island: Indian self-determination and the rise of Indian activism.* Urbana: University of Illinois Press.

Johnson-Cartee, K. S., & Copeland, G. A. (1997). *Inside political campaigns: Theory and practice.* Westport, CT: Praeger.

Jones, J. L. (2002a). Performance ethnography: The role of embodiment in cultural authenticity. *Theatre Topics, 12,* 1-15.

Jones, J. L. (2002b). Teaching in the borderlands. In N. Stucky & C. Wimmer (Eds.), *Teaching performance studies* (pp. 175-190). Carbondale: Southern Illinois University Press.

Jones, T. S., & Bodtker, A. (1998). A dialectical analysis of a social justice process: International collaboration in South Africa. *Journal of Applied Communication Research, 26,* 357-373.

Jørgensen, C. (1998). Public debate—An act of hostility? *Argumentation, 12,* 431-443.

Kahn, R., & Kellner, D. (2004). New media and internet activism: From the "battle of Seattle" to blogging. *New Media & Society, 6,* 87-95.

Kaplan, F. F. (Ed.). (2006). *Art therapy and social action.* Philadelphia: J. Kingsley.

Keck, M. E., & Sikkink, K. (1999). *Activists beyond borders: Advocacy networks in international politics.* Ithaca, NY: Cornell University Press.

Kellner, D. (1990). *Television and the crisis of democracy.* Boulder, CO: Westview Press.

Kellner, D. (1995). *Media culture: Cultural studies, identity, and politics between the modern and the postmodern.* New York: Routledge.

Kemmis, S., & McTaggart, R. (2005). Participatory action research: Communication action and the public sphere. In N. K. Denzin & Y. S. Lincoln (Eds.), *The Sage handbook of qualitative research* (3rd ed., pp. 559-603). Thousand Oaks, CA: Sage.

Kennedy, D. (1997). *Academic duty.* Cambridge, MA: Harvard University Press.

Kerr, H. P. (1959). The rhetoric of political protest. *Quarterly Journal of Speech, 45,* 146-152.

Kershaw, B. (1992). *The politics of performance: Radical theatre as cultural intervention.* New York: Routledge.

Kibler, R. J., & Barker, L. L. (Eds.). (1969). *Conceptual frontiers in speech-communication: Report of the New Orleans Conference on Research and Instructional Development.* New York: Speech Association of America.

Kielbowicz, R. B., & Scherer, C. (1986). The role of the press in the dynamics of social movements. In K. Lang & G. E. Lang (Eds.), *Research in social movements, conflicts and change* (Vol. 9, pp. 71-96). Greenwich, CT: JAI Press.

Kim, J., Wyatt, R. O., & Katz, E. (1999). News, talk, opinion, participation: The part played by conversation in deliberative democracy. *Political Communication, 16,* 361-385.

Klope, D. C. (1994). Creationism and the tactic of debate: A performance study of guerrilla rhetoric. *Journal of Communication & Religion, 17,* 39-51.

Knight, G., & Greenberg, J. (2002). Promotionalism and subpolitics: Nike and its labor critics. *Management Communication Quarterly, 15,* 541-570.

Korza, P., & Bacon, B. S. (Eds.). (2005). *Art, dialogue, action, activism: Case studies from animating democracy.* Washington, DC: Americans for the Arts.

Kosokoff, S., & Carlmichael, C. W. (1970). The rhetoric of protest: Song, speech, and attitude change. *Southern Speech Journal, 35,* 295-302.

Kowal, D. M. (2000). One cause, two paths: Militant vs. adjustive strategies in British American women's suffrage movements. *Communication Quarterly, 48,* 240-255.

Kreps, G. L. (1989). A therapeutic model of organizational communication consultation: Application of interpretive field methods. *Southern Communication Journal, 55,* 1-21.

Kreps, G. L., Frey, L. R., & O'Hair, D. (1991). Applied communication research: Scholarship that can make a difference. *Journal of Applied Communication Research, 19,* 71-87.

Kurpius, D. D., & Mendelson, A. (2002). A case study of deliberative democracy on television: Civic dialogue on C-SPAN call-in shows. *Journalism & Mass Communication Quarterly, 79,* 587-601.

Kuypers, J. A. (2000). Must we all be political activists? *American Communication Journal, 4*(1). Retrieved June 24, 2006, from http://acjournal.org/holdings/vol4/iss1/special/kuypers.htm

Lampert, K. (2005). *Traditions of compassion: From religious duty to social activism.* New York: Palgrave Macmillan.

Lange, J. (1984). Seeking client resistance: Rhetorical strategy in communication consulting. *Journal of Applied Communication Research, 12,* 50-62.

Lawton, W. (1968). Thoreau and the rhetoric of dissent. *Today's Speech, 16*(2), 23-25.

Lemish, D. (2002). Gender at the forefront: Feminist perspectives on action theoretical approaches in communication research. *Communications: The European Journal of Communication Research, 27,* 63-78.

Lengel, L. B. (1998). Researching the "other," transforming ourselves: Methodological considerations of feminist ethnography. *Journal of Communication Inquiry, 22,* 229-250.

Levinas, E. (1969). *Totality and infinity* (A. Lingis, Trans.). Pittsburgh, PA: Duquesne University Press. (Original work published 1961)

Levine, P., Fung, A., & Gastil, J. (2005). Future directions for public deliberation. *Journal of Public Deliberation, 1*(1), Article 3. Retrieved June 28, 2006, from http://services.bepress.com/cgi/viewcontent.cgi?article=1003&context=jpd

Lewis, J. (1999). Reproducing political hegemony in the United States. *Critical Studies in Mass Communication, 16,* 251-267.

Lewis, J. (2001). *Constructing public opinion: How political elites do what they like and why we seem to go along with it.* New York: Columbia University Press.

Leyland, W. (Ed.). (2002). *Out in the Castro: Desire, promise, activism.* San Francisco: Leyland.

Lomas, C. W. (1960). The agitator in American politics. *Western Speech, 24,* 76-83.

Lomas, C. W. (1963). Agitator in a cassock. *Western Speech, 27,* 14-26.

Lubin, D. M. (1994). *Picturing a nation: Art and social change in nineteenth-century America.* New Haven, CT: Yale University Press.

Madison, D. S. (2005a). *Critical ethnography: Method, ethics, and performance.* Thousand Oaks, CA: Sage.

Madison, D. S. (2005b). Critical ethnography as street performance: Reflections of home, race, murder, and justice. In N. K. Denzin & Y. S. Lincoln (Eds.), *The Sage handbook of qualitative research* (3rd ed., pp. 537-546). Thousand Oaks, CA: Sage.

Madison, D. S. (2006). Staging fieldwork/performing human rights. In D. S. Madison & J. Hamera (Eds.), *The Sage handbook of performance studies* (pp. 397-418). Thousand Oaks, CA: Sage.

Makau, J. M. (1996). Notes on communication education and social justice. *Communication Studies, 47,* 135-141.

March, J. G. (1991). Organizational consultants and organizational research. *Journal of Applied Communication Research, 19,* 20-31.

Markowitz, L. (2000). *Worker activism after successful union organizing.* Armonk: NY: M. E. Sharpe.

Martin, H. H. (1966). The rhetoric of academic protest. *Central States Speech Journal, 17,* 244-250.

Mattson, K. (2002). Do Americans really want deliberative democracy? *Rhetoric & Public Affairs, 5,* 327-329.

Mauch, C., Stolzfus, N., & Weiner, D. R. (Eds.). (2006). *Shades of green: Environmental activism around the globe.* Lanham, MD: Rowman & Littlefield.

McAdam, D. (1996). The framing function of movement tactics: Strategic dramaturgy in the American civil rights movement. In D. McAdam, J. D. McCarthy, & M. N. Zald (Eds.), *Comparative perspectives on social movements: Political opportunities, mobilizing structures, and cultural framings* (pp. 338-355). New York: Cambridge University Press.

McBurney, J. H., & Hance, K. G. (1939). *The principles and methods of discussion.* New York: Harper & Brothers.

McCall, M. M. (2000). Performance ethnography: A brief history and some advice. In N. K. Denzin & Y. S. Lincoln (Eds.), *Handbook of qualitative research* (2nd ed., pp. 421-433). Thousand Oaks, CA: Sage.

McCaughey, M., & Ayers, M. D. (Eds.). (2003). *Cyberactivism: Online activism in theory and practice.* New York: Routledge.

McChesney, R. W. (1999). *Rich media, poor democracy: Communication politics in dubious times.* Urbana: University of Illinois Press.

McChesney, R. W. (2004a). Media policy goes to main street: The uprising of 2003. *Communication Review, 7,* 223-258.

McChesney, R. W. (2004b). *The problem of the media: U.S. communication politics in the twenty-first century*. New York: Monthly Review Press.

McEdwards, M. G. (1968). Agitative rhetoric: Its nature and effect. *Western Speech*, *32*, 36-43.

McGee, J. J. (2003). A pilgrim's progress: Metaphor in the rhetoric of Mary Fisher, AIDS activist. *Women's Studies in Communication*, *26*, 191-213.

McGuire, M., & Slembeck, E. (1987). An emerging critical rhetoric: Hellmut Geissner's *Sprechwissenschaft*. *Quarterly Journal of Speech*, *73*, 349-358.

McHale, J. P. (2004). *Communicating for change: Strategies of social and political advocates*. Lanham, MD: Rowman & Littlefield.

McHale, J. P. (Producer/Director), Wylie, R. (Producer/Editor), & Huck, D. (Producer/Assistant Editor). (2002). *Unreasonable doubt: The Joe Amrine case* [Videotape]. (Available from Hampton Press)

McKerrow, R. E. (1989). Critical rhetoric: Theory and praxis. *Communication Monographs*, *56*, 91-111.

McKerrow, R. E. (1991). Critical rhetoric in a postmodern world. *Quarterly Journal of Speech*, *77*, 75-78.

McKerrow, R. E. (1993). Critical rhetoric and the possibility of the subject. In I. Angus & L. Langsdorf (Eds.), *The critical turn: Rhetoric and philosophy in postmodern discourse* (pp. 51-67). Carbondale: Southern Illinois University Press.

McNiff, J., & Whitehead, J. (2002). *Action research: Principles and practice* (2nd ed.). New York: RoutledgeFalmer.

McNiff, J., & Whitehead, J. (2006). *Action research: Living theory*. Thousand Oaks, CA: Sage.

Meehan, E. R, & Riordan, E. (Eds.). (2001). *Sex and money: Feminism and political economy in the media*. Minneapolis: University of Minnesota Press.

Meikle, G. (2002). *Future active: Media activism and the internet*. New York: Routledge.

Melcher, C. (1995). Non-expert expertise: Chronicling the success of AIDS and breast cancer activists. In S. A. Jackson (Ed.), *Argumentation and values: Proceedings of the Ninth Speech Communication Association/American Forensic Association Conference on Argumentation* (pp. 356-361). Annandale, VA: Speech Communication Association.

Merriam-Webster Online. (2006). *Activism*. Retrieved May 15, 2006, from http://www.m-w.com/dictionary/activism

Meyers, R. A., & Brashers, D. E. (2002). Rethinking traditional approaches to argument in groups. In L. R. Frey (Ed.), *New directions in group communication* (pp. 141-158). Thousand Oaks, CA: Sage.

Mienczakowski, J. (1995). The theatre of ethnography: The reconstruction of ethnography into theatre with emancipatory potential. *Qualitative Inquiry*, *1*, 360-375.

Miller, G. R. (1995). "I think my schizophrenia is better today," said the communication researcher unanimously: Some thoughts on the dysfunctional dichotomy between pure and applied communication research. In K. N. Cissna (Ed.), *Applied communication in the 21st century* (pp. 47-55). Mahwah, NJ: Erlbaum.

Miller, G. R., & Sunnafrank, M. J. (1984). Theoretical dimensions of applied communication research. *Quarterly Journal of Speech*, *70*, 255-263.

Monks, R. A. G. (1999). *The Emperor's nightingale: Restoring the integrity of the corporation in the age of shareholder activism.* Reading, MA: Perseus Books.

Montgomery, D., Wiseman, D. W., & DeCaro, P. (2001). Toward a code of ethics for organizational communication professionals: A working proposal. *American Communication Journal, 5*(1). Retrieved July 3, 2006, from http://acjournal.org/ holdings/vol5/iss1/special/montgomery.htm

Morley, D. (1980). *The nationwide audience.* London: British Film Institute.

Morley, D. (1992). *Television, audiences, and cultural studies.* New York: Routledge.

Mosco, V. (1996). *The political economy of communication: Rethinking and renewal.* Thousand Oaks, CA: Sage.

Muir, C. (1996). Using consulting projects to teach critical-thinking skills in business communication. *Business Communication Quarterly, 59*(4), 77-87.

Mumby, D. K. (1993). Critical organizational communication studies: The next 10 years. *Communication Monographs, 60,* 18-25.

Murphy, T. A. (2004). Deliberative civic education and civil society: A consideration of ideals and actualities in democracy and communication education. *Communication Education, 53,* 74-91.

Neal, L. (1968). The Black arts movement. *TDR: The Drama Review, 12*(4), 29-39.

Nielsen, J. M. (Ed.). (1990). *Feminist research methods: Exemplary readings in the social sciences.* Boulder, CO: Westview Press.

Noakes, J. A., & Wilkins, K. G. (2002). Shifting frames of the Palestinian movement in US news. *Media, Culture & Society, 5,* 649-671.

Novek, E. (1999). Service is a feminist issue: Transforming communication pedagogy. *Women's Studies in Communication, 22,* 230-240.

Novek, E. (2005). "The devil's bargain": Censorship, identity and the promise of empowerment in a prison newspaper. *Journalism: Theory, Practice & Criticism, 6,* 5-23.

O'Hair, D., Kreps, G. L., & Frey, L. R. (1990). Conceptual issues. In D. O'Hair & G. L. Kreps (Eds.), *Applied communication theory and research* (pp. 3-22). Hillsdale, NJ: Erlbaum.

Oleson, V. (2005). Early millennial feminist qualitative research: Challenges and contours. In N. K. Denzin & Y. S. Lincoln (Eds.), *The Sage handbook of qualitative methods* (3rd ed., pp. 235-278). Thousand Oaks, CA: Sage.

Oliver, P. E., & Myers, D. J. (1999). How events enter the public sphere: Conflict, location, and sponsorship in local newspaper coverage of public events. *American Journal of Sociology, 105,* 38-87.

Olomo, O. O. O. (2006). Performance and ethnography, performing ethnography, performance ethnography. In D. S. Madison & J. Hamera (Eds.), *The Sage handbook of performance studies* (pp. 339-345). Thousand Oaks, CA: Sage.

Olson, K. M., & Olson, C. D. (2003). Problems of exclusionary research criteria: The case against the "usable knowledge" litmus test for social justice communication research. *Communication Studies, 54,* 438-450.

Online Etymology Dictionary. (2006). *Theory.* Retrieved May 15, 2006, from http://www.etymonline.com/index.php?term=theory

Ono, K. A., & Sloop, J. M. (1992). Commitment to "telos"—A sustained critical rhetoric. *Communication Monographs, 59,* 48-60.

Palczewski, H. (2001). Cyber-movements, new social movements, and counter-publics. In R. Asen & D. C. Brouwer (Eds.), *Counterpublics and the state* (pp. 161-186). Albany: State University of New York Press.

Palmeri, T. (2006). Media activism in a "conservative" city: Modeling citizenship. In O. Swartz (Ed.), *Social justice and communication scholarship* (pp. 149-173). Mahwah, NJ: Erlbaum.

Park-Fuller, L. (2003). Audiencing the audience: Playback Theatre, performative writing, and social activism. *Text and Performance Quarterly, 23,* 288-310.

Pearce, K. A., & Pearce, W. B. (2001). The Public Dialogue Consortium's school-wide dialogue process: A communication approach to develop citizenship skills and enhance school climate. *Communication Theory, 11,* 105-123.

Pearce, K. A., Spano, S., & Pearce, W. B. (in press). The multiple faces of the Public Dialogue Consortium: Scholars, practitioners, and dreamers of better social worlds. In L. R. Frey & K. N. Cissna (Eds.), *Handbook of applied communication.* Mahwah, NJ: Erlbaum.

Pearce, W. B. (1998). On putting social justice in the discipline of communication and putting enriched concepts of communication in social justice research and practice. *Journal of Applied Communication Research, 26,* 272-278.

Pearce, W. B., & Pearce, K. A. (2000a). Combining passions and abilities: Toward dialogic virtuosity. *Southern Communication Journal, 65,* 161-175.

Pearce, W. B., & Pearce, K. A. (2000b). Extending the theory of the coordinated management of meaning (CMM) through a community dialogue process. *Communication Theory, 10,* 405-423.

Peeples, J. A. (2003). Trashing South-Central: Place and identity in a community-level environmental justice dispute. *Southern Communication Journal, 69,* 82-95.

Pestello, F. G., Saxton, S. L., Miller, D. E., & Donnelly, P. G. (1996). Community and the practice of sociology. *Teaching Sociology, 24,* 148-156.

Peterson, K. (2006, August 3). *Wash., New York say no to gay marriage.* Retrieved August 22, 2006, from http://www.stateline.org/live/ViewPage.action?site NodeId=136&languageId=1&contentId=20695

Pezzullo, P. C. (2001). Performing critical interruptions: Stories, rhetorical invention, and the environmental justice movement. *Western Journal of Communication, 65,* 1-25.

Pezzullo, P. C. (2003). Resisting "National Breast Cancer Awareness Month": The rhetoric of counterpublics and their cultural performances. *Quarterly Journal of Speech, 89,* 345-365.

Phillips, G. M. (1992). They do it for the money. *Journal of Applied Communication Research, 20,* 219-224.

Pickerill, J. (2003). *Cyberprotest: Environmental activism online.* New York: Manchester University Press.

Pilotta, J. J., McCaughan, J. A., Jasko, S., Murphy, J., Jones, T., Wilson, L. et al. (2001). *Communication and social action research.* Cresskill, NJ: Hampton Press.

Pingree, R. J. (2006). Decision structure and the problem of scale in deliberation. *Communication Theory, 16,* 198-222.

Pini, B., Brown, K., & Previte, J. (2004). Politics and identity in cyberspace: A case study of Australian women in agriculture online. *Information, Communication & Society, 7,* 167-184.

Plax, T. G. (1991). Understanding applied communication inquiry: Researcher as organizational consultant. *Journal of Applied Communication Research, 19,* 55-70.

Poe, S. D. (2002). Technical communication consulting as a business. *Technical Communication, 49,* 171-180.

Pollock, M. A., Artz, L., Frey, L. R., Pearce, W. B., & Murphy, B. A. O. (1996). Navigating between Scylla and Charybdis: Continuing the dialogue on communication and social justice. *Communication Studies, 47,* 142-151.

Quigley, D., Sanchez, V., Handy, D., Goble, R., & George, P. (2000). Participatory research strategies in nuclear risk management for native communities. *Journal of Health Communication: International Perspectives, 5,* 305-331.

Rakow, L. F. (2005). Why did the scholar cross the road? Community action research and the citizen-scholar. In S. H. Priest (Ed.), *Communication impact: Designing research that matters* (pp. 5-17). Lanham, MD: Rowman & Littlefield.

Real, M. (1984). Debate on critical theory and the study of communications: A commentary on ferment in the field. *Journal of Communication, 34*(4), 72-80.

Reason, P., & Bradbury, H. (Eds.). (2001). *Handbook of action research: Participative inquiry and practice.* Thousand Oaks, CA: Sage.

Reber, B. H., & Berger, B. K. (2005). Framing analysis of activist rhetoric: How the Sierra Club succeeds or fails at creating salient messages. *Public Relations Review, 31,* 185-195.

Redding, C. (1979). Graduate education and the communication consultant: Playing God for a fee. *Communication Education, 28,* 346-352.

Reed, T. V. (2005). *The art of protest: Culture and activism from the civil rights movement to the streets of Seattle.* Minneapolis: University of Minnesota Press.

Reinharz, S. (with Davidman, L.). (1992). *Feminist methods in social research.* New York: Oxford University Press.

Rhoads, R. A. (1998). *Freedom's web: Student activism in an age of cultural diversity.* Baltimore: John Hopkins University Press.

Ristock, J. L., & Pennell, J. (1996). *Community research as empowerment: Feminist links, postmodern interruptions.* New York: Oxford University Press.

Rogers, E. M. (1994). *A history of communication study: A biographical approach.* New York: Free Press.

Rojecki, A. (1999). *Silencing the opposition: Antinuclear movements and the media in the Cold War.* Urbana: University of Illinois Press.

Rojecki, A. (2002). Modernism, state sovereignty and dissent: Media and the new post-Cold War movements. *Critical Studies in Media Communication, 19,* 152-171.

Rosenfield, L. W. (1983). Ideological miasma. *Central States Speech Journal, 34,* 119-121.

Rude, L. G. (1969). The rhetoric of farmer labor agitators. *Central States Speech Journal, 20,* 280-285.

Rushing, J. H., & Frentz, T. S. (1991). Integrating ideology and achetype in rhetorical criticism. *Quarterly Journal of Speech, 77,* 385-406.

Ryan, C. (1991). *Prime time activism: Media strategies for grassroots organizing.* Boston: South End Press.

Ryan, C. (2005). Successful collaboration: Movement building in the media arena. In D. Croteau, W. Hoynes, & C. Ryan (Eds.), *Rhyming hope and history: Activists, academics, and social movement scholarship* (pp. 115-136). Minneapolis: University of Minnesota Press.

Ryan, C., Carragee, K. M., & Meinhofer, W. (2001). Theory into practice: Framing, the news media, and collective action. *Journal of Broadcasting & Electronic Media, 45,* 175-182.

Ryan, C., Carragee, K. M., & Schwerner, C. (1998). Media, movements, and the quest for social justice. *Journal of Applied Communication Research, 26,* 165-181.

Ryfe, D. M. (2002). The practice of deliberative democracy: A study of 16 deliberative organizations. *Political Communication, 19,* 359-377.

Ryfe, D. M. (2005). Does deliberative democracy work? *Annual Review of Political Science, 8,* 49-71.

Said, E. (1989). Representing the colonized: Anthropology's interlocutors. *Critical Inquiry, 15,* 205-225.

Salter, L. (2004). Structure and forms of use: A contribution to understanding the "effects" of the internet on deliberative democracy. *Information, Communication & Society, 7,* 185-206.

Sanchez, J., & Stuckey, M. E. (2000). The rhetoric of American Indian activism in the 1960s and 1970s. *Communication Quarterly, 48,* 120-136.

Sandmann, L. R., & Lewis, A. G. (1991). Land grant universities on trial. *Adult Learning, 3,* 23.

Sanford, V., & Angel-Ajani, A. (Eds.). (2006). *Engaged observer: Anthropology, advocacy, and activism.* New Brunswick, NJ: Rutgers University Press.

Santiago, C. D. (1972). *A century of activism.* Manila, The Philippines: Rex.

Schiller, H. I. (1989). *Culture, Inc.: The corporate takeover of public expression.* New York: Oxford University Press.

Schiller, H. I. (1996). *Information inequality: The deepening social crisis in America.* New York: Routledge.

Schoening, G. T., & Anderson, J. A. (1995). Social action media studies: Foundational arguments and common premises. *Communication Theory, 5,* 93-116.

Schragge, E. (2003). *Activism and social change: Lessons for community and local organizing.* Orchard Park, NY: Broadview Press.

Schramm, W. (1997). *The beginnings of communication study in America: A personal memoir* (S. H. Chaffee & E. M. Rogers, Eds.). Thousand Oaks, CA: Sage.

Scott, R. L., & Smith, D. K. (1969). The rhetoric of confrontation. *Quarterly Journal of Speech, 55,* 1-8.

Seaton, C. E. (1996). *Altruism and activism: Character disposition and ideology as factors in a blockade of an abortion clinic: An exploratory study* (2nd ed.). Lanham, MD: University Press of America.

Seibold, D. R. (1995). *Theoria* and *praxis:* Means and ends in applied communication research. In K. N. Cissna (Ed.), *Applied communication in the 21st century* (pp. 23-38). Mahwah, NJ: Erlbaum.

Seibold, D. R. (2000). Applied communication scholarship: Less a matter of boundaries than of emphases. *Journal of Applied Communication Research, 28,* 183-187.

Sender, K. (2001). Gay readers, consumers, and a dominant gay habitus: 25 years of the *Advocate* magazine. *Journal of Communication, 51,* 73-99.

Sheffield, A. D. (1926). *Creative discussion: A statement of method for leaders and members of discussion groups and conferences* (3rd ed.). New York: American Press.

Shepherd, C. (1998). *A study of the relationship between style I art and socio-political change in early mediaeval Europe.* Oxford, England: British Archaeological Reports.

Shi, Y. (2005). Identity construction of the Chinese diaspora, ethnic media use, community formation, and the possibility of social activism. *Continuum: Journal of Media & Cultural Studies, 19,* 55-72.

Shoemaker, P. J. (1984). Media treatment of deviant political groups. *Journalism Quarterly, 61,* 66-75, 82.

Shotter, J. (1997). On a different ground: From contests between monologues to dialogic contest. *Argumentation, 11,* 95-112.

Sirianni, C., & Friedland, L. (1997, January/February). Civic innovation and American democracy. *Change,* pp. 14-23.

Smith, D. H. (1967). Social protest . . . and the oratory of human rights. *Today's Speech, 15*(3), 2-8.

Smith, J., McCarthy, J. D., McPhail, C., & Augustyn, B. (2001). From protest to agenda building: Description bias in media coverage of protest events in Washington, D.C. *Social Forces, 79,* 1397-1423.

Smith, R. A., & Siplon, P. D. (2006). *Drugs into bodies: Global AIDS treatment activism.* Westport, CT: Praeger.

Sobnowsky, M. J., & Hauser, E. (1998). Initiating or avoiding activism: Red ribbons, pink triangles, and public argument about AIDS. In W. E. Elwood (Ed.), *Power in the blood: A handbook on AIDS, politics, and communication* (pp. 25-38). Mahwah, NJ: Erlbaum.

Sowards, S. K., & Renegar, V. (2004). The rhetorical functions of consciousness-raising in third wave feminism. *Communication Studies, 55,* 535-552.

Spano, S. (2001). *Public dialogue and participatory democracy: The Cupertino community project.* Cresskill, NJ: Hampton Press.

Spano, S. (2006). Theory and practice in public dialogue: A case study in facilitating community transformation. In L. R. Frey (Ed.), *Facilitating group communication in context: Innovations and applications with natural groups: Vol. 1. Facilitating group creation, conflict, and conversation* (pp. 271-298). Cresskill, NJ: Hampton Press.

Sprague, J. (2005). *Feminist methodologies for critical researchers: Bridging differences.* Walnut Creek, CA: AltaMira Press.

Staggenborg, S. (1991). *The pro-choice movement: Organization and activism in the abortion conflict.* New York: Oxford University Press.

Stengrim, L. (2005). Negotiating postmodern democracy, political activism, and knowledge production: Indymedia's grassroots and e-savvy answer to media oligopoly. *Communication & Critical/Cultural Studies, 2,* 281-304.

Stevenson, M. R., & Cogan, J. C. (Eds.). (2003). *Everyday activism: A handbook for lesbian, gay, and bisexual people and their allies.* New York: Routledge.

Stewart, C. K. (1991, November). *Research in organizational communication.* Paper presented at the meeting of the Speech Communication Association, Atlanta, GA.

Stewart, J. (1983). Reconsidering communication consulting. *Journal of Applied Communication Research, 11,* 153-167.

Stockdill, B. C. (2003). *Activism against AIDS: At the intersection of sexuality, race, gender, and class.* Boulder, CO: Lynne Rienner.

Strine, M. S. (1991). Critical theory and "organic" intellectuals: Reframing the work of cultural critique. *Communication Monographs, 58,* 195-201.

Strine, M. (1992). Art, activism, and the performance (con)text: A response. *Text and Performance Quarterly, 12,* 391-395.

Stringer, E. T. (1999). *Action research* (2nd ed.). Thousand Oaks, CA: Sage.

Stucky, N. (2006). Fieldwork in the performance studies classroom: Learning objectives and the activist curriculum. In D. S. Madison & J. Hamera (Eds.), *The Sage handbook of performance studies* (pp. 261-277). Thousand Oaks, CA: Sage.

Sunwolf. (2006). Empathic attunement facilitation: Stimulating immediate task engagement in zero-history training groups of helping professionals. In L. R. Frey (Ed.), *Facilitating group communication in context: Innovations and applications with natural groups: Vol. 1. Facilitating group creation, conflict, and conversation* (pp. 63-92). Cresskill, NJ: Hampton Press.

Sussman, L. (1982). OD as muddling: Implications for communication consultants. *Communication Quarterly, 30,* 85-91.

Swan, S. (2002). Rhetoric, service, and social justice. *Written Communication, 19,* 76-108.

Swartz, O. (1997). *Conducting socially responsible research: Critical theory, neopragmatism, and rhetorical inquiry.* Thousand Oaks, CA: Sage.

Swartz, O. (2004). Partisan, empathic and invitational criticism: The challenge of materiality. *Ethical Space: The International Journal of Communication Ethics, 1,* 28-33.

Swartz, O. (2005). *In defense of partisan criticism.* New York: Peter Lang.

Swartz, O. (Ed.). (2006). *Social justice and communication scholarship.* Mahwah, NJ: Erlbaum.

Taylor, P. (2003). *Applied theatre: Creating transformative encounters in the community.* Portsmouth, NH: Heinemann.

Tenopir, C., & King, D. W. (2000). Towards electronic journals: Realities for scientists, librarians, and publishers. *Psycoloquy, 11*(84). Retrieved May 15, 2006, from http://psycprints.ecs.soton.ac.uk/archive/00000084/#html

Theodore, A. (2002). "A right to speak on the subject": The U.S. women's antiremoval petition campaign, 1829-1831. *Rhetoric & Public Affairs, 5,* 601-624.

Thomas, J. (1993). *Doing critical ethnography.* Newbury Park, CA: Sage.

Thousands march for immigrant rights: Schools, businesses feel impact as students, workers walk out. (2006, May 1). Retrieved May 12, 2006, from http://www.cnn.com/2006/US/05/01/immigrant.day/index.html

Toc, H. (1971). "I shot an arrow in the air . . .": The performing arts as weapons of social change. *Journal of Communication, 21,* 115-135.

Toch, H. H., Deutsch, S. E., & Wilkins, D. M. (1960). The wrath of the bigot: An analysis of protest mail. *Journalism Quarterly, 27,* 173-185.

Tuchman, G. (1978). *Making news: A study in the construction of reality.* New York: Free Press.

Turner, V., & Turner, E. (1982). Performing ethnography. *TDR: The Drama Review, 26,* 33-50.

Turner, V., & Turner, E. (1988). Performance ethnography. In V. Turner, *The anthropology of performance* (pp. 139-155). New York: Performing Arts Journal.

Ugwu, C. (Ed.). (1995). *Let's get it on: The politics of Black performance.* Seattle, WA: Bay Press.

Van de Donk, W., Loader, B. D., Nixon, P. G., & Rucht, D. (Eds.). (2004). *Cyberprotest: New media, citizens, and social movements.* New York: Routledge.

van Erven, E. (1992). *The playful revolution: Theatre and liberation in Asia.* Bloomington: Indiana University Press.

Varallo, S. M., Ray, E. B., & Ellis, B. H. (1998). Speaking of incest: The research interview as social justice. *Journal of Applied Communication Research, 26,* 254-271.

Wander, P. (1983). The ideological turn in modern criticism. *Central States Speech Journal, 34,* 1-18.

Wander, P. (1984). The third persona: An ideological turn in rhetorical theory. *Central States Speech Journal, 35,* 197-216.

Wander, P., & Jenkins, S. (1972). Rhetoric, society, and the critical response. *Quarterly Journal of Speech, 58,* 441-450.

Warren, K. B. (1998). *Indigenous movements and their critics: Pan-Maya activism in Guatemala.* Princeton, NJ: Princeton University Press.

Weiss, A. (2002). *Principles of spiritual activism.* Hoboken, NJ: KTAV.

Weissberg, R. (2005). *The limits of civic activism: Cautionary tales on the use of politics.* New Brunswick, NJ: Transaction.

Welsh, S. (2002). Deliberative democracy and the rhetorical production of political culture. *Rhetoric & Public Affairs, 5,* 679-708.

West, M., & Gastil, J. (2004). Deliberation at the margins: Participant accounts of face-to-face public deliberation at the 1999-2000 world trade protests in Seattle and Prague. *Qualitative Research Reports in Communication, 5,* 1-7.

Whedbee, K. E. (2003). The tyranny of Athens: Representations of rhetorical democracy in eighteenth-century Britain. *Rhetoric Society Quarterly, 33*(4), 65-85.

Whedbee, K. E. (2004). Reclaiming rhetorical democracy: George Grote's defense of Cleon and the Athenian demagogues. *Rhetoric Society Quarterly, 34*(4), 71-95.

Whillock, R. K. (1989). Political empiricism: The role of a communication scholar as a consultant for one mayoral election. *Southern Communication Journal, 55,* 55-71.

Wigginton, E. (Ed.). (1991). *Refuse to stand silently by: An oral history of grass roots social activism in America, 1921-64.* New York: Doubleday.

Williams, D. C., Ishiyama, J. T., Young, M. J., & Launer, M. K. (1997). The role of public argument in emerging democracies: A case study of the 12 December 1993 elections in the Russian Federation. *Argumentation, 11,* 179-195.

Williams, R. (1975). *Television: Technology and cultural form.* New York: Schocken Books.

Wolfe, C. (1997). *Judicial activism: Bulwark of freedom or precarious society?* (rev. ed.). Lanham, MD: Rowman & Littlefield.

Wood, J. T. (1995). Theorizing practice, practicing theory. In K. N. Cissna (Ed.), *Applied communication in the 21st century* (pp. 181-192). Mahwah, NJ: Erlbaum.

Wood, J. T. (1996). Social justice research: Alive and well in the field of communication. *Communication Studies, 47,* 128-134.

Yoder, J. (1969). The protest of the American clergy in opposition to the war in Vietnam. *Today's Speech, 17*(3), 51-59.

Young, I. M. (2000). *Inclusion and democracy.* New York: Oxford University Press.

Zald, M. (1996). Culture, ideology, and strategic framing. In D. McAdam, J. D. McCarthy, & M. N. Zald (Eds.), *Comparative perspectives on social movements: Political opportunities, mobilizing structures, and cultural framings* (pp. 261-274). New York: Cambridge University Press.

Zoller, H. M. (2005). Health activism: Communication theory and action for social change. *Communication Theory, 15*, 341-364.

PART I

Promoting Public Dialogue, Debate, and Discussion

1

PROMOTING DELIBERATIVE DEMOCRACY THROUGH DIALOGUE

Communication Contributions to a Grassroots Movement for Truth, Justice, and Reconciliation

Spoma Jovanovic

Carol Steger

Sarah Symonds

Donata Nelson

University of North Carolina at Greensboro

The public sphere is the locus of a discussion potentially engaging everyone so that the society can come to a common mind about important matters. This common mind is a reflective view, emerging from critical debate, and not just a summation of whatever views happen to be held in the population. So it has a normative status: government ought to listen to it.

—Taylor (1995, p. 263)

On November 3, 1979, members of the Communist Workers Party gathered in Greensboro, NC to organize textile mill workers and protest the growing influence of the Ku Klux Klan (KKK) in the area. In an African American community on the east side of town where approximately 30 Blacks and Whites were beginning to assemble for a march, the social protest was brought to a screeching halt by a 9-car caravan of 35 KKK and neo-Nazi members who drove in and began shooting into the crowd. Five people were killed that day, and another 10 wounded.[1] As four television stations captured the bloody details on videotape, onlookers took cover the best they could. Six Klan and neo-Nazi members were charged with first-degree murder, but two criminal trials resulted in acquittals for all of the accused, leading some people to question the validity of a judicial system that could find these men innocent despite substantial evidence to suggest otherwise. Finally, a third civil trial found the police and members of the hate groups liable for one of the deaths, requiring payment of $395,000 to the survivors.

These facts of our community's tragedy are ones that are widely accepted in Greensboro. However, the stories that evolved to explain how the incident occurred, who was involved, who was to blame, and what Greensboro should have done in response to this incident, are issues our community struggles with decades later. That is, the way in which we talk about what happened, or do not, remains a source of discomfort, confusion, and conflict.

The dominant narrative, the one most widely circulated in the local media and endorsed by the city's leaders, is that on November 3, 1979, two extremist groups from outside the city collided in an unfortunate, violent shootout. In this version of the story, culpability for the deaths and subsequent shame brought to Greensboro falls squarely on the shoulders of radical individuals who were not really members of the community (Wheaton, 1987). An alternative narrative, voiced by the survivors and their supporters, although largely ignored by those in power, is that this massacre of community members was planned with the knowledge of local law enforcement agencies and that the victims were deprived of their constitutional right to protection in assembling to express their views. This alternative story tracks the cultural and social history of the community to expose the chronic economic and racial injustices that the police and city leaders tacitly encouraged (Waller, 2002).

Marty Nathan, wife of slain march organizer Dr. Michael Nathan, declared that the protesters' constitutionally protected free speech was violated:

> We were hated, all of us were, for what we were doing. If you are in the faces of others, looking at deep structures of power, the principalities won't like you. In an attempt to liberate ourselves from racial and eco-

nomic injustice, enemies were made. Those enemies snuffed us out on November 3, 1979. We were left bereft, with no capability to fight back on our own. We had no jobs and we were living in poverty. (personal communication, November 1, 2003)

Greensboro, NC is a city today not unlike many others across the nation where people fill their days with family life, work or school, and socializing. In Greensboro, we point proudly to our distinguished levels of charitable giving and volunteerism; we flinch at our low levels of social trust and near-absent political protest that was once a model for the nation.[2] When carnage strikes, as it did in Greensboro in 1979, the wounds left behind scar not only the individuals involved but an entire community. The significance of the past for the city today is reflected in the lingering racial and economic tensions that grip Greensboro. To repair the damage to the fabric of community relationships caused by the polemical quality of discourse about the events leading up to and following November 3, a diverse collection of citizens organized in 2003 to seek a different kind of resolution from what the local government offered in 1979 and the state and federal judicial systems decided later; their search was for truth and community reconciliation.

This group of spirited people organized themselves into the Greensboro Truth and Community Reconciliation Project (GTCRP). They hoped to initiate dialogue about November 3, 1979, that would take into account all of the relevant factors, many of which never were entered into public record or public conversation over the years.[3] Among those who met regularly in this collaborative effort were local, progressive political and faith-based leaders, concerned citizens, survivors of the catastrophe, college professors, student activists, and national figures prominent in a variety of social justice issues.

We, as communication scholars teaching and learning at the University of North Carolina at Greensboro (UNCG) and as residents of the Greensboro community, were among those deeply disturbed by the tragedy we did not know about in 1979 but came to learn of in 2003. We joined with others working to expose the hidden legacy of Greensboro, with our involvement focused primarily on community organizing and education efforts. We wanted to see, in particular, if the promise of dialogue would result in a viable method to positively address our community's ills (see also Adams, Berquist, Dillon, & Galanes, this volume). Thus, we joined hands with those hoping to glean the wisdom and informed activism that comes from critical inquiry, time, and reflection.

In this chapter, we examine our communication activism with the GTCRP from January 2003 to July 2004. We begin with the details of our research agenda, followed by a discussion of the democratic and philosophical theories that influenced our gaze and involvement in this initiative for community dialogue. We then describe the role and function of the GTCRP and the community response to it, followed by a consideration of how communication scholarship intersects with concerns for social justice. Recognizing that this type of work is fraught with challenges, we subsequently share difficulties and tensions we faced in performing our communication activism. Finally, we conclude the chapter with a discussion of important lessons learned from our labor in the field as fodder and inspiration for those who would engage in this type of scholarly, pragmatic work for boldly affecting what demands our collective attention and action.

OUR SOCIAL ACTION RESEARCH PLAN

Our work with the GTCRP began in a graduate seminar entitled "Communication and Social Change" taught by the first author, Spoma Jovanovic. Recognizing that change can be initiated both within established community institutions and by new grassroots coalitions, this course encouraged students to actively seek out organizations, groups, and individuals striving to enact community change. Thematically, the course was designed to address six broad areas: ethics, social justice, democratic theory, the individualism-collectivism tension, the role of communication in community formation, and the moral imperative of social action research. After considering four potential community projects, the 16 class members eventually decided to work with the GTCRP, which was establishing its identity at precisely the time the class was beginning. The GTCRP's first public announcement of activity in the local newspaper captured the students' attention and interest. Furthermore, the GTCRP alone, among the projects considered, involved a politically contested understanding of community values.

A group of six graduate students and their faculty advisor (Jovanovic) remained involved in the project beyond the completion of the semester-long class. That number eventually dropped to three active students and, finally, to one after 18 months of community work.[4]

Understanding how knowledge is constructed requires examining the communication code(s) at work among community members. This code represents often-unarticulated assumptions that operate to determine the range of communication alternatives and meanings within a social system (Pilotta et al., 2001). Understanding the code, and what it both enables and constrains, highlights the political, contested nature of communication.

We believed that to understand the Greensboro community, its code(s), and its values, we needed to engage in ethnographic research. Accordingly, we logged over 1,000 hours of observation, participation, and other research on this project. We became familiar with historical records and media representations of the 1979 event. We attended and participated in open house events held at local public libraries and other sites that introduced the GTCRP to the citizens of Greensboro. In addition, we met with all the principal leaders of the project, attended bimonthly local task force meetings, interviewed many of the task force members, and sought out city and county officials who opposed the project. We also contributed time to fund-raising, promotion, strategic planning, web design and development, and survey efforts related to the project. Throughout our study of this project devoted to social justice, we attempted to "do" justice to our commitment to employing practices that treat people with a deep respect for their knowledge and contributions (Altheide & Johnson, 1997).

As communication scholars committed to community activism, we set out to lend credibility to the project in the ways we could; namely, by using our communication knowledge and resources to (a) influence community-building by inspiring public trust and accountability in the community by encouraging transparent processes of dialogue, (b) create networks among citizens and institutions within the community, (c) be recognized as active participants in addressing our community's concerns, and (d) have our work endorsed by recognized community leaders and media representatives (Pilotta et al., 2001).

Underlying this type of social action research is an approach that honors a dialogic partnership with community members. For this project to succeed, that partnership would need to delve sincerely into lingering community issues.

First, by attending the regularly scheduled local task force meetings and training sessions for their members, and then by going to community presentations and conducting interviews, as previously described, we became educated about the event and the community response in 1979 and over the course of the years following it. As in learning about most contested narratives, the story of November 3, 1979, unfolded gradually, and we integrated discrete bits of information and perspectives into our knowledge base over the duration of our involvement. We heard the facts and, more, we learned to appreciate the passions that fueled the effort. A local task force member, recognizing that this process was, for all of us, rooted in sustained inquiry and personal commitment, said, "Facts may not get us where we want to go. The personal, emotional, and spiritual journeys we take will be what inspire the compassion and understanding needed."

Our research team consulted with the GTCRP on a number of community outreach projects intended to improve the message of the grassroots program. In particular, several communication students worked together to establish a logo and web site for the GTCRP that became a vital community resource. The web site (www.gtcrp.org) provided background material on the project, a complete listing of all the project's main documents, announcements of upcoming events, media information, contact information, volunteer opportunities, and links to other related sites.

The need to create effective documents that explained the project's process and asked for community support was essential for the GTCRP's community education mission. Many of those documents were reviewed not only by local task force members but also by our team of communication scholars. We drafted, edited, and reviewed dozens of documents, resolutions, and media materials, attempting to have the documents best communicate the ambitions of the project by critical consideration of their words, flow, and tone.

For instance, *A Call for Dialogue: Greensboro, North Carolina's Opportunity to Move toward Wholeness*, a 16-page booklet, was written by one of the student members of our research team to explain the connection between the quality of Greensboro's civic relationships and the communication strategies used to deal with the issues surrounding the events of November 3, 1979 (Steger, 2004). The hope underlying this booklet was that citizens would recognize the value of sharing perspectives, engaging in community deliberation, and building deeper understanding across their differences. This booklet was made available to the public free of charge, with printing costs paid by donations collected from local task force members, other community members, the local library, and several organizations committed to fostering community conversation on the topic.

Media advocacy was another important task of our research team. Members of the GTCRP claimed that a media blockade was keeping news of the process away from the citizens of Greensboro. Our research team recognized the need to initiate dialogue between community and media members to consider the local media's communication choices, the community climate they helped to create through their rhetorical construction of the event, and a reckoning of their treatment of the victims. To begin the process, we hosted at UNCG a 2-hour public discussion with three journalists on reporting practices in 1979 and in 2004 that supported or diffused community participation and avenues for community-media collaboration. Winston Cavin, a reporter on the scene in 1979 who took cover behind a parked car to avoid the gunfire, said at that public discussion, "I think the GTCRP is a good idea. November 3, 1979 is the elephant in the living room. *Any* attempt to try and understand and come to resolution is good for the city." Jim Schlosser, another reporter who covered the 1979 shootings and a columnist today for the local daily newspaper, Greensboro's *News and Record*, added, "I think our newspaper ought to do an investigation again." However, Charles Davenport, a columnist for the same newspaper, disagreed, asking, "Why put out the impression that Greensboro is racist? This is ancient history and there is no legitimate reason to bring it up." Throughout the evening, questions, challenges, and explanations moved swiftly among media personnel, survivors, college students, and other community members as they sorted through stories of personal and professional experiences with the November 3, 1979 event.

As the discussion came to a close, survivor Joyce Johnson held out a conciliatory hand, asking for cooperative action for the future despite the sometimes heated exchanges that characterized the evening. The three media panelists had called November 3, 1979, a "gang war" and "a clash of ideological zealots," and they characterized the organizers in 1979 as suffering from "liberal guilt" and compared them to "Muslim extremists." Johnson, who had listened quietly most of the evening, rose proudly at the end and said, "Yes, I have a point of view, but can we talk about that together? Are you willing to risk understanding me to make the community better?" As the media panel concluded, contact information was exchanged between journalists and survivors, signaling a step toward the improved media relations that would follow.

Some members of our research team also developed a survey questionnaire to assess community members' knowledge of the 1979 event and the GTCRP. The questionnaire was distributed to citizens at local malls, economic development group meetings, area schools, churches, and other venues where citizens circulated. Survey collectors, 20 upper division undergraduate students who were studying this event as part of another communication course, were instructed to gather data from as diverse an audience as possible based on race, gender, and education level. Within a week's time, more than 300 questionnaires were completed. The survey data were analyzed and shared with the GTCRP to use as a benchmark for future assessment work. Our sample included respondents who were 67% White, 30% African American, and 3% other, with just over 73% who had lived in Greensboro for less than 5 years. More than 56% were unaware of the 1979 incident, 82% had not heard of the GTCRP (not surprising as the project still was relatively new), and 90% were unaware that there was a ruling of liability in at least one of the deaths. Importantly, 79% of those surveyed supported the community's effort to seek truth and reconciliation regarding the events of November 3, 1979.

Other research team members were active in a college student mobilization drive to introduce the historical and current significance of November 3, 1979, to the six Greensboro colleges and universities. These communication students attended local discussion groups aimed at attracting some of the 24,000 college students in the area, met with campus leaders and student body presidents to discuss the project, made guest presentations in classrooms, participated in the launch of an official student task force, and organized a community-wide meeting on one of the local college campuses. According to all involved, this mobilization drive was very successful at garnering student support and inspiring a new generation of citizens to com-

munity activism. Survivor Nelson Johnson, one of the key organizers of the
GTCRP, reflected at a meeting of the local task force on youth involvement
in the project's initial year of work:

> Our goal has been to get the student youth base more organized. We had
> 150 people, mainly youth, at a recent evening event. We've had work-
> shops for and with our youth, and college students from the area have
> come to us to hear more and learn more. We count this as a break-
> through in our organizing efforts.

To find the stories behind the story (see Swan, 2002) of November 3,
1979, we interviewed local task force members and others involved in the
events of that day. These interviews provided a vehicle for community members to speak about their motivations, understandings, and hopes for the
project. At the same time, the process of collecting these narratives built
important community-university relationships based on trust, time, and
conversation. The interviews, many of which were written up as sensitive
testimonies of hope and despair, were posted on the GTCRP web site with
the permission of interviewees. One African American male survivor sadly
told a student that the power structures in Greensboro "assassinated my
character because I was friends with members of the Communist Workers
Party. They kept me from getting work, and the police harassed me." A protester in 1979 who was not wounded physically but shaken in every other
way saw the event as part of a larger cultural condition:

> The world during that period of time was in a lot of social upheaval.
> There was a huge uprising going on in Iran at the time and there were
> successful socialist revolutions in places like Ethiopia. I am sure that
> there was a sense . . . that it was all getting out of line. How much they
> intended as an effort to put people back in their place, how conscious
> that was, is not exactly clear.

Most of the students who conducted the interviews commented on the
value of talking to key participants in a major political event. The students
appreciated and were inspired by the opportunity to record the stories of
these individuals who had lived through adversity, yet remained committed
to the community that had brought them pain.

Finally, we launched an outreach program through a university-wide
dialogue project. With internal funding provided by the College of Arts and
Sciences at UNCG to bring speakers to the campus, an interdisciplinary team
was assembled, of which we were a part, to commence a sustained critical
inquiry into November 3, 1979, the work of the GTCRP, and the response

of community leaders. The Ashby Dialogue series, entitled "Greensboro's Hidden Legacy: The Impact of November 3, 1979 on the City Today," brought together over 450 students, faculty, and community members. The series was planned to feature local and national experts and the survivors at monthly programs. The chief civil trial lawyer provided a lesson on the legal intricacies surrounding the tragedy, including the prosecution's argument that the local police and federal officials knew in advance that violence would erupt that day. Another lawyer, who had defended a Klansman, and a police investigator shared films, charts, and other evidence used in the criminal trials. An expert on worldwide truth and reconciliation commissions participated, as did academic commentators, speaking about the economic ramifications, sociological implications, and spiritual/religious responses to November 3, 1979. The university dialogue was designed to provide an independent, yet tandem process to the GTCRP that could bring together supporters and opponents of the process. Although most of the 14 speakers were supportive of the GTCRP (many opponents declined repeated invitations to speak), at least five were skeptical of the GTCRP but agreed to participate because they trusted that the university-sponsored event would feature an impartiality they presumed was missing from the GTCRP movement.

THEORETICAL INFLUENCES ON THIS COMMUNICATION ACTIVISM

Our communication activism throughout this project has been grounded in the works of two scholars: Iris Marion Young and Emmanuel Levinas. Young (2000) offered a critical theory for inclusive political communication that seeks the involvement of marginalized groups and strives for justice through deliberative means. Young's political theory is complemented by the ethics philosophy of Levinas (1961/1969), who called for recognizing the other (i.e., the cast aside, the marginalized) as the basis for a more just world. For Levinas, the self is bound by a relationship to the other that is absolute in its responsibility; the other calls forth a response from the self that is neither neutral nor distant but, rather, compassionate and involved. Both of these theoretical perspectives are explained next in more detail.

Young's Political Theory: Inclusion, Community, and Democracy

Our research team applied the concepts derived from Young's (2000) "communicative democracy" in our work in Greensboro. Young recognized the value of a deliberative model of democracy in which personal preferences are transformed into social reasons through argumentation that considers others' views and aims for collective wisdom. Yet, she realized that argumentation alone will not suffice for two primary reasons. First, arguments require shared assumptions, but some conflicts, such as the differing narratives surrounding November 3, 1979, lack shared understanding. Second, focusing on arguments alone often brings with it the exclusion of style and idiom, disallowing, in particular, embodied forms of expression and emotion. This leads to the exclusion of ideas based not on the *value* of their content but on *how the content is expressed.* A norm of order privileges the status quo and excludes disruptive expression that seeks to gain recognition for an alternative point of view. We agreed with Young's call for democracy and justice that relies on diverse, discussion-based modes of communication—specifically, the greeting, narratives, and rhetoric.

The *greeting* is a public acknowledgement of another that invites *particular* individuals or social groups—especially those having differing perspectives, interests, or social locations than the status quo—to be included in public discussions. The greeting, in effect, calls on us to be accountable to others through a process of welcoming, listening, and taking seriously others' opinions. As a discursive sign of inclusivity, the greeting upholds the requirement of democratic legitimacy that "all those affected by decisions should be included in discussions" (Young, 2000, p. 61). The greeting, thus, helps to set the stage for parties to engage each other as dialogic partners.

The use of *narratives,* or stories, offers an important opportunity for people to contribute to their community's construction of knowledge. Narratives are especially helpful for those who are marginalized and whose discourse may be misunderstood, devalued, or altered to fit the dominant thinking (see Arnett & Arneson, 1999; Goodwin, 1990; Polkinghorne, 1988; Reissman, 1993; Young, 2000), because storytelling can foster understanding by presenting human experiences that challenge the hegemonic condition and express the particularity of individual experience. As Zeb ("Z") Holler, a retired Presbyterian minister and co-chair of the GTCRP local task force, pronounced, "As divided as we are [in the city of Greensboro], the more stories and more diverse the perspectives that can be teased out, the greater the possibility to see who we are." Honoring the stories offered by all the representative groups of Greensboro's community was seen as the beginning of a new community rhetoric.

Young (2000) defined *rhetoric,* the third inclusion mode, as the effect of messages on an audience. We, as communication scholars, define it to also include the messages' content, speakers' emotions, and speakers' performances. We rely on rhetoric that is inclusive, situated, affective, and effective to help citizens move from reason to judgment, and from thinking to committed action based on that judgment.

Applying Young's (2000) theory of communicative democracy to Greensboro, members of the GTCRP organized a panel of 15-20 members who would consider nominations and then select seven Truth and Reconciliation Commissioners, by extending a greeting and invitation to conservative and liberal groups, White and Black faith-based organizations, business and labor associations, government agencies (e.g., police associations) and grassroots councils, and other community stakeholder groups.[5] A local task force member acknowledged that there might be groups that would not want to be involved, such as the Sons of Confederate Veterans and United Daughters of the Confederacy, but that the job of the task force was to make a sincere attempt to recognize, respect, and validate the right of such groups to be involved in the community-wide process if they so chose.

Levinas's Ethics

The second scholarly work grounding our communication activism in Greensboro was the ethics philosophy of Levinas. Levinas's thought is anchored in the recognition of the imperative issued by the other in the call, "Thou shall not kill." Levinas viewed that call not only in terms of physical murder being unethical but also with respect to the type of killing that gradually and slowly denies the other person significance in the world. That this type of killing is oftentimes housed within the abode of indifference is no coincidence. As Surber (1994) explained:

> Beginning with a simple turn away from the face of the Other, I may come, "by degrees," simply to ignore the appellations of the Other, later to discredit the Other's discourse, then to deprive the Other of any "right" to discourse, and finally to regard the Other as unworthy of its very existence since, deprived of discourse, "it" can no longer appear to me as an "ethically relevant" Other. (p. 309)

Many of the survivors of November 3, 1979, say that they were objectified in the media, the court trials, and the community. Survivor Sally Bermanzohn explained that she wrote the book, *Through Survivors' Eyes: From the Sixties to the Greensboro Massacre* (2003), to counter the lingering negative views in the community toward those who protested in 1979. As she claimed, "My motivation was to have six survivors tell the story of their lives and to show that they are humans. We were dehumanized by the media and the courts" (personal communication, October 30, 2003). The names of those who died that day were erased from public memory, replaced instead by labels such as "commies," "agitators," and "combatants." Even a small plaque that was a tribute to those who died that day eventually was removed or stolen from the site of the shootings when a new housing development was located there. Forgetting that day, place, and the people who died there, who embodied a deep "activist and idealist spirit" (Waller, 2002, p. xvi), represents for the survivors a lack of response to their call.

Communication for Levinas (1982/1985), then, is centered on the response: "It is discourse and more exactly, response or responsibility which is this authentic relationship" (p. 88). He viewed ethics as response-ability, not as right versus wrong. Ethics is a calling for a response to what the other is requesting or calling for, not to what *we* think the other needs: "The other as other here is not an object which becomes ours or which becomes us, to the contrary, it withdraws into its mystery" (p. 67).

Many people in Greensboro felt that stories inconsistent with the dominant narrative never were adequately acknowledged by the community. They sensed that government officials and the media worked together behind the scenes to silence advocates who raised troubling issues or highlighted the unflattering conditions in Greensboro at the time. They wanted a response that recognized what had been denied—truth and reconciliation.

SEEKING SOCIAL CHANGE

The relevance of this citizen-based effort from a communication perspective was the opportunity to examine and contribute to an alternative community narrative aimed at producing social change. GTCRP co-chair Z Holler was hopeful that Greensboro could demonstrate through this project how people of differing perspectives could assemble for the purpose of engaging in dialogue, without fear, to promote peaceful community change. As Holler said, "If we can show people how to deal with dissident struggles in a community, if we can listen to those on the other side of the divide, then it's a bellwether of extraordinary significance" (personal communication, February 21, 2003).

Other communities across the United States and throughout the world grapple with numerous social problems, looking for effective models to negotiate among competing claims for justice. To them, Greensboro offered a ray of hope for a new approach to communication in the 21st century.[6]

Patterned loosely after the South African Truth and Reconciliation Commission,[7] the GTCRP began with the hope of bringing truth, justice, and healing to a city divided on whether such an initiative was necessary. Work in earnest began on receipt of a $330,000 grant from the Andrus Family Fund in New York City, a private foundation committed to restorative justice and community reconciliation. With financial support in hand, the project's members sought to involve local citizens, national civil rights supporters, and international reconciliation experts in a quest to uncover the stories buried over the years by ideological warfare and fear. It was the project's hope that, in doing so, the future of Greensboro would be more financially and socially prosperous for all citizens. The goal was to launch a thorough investigation more broad than that which judicial review allowed. As survivor Nelson Johnson explained:

> One thing we have to do is convey this is driven by love not fear for this city. We need to promote a vision of hope and diversity. We need to teach our children the mistakes we made. No one can be proud of what happened on November 3, 1979.

The truth-finding task was designed, in turn, to lead to the crafting of a community response inclusive of many of the facts previously discredited or disallowed. By including more information than that which had previously been considered, and by distinguishing fact from community myth, the proponents of the process saw the potential of generating a new level of creativity and collaboration among social classes, religious organizations, and labor groups that would provide a model for other cities to follow in examining past wrongs. Steve Simpson, executive director of the North Carolina office of the National Conference for Community and Justice, said of Greensboro, "The biggest problem in this community is that we don't talk honestly. In some cases, we are historically inaccurate."

One problem that is not talked about honestly in Greensboro is race, which is a persistent issue in this community. An economic development report commissioned by the city's local foundations concluded that unless the citizens of Greensboro were willing to confront long-standing and complex racial divisions through open and honest communication, the city would be unable to move forward in attracting new business and industry to the area (McKinsey & Company, 2000).

Greensboro, the third-largest city in North Carolina, has approximately 224,000 residents, divided into two dominant racial groups: Whites, comprising 55% of the population, and Blacks, amounting to 37% (U.S. Census Bureau, 2000b). In addition, there is a rapidly growing immigrant population in Greensboro comprised of refugees and other settlers who identify themselves as Hispanic/Latino/a, Asian, African, and Eastern European. The median household income is $23,340 (U.S. Census Bureau, 2000a), the unemployment rate is 6.4%, and those living below the poverty line account for 12.3% of the population (U.S. Census Bureau, 2000b). The GTCRP sought to bring together the disparate racial, ethnic, and economic factions of the community through a process pointed at reconciliation, not further retribution.

The GTCRP proposed to accomplish its mission using four strategies to: (a) educate the community about November 3, 1979, and the truth and community reconciliation process over the course of approximately 3 years; (b) establish a volunteer Truth and Reconciliation Commission by an independent selection panel comprised of more than a dozen stakeholder groups, a process requiring approximately 9 months; (c) fund an investigation of November 3, 1979, by the commission, anticipated to take an additional 18-24 months; and (d) facilitate a year-long community dialogue following the release of the commission's findings.

Even with the coordinated efforts of White and Black citizen activists, the support of 5,000 community members who signed petitions urging the Greensboro City Council to support the endeavor, and the endorsement of the local newspaper's editorial staff, the GTCRP faced opposition. Other community members, political leaders, and some local academics were not so eager to engage in this dialogue, fearing that talk about lingering racial tensions, suspected local and federal government complicity in that tragic event, labor unrest, and renewed charges of civil rights violations would effectively drive away economic opportunities the city badly needed. They worried that the conversation would not achieve the level of honesty needed to obtain reconciliation and, instead, would create greater pain and division among the city's residents. The mayor said he spoke for most of the city's residents when he declared that we should "put the event behind us" and recognize that the city today is a very different place than it was in 1979.

The objections from top-level officials reflected what rhetorical scholars of social change movements recognize as a governing principle to maintain control: "Decision makers must assume that the worst will happen in a given instance of agitation" (Bowers, Ochs, & Jensen, 1993, p. 47). The corollary to that principle is equally important: "Decision makers must be prepared to repel any attack on the establishment" (Bowers et al., p. 47).

A newspaper reporter who asked 10 local residents about their views of the GTCRP found those citizens evenly split on the matter ("The Public Pulse," 2003). Of those against the project, a political science professor said, "In general, I oppose committees like this. I believe they have negative outcomes"; an ophthalmologist added, "It would be helpful to lay this issue to rest"; and a sales manager exclaimed, "It is definitely time to move on" ("The Public Pulse," p. H3). Those supporting the initiative, however, believed that discussion of the past was a positive move for the future. Both African American males interviewed by the newspaper reporter pointed to the project as a worthy endeavor: one, a network engineer said, "In order for Greensboro to move into the future, we have to resolve any doubts about the past"; the other, a technology manager, added, "This committee should be one that would find out how a law enforcement department could let this happen" ("The Public Pulse," p. H3).

The groundbreaking work of this project was built on some of Greensboro's past successes at lessening racial and class inequalities.

Numerous grassroots programs started by citizen groups to benefit under-resourced groups are well established in Greensboro. For instance, the Greensboro Housing Coalition was created to advocate for affordable housing, and its volunteers recently inventoried the entire city's rental housing to benchmark persistent problems in an attempt to end substandard housing in the city; the Women's Resource Center of Greensboro was established to empower women to realize their economic and educational potential; the Triad Health Project provides emotional and practical support to individuals living with HIV and/or AIDS; and the Beloved Community Center was started with the mission of providing social, spiritual, and economic assistance to poor people.

Still, there is an ever-widening divide between the rich and the poor in Greensboro. School segregation is the result of residential housing patterns that divide the city's deteriorating east side, populated primarily by African Americans, from the more prosperous, White, suburban west side. The city's loss of textile factories has left many laborers without opportunities for meaningful work. In terms of employment, education, and housing, the African American population has been most adversely affected, with an unemployment rate approximately double that of Whites in the area (U.S. Census Bureau, 2000b). The racial chasm is further complicated by the influx of numerous ethnic groups that vie for the limited resources in the area.

The disparity among races surfaces in healthcare, as well. The North Carolina State Center for Health Statistics (2003) reported that the area's infant mortality rate (deaths during the first year of life per 1,000 live births) is 5.9 for White children and 14.0 for minority children. Although Greensboro has a nonprofit organization dedicated to helping uninsured residents, its facilities need to be doubled or tripled to accommodate the current need, said ex-mayor and GTCRP co-chair Carolyn Allen.

As a result of a complicated list of economic and social troubles, the city's leaders have scrambled to find hope. Their focus of late has been on developing and marketing amenities to draw new business to the area. Consequently, a new downtown baseball stadium was privately financed; a nonprofit group, Action Greensboro, was formed by local foundations and corporate executives to pool money and talent to attract new jobs to the area; numerous economic development groups have been established to build on the success of attracting a Federal Express hub to the area; and businesses have joined together to provide incentives to teachers and schools for improving standardized educational test scores.

Although many efforts are underway to improve the quality of life in Greensboro through social and economic programs and partnerships, there remains among some community members a reluctance to confront the root racial and class disparity issues. Gayle Fripp, a resident of Greensboro since

1959, and an author of several books on Greensboro's history, explained the situation when she addressed the students in the graduate seminar that launched our work with the GTCRP:

> Civil rights [in Greensboro] came to a halt because of the fear of retaliation. From the White, liberal perspective, there was fear of being associated with communists. From the Black perspective, people were afraid of retribution, more violence, and losing their jobs. Soon after the event [November 3, 1979], we dropped cross-town busing.

Dealing with root causes of racial and economic injustices is more difficult and potentially less financially rewarding than introducing new programs to attract jobs to the area. Business and community leaders question how difficult truths can be faced in a way that demonstrates community-wide hope for a better future rather than highlight failed past attempts. How, they ask, does bringing up messy and awful events of the past lure new, needed business to the area? The response has been to funnel money and talent toward less controversial programs and to leave behind critical, public discussion of the painful past.

What virtually everyone agrees with, however, is that the ample evidence collected since November 3, 1979—in the three trials that followed and numerous books that were written about the confrontation—showed that day to be the result of one communication failure after another. It is reasonable, then, to conclude that the communication processes themselves warrant change through a sustained and deep inquiry by the citizens, political institutions, social groups, and business organizations of the community. Survivor Nelson Johnson is convinced that communication is the key to community building and reconciliation:

> This is a struggle to have a discussion and to introduce a new story to replace a distorted one. All the critiques have been about motive and intent, not November 3, 1979. Human language itself is part of a force that brings into being certain things. The deceptive, distorted memory undergirds a life that is painful for many people. There's a potential here to stand and rise and be a wonderful, powerful community.

SOCIAL JUSTICE SUPPORTS AND DISRUPTS COMMUNITY DEVELOPMENT

Like some other scholars in the communication discipline, we regard the use of communication scholarship to further an activist agenda of social justice as an imperative of democratic life (see, e.g., Artz, 2001; Conquergood, 1991; Fiske, 1991; Frey, Pearce, Pollock, Artz, & Murphy, 1996; Pearce, 2002; Ryan, Carragee, & Schwerner, 1998; Wood, 1996). For us, social justice seeks to recognize the needs of all citizens, not just some, to ensure that the powerful and underresourced alike benefit equally from laws, cultural norms, and institutional practices. As Reisch (2002) explained, "Our understanding of social justice is inextricably connected to our definition of terms like equality and freedom, and to sweeping policy questions about the relative responsibilities and obligations of individuals and society" (p. 343). Furthermore, our project team recognized the need for considering and discussing the interplay of ethical and political concerns in public deliberations and collective decision making. We sought in our community work to advance an agenda of social change wherein conspicuously absent voices are brought into public life, granting full consideration to those perspectives alongside mainstream rhetoric. In doing so, there is the opportunity to consider not only pressing issues that demand public policy choices but also to examine how those issues are framed in the first place (as political, moral, or economic, for instance) and the directional flow of discourse that transforms passive or silent consumers and audience members into active citizens (Pearce, 2002). For these reasons, we did not hesitate to join the efforts of the GTCRP.

The GTCRP organized itself around the interplay of race, class, and civil rights that characterized November 3, 1979. The organizers saw, however, that their work had implications beyond the boundaries of a single event to include an honest assessment of the current cultural conditions that permeate not only this one city but an entire nation. Many of the local task force members also are involved in educational reform, homelessness prevention, immigration concerns, and challenging racism.

Dr. Marty Nathan, whose husband was killed on November 3, 1979, lives today in Massachusetts but has an enduring commitment to continue the work started in Greensboro decades ago and sees its connection to other social issues. She explained her involvement then and now to members of the Greensboro community on the 24th anniversary of the killings:

> We were working in mills to end sexual harassment, get better wages, and improve working conditions. There's no way to look at the Greensboro Massacre and stick to Greensboro—it's bigger. Sexism, religious domination, and corporate domination all intersect with the haves and have nots, and war and peace. The powers and principalities of Greensboro are an echo of what is all around us.

Through a process that sought to involve a wide cross-section of the population, the GTCRP sought to change Greensboro's traditional approach to problem solving, in which only a select few individuals established and carried forward agendas for the future. A paternalistic White elite had dominated Greensboro, operating to avoid conflict, preserve class divisions, and maintain the divided racial status quo (Chafe, 1980).[8] To guide an alternative discourse effort, one that could unite varying class and racial groups, the Greensboro Truth and Community Reconciliation Project (2003a) drafted "The Declaration" to espouse the purpose and intentions of the group. The Declaration, which was printed in the local newspaper and distributed widely, said:

> We believe that by helping to clear up lingering confusion, division, and ill feelings and by promoting reconciliation among individuals, sectors, and institutions within our community, the project will transcend the hurtful legacy of events of November 3, 1979. It is our conviction that this undertaking will go a long way in both healing long-standing wounds and opening new possibilities for Greensboro to become a better, more just and compassionate city.

GTCRP members anticipated that their communication activities would lead to reconciliation and proposals for restorative justice by involving large groups of people together in dialogue. Survivor Nelson Johnson explained that reconciliation *was* the process of dialogue. Lewis Pitts, the attorney for the survivors in the third civil trial, defined *reconciliation* as the coming together of all involved parties, in dialogue, to share how they contributed to the problem, as well as the injuries they suffered as a result. Survivor Sally Bermanzohn admitted that reconciliation has many layers and levels: "I see it as a community process that requires dialogue and give and take" (personal communication, October 31, 2003). The key was that dialogue still was possible, in large part, because the people involved in 1979, as well as interested newcomers, could share their stories, concerns, and hopes for the future.

To engage the community in this difficult conversation required a strategic plan. First, as GTCRP co-chair Z Holler explained, dialogue would need to begin with all-inclusive meetings and e-mails among GTCRP supporters to define a truth and community reconciliation process that could be defensible as fair and above reproach. Second, the GTCRP recognized the need to educate the community at large before moving to the third task of involving large groups of people in dialogue together over time. The fourth task, as the initial plans proposed, was to keep communication with the community from becoming defensive and to focus on supporting a good process rather than overwhelming citizens with facts contradictory to the current community narrative.

Certainly, the risks associated with this project were real and the stakes were high for the community of Greensboro. Proponents of the project worked tirelessly to answer critics' charges and questions. Would the pursuit of "truth," the raising of profound questions of responsibility, and a dialogic reckoning of history actually enable the members of this community to confront (arguably, again) and transcend issues of race and class? Would this community-wide examination, if it could capture the interest and imagination of its citizens, really lead to learning, healing, and reconciliation? What, if anything, would keep the fiery, yet somewhat dormant racial and economic tensions in the community from being fanned into a frenzy? How could those initiating social change processes in Greensboro prevent moving a community from a carefully constructed pattern of civility to one of rancor and recrimination if the "truth" could not be agreed on by those involved?

The Nexus of Communication and Community

At the core of this process of truth and reconciliation, then, were questions centrally involving community and communication: Could this community survive a dialogue involving the rhetoric of hate groups and communists? Could the community thrive as it questioned police practices, judicial processes, and government obligations? In short, could this community benefit from talking about the past?

Community, as scholars have noted, is not so easily defined according to a set list of criteria but is more fully conceived as an outgrowth of communication according to some combination of locality, identity, social accomplishment, emotional connections, organizational structure, and ideological bases (see, e.g., Adelman & Frey, 1997; Arnett, 1986; Bauman, 2001; Friedland, 2001; Pilotta et al., 2001; Shepherd & Rothenbuhler, 2001; Swan, 2002; Young, 2000; Zoller, 2000). Popular conceptions of community often juxtapose individuality against collectivity in a creative tension that needs to be resolved. However, constructive use and management of that tension, rather than its resolution, may be the best chance for an ethical and just vision of community, as communities themselves most often involve difference and difficulty rather than commonality and ease (Rothenbuhler, 2001). Recognizing, accepting, and managing the tension is a hopeful endeavor, as Bauman (2001) explained:

> The argument between security and freedom, and so the argument between community and individuality, is unlikely ever to be resolved and so likely to go on for a long time to come; not finding the right solu-

tion and being frustrated by the one that has been tried will not prompt
us to abandon the search—but to go on trying. Being human, we can
neither fulfill the hope nor cease hoping. (p. 5)

The GTCRP sought to promote this sense of community with respect
to reconciliation of individual culpability and collective responsibility for
the November 3, 1979, tragedy. Shifting the discourse to extend beyond
individual responsibility on the part of the KKK and the Communist
Workers Party to the city's practices and involvement, however, was a direct
challenge to the city's desire to close the history book on that tragedy.

Communication scholars recognize that communities are realized in
and through talk (e.g., Adelman & Frey, 1997) and shaped by the systems,
cultures, and histories that constitute our collective life (e.g., Artz, 2001).
When adversity hits, as it did in Greensboro, what follows "illuminate[s] the
arbitrariness of . . . naming and framing, presenting alternative possibilities
for assigning guilt and responsibility" (Rakow et al., 2003, p. 39). The
GTCRP's activities, as social and political acts of resistance to the dominant
narrative, were squarely intended to persuade the community that
Greensboro should "reopen the endings of the stories previously told"
(Pezzullo, 2001, p. 15). In doing so, the hope was that a new ending could
be authored by city officials, survivors, *and* other community members to
account for the struggle for social justice started by the activists in 1979.

Past communication research provides examples of how the inclusion of
diverse voices in community-planning efforts can be accomplished. For
example, at an agency for battered women where members were committed
to rejecting masculinist ways of handling difference, Ashcraft (2000) found
that the staff attempted to empower paid employees and members by engaging in various modes of open and improvised communication strategies.
Self-reflexivity, a willingness to name and encounter conflict, and an engagement in self- and mutual criticism led to thoughtful adjustments to organizational structures. The result was the creation of an environment where
opposing views could be negotiated successfully into a "mutually acceptable
balance" (Ashcraft, p. 91). In another community studied by Hafner (2001),
"The Wall," which was developed in cyberspace in 1985, smart, liberal baby
boomers shared their views about this online community, with some members establishing an "electronic persona" that provided a platform for the
otherwise "shy, self-conscious, or socially awkward to wield power, to com-
mand respect and gain popularity" (p. 57). As a final example, in a Northern
California community where environmentalists and loggers squared off,
Ruud and Sprague (2000) found that focusing on the different expertise each
side brought to the conversation actually elucidated the underlying values
important to each side and, thereby, reduced the need to resort to myths and
stereotypes in language choice. In all these instances, the avowed goal was to

seek out, beyond the dominant voices, the many varied voices that can contribute to community.

Constructing a New Community Narrative

The GTCRP members maintained that previous attempts to examine November 3, 1979, fell short of collectively addressing the deep social concerns that many community members still had about that event. Survivor Signe Waller explained that the purpose of the protesters' actions in 1979 remained the same in the 21st century: "To awaken people to hope that we can transform society to become more just. Education and organizing are just the tactics we use." Supporters of the GTCRP initiative claimed that the judicial system provided an unsatisfying analysis of the situation, and that a full reckoning of the event required a more broad-based form of inquiry. Doing so more than 20 years later, however, was a questionable endeavor for some people.

Critics claimed that event participants' memories had faded, providing even less conclusive evidence to point to any wrongdoing by police or government officials. One current city councilwoman explained that like a bull's-eye target, the further one moves away from an event, the less likely a person is to remember the facts and actual happenings. She suggested that with time, memories create something very different than what really happened. Thus, the argument continued, there was no value in reconstructing the events and stories surrounding November 3, 1979. Instead, this councilwoman urged citizens to tackle pressing problems currently existing in Greensboro, such as the closing of factories and the need to recruit new and varied companies to the area.

Supporters of the project, however, countered that the passage of time was helpful to a process of dialogue, as people who once feared for their jobs or retribution by the KKK could now more readily share their stories. Willena Canon, a survivor of November 3, described the scene in 1979 as one full of justified worry: "That day, my sister was so nervous but went out and hugged Nelson Johnson [a main coordinator of the Communist Workers Party activities and now pastor of a local church and key organizer of the GTCRP]. That picture was in the paper and then she got fired from her daycare job. It was hard for people to support this."

Another survivor, Portia Shipman, was in high school in 1979 and a member of the Communist Workers Party. The shootings scared her, but what scared her more was the reaction of the city afterwards when nothing good was said publicly about the protest organizers and their goals. She responded by refusing to speak or even think about November 3, 1979, until the formation of the GTCRP more than 20 years later. As she explained:

I'm still suffering. I didn't come out of the closet until last year. I tried
to bury it, but I'm tired of holding back. I don't care about what people
will say about me anymore. Now, I care about my granddaughters being
able to speak their minds. Let's educate, formulate, and resuscitate what
happened in 1979.

The GTCRP, recognizing the need to establish credibility for its mission, relied on its prominent co-chairs of the local task force and other progressive citizens who used their influence to build support across many sectors of the community. Carolyn Allen, co-chair of the GTCRP and former
Greensboro mayor, expressed high hopes for the process of dialogue:

> The development of stereotyped images will be, if not destroyed, at least
> shaken up a bit. The commission's report should provide a basis for an
> ongoing, community discussion. We'll have the opportunity to develop
> trust where there has been none. Throughout, we'll have the opportuni-
> ty to develop new forms of communication.

Reaching out to the community in this manner was important, for as
Pearce (2002) claimed:

> Minority voices in this country are excluded from the public conversa-
> tion not only because of the race, creed, or economic level of the speak-
> er, but also because what they say does not fit into the larger, usually
> unspoken story that serves as a context for what is heard . . . [and,
> hence,] what they have to say appears foolish and, because of this, is not
> heard or responded to. (p. 31)

The survivors of November 3, 1979, wanted to engage the evidence that
suggested federal and local authorities were well aware of the Klan-Nazi
plans and chose not to protect a politically radical group (Waller, 2002). To
do so, activists desired to initiate conversations throughout Greensboro in
ways that reflected "new depths of community values . . . modeling new vis-
tas of democracy for our nation" (Greensboro Truth and Community
Reconciliation Project, 2003a). The task was not just to suggest that the
dominant narrative be changed; all of the data we collected, and the experiences shared by local task force members, indicated a real need to educate
the citizenry about the events of November 3, 1979, that had been silenced.
A year after the GTCRP had been operating, holding community events,
and gaining some media recognition, there still was much work to be done,
as suggested by a local task force member:

> I went to a neighborhood just outside the city limits and of the 25 signatures I collected on the petition, and the 30 homes I visited, not one person knew about this group [the GTCRP]. I want to host a community event and read the booklet [*A Call for Dialogue*].

The often-repeated desire by the agents for social change was to be inclusive and respectful of others, but staying committed to that vision sometimes was challenging. For example, as documents were drafted to invite public participation, the language sometimes required editing to eliminate inflammatory or prejudiced rhetoric. At the heart of this project was a conviction on the part of the GTCRP activists that the power elite of Greensboro brokered a story that fractured a community to locate blame elsewhere, away from the governmental institutions. That critical conviction, whether accurate or not, had the potential to distance others in the community who did not assume the same level of mistrust. At several local task force meetings, the members debated the merits of the following paragraph presented as a draft in the proposed Mandate for the Greensboro Truth and Reconciliation Commission:

> We can assume that none will be found completely blameless, yet simply finding that all have blame would not satisfy this Commission's mandate to look deeply beneath the surface of the events to find their causes. (Greensboro Truth and Community Reconciliation Project, 2003b)

The paragraph originally was written to recognize that the memory of November 3, 1979, had been defined in the local culture in ways that were contrary to the available facts. As a task force member explained, "We don't want to assign blame; we want to recognize the root causes of the problem and, therefore, identify where responsibility lies." A rabbi in the group, however, expressed reservations, saying, "I agree ethically, but strategically, the language is a problem." He noted that in establishing that the Truth and Reconciliation Commission presumably would find some parties more responsible than others for the tragedy that day, there was, in fact, a specific agenda being presented and a prejudice being imposed on the process.

Eventually, the paragraph was eliminated from the GTCRP Mandate and replaced with the following one that the group members agreed reflected more accurately the intent of their work:

> In addition to exploring questions of institutional and individual responsibility for what happened, as a necessary part of the truth-seek-

ing process we urge the Commission to look deeply into the root causes and historical context of the events of November 3, 1979.
(Greensboro Truth and Community Reconciliation Project, 2003b)

The key distinction drawn in the second and final version of the paragraph
is that the local task force members reminded themselves that the Truth and
Reconciliation Commission was designed to be an independent body, not
beholden to anyone, not even to the vision of the activists themselves.

CHALLENGES TO OUR COMMUNICATION ACTIVISM

The GTCRP attempted to put into action what Young (2000) and Levinas
(1961/1968) suggested in their views of justice and ethics, particularly
regarding processes for including others who have been marginalized in a
democracy/community. As the GTCRP considered how to involve others in
its quest for truth, justice, and reconciliation, one local task force member
reminded the others that the panel that would select the Truth
Commissioners needed to be a group that the community saw as credible
and diverse:

> We're not looking for a centrist group but, rather, a group that repre-
> sents all the interests of the community. The idea is that someone could
> look at the list of selection panel members and say, "My voice is repre-
> sented there by someone."

The continuing challenge for the GTCRP, therefore, was to be attentive to
the myriad needs in the community and include people who would both
support and criticize the process of dialogue in an effort to involve as wide
a community base as possible.

Considering communication theory and its relationship to community
practice led us to offer suggestions for increasing citizen involvement in
and improving public dialogue about the events of November 3, 1979.
After 18 months, some citizens came to recognize that, as members of a
shared community, we all played a part in the tragedy and its aftermath.
John Young, active in the local task force and other programs for social justice, remarked:

> We and our community failed on that day. So I would like us all to
> accept blame for November 3, 1979, and realize that we are all in need
> of forgiveness for the horror that occurred. Our indifference, our anger,

our arrogance, our racism, and our separation from each other as human beings were all part of the tragedy of November 3.

Still, progress has been slow, as many newspaper editorials and citizen comments have shown. One citizen said that she hears people grumble about the need to talk: "They tell me this is about a few bitter people who will just have to get over it. Besides, they say, they'll all be dead in 10 years." Given this situation, we specifically look here at how to overcome opposition from those who have no interest in participating in a dialogic process and how norms of southern U.S. civility can sidetrack substantive discussions that necessarily involve moral conflict.

Overcoming Opposition to Dialogue

Greensboro had a reluctant government in 1979 and another one decades later concerning the discussion of November 3, 1979. Key city officials disregarded invitations to visit or join the local task force. A councilwoman, who pledged to spend 30 minutes a day working against the project because she feared a negative economic impact on the community, stated her many concerns:

> This project is opening an old wound. I believe it will bring further polarization to the city. This project assumes that all we have done [in Greensboro] is not worth anything. We've really made strides. We are in bad economic times and there is no hope for it to be better. So anything we do to hurt us is really bad. I do think it's important to know about your past. However, learning about the past is very different than holding public trials.

Among our greatest hurdles, then, was convincing people that to talk about a difficult past did not have to include divisive conflict.

Our research team worked with those who were willing to share their views and kept the door open to those who were not by maintaining relationships and continuing to invite them to enter the conversation if and when they were ready to do so. For instance, the mayor, who did not meet with the GTCRP, met with us twice at a local coffeehouse to discuss the project and his reticence to offer public support for it. Those conversations brought forth many new understandings, including his concern that there existed an ulterior motive on the part of the survivors who were GTCRP members. He pointed to the term "accountability" in the GTCRP Mandate, saying that it implied judicial recrimination for wrongdoing. Because we had attended most local task force meetings and been involved in the drafting of that document, we were able to share with him our understanding of how the term was being used—namely, as a means by which citizens of Greensboro could see themselves as part of a culture that allowed the tragedy to unfold and subsequently get narrated as it did.

After the GTCRP had been in existence for 18 months, the mayor still was not overtly supportive of it. However, he did name a district court judge to sit on the selection panel that chose the Truth Commissioners. In addition, two board members of the city's Human Relations Commission took an active role in the local task force activities.

The coverage by the daily newspaper and television stations, with the notable exception of a newspaper editorial endorsing the project, had been lukewarm to the GTCRP activities. The city's weekly African American newspaper and National Public Radio affiliate had been more sympathetic to the GTCRP goals, but their audiences amounted to less than 10% of the readership and viewing audiences of the mainstream media sources. There were many times that the daily newspaper simply passed on opportunities to write stories detailing the initiative—the first of its kind in this country—and its progress. Following our public discussion with journalists at the Ashby Dialogue, described previously, the local task force co-chairs and survivors of November 3, 1979, secured a meeting with daily newspaper personnel to detail their concerns. Afterwards, the newspaper coverage improved dramatically, not only in terms of the number of stories but also in the breadth of the coverage. Details of the truth and community reconciliation process were announced, press releases from the GTCRP were used as the basis of several stories, and reporters sought out residents of the low-income neighborhood where the shootings occurred.

Concurrent with the efforts to work with the local media, a press relations manager was hired by the GTCRP to secure regional and national media attention. When stories appeared in the *Philadelphia Inquirer, USA Today, Atlanta Journal-Constitution*, and other newspapers around the country, the editor of Greensboro's business journal commented, "I didn't know this project was the first of its kind in the United States," to which a GTCRP member replied, "That's what I've been trying to tell you all along." It took the attention of others, outside the community, to shed light on what was happening in the community.

How Norms of Southern U.S. Civility Challenge an Effort of This Type

Chafe (1980), a historian at Duke University, wrote that for the past 100 years, Greensboro has given civility top priority, even above civil rights.

Chafe found that in Greensboro, as in much of the U.S. South, there circulated a series of implicit assumptions and modes of relating based on several beliefs of the dominant White community that have been all the more powerful precisely because they are so elusive. Among those beliefs in Greensboro are that conflict inherently is bad and that any action has to be agreed on by everyone involved. Chafe documented that in Greensboro, White leaders thought that civility should govern all relationships, and good manners were more important than substantial action.

We argue that "civility" all too often has been used in Greensboro to mask, hide, and cover up important views and positions. Within such a perspective of civility, ideas that are defined as "radical" have been thwarted either by excluding them from public discourse or denying that there is support for that perspective beyond a "deviant" individual or social group (Jovanovic, 2002). Maintaining a community discourse that highlights rather than covers up a multiplicity of views, even when some of those views are deemed radical or extremist, is important for dialogue and social change. Thus, examining the extreme boundaries of an issue to affect change rather than to defend the status quo, can be a beneficial discourse strategy. Mouffe (2000) argued convincingly that if we do not open up spaces for conflicting discourses more effectively, the likely alternative is physical violence and war.

We found the norm of civility to be deeply entrenched and pervasive in Greensboro, permeating the discussion, or lack of needed discussion, on many other issues besides this 1979 event. However, we believed that there was hope in promoting communicative practices to change prevailing ways of knowing and understanding toward options that are more inclusive. Derrida's (1982) discussion of difference reminded us that there are vast opportunities inherent in language. As Manning (2001) explained:

> The play of our thinking within every discourse is limited, hedged in by the terms within that field of discourse. . . . There is no cosmic rule forcing us to stay within the boundaries of the terms we inherit within any particular field of discourse. Language, in fact, with its infinite capacity to generate more and more difference, provides the way to break beyond the established boundaries and think in new, broader, and more open ways. (p. 145)

Breaking through the confines of civility that are culturally created, yet subject to contestation through discourse, was the challenge we faced. We learned to ask questions often, remind one another to resist the temptation to reduce complex social issues to right/wrong dichotomies, and invite contradictory views into conversation by reaching out to reluctant community members.

TENSIONS IN PERFORMING
COMMUNITY ACTION

Communication research that answers the call of ethics for the purpose of community action is the basis for scholarly endeavors that seek to make known important social concerns and transform unjust ones. Denzin and Lincoln (2000) described the "seventh moment of qualitative research" as one in which researchers move beyond description and criticism toward concern for moral discourse that necessarily involves discussions of democracy, race, gender, class, freedom, and community as ethical points. We experienced the compelling movement of our inquiry toward a synchronicity of ethical, political, and spiritual questions. We wondered about the possibilities and limitations of communication as we heralded its virtues, the influence of social relationships on the self and other as we questioned our level of involvement, and the considerations of interaction in terms of those with whom we spoke and what we discussed with them (Bochner & Ellis, 1999; see also Walker & Curry, Volume 2).

This project was an ideal one for us in that it focused on talk as the gateway to community healing and reconciliation. The role of communication in reconstructing the community of Greensboro was recognized by the grassroots movement, as people saw that by engaging in a new kind of discourse, they could produce a new community narrative attuned to understanding and care. The success of this project held promise for a new kind of community—one in which members would work together to manage lingering tensions through dialogic communication. We were hopeful of the possibilities for success, but not without a dose of skepticism. Early on in the process, we saw instances of talk that never moved to the intended action. For instance, we had secured a verbal agreement from one city official to discuss in a public forum the ramifications of November 3, 1979, but once that event was organized, the official declined to participate. In fact, Greensboro has a history of this "rhetoric of good intentions" followed by inaction (Chafe, 1980, p. 118). This condition is indicative of nearly all movements for social change that solicit the support of established leaders and organizations in the community. As Stewart, Smith, and Denton (2001) explained:

> Institutions, no matter how tolerant and understanding they may seem or want to be, can accept only minor challenges to norms, values, and their legitimacy. They cannot sustain a loss to uninstitutionalized forces and still maintain their authority, credibility, and control over constituencies. (p. 17)

Working both outside the structures of power for change and within those same structures for political reform seemed prudent. However, maintaining trust and ongoing conversation among all the parties proved to be difficult.

Recognizing the simultaneous need for cooperation and the desire to express dissent with the status quo, we questioned where our obligations began and ended with the community we were studying and of which we were members. We wondered how committed we were to the process and what influence our research agenda had on our motivation. We questioned how far we would go in voicing views that might invite disapproval from community leaders and/or the grassroots organization. We were mindful that we had the luxury of pulling out of the fray at a moment's notice.

Specifically, we pondered what it meant to the project and our activism that we initially declined membership on the local task force, despite numerous requests from members to join. We reasoned that we would be more valuable to the project by remaining somewhat outside the process (at least to external eyes) and, thereby, providing a certain legitimacy through our academic affiliation. Although we believed this, we also recognized that in not publicly aligning with the project as members of the local task force, we retained a certain "safety," both personally and professionally.

We were not the first to express hesitation with becoming formal allies with the survivors. Following November 3, 1979, there were many supporters of the victims who organized themselves into separate groups so as not to be associated with the Communist Workers Party. Although support was expressed from a number of these groups for the survivors, there never was a strong collective voice that expressed dissent with the dominant narrative that focused on the conflict between two outside, agitator groups. Through the years, the survivors claimed that their alternative narrative was not heard, a narrative that put the spotlight on the role of official agencies, and their informants, in carefully orchestrating the activities that resulted in physical deaths and character assassinations of surviving workers attempting to promote social and economic justice.

This matter of membership on the local task force shows that we were experiencing a dialectic in our researcher identities, drawing on both deconstructive practices to critique discursive moves and reconstructive activities to suggest alternative discourses aimed at building bridges among various community interests (Giroux, 2001). Thus, balancing our desire to be associated with the project and our recognition of the value of remaining outside of it became the subject of many of our research team conversations (see also Crabtree & Ford, this volume). Foremost in our plans was working to not further polarize our community by aligning too publicly with anything beyond the process of dialogue itself. In doing so, we were able to talk to police officers, public officials, and business representatives who saw our inquiry as one steeped in education more than persuasion. Eventually, the issue of membership became a moot point as the local task force transformed itself from a membership-based body into a bimonthly gathering place where attendance was open to all, and all in attendance were welcome to contribute to the conversation and planning activities.

More critically, we questioned our resolve to do what we were advocating others to do: to take a stand on the important political and ethical concerns arising from the community response to November 3, 1979, and its aftermath. Over time, two of us (Steger and Jovanovic) emerged as among the approximately 30 people in the community whom many could point to as recognized supporters of the GTCRP. The two of us exposed ourselves to the scrutiny of others, difficult as that was, which proved to be a turning point in our research process because once we were "known" for our role in the project, we stood even more proudly for our belief in dialogue as a means for achieving social justice in the community. We faced friends and acquaintances at civic, religious, and social functions who questioned our allegiance and time spent with such a controversial project (see also Esrock, Hart, & Leichty, this volume). We learned to respond to them in ways consistent with our theoretical perspectives, ethical sensibilities, and strategic knowledge. We listened first, before we advocated for the process of dialogue, shared developments and successes of the GTCRP, and asked modest questions of our own to learn from those who were willing to speak to us.

From the beginning of our research, members of the local task force knew of our scholarly interests and personal commitment to activism. Over time, Steger and Jovanovic remained involved with the GTCRP by way of drafting documents, advocating in the community, writing grants, and soliciting university involvement and support. For every large event or strategy session, we were viewed as part of the local task force team.

LESSONS LEARNED ABOUT COMMUNICATION ACTIVISM

We learned several important lessons about communication activism as we worked with the GTCRP. The first of these lessons we offer to those involved in community conflict; the latter lessons are intended for communication researchers as they consider forays into activist research.

First, community dialogue is facilitated by a 3-pronged approach of educating, organizing, and questioning. Focusing on an educational appeal has the advantage of motivating the uninitiated by challenging, not vilifying, the status quo. The GTCRP's focus was to uncover stories and establish a ground for community reflection that could lead to reconciliation rather than to protest against and alienate others. We saw that the more people know about the facts and stories surrounding a controversial subject, the stronger is their moral resolve to address that subject with compassion and justice. Organizing people in a community initiative, we learned, requires no less than a massive one-on-one campaign. We operated daily with the help of high-tech communication media, but we found that those media simply were inadequate to move people to action. E-mail announcements, flyers, web page information, and newspaper publicity could accomplish much in terms of sharing information, but it was the personal telephone calls, private conversations, and appeals for support in face-to-face encounters that yielded the best results, whether that was in securing new attendees at the local task force meetings, recruiting student volunteers, or getting time to speak at local organization meetings (see the discussion of communication forms for activism in McHale, Volume 2). Finally, dialogue requires a commitment to discovering something new and, thereby, opening ourselves up to the possibility of transformation (Arnett, 1986). We found that responding to citizens' inquiries with questions of our own created a way to open up a deeper discussion than offering answers alone could provide. Furthermore, doing so kept that discussion going and allowed for new understandings to emerge (Manning, 2001). It also enabled citizens to examine the perspectives and underlying assumptions on which their original questions were based (Kellett & Dalton, 2001).

Because much of our communication research activity was spent with the organizers of the GTCRP, we saw how supporters came to know one another and developed their commitment to the project. At first, supporters were asked to comment on the process and give feedback on documents being written. Over time, various members volunteered to do more. One drafted a petition to urge the Greensboro City Council to support the GTCRP, and at least a dozen others volunteered to walk door-to-door in neighborhoods all over Greensboro collecting signatures in support of the petition. Many of the volunteers introduced the GTCRP to their local churches through the showing of a 17-minute videotape documenting the events of November 3, 1979, and the subsequent formation of the GTCRP, or in leading a discussion about the project at adult Sunday school classes. Throughout this process, supporters of the GTCRP reflected on their activities and made appropriate changes as they moved forward with plans for future events.

When a march was planned for the 25th anniversary commemoration of the November 3, 1979 event, several special meetings were called specifically to address the conflict that emerged in the group over whether the march would further the goal of reconciliation or derail it by inviting protest rhetoric into a process espousing collaboration. At the first meeting, 30 people, half Black and half White, voiced their views and concerns in a 3-hour discussion about the proposed march. One White male who owned a bar in

1979 and witnessed firsthand the intimidation by Klan members who visited his business said, "If it appears that we're trying to finish the job of the
Communist Workers Party, we'll lose people who are just signing on to this
process of truth and reconciliation." An African American woman, who was
4 years old in 1979, countered, "The convenience of dealing with this issue
[the march] to make it appealing to all groups offends me. You don't need
them anyway. On November 3, 1979, no one considered how convenient it
was for five people to die."

At a later meeting, some people expressed concern that a march might
interrupt the truth and reconciliation process in a way that would permanently damage the potential for community healing. A retired, White physician explained his views:

> First, I have a great deal of respect for the agony the date November 3
> brings. Second, the 25th anniversary is a huge milestone. Third, the
> Truth Commission needs to be insulated from controversy surrounding
> the march. Even a candlelight vigil could be construed as a disturbance.

Others argued that the tension a march would create was exactly the next
step needed to continue educating the public. A White male active in social
protest in the 1970s and now involved in diversity and leadership issues as a
city employee offered his perspective:

> I think the march is a good idea for a lot of reasons. If we trust the Truth
> and Reconciliation Commissioners, they're insulated by their own
> integrity. We keep saying there will be people turned off by a march, but
> there will be people turned on by a march. If the people who died were
> here today, they'd be doing this.

Eventually, most participants agreed to allow those in favor of a march to
plan one. The supporters of the march enthusiastically agreed to incorporate
all of the concerns raised in the discussion in future planning processes.

When the 25th anniversary march was held, approximately 700 people
from Greensboro, other cities in North Carolina, and from states along the
eastern U.S. seaboard participated, along with 300 police officers, walking
shoulder-to-shoulder along the 2.1-mile route (Collins, 2004). According to
the marchers' accounts (we did not attend), it was a joyful celebration that
turned "tragedy into triumph" with song, celebratory speeches, and renewal of friendships (on the need for communication activism to be joyful, see
Hartnett, this volume). Liz, a White, female college student said of the experience, "I felt a baton was being passed down to our generation. I saw the
beauty that comes out of struggle." The retired physician who previously

was against the march added how his change of heart was indicative of the type of change Greensboro needed. He attended the march, was featured in a photograph that ran on the front page of the daily newspaper, and had this to say about his experience: "Some of you were here the day when the march was decided. I voiced reservations then. The challenge for me was to keep open and to realize how great something like this could be."

A second lesson we learned is that communication about November 3, 1979, or any major conflict, constantly needs to be directed back to the root issue—in this case, the violation of constitutional rights. We witnessed the tendency of people to drift toward other issues of their own design, using the topic of conversation only as a springboard for advancing their agendas. Other times, we saw people wanting badly to believe that our institutions of power are beyond reproach. Questioning those institutions was more difficult than pointing the finger of blame at individuals, be that the mayor or an activist. We found that it was very difficult for citizens to see the wider, deeper structural conditions in the city that needed attention in 1979, and 25 years later, remain contested matters, such as the imbalance in the allocation of resources, the impact of not having a living wage, and the persistent effects of racism. The challenge for this community, then, was to focus on what are the patterns of power and privilege that shape the possibilities for the expression or suppression of various stakeholder views.

Third, wide involvement, even by those who are against a social change project, is the best way to assure that the process is kept honest and true to its goals. We recognize that there always will be those who feign silence in an attempt to discredit a grassroots effort. We have, in fact, been culturally organized by society not to rebel (Goodwyn, 1978). However, when the momentum builds for examining a social issue, as it did for the events of November 3, 1979, in Greensboro, it behooves detractors and supporters alike to express their views publicly as a demonstration of support for our democratic way of life (see Hartnett, this volume; Palmer, this volume). By getting involved, citizens not only monitor the process but also help to shape it. Their concerns can and should be discussed, bringing forth new possibilities for how to attend to them. One citizen captured the spirit of our views when he said that it was "unconscionable" that some civic leaders refused to participate in a process that so many members of the community wanted.

Fourth, it is imperative that researchers and community activists focus continually on ethics as they observe and play a part in a process as controversial as this one. There was a poignant moment during a community presentation by one of the survivors, Signe Waller, when she shared her continuing struggle to move toward a spiritually based approach to reconciliation that honors the connection of all individuals, and away from a partisan-based cynicism that pits one side against the other. This position was echoed by others who once were 1960s activists, ready to fight for justice and fairness in society. The desire for the same ideals continues, but among these activists there is a softer view that has emerged, one that recognizes that when people have the opportunity to talk about important issues, there is hope for better public actions.

The fifth lesson is that dialogue can, in fact (not just in theory), have a positive effect on community relations (see Adams et al., this volume). Greensboro's mayor demonstrated tangible shifts in his actions toward the GTCRP, due, in part, to two extended conversations with us and likely other talks with community members. Initially, the mayor did not think that this project warranted discussion in the community, had not accepted invitations to attend the local task force meetings, and had expressed, in an interview published in *Newsweek*, his fear that this project would turn into a witch hunt (Cose, 2003). Six months later, he made his first public appearance to listen to and discuss the purpose of the GTCRP at a City of Greensboro Human Relations Commission meeting. Afterwards, the mayor was invited by a key GTCRP leader to discuss the project privately, in more detail. The mayor told the leader, on accepting the invitation, that some of his comments might have been taken out of context and suggested that "we're not as far apart as you might think." Equally important, he agreed to appoint a representative to the Truth Commissioners' selection panel. That movement is reason enough for communication scholars to not only pay attention to processes that promote dialogue but also to encourage, support, and assist in their development.

The final lesson we learned is that creating the conditions for high-quality dialogic processes requires time—lots of it. Grassroots groups have to balance the need for generating enough tangible results to attract and retain members with the recognition that despite such results, other people will require even more time to make the decision to join a movement for social change. After much discussion at one meeting about whether to move forward without the full support of key community leaders, one local task force member proposed an idea that brought a rousing expression of consensus from the other members. She said, "It will take as long as it takes. We put together a calendar, but we're talking about a process of building community." She recognized, as did others, that soliciting support for the GTCRP involved a much larger concern—collaboration among groups that never before had worked together. It was a mammoth task, and one that the local task force members realized required time and patience. Time, we found, was not the enemy; it was the gift that enabled citizens to pursue much-needed conversations. Communication and community building, these activists for social change found, and we witnessed, are ongoing achievements that require collective interest in talking about the past, engaging the present, and planning for the future.

CONCLUSION

The GTCRP is far from being done with its work, yet the results have been encouraging to date. A selection panel, representing a broad cross-section of the community, completed its work and named seven Truth Commissioners. It is a welcomed surprise to the local task force members that although the GTCRP often has been critiqued in the daily newspaper, not a single letter to the editor appeared criticizing the character or charter of the Truth Commissioners.[9] Five thousand signatures were collected on petitions asking the Greensboro City Council to support the project, and publicity about the project increased within Greensboro and exploded on the national and international scenes.

As the Truth Commissioners began their work in June 2004, the GTCRP continued its efforts to educate the public about November 3, 1979, and the process of truth and community reconciliation. Many people recognized that in the coming months and years, it is likely that opposition to this process will intensify. Survivor Nelson Johnson forecasted that there are those who fear that the project could unearth unpleasant findings about city officials and who may attempt to discredit the GTCRP, as has been the pattern throughout history whenever the status quo is successfully challenged (personal communication, May 15, 2004).

Because the GTCRP involves a dialogic communication process, the results cannot be predetermined nor guaranteed. With several years remaining, its proponents continue to work hard at creating an environment conducive to dialogue, recognizing that they have no ability to predict what the outcome will be other than the publication of a report by the Truth Commission. If the pursuit of truth reveals relevant information not previously embraced and changes some perspectives about November 3, 1979; if we all learn how to better get along with each other, even as we disagree about the facts surrounding our history; if the truth and community reconciliation process can provide alternative interpretations never before considered; and if the project can heighten community awareness about the shared duty of government and citizens to create their future, then the GTCRP will have been successful.

Our communication activism, fueled by the theories of Young (2001) and Levinas (1961/1969), compels us not only to write about social change efforts but to participate fully in them with a concern for including voices that have been silenced and extending our responsibility to others who share our social world. Our activism with the GTCRP was specifically intended to give rise to the importance of dialogue, influenced, in part, by the work of Freire (2000), who stated that language is an ideological concern as much as a linguistic matter: "If it is in speaking their word that people, by naming the world, transform it, dialogue imposes itself as the way by which they achieve significance as human beings. Dialogue is thus an existential necessity" (p. 88). Like Freire, who advocated for revolutionary and transformative pedagogy, we acted on an impulse to speak out for social change that moved us into the center of our community's discourse struggle. We did so, not with certainty but with a desire to listen and engage with the many stories of our community and reflect on what we were learning. We did so with an appetite to teach others, too, of our new knowledge gained through dialogue.

We see communication activism as inherently an act of care that pulls us toward others who struggle to realize the full potential of democracy and community, inspired by a quest for critical knowledge and informed by personal experiences. Above all else, we see communication as an act of love. As Freire (2000) said:

> Dialogue cannot exist . . . in the absence of a profound love for the world and for people. . . . . Because love is an act of courage, not of fear, love is a commitment to others. No matter where the oppressed are found, the act of love is commitment to their cause—the cause of liberation. And this commitment, because it is loving, is dialogical. (p. 89)

Researching, writing, teaching, and learning are our modes of communication activism in Greensboro. Integrating our academic pursuits with our ethical and political concerns enabled us to influence community leaders and citizens through a process of critical reason, a passion for social justice, and a commitment to dialogue. It is that combination of scholarship and activism that communicates creative, exciting possibilities to mobilize people for truth, reconciliation, and constructive community change.

NOTES

1. Four of the five people killed were union organizers in the textile mills. All five people recognized the KKK as a formidable obstacle to bringing Whites and Blacks together to protest deplorable working conditions. Textile workers were exposed to dangerously high levels of cotton dust (leading to brown lung disease), yet received few or no health, retirement, and sick-day benefits (Waller, 2002). North Carolina, as Wheaton (1987) noted, "has historically ranked at or near the bottom of the national scales for average wages and for percentage of unionized workers" (p. 15). Those killed were Cesar Cauce, a Cuban immigrant who graduated *magna cum laude* with a degree in history from Duke University; Dr. Michael R. Nathan, a pediatrician who served predominantly Blacks and poor residents in North Carolina; William E. Sampson, who, with a master's degree from Harvard Divinity School, left medical school only a few months before graduation to work at a textile mill; Sandra Neely Smith, who,

on graduating from Greensboro's Bennett College as student body president, abandoned her dreams to be a nurse to work in a textile mill; and Dr. James M. Waller, who left the practice of medicine to become a textile mill worker and union local president.

2. According to a 2000 national survey designed and implemented by Harvard University, Greensboro ranked second out of 40 U.S. cities in volunteering and charitable giving, 25th in social trust, 21st in interracial trust, and 34th in informal social interaction among neighbors, coworkers, and friends (Social Capital Community Benchmark Survey, 2001). In terms of political activities, which include protests and grassroots efforts, the area ranked 36th (Community Foundation of Greater Greensboro, 2001). This ranking of political activities is particularly disturbing in light of Greensboro's distinguished role in the U.S. South for vigorous antislavery activity (Chafe, 1980) and, later, for launching the national sit-in movement for desegregation of public facilities, when, in 1960, four Black students from North Carolina Agriculture and Technical College demanded equal service with White persons at the lunch counter of the local Woolworth's store.

3. The formation of the GTCRP was the latest of numerous attempts to engage the citizens and political institutions of Greensboro in public conversation about November 3, 1979. Initially, the three trials extending to 1985 served as the subject for media analysis for public consumption. A half-dozen filmmakers produced documentaries about the event, several of which aired on national television, and Emily Mann wrote and directed a play, *Greensboro: A Requiem*, that premiered in Princeton, NJ in 1996. Throughout the years, the survivors organized various public events on the anniversary of the incident.

4. Although all 16 students in the Communication and Social Change class were invited to write with the professor for publication, only three chose to participate in that endeavor and are included as coauthors of this chapter. We are particularly grateful to fellow students Drewry Sackett, Cara Michele Forest, and Dana Carter, who were among those who contributed many hours of service to the GTCRP and provided invaluable insight into its communication processes before we undertook the writing of this chapter. Some of their ideas, work products, and reflections are included in our analysis.

   After the first 18 months of our work was completed, Carol Steger and Spoma Jovanovic remained active participants in this process for social change. Among the main challenges for student involvement in a process such as this are competing demands for time, loss of interest once class discussions and assignments are no longer routine, and, in at least one case, "burnout" from the many hours spent in cycles of hope and disappointment about what could be accomplished.

5. The following groups and organizations (listed alphabetically) each appointed a person to serve on a community panel that met weekly for 3 months to select the seven Truth and Reconciliation Commissioners from 67 nominations forwarded by the community:

   - Chancellors and presidents of the six colleges and universities in Greensboro

- Chairs of the student bodies of five of the city's colleges and universities
- The Greensboro Mayor's Office
- Greensboro Neighborhood Congress (a citywide alliance of neighborhoods)
- Greensboro Truth and Community Reconciliation Project
- Guilford County Democratic Party
- Guilford County Republican Party
- The Jewish community
- The Muslim community
- National Association for the Advancement of Colored People
- The National Conference for Community and Justice
- The Pulpit Forum/African American churches
- Traditional Catholic, Protestant, and independent churches
- The Triad Central Labor Council (an AFL-CIO union organization)

6. Among the cities that watched Greensboro's effort to launch a truth and community reconciliation process were Memphis, TN, Philadelphia, PA, and Marion, IN, cities that also were trying to heal a history of civil rights and racial violations.

7. The South African Truth and Reconciliation Commission was established by the South African Parliament to investigate abuses resulting from Apartheid rule over a period of 45 years. With a staff totaling 300 and a budget of $45 million, the operation was, by far, the largest of its kind in history (Hayner, 2002). The commission was established to move South Africa from a period of tyranny and chaos to the beginning of a democratic state by exposing the violence committed during apartheid and then reconciling with those ghosts and enemies of the past (Tutu, 1997).

   In Greensboro, as in South Africa, the work for truth and community reconciliation advanced with a spiritual grounding, one in which forgiveness and healing were the goals once the truth could fully be ascertained. GTCRP supporters forecasted that the Truth Commission would issue a report requiring institutional change within business and government bodies. However, the Greensboro initiative differed significantly from the South African model and other truth commissions in three ways: (a) the Greensboro project had no subpoena power, (b) the effort was not sanctioned by any governmental body, and (c) the focus in Greensboro was on one specific event rather than a pattern of abuses over a period of time.

8. A look at Greensboro's history, says Chafe, reveals a strong pattern of civility characterizing all relationships. Space was carved out in public venues to listen to opposing views, but then little follow-up action resulted. Blacks and Whites would negotiate, for instance, for better education for minority students, but then inaction would follow. When civility failed, as it did numerous times in Greensboro's history, violence followed, only to be contained again through unmet promises for change until the next confrontational episode.

9. As of this writing, there has been little public reaction to the Truth Commissioners beyond what was evident at the swearing-in ceremony, where 500 people gathered to celebrate the naming of the seven commissioners from

the 67 nominations received from community members. The commissioners are: Cynthia Brown of Durham, NC, a grassroots organizer and one-time candidate for U.S. Senate; Patricia Clark of New York, executive director of the Fellowship of Reconciliation; Muktha Jost of Greensboro, assistant professor at North Carolina A&T State University; Angela Lawrence of Greensboro, a community activist involved in education and neighborhood development; Robert Peters of Greensboro, a retired corporate attorney; Reverend Mark Sills, executive director of Greensboro's Faith Action International House; and Barbara Walker of Greensboro, a retired manager with Wrangler Corporation and former board president of Greensboro's Young Women's Christian Association (YWCA).

REFERENCES

Adelman, M. B., & Frey, L. R. (1997). *The fragile community: Living together with AIDS*. Mahwah, NJ: Erlbaum.

Altheide, D. L., & Johnson, J. M. (1997). Ethnography and justice. In G. Miller & R. Dingwall (Eds.), *Context and method in qualitative research* (pp. 172-184). Thousand Oaks, CA: Sage.

Arnett, R. C. (1986). *Communication and community: Implications of Martin Buber's dialogue*. Carbondale: Southern Illinois University Press.

Arnett, R. C., & Arneson, P. (1999). *Dialogic civility in a cynical age: Community, hope, and interpersonal relationships*. Albany: State University of New York Press.

Artz, L. (2001). Critical ethnography for communication studies: Dialogue and social justice in service-learning. *Southern Communication Journal, 66*, 239-250.

Ashcraft, K. L. (2001). Feminist organizing and the construction of "alternative" community. In G. J. Shepherd & E. W. Rothenbuhler (Eds.), *Communication and community* (pp. 79-110). Mahwah, NJ: Erlbaum.

Bauman, Z. (2001). *Community: Seeking safety in an insecure world*. Cambridge, United Kingdom: Polity Press.

Bermanzohn, S. (2003). *Through survivors' eyes: From the sixties to the Greensboro massacre*. Nashville, TN: Vanderbilt University Press.

Bochner, A. P., & Ellis, C. (1999). Which way to turn? *Journal of Contemporary Ethnography, 28*, 485-499.

Bowers, J. W., Ochs, D. J., & Jensen, R. J. (1993). *The rhetoric of agitation and control* (2nd ed.) Long Grove, IL: Waveland Press.

Chafe, W. H. (1980). *Civilities and civil rights: Greensboro, North Carolina, and the Black struggle for freedom*. New York: Oxford University Press.

Collins, E. (2004, November 14). Justice marches on. *News & Record* (Greensboro, NC), pp. B1-B2.

Community Foundation of Greater Greensboro. (2001, March 1). *Social capital community survey shows area's strengths and needs for improvement*. Retrieved September 30, 2003, from http://www.cfgg

Conquergood, D. (1991). Rethinking ethnography: Towards a critical cultural politics. *Communication Monographs, 58*, 179-194.

Cose, E. (2003, June 2). How to mend a massacre. *Newsweek*, p. 41.

Denzin, N. K., & Lincoln, Y. S. (2000). Introduction: Entering the field of qualitative research. In N. K. Denzin & Y. S. Lincoln (Eds.), *Handbook of qualitative research* (2nd ed., pp. 1-17). Thousand Oaks, CA: Sage.

Derrida, J. (1982). *Positions* (A. Ball, Trans.). Chicago: University of Chicago Press.

Fiske, J. (1991). Writing ethnographies: Contribution to a dialogue. *Quarterly Journal of Speech, 77*, 330-335.

Freire, P. (2000). *Pedagogy of the oppressed* (30th anniversary ed.; M. B. Ramos, Trans). New York: Continuum.

Frey, L. R., Pearce, W. B., Pollock, M. A., Artz, L., & Murphy, B. A. O. (1996). Looking for justice in all the wrong places: On a communication approach to social justice. *Communication Studies, 47*, 110-127.

Friedland, L. A. (2001). Communication, community, and democracy: Toward a theory of communicatively integrated community. *Communication Research, 28*, 358-391.

Giroux, H. A. (2001). *Public spaces, private lives: Beyond the culture of cynicism.* Lanham, MD: Rowman & Littlefield.

Goodwin, M. H. (1990). *He-said-she-said: Talk as social organization among Black children.* Bloomington: Indiana University Press.

Goodwyn, L. (1978). *The populist movement: A short history of the agrarian revolt in America.* New York: Oxford University Press.

Greensboro Truth and Community Reconciliation Project. (2003a). *The declaration* [Brochure]. Greensboro, NC: Local Task Force & National Advisory Committee.

Greensboro Truth and Community Reconciliation Project. (2003b). *Mandate for the Greensboro Truth and Reconciliation Commission* [Brochure]. Greensboro, NC: Local Task Force & National Advisory Committee.

Hafner, K. (2001). The well: Life, death, and social norms in the seminal online community. *Responsive Community, 11*, 52-61.

Hayner, P. B. (2002). *Unspeakable truths: Facing the challenge of truth commissions.* New York: Routledge.

Jovanovic, S. (2002, October). *Civil rights is not a Black and White issue . . . or is it?* Paper presented at the meeting of the Carolinas Communication Association, Greensboro, NC.

Kellett, P. N., & Dalton, D. G. (2001). *Managing conflict in a negotiated world: A narrative approach to achieving dialogue and change.* Thousand Oaks, CA: Sage.

Levinas, E. (1969). *Totality and infinity* (A. Lingis, Trans.). Pittsburgh, PA: Duquesne University Press. (Original work published 1961)

Levinas, E. (1985). *Ethics and infinity* (R. A. Cohen, Trans.). Pittsburgh, PA: Duquesne University Press. (Original work published 1982)

Manning, R. J. S. (2001). *Beyond ethics to justice through Levinas and Derrida: The legacy of Levinas.* Quincy, IL: Franciscan Press.

McKinsey & Company. (2000). *Building consensus for Greensboro's future: Discussion report.* Retrieved October 27, 2003, from http://www.weaverfoundation.com/report1.pdf

Mouffe, C. (2000). *The democratic paradox.* New York: Verso.

North Carolina State Center for Health Statistics. (2003). *2003 infant mortality statistics for North Carolina.* Retrieved June 6, 2004, from http://www.schs.state.nc.us/SCHS/deaths/ims/2003

Pearce, W. B. (2002). Toward a national conversation about public issues. In W. F. Eadie & P. E. Nelson (Eds.), *The changing conversation in America: Lectures from the Smithsonian* (pp. 13-37). Thousand Oaks, CA: Sage.

Pezzullo, P. C. (2001). Performing critical interruptions: Stories, rhetorical invention, and the environmental justice movement. *Western Journal of Communication, 65*, 1-25.

Pilotta, J. J., McCaughan, J. A., Jasko, S., Murphy, J., Jones, T., Wilson, L. et al. (2001). *Communication and social action research*. Cresskill, NJ: Hampton Press.

Polkinghorne, D. E. (1988). *Narrative knowing and the human sciences*. Albany: State University of New York Press.

Rakow, L. F., Belter, B., Dyrstad, H., Hallsten, J., Johnson, J., & Indvik, K. (2003). The talk of movers and shakers: Class conflict in the making of a community disaster. *Southern Communication Journal, 69*, 37-50.

Reisch, M. (2002). Defining social justice in a socially unjust world. *Families in Society, 83*, 343-354.

Reissman, C. K. (1993). *Narrative analysis*. Newbury Park, CA: Sage.

Rothenbuhler, E. W. (2001). Revising communication research for working on community. In G. J. Shepherd & E. W. Rothenbuhler (Eds.), *Communication and community* (pp. 159-179). Mahwah, NJ: Erlbaum.

Ruud, G., & Sprague, J. (2000). Can't see the [old growth] forest for the logs: Dialectical tensions in the interpretive practices of environmentalists and loggers. *Communication Reports, 13*, 55-66.

Ryan, C., Carragee, K. M., & Schwerner, C. (1998). Media, movements, and the quest for social justice. *Journal of Applied Communication Research, 26*, 165-181.

Shepherd, G. J., & Rothenbuhler, E. W. (Eds.). (2001). *Communication and community*. Mahwah, NJ: Erlbaum.

Social Capital Community Benchmark Survey. (2001, March 1). Retrieved July 17, 2004, from http://www.cfsv.org/communitysurvey/nc3c.html

Steger, C. E. (2004). *A call for dialogue: Greensboro, North Carolina's opportunity to move toward wholeness*. Greensboro: University of North Carolina at Greensboro, Department of Communication.

Stewart, C. J., Smith, C. A., & Denton, R. E., Jr. (2001). *Persuasion and social movements* (4th ed.). Prospect Heights, IL: Waveland Press.

Surber, J. P. (1994, Fall). Kant, Levinas, and the thought of the "other." *Philosophy Today*, pp. 294-316.

Swan, S. (2002). Rhetoric, service, and social justice. *Written Communication, 19*, 76-108.

Taylor, C. (1995). *Philosophical arguments*. Cambridge, MA: Harvard University Press.

The public pulse. (2003, February 9). *News & Record* (Greensboro, NC), p. H3.

Tutu, D. M. (1999). *No future without forgiveness*. New York: Doubleday.

U.S. Census Bureau. (2000a). *Median household income in 1999 (dollars)*. Retrieved July 18, 2004, from http://factfinder.census.gov/home/saff/main.html?_lang=en

U.S. Census Bureau. (2000b). *Profile of general demographic characteristics: 2000*. Retrieved July 18, 2004, from http://factfinder.census.gov/home/saff/main.html?_lang=en

Waller, S. (2002). *Love and revolution: A political memoir: People's history of the Greensboro massacre, its setting and aftermath.* Lanham, MD: Rowman and Littlefield.

Wheaton, E. (1987). *Codename GREENKIL: The 1979 Greensboro killings.* Athens: University of Georgia Press.

Wood, J. T. (1996). Social justice research: Alive and well in the field of communication. *Communication Studies, 47,* 128-134.

Young, I. M. (2000). *Inclusion and democracy.* New York: Oxford University Press.

Zoller, H. M. (2000). "A place you haven't visited before": Creating the conditions for community dialogue. *Southern Communication Journal, 65,* 191-207.

2

PUBLIC DIALOGUE AS COMMUNICATION ACTIVISM

Lessons Learned From Engaging in Community-Based Action Research

Carey Adams
Charlene Berquist
Randy Dillon
Gloria Galanes
Missouri State University

In 1994, an alliance of leaders in Springfield, MO, known as The Good Community Committee, organized a citywide forum to discuss civic virtues the community should embrace as guiding principles. Having formed originally as a volunteer effort to address issues of violence in the community, this group of 40 education, business, and civic leaders turned its attention to what might be agreed on as the basis of a "good" community. The discussion, however, derailed when vocal religious and social conservatives attacked the advocated virtue of "tolerance" as a code word for approving lifestyles they viewed as objectionable. The ensuing argument demonstrated very little tolerance from either side, and some 10 years later, no one has been bold enough to propose returning to the task of discussing, let alone reaching agreement on, common community values. Although this reluctance may be due, in part, to community members' belief that agreement probably is not possible, it also may be due in larger measure to their feeling that disagreement is just too painful.

Dialogue amidst difference, however, is critical to contemporary civic life. Rothenbuhler (2001) described "community" as "a container of difference" (p. 169) and Adelman and Frey (1997) claimed that "communication is the primary social process . . . that creates space [in a community] for multiple and oppositional voices to be heard" (p. 106). If homogeneity and agreement are necessary prerequisites for joint community action, such action will be very slow in coming. Joint action is a better model for civic life, yet joint action requires forms of communication that are not predicated on the assumption that participants either begin or end with common views of the world.

The experience of The Good Community Committee illustrates the importance of undergirding community activism with the necessary communication infrastructure that makes joint action possible. The community itself is situated in the Ozarks region of southwest Missouri and encompasses the urban center of Springfield and the surrounding suburbs and rural areas that make up Greene County. The community predominately is White and conservative and often is referred to as the "buckle" on the nation's Bible belt. Members of The Good Community Committee recognized the need for public participation in setting an agenda for civic renewal, but they overestimated community participants' ability and willingness to dialogue productively in the presence of deeply divided factions, distrust, and even open hostility. Although change proponents often are critical of efforts that are "all talk and no action," elucidation of the ways in which talk *is* action and the role that talk plays in making other action possible is a key responsibility of communication activists (see also Jovanovic, Steger, Symonds, & Nelson, this volume). In this chapter, we present three examples of dialogue as communication activism with which we have been involved and the lessons we have learned from those projects about activism, action research, and practical theory. We first explain our view of public dialogue, including its grounding in the coordinated management of meaning theory, as a vehicle of communication activism. We then detail the three extensive public dialogue projects and examine the practical effects that dialogue has had in those contexts and the lessons we have learned.

PUBLIC DIALOGUE AS PRACTICAL THEORY

Activism generally is understood as action that attempts to bring about some type of societal change. We commonly associate particular forms of communication with activism, including protests, political rhetoric, demonstrations, lobbying, debate, propaganda, and mobilization of media resources. These all are very public forms of communication, but there is another sense in which "public" communication is understood to include dialogue at a more interpersonal local level. This is the approach taken by the Public Dialogue Consortium (PDC), as articulated by its members (see, e.g., K.A. Pearce & Pearce, 2001; W. B. Pearce & Pearce, 2000; Spano, 2001).

The primary goal of the PDC is "to improve the quality of public communication" (K. A. Pearce & Pearce, 2001, p. 105). This goal is pursued by working to create contexts in which dialogue is possible where otherwise it would not have been. This gap between the possible and the impossible is bridged by an analysis of the specific communication context using an interpretive framework based on the theory of coordinated management of meaning (CMM).

In CMM terms, people manage their interactions with others using coordination and coherence (for reviews of CMM, see Barge & Pearce, 2004; W. B. Pearce & Cronen, 1980; W. B. Pearce & Pearce, 2000). *Coordination* refers to the meshing of individuals' rules for action and meaning to bring about a mutually desired outcome; *coherence* is the process of making sense of what one observes. Successful coordination with others does not require that everyone share the same meanings or interpretations of referents, only that individuals be able to predict others' actions sufficiently to carry out a line of action (W. B. Pearce & Cronen, 1980). Emerging from the conversations in which they have been and are immersed, people negotiate rules for interpreting actions (constitutive rules) and for guiding actions (regulative rules). Regulative rules aid persons in deciding what types of acts should follow other types of acts (prefigurative and contextual forces), and such rules suggest what acts logically should lead to other acts or outcomes (practical and implicative forces). These constellations of rules constitute interpersonal systems of meaning that must be coordinated with others and, in turn, those attempts at coordination may reinforce and/or bring about changes in interpersonal rules.

Also central to CMM is the concept of "nested hierarchies of contexts." Briefly, these levels of context include (a) content (verbal and nonverbal behaviors), (b) speech acts (expressed and perceived intent of communicative behaviors), (c) episodes (the "kinds" of interactions in which participants believe themselves to be engaged), (d) relationships (how participants define their relations to particular others), (e) life scripts (participants' identities or self-concepts), and (f) sociocultural patterns (customs and interpretations that characterize the larger cultural background[s] in which communication occurs). Any of these levels may serve to contextualize other levels. For instance, individuals gathered to discuss how to improve education in their community might approach the discussion as a debate (episode) in which they need to argue persuasively for their ideas; within that context, the statement of an opposing viewpoint is understood as a challenge to the validity of one's position (speech act), requiring a refutation of the opposing view (regulative rule).

Individuals' abilities to engage in dialogue are constrained and/or enabled by their interpretations of the context and the available resources and practices they employ in managing their interactions in that context (W. B. Pearce, 1989). Put in these terms, public dialogue practitioners seek to create contexts wherein coordination is possible, even where mutual coherence (i.e., agreement) is unlikely. In public dialogue events, this is accomplished by purposively shaping people's definitions of the context and imposing and enforcing certain "rules" for communication.

Several scholars have described public dialogue as a context where differences are welcomed and where participants are encouraged to remain in the "tension" between holding their position and being open to the viewpoints of others (see W. B. Pearce & Pearce, 2000; Stewart & Zediker, 2000). K. A. Pearce (2001) explained that public dialogue facilitation is a complex process that encompasses three phases: strategic process design, event design, and event facilitation. *Strategic process design* focuses on bringing together the multiple stakeholders involved in an issue and working with them to develop the project outline and identify the project's long-term goals. The specific *event design* may take many forms but, ultimately, as Spano (2006) explained, "the design of a given dialogue event is shaped by its placement within the overall strategic process" (p. 306). *Event facilitation* requires the enactment of multiple communication skills, including leading with curiosity and wonder, active listening, enriching the conversation, and recording the conversation.

Leading with curiosity and wonder requires the public dialogue facilitator to assume a neutral stance and display genuine interest in the opinions of all participants. *Active listening* involves both verbal and nonverbal expressions by the facilitator that indicate to participants that they are heard and understood. K. A. Pearce and Pearce (2001) underscored the power of active listening when they acknowledged its rarity and explained that "in its absence most people are unwilling or unable to participate in rich conversation" (p. 113). *Enriching the conversation* includes the use of strategic and appreciative questioning (Cooperrider, 1986), as well as strategies of reflection and reframing. Wilmot and Hocker (2001) described "reframing" as a constructive way to redescribe a problem or issue "with the goal of changing perceptions and positions from negative and fixed to more positive and flexible" (p. 259); as such, reframing is a critical facilitation strategy that helps to expand the range of participants' perceptions and communication choices. The final communication skill required of facilitators is *recording the conversation* (e.g., via audio recordings or handwritten notes), which plays an important role in the dialogue itself by validating the importance of what is said.

Together, these practices are designed to encourage dialogue and provide a public space in which participants feel safe sharing their "stories," are encouraged to fully listen to the stories of others, and feel free to acknowledge and explore differences. The specific forms these communicative practices take in each of the three dialogue projects are articulated in more detail later in the chapter.

The PDC's notion of *practical theory* resonates with what others have described as "action research" (Greenwood & Levin, 2000) and *"praxis"* (Stewart & Zediker, 2000). In his preface to a special issue of *Communication Theory* devoted to examples of practical theory, Barge (2001) claimed that "practical theory should improve the lives of people and have applicability for enhancing their capacity for action" (p. 6). The communication activism that we seek to promote through public dialogue is rooted in the contention that talk is action, and in the belief that equipping communities with appropriate communication knowledge and tools enhances their capacity for further activism.

Understood this way, public dialogue serves as a link (often a *missing* link) between the goals of communication activism and the accomplishment of social change. Stewart and Zediker (2000) interpreted Aristotle's notion of *praxis* as a science in which the "end is not to produce a specific product but to realize some morally worthwhile good" (p. 229). These scholars used this definition of *praxis* to present dialogue as a practice that promotes communication that is qualitatively different from other forms, such as debate and discussion. W. B. Pearce and others (e.g., Barge, 2002; Shepherd, 2001; Wheatley, 2002) similarly have advocated for dialogue as an alternative to other forms of communication for facilitating democracy and community action. Our experience coincides with W. B. Pearce and Pearce's (2000) treatment of talk "as a form of action, not as a substitute for it" (p. 408). Our experience also is that public dialogue scholars and practitioners have much to contribute to effective community activism.

Our theoretical understanding, research practices, and practical application of public dialogue have evolved over a 2-year period based on our communication activism projects. Barge (2001) suggested three approaches to practical theory: mapping, engaged reflection, and transformative practice. These three approaches differ in the extent to which investigators become reflexively and mutually engaged with the people who are co-participants in the research. In retrospect, we see that our public dialogue work has progressed through each of these approaches and, at times, has reflected elements of all three.

We began our first project, the Every Kid Counts Initiative, as a straightforward application of existing public dialogue theory and technique to a practical challenge. As Barge (2001) described this "mapping" process, we intended in that project to "assume a third-person perspective toward communication . . . [to] map and describe the unfolding communication process and develop the guiding concepts, normative prescriptions, and rules that persons should use to perform the practice well" (p. 7). Our continuing experience with the Every Kid Counts Initiative and the development of a second project regarding meeting the needs of older adults required "engaged reflection" to adapt our techniques and recalibrate our conceptions of public dialogue and CMM theory. Finally, we are aware in our most recent project, the Raise Your Voice campaign, of our pronounced openness to the communities with which we are engaged, and we find theory, research, and application interacting in ways that Barge (2001) described as "transformative practice." We now turn to a description of these three communication activism projects.

EVERY KID COUNTS INITIATIVE

Our first communication activism project involving public dialogue already had an activist agenda in place. The Every Kid Counts Initiative was developed in response to information compiled by the county health department that pointed to disturbing trends about the quality of life for youth in Springfield, MO, including increasing rates of school dropouts, youth violence, youths in trouble with the law, teen pregnancy, and a growing need for foster care. Several people in the community, including members of The Good Community Committee, which had continued to function over the years since the first citywide forum in the mid 1990s, believed that it was imperative to turn the situation around. Because problems of youth directly or indirectly involved the entire community, the Every Kid Counts Initiative hoped to begin a widespread discussion about the needs of youth.

As The Good Community Committee sought ways to engage the community in a discussion about youth issues, the College of Arts and Letters and the Department of Communication at Missouri State University, of which we are faculty members, invited W. Barnett Pearce and Kimberly Pearce, founding members of the PDC, to present their cutting-edge public dialogue work integrating theory with practice at the Fall 2001 College Lecture Series. In addition to showcasing their work via lecture, members from the Department of Communication hoped to provide a demonstration of public dialogue for the local community. The question, then, became: What would be the topic for this public dialogue? At this juncture, our agenda and that of the Every Kid Counts Initiative merged.

As communication scholars and activists, we believed that public dialogue was a way to engage with the community to "democratize research," described by Greenwood and Levin (2000) as taking "skills outside the university to collaborate in broader knowledge-generation and evaluation processes as professional researchers and supporters of collaborative research processes" (p. 103). To build our knowledge of the Every Kid Counts Initiative and the individuals involved, as well as to set the tone for a collaborative partnership, Dillon and Galanes volunteered to serve on work groups established for the initiative. By doing so, we demonstrated our commitment to the issue and established our "in" to the community. According to Barge's (2001) definition of practical theory, however, we still very much viewed our involvement as the application of existing theory and practice to a specific situation. We had not yet come to appreciate the extent to which public dialogue would require reflection and reflexivity on our parts.

Over the next several months of discussing the Every Kid Counts Initiative in small work groups, we gradually introduced the possibility of conducting public dialogues as a way to encourage diverse voices from the community to weigh in on youth issues. One of the early enthusiasts for the value of public dialogue was the chair of The Good Community Committee, who was instrumental in helping to persuade others that it was time to introduce the Every Kid Counts Initiative to a wider audience and that public dialogue was the best method to do so. Particularly compelling for many committee members was the opportunity to learn the techniques and skills associated with promoting public dialogue via the PDC model, and the focus of that method on *appreciative inquiry*, which Spano (2001) described as a process of "identifying positive resources—what works best in the community—and [using] these results . . . as a frame for creating some future course of action" (p. 40). In this way, "The goal of appreciative inquiry, then, is not to circumvent difficult issues, but rather to reframe them in a constructive manner" (p. 40). This focus was especially appealing to those who remembered the earlier forum on civic values, described previously, that erupted into a mean-spirited shout-fest about whether tolerance should be a community value.

By August 2001, the ground was prepared for The Good Community Committee and its Every Kid Counts Initiative to utilize public dialogue as the vehicle for engaging in widespread community discussion about the needs of youth. The goal of the demonstration project was to teach members of the campus and community how difficult and controversial issues could be discussed effectively with multiple voices contributing to the discussion.

The first "Every Kid Counts" public dialogue occurred on October 10, 2001. Preparation took 8 months and included four stages. Stage One, planning, involved extensive conversations with members of The Good Community Committee to identify initial youth issues to get the public dialogue participants started and develop the promotional plan for the event. Stage Two consisted of 2 days of training facilitators and designated listeners/note-takers. These individuals were students and faculty from Missouri State University, members of The Good Community Committee, and other interested individuals in the community. Conducted by Barnett and Kim Pearce, this training involved role-plays of the dialogue process and attention to the "micro skills" of communication facilitation, such as listening appreciatively to encourage the expression of divergent viewpoints. Stage Three was the public dialogue demonstration itself. A brochure publicizing the public dialogue event went out to Springfield community groups, including city government offices, churches, nonprofit agencies, schools, police, and healthcare organizations. In addition, those participating in the work groups established for the Every Kid Counts Initiative and the members of The Good Community Committee were invited to participate in the public dialogue. The nearly 100 individuals who attended were divided into facilitated groups of 6-8 people; they were encouraged by the facilitators to present their views about the needs of local youth and how well the community was meeting those needs. During discussion, the assigned note-taker recorded the information, which was later compiled into a summary report and mailed to all who attended and facilitated the dialogue. Videotaping and audiotaping were used not only for purposes of confidentiality but also because it was emphasized that the recording of *what* was said in public was more important than *who* in particular said it. Stage Four involved widening the discussion by planning for and conducting additional dialogues in the community in the months following the initial public dialogue.

Although this first Every Kid Counts public dialogue event was widely publicized and attended by several university students and community members working with youth, including members of The Good Community Committee, it was clear that more community input was needed from particular constituent groups—most notably, youths were underrepresented at this initial dialogue. We subsequently conducted public dialogues in schools, libraries, churches, senior citizens centers, and other places where people congregate. These follow-up events involved diverse populations, including middle and high school students, minority groups, business and education leaders, neighborhood betterment groups, social service providers, and senior citizens. We ultimately ended up talking with 317 participants in 41 separate dialogue groups in 13 different sites; 253 of these participants were youth. We received substantial support from our school district administrators, who helped us to schedule group interviews with youth during school time. We also spoke to middle school and high school students from schools throughout the city and in the county. We included students attending an alternative school for those with special concerns (e.g., teen parents whose children are cared for on school premises) and young people at a drop-in center designed especially to serve homeless youth. In addition to young people, we spoke with a variety of adult community groups that included youth agency service workers and a neighborhood betterment association. The information we compiled from those conversations highlighted the needs identified by both young people themselves and others, and we were surprised by the substantial agreement between youth and others about what young people need. These needs included more safe fun places for youth; the need for youth to have adult mentors; the need to support and provide information about the assets the community already had in place for youth (including faith-based organizations, social service agencies, and school-based and governmental programs); and the need to recognize the good that youth do for the community instead of only concentrating on the negative.

Public dialogue often is said to be "learnable, teachable, and contagious" (Griffin, 2000), and this was our experience with the Every Kid Counts public dialogue, as the students from our university courses who participated developed a passion and enthusiasm for both the public dialogue method and the Every Kid Counts Initiative. Our students were instrumental in helping to make these public dialogues a success as they made particularly good facilitators, in part, because they were relatively close in age to the youth participants. For many middle school and high school students, being in a public dialogue led by a college student was "cool." In addition to the Every Kid Counts public dialogues, several of our students have gone on to help with the training and facilitation of other public dialogue efforts in the community (the Older Adults and the Raise Your Voices projects that are explained later in this chapter). The training in and facilitation of these public dialogues provided these university students with invaluable life skills in interviewing, conflict management, appreciative inquiry, and listening, and no one realized this more than our students.

We agree with W. B. Pearce and Pearce (2000) that public dialogue allows people to focus their "efforts on creating conversations where they otherwise would not have existed and shaping these conversations in specific ways" (p. 408). The Every Kid Counts public dialogues gave members of the community an opportunity to engage in a discussion of youth issues that might not have occurred otherwise, and they brought into that discussion a wide range of community voices, including voices not often heard, such as those of youth and seniors.

The Every Kid Counts public dialogues have produced several tangible results. The information compiled from the discussions clearly supported the perception that there were substantial gaps between what youth need and what they actually were receiving, including the need to be more proactive than reactive and the recognition that youth need to be involved in community initiatives targeted for youth. This discussion was framed as a public health issue: Unless the community attended more vigilantly to the needs of its youth, the community increasingly would experience youth with severe physical, emotional, and social problems that would end up affecting the entire community. To continue focusing the community's attention on the needs of youth, a nonprofit organization called Every Kid Counts was formed, which was designed not as a direct service provider but as a catalyst to encourage other agencies and the community at large to pay better attention to youth. The organization was housed in the Greene County Health Department and funded at a minimal level through grants and in-kind contributions from the city. Since its initial formation, a full-time director has been hired and the organization itself has evolved, as of February 2006, and with the approval of City Council, to become the Mayor's Commission on Children, with its director now funded by the city. This move will provide stable funding, which, in turn, will allow its director to concentrate on being preemptive—preventing problems such as youth violence and delinquency, abuse, lack of foster care, high rates of teenage pregnancy, and dropping out of school from occurring in the first place. It is too early to point to tangible successes of this endeavor, but its status as a commission suggests that youth issues and primary prevention of problems are being recognized as worthy of the entire community's attention.

Our work with public dialogue for the Every Kid Counts Initiative enabled us to begin the mapping process that Barge (2001) described as one of the approaches to practical theory. For Missouri State University's Department of Communication, it enabled faculty and students to assume more visible roles in the local community by applying communication theories, principles, and practices to real-life challenges. Public dialogue, in this case, allowed participants, including us, to engage in communication activism for the purpose of imagining and enacting possible futures (Spano, 2001) for our community. In conducting additional public dialogues with community groups and with youth, in particular, we increasingly found ourselves in "engaged reflection." We had to adapt our approach to public dialogue, including the rewording of questions to honor the language of the participants. If we wanted to hear from those in the community whose voices are not often heard or valued, we had to go to their schools, places of worship, and other places where these individuals and groups congregate and feel safe because they would not come to a community-wide event, such as a public dialogue, that took place on a university campus. The lessons gained in theoretical understanding, research practice, and the application of public dialogue with the Every Kid Counts Initiative helped to prepare us for future public dialogues.

OLDER ADULTS PROJECT

Our work with the Every Kid Counts Initiative came to the attention of an individual with links to several community betterment associations in Springfield, MO. He saw the potential of public dialogue to address a variety of issues important to that community and asked whether we would be willing to help the Community Foundation of the Ozarks (CFO) in its mission to improve the lives of older adults. CFO administers a $50,000 annual endowment earmarked for improving the lives of older adults, but staff members had been frustrated because the small, limited requests from community agencies working with older adults did not seem to be producing the synergistic, comprehensive improvements they envisioned. For example, CFO routinely granted money for senior centers to buy equipment, such as computers, pool tables, and televisions. However, the more serious and complex needs of older adults, such as the availability of shopping, transportation, and low-cost repair services to enable seniors to remain in their homes for as long as possible, went largely unaddressed or, if addressed, were done so in a piecemeal fashion by a myriad of agencies that forced seniors to navigate bureaucracies that were nearly impossible to figure out. Missouri State University Department of Communication representatives met with the committee charged with disbursing these funds and talked through the CFO's goals and hopes for a public dialogue project.

The first event scheduled as part of what we came to call the Older Adults Project was a public dialogue designed specifically for representatives of agencies that provide services for older adults. These professionals held unique perspectives about older adults' needs, and their voices needed to be included. The design of this event turned out to be crucial; this first public dialogue of the Older Adults Project succeeded, in large part, because public dialogue explicitly does *not* seek consensus among participants. Anticipating that turf issues would arise, we asked attendees to participate in an exercise designed to encourage them to picture what constitutes successful aging, as a kickoff to the public dialogue itself. We also planned the dialogue questions carefully to encourage participants initially to share what their agencies did and give them time to recognize their common goals. This succeeded better than we could have imagined, as individuals' energies were spent exploring their common concerns instead of defending their territory. We learned, to our surprise, that these agency representatives did not know each other, did not know in any detail what the other agencies did, and did not meet regularly to discuss their common concerns. To our delight, this group, calling itself SeniorLink, has continued to meet monthly with coordination help from a CFO staff member.

Public dialogue encourages as many voices as possible to be heard from directly, and our intention, from the outset of this project, was to talk to many older adults in different types of circumstances. We needed student and faculty help to accomplish this goal. We had learned from the Every Kid Counts Initiative how helpful students could be as public dialogue facilitators, but we wanted to find some means of rewarding students in tangible ways rather than relying on them to volunteer. To these ends, we developed an applied communication research course, taught by Galanes, that had two goals: (a) providing students with opportunities to engage in applied communication research using public dialogue as a primary research tool and (b) providing the CFO with information to help its efforts to improve the lives of older adults. In addition to using public dialogue as a research tool, we also incorporated individual appreciative interviewing (Cooperrider, 1986; Cooperrider & Srivastva, 1987; Johnson & Leavitt, 2001) as a secondary compatible method. Public dialogue participants, by definition, are mobile enough to come to public settings, but we also wanted to hear from homebound older adults who were unable to attend a traditional public dialogue. These techniques of public dialogue coupled with individual interviewing were paired successfully in the PDC's Cupertino project (see W. B. Pearce & Pearce, 2000; Spano, 2001) and we employed them similarly here.

The applied communication research course was designed to encourage flexible participation in this project on the part of students. It was offered for credit to both graduate and undergraduate students, was open to students from all majors, and was adaptable such that interested students and faculty who wanted to participate in the project, but did not want course credit, could be involved as much as their schedules permitted. The public dialogue training of these students, conducted by Berquist, Dillon, and Galanes, took place during two class periods early in the semester. The initial set of nine dialogue questions was developed during the training. These questions asked older adults about things such as what was most important to them in their lives; what people, places, or situations made their lives better or more difficult; what their top concerns were; and what the role of the community should be in helping to meet their needs. Based on their disciplinary perspective, gerontology students enrolled in the course encouraged us to use the term "older adults" instead of our original term of "senior citizens," a change we appreciated and adopted.

A CFO staff member scheduled the public dialogues at senior centers, support group meetings (Alzheimer's, stroke, and diabetes groups), a church, a neighborhood association meeting, and two community centers. In all, we went to 11 different settings where older adults (primarily) congregated and spoke with 201 individuals. One of the most important lessons the students learned was the need to be flexible; at only two of these settings was the public dialogue process followed as designed, with the entire group first listening to overall instructions and smaller groups then forming in an orderly way for the group dialogues. For example, in several senior centers, students had to recruit groups of older adults already engaged in an activity and persuade them to participate. In other instances, older adults refused to sign the informed consent forms that explained the purposes of the public dialogues (mistrust of government agencies runs high in southern Missouri) but, at the same time, eagerly participated in the discussions. At the conclusion of each dialogue, specific students were asked to type the flipchart notes in a common format and to send them to Galanes. In this way, the primary data—the flipchart notes—were kept current.

The individual interviews presented unique challenges. With no list of homebound older adults from which to select a sample, we worked with the coordinator of the Walking Books Program of our county-wide library system, which utilizes volunteers to deliver books every 2 weeks to homebound individuals, most of whom are older adults. Because of privacy issues, permission first had to be obtained from the Walking Books recipients, which was accomplished with the help of the delivery volunteers, most of whom had developed close relationships with their clients. The coordinator of the program then compiled a list of individuals willing to be interviewed, and our students scheduled interviews with them in their homes at mutually convenient times. In addition, we arranged for a student to accompany the coordinator of the meal delivery programs on several deliveries. This entire process took considerable time. Students were encouraged to work in pairs so that one of them could be free to take notes, but scheduling constraints resulted in a number of students working alone. The same questions were asked during the individual interviews as had been asked during the public dialogues. Student interviewers typed their summaries of the 23 interviews conducted as soon as was possible and sent them to Galanes. In all, we talked to 224 participants, most of them older adults, from throughout Greene County.

Even with a diligent effort on everyone's part, the sample of older adults who participated in the public dialogues and individual interviews was not fully representative of the community. For instance, no Latinos/as could be persuaded to participate, and only one group of African American older adults engaged in a public dialogue, a group that posed significant challenges to the students and faculty members who facilitated the dialogue. In particular, a number of African American individuals at that public dialogue wanted to talk about and share their experiences with racism in Springfield. We made an on-the-fly decision to allow that dialogue to take us wherever the participants wanted to go. Thus, even though our prepared public dialogue questions were not all addressed, we learned a lot about the perspectives of African Americans in Springfield, and students learned, again, that some of the most interesting findings that result from public dialogue are those that are unexpected. For example, it surprised our students, many of whom were lifelong Springfield residents, that African American men still experience the

indignity of being called "boy" and that African Americans still are routinely ignored as they wait for service in public places such as restaurants and
retail stores. Our students began to understand why several African
American participants were reluctant to participate in activities at their local
senior centers, where the clientele overwhelmingly are Caucasian.

Throughout the entire semester, discussion in the applied communication research class focused on what we were learning about older adults and
the process of applied research, what themes were emerging from the public
dialogues and individual interviews, and what issues we wanted to highlight
for the CFO. At the end of the semester, course instructor Galanes, with the
help of a graduate student, compiled a report summarizing the information
and presented the findings to the CFO's Older Adult subcommittee, as well
as to the entire foundation board.

The last step in the Older Adults Project occurred during the subsequent semester. The findings from our report had revealed six issues of
greatest importance in improving the lives of older adults: healthcare, transportation, housing, finances, loneliness, and awareness of and access to existing services. The CFO wanted to develop a request for funding proposal
(RFP) that encouraged collaboration among agencies in addressing one or
more of these issues. The CFO staff, in collaboration with Berquist and
Galanes, developed a 5-hour workshop for SeniorLink representatives that
focused on issues of collaboration, including identifying opportunities for
and barriers to collaborative efforts in addressing the most critical needs of
older adults.

There have been several specific tangible outcomes of this project. First,
as mentioned earlier, SeniorLink, the organization formed by participants at
our first public dialogue, continues to meet. The primary purpose of
SeniorLink is sharing information, but the personal contacts established and
maintained through it have enabled several agencies to collaborate with
respect to offering services to older adults. Second, the CFO rewrote its
RFP to focus specifically on the areas identified by our public dialogues as
being most problematic for older adults—in particular, the issue of awareness of and access to existing services. The RFP was announced in early Fall
2003, about 10 months after we presented our report on older adults to the
CFO. The grant, for $100,000 over a 3-year period, was awarded in Spring
2004 to the Southwest Missouri Office on Aging (SWMOA). SWMOA's
proposal involved collaboration among several other agencies, including the
Alzheimer's Association, two home-care services, the Older Adults
Transportation Service, the Retired Senior Volunteer Program, the local
library system, a local hospital, and SeniorLink, to which most of the collaborating partners now belong. Designed to increase awareness of and access
to services, among other things, the grant will be used to fund a full-time
staff person working with volunteers to serve as a first line of information

and referral for seniors who need services. Missouri State University Communication Department faculty will continue to be involved by helping SWMOA to assess the effectiveness of its efforts.

In each of the elements of the Older Adults Project, it is easy to see the way in which discipline-specific knowledge and techniques were used as action research to attempt to improve the lives of older adults. The public dialogue process, individual appreciative interviews, and communication training techniques that we employed on behalf of the CFO helped to channel the community's energy along directions most likely to be helpful for older adults. For university students who participated, the process was invaluable for learning about communication theory, research, and practice. This project, particularly the specially designed course, met what Greenwood and Levin (2000) claimed is the challenge for universities: "to turn away from conventional lecturing to learning situations based on the search for solutions to real-life, open-ended problems" (p. 86). Understanding issues of access to services for this critical population, collaboration with key community partners, and mutual benefits both to the department and to the community all resulted from this project. Moreover, the Older Adults Project propelled our understanding of public dialogue beyond the mapping process that Barge (2001) described and that predominated during the Every Kid Counts Initiative. We entered the world of older adults much more fully than we had the world of youth; consequently, our eyes were opened in ways that surprised and sometimes overwhelmed us. We practiced "engaged reflection" in that we consciously discussed and adapted our methods and approaches to achieve our research goals. We also sought to enhance our understanding of the world of older adults, but stating that does not begin to convey the emotions we experienced, crying together in class, as we listened to and later discussed the stories of loneliness, fear, and courage we heard. In retrospect, we were becoming prepared to experience public dialogue as a transformative practice.

RAISE YOUR VOICE—STUDENT ACTION FOR CHANGE CAMPAIGN

In August 2002, we were asked by the director of the Missouri Campus Compact, a national coalition of colleges and universities committed to integrating civic involvement into higher education, to contribute our expertise in public dialogue to a newly formed Campus Compact initiative entitled Raise Your Voice—Student Action for Change Campaign. The previous October, the director of this initiative observed the Every Kid Counts public dialogue demonstration held on the Missouri State University campus and had interviewed Barnett and Kimberly Pearce for a local public affairs television program. Impressed with the structure of this form of public dialogue and the communication skill training underlying the process, he believed it was the ideal vehicle to teach college and university students in Missouri to effectively participate in the Raise Your Voice Campaign.

The Raise Your Voice Campaign, a multiyear civic engagement project sponsored by Campus Compact and funded by a grant from the Pew Charitable Trusts, was conceived in response to issues highlighted in the March 2001 Wingspread Summit held at the Johnson Foundation in Racine, WI. Convened by Campus Compact to explore college and university students' perceptions of and participation in public life, the summit brought together a diverse group of 33 students from 27 colleges and universities to discuss their views on political life and civic engagement. Greenleaf (1978) observed that each generation crafts its version of democracy and civic involvement and develops tools with which it can fashion, activate, and accommodate that democracy. Consistent with Greenleaf's observations, conclusions of the Summit painted a picture of students who defined democratic participation and civic engagement as an individual responsibility reflected in personal grassroots endeavors. Whereas traditional political participation often is characterized by voting, involvement in political parties, and lobbying, these students articulated their engagement through volunteerism and community service. They felt largely disenfranchised from traditional political life and misunderstood by those who viewed political and civic engagement through a more traditional lens. Campus Compact believed that these conclusions underscored the need to further explore students' perceptions of civic engagement and encourage students to develop a political voice and space for that voice to be heard.

The Raise Your Voice Campaign was created to provide this space by engaging students at colleges and universities throughout the United States in conversations about civic engagement and the social and political issues important to them. Campus Compact and the Pew Charitable Trusts recognized that creating opportunities for students to talk about civic engagement, in itself, was a form of activism, but they also believed that this talk would serve as a catalyst for future action. The central goals of the campaign were, through talk, to ignite in students a passion for public life and to equip them with skills to articulate their passion through activism and civic engagement.

The director of the Missouri Campus Compact and the state coordinator of the Raise Your Voice Campaign saw a natural fit between these goals and public dialogue. They believed that teaching students and faculty mentors about public dialogue techniques would provide an organizing framework for Missouri's Raise Your Voice Campaign efforts. We agreed with their assessment and, over the next several months, we collaborated in an extensive planning process to educate university students and faculty throughout the state in the method and skills of public dialogue.

There were three major goals for the Missouri Raise Your Voice Campaign. The first was to teach student leaders and faculty mentors how to plan and conduct public dialogues on civic engagement issues at their respective campuses. The second was to prepare students to take part in a public dialogue at the State Capitol in Jefferson City, MO, to launch the Raise Your Voice Campaign in Missouri and coincide that event with the National Campus Compact's "Week of Action" in February 2003. This kickoff event would be one of many activities around the country that would provide university students with an opportunity to discuss civic engagement and the public issues that were important to them. The third, less obvious but equally important, goal was to provide students with communication skills, as well as an understandable and adaptable method that they could use to transcend the immediate context and engage in future activism.

Along with our Campus Compact colleagues, we determined that the best way to accomplish all three goals was to conduct 2-day-long public dialogue training sessions on consecutive Saturdays in early 2003. These sessions included an overview of the goals of the Raise Your Voice Campaign, an explanation of the public dialogue method, and a description and demonstration of the communication micro-level skills used in public dialogue. Because students (and faculty mentors) were being asked to organize and conduct dialogues on their campuses, we scheduled into the sessions (what we thought was) ample time for role-plays, practice dialogue sessions, and debriefings at various points throughout the day. Documenting campus conversations about civic engagement was a stipulation of Pew's funding; hence, we also explained how information from each public dialogue was to be summarized on a flipchart, compiled in a consistent format, and made available on the Missouri Campus Compact web site.

The first public dialogue session occurred on Saturday, January 25, 2003, on the campus of Saint Louis University. The session was facilitated by us, as well as by graduate and undergraduate students who had participated in our previous public dialogue projects. We were also assisted by student leaders of the Raise Your Voice Campaign in Missouri. Twenty-two students and faculty mentors representing five colleges and universities participated. At the conclusion of the session, we asked participants to evaluate in writing the effectiveness of the training and talk with us about specific ways to improve it. This collaborative element of the training was important and led us to make several changes in the training we conducted the following weekend in Kansas City, MO. In particular, participants told us that they needed a clearer picture at the beginning of the session of what a public dialogue should look like. They were enthusiastic about the skills of facilitation but wanted more opportunities to practice and receive feedback about these skills. Participants also said that "civic engagement" was such a broad and multifaceted concept that it required greater focus and specificity. Finally, we realized that the dialogue questions we had created to generate discussion about civic engagement needed to be created by the students themselves to resonate with their lived experiences. This process of soliciting feedback from participants about the structure of the session and the wording of public dialogue questions, described by Barge (2001, p. 8) as "tacking back and forth between abstract concepts and the particular situation," was invaluable and allowed us to significantly refine the subsequent public dialogue training in Kansas City, MO.

The first opportunity to watch students use the public dialogue facilitation skills they had learned came on February 20, 2003, when approximately 200 students from across the state of Missouri converged at the Missouri State Capitol in Jefferson City to participate in a public dialogue on civic engagement. In the morning, students observed legislative sessions of the Missouri House of Representatives, where they were recognized from the floor by the Missouri Senate. After lunch, students who had attended one of the previous dialogue training sessions were assigned to facilitate or take notes for one of several small group discussions. These discussion groups, with approximately 8-10 students, were held in separate rooms in the State Capitol building, and then all participants came together on the floor of the House of Representatives to report on these group discussions. Legislators were invited to observe the students as they discussed in the small groups their experiences with and opinions about civic engagement.

The Jefferson City public dialogue was the culminating event of a year-long planning and training process. It also was the first of many public dialogues that students and faculty mentors trained in the process would be coordinating in the future at universities throughout Missouri. In addition, students from across Missouri conducted a second dialogue at the State Capitol on February 12, 2004, which was similar to the one conducted the year before.

We recognized at the onset that several features distinguished the planning and executing of this dialogue project from the Every Kid Counts Initiative and the Older Adults Project previously explained. The most pronounced difference was that transformative practice was infused throughout the Raise Your Voice Campaign. Barge (2001) explained that "practical theorizing from [a transformational] perspective takes seriously the need to honor the interests of the community members and to engage in theorizing practices that transform the abilities and practices of individuals to make their lives better" (p. 9). In the two previous projects, we understood the importance of identifying key players and working collaboratively to use the method of public dialogue to explore an existing issue or problem. In the Raise Your Voice Campaign, however, the dynamic of collaboration changed, such that to fulfill the goals of the campaign, we needed to work with students from across Missouri to create a process wherein they could take the public dialogue method and the communication skills inherent in that method and apply them in the present to talk about civic engagement and use them in the future as a catalyst for activism in ways that we could not anticipate.

The goal of using the public dialogue training sessions as a vehicle to educate students in communication skills and provide them with a structure to promote activism and civic engagement is beginning to be realized on several college and university campuses in Missouri. Public dialogues have been conducted by Campus Compact student leaders for the purpose of facilitating discussions and initiating civic engagement projects, such as blood drives, mentoring programs for homeless and at-risk children, building projects for Habitat for Humanity, and several events surrounding the 2004 presidential elections. Public dialogues also have been convened on several campuses to promote discussion between students and faculty of different religious faiths, racial and ethnic heritage, and political and social viewpoints.

LESSONS LEARNED ABOUT COMMUNICATION ACTIVISM

People frequently assume that although talk may, at times, necessarily precede action, talk is not itself action. People become frustrated with what they perceive to be "just talk" for several reasons. Often, talk does not lead to any noticeable change in what people believe to be undesirable circumstances. Sometimes, people equate productive discussion with the advancement of their own agenda. Frequently, conversations entail more talking *at* one another than *with* one another, which certainly can leave all parties feeling as if no progress has been made.

We contend that the reason so many people believe that talk is not action is because they have experienced so much bad talk. *Webster's College Dictionary* defines *action* as "practical, often organized activity undertaken to deal with or accomplish something." Given that people have experienced so much talk that is impractical, disorganized, and unproductive, is it any wonder that they would conclude that talk is not necessarily action?

Our experiences with public dialogue provide powerful arguments for embracing talk as a form of communication activism. Here we review these arguments, as well as the "affordances and constraints" (Cronen, 2001, p. 24) created by theoretically informed communication activism.

Talk, enacted in a context of appreciation and respect, potentially is an important form of action if participants have never been able to talk in this way before, if they are talking with people to whom they have never talked, and if they are saying and hearing things that have not been said or heard before. This was the case in each of the public dialogues we described. It certainly is the case that such talk may be viewed as a necessary first step toward further action, but we must not overlook the accomplishment that talk itself represents in these cases. Recall the example of the "tolerance" forum from the beginning of this chapter. If participants had been able to openly express and hear alternative points of view, that would have been a significant step forward, regardless of whether consensus was sought or achieved.

Each of the projects we described, like other public dialogues (see K. A. Pearce & Pearce, 2001; W. B. Pearce & Pearce, 2000; Spano, 2001, 2006; see also Jovanovic et al., this volume), extended over months and even years. Rather than one-shot conversations, they literally were campaigns of talk, as carefully planned and orchestrated as any activist demonstration or protest. The contents of each dialogue were documented, and the reports of the entire process were fed back to participants and distributed publicly. Although every discussion in each public dialogue event constituted action, making the dialogues available for ongoing conversation and other forms of action brought these projects further into the realm of activism.

Furthermore, our roles were not limited to merely recording, transcribing, and summarizing the talk of others. As co-participants with community members, and being community members ourselves, we actively shaped and were affected by the public dialogue process. In addition to providing the training for facilitators and establishing the rules for the public conversations, we put significant effort into framing the discussion issues and questions. Effective framing made it possible for participants to think and speak of issues in new ways and avoid unproductive patterns of thought and interaction. As Mayer (2000) argued, conflict between parties "often requires changing the *story line*, the dramatic views people have of a conflict or problem. . . . The process of reframing is an action that must precede subsequent action" (p. 137). This was true in our first Older Adults dialogue event involving representatives from different service agencies. Having been invited to participate by a community foundation that was a potential or current funding source, with participants being accustomed to competing with one another for scarce resources, they reasonably could have approached the dialogue as an opportunity to jockey for position or viewed their attendance as a way to curry favor with a grant source. Although we cannot say with certainty how things would have turned out otherwise, we believe that our framing strategies as facilitators were at least partly responsible for the productive tone and outcome of that event.

On a broader level, the language and practice of public dialogue has provided an accessible and applicable vocabulary for talking with communities about the role of communication in activism. As W. B. Pearce and Pearce (2000) wryly acknowledged, community members care not at all about the theoretical underpinnings of public dialogue, nor are they concerned with the implications of such projects for communication theory and research. They do, however, have an intuitive grasp of the value of dialogue. Furthermore, their prior experiences with trying to facilitate community-wide communication typically have taught them that this is more difficult than it appears. As community leaders and citizens see public dialogue lead to the types of exchanges and cooperation that they seek, they gain appreciation for the theory and professional practice that can make such dialogue possible.

This common ground between academics and communities, between "town and gown" as it were, is but one positive outcome of these public dialogues. Briefly, we point to several others:

- As individuals, we each are more active in community service, and as an academic unit, our department now has a more developed culture of service to on-campus and off-campus constituencies. Such involvement can lead to fragmented efforts that are not joined toward specific goals in teaching, scholarship, and service; however, public dialogue integrates our passions for teaching, research, and service in ways that simultaneously have (a) created learning opportunities for our students, (b) resulted in published scholarship, and (c) provided significant service to our community.
- Public dialogues, in general, and CMM theory, more specifically, have been the conceptual center for multiple activist projects by us and our colleagues, providing frameworks for both research and activism that truly is programmatic. From a professional, academic standpoint, we believe it is critical that a communication activist agenda be grounded in and provide opportunities for advancing the communication discipline.
- Our theoretically informed activism has produced positive public relations for our department in all the right ways and for all the right reasons. We have formed partnerships that demonstrate the kind of relevance that universities can and should have for their communities (Greenwood & Levin, 2000).

Activist research also presents challenges that differ from more traditional, detached research. For example, student and community involvement in these projects was enthusiastic and intense, sometimes outpacing our states of readiness. The involvement of these groups, and the ambiguous nature of the projects during their development, required us to engage those participants more directly in the research process than we expected. This type of collaboration involves relationships that have long-term and unpredictable trajectories. Along with the many benefits of such relationships, we learned that there also is potential for being drawn into unanticipated levels of commitment, for the demands of community activists do not subside with the completion of a single research project. Whether due to their passions, ours, or both, we can find ourselves torn between our professional goals and responsibilities and those of an activist agenda.

Engaging in activism with communities also means relinquishing exclusive control over the conduct and consequences of our research. In some ways, this work is similar to the conduct of proprietary research for a corporate client. However, although a corporate client may place restrictions on one's research and control the use of its results, usually the client does not participate collaboratively to the extent that people do in a community activist project such as public dialogue. One disadvantage of the accessibility of public dialogue as a concept, for example, is that people may overestimate their understanding and mastery of the process. If our skill makes public dialogue appear easy, others may begin to think that it is easy and that anyone can do it. Even when participants genuinely are skilled and sincere, it can be difficult to "let go" of our work and watch others apply it in ways that we might not have anticipated nor approve. We experienced this especially in working with the Raise Your Voice Campaign, when students on our campus and elsewhere became excited by the possibilities of public dialogue and began facilitating their own events in unique ways. This certainly was in line with the goals of the campaign, although it was difficult to see the label "public dialogue" applied to these events given that they did not necessarily conform to our understanding of the concept.

CONCLUSION

Our long-term objective is to build the capacity of citizens to use public dialogue as a means of expressing differences, coordinating joint action, and making decisions that affect their community. In public dialogue, individuals experience communication in new ways and hopefully acquire perceptual and behavioral skills that enhance their communication in other contexts. At the same time, the community-level focus of public dialogue in the strategic design of the process and specific events conducted contextualizes individual experiences and makes the learning experience communal as well as personal. Public dialogue, thus, can change the ways in which community members speak and listen to one another. In some cases, it makes talk possible where no ability to engage in talk existed before. We continue to be excited and challenged by the possibilities afforded by public dialogue. Our long-term goal is to persuade communities that talk, or at least certain types of talk, is action, and that public dialogue is a valuable way of raising talk to the level of action and action to the level of dialogue.

REFERENCES

Adelman, M. B., & Frey, L. R. (1997). *The fragile community: Living together with AIDS*. Mahwah, NJ: Erlbaum.

Barge, J. K. (2001). Practical theory as mapping, engaged reflection, and transformative practice. *Communication Theory, 11,* 5-13.

Barge, J. K. (2002). Enlarging the meaning of group deliberation: From discussion to dialogue. In L. R. Frey (Ed.), *New directions in group communication* (pp. 159-178). Thousand Oaks, CA: Sage.

Barge, J. K., & Pearce, W. B. (2004). A reconnaissance of CMM research. *Human Systems: The Journal of Systemic Consultation and Management, 15,* 13-32.

Cooperrider, D. L. (1986). *Appreciative inquiry: Toward a methodology for understanding and enhancing organizational innovation.* Unpublished doctoral dissertation, Case Western Reserve University, Cleveland, OH.

Cooperrider, D. L., & Srivastva, S. (1987). Appreciative inquiry in organizational life. In R. W. Woodman & W. A. Pasmore (Eds.), *Research in organizational change and development* (Vol. 1, pp. 129-169). Greenwich, CT: JAI Press.

Cronen, V. E. (2001). Practical theory, practical art, and the pragmatic-systemic account of inquiry. *Communication Theory, 11,* 14-35.

Greenleaf, R. K. (1978). *The leadership crisis: A message for college and university faculty.* Newton Center, MA: Robert K. Greenleaf Center.

Greenwood, D. J., & Levin, M. (2000). Introduction to action research: Social research for social change. In N. K. Denzin & Y. S. Lincoln (Eds.), *Handbook of qualitative research* (2nd ed., pp. 85-106). Thousand Oaks, CA: Sage.

Griffin, E. (2000). *Conversations with communication theorists* [videotape]. Boston: McGraw-Hill.

Johnson, G., & Leavitt, W. M. (2001). Building on success: Transforming organizations through an appreciative inquiry. *Public Personnel Management, 30,* 129-136.

Mayer, B. S. (2000). *The dynamics of conflict resolution: A practitioner's guide.* San Francisco: Jossey-Bass.

Pearce, K. A. (2001). *Facilitating dialogic communication: Basic facilitation training manual.* San Francisco: Public Dialogue Consortium.

Pearce, K. A., & Pearce, W. B. (2001). The Public Dialogue Consortium's school-wide dialogue process: A communication approach to develop citizenship skills and enhance school climate. *Communication Theory, 11,* 105-123.

Pearce, W. B. (1989). *Communication and the human condition.* Carbondale: University of Southern Illinois Press.

Pearce, W. B., & Cronen, V.E. (1980). *Communication, action, and meaning: The creation of social realities.* New York: Praeger.

Pearce, W. B., & Pearce, K. A. (2000). Extending the theory of the coordinated management of meaning (CMM) through a community dialogue process. *Communication Theory, 10,* 405-423.

Rothenbuhler, E. W. (2001). Revising communication research for working on community. In G. J. Shepherd & E. W. Rothenbuhler (Eds.), *Communication and community* (pp. 159-174). Mahwah, NJ: Erlbaum.

Shepherd, G. J. (2001). Community as the interpersonal accomplishment of communication. In G. J. Shepherd & E. W. Rothenbuhler (Eds.), *Communication and community* (pp. 25-35). Mahwah, NJ: Erlbaum.

Spano, S. (2001). *Public dialogue and participatory democracy: The Cupertino community project.* Cresskill, NJ: Hampton Press.

Spano, S. (2006). Theory and practice in public dialogue: A case study in facilitating community transformation. In L. R. Frey (Ed.), *Facilitating group communication in context: Innovations and applications with natural groups: Vol. 1. Facilitating group creation, conflict, and conversation* (pp. 271-298). Cresskill, NJ: Hampton Press.

Stewart, J., & Zediker, K.E. (2000). Dialogue as tensional, ethical practice. *Southern Communication Journal, 65,* 224-242.

Wheatley, M. J. (2002). *Turning to one another: Simple conversations to restore hope to the future.* San Francisco: Berrett-Koehler.

Wilmot, W., & Hocker, J. (2001). *Interpersonal conflict* (6th ed.). New York: McGraw-Hill.

3

ASSESSING THE CIVIL RIGHTS HEALTH OF COMMUNITIES

Engaged Scholarship Through Dialogue*

Mark P. Orbe

Western Michigan University

The legacy of the 1960s civil rights movement is embedded within the history of the United States itself. In light of the advances made as a result of the movement, civil rights advocates are faced with the challenge of a general public that now questions the movement's continued relevance to life in the 21st century (Huesca, 2001). Some people regard civil rights organizations as no longer necessary, whereas others criticize the effectiveness of those

*The Civil Rights Health (CRH) Project described in this chapter was supported through two grants, one from the Michigan Department of Civil Rights (MDCR) and another from Detroit Entertainment LLC. In reporting on the success of this project, I would also like to acknowledge the synergistic teamwork of MDCR civil rights professionals, community members across the state of Michigan, and the interdisciplinary research team of faculty and graduate students.

organizations in addressing the changing needs of constituents (Stewart, 1997; Wilkins, 2000). Civil rights organizations, in turn, are involved in a constant struggle to utilize existing antidiscrimination laws to reflect the needs of a constantly changing society—something that contributes to the general perception that they are out of touch with changing public needs. This chapter describes a recent communication activism project that was designed to engage various communities in collaborations that ultimately could be used to strengthen efforts to ensure basic civil rights for all.

For the past 3 years, I have offered leadership to a team of university researchers who have been working in partnership with the Michigan Department of Civil Rights and local communities across the state of Michigan on a civil rights health project. The explicit goal of this project was to "provide a meaningful, non-judgmental, community-based assessment instrument that allows individual communities to systematically discern the state of civil rights health in their respective communities" (Michigan Department of Civil Rights, 2003b, p. vii). This project serves as a prime example of the benefits that derive from *engaged scholarship*, a descriptor that refers to projects where research, teaching, and service become inseparable from efforts to address important social issues (Applegate, 2001).

In this chapter, I highlight specific ways in which the Civil Rights Health (CRH) Project represents a form of communication activism—one that illustrates how a network of local communities, government representatives, and communication scholars successfully worked together to enhance the civil rights health of various communities. Specifically, I first provide a brief description of the CRH Project. I then explain how a communication theory—co-cultural theory—served as an important foundation for the project. The third section highlights how phenomenological methods were used to inductively uncover diverse voices that typically have been muted during civil rights discussions. Within both the second and third sections, I illustrate the centrality of communication theory and research methods by referring to particular aspects of the CRH Project. Finally, I conclude the chapter with a discussion of several challenges faced in the latest community to implement the CRH Project and focus on those challenges as specific points of analyses to reflect on the challenges of communication activism generally.

THE CIVIL RIGHTS HEALTH PROJECT

In July 1998, the Michigan Department of Civil Rights (MDCR) was approached by the Community Uniting for Peace (CUP), an operating entity of the Muskegon County Cooperating Churches, to conduct a major research assessment project in Muskegon County on racial-ethnic relations and equity issues. This assessment was intended to help determine civil rights and related challenges in areas such as employment, education, housing, health, economics, and law enforcement. Ultimately, the goal of this assessment was to stimulate strategic planning in regard to specific civil rights issues, as well as to set benchmarks by which future progress could be measured. The MDCR acknowledged the potential value of the assessment project and expressed its interest in participating in the development of the project for use by communities throughout the state. It was recognized from the onset that additional resources beyond those that MDCR could provide would be required to conduct the type of comprehensive assessment as envisioned by CUP.

During the summer of 1999, MDCR began an expanded liaison community initiative to enhance its service delivery, in terms of education and antidiscrimination protection, to specific communities throughout the state. Meetings were convened with municipal and county officials and administrators in 23 Michigan communities, including Muskegon. These meetings generated discussions about common issues and concerns regarding civil rights and provided opportunities to assess the potential for shared resources and collaborative partnerships to address civil rights problems (for an asset-based approach to community organizing, see Herman & Ettema, Volume 2). These meetings confirmed that these communities were experiencing common challenges related to economic development, workforce diversity, fair housing, public safety, and hate crimes. It became even more apparent that the development of a meaningful, nonjudgmental, progressive assessment process, in light of projected demographic shifts, was a step in the right direction. Subsequently, MDCR approached me to explore opportunities for a collective partnership with Western Michigan University for the purpose of securing expertise, support, and resources to develop an assessment instrument that could be used as a model to measure the civil rights health of any community in the state. The focus for community-based discussions was to develop a process for determining and evaluating the current status of equity that could be utilized to change the civil rights health of those and other communities.

Over a 1-year period (September 2000-September 2001), our university research team—ranging from 3-6 persons—worked with three different pilot communities to launch the CRH Project. In particular, we collaborated with a committee in each community that served to organize each respective project. These local groups were representative of each community and were comprised of city officials, community activists, and leaders from the corporate, education, financial, and social service sectors. Based on the decisions made by each community-based committee, a process was outlined whereby our research team would work within the community to investigate community members' perceptions of current civil rights health. To produce an assessment model that would be relevant to all communities, a conscious decision was made to initially work with three different types of communities in terms of demographic composition. Thus, for instance, the city of Pontiac was chosen because it was a mid-sized, "majority-minority" city (with approximately 75% people of color) that was struggling financially. At the other end of the spectrum, Midland was a small, predominantly White (96%) city where the median income figures were twice as much as Pontiac. The third community, Muskegon County, fell in between these two communities, both in terms of racial-ethnic diversity and economic status.

The CRH Project was grounded in several assumptions, each of which was recognized as a core value associated with the initiative: (a) Civil rights challenges, at some level and in varying degrees, are present in every community; (b) the ways in which civil rights issues play out in communities are simultaneously similar and different; (c) all those involved in the CRH Project are positioned, in a variety of ways, as members of one or more communities; (d) all those involved in the CRH Project are invested in achieving human dignity for all; (e) the goal of the CRH Project was not to bring "answers" to communities but to collaborate with them so that "answers" could be self-generated within the context of these very communities; (f) the best vantage point to empower self and others is where the theoretical, experiential, and practical meet as one; and (g) the value of the work associated with the CRH Project is in the process(es), as much as in the outcome(s) (Michigan Department of Civil Rights, 2003b).

As stated earlier, the objective of the CRH Project was to create and promote the use of a meaningful, nonjudgmental, community-based assessment model that would help to systematically discern the state of civil rights health in communities for the purpose of enacting future social change. In addition to this macro-level goal, several more micro-level goals were identified: (a) to bring people, across their respective communities, together to discuss civil rights issues; (b) to raise awareness within these communities in terms of how civil rights issues affect various aspects of people's lives; (c) to create a collaborative effort whereby various sectors of the community (e.g., business, education, social services, and faith-based organizations) could invest in a self-assessment process; and (d) to play an important role in a process that could ultimately enhance the civil rights health of these communities (Michigan Department of Civil Rights, 2003b).

With these assumptions and goals in mind, our research team began to collect descriptions of civil rights health from various perspectives in the three different pilot communities identified. In addition to reviewing existing reports related to civil rights issues, the data were generated through one public forum (lasting 2.5-4 hours) and 7-10 focus groups (lasting 45-75 minutes) at each site. Over the 1-year period, our research team met with close to 300 persons via these two communicative forms of data collection. All of the public forums and focus group discussions were audiotaped, transcribed, and analyzed, and individual reports of the analyses that were designed to inform strategic planning on civil rights-based initiatives were given to each community.

One of the specific outcomes of the CRH Project was the creation of a resource manual (Michigan Department of Civil Rights, 2003b) available to communities interested in assessing their civil rights health. This document drew on the experiences of each pilot community to describe a detailed framework to assist community members on how to decide, organize, plan, and facilitate a civil rights health self-assessment. It also provided guidance for writing up the findings of the self-assessment and how such a report might be utilized within community-based strategic planning (for an overview of the resource manual, see the Appendix). In 2002, a draft of this resource manual was used to facilitate a CRH assessment in a fourth Michigan community. Prior to discussing the outcomes of this particular community assessment (see the final section of this chapter), it is important to explain how the project as a whole was informed by the tenets of co-cultural theory and phenomenological inquiry.

UTILIZING A CO-CULTURAL THEORETICAL FRAMEWORK

Co-cultural theory provided an important theoretical foundation to help CRH Project organizers maximize ways in which community members discussed their experiences with civil rights health. To explicate the connection between this theory and the logistics of the CRH Project, I first outline the basic tenets of co-cultural theory and then discuss how they were applied to various aspects of the project.

Co-Cultural Theory

Co-cultural theory, as described by Orbe (1998a), assists in understanding how persons who are traditionally marginalized in dominant societal structures communicate in their everyday lives. Grounded in muted group theory, which argues that dominant groups in society silence the voices of others (see, e.g., Kramarae, 1981), and standpoint theory, which asserts that social group membership leads to varying perceptions of reality (see, e.g., Smith, 1987), co-cultural theory is derived from the lived experiences of a variety of "nondominant" or co-cultural groups, including people of color, women, persons with disabilities, gays/lesbians/bisexuals/transgendered

(GLBT) individuals, and those from a lower socioeconomic background. Focusing on the lived experiences of these groups, co-cultural theory begins from two epistemological assumptions: (a) Although representing a widely diverse array of lived experiences, co-cultural group members share a similar positioning of being marginalized within society; and (b) to negotiate oppressive dominant forces and achieve any measure of success, co-cultural group members must develop a level of consciousness that leads to adopting certain communication orientations in their everyday interactions.

Co-cultural theory utilizes a number of concepts to provide insight into the communication processes of those typically marginalized in dominant societal structures. However, the following statement summarizes the primary idea behind cocultural theory:

> Situated within a particular field of *experience* that governs their perceptions of the *costs and rewards* associated with, as well as their *capability* to engage in, various communicative practices, co-cultural group members will adopt certain communication orientations — based on their *preferred outcomes* and *communication approaches* — to fit the circumstances of a specific situation. (Orbe, 1998a, p. 18)

This description of co-cultural communication, as explained previously, contains the term *communication orientation*, a concept that refers to specific stances (e.g., assertive accommodation) that underrepresented group members assume during their everyday interactions. Each communication orientation is primarily situated within a specific preferred outcome (assimilation, accommodation, or separation) and communication approach (nonassertive, assertive, or aggressive), but it also is directly influenced by four other factors (field of experience, perceived costs and rewards, capability, and situational context). Given these issues, co-cultural theory suggests that underrepresented group members can assume one or more communication stances during their everyday interactions with others, which is done with a significant amount of consciousness given their marginalized positionality.

In this regard, co-cultural theory lends insight into the processes by which co-cultural group members negotiate their "cultural differentness" with others (both with those who are like and unlike themselves). For researchers and practitioners interested in the experiences of underrepresented group members, co-cultural theory offers a framework for understanding the processes by which such individuals come to select how they are going to interact with others in various interpersonal, group, and organizational contexts (see Buzzanell, 1999; Fox, Giles, Orbe, & Bourhis, 2000; Greer-Williams, 2000; Harter, Berquist, Schuette, & Redepenning, 2001; Lapinski & Orbe, 2002; Orbe, 1998b; Phillips-Gott, 1999), including how citizens participate in public discussions (Miura, 2001). Although the research cited here focused on a variety of cultural groups within different settings, each study was grounded in the assumptions inherent in co-cultural theory. In terms of the CRH Project, as explained next, co-cultural theory served as an important conceptual foundation for organizers who were concerned with maximizing community discussions in which individuals from diverse backgrounds would come together and discuss their experiences with civil rights issues.

A Co-Cultural Theoretical Foundation for Civil Rights Health Assessment

As discussed in the opening section of this chapter, two of the stated goals of the CRH Project were to "bring people, across their respective communities, together to discuss civil rights issues" and "raise awareness across the community in terms of how civil rights issues affect various aspects of people's lives" (Michigan Department of Civil Rights, 2003b, p. 2). Given existing gaps in how different groups perceive civil rights ("Blacks, Whites," 2001), one can see the importance of creating public discourse environments where all voices can be heard and ideally engaged in dialogue. As such, a co-cultural theoretical foundation was important in acknowledging ways that traditional structures marginalized the voices of certain community members.

Accordingly, the primary contribution that co-cultural theory made to the CRH Project was to provide organizers with a theoretical framework that encouraged recognition and respect of the "Other." For example, through applications of the theory, organizers, as well as participants, came to understand the direct and indirect means by which a person's field of experience influences how he or she communicates about civil rights issues. In the most ideal scenario, participants also came to understand concerns surrounding this topic in the context of specific costs and rewards that inform said comments. On a more practical level, co-cultural theory helped CRH Project planners to recognize the situational context as a key factor in how people engage in civil rights discussions. For example, over time, the CRH steering committee came to recognize that having discussions occur within familiar community locations (e.g., at community centers and churches) maximized the participation and contribution of underrepresented group members. A multitude of other logistical decisions—such as time, place, who was invited, the availability of daycare, and whether the location was accessible to persons with disabilities—also affected the ability of other community members to participate in meaningful ways. As one can see from the brief description provided here, co-cultural theory provided a useful framework (e.g., concepts, structures, and a model) for creating an environment where productive civil rights discussions could be maximized.

Several specific factors illustrate the particular ways in which co-cultural theory was used to inform the CRH Project. According to co-cultural theory, two particular factors—preferred outcome and communication approach—intersect to form a specific communication orientation for members of marginalized groups. *Preferred outcome* is defined as the ultimate effect desired by an individual in a co-cultural communication context; in essence, it includes a conscious or unconscious answer to the question, "What communication behavior will lead to the effect that I desire?" (Orbe, 1998a, p. 89). As alluded to earlier, responses to this question typically take one of three forms: (a) *assimilation* (striving to fit in with dominant members and structures), (b) *accommodation* (working with dominant group members to alter existing structures), or (c) *separation* (working outside dominant group structures to form collective action as a means to invoke change).

As articulated previously, one of the short-term goals of the CRH Project was to bring people from diverse backgrounds together to share their perceptions, concerns, and experiences with civil rights issues. Although this was an admirable goal, many of the community organizers did not recognize that participants would bring different preferred outcomes to the civil rights dialogues. In fact, the existence of divergent—sometimes opposing—preferred outcomes in some discussions resulted in increased tension between groups. For instance, one public forum attracted over 70 residents, all but one of whom were African American or Latino/a. Within this particular context, some of the people of color were representatives of different organizations (e.g., the Urban League or the National Association for the Advancement of Colored People) that had longstanding working relationships with the MDCR. However, others at the public forum who did not have these previous relationships took a more confrontational approach to civil rights issues and perceived those individuals with such relationships as being "sell-outs." This dynamic produced a clear tension between participants who had "different agendas." In terms of co-cultural theory, facilitators were able to understand how this scenario was rooted in different preferred outcomes that needed to be acknowledged. Accordingly, facilitators enacted strategies whereby participants could recognize the value in each desired result and the ways in which they ultimately overlap in concrete ways (e.g., identifying common goals articulated by different speakers and simultaneously recognizing various means to accomplish those goals).

Another co-cultural theoretical concept that provided an important foundation to the CRH Project was *communication approach*. According to Orbe (1998a), three primary communication approaches are used by co-cultural members with both dominant group and other co-cultural group members. *Aggressive communication* consists of those communicative practices perceived by the other person to be hurtfully expressive, self-promoting, and assuming control over the choices of others. At the other extreme, *nonassertive communication* includes behavior by individuals that is seemingly inhibited, nonconfrontational, and that puts the needs of others before their own. As a middle point, *assertive communication* involves a balance between aggressive and nonassertive communication, whereby self-enhancing, expressive behavior takes into account the needs of both self and others.

Similar to what happened regarding participants' preferred outcome, the diversity of communication approaches demonstrated within the public forums and focus group discussions sometimes created potentially difficult dialogues. This was most often the case when certain participants, including some facilitators, were uncomfortable with others who used — in their estimations — an inappropriate communication approach. For instance, in one public forum, several individuals took turns at the microphone to describe civil rights issues in their community. The first few people focused on the positive things going on within the community and included comments about "how great it was to live in a community where people cared about one another." In these persons' views, the civil rights issues that did exist were relatively minor and not comparable to the more positive things happening. Subsequent speakers, however, took issue with such a "glowing account" of things and criticized earlier speakers for putting the needs of the majority above their own by not wanting to "rock the boat." Before long, multiple subsequent speakers at the community meeting were focusing more on other speakers' comments than they were on the issues at hand. Consequently, unproductive discussions that lost focus on the topic at hand emerged when different communication approaches were criticized as being ineffective in drawing attention to civil rights issues. What was disregarded in this exchange was the realization that all communication approaches typically are necessary to ensure that others will actually receive the information. In other words, effective communication requires attention beyond initial perceptions of the forcefulness of one's comments. Co-cultural theory, thus, provided a framework to discuss these issues openly and productively.

PHENOMENOLOGICAL INQUIRY

To meet the CRH Project's objectives, a phenomenological methodology was used to facilitate the public forums and focus group discussions. Co-cultural theory and phenomenology have been used together in past communication research (Orbe, 1998a) and served as a powerful combination of applied theory and research methods for this project. In this section, I explain the basic ideas associated with phenomenological inquiry and its utility to this project.

Phenomenology is the name for the historical movement inaugurated in Germany by a number of scholars, including Husserl, Heidegger, and Jaspers, and continued in France by Merleau-Ponty and Sartre (for a review, see Husserl, 1900/1970, 1964; Lanigan, 1979; Merleau-Ponty, 1968). From such beginnings, phenomenology has developed into a human science approach to qualitative thematic analysis that has been successfully used by education (e.g., van Maanen, 1990), sociology (e.g., Garfinkel, 1967; Schutz, 1973), and communication researchers (Lanigan, 1979; Nelson, 1989; Orbe, 1998a) to gain understanding regarding the phenomenon under investigation from co-researchers that is approached in an open, unconstricting manner.

Hermeneutic phenomenology is the study of the lifeworld (*lebenswelt*), the world as we immediately experience it prereflectively, rather than as we conceptualize or theorize it (Husserl, 1970). In other words, phenomenology attempts to focus on the preconscious experiences of how a person relates to the lived world she or he inhabits (*Zeitgeist*) (Lanigan, 1988). Given this focus, phenomenology was especially useful to the CRH Project's attempt to inductively explore how diverse citizens experienced civil rights issues in their everyday lives. Orbe (2000) made the productive link between phenomenology and race/ethnicity explicit when he argued that the two can work together effectively to produce scholarship that centralizes the communication of co-cultural group members without generalizing in-group differences. Given the diversity of civil rights experiences within any one protected class, this was a key principle for the organizers of the CRH Project.

To engage in phenomenological studies, researchers follow a 3-step process: (a) gathering descriptions of lived experiences, (b) reviewing these descriptions to reveal essential themes, and (c) interpreting and analyzing these themes. This process, as described by Nelson (1989) and van Maanen (1990), allows researchers to report their findings in ways that capture the essence of participants' experiences. The next section describes how these phenomenological procedures informed the organization and structure of the public forums and focus group discussions, as well as the analysis of citizens' comments collected via these two data-collection strategies.

The Value of Phenomenological Inquiry in the Civil Rights Health Project

Phenomenological research, unlike traditional social-scientific research methodologies, is not concerned with obtaining a random sample of participants (van Maanen, 1990); instead, the focus is on collecting descriptions of diverse lived experiences until no new information appears to be forthcoming. In terms of the CRH Project, local community organizers recruited participants for the public forums and focus group discussions. Through a synergistic planning process, conscious attention was paid to see that as many sectors of the community as possible were engaged in the project. For some committees, this meant that organizers reflected the diversity of the community, whereas others worked diligently to be sure that our research team—which also attempted to reflect the diversity of the different communities—met with representatives from various segments of the community.

To apply the phenomenological methodology to the CRH Project, a number of steps were taken. First, a public forum facilitated by members of our research team in each community was employed to inductively explore general civil rights issues. Once an initial analysis of the information collected from this forum was conducted, focus groups were held with the intended purpose of gaining specific insight into the particular community issues that had been raised during the public forums. This structural element reflected the beginning of the second stage of phenomenological inquiry—reduction. Consequently, the focus groups allowed our research team to obtain more specificity regarding the initial themes discovered from the public forums. In addition, the focus groups provided important feedback about, and clarification of, those very themes, something that stimulated a further reduction of major civil rights themes.

To understand this process, some description regarding the focus groups is warranted. Lasting approximately 45-75 minutes, focus group discussions used an interview guide (topical protocol) to generate a conversation about community civil rights issues. Consistent with the thematic analysis associated with phenomenology, open-ended and broadly structured questions were used to focus participants' attention on issues that they regarded as most significant. Once general introductions were facilitated, opening questions included prompts such as, "What are some of the specific civil rights issues in this community?" "Are these the same across the community or specific to certain areas or protected groups?" "What existing programs or efforts deal with these issues?" "If you could identify the largest civil rights challenge in the community, what would it be?" "In the long run—with money, time, and resources not being an issue—what do you think needs to be done with this challenge?" "For those who have some history in the community, what do you think has been the biggest improvement in terms of civil rights?"

As alluded to earlier, Stages 2 and 3 of the phenomenological process (reduction and interpretation of experiences) begin during Stage 1 (collection of lived experiences). In this regard, the process reflects more of a spiral than traditional, linear forms of research (Nelson, 1989). In addition, inherent in phenomenological inquiries are specific techniques that researchers use to address their subjectivities and tendency to give a hypervisibility to certain participants' voices over others. Space limitations do not allow for an in-depth treatment of each of these aspects of phenomenology; however, I discuss the crucial role that one technique—imaginative free variation—played in the CRH Project.

Imaginative free variation is a phenomenological technique that helps researchers to focus on the centrality of each theme in relation to the essence of the phenomenon under investigation (Lanigan, 1979). Specifically, this technique facilitates a process by which researchers can isolate a particular theme and determine its affiliation to the phenomenon under exploration. Nelson (1989) described the process of imaginative free variation in this way:

> Through the techniques of imaginative free variation, which contextualizes various features of the phenomenon within the whole, and which allows for comparison and contrast, a pattern of experience emerges. With it emerges the shape of the phenomenon as it is attended to in experience. (p. 235)

For the CRH Project, imaginative free variation played a key role in identifying those themes that were essential to civil rights issues in the various communities and simultaneously recognized those points of analyses that were incidental or happenstance (van Maanen, 1990). Feedback about the initial themes, offered by a network of community members and civil rights professionals (who served on area-site committees), also was instrumental in fine-tuning the themes discussed in the final report written for each community.

In short, phenomenology was an important methodological framework for the CRH Project. Not only did it lend itself to a discovery-oriented approach to researching the issue of community civil rights but it also provided the researchers with clear structural techniques to recognize sometimes less-visible issues that go unexplored in traditional research practices (e.g., revelatory phrases that were uttered by one or two focus group participants). Finally, phenomenology, with its recognition of the ways in which perceptions of reality are specific to a particular time and space, stresses research activities that are open-ended and not finalized. Given the changing nature of civil rights issues in and among different communities, such an approach was especially important to the CRH Project. This point is crucial because some communities may attempt to utilize the CRH Project as an instant solution to addressing multidimensional, complex issues, something that is not in line with its objective. Promoting an understanding of phenomenological research as an ongoing process, as articulated later, helps communities to recognize that an easy solution is unlikely. As Orbe (2000) explained:

> Phenomenological inquiry never positions itself as arriving at a definitive set of conclusions. In this regard, a "final" answer is never accomplished; instead the researcher is always left asking, "What have I missed?" Given the intricate complexities of intercultural research [and civil rights], such a constantly ambiguous standpoint can be especially productive as we seek understanding in a new millennium. (p. 618)

FACILITATING THE CRH PROJECT: OPPORTUNITIES AND CHALLENGES

The research just described in these three pilot communities was used to produce a CRH Resource Manual, the objective of which was to provide a guide for groups interested in facilitating a CRH assessment in their communities. In 2002, Kalamazoo, a mid-sized community in Michigan, was chosen by a statewide steering committee as the first site to utilize the newly created manual. This final section describes the assessment process for Kalamazoo and highlights several challenges that were faced by organizers.

CRH Project in Kalamazoo

Kalamazoo, MI, the fourth community in which a CRH assessment was facilitated and the first to utilize the newly created manual, was selected for inclusion in this project for two primary reasons. First, it was located in the southwestern part of Michigan, a geographical area that previously had not been included. Second, it represented a type of community that had not been included in the three pilot communities—a "college town" with a strong private business sector (e.g., a diverse industrial base). According to the 2000 U.S. Census (see Michigan Department of Civil Rights, 2003a), Kalamazoo had a population of 238,603, of which 83.5% were White, 9.6% African American, 2.6% Hispanic, 1.9% Asian/Pacific Islander, and .5% Native American. Although the community's overall economic picture was generally positive, several recent mergers and plant closings had resulted in a substantial loss of jobs.

The area-site committee for Kalamazoo's assessment was co-chaired by an elected city official and the chief executive officer of a national, community-based organization, and it included a dozen members of the community who volunteered from local churches, government agencies, and community-based organizations. Given the shifting economic situation in the community, the area-site committee decided that the focus of the assessment would be on employment generally, and specifically on discrimination issues within various business sectors of the employment arena. According to Michigan state law, civil rights laws prohibit discrimination based on religion, race, color, national origin, sex, age, marital status, familial status, disability, height, weight, and arrest record. In addition to these issues, the area-site committee was interested in assessing any discrimination against groups unprotected by the current statute, including those based on socioeconomic status and sexual orientation.

Across the span of 4 months (July-November, 2002), data collection for the CRH assessment was completed. This procedure included a content analysis of local media's coverage of civil rights issues, as well as a thorough review of existing local reports and documents related to civil rights as identified by the area-site committee—all of which was completed by our research team. However, the crux of the data, as outlined by the CRH Resource Manual, was collected through a public forum and several focus group discussions.

On July 29, 2002, a civil rights health public forum was held at the Kalamazoo city hall. This event was widely publicized via coverage by local radio and television stations; in addition, letters of invitation were sent to a large list of individuals and organizations identified by the area-site committee. To facilitate maximum attendance and participation, this 3-hour open meeting was divided into two sections, 4:00-5:30 p.m. and 5:30-7:00 p.m., so that participants could come and go without a commitment to stay for the entire 3 hours. Approximately 75 people attended this meeting. During the meeting, our research team was able to collect data regarding individuals' perceptions of civil rights related to employment through three means: (a) comments shared publicly at the forum, which were taped and transcribed; (b) comments shared through one-on-one private interviews that we conducted with participants; and (c) written comments submitted anonymously. All of this information was reviewed to generate general insight into the civil rights issues particular to Kalamazoo.

We then facilitated nine focus group discussions across Kalamazoo on August 20-21, 2002. To maximize participation of various community members, these discussions were held at many locations, including local churches, community centers, and organizations. Over the course of this 2-day period, over 66 community members participated in focus group discussions, providing rich information regarding their perceptions of civil rights issues in the community. Group discussions, organized with respect to particular demographic characteristics of the participants, were facilitated with the following foci: (a) disability issues, (b) youth issues, (c) older worker issues, (d) women's issues, (e) GLBT issues, (f) African American issues, (g)

Hispanic/Latino/a issues, (h) low-income issues, and (i) faith-based issues. Focus groups were co-facilitated by the author and one other member of the research team and followed the same phenomenologically based topical protocol described previously. Like the public forum, these sessions—ranging from 40-75 minutes in length—were taped, transcribed, and later analyzed.

On February 5, 2003, a press conference was held in which a report describing the civil rights health of Kalamazoo was released to the public by selected members of the area-site committee, including myself as director of the research team. Attended by various community members, in addition to the local press, the press conference was immediately followed by a panel discussion of the area-site committee members' reactions to the report. The 57-page report highlighted specific issues of discrimination faced by various groups in the community. The report also summarized several thematic conclusions regarding Kalamazoo's civil rights health generally, including: (a) employment issues affect, and are affected by, all other areas of civil rights; (b) despite current laws prohibiting it, discrimination in employment practices is common, but because discrimination is subtle and complex, it is difficult to prove; (c) civil rights laws are an important foundation, but are not enough; (d) for many individuals, filing a civil rights complaint is not perceived as an option due to the negative consequences of being labeled as a troublemaker; (e) businesses must address civil rights health issues to maximize their most important resource—people; (f) perception is a key element in studying civil rights health and should be studied alongside statistical facts; and (g) effective efforts for increasing Kalamazoo's civil rights health must acknowledge how intersections of identity affect one's experience in the workplace.

As one might expect, the CRH report generated significant attention from those in city and county government entities, the business sector, and the local media. Currently, the area-site committee has officially disbanded and transitioned into a strategic planning committee that has the explicit objective of mobilizing existing community organizations to participate in a process whereby specific findings of the report can serve as benchmarks to generate actions plans for future success. I currently serve on the strategic planning committee that intends to function as an umbrella organization for existing groups committed to fostering social change regarding the issues addressed in the Kalamazoo CRH report.

Civil Rights Health Challenges

The CRH assessment process in Kalamazoo, and as outlined in the resource manual (Michigan Department of Civil Rights, 2003b), benefited greatly from the lessons learned from the three pilot sites. Specifically, the statewide steering committee was able to identify, discuss, and analyze the different issues involved as they arose. Consequently, after the resource manual was written, I was able to offer insight on how communities could proactively address potential problems during the assessment-planning stages. These issues notwithstanding, the CRH assessment in Kalamazoo still faced several challenges that I suggest are inherent to many forms of engaged scholarship and communication activism. Here, I briefly discuss five of the more prominent challenges: (a) individual, oftentimes competing, agendas; (b) sustained community participation; (c) negotiating tensions between processes and outcomes; (d) creating meaningful processes and outcomes with long-term impact; and (e) facilitating social change.

Individual, oftentimes competing, agendas. Although the general idea of a civil rights assessment has been explored previously by the U.S. Justice Department, the initial stimulus for the CRH Project in Michigan was generated by a proposal submitted by a faith-based organization in the western part of the state. When this community (Muskegon County) was selected as one of the pilot sites for the project, it became clear that members of the area-site committee had different ideas about what should be accomplished through the project. For instance, some city officials and agency representatives were less interested in an honest self-assessment, wanting, instead, to use the process to highlight the positive things that existed in their community (for many, this meant focusing on what their particular organization was doing in the area of civil rights). A few community members wanted the project to uncover blatant, as well as subtle, forms of discrimination throughout their community; their primary objective was to gain evidence that could be used to successfully confront companies to change existing policies (e.g., hiring). Others, however, were true to the reflective nature of the self-assessment process and saw the project as a means to collaboratively work together for positive change in their community. The challenge for CRH organizers was to acknowledge all of these individual agendas but also to persuade community group members to not allow competing agendas to take away from the overall objective of the project.

Similar challenges arose in two of the three pilot sites. In Kalamazoo, this tension became most apparent during initial planning for the CRH assessment. As mentioned previously, the area-site committee decided to focus on employment issues; however, this decision was achieved only after much discussion. Each of the community pilot sites had taken a general approach to the assessment that included collecting data regarding employment, housing, public accommodation, education, and other important matters. However, the area-site committee members in Kalamazoo realized that a more focused approach would be more beneficial to them, so they engaged in discussions to see what that focus might be; potential areas that they identified included housing discrimination, police-community relations, health-care gaps among racial-ethnic groups, access to capital, and hate crimes. However, a point of contention emerged between a couple of area-site committee members whose personal/political/professional agendas clashed concerning the inclusion of gays and lesbians in the assessment process. One member explicitly pushed the committee to focus on access to capital, partly because it presumably would exclude the GLBT community (e.g., based on the person's belief than gays and lesbians have higher income levels than their heterosexual counterparts). Other members, including a woman who was executive director of a local GLBT resource center, insisted that GLBT issues, although not currently protected under state law, be included. After much discussion, and largely due to the positive relationships established between committee members, the committee decided to focus on employment issues (which represented a consensus position). Such a productive solution was only possible, I believe, because of committee members' dedication and commitment to the potential of the project. Consequently, future sites interested in facilitating the CRH Project in their communities should devote considerable attention to attracting community members to the area-site committee who have considerable commitment to the issue of civil rights.

Sustained community participation. To be successful, any effort that relies on unpaid volunteers must work diligently to sustain the active participation of its core workers. Within the structures of the CRH Project, only the members of the research team were compensated for their efforts; all others either volunteered their time or participated as part of their work duties. The challenge of getting—and keeping—people involved in such a huge undertaking was present at each of the pilot sites; in fact, this was probably the largest challenge for two of the three sites. In both pilot communities with a fairly large area-site committee (10-15 members each), several meetings were held at which only 2-3 people showed up. Such, however, was not the case in Kalamazoo.

In Kalamazoo, initial organizers worked diligently to invite a wide array of individuals to the first orientation meeting. At this initial meeting, a dozen or so persons committed to serving on the area-site committee and others agreed to serve in various capacities (e.g., strategic planning). Although a few of these individuals participated in sporadic ways, the vast majority of area-site committee members (about 8-9) participated actively throughout the duration of the project. This level of participation appeared to be due to several conditions. First, clear expectations, duties, and responsibilities were outlined in the CRH Resource Manual, and, consequently, individuals could make an informed decision regarding their ability to commit to the project; such was not the case during the projects in the pilot communities used to develop the manual. Second, the timeline for the project had been established, enabling individuals to see that their commitment was clearly defined and relatively quick (6 months, start to finish), and adhering to this timeline undoubtedly assisted in sustaining participants' involvement. The third and final contributing factor to Kalamazoo's ability to maintain an active area-site committee related to the leadership styles of the two co-chairs. Both women worked in organizations whose mission was aligned to that of the project. Hence, working with the CRH Project was seen by these women as a part of their formal duties (e.g., one co-chair incorporated the project into the annual objectives of her organization). As explained earlier, the area-site committee has started the transition into a strategic planning team and has faced the challenge of sustaining participation. As the time commitment to the project extends beyond the assessment phase, members will need to continue to address this issue by widening the circle of individuals interested in advocating for greater equity across the community.

Negotiating tensions between processes and outcomes. In addition to the challenge of having multiple, competing agendas present within the CRH Project's planning and implementation, a related, but different, challenge exists when researchers, organizers, and participants regard the value of a project in contrary ways. The author's experiences within the different communities involved in this project revealed that two opposing viewpoints typically were evident. For some people, the report was the valued goal of the CRH assessment. For these individuals, getting the data collected, analyzed, and written up was a means to the end (with many seeing it and not the change it could generate as *the* solution to existing problems). Consequently, most of their efforts were geared toward completion of the report. For others, however, the value of the CRH assessment was in the process itself; although the report was a valuable outcome, it simply reflected one point in an ongoing process of addressing civil rights issues. These individuals were much more likely to remain committed to the intricacies of the planning activities and appreciate discussions that resulted in no clear decision making. As one might expect, having an area-site committee with individuals whose perspectives were grounded in each of these values was difficult to manage in a way that led all parties to view the project as worthwhile.

The question that remains is where the ultimate value of engaged communication activist scholarship, such as that which was facilitated through the CRH Project, lies. As articulated earlier, one of the core assumptions of this project was that "the value of the work associated with the CRH Project is in the process, as much as the outcome(s)" (Michigan Department of Civil Rights, 2003b, p. 2). The ultimate goal, then, is to have participants understand the value of both the processes and the outcomes. However, getting all participants to adopt this perspective—especially those whose professional lives are driven by "the bottom line" or "outcome measures"—remains a challenge.

Creating meaningful processes and outcomes with long-term impact. Another challenge inherent to communication activism, such as the CRH Project, involves the ability to have a long-term impact. The CRH Resource Manual features an entire section on the steps that communities can take once a civil rights health report is completed and disseminated. However, the procedures for this post-assessment work are significantly less structured in comparison to other areas of the manual. To date, the largest criticism of the CRH Project has focused on what has happened, or has not happened, following the completion of the assessment. This was most apparent in the pilot site of Midland, where both co-chairs left the community to take advantage of professional opportunities. For this community, the absence of these individuals, who were committed to the project, has created a major hurdle in advancing any type of strategic planning.

This problem, however, has not been the case for Kalamazoo. One of the original area-site committee co-chairs has committed to providing leadership to the strategic planning group, and another committee member has volunteered to serve as co-chair. In addition, a core group of committee members has continued to work with the project and are excited about recruiting new members. The challenge of facilitating a long-term impact, however, is still very real. Although the nonjudgmental, descriptive nature of the report provided significant insight into civil rights issues in Kalamazoo, it lacked specific recommendations that some area-site committee members thought were crucial to guiding post-assessment efforts. In addition, planning efforts are largely constrained due to a lack of funding, even with respect to meeting the small costs associated with monthly committee meetings. Finally, as time passes, the committee will be challenged to sustain the community's interest in the project. Although many of the CRH organizers in Kalamazoo found the project personally, socially, and professionally meaningful, they must now convince those external to the project of the potential impact that it could have on the overall well-being of the community.

Facilitating social change. Within this chapter, in some significant detail, the central role that community-based discussions served in the CRH Project has been described. As the director of the research team, my leadership activities included overseeing the collection, transcription, and analysis of diverse experiences regarding civil rights issues across the four different communities that participated in the project. The final, official responsibility of our research team was the preparation and presentation of a final report for each community. As outlined in the CRH Resource Manual, once the report was delivered, the area-site committee then assumed responsibility to engage the larger community in a strategic planning process whereby specific aspects of the report could be addressed. In this regard, the assessment process was designed to utilize dialogue as a means to enhance understanding of community members' diverse experiences and facilitate social change within each respective community (for additional studies and discussion of dialogue as a means of social change, see Adams, Berquist, Dillon, & Galanes, this volume; Jovanovic, Steger, Symonds, & Nelson, this volume).

Within each community, evidence exists that points to particular ways in which the assessment process and report facilitated changes in policy and procedures. One example is the extended liaison initiative that the MDCR instituted, in part, as a response to citizens' concerns about the closing of a civil rights office in the city of Pontiac, MI. Although budgetary limitations did not permit reopening the office, a new program was established in which civil rights representatives were assigned to expand outreach activities to underserved communities, including Pontiac. This program serves as one example—others also exist—of how the CRH Project enhanced the MDCR's ability to effectively serve the people of Michigan. Yet, an explicit goal of the initiative also was to generate social change at the individual community level. At the time of writing this chapter, it remains unclear if the project will have any long-term consequences with regard to particular actions taken by each community.

A significant barrier to utilizing the CRH Project to facilitate social change in each community is related to the shifting of responsibility from the MDCR and research team to the area-site committee. Within the structure of the project, the MDCR assisted in the creation and initial work of each area-site committee, and our research team then was primarily responsible for all aspects of completing the actual assessment. Following the presentation of the final document, each area-site committee was then responsible—without the direct involvement of the MDCR or research team—for using the guidelines within the CRH Resource Manual to create and implement a strategic plan. Within the three pilot communities that facilitated a CRH assessment, each area-site committee struggled with maintaining sufficient momentum to effectively create and implement a strategic plan. For some, this struggle was tied to a lack of clear, committed leadership on the area-site committee; for others, it was directly tied to a lack of resources needed to advance the work of the initiative. The first community to benefit from the established model, Kalamazoo, appears to be best positioned to advance beyond the barriers that occur with the transition of responsibility, for, as described earlier, this community has maintained an active group of people who remain committed to utilizing the CRH Report to create specific action plans.

CONCLUSION

In light of changing demographics and ideological values, civil rights advocates are constantly challenged to discover ways in which they can work to promote equality in a society that varies in its understanding of and commitment to social justice issues. This chapter outlined specific ways in which communication theory, research, and methods can enhance the effectiveness of a network of community members, academicians, and state employees, who are committed to addressing the important social issue of civil rights in their communities. To this end, the concepts of engaged scholarship (Applegate, 2001) and communication activism as prototypes of the value of networking within and among different segments of the population were used.

According to some people—especially members of the general public who are unfamiliar with scholarly work—theory, research, and methods are regarded as abstract, philosophical, and intellectual pursuits with little practical value to everyday life. However, as described throughout this 2-volume set, this is definitely not the case. Within the CRH Project, co-cultural theory provided an important foundation to help organizers and facilitators maximize ways in which people discussed their experiences with the civil rights health of their communities. In equally important ways, phenomenology served as an invaluable research methodology that produced an inductive, open, and inclusive process of discovery. This chapter, hopefully, has highlighted the productive ways in which communication theory and research can be used to promote communication activism. Creating opportunities for community dialogue, thus, is one means to facilitate understanding toward the larger goal of social change. It is equally important to recognize, however, that talk cannot serve as a replacement for other action (Zoller, 2000).

In closing, scholars have traditionally differentiated between two types of research: basic (or pure) research that tests theory and applied research that seeks to solve practical problems (see, e.g., O'Hair, Kreps, & Frey, 1990). Communication researchers who embrace the position of an engaged scholar committed to communication activism transcend the limitations of this problematic dichotomy. Engaged scholarship, such as that which occurred within the context of the CRH Project, tests the value of theory through applications that seek solutions to practical problems—in this case, the important issue of promoting civil rights health amidst a changing society. Ideally, such communication activism is a process whereby a network of individuals engages in a mutually beneficial partnership in which all parties contribute to and gain from the experience.

APPENDIX
CIVIL RIGHTS HEALTH:
A COMMUNITY-BASED ASSESSMENT

Objective: To provide a meaningful, nonjudgmental, community-based assessment instrument that allows individual communities to systematically discern the state of civil rights health (CRH) in their respective communities

Step 1: Deciding to Conduct a CRH Assessment
- Create a community profile
- Identify key community issues related to civil rights
- Evaluate community support for a CRH assessment
- Gain commitment from "key players" across the community

Step 2: Organizing a CRH Assessment
- Foster meaningful community involvement
- Utilize new/existing coalitions
- Create a local CRH committee
- Establish CRH assessment focus
- Identify research resources

Step 3: Planning a CRH Assessment
- Creating a timeline
- Preparing the research team
- Locating existing documents
- Planning the public forums
- Planning the focus group discussions
- Promoting local media coverage

Step 4: Facilitating a CRH Assessment
- Existing documents
- Public forums
- Focus group discussions
- Follow-up data collection

Step 5: Creating the CRH Assessment Report
- Document the process
- Transcription
- Thematization process
- Utilize existing documents

Step 6: Utilizing the CRH Assessment Report
- Document distribution
- Public presentation(s)
- Additional data collection
- Community-based strategic planning
- Promising practices

REFERENCES

Applegate, J. L. (2001, September). Engaged graduate education: Skating to where the puck will be. *Spectra*, pp. 2-5.

Blacks, Whites further apart in perceptions. (2001, July 11). *Kalamazoo Gazette*, pp. A1-A2.

Buzzanell, P. M. (1999). Tensions and burdens in employment interviewing processes: Perspectives of non-dominant group members. *Journal of Business Communication, 36*, 143-162.

Fox, S., Giles, H., Orbe, M., & Bourhis, R. Y. (2000). Interability communication: Theoretical perspectives. In D. O. Braithwaite & T. L. Thompson (Eds.), *Handbook of communication and people with disabilities: Research and application* (pp. 193-222). Mahwah, NJ: Erlbaum.

Garfinkel, H. (1967). *Studies in ethnomethodology.* Englewood Cliffs, NJ: Prentice-Hall.

Greer-Williams, N. (2000, November). *Diversity and organizations: A smooth mixture.* Paper presented at the meeting of the National Communication Association, Seattle, WA.

Harter, L. M., Berquist, C. A., Schuette, S., & Redepenning, M. (2001, April). *Voices without homes: Exploring homeless narratives from a co-cultural perspective.* Paper presented at the meeting of the Central States Communication Association, Cincinnati, OH.

Huesca, R. (2001). Conceptual contributions of new social movements to development communication research. *Communication Theory, 11*, 415-433.

Husserl, E. (1964). *The idea of phenomenology* (W. P. Alson & G. Nakhnikian, Trans.). The Hague, Netherlands: Martinus Nijhoff.

Husserl, E. (1970). *Logical investigations* (J. N. Findlay, Trans.). London: Routledge and Kegan Paul. (Original work published 1900)

Kramarae, C. (1981). *Women and men speaking: Frameworks for analysis.* Rowley, MA: Newbury House.

Lanigan, R. L. (1979). The phenomenology of human communication. *Philosophy Today, 23*, 3-15.

Lanigan, R. L. (1988). *Phenomenology of communication: Merleau-Ponty's thematics in communicology and semiology.* Pittsburgh, PA: Duquesne University Press.

Lapinski, M., & Orbe, M. (2002, July). *Measuring the components of co-cultural theory.* Paper presented at the meeting of the International Communication Association, Seoul, South Korea.

Merleau-Ponty, M. (1968). *The visible and the invisible* (C. Lefort, Ed.; A. Lingis, Trans.). Evanston, IL: Northwestern University Press.

Michigan Department of Civil Rights. (2003a). *Civil rights health: A community-based assessment in Kalamazoo County.* Lansing, MI: Author.

Michigan Department of Civil Rights. (2003b). *Civil Rights Health Resource Manual: A community-based assessment.* Lansing, MI: Author.

Miura, S. Y. (2001). New identity, new rhetoric: The Native Hawaiian quest for independence. *Journal of Intergroup Relations, 28*(2), 3-16.

Nelson, J. (1989). Phenomenology as feminist methodology: Explicating interviews. In K. Carter & C. Spitzack (Eds.), *Doing research on women's communication: Perspectives on theory and method* (pp. 221-241). Norwood, NJ: Ablex.

O'Hair, D., Kreps, G. L., & Frey, L. R. (1990). Conceptual issues. In D. O'Hair & G. L. Kreps (Eds.), *Applied communication theory and research* (pp. 3-22). Hillsdale, NJ: Erlbaum.

Orbe, M. P. (1998a). *Constructing co-cultural theory: An explication of culture, power, and communication.* Thousand Oaks, CA: Sage.

Orbe, M. P. (1998b). An "outsider within" perspective to organizational communication: Explicating the communicative practices of co-cultural group members. *Management Communication Quarterly, 12,* 230-279.

Orbe, M. P. (2000). Centralizing diverse racial/ethnic voices in scholarly research: The value of phenomenological inquiry. *International Journal of Intercultural Relations, 24,* 603-621.

Phillips-Gott, P. C. (1999, November). *African American communication, organizations, and assimilation: A co-cultural perspective.* Paper presented at the meeting of the National Communication Association, Chicago, IL.

Schutz, A. (1972). *The phenomenology of the social world* (G. Walsh & F. Lehnert, Trans.). London: Heinemann Educational Books.

Smith, D. E. (1987). *The everyday world as problematic: A feminist sociology of knowledge.* Boston: Northeastern University Press.

Stewart, C. J. (1997). The evolution of a revolution: Stokely Carmichael and the rhetoric of Black power. *Quarterly Journal of Speech, 83,* 429-446.

van Maanen, M. (1990). *Researching lived experience: Human science for action sensitive pedagogy.* Albany: State University of New York Press.

Wilkins, K. G. (2000). Introduction. In K. G. Wilkins (Ed.), *Redeveloping communication for social change: Theory, practice, and power* (pp. 1-4). Lanham, MD: Rowman & Littlefield.

Zoller, H. M. (2000). "A place you haven't visited before": Creating the conditions of community dialogue. *Southern Communication Journal, 65,* 191-207.

4

THE URBAN DEBATE LEAGUE RHETORICAL VISION

Empowering Marginalized Voices for Leadership and Activism

Donald C. Shields

University of Missouri—St. Louis;
University of Missouri—Kansas City

C. Thomas Preston, Jr.

Gainesville State College

The relationship between public policy debate and the furtherance of democracy and democratic values is a long-established one dating to Greece in the 5th century, BCE. Modern policy debate entails a rigorous and passionate discussion about change in the polity and how that change may be achieved. Through such discussions, the democratic values of awareness, liberty, opportunity, and openness are reinforced. Studies by Chaffee (1978), Drew and Weaver (1991), Lemert (1993), and Morello (1988) have shown, for instance, that televised presidential debates contribute to the maintenance of democracy by informing voters about public policy, candidate qualities, and campaign issues. Thus, within a democracy, the development of argumentative skills for both making and evaluating arguments serves the electorate well. Concomitantly, communication scholarship is replete with studies that view the development and improvement of argumentative skills as being beneficial to individuals. Useful skills range from those that are argument specific, such as good reasoning, documentation, refutation, and critical thinking, to general communication skills, including assertiveness, persuasiveness, and willingness to argue for one's positions.

Beginning more than 50 years ago, scholars reported studies that demonstrated the value of educational training in argumentation. For example, Brembeck (1949) found that college students who received training in argumentation improved significantly in critical thinking over an untrained matched group. Krumboltz (1957) noted that business executives who had been trained as debaters made more money than those who had not. McBath (1963) reported a survey indicating that, at the time, 62.5% of government leaders—including members of the U.S. Congress, senators, governors, cabinet members, and Supreme Court justices—had participated in school debate; of these, 90% indicated that their experience had helped their careers either "greatly" or "invaluably." Other studies have shown that training in argumentation transfers to other aspects of the real world. Semlak and Shields (1977), for instance, found that community leaders, after watching both trained and untrained people arguing value questions in celebration of our nation's bicentennial, rated those participants with debate experience comparatively higher in analysis, delivery, and organization. Hirokawa (1985) demonstrated that discussion groups that more competently performed the functions of analyzing a problem and assessing the advantages and disadvantages of each proposed solution were evaluated as reaching higher quality decisions as compared to groups that did not perform these functions well. Infante and Gordon (1987) reported that people with the ability to make high-quality arguments were perceived as more competent than those who were not able to do so in superior-subordinate work situations. Canary, Brossman, Brossman, and Weger (1995) reported that "communicators using complex arguments" were "seen as more instrumentally effective than communicators using simple arguments" (p. 183). D. Johnson and Sellnow (1995) found that organizational managers' ability to construct both forensic (legal) and deliberative (public policy) arguments were intrinsic to organizational crisis management. On the basis of these and other studies, Cragan and Shields (1998) concluded that "the ability to use rational argumentation theory is one of the hallmarks of an educated person" (p. 66).

Within the educational context, the acquisition of rational argumentation and debate skills has consistently been shown to be useful to both communication majors and others across the undergraduate curriculum (see

Allen, Berkowitz, Hunt, & Louden, 1999; Allen, Berkowitz, & Louden, 1995; Anderson, Schultz, & Courtney, 1987; Barfield, 1989; Breger, 1998; Colbert, 1993, 1994; Crenshaw, 1998; Infante & Gordon, 1989; Madrid, 1999; McCroskey, 1962; Myers, 1998; Rancer, Kosberg, & Baukus, 1992; Roberto & Finucane, 1997; Sanders, Wiseman, & Gass, 1994; Semlak & Shields, 1977; Wade, 1998; Ziegelmueller, 1998). The Vashon Interdisciplinary Project for Education Reform (2002), a science education project hosted at the University of Missouri (UM)—St. Louis, even linked the development of argumentative skills to effective learning of scientific concepts and skills. Because of such findings, G. A. Fine (2001) argued that "debate should be part of American education. . . . It would be naive to suggest that debate and rhetorical training could save the American republic, although some debaters would make that claim passionately. They might be right. The naive may be visionary" (pp. 250-251). Regardless of the research or the naivete behind the claim, the educational benefits of communication skills enhancement seems clear: Those students who are educated in argumentation skills are better equipped communicatively to function in the economic, political, and social domains in which they will participate as adults.

Due to eroded tax bases and insufficient budgets, until the late 1990s, within most major U.S. cities, intensive education in argumentation was unavailable to at-risk and underserved persons attending public schools. This created an inequity in the education in argumentation received by inner-city students vis-à-vis their counterparts at suburban schools. The solution posited to eliminate this discrepancy was the establishment of urban debate leagues (UDLs). UDLs promote debate as a component of the regular high school classroom curriculum by organizing interscholastic debate as an academic competition so that urban youth who have for so long been denied the powerful academic benefits of debate can be offered this valuable learning tool. UDLs, thus, aim to eliminate a particular form of educational and social inequality and have a positive academic impact on the entire urban public school systems within which they function as they prepare students to engage more fully within our democratic society.

We were co-principal investigators on a 3-year grant from the Soros Foundation's Open Society Institute of New York (OSI) that supported the founding of the Urban Debate League—St. Louis (hereafter, SLUDL), one of 16 leagues across the nation funded by OSI that provided argumentation education, coaching, and tournament participation opportunities for disadvantaged, inner-city high school students and their faculty. In St. Louis, Preston served as the primary administrator for the OSI grant and the SLUDL project; Shields served as an unpaid advisor on project activities and research investigations. The grant project was designed first to serve as a community-activist intervention to address the discrepancy in debating skills between urban public school students and suburban school students and, second, to enhance the ability of inner-city youths to contribute to a democratic society by affording them new opportunities to empower themselves by learning and practicing debate and argumentation skills. The Communication Arts Facilitator for the St. Louis Public Schools (John Grant the first 2.5 years and Paulette Kirkwood late in the third year) provided matching district funds to help secure the OSI grant and coordinated the district's effort in conjunction with the co-investigators. To explain how this community-activist intervention served to address these concerns both across the nation and in St. Louis, MO, we (a) provide an overview of the theory—symbolic convergence theory—that guided this intervention and the UDL rhetorical vision, (b) examine the benefits of and reactions to the UDL movement, and (c) present a case study of the SLUDL intervention as an extended exemplar of this national community-activist movement.

OVERVIEW OF SYMBOLIC CONVERGENCE THEORY AND THE URBAN DEBATE LEAGUE RHETORICAL VISION

In this section, we first set out those aspects of symbolic convergence theory relevant to the project and then elaborate on the UDL's rhetorical vision. Second, we characterize the adherents who comprise the UDL vision's rhetorical community. Third, we detail the interventions needed to ignite participation in this rhetorical vision, raise the consciousness of vision adherents, sustain their participation in the vision, and carry out the necessary actions within the school districts.

Symbolic Convergence Theory

Symbolic convergence theory (SCT) provides an account of how the consciousness of a collectivity of people is created, raised, and sustained by involving them in a composite drama—called a *rhetorical vision*—that comes to represent their symbolic reality (Bormann, 1972, 1985; Bormann, Cragan, & Shields, 1994, 1996, 2001, 2003; Cragan & Shields, 1981, 1992, 1995a, 1995b, 1998, 1999; Csapó-Sweet & Shields, 2000; Shields, 2000; Shields & Preston, 1985). Rhetorical visions may be created with an underlying deep structure reflecting a primarily *righteous* (the correct way), *social* (the humane way), or *pragmatic* (the expedient way) of depicting reality (Bormann et al., 1996, 2001; Cragan & Shields, 1981). More specifically, SCT explains the effects on people of dramatizing messages that contain heroes and villains, plot or action lines, and scenic descriptions. Such dramatized messages, called *fantasy themes*, provide meaning, emotion, and value within the words comprising the fantasy and, thereby, provide motive for both individual and collective human action.[1] Cragan and Shields (1998, 1999) noted that the communicative force of fantasy flows from communicators (*fantasizers* at the individual level and *rhetorical communities* at the collective level) communicating (*fantasy sharing* and *fantasy chaining*) by presenting messages (*fantasy themes, symbolic cues, fantasy types, sagas,* and *rhetorical visions*) propagated (grown and spread) by way of a medium (*group* and/or *public sharing*) affected by a communication dynamic (*righteous, social,* and *pragmatic master analog* deep structures of rhetorical visions) and evaluated for *fantasy theme artistry, rhetorical vision reality links,* and *shared group consciousness*. Thus, we used SCT to capture, describe, and depict the UDL rhetorical vision and to guide our efforts at raising the consciousness of the youth participating in the SLUDL program.

The Urban Debate League Rhetorical Vision

The specific UDL composite drama that entwined a large group of people into a common symbolic reality was succinctly encapsulated by Mitchell (1998):

> The transformative dimension of debate pedagogy can be pursued in outreach efforts designed to share debate with traditionally underserved student populations and communities. With recognition of the emancipatory potential of critical thinking and oral advocacy skills in hand, students and teachers trained in argumentation are today transforming debate practice into a tool of empowerment by collaborating with students who are systematically denied opportunities for engaging in exciting, rewarding, and powerful intellectual activities in their school. Debate outreach efforts carry political significance because they counter unequal treatment of the educational system, a major root of inequality in our society. (pp. 50-51)

The 2000 annual report on the OSI U.S. programs (Open Society Institute, 2000) also included a statement that concisely depicts the UDL rhetorical vision:

> The program gives young people the tools to express themselves, command attention with words, and respond effectively to the arguments of those who may disagree with them. Debate develops critical thinking, academic research, and communication skills, and increases self-confi-

dence. Students who debate often receive better grades than those who do not participate in debates, and are more likely to continue in post-secondary education. (p. 35)

The 2003 annual report on the OSI U.S. programs (Open Society Institute, 2003) elaborated on this rhetorical vision, noting that "the purpose of debating leagues goes beyond honing public speaking skills and promoting discussion" (p. 48). In addition, "formal debate training is one of OSI's strategies for developing the critical-thinking and analytical skills that are so vital to the democratic participation of young people" (p. 47). The 2003 report concluded about the vision that:

> During the past several years, the urban debate leagues sponsored by Youth Initiatives in cities across the country have played a critical role in encouraging young people from low-income and minority communities to develop their academic and political power. (p. 48)

One of the technical concepts within SCT is that of the *fantasy type*, a stock scenario that explains new events in a well-known dramatic form (Bormann, 1977). The fantasy type that served to energize the UDL vision was the great *gap* between those who possess competent communication skills and those who do not. Whether such a gap is called a "missile gap," as the Democratic Party candidate for President of the United States, John F. Kennedy, labeled the U.S. defense preparedness vis-à-vis the U.S.S.R. in 1960 (see Blum et al., 1963), or a "knowledge gap," as diffusion-of-innovation researchers labeled the gap that occurs between the "haves" and the "have-nots" when new technologies are invented (see the "digital divide" discussion in Herman & Ettema, Volume 2), the importance of the gap fantasy type is that it centers on a felt need to address the inequality (Donohue, Tichenor, & Olien, 1975; McAnany, 1984). Thus, those who accept and become entwined in "gap rhetoric" become predisposed—motivated by their rhetoric—to search for and act on ways to close the gap.

The UDL experience sought to close just such a gap in argumentative skills. One of the rhetorical vision's central plot lines envisioned empowerment for the have-nots through debate education and competition; that is, the enhancement of argumentative skills through education and practice. Another plot line envisioned such empowerment as coming through the fantasy type of the spin-off benefits of such education: better grades, less physical violence in the schools, improved graduation rates, and increased interest in attending college. A final central plot line foresaw enhanced civic engagement with issues being debated, thereby making a contribution to democratic society.

These UDL rhetorical vision plot lines are, in actuality, closely entwined with a theory of education espoused by Paulo Freire (1970, 1985, 1994, 1997, 1998), the famous education reformer from Brazil. Freire's ideas provide the philosophy undergirding many educational programs in the United States (see Gadotti & Torres, 2003), and they often were used by UDL program directors to support the UDL's vision, goals, and activities (see, e.g., Mitchell, 1998; Wade, 1998; Warner & Bruschke, 2001). In particular, Freire's educational rhetorical vision provided two major plot lines for the UDL rhetorical vision that became the criteria for evaluating the success of the UDLs: (a) *engagement* (through dialogue) with the problems that confront the marginalized and (b) *empowerment* of participants (as an outcome of that dialogue) that enables the marginalized to recognize and improve their situation.[2] These Freirian plot lines manifested themselves within the UDL, as mentioned previously, as personal empowerment through education in debate, a substitute for violence, and an increased civic engagement by promoting interest in the policy issues of a democracy. As Galston (1996) noted, at its most basic level, social policy should focus on "empowering poor people to do the things that the more affluent can already do, aim at spreading the power around a bit more . . . and do so where it matters most, in people's control over their own lives" (p. 164).

The seeds germinating into the UDL's empowerment rhetorical vision were planted by some early activists, and across the years, the characters (*dramatis personae*) within the UDL's rhetorical vision have included heroes, villains, and a number of supporting players. The activists began surfacing in two distinct urban locales. The initial fantasizers came from Emory University's Barkley Forum debating society, who sought to address inequality of debate opportunities in Atlanta's urban high schools by starting the Atlanta UDL in 1985. Faculty members of the Department of Communication at Wayne State University also are often credited with beginning a similar interscholastic debate program in Detroit in 1984. Both universities started these interscholastic debate programs by having members of their college debate teams assist urban high schools in beginning small interscholastic debate programs in which participants engaged in short (often 3-round instead of the typical 6-8-round) debate tournament events. A few years later, the Improving Mentor Practices and Communication Techniques Coalition (IMPACT Coalition), involving several university debate programs, former collegiate debaters, and community activists, started a similar program in New York City.

The central plot line or goal of these three initial programs aimed not to create further dependence for assistance on the part of the participating marginalized communities but, rather, to enable these communities to produce the tools needed to empower themselves to develop and run their own interscholastic debate leagues. As Freire (1970) argued:

False charity constrains the fearful and subdued . . . [whereas] true gen-
erosity lies in striving so that these hands—whether of individuals or
entire peoples—need be extended less and less in supplication, so that
more and more they become human hands which work and, working,
transform the world. (p. 45)

From such a modest goal, a full-blown rhetorical vision evolved as others around the country became caught up in and helped to embellish and
flesh out the vision. The model of the Atlanta, Detroit, and New York City
efforts involved the developmental plot line of building the leagues on a
school-by-school, principal-by-principal, and teacher-by-teacher basis.
Across the nation, each league's founders—directors of college debate programs in urban areas who took up the UDL mantle—worked with other
interested individuals in their area to build the leagues. As soon as a new
school came on board, high school coaches, often from disciplines other
than communication, were brought on board and taught through summer
debate institutes and league meetings held throughout the school year.
Students from the sponsoring university or universities in each urban area
volunteered to coach the high school students and host and judge the tournaments, until the newly recruited high school teacher/coach felt confident
enough to do all of the coaching and tournament scheduling on his or her
own. In this manner, building vision participation began almost immediately. Adherents to the vision of creating debate opportunities—such as those
in the underserved areas of Atlanta, Detroit, and New York City—began to
increase, and proponents of the model began to surface elsewhere.

At this point, a new player who also had a vision entered the dramatic
action. The OSI, under the umbrella of the Soros Foundation (billionaire
George Soros's philanthropic foundation), wanted both to serve and
empower marginalized communities to participate more fully within U.S.
democratic society. Having witnessed the successes of the IMPACT
Coalition in New York City and the UDL in Atlanta, the OSI brought into
the vision the belief that underserved communities in the inner city could,
through debate, develop high school graduates capable of improving their
condition. The OSI subsequently began a grant-funding program to establish UDLs in cities across the United States. As the National Association of
Urban Debate Leagues' (2004, ¶ 4) organizing principles suggested, the
Soros Foundation, through its urban debate program, sought to "institutionalize competitive policy debate programs, particularly in urban high
schools" across the United States. Accepting the vision's legitimizing sanc-
tioning agent of eventual independence of such funded programs, the OSI
requested grant proposals from universities in urban areas where seed
money could help UDLs to begin, with that seed money extended in each
city for a period of up to 3 years. Table 4.1 provides an example of the

parameters—the types of interventions funded and the primary activities—of these grants. The goal of an intervention was "to provide urban youth with the academic and social tools they need in order to become engaged and responsible citizens" (National Association of Urban Debate Leagues, 2004, ¶ 7).

Such goals are grounded in Freire's vision for education. Throughout his writings, Freire stressed the importance of dialogue among persons in different locations experiencing similar social and political pressures. Within the United States, we might ask, what does inequality in Atlanta mean for inequality in New York City or elsewhere? Recognizing that debate spurs dialogue and that cities could work together, the initial fantasizers worked quickly to spread the UDL rhetorical vision. Thus, the vision spread rapidly beyond Atlanta and New York City. UDLs—aided by OSI grants—began surfacing at the rate of two or more per year in Baltimore, Birmingham, Chicago, Detroit, Kansas City, Newark, Providence, Los Angeles, St. Louis, San Francisco, Seattle, and Washington, DC (National Association of Urban Debate Leagues, 2003). In a few other cities, such as Louisville, KY, vision participants found the model so exemplary and com-

TABLE 4.1. Urban Debate League—St. Louis Projects and Interventions Funded

---

- Travel for league directors, selected high schools teachers, and administrators in grantee and prospective grantee cities to attend development conferences, such as the annual Ideafest Conference in New York City designed to raise participants' consciousness and commitment to the national UDL vision; travel to national communication conventions was funded for those presenting papers concerning the activities of the UDLs
- Summer educational institutes for new debate coaches, as well as local institutes for each city
- Funding for returning UDL students to attend national-caliber debate institutes, accompanied by supervising teachers and, in some instances, for local league administrators visiting institutes to assess the fit between that institute and the league students
- Small stipends for college debate students to visit schools on a regular basis and help educate teachers to coach their teams, with the goal of teachers becoming independent
- In the first years of the grant, resources for meeting the logistical needs of hosting the tournaments during the school year, as well as day-to-day copying expenses
- Salaries for a league administrator
- Release time in terms of class buyouts to grantees to plan, administer, and evaluate the program

---

pelling that they implemented it without waiting for grant funding. In 2001, Springfield, IL, with the help of Mount Holyoke College, implemented the model using a Lincoln-Douglas, 1-person debate program rather than the 2-person teams of most scholastic debate models. Often, within each location, the grants engendered activity in multiple school districts and even crossed state and county lines. By the year 2000, the number of inner-city public schools engaged in policy debate exceeded 150 and reached a student participation rate of more than 2,000 per year (Snider, 2000); in 2003, 4,000 students from 227 high schools and 50 middle schools took part (Heinz Center, 2004). Across the years, more than 12,000 high school students, largely disadvantaged minority students, have participated in UDL debate (Bruschke, 2003).

Beginning in 2000, the National Association of Urban Debate Leagues (NAUDL), located in Chicago, began operating to assist the individual UDLs. After the OSI's initial 3-year funding period ended, all of the UDL programs continued despite sometimes undergoing a metamorphosis. For example, in some cities, such as Kansas City, MO, the post-grant UDL continued through the sponsorship of the UM—Kansas City; in other cities, such as New York City, civic organizations teamed up with the school district to help ensure sustainability; and in still other cities, such as Chicago, Detroit, Newark, and St. Louis, the school district(s) assumed responsibility. For 2003, NAUDL secured support from the Heinz Center (a nonprofit institution dedicated to improving the scientific and economic foundation for environmental policy), which, for example, provided copies of its books and reports on coastal and ocean policy to the 277 urban high schools and middle schools that participated in the UDL that year (Heinz Center, 2004). Also attesting to the viability of the vision, in Spring 2004, Austin, TX, became the 16th city to adopt the UDL model, with 14 high schools from 3 school districts agreeing to participate for the 2004-2005 school year with the assistance of district funds and the coaching of debaters from the University of Texas—Austin and the University of Texas—San Marcos.

BENEFITS OF AND REACTIONS TO THE URBAN DEBATE LEAGUE MOVEMENT

As we describe benefits of and reactions to the UDL movement nationally, we simultaneously can establish that the UDL vision spread and was adopted by many new communities and affected both those communities and the interscholastic policy debate circuit. Although much of the assessment of the long-term political and economic effects of the UDL movement on participants lies in the future, given that the UDLs only became national in the late

1990s, there is a growing body of evidence that supports the claims that the UDL vision has attracted a large rhetorical community and that UDL participants—mentors, students, and teachers alike—have been profoundly affected by the experience. As early as 1998, Mitchell noted that "recently published literature suggests that the UDL initiatives are meeting with great success in stimulating new debate circuits and bringing debaters from diverse backgrounds together in a variety of pedagogical milieu" (p. 51). Such evidence includes empirical data on participation patterns, successes, and specific effects, and anecdotal and testimonial data from administrators, mentors, students, and teachers (Barber, 1998; Breger, 1998; Lynn, 1998). In this section, we review and update such data. Later, as a postscript, we report the general response of the initial sponsor, the OSI, to the project's outcomes.

We begin with some of the findings of Melinda F. Fine, the OSI's independent evaluator in 1999 for the UDL in New York City. Using open-ended questions, M. F. Fine (1999) surveyed several hundred UDL participants about their attitudes. She found that New York City high school students felt empowered and engaged after participation in the UDL because "they have something useful to say, and because they feel more articulate in saying it" (p. 61). She also noted that UDL participation "appears to strengthen students' ability to persevere, remain focused, and work toward challenging goals" (p. 62). In addition, she found an explicit connection between UDL participation and violence reduction based on the debaters assigning a "higher value to resolving their conflicts through dialogue rather than force" (p. 64). She also noted that the students reported a newfound ability to "stand back, reflect on their arguments, frame them more powerfully, and communicate without conveying an aggressive energy that might prohibit productive exchange" (p. 64). In Freirian terms, debaters saw themselves as empowered subjects rather than debilitated objects in political dialogue, sometimes for the first time in their school experience.

High school students in various UDL cities responded in support of the vision's plot line by evidencing debate and other communication skills that met and, in some cases, surpassed the skills held by suburban students whose debate programs had been well established. Eric Wilcox, coach at California's Balboa High School, said, "The goal is to shape a better-rounded student by facilitating critical thinking, public speaking, note-taking and research abilities, the very skills . . . most lacking in public school students," and he went on to stress that the UDL is "helping them at every level—oral, written and reading, not to mention critical thought" (cited in Estrella, 2002, ¶ 12). A UDL student at Chicago's De Sable High School affirmed Wilcox's view: "It challenges your mind. It forces you to think critically. I think debate is something that everybody needs in society" (cited in Keoun, 2000, p. 3). A student from Seattle's UDL noted, "If you're good at debating I think you could become a good attorney. That's what attorneys do, is debate" (cited in Ervin, 2001, ¶ 34).

The UDL experience also helped students formerly apprehensive about jumping into debate to become more confident and engaging. For example, students from the New York City UDL reflected on the impact of their interactions with suburban high school students: "The way I used to think about them and they used to think about me, once you get together, that's abolished. At first I thought, 'they're so snotty'; but they weren't snotty, they were cool" (cited in Bahrampour, 2000, p. B14). Another student added, "Debate is like a link to different places" (cited in Bahrampour, p. B14). Still another student, reporting on the Atlanta UDL, said, "We lost every round. It was pitiful, but you've got to lose to learn" (cited in Ghezzi, 2002, p. B1). Through the opportunities for engagement and empowerment offered by the UDLs, the "debate knowledge gap" became something to work toward closing rather than an experience to fear.

The newfound confidence evidenced by the urban debaters reflects years of research on the positive effects of training in argumentation and debate. For example, in 1975-1976, the National Communication Association sponsored a program—funded by the National Endowment for the Humanities and matching contributions from donors in the private sector—to encourage U.S. Americans (high school and college students and adults) to engage in debate on the values that made our country great. Semlak and Shields (1977, p. 194), reporting on their empirical study of that program, discovered that of all the participants, those with debate training and experience were "significantly better at employing three communication skills (analysis, delivery, and organization)" than those participants without such educational training and experience. Barfield (1989) later reported that high school students' participation in competitive debate correlated positively with significant gains in their cumulative grade point average. Bellon (2000), reviewing recent studies concerning the effects of debate, concluded that debate experience improved students' ability to communicate, conduct research, think quickly and critically, construct arguments, and transfer these skills successfully to other settings, such as other classes. Finally, Littlefield (2001), in a study of 629 high school debaters, showed that students also perceived improvement in these areas as a major outcome of their participation in interscholastic debate.

Thus, it should not come as a surprise that several empirical investigations confirmed that these same skills improved among the UDL students. For example, Blair (2003) quoted Les Lynn, the Executive Director of the NAUDL, as saying that "more than 25 students have gone to college toting debate-related scholarships; hundreds of others gained admission to schools in large part because of their achievements in the competition" (p. 22). Blair also reported that Tracy Carson, then a 20-year-old junior attending

Northwestern University on a full scholarship, had participated in the UDL from Chicago's Morgan Park High School, and "made history when she became the first Chicago Public School alum to win a major national college debate tournament in decades" (p. 22).

Carson (2003), the UDL debater mentioned by Blair (2003), noted that participation in the UDL gets students more interested in college and careers that demand college degrees. Importantly, and in part thanks to the success of the UDLs in improving college preparatory skills, more than 60 U.S. universities presently offer scholarships specifically targeted for UDL alumni. Reflecting outcomes reported across the nation, Mueller (2000) depicted the effects of the UDL on Tommie Shaw, a St. Louis student and captain of Cleveland Naval Academy's high school debate team:

> "My grades have gotten better, and my study skills have gotten better," said Tommie, a senior who plans to pursue a pre-law program at either West Point or Tulane University. Tommie's research and note-taking skills have improved dramatically as a result of preparing for policy debates about Medicare, education, federalism, and war. He looks forward to using his debate skills as a lawyer some day in a courtroom. (p. 1)

In another study, Arbenz and Beltran (2001) discovered that although Latinas participating in Southern California's (Greater Los Angeles) UDL won only 39% of the ballots judges cast, they found no significant speaker-point or award-recognition differences between them and other UDL participants. Arbenz and Beltran also noted the potential for the UDLs to empower Latinas by educating them to argue the pros and cons of policy decision making. In addition, Warner and Bruschke (2001), in a study of the New York City UDL, noted that the sheer number of urban schools and debaters participating in the league gave it the potential to become a dominant force for empowering disadvantaged youths in that city. Indeed, Bahrampour (2000) reported that in just the second year of the New York City UDL:

> An Urban Debate League school, Grace H. Dodge Vocational in the Bronx, was the junior varsity state champion. Last year [1999], Franklin K. Lane High School came in third all around in the state, with fourth and fifth positions also taken by Urban Debate League schools. (p. B14)

In another study, Gregory and Alimahomed (2001, p. 18) noted that the UDL opens "a rhetoric of possibility [that] can influence the inner ethics of the individual. By personalizing travesties of humans [through the use of argument], the debate community sees the grim reality of certain areas of the world—and this opens up new possibilities" for personal empowerment.[3] For example, as a UDL debater, Daymean Lewis, age 15, told Bahrampour (2000), "You get familiarized with what's going on in your society and you just get this tone in your voice, you feel more forceful, that you can do anything" (p. B14). This outcome clearly fits the empowerment vision of the UDLs, in which, in an ideal world, self-empowerment supplants the "White man's burden" view of the world. As Madrid (2000), the project director of the SLUDL, stated in a letter to participating students, "Be proud of who and what you are, love yourself so much that you are willing to develop fully the talents that are within you" (p. 3). Madrid also encouraged such attitudes in his instructions to judges at the SLUDL tournaments. Small wonder, then, that after only 2 years of competition, and as we explain in more detail in the case study section of this chapter, the SLUDL students became more willing to argue (Preston & Shields, 2003). This willingness by students to argue is a prerequisite to full student participation in what Freire (1970) would term a "critical and liberating dialogue," which presupposes action and "must be carried on with the oppressed at whatever the stage of their struggle for liberation" (p. 65). With the UDL nationally, this dialogue not only took place in debate rounds but in institutes, idea exchanges, and tournaments as participants from different cities came together.

Such outcomes indicate that as the UDL participants improved their debating proficiency and began to catch up with their suburban counterparts, their improved debate records both validated the self-empowering elements of the UDL rhetorical vision and fulfilled its plot-line prophecy that the debate knowledge gap would narrow between inner-city and suburban schools through educational training in debate. As presented below, a preliminary report of a NAUDL-sponsored evaluative study demonstrated improved reading skills among UDL participants versus nonparticipants ("New National Study," 2004). In the SLUDL project, teams began making elimination rounds in the novice division of suburban tournaments by the end of the first year, a SLUDL student was a top speaker at a national debate institute in the second summer, a SLUDL graduate won a debate scholarship at Emory University in the third year, and in the fourth year, a SLUDL team went through six rounds at the Eastern Missouri National Forensic League Championship and SLUDL teams were regularly winning awards at county-sponsored tournaments. In the fifth year, 2 full years after the elimination of OSI funding, debate teams from three SLUDL high schools were regularly in elimination rounds in suburban high school tournaments, and teams from other SLUDL programs placed periodically.

In terms of academic achievement, the UDL students' reports about their experiences reflect what has long been known about debating: When students formulate arguments and orally defend those arguments in a formal debate setting, they also are better prepared to make arguments in less rigorous assignments, such as in term papers. Ghezzi (2002) reported on a UDL debater named Anthony, who lived with his great-grandmother and liked debate because it kept him busy after school:

> "Kids don't play outside in my neighborhood, because there are no sidewalks." But he has gotten much more out of debate. At camp, he carries a small dictionary to look up new words he doesn't know. "I'm always looking up new words and new things," he said, adding that he often is asked to speak at school functions. (p. B1)

As vocabularies improve as a result of UDL participation, so do school grades. Bahrampour (2000) reported that "the UDL debaters have also seen their grades rise and discipline problems fall" (p. 1). Morris (2002) confirmed this conclusion in her report on the Baltimore UDL, noting that "self-respect, then grades, improved" (p. 50). Students, teachers, and administrators alike also have reported increased student academic performance. A student in the New York City UDL who had failed classes before said, "I got a 91 on my report card in English" (cited in Bahrampour, 2001, p. B14). Tinajero (2003), a teacher and school board member from Fullerton-Union High School in Los Angeles, noted that her UDL students "have gained better study habits and learned how to write complicated, research-based essays" (¶ 9). Administrators also confirm the impact that participation in the UDL has on students' academic performance. Hawkins (2003), the Principal at Lincoln Prep High School in Kansas City, MO, noted that his school's UDL debaters are the leaders at that school and indicated "they excel in classroom discussions and set a tone of academic excellence that resonates throughout the school" (¶ 4). He also said that although "the team only works with a couple dozen students out of the entire student body, the preparation and rigor that they [the debaters] bring to their classrooms set the standards that other students strive to meet" (¶ 4). In a similar vein, Maddox (2003), a consultant to the Atlanta public schools, reflected, "I've seen the reading scores of students jump two and three grade levels in a single semester" (¶ 5). This result reflects the close connection that Freire noted between literacy and political empowerment. To the extent that the UDL experience seemed to help literacy, it further stimulated empowerment.

As of November 2003, Linda Collier, Associate Professor and Director of Forensics at UM—Kansas City, had completed data-gathering in a nationwide evaluation of UDL participation funded by OSI, the UM Research Board, and the Center for the City at UM—Kansas City. Collier's study was designed to measure, among other things, the impact of UDL participation on student academic performance. Collier collected the data on-site in five cities. Initial preliminary findings were released on the NAUDL web site on May 20, 2004. NAUDL reported from Collier's study, named "Arguments for Success," that debate "dramatically boosts reading skills of at-risk urban high school students" ("New National Study," 2004, ¶ 1). Collier compared 209 UDL debaters and 212 nondebaters from 27 urban high schools in five cities on their pretest and posttest scores on a standardized reading test designed to meet the U.S. requirements of the No Child Left Behind legislation. NAUDL indicated that "the reading scores of all students improved over the school year, but debaters improved by 25% more than non-debaters" ("New National Study, ¶ 7).

Perhaps the following narrative of a UDL alumna, who attended Northwestern University, best summed up the impact of the UDL:

> I credit my experience in the Urban Debate League with setting me up to succeed. First, it made attending Northwestern seem like a very real possibility, since I debated on campus and attended the summer institute while in the UDL. Second, it helped prepare me to submit a successful application. I learned how to organize my ideas for an essay. Debate sharpened my reading, writing, speaking and thinking skills, improving my grades and SAT scores. Third, I entered college with more self-confidence than many of my peers, even here [at Northwestern]. I can speak in front of other students, and often out-perform the most talented of them. The UDL's are a really good college prep program. (cited in Carson, 2003, ¶ 7)

Other published stories provide accolades detailing the positive effects of the UDL on urban students, with most of those effects coming in the form of engagement and empowerment (see Bahrampour, 2000; Blair, 2003; Ervin, 2001; Ghezzi, 2002; Keoun, 2000; Morris, 2002; Mueller, 2000; Ruenzel, 2002). Wade (1998) noted that debate promotes engagement: "A contest round reverses the narration pattern of traditional education. [In debate,] the student speaks to the teacher referencing information that reflects an understanding of concrete knowledge grounded in research" (pp. 63-64). Warner and Bruschke (2001) stressed how debate promotes empowerment because:

> Students must engage in a public speaking event, face the challenges of their opponent, and then immediately receive evaluation by a judge . . . [and then] students who can face and overcome these challenges and those fears are seldom afraid of the public dialogue in any other context, be it a political rally, city board meeting, electoral campaign, legal proceeding, or town hall meeting. (p. 17)

Hence, students at all levels feel more engaged and empowered through learning about argumentation and participating in debate. For thousands of high school, inner-city debaters, engagement and empowerment have been the crowning benefits of their participation in the UDL rhetorical vision.

THE ST. LOUIS CASE STUDY: A VISION OF ENGAGEMENT AND EMPOWERMENT

Given the preceding discussion of engagement and empowerment, our case study focuses on the extent to which the 1998-2001 educational activities of the SLUDL promoted engagement and empowerment for its participants.[4] We begin by describing the structure of the SLUDL with respect to who did what, when, where, and with what results during our 3-year involvement with the OSI grant in St. Louis. We then assess these results with respect to engagement and empowerment of the SLUDL participants.

Structure of the St. Louis Urban Debate League

The SLUDL essentially involved four elements: high school students, teachers, school administrators, and university personnel. We explain each of these elements below.

High school students served as the focus of the SLUDL; first, in 1998, students from the St. Louis public schools (80% African American), and then students were added from the Normandy schools for 2000-2001 (99% African American). Normandy is directly adjacent to St. Louis City, although it is technically in St. Louis County and not the city. During the 3-year period of the grant, high school students from these districts attended SLUDL-sponsored tournaments and were encouraged to attend existing local debate workshops held by the sponsoring college(s).

In 1998, no high school students engaged in debate in the St. Louis public schools, although a city speech championship that offered some nondebate speaking events at one meet had been established a few years earlier. In Spring 1998, five high schools—Beaumont, Soldan, Cleveland, Metro, and Central Visual and Performing Arts—participated in the Barbara Jordan Youth Debates on a health topic in a pilot program sponsored by the Kaiser Foundation and held in conjunction with the Department of Communication's involvement in the UM—St. Louis Bridge Program to inner-city schools. This pilot program was directed by Preston and taught with the assistance of the UM—St. Louis Debate Team. These five public high schools helped to form the foundation of the SLUDL once we had applied for the OSI grant with the endorsement of the St. Louis public school district. In each of the 3 years of the grant, more than 100 students per year from at least 10 different high schools participated in the SLUDL tournaments. In addition, over the course of the grant, more than 100 students attended debate institutes in either St. Louis or other cities. Another 75 students participated in the UM—St. Louis Bridge Program across the 3-year period (see Table 4.2).

High school teachers, as part of the school district's matching funds for obtaining the grant, participated in the project. The district paid for two teachers per school to be assigned to the SLUDL. Thus, with 11 schools administered under the District's Communication Arts Division, that Division pre-selected the 22 teachers for SLUDL. Of these 22 teachers, 18 came on board with no debate experience as either a participant or as a teacher. These 18 teachers were trained as coaches in Summer 1998, in a course, Communication 392: Administration of Co-curricular Activities, offered by the Communication Department at UM—St. Louis. The course emphasized and followed a standard 2-person cross-examination debate curriculum developed at Emory University for training debate coaches. The course also allowed teachers from different schools to network and engage in dialogue concerning conditions at their schools.

Although some of the 22 teachers had a Missouri teaching certificate qualifying them to teach high school speech and theater, again, only four of them had debate coaching experience. Prior to the SLUDL grant, five of the schools had participated in the Barbara Jordan Youth Debates on a health topic in 1998, and those participants had been educated in the basics of debate in a series of day-long workshops offered by UM—St. Louis's Department of Communication to prepare for the St. Louis City qualifying

TABLE 4.2. Student Participation in the Urban Debate League—
St. Louis, 1998-2001

Year	Students in Tournaments	Students at Home Institutes	Students at Away Institutes
1998-1999	93	39	-
1999-2000	106	40	28
2000-2001	108	39	21

Note. Total participation does not equal the total of the columns and rows because some students debated for 2 and even 3 years and attended more than one debate institute.

tournament in that activity. All teachers were offered three separate opportunities for learning how to become a debate coach. One opportunity took
the form of scholarships funded by OSI to take the Communication 392
summer credit course at UM—St. Louis described previously. To earn that
credit, the teachers, in addition to attending the course, worked in a 2-week
UM—St. Louis Gateway Debate Institute for incoming SLUDL high school
students. In addition, the teachers, for their in-class assignments, participated in debates themselves on the 1998-1999 national high school debate resolution concerning whether U.S. foreign policy should limit the use of
weapons of mass destruction. SLUDL teachers were encouraged as coaches
to engage in dialogue both with each other and with the students about the
significance of this topic to them and to their students, to make the topic as
personally meaningful as possible. A second opportunity, cosponsored by
UM—St. Louis's Department of Communication and debate squad, the
OSI, and the St. Louis school district, occurred at the beginning of each
year's day-long kickoff celebration. Every school and more than 100 students attended that celebration, which featured specialized teacher and student topic workshops, lectures, and a demonstration student debate with
critiques offered by college debate coaches. The third debate educational
opportunity consisted of an hour-long session held before the beginning of
each SLUDL tournament, in which high school teachers and volunteer
judges were given instructions on how to (a) conduct each of the 2-person
policy question debate rounds they would observe that day, (b) engage in
dialogue with the students after the round, (c) award speaker points and
assign wins by the criteria for 2-person policy debate, and (d) implement
specific educational goals of the day's 3-round tournament. A unique and
empowering aspect of the SLUDL was the educational training of high
school teachers in how to administer a tournament and involve their students in that administration. This training involved hands-on experience in
operating debate tournaments, including taking entries, scheduling rounds
and teams, assigning rooms, assigning judges, collecting ballots, tabulating
results, and conducting awards ceremonies. By the middle of the grant's second year, the high school teachers were running tournaments independent
of instruction from college personnel. In short, through educational training, the high school teachers were empowered to take on an increasing
amount of the administrative responsibility for hosting the SLUDL debates.

School district personnel helped throughout the life of the grant. The
Communication Arts Division of the district and the communication coor-
dinators for the district served four functions. First, the Division furnished
equipment, including a computer, for the use of every debate team in the district. Second, the Division both selected and paid the teachers who served as
debate coaches. Third, the district, in coordination with UM—St. Louis and,
in subsequent years, Webster University and Washington University as

cosponsors, paid for an increasing amount of the transportation to enable students without transportation to attend the SLUDL debate tournaments at city high schools during the first year, tournaments at the suburban county high schools during the second and third years, and various in-city and out-of-city debate workshops and institutes held across the years. Fourth, the district worked with the principals of each school to make sure that logistics, such as room access, building security, and janitorial services, were arranged for each SLUDL meet. Overall, the St. Louis District and, during the third year, the Normandy School District worked closely with us, the SLUDL grant staff, the high school teachers, and the league administrators to ensure smooth logistics for the hosting of the SLUDL events at the high schools.

University staff and others also contributed throughout the life of the grant. The personnel at this level included the two of us as grantees, the paid SLUDL project director, local university debate coaches, college debate students, and community volunteers. A community board—consisting of the grantees; directors of debate at Webster University, Washington University, and UM—St. Louis; teacher and parent representatives; and community representatives—met monthly to help coordinate the activities. Students on the local university debate teams, hired with grant money, helped the participating high schools' new coaches. In addition, university students, coaches from existing high school programs (when available), community activists, parents, and attorneys assisted in judging the tournaments. Coaches from existing suburban high schools also participated in the development of the league; their help ranged from hosting and mentoring UDL schools in the very first year to attending a national OSI-NAUDL Ideafest meeting to judging debates.

The university staff consisted of four groups of people: (a) the grantees (both of us and Barbara Holt, Director of the Bridge Program for outreach at UM—St. Louis the first year, with Scott Jensen, Director of Forensics at Webster University, and Jennifer Rigdon, Director of Forensics at Washington University, receiving smaller OSI grants for the third year to reimburse some of their staff members who contributed to the league); (b) SLUDL's Project Director, Madrid; (c) part-time staff assistants hired by UM—St. Louis the first 2 years and by Washington University and Webster University the third year to help coordinate volunteers and to serve as coaches at the summer Gateway Debate Institute held at UM—St. Louis the first 2 years and at Webster University the third year; and (d) college debate students from the three universities that contributed students each year, who were either paid part time or who volunteered. The college debaters helped each high school program by providing assistant coaching, institute counseling when attending various debate institutes, and judging at various SLUDL events during the term of the grant.

Preston conducted the first-year teacher training summer institute by following the Emory University curriculum furnished by the Barkley Forum. In addition, working with Jensen and Holt beginning the first year, and Rigdon beginning the third year, he applied for supplemental grants and coordinated the fund-raising efforts of the league, including the money raised each year by the UM—St. Louis debate program for the SLUDL. Together, we worked closely with OSI in procuring a continuation of the grant for each of the 3 years. Preston took primary responsibility for preparation of the mid-year and annual reports to OSI and the other granting agencies. Throughout the process, Shields served as an unpaid co-investigator, advisor, and coauthor of the grant.

Madrid coordinated the pedagogical efforts for the SLUDL. First, he designed curriculum for the debate educational sessions for the first 2 years of the grant and worked with the other university partners to refine the curriculum during the last year. As well, he outlined the parameters of each year's debate topic, developed and coordinated distribution of the core evidence file for the league, and worked closely with students at the summer institutes to select and limit the topic areas of emphasis for the novice divisions each year. He also encouraged varsity teams to choose case ideas that represented social issues of relevance and of interest to them and the communities they represented. Thus, on the 1999-2000 debate resolution— "RESOLVED: That the federal government should establish an education policy to increase significantly academic achievement in secondary schools in the United States"—Madrid encouraged argument about the pros and cons of issues, such as standardized test scores and retention and graduation rates, that might affect people in the inner city in regard to this education topic. He also developed, distributed, collected, and reviewed applications for the student summer institute scholarships. Each application involved an assessment of a student's SLUDL debating records, academic performance, and the review of letters of recommendation written by at least one debate coach and one teacher who was not a debate coach. In addition, Madrid developed the curricula for the year-round coaches' training sessions, although he began sharing some of those duties with the high school debate coaches during the third year. In addition, he arranged for scholarships at several prestigious national debating institutes.[5] He also visited these institutes periodically to assess them and advocate for the special educational needs of the SLUDL students who attended these institutes. His assessments, used in the placement of students in future years, checked the match of an institute's pedagogical methods with those of the UDL rhetorical vision to ensure consistency with the Freirian principles of students as subjects rather than as objects.

Part-time staff assistants were hired for several purposes. At UM—St. Louis, throughout the life of the grant, a person was hired to coordinate all of the league's publicity efforts, which included writing press releases for the local media, creating programs for each tournament, and preparing and publishing the successful newsletter *The Urban Debater*. The newsletter served as an important repository for dialogue about the SLUDL and came to be a model that other cities emulated. The newsletter contained stories that focused on the students and provided them with opportunities to relate their SLUDL debate experiences. It also encouraged teachers to share their concerns about the SLUDL in a forum section. Finally, it provided a way for us to recognize the efforts of students, parents, and teachers in the successful implementation of the SLUDL. The newsletter, distributed to students, teachers, principals, volunteers, parents, other UDLs, and cosponsoring organizations, promoted the SLUDL and heightened awareness among its participants and other interested parties.

The part-time assistants also developed both an information packet and a brochure about the SLUDL to assist in grassroots fund-raising efforts. During the third year, assistants, through the grant, were hired part time at Webster University and Washington University to help coordinate students from those institutions, who, in turn, helped to coach some of the high school squads. Each year, money was allocated both from funds raised by the UM—St. Louis debate program and the OSI grant to bring in part-time staff for both the summer Gateway Debate Institute and the beginning-of-the-year kickoff celebration and workshop. These staff members included graduate students and debaters from area colleges and universities, as well as experienced teachers from other successful UDL programs around the nation who served as guest speakers. These different voices provided the type of intercity dialogue that Freire advocated throughout his writings, and the sharing of similar experiences proved useful and helpful in the development of the SLUDL.

Results of the Coordinated Effort

Student involvement and engagement within the organizational framework just described began almost immediately. The SLUDL furnished four opportunities for students to engage in debating through participation in (a) summer debate workshops at UM—St. Louis the first year and at national summer institutes the last 2 years; (b) community debates before real audiences, such as those that took place at year-end awards presentations, at the Gateway Mock trial institute, and before the membership of the St. Louis chapter of the Urban League; (c) demonstration debates at the summer institutes and the kickoff workshop at the beginning of each school year; and (d) six interscholastic SLUDL debate tournaments held during the first year, then at both the SLUDL and the suburban high school tournaments in the second and third years, and, finally, in some cases, at national circuit debate tournaments by the third year of the grant. An ongoing assessment of the intensity and value of the high school students' participation was carried out by us throughout the 3-year life of the grant. That assessment involved four dimensions: (a) the number of students participating in workshops, (b) the number of students entering debate tournaments, (c) the degree of student retention in the program, and (d) the degree of change reflected in students' basic debate competence and willingness to argue.

In Summer 1998, 48 students were recruited—beginning in May—to attend the June 29-July 11 Gateway Debate Institute held at UM—St. Louis. Of those students, 18 finished the institute tournament, with an additional 21 finishing the debate class in the workshop sponsored from June-July in the Bridge Program. Nine students dropped out at some point during the institute or institute tournament for varying personal reasons, ranging from a death in the family to being needed at home to getting a summer job. In Fall 1998, about 85 students from 11 high schools attended the 1-day kick-off celebration and debate workshop. The students from the summer institute and kickoff workshop formed the core SLUDL group for 1998-1999, with 93 students from 11 schools participating at the six SLUDL novice tournaments. Although only 93 students debated during the school year, 132 students in all participated in debate from the summer institute through the fall kickoff workshop and the six academic calendar tournaments.

In 1999-2000, 28 students attended debate institutes away from St. Louis and 25 attended the novice SLUDL home institute, with 17 competing in and completing the novice tournament. Forty-four students participated in the varsity division during the regular season tournaments and 62 new students participated in the novice division, for a total of 106 debate participants during that year. Adding the participants who debated at the summer institute and the kickoff workshop to this number, about 150 students participated in SLUDL debate activities during 1999-2000.

For 2000-2001, 21 students attended top-notch national away summer debate institutes and 39 attended the home SLUDL summer institute. The excitement generated by such attendance resulted in 25 SLUDL students participating in the varsity divisions for 2000-2001 and 83 newcomers participating in novice divisions. Adding the participants who debated at the summer institutes and the kickoff workshop to those who debated during the school year, 165 students participated in SLUDL activities for the year 2000-2001.

Although adding the totals of actual SLUDL tournament debaters across the 3-year period sums to 307, due to the retention of many students for their second and third year of debate, only 238 different students competed in SLUDL debate tournaments during the grant period. As could be anticipated from the results of earlier studies about the effects of learning argumentation skills on students' lives, as we demonstrate next, this level of participation affected both students and teachers alike.

Empowerment through Engagement

Across the 3 years of the grant, 238 students from the 12 high schools (the 11 St. Louis public schools and the one Normandy school), which prior to 1998 did not offer any interscholastic debate, received both education and practice in such debate. During that time frame, we conducted two initial studies of students in the SLUDL using a debate competence measure and a willingness-to-argue measure. Those studies were conducted using a posttest-only design conducted at the end of each year that was compared to an availability sample of non-SLUDL inner-city students obtained from students not involved in debate activities. The nondebaters were high school students of similar backgrounds who were attendees of the UM—St. Louis Bridge Program. Results of the comparison indicated that students who participated in debate through the SLUDL gained more competence in two dimensions of debate related to engagement and empowerment as compared to nondebaters. For example, applying Infante and Rancer's (1982) willingness-to-argue scale at the 1999 kickoff celebration, Preston and Shields (2003) discovered that 44 students with SLUDL experience (gained by debating in 1998-1999) indicated a significantly higher willingness to argue ($M = 16.09$) than 106 respondents self-reporting no debating experience ($M = 7.79$). Thus, experienced SLUDL high school students—as speculated would occur by the earlier qualitative analyses of the UDL experience offered by Wade (1998) and Warner and Bruschke (2001)—became significantly less reticent about arguing in front of an audience through debate participation. We also believe that the SLUDL-educated students became better at arguing than their untrained counterparts. Preston (2004), by developing a newly created basic debating competence scale (which achieved a Cronbach's alpha of .80 when tested for reliability), discovered that:

> testing whether differences in fundamental debate knowledge exist between debaters with competition experience from year one ([$n = 21$] mean score = 53.92) differed from those [high school students] without experience ([$n = 27$] mean score = 12.93) indicated a significant difference (40.99). This difference was highly significant because in using the .05 level of probability as our cut-off point, the expected result would be a much smaller difference [$t(48) = 3.56$, $p < .05$]. (p. 7)

Preston (2004) also conducted a correlational analysis of debate competence scores and institute and tournament attendance, finding that debating competence scores for the 48 students were more highly correlated with a year of debate education and experience, $r = .74$, than with year in school, magnet school attendance, or institute attendance. Thus, willingness to argue and debate competence—two essential prerequisites for students to become engaged and, hence, empower themselves—were found to increase for students participating in the SLUDL.

We also collected self-reports of the SLUDL students from selected interviews and institute and workshop evaluation forms open-ended questions, as well as reports of the national UDL students from a qualitative analysis of newspaper articles, web pages, and newsletters. Our qualitative analysis of these data uncovered five dominant fantasy themes concerning empowerment. First, students believed that the SLUDL experience helped them in general to be more politically engaged. Across the 3-year grant period, they debated questions about foreign policy and the control of weapons of mass destruction; privacy protection and the security of employment and medical records, or the legality of search-and-seizure investigations; and education policy with respect to the best means of increasing academic achievement. As a result of their participation, the students appeared to gain a newfound sense of how debate had helped them to become more engaged. As one student put it, "Participating in debate, speaking in front of an audience, and saying what I want to say about important topics, that's just great." Another student said, "When I debate, the grown-ups have to listen to me." Second, students also claimed that the experience helped them in school, with remarks such as, "It made me a better overall student" and "My friends in classes were asking me how to get better at studying." Third, they viewed themselves as being better able to engage with and talk to other students, which was reflected in comments such as, "It made me eager to learn and compete with students like me" and "I really enjoyed the sense of 'family' that the debate squad and the other SLUDL participants provided." Fourth, the students felt empowered to go to college. For example, a female student said, "I think I'm much more confident and that made me think I could do well in college"; another female student claimed, "I'm going to Harris-Stowe [a state-supported teacher's college in St. Louis] to become a teacher!"; and a third student noted that the SLUDL experience helped her to realize her potential and led her to "choose to attend college." Fifth, students became more politically active. The SLUDL students also were cognizant of the empowering effects of their participation. For example, one student noted that "the SLUDL experience changed my life; it made me more aware, and concerned, and involved." Her mother confirmed the change, indicating that the experience "really brought my daughter out of her shell." As well, several times during 2001-2002, the year after the 3-year grant ended, the league's Project Director, Madrid, accompanied parents and students to speak before the St. Louis School Board to urge continued support for the

SLUDL, which, for 2002-2003 and 2003-2004, was funded by the St. Louis School District. In addition, as of October 2004, 5 of the 12 SLUDL schools had formed active chapters of the National Forensic League (NFL), the oldest and most-respected interscholastic debating society in the United States, which has for 40 years been dominated by suburban high schools.

Because the students who started as novices in 1998-1999 would, as of this writing, only be completing their first year of college, it is difficult to say empirically if they are now more politically engaged than those who did not debate. Certainly, as evidenced by their participation in SLUDL, many were involved in the essential part of the debate process that empowered them to invent, clarify, and amplify their viewpoint in public forums. Thus, although to date the evidence for the influence of the SLUDL experience has focused on individual outcomes linked to educational achievement, and that evidence is most convincing, it will await posterity for an evaluation of whether and how the SLUDL experience contributed to increased levels of civic and political engagement.

Nonetheless, we would be remiss not to report that the careers of teachers also were enhanced by the SLUDL experience. The Director of Debate, Kathy Gregory, at Meda P. Washington Education Center (the St. Louis School District's alternative school for expectant mothers), went on to win two grants from the Kaiser Family Foundation to continue the Barbara Jordan Debate Program in St. Louis for 2002 and 2003, and she also received a grant to purchase a copier for her school. Soldan High School's program became independent early in the second year of the SLUDL, and its Director, Harry Kumke, continues to host a Greater St. Louis high school speech tournament each year, with schools from the county, along with inner-city schools, competing. Students at Soldan High School also are now actively involved in speech and debate tournaments throughout the state of Missouri. In addition, Kumke currently serves on the Board of Governors for the Speech and Theatre Association of Missouri. Lyn Nicolay, the Director of Forensics at the Central and Visual Performing Arts High School, has had debaters attend national circuit tournaments and workshops since the grant period ended. Anthony Grobe, who started the program at an alternative inner-city high school, the King Tri-A Academy, has moved to another SLUDL school, the Cleveland Naval ROTC program, where his debate teams have continued to enjoy success at county meets. Frank Richter, the Director of Debate at Vashon High School, engaged his debate students in a science program with the Department of Biology at UM—St. Louis, and hosts an audience debate on a genetic or other biology topic each March for high school students that has won acclaim from the sponsoring university's science program (Granger, 2002). These and other league teachers have attended national debate institutes, and two of them continue to be invited to attend the NAUDL's Ideafest conference each year.

Naturally, there have been some spin-off results of the SLUDL grant. For example, Ed Taylor, who started the debate program at Cleveland Navel Academy, was hired recently as Director of Forensics at Oakville High School, a large, established suburban high school. Dennis Kane, who completed Communication 392 and served as a volunteer judge as a speech and teacher trainee at UM—St. Louis, now directs a highly successful debate program at Marquette High School in suburban St. Louis County that boasts a squad of more than 100 students. Since the SLUDL grant ended, Marquette has sent many students to the NFL's national tournament and continues to enjoy a SLUDL-style coaching partnership with Webster University. Overall, the activities offered by the SLUDL, such as Communication 392 and the urging of its members to become involved in the Speech and Theatre Association of Missouri, have benefited these people and others with enhanced networking opportunities.

Of course, during the first 3 years of the SLUDL, teachers did express some frustration, mainly over issues such as the increased pressures that coaching debate placed on their time in addition to their other duties and their lack of day-to-day control over their program. At times, they complained directly to visiting OSI personnel that they did not feel in control, as if the experience were controlling them rather than the other way around, but such comments began to subside after the first year of the grant. By the end of the 3-year period, participants were eagerly running their own debate tournaments, selecting away tournaments to attend, and choosing the debate events in which their students entered. By the time UM—St. Louis cosponsored and hosted the Barbara Jordan tournament in the winter of 2003, it was taken for granted by us that the teachers ran their own tournaments. Teachers and former SLUDL students also provided the core of counseling at the local summer 2003 SLUDL institute held at Webster University.

Despite some of its growing pains and shortcomings, the SLUDL initiative ultimately succeeded in confirming that excellent educational opportunities come from an activity based on a rhetorical vision that seeks to offer empowerment opportunities to both educators and students alike through engagement with interscholastic policy debate. In addition to the results documented here, during the grant period, the gap between debating opportunities was reduced directly, as the number of students from the city who were involved at the beginning of 1998 was zero when compared to opportunities in the suburban areas. In addition, the urban schools went from no national exposure in debate to students attending national debate institutes, participating in national forensics tournaments, and maintaining their debate programs. Moreover, participation in the SLUDL increased students' argumentative competence and their willingness to argue. Finally, although we did not receive permission to track grades at the time of the grant, testimonials indicated that students felt empowered in the classroom and, thereby, more capable of meeting the challenges of their other schoolwork. However, as seen in the preliminary findings of the post-hoc Collier evaluation study that involved the SLUDL debaters within her sample, the students' scores on a standardized reading test did improve 25% more than those without the SLUDL experience ("New National Study," 2004). Moreover, as we noted earlier, schoolwork begins to look easier to a student who has had to defend his or her arguments in a formal debate. Student and teacher commentaries also indicated improvements in students' study habits, writing ability, and grades. Such improvements were due, in large part, from the lessons learned through students' participation in the SLUDL rhetorical vision.

LESSONS LEARNED

Although the UDL vision has been largely a success, three important lessons have been learned in terms of how to perpetuate rhetorical visions concerned with reducing gaps between the haves and have-nots. First, there is a tension between the need to work from the "bottom up" and the need for administrative support. In the case of the SLUDL, the league formed quickly when a communication arts supervisor within the district decided the program would start in all of the district's schools. Just as quickly, when a district-wide restructuring took place, as was the case recently in St. Louis after the termination of the OSI grant, uncertainty about continuing the SLUDL experience reared its ugly head in the debate programs. For example, league competition, due to the decline in monetary support for coaches, lessened. We concluded that, even when leagues start well due to strong central administration support, planning for strong grassroots programs at the principal-teacher level is essential for the sustainability of debating programs that can and must survive changes in the district infrastructure. Programs that became more independent, such as Soldan and Cleveland Naval, showed the most promise to survive the current district reshuffling.

Second, most of the UDLs initially adopted the traditional rational argument theory (see Cragan & Shields, 1998) evidentiary approach to policy debating as a means of implementing the new debate programs along with debate on the national high school topic. Perhaps, rather than adopting the national high school topic as a strict rule, more experimentation in alternative topics, or topics dealing with issues to which the debaters might more closely relate, could have had more direct impact on the students' ability to engage in political dialogue. The Barbara Jordan Youth Debates on Health, to a certain extent, provided another alternative for some students, but even then, debating healthcare issues was as much related to Kaiser's concern with health issues as it was to the students' choice. Although students did have a degree of freedom in the issues they discussed in policy debate, particularly as they developed their unique cases and negative refutations, it might be that empowering students and teachers to choose alternative topics and approaches and debate in an intramural fashion within each school rather than travel to tournaments to debate a variety of schools could have resulted in more sustainability in years when budgets and grants are scarce. Indeed, empowering local teachers and students to choose their own topics might also be more in line with Freire's notion that they constitute empowered subjects themselves rather than objects expected to imitate what is done in more affluent schools. Of course, we will not know the answer to such speculation until a new initiative is developed and tested directly against the positive outcomes of policy debate in interscholastic competition. In the meantime, the SLUDL and the national UDL movement can attest to the benefits they have provided regarding engagement and empowerment of our nation's urban youth as they debate the national high school topic.

Third, SCT's evaluative concept of *rhetorical vision reality link* (Cragan & Shields, 1995a, 1998) did provide a powerful way of evaluating the capability of a rhetorical vision to prompt action. As we saw earlier, for the participants in the vision, the meaning, emotion, value, and motive for action embodied by the UDL rhetorical visions prompted them to take action and launch the SLUDL. That same rhetoric, when confirmed by the reality link of the anecdotal and social-scientific studies demonstrating skills improvement, served to sanction and legitimize the UDL experience. We believe those benefits will, in turn, provide the reality links that sustain the vision of engagement and empowerment and warrant the activism that will ensure that the SLUDL and UDL-type interscholastic debate will continue.

CONCLUSION

Gara LaMarche, representing the George Soros Foundation, in a May 23, 2002 letter, reminded the OSI participating U.S. programs, communities, and friends that the urban debate program was one of the two foundation programs that "have always operated with a finite time horizon" (¶11). Thus, the OSI-sponsored UDLs were coming to an end. In October 2003, the OSI's Youth Initiative Director, Erlin Ibreck (2003), spoke glowingly of the UDL program's legacy:

> The Urban Debate Program, which spearheaded the expansion of a movement to bring formal debate programs to urban high schools, was modeled on a design that provided up to four years funding for urban debate leagues. The leagues replicated a successful model that developed partnerships between school districts, academic institutions and

other community stakeholders with the purpose of leveraging public and other private support to institutionalize urban debate in school systems. . . . Our remaining program funds are designated for final support to several grantees. The launching of a national umbrella organization for urban debate [NAUDL] and support for a preliminary study on the effects of debate [Collier], are also part of OSI's legacy to this movement. Over the next several months we will be exploring ideas for an evaluation of the grant-making program. (¶ 3)

As noted previously, the launching of the Austin UDL recently brought the number of OSI-funded programs to 16, as of Fall 2004.

POSTSCRIPT

For us, the legacy of the SLUDL is that debate lives on in the city schools. For students at some of the 12 participating high schools, it lives as they host and compete in city tournaments; for others, it lives as they continue to discover ways to work with NAUDL to advocate a balance between school district support and the need to become more independent programs; and for still others, it lives through participation and competition in the Barbara Jordan Youth Debates, National Forensic League tournaments, audience debates on scientific topics at biology symposia, the St. Louis Urban League's public debates, and suburban debate tournaments. Each of these opportunities illustrates that interscholastic debate can live in St. Louis with some school district and private support rather than grant support. Thus, the communication activism prompted by the messages contained in the SLUDL rhetorical vision lives on independently.

NOTES

1. SCT posited the impact of emotion on human action from its onset (Bormann, 1972), and interpersonal scholars, such as S. M. Johnson and Greenberg (1994), V. S. Johnson (1999), and Planalp (2003), have recently established that one hallmark of emotions is their link as motivators to human action.
2. Freire (1970) equated traditional lecture-testing approaches to education with a "banking" system that seeks to "deposit" information into students' minds with the goal of "withdrawing" it later. Freire contrasted this approach to learning with a "problem-posing approach" that stressed the need for engagement: "Whereas banking education anesthetizes and inhibits creative power, problem-posing education involves a constant unveiling of reality. The former attempts

to maintain the *submersion* of consciousness; the latter strives for the *emergence* of consciousness and *critical intervention* in reality" (p. 81). Freire also explained that the outcome of such dialogic education was commitment to learning and empowerment through "education as the practice of freedom—as opposed to education as the practice of domination" (p. 81). As Freire noted, "Students . . . posed with problems relating to themselves in . . . and with the world . . . feel increasingly challenged. . . . Their response to the challenge evokes new challenges, followed by new understandings; and gradually the students come to regard themselves as committed" (p. 81; see also Harter, Sharma, Pant, Singhal, & Sharma, Volume 2; Rich & Rodríguez, Volume 2).

3. An example of the possibilities for diversity in approach and empowerment occurred when the University of Louisville's debate program adopted a narrative form of argument that borrowed from rap music to make its points about weapons of mass destruction during the 2001-2002 debate year. Reporting on this new communication phenomenon, Coomes (2002) wrote:

> Seven-eighths black, five-eighths female and 100% committed to challenging elitist orthodoxy, the University of Louisville debate team has seized college debate by the scruff of its ivory neck and shaken the stuffing out of the status quo. (¶11)

For Coomes (2002), traditional collegiate debate has far to go to achieve the racial and idea diversity achieved regularly at UDL tournaments. As Coomes reported, "The bad news is old news: Of the 218 debaters who competed at Pepperdine [at the Cross Examination Debate Association Nationals], only six were African American and half of them were from the U[niversity] of L[ouisville]" (¶ 28). However, for Coomes, the high national ranking of Louisville's team demonstrated that a knowledge gap also can occur in reverse, with students from urban areas teaching students from other areas new ideas about how best to debate.

4. The St. Louis City and Normandy School Districts both face special challenges. According to a ranking by Missouri Kids Count (2003), since 1995, the St. Louis city schools have ranked 115 out of the 115 counties in Missouri in 10 socioeconomic quality categories. By contrast, suburban St. Louis County has ranked in the top 18 or higher, and the adjacent St. Charles County has ranked in the top 4 during this period. Similarly, St. Louis City led the state in dropout rates and percentage of students reliant on free or reduced-price lunches. The Missouri Department of Elementary and Secondary Education (2004) provided data that further reveal the stark contrasts. In 2000, during the height of our involvement with the SLUDL, the average American College Test (ACT) score among Normandy students was 16.5, and the average score among St. Louis City students was 18.1, whereas the state average was 20.9. At the same time, the percentage of Normandy school district high school graduates going on to attend 4-year colleges was 38.0, whereas the percentage of St. Louis city district graduates was 22.7; the average for Missouri was 38.5%.

5. The institutes included those sponsored by Baylor University, California State University—Fullerton, the Chicago Debate Commission (Northwestern University), Emory University, University of Iowa, Michigan State University,

the University of Michigan, UM—Kansas City, the University of Vermont, and Wake Forest University.

REFERENCES

Allen, M., Berkowitz, S., Hunt, S., & Louden, A. (1999). A meta-analysis of the impact of forensics and communication education on critical thinking. *Communication Education, 48,* 18-30.

Allen, M., Berkowitz, S., & Louden, A. (1995, Fall). A study comparing the impact of communication classes and competitive forensic experience on critical thinking improvement. *Forensic of Pi Kappa Delta,* pp. 1-8.

Anderson, J., Schultz, D., & Courtney, C. (1987). Training in argumentativeness: New hope for nonassertive women. *Women's Studies in Communication, 10,* 58-66.

Arbenz, C., & Beltran, S. (2001, February). *Empowering Latinas through debate: An analysis of rates of success at SCUDL tournaments of Latina debaters.* Paper presented at the meeting of the Western States Communication Association, Coeur d'Alene, ID.

Bahrampour, T. (2000, October 13). Resolved: That high school debate is back. *The New York Times,* p. B-14.

Barber, I. (1998, Summer). Agreeing to disagree. *Open Society Institute News,* pp. 14-15.

Barfield, K. D. (1989). A study of the relationship between active participation in interscholastic debating and the development of critical thinking skills with implications for school administrators and instructional leaders. *Dissertation Abstracts International,* 50-09A: 2714.

Bellon, J. (2000). A research-based justification for debate across the curriculum. *Argumentation and Advocacy, 36,* 161-176.

Blair, B. (2003, March). Voices of reason: Once an activity confined to wealthy suburban schools, debate is embraced by a new breed of inner-city competitors. *Chicago Magazine,* p. 22.

Blum, J. M., Catton, B., Morgan, E. S., Schlesinger, A. M., Jr., Stampp, K. M., & Woodward, C. V. (1963). *The national experience: A history of the United States.* New York: Harcourt, Brace & World.

Bormann, E. G. (1972). Fantasy and rhetorical vision: The rhetorical criticism of social reality. *Quarterly Journal of Speech, 58,* 396-407.

Bormann, E. G. (1977). Fetching good out of evil: A rhetorical use of calamity. *Quarterly Journal of Speech, 63,* 130-139.

Bormann, E. G. (1985). Symbolic convergence theory: A communication formulation. *Journal of Communication, 35*(4), 128-138.

Bormann, E. G., Cragan, J. F., & Shields, D. C. (1994). In defense of symbolic convergence theory: A look at the theory and its criticisms after two decades. *Communication Theory, 4,* 259-294.

Bormann, E. G., Cragan, J. F., & Shields, D. C. (1996). An expansion of the rhetorical vision concept of symbolic convergence theory: The Cold War paradigm case. *Communication Monographs, 63,* 1-28.

Bormann, E. G., Cragan, J. F., & Shields, D. C. (2001). Three decades of developing, grounding, and using symbolic convergence theory. In W. B. Gudykunst (Ed.), *Communication yearbook* (Vol. 25, pp. 271-313). Mahwah, NJ: Erlbaum.

Bormann, E. G., Cragan, J. F., & Shields, D. C. (2003). Defending symbolic convergence theory from an imaginary Gunn. *Quarterly Journal of Speech, 89,* 366-372.

Breger, B. (1998). Building open societies through debate. *Contemporary Argumentation and Debate, 19,* 66-68.

Brembeck, W. L. (1949). The effects of a course in argumentation on critical thinking ability. *Speech Monographs, 16,* 177-189.

Bruschke, J. (2003, November). *The role of institutional constraint in the success of debate outreach.* Paper presented at the meeting of National Communication Association, Miami Beach, FL.

Canary, D. J., Brossman, J. E., Brossman, B. G., & Weger, H., Jr. (1995). Toward a theory of minimally rational argument: Analysis of episode-specific effects of argument structures. *Communication Monographs, 62,* 183-212.

Carson, T. (2003). *What people are saying about urban debate.* Retrieved October 26, 2003, from http://www.naudl.org/endorsements

Chaffee, S. H. (1978). Presidential debates—are they helpful to voters? *Communication Monographs, 45,* 330-346.

Colbert, K. (1993). The effects of debate participation on argumentativeness and verbal aggression. *Communication Education, 42,* 206-214.

Colbert, K. (1994). Replicating the effects of debate participation on argumentativeness and verbal aggression. *Forensic, 79,* 1-13.

Coomes, M. (2002, December 1). Talk smart: Top-rated U of L debate team uses a dash of hip-hop to get its points across. *Louisville Courier-Journal.* Retrieved September 30, 2003, from http://www.courier-journal.com/features/2002/12/20021201.html

Cragan, J. F., & Shields, D. C. (1981). Uses of Bormann's rhetorical theory in applied communication research. In J. F. Cragan & D. C. Shields (Eds.), *Applied communication research: A dramatistic approach* (pp. 31-42). Prospect Heights, IL: Waveland Press.

Cragan, J. F., & Shields, D. C. (1992). The use of symbolic convergence theory in corporate strategic planning: A case study. *Journal of Applied Communication Research, 20,* 199-218.

Cragan, J. F., & Shields, D. C. (1995a). *Symbolic theories in applied communication research: Bormann, Burke, and Fisher.* Cresskill, NJ: Hampton Press.

Cragan, J. F., & Shields, D. C. (1995b). Using SCT-based focus group interviews to do applied communication research. In L. R. Frey (Ed.), *Innovations in group facilitation: Applications in natural settings* (pp. 233-256). Cresskill, NJ: Hampton Press.

Cragan, J. F., & Shields, D. C. (1998). *Understanding communication theory: The communicative forces for human action.* Boston: Allyn and Bacon.

Cragan, J. F., & Shields, D. C. (1999). Translating scholarship into practice: Communication studies reflecting the value of theory-based research to everyday life. *Journal of Applied Communication Research, 27,* 92-106.

Crenshaw, C. (1998). Sharing the gift of debate: Notes from the Tuscaloosa Debate League. *Contemporary Argumentation and Debate, 19,* 80-84.

Csapó-Sweet, R., & Shields, D. C. (2000). Explicating the saga component of symbolic convergence theory: The case of Serbia's Radio B92 in cyberspace. *Critical Studies in Media Communication, 17,* 318-333.

Donohue, G. A., Tichenor, P. J., & Olien, C. N. (1975). Mass media and the knowledge gap: A hypothesis reconsidered. *Communication Research, 2,* 2-23.

Drew, D., & Weaver, D. (1991). Voter learning in the 1988 presidential election: Did the debates and the media matter? *Journalism Quarterly, 68,* 27-37.

Ervin, K. (2001, March 26). Student debates prompt cheers: Program makes a comeback. *Seattle Times.* Retrieved October 26, 2003, from http://archives.seattletimes.nwsource.com/cgi-bin/texis.cgi/web/vortex/display?slug=debate26m&date=20010326&query=Ervin

Estrella, C. A. (2002, February 15). Open to debate: Forensics program helps disadvantaged students gain critical-thinking skills. *San Francisco Chronicle,* p. 1. Retrieved December 2, 2002, from http://sfgate.com/cgi-bin/article.cgi?file=/chronicle/archive/2002/02/15/EB126466.DTL

Fine, G. A. (2001). *Gifted tongues: High school debate and adolescent culture.* Princeton, NJ: Princeton University Press.

Fine, M. F. (1999, June). *"My friends say, 'Debater girl! Why are you always debating with me?'": A study of the New York Urban Debate League.* Unpublished report submitted to the Open Society Institute, 400 West 59th Street, New York, NY 10019.

Freire, P. (1970). *Pedagogy of the oppressed* (M. B. Ramos, Trans.). New York: Herder and Herder.

Freire, P. (1985). *The politics of education: Culture, power, and liberation* (D. Macedo, Trans.). South Hadley, MA: Bergin and Garvey.

Freire, P. (1994). *Pedagogy of hope: Reliving* Pedagogy of the oppressed (R. R. Barr, Trans.). New York: Continuum.

Freire, P. (1997). *Pedagogy of the heart* (D. Macedo & A. Oliveira, Trans.). New York: Continuum.

Freire, P. (1998). *Pedagogy of freedom: Ethics, democracy, and civic courage* (P. Clarke, Trans.). Lanham, MD: Rowman and Littlefield.

Gadotti, M., & Torres, C. A. (2003). *Paulo Freire: A homage.* Retrieved October 26, 2003, from http://www.gseis.ucla.edu/cide/projects/Torres.pdf

Galston, W. (1996). *To empower people from state to civil society.* Washington, DC: American Institute Press.

Ghezzi, P. (2002, June 24). Good learning talked up at Emory: Urban students make statement with debate. *Atlanta Journal-Constitution,* p. B1.

Granger, C. (2002). *Vashon Interdisciplinary Project for Education Reform.* Retrieved June 3, 2003, from http://www.umsl.edu/~sep/viper.htm

Gregory, J., & Alimahomed, K. (2001, February). *Narrative voice and the urban debater: An investigation into empowerment.* Paper presented at the meeting of the Western States Communication Association, Coeur D'Alene, ID.

Hawkins, H. (2003). *What people are saying about urban debate.* Retrieved October 26, 2003, from http://www.naudl.org/endorsements

Heinz Center. (2004). Heinz Center and urban debate leagues. *Crossroads, 1*(1), 1-8.

Hirokawa, R. Y. (1985). Discussion procedures and decision-making performance: A test of the functional perspective. *Human Communication Research, 12,* 203-224.

Ibreck, E. (2003, October 1). *Report from youth initiatives director.* Retrieved November 1, 2003, from http://www.soros.org/initiatives/youth/articles_publications/articles/changes_20031001

Infante, D. A., & Gordon, W. I. (1987). Superior and subordinate communication profiles: Implications for independent-mindedness and upward effectiveness. *Central States Speech Journal, 38,* 73-80.

Infante, D. A., & Gordon, W. I. (1989). Argumentativeness and affirming communicator style as predictors of satisfaction/dissatisfaction with subordinates. *Communication Quarterly, 37,* 81-90.

Infante, D. A., & Rancer, A. S. (1982). Conceptualization and measure of argumentativeness. *Journal of Personality Assessment, 46,* 117-125.

Johnson, D., & Sellnow, T. (1995). Deliberative rhetoric as a step in organizational crisis management: Exxon as a case study. *Communication Reports, 8,* 54-60.

Johnson, S. M., & Greenberg, L. S. (1994). *The heart of the matter: Perspectives on emotion in marital therapy.* New York: Brunner/Mazel.

Johnson, V. S. (1999). *Why we feel: The science of human emotions.* Reading, MA: Perseus Books.

Keoun, B. (2000, January 21). War of words inspires students to succeed. *Chicago Tribune,* Metro Chicago Sec., p. 3.

Krumboltz, J. D. (1957). The relation of extracurricular participation to leadership criteria. *Personnel and Guidance Journal, 35,* 307-314.

LaMarche, G. (2002, May 23). *A letter to the OSI U.S. programs community and friends.* Retrieved November 1, 2003, from http://www.soros.org/resources/articles_publications/articles/letter_20020523

Lemert, J. B. (1993). Do televised presidential debates help inform voters? *Journal of Broadcasting & Electronic Media, 37,* 83-94.

Littlefield, R. S. (2001). High school student perceptions of the efficacy of debate participation. *Argumentation and Advocacy, 38,* 83-97.

Lynn, L. (1998). Debating funding, funding debating: The Chicago Debate Commission's tale of two cities. *Contemporary Argumentation and Debate, 19,* 72-75.

Maddox, B. (2003). *What people are saying about urban debate.* Retrieved October 26, 2003, from http://www.naudl.org/endorsements

Madrid, A. (1999). Urban Debate League—St. Louis: A project manager's perspective. *Speech and Theatre Association of Missouri Journal, 29,* 80-83.

Madrid, A. (2000). Letter to the St. Louis urban debate league. *Urban Debater, 2*(4), 3.

McAnany, E. G. (1984). The diffusion of innovation: Why does it endure? *Critical Studies in Mass Communication, 1,* 439-442.

McBath, J. H. (1963). *Argumentation and debate: Principles and practices* (rev. ed.). New York: Holt, Rinehart, and Winston.

McCroskey, J. C. (1962). The effect of college speech training on academic marks. *Register of the American Forensic Association, 10,* 6-11.

Missouri Kids Count. (2003). *Data book* [Table]. Retrieved October 15, 2004, from http://www.oseda.missouri.edu/kidscount/03/county_rankings_2003.pdf

Missouri Department of Elementary and Secondary Education. (2004). *Educational performance data: American College Test and graduation analysis* [Tables].

Retrieved October 15, 2004, from http://dese.mo.gov/planning/pro-file/096109.html (Normandy School District) and from http://dese.mo.gov/planning/profile/115115.html (St. Louis City School District)

Mitchell, G. R. (1998). Pedagogical possibilities for argumentative agency in academic debate. *Argumentation and Advocacy, 35,* 41-60.

Morello, J. T. (1988). Argument and visual structuring in the 1984 Mondale-Reagan debates: The medium's influence on the perception of clash. *Western Journal of Speech Communication, 52,* 277-290.

Morris, H. (2002, July 17). League of their own: Inner-city debate teams are on the rise, and they're bringing student achievement with them. *U.S. News and World Report,* pp. 50, 52.

Mueller, M. (2000, February 21). Debate league students are gaining essential skills. *St. Louis Post Dispatch* (West Post), p. 9.

Myers, S. A. (1998). Instructor socio-communicative style, argumentativeness, and verbal aggressiveness in the college classroom. *Communication Research Reports, 15,* 141-150.

National Association of Urban Debate Leagues. (2003). *About the local sites.* Retrieved June 1, 2003, from http://www.urbandebate.org/members

National Association of Urban Debate Leagues. (2004). *Organizing principles.* Retrieved July 20, 2004, from http://www.naudl.org/orgprinciples

New national study shows debate boosts urban student achievement. (2004). Retrieved June 7, 2004, from http://www.urbandebate.org/newsStory?id=52

Open Society Institute. (2000). *U.S. programs annual report.* New York: Author.

Open Society Institute. (2003). *U.S. programs annual report.* New York: Author.

Planalp, S. (2003). The unacknowledged role of emotion in theories of close relationships: How do theories feel? *Communication Theory, 13,* 78-99.

Preston, C. T., Jr. (2004, November). *Debate institute education, urban debate league experience, and fundamental argumentative competence: Impacts on retention and success in first- and second-year UDL students.* Paper presented at the meeting of the National Communication Association, Chicago, IL.

Preston, C. T., Jr., & Shields, D. C. (2003, October). *The impact of urban debate league training and experience on willingness to argue among high school students.* Paper presented at the meeting of the International Debate Educational Association, Dubrovnik, Croatia.

Rancer, A. S., Kosberg, R. L., & Baukus, R. A. (1992). Relations between argumentativeness and belief structures about arguing. *Communication Education, 37,* 37-47.

Roberto, A. J., & Finucane, M. E. (1997). The assessment of argumentativeness and verbal aggressiveness in adolescent populations. *Communication Quarterly, 45,* 21-36.

Ruenzel, D. (2002, April). Making themselves heard: How can low-income kids break away from failure and get folks to recognize their hidden talents? At California's Kennedy High and a dozen other schools nationwide, the answer's simple: Join the debate team. *Teacher Magazine,* pp. 1-2.

Sanders, J. A., Wiseman, R. L., & Gass, R. H. (1994). Does teaching argumentation facilitate critical thinking? *Communication Reports, 7,* 27-35.

Semlak, W. D., & Shields, D. C. (1977). The effect of debate training on students' participation in the bicentennial youth debates. *Journal of the American Forensic Association, 13*, 194-196.

Shields, D. C. (2000). Symbolic convergence and special communication theories: Sensing and examining dis/enchantment with the theoretical robustness of critical autoethnography. *Communication Monographs, 67*, 392-421.

Shields, D. C., & Preston, C. T., Jr. (1985). Fantasy theme analysis in competitive rhetorical criticism. *National Forensic Journal, 3*, 102-115.

Snider, A. C. (2000, December 8). *Urban debate leagues college placement project.* Retrieved November 1, 2003, from http://www.ndtceda.com/archives/200012/0181.html

Tinajero, S. (2003). *What people are saying about urban debate.* Retrieved October 26, 2003, from http://www.naudl.org/endorsements

Vashon Interdisciplinary Project for Education Reform. (2002). Retrieved June 1, 2003, from http://www.biologie.uni-hamburg.de/b-online/ibc99/missouri/viper.htm

Wade, M. M. (1998). The case for urban debate leagues. *Contemporary Argumentation and Debate, 19*, 60-65.

Warner, E., & Bruschke, J. (2001, February). *Gone on debating: Competitive academic debate as a tool of empowerment for urban America.* Paper presented at the meeting of the Western States Communication Association Convention, Coeur d'Alene, ID. Retrieved, June 1, 2003, from http://www.mtholyoke.edu/acad/programs/wcl/deal/warner.pdf

Ziegelmueller, G. W. (1998). The Detroit experience. *Contemporary Argumentation and Debate, 19*, 85-88.

5

"YOU ARE FIT FOR SOMETHING BETTER"

Communicating Hope in Antiwar Activism

Stephen John Hartnett

University of Illinois

> You need to know that you are fit for something better than slavery and cannon fodder. . . . You need to know that it is for you to know something about literature, and about science, and about art. You need to know that you are on the edge of a great new world.
>
> —Eugene Victor Debs (1918a, p. 26)

I open with Debs's visionary plea to indicate that I hope in this chapter both to celebrate the ways my fellow antiwar communication activists embodied Debs's courage in the days leading up to the war on Iraq and demonstrate some of the important rhetorical lessons our movement may learn from our forebears. Debs spoke the words just quoted on June 16, 1918, in Canton, Ohio, as part of a tour arranged to protest the United States entering World War I and its passing of the Sedition Act, the May 16, 1918 supplement to the June 15, 1917 Espionage Act. Like the Uniting and Strengthening America by Providing Appropriate Tools Required to Intercept and Obstruct Terrorism Act (2001, the Patriot Act), the Espionage and Sedition Acts were seen by critics as grave wartime infringements on civil liberties, in general, and the First Amendment of the U.S. Constitution, in particular.[1] Coming out of retirement in the hope of getting arrested so that he could take his arguments against the war and the Sedition and Espionage Acts before the courts, Debs received his wish shortly after giving his Canton speech. His arrest was a foregone conclusion, for it was known that the U.S. Attorney for Northern Ohio, E. S. Wertz, was so intent on arresting the most-prominent U.S. antiwar activist and defender of civil liberties that he assigned a stenographer to record Debs's Canton speech (see Ginger, 1949; Salvatore, 1982).[2]

Debs left Wertz with little choice that day, as he delivered a robust anti-war oration that ranks among our nation's finest examples of sermonic rhetoric. Although Debs spoke repeatedly, as witnessed in the earlier quotation, of hope, commitment, and the struggle for a better America, much of his speech was a scathing indictment of the men who had driven the country into the bloody ditch of WWI. Debs (1918a) railed against "corporation lawyers and cowardly politicians" (p. 5); lambasted former President Theodore Roosevelt as the friend, political ally, and hunting partner of "Kaisers and Czars and Emperors" (p. 8); denounced the war profiteering of "our plutocracy" (p. 10), the aristocratic "Wall Street gentry" (p. 10), and every "tyrant who has wrapped himself in the cloak of patriotism, religion, or both" (p. 10), lumping them all together as "these autocrats, these tyrants, these red-handed robbers and murderers" (p. 13); and singled out financier John D. Rockefeller's loans to England and France—which we now know were a significant reason for the United States entering the war[3]—as little more than "blood-stained dollars" (p. 17). These stinging denunciations were interwoven, however, with utopian visions of a better nation, one cleansed of its sins and transformed "from despotism to Democracy. . . . From slavery to freedom!" (p. 32). Debs, thus, delivered what can only be called a *jeremiad*, a fiery sermon merging political critique, blistering moralizing, and idealistic dreaming (see Bercovitch, 1978; Bostdorff, 2003), which amounted to a passionate anti war speech the likes of which most U.S. Americans—given today's muzzled and moronic standards of public address (see McChesney, 1999, 2004; Rampton & Stauber, 2003; Stengrim, 2005)— never will hear.[4]

In fact, prior to the March 2003 invasion of Iraq, the U.S. political establishment's response to the march toward war was cowardly silence. In his melancholy U.S. Senate speech of February 12, 2003, Senator Robert Byrd, one of the only establishment figures to raise a voice in protest, lamented his colleagues' bewildering abdication of duty:

> On this February day, as this nation stands at the brink of battle, every American on some level must be contemplating the horrors of war. Yet this chamber is, for the most part, silent—ominously, dreadfully silent. There is no debate, no discussion, no attempt to lay out for the nation the pros and cons of this particular war. There is nothing. (¶ 1-2)

Later in that same speech, Byrd remarked on the fact that his colleagues had left the Senate "hauntingly silent," enabling the nation to "sleepwalk through history" (¶ 19-20). Silence, ominous dreadful silence, there is nothing, no debate, no discussion, hauntingly silent, sleepwalking through history—I can imagine Debs rolling in his grave at the prospect of his beloved and boisterous nation being described in such quiescent terms, for Debs tried to warn us 88 years ago that the march toward war always tramples the truth and silences free speech and, thereby, makes the world's best democracy less democratic.

Indeed, commentators have observed that the United States' post-9/11 deadly triumvirate of the war on terror, war in Afghanistan, and war on Iraq has resulted in mass-produced lies (see Hartnett & Stengrim, 2004; Rampton & Stauber, 2003; "The Daily Mis-lead," 2003), suppressed civil liberties (see Cole & Dempsey, 2002; Hartnett, 2002b; the reports from the groups and organizations listed in Section C of the Appendix), and wasted international goodwill for the United States (see Bernstein, 2003; Weisman, 2003). Given the fact that Afghanistan is sliding back into anarchy, with warlords running much of that tortured nation (see Bearak, 2003; Gall, 2003; Rhode, 2003b), and that post-war Iraq is a disaster of inexpressible proportions,[5] an increasing chorus of scholars, activists, and even establishment figures argues that post-9/11 U.S. foreign policy is misguided and doomed to fail. When I think of President George W. Bush, then, I cannot help but recall Debs (1918a), his temples bulging, his hands open, and his voice hoarse from shouting warnings to the world, prophesying how "every move he makes," referring to Rockefeller, but offering a line as pertinent to President Bush, "hastens the coming of his doom" (p. 16).

However, whereas Debs spoke to and for a small segment of U.S. Americans, and whereas Senator Byrd was one of the few elite figures with the courage to question a complacent prewar Congress, I demonstrate in this chapter that the antiwar movement responded admirably to the push for war on Iraq, and despite the corporate media either misrepresenting or ignoring our efforts, we filled America's streets, churches, parks, and airwaves with energetic and thoughtful messages. Feeding off this energy, I propose that the fate of our nation hinges on the rhetorical question of how to demonstrate to our neighbors—both domestic and international—that the push for empire undermines the promises and practices of democracy. My arguments are based largely on my experiences in Champaign-Urbana, IL, where I am among the founders of the Teachers for Peace and Justice (TFPJ) and a frequent participant in and supporter of the work of the Anti-War Anti-Racism Effort (AWARE) and the Progressive Resource Cooperative (PRC), all of which have been waging tireless yet remarkably cheerful campaigns for peace. This chapter, thus, functions both as a loving tribute to my fellow activists and as a scholarly attempt to examine the possibilities and limitations of communication activism in an age of terrorism, war, and empire.

My arguments are fueled by the hope that Debs was right: That if we come together to voice our concerns and commitments, perhaps we may be "on the edge of a great new world." To support this goal, I offer three sections of analysis. First, I examine the connections among globalizing capitalism, empire, and the recent wars fought by the United States to provide necessary historical and political foreground for thinking critically about post-9/11 U.S. foreign policy. Second, based on my participation in the activities of TFPJ, AWARE, and PRC, I outline four guiding theses and six thematically organized sets of examples illustrating communication strategies for reclaiming democracy from empire. Third, I reflect on some of the difficulties encountered in the political events described here and convey some of the existential commitments fueling antiwar activism. The theme of building community is woven throughout this chapter, demonstrating that I am advocating not only for participating in movements that focus on specific political goals but also in making a commitment to activism as a lifestyle, a way of being in the world. If readers find my arguments persuasive, I hope they use the resource guide offered in the Appendix (co-authored by Laura Stengrim) as a helpful source of information for their scholarship and activism.

THINKING HISTORICALLY ABOUT GLOBALIZATION, TERRORISM, AND WARS OF EMPIRE

Following the attacks of September 11, 2001, President Bush sought to justify the use of unilateral, preemptive U.S. military action. Conflating Afghanistan, Iraq, and a host of other rogue states and terrorists into one catch-all "axis of evil" in his January 29, 2002 State of the Union Address, delivered just 4 months after 9/11, President Bush (2002a) proposed that the United States forego entangling alliances and, instead, strike where and when it chooses in the name of self-defense. In the September 2002 *National*

Security Strategy of the United States (*NSSUS*), the text articulating "the Bush doctrine," President Bush warned that "we will not hesitate to act alone, if necessary, to exercise our right of self-defense by acting preemptively" (p. 6). The *NSSUS* referred to this right to act preemptively as part of a larger strategy of "anticipatory action" (p. 15), by which enemies will be attacked "before they are able to threaten or use WMD [weapons of mass destruction] against the United States" (p. 14). Overturning 50 years of deterrence theory and multilateral security agreements, and returning again and again to 9/11 as the event catalyzing these transformations in U.S. foreign policy, the President's arguments in both the *NSSUS* and his State of the Union Address called for an American empire in which international security supposedly would be achieved by unilateral U.S. actions. Hartnett and Stengrim (2004, 2006a, 2006b) have demonstrated that the major premises used to justify this new American empire are lies that have cost many innocent lives, subverted the constitutional process of checks and balances, wasted numerous tax dollars, committed U.S. troops to bloody quagmires, left both Afghanistan and Iraq devastated and lawless, and squandered the world's post-9/11 goodwill toward the United States, leaving our nation feared now more than ever and, hence, more likely than ever to be the target of terrorist vengeance. Thus, although post-9/11 U.S. foreign policy appears determined to build a unilateral American empire, the results so far clearly have failed.

Assuming that the wars in Afghanistan and Iraq are but the first two steps in fighting what the preface to the *NSSUS* (2002) called "a global enterprise of uncertain duration" (p. iii), and clearly recognizing that wars of military aggression are hard to sell to the public, President Bush has supplemented his arguments regarding terrorism, WMD, and the use of unilateral preemptive military force with a series of more broadly construed reasons for unrestrained U.S. power. Practicing the rhetorical art of appropriation, President Bush has employed well-established theological, historical, and economic arguments to promise that because the United States is God's agent of redemption, it will win the battle against evil and correct the course of history. For example, President Bush's theological comments demonstrate that even though he argued for the war in Iraq on the basis of charges about WMD and terrorism, his speeches were infused with a religious, even evangelical fervor. Indeed, the President spoke repeatedly of a struggle between good and evil, healing the world by ridding it of sin, and spreading values blessed by God. Similarly, whenever the President invoked history, he did so in a millennial fashion, portraying current events as a preordained unfolding of God's vision. President Bush, thus, merged evangelical theology and millennial history to create a sermonic vision of a world on the brink of disaster yet salvageable through heroic good deeds. Collapsing geopolitical complexities and flattening historical legacies, the President's theological and millennial visions offered a fairy tale of the United States as a benevolent nation carrying God's fight to redeem the world from evil. According to such claims, the United States will be an Empire of Goodness (see Bush, 2001, 2002a, 2002d, 2002e, 2002f, 2003b, 2003c; for critiques, see Bostdorff, 2003; Hariman, 2003, Hartnett & Stengrim, 2006a; McDaniel, 2003; J. Murphy, 2004).

Moreover, the President and his supporters have argued that this triumph of a Good Empire over an Evil Axis will be won not through aggression—although there will be much of that—but by promulgating righteousness, *primarily in the form of free markets*. Claiming that globalizing free markets inevitably produce economic opportunity, political reform, and judicial fairness—and implying perhaps even Christian religious conversion—the President has portrayed unfettered U.S.-style capitalism as the *only* model for continued world development (see Bush, 2002a, 2002b, 2002c, 2003a, 2003b). In fact, the opening sentence of the *NSSUS* (2002) proclaimed that all of history points to the triumph of "freedom, democracy, and free enterprise" (p. iii), and its closing sentence stated that the future security of the United States "comes from" the nation's "entrepreneurial energy" (p. 31). Therefore, the *NSSUS*, the "Bush doctrine," begins and ends with the understanding that democracy *is* capitalism and that capitalism *is* democracy. For President Bush and his supporters, globalizing free markets and the use of unilateral military force go hand-in-hand—they are the one-two punch of the new American empire (see Falk, 2003; Kellner, 2003; Lapham, 2002; Nye, 2002).[6]

Scholars and activists alike should be careful, however, not to jump to hasty conclusions about the future success of this post-9/11 U.S. empire building, for the historical record offers some sobering considerations regarding the deep connections among those who champion "free markets," those who pursue empires via military force, and those who claim to defend the best interests of civilization. For example, to comprehend our current moment of globalization and empire and, thereby, situate recent claims about freedom and democracy, free trade and globalization, and 9/11 and its subsequent wars within narratives that pre-date 9/11, I turn briefly to Hobson's (1902) exposé of the corruption and cronyism driving the British Empire. In his chapter heading of "Economic Parasites of Imperialism," Hobson offered this poignant observation:

> Seeing that the imperialism of the last three decades is clearly condemned as a business policy, in that at enormous expense it has procured a small, bad, unsafe, increase of markets, and has jeopardized the entire wealth of the nation in rousing the strong resentment of other nations, we may ask, "How is the British nation induced to embark upon such unsound business practices?" The only possible answer is that the business interests of the nation as a whole are subordinated to those of cer-

tain sectional interests that usurp control of the national resources and use them for their private gain. (p. 51)

The 21st-century world of President Bush's wars in Afghanistan and Iraq, of course, is fundamentally different from the one that saw British forces circling the globe at the start of the 20th century; nonetheless, Hobson's (1902) study rings true. In fact, in offering a critique as applicable to the crony capitalism driving the reconstruction of Iraq in 2006 as it was to the British empire of 1902, Hobson argued that the usurpation of national resources for private gain produces catastrophic consequences on both domestic and international levels.[7]

Domestically, the rise of imperialism's economic parasites means that "certain definite business and professional interests feeding upon imperialistic expenditure, or upon the results of that expenditure, are set up in opposition to the common good" (Hobson, 1902, p. 53). Because of imperialism, domestic programs languish, political accountability suffers, and, as elucidated so clearly by Hobsbawm (1987), norms of cosmopolitan internationalism slide toward chauvinism, exceptionalism, and xenophobia. As Hobsbawm observed of the decade preceding WWI, empire-hungry elites did not stress "glory and conquest, but that 'we' were the victims of aggression" by a foggy "they" that "represented a moral threat to the values of freedom and civilization which 'we' embodied" (p. 163). Internationally, Hobson (1902) argued that the triumph of these same forces means "the use of the machinery of government by private interests . . . to secure for them economic gains outside their country" (p. 100). Put simply, the commercial interests of Hobson's usurpers transform "the machinery of government" into a war-making, nation-conquering battering ram to topple foreign barriers to profitability. Taken together, these entwined consequences point to an assault not only on the political sovereignty and market autonomy of foreign nations but on the sense of representational government, decision-making transparency, and pursuit of the general welfare that render democracy (even the diluted British version of the early 20th century) legitimate. For Hobson and Hobsbawm, then, imperialism is toxic: It compromises the State's ability to govern at home, drains the treasury, fuels racism and militarized versions of nationalism, and enriches a class of political and economic parasites at the cost of the "common good."

Hobson (1902) and Hobsbawm (1987) also demonstrated that the push for empire at the close of the 19th and opening of the 20th centuries created a cascading series of foreign enemies, turning the emissaries of empire into walking targets for those who resented the political, economic, and cultural encroachments of foreigners. Linebaugh and Rediker's (2000) analysis is especially powerful in this regard, for it demonstrates how the earliest thrusts of the British empire into the New World, beginning with attempts to establish colonial-capitalist outposts in the late-16th and early-17th centuries, triggered waves of ship mutinies, slave rebellions, counter-imperial insurgencies, roving bands of criminals and pirates, and other forms of violence that likely would fall under today's heading of terrorism. Reading Hobson, Hobsbawm, Linebaugh and Rediker, and other critics of previous empires, thus, makes it painfully evident that 9/11, despite the stunning originality of the method and the staggering death toll from the attacks, was not so much an inexplicable and random event as yet another in a long series of violent backlashes against empire.[8]

The fact that the fury of 9/11 was directed at the World Trade Center and the Pentagon underscores this argument, for it demonstrates how the attacks were directed at the twin pillars of U.S. power: leadership in globalizing free markets and unrivaled military dominance. The symbolism of these targets is so obvious, and the powers they represent so ubiquitous yet mundane for many U.S. Americans, that a surprising number of observers have acted as if the attacks predominantly were symbolic rather than opening salvos in a strategic war against Western globalization (the twin towers) and U.S. empire (the Pentagon). Thus, to prevent ourselves from falling into the trap of seeing the world through jaded eyes, through the culturally sanctioned form of historical blindness discussed earlier, I suggest that thinking critically about our communication activism options in post-9/11 America entails situating our country's recent wars within the histories of globalizing capitalism, expanding empires, and the many forms of violence they inevitably produce.

As a rhetorical critic, I am particularly concerned with addressing the ways that elites have sought to decouple the violence of war, economic domination, and cultural conquest from any sense of historical, economic, or political causality. It is especially important in this regard to notice how the chant of "free trade" has been remarkably persuasive for justifying globalization and pursuing empire (see Palmer, this volume). Indeed, although there are a dizzying number of theories, histories, and definitions bidding to explain the now-ubiquitous (and deeply confusing) notions of globalization and empire (see Barber, 1995; Falk, 1999; Greider, 1997; Hartnett & Stengrim, 2006a; Jameson & Miyoshi, 1998; Singer, 2002; Stengrim & Hartnett, 2004; Stiglitz, 2003; Waters, 2001; Wood, 2003), my research demonstrates that from the earliest moments of international trade, national conquest, and cultural exchange, capitalist elites and their political allies used varying notions of free trade to justify their imperialist actions.

For example, from as early as the Dutch commercial empire of the mid-17th century, globe-trotting capitalists—sometimes acting as official servants of the state, hired mercenaries, or adventurers whose initial forays would lead to later State intervention—have linked notions of free trade and international law to explain their right to exploit the raw materials and labor forces of foreign markets. Consider the British, who initially did not have the manpower to invade the New World with formal armies in the late-17th and early-18th centuries, meaning, according to Armitage, that the State "led from behind and *allowed private enterprise to bear the burdens of conquest and settlement*" (cited in Colley, 2004, p. 155; italics added). Moreover, although their triumph in the Seven Years War (begun in 1756) launched the British on an unprecedented course of globalizing colonization, it would not be long before their defeat at the hands of revolutionary Americans (and their allies, the French, Dutch, and the Spanish, each of whom waged war against the British in far-flung colonies) demonstrated that profits would be better pursued not by setting up colonial administrations but by leveraging economic power via what Colley (2004) called the "cheap and indirect version of empire" (p. 155). In fact, Cain (1980, p. 19) argued that by the 19th century, "free trade imperialism" had become Britain's strategy for continued international domination. Cain noted, however, that "free trade was seen as a weapon . . . and when it did not seem to answer to their needs it was not supported" (p. 20). Indeed, the rapidity with which free trade champions could become either ardent protectionists or aggressive colonizers suggests that the earliest proponents of free trade were less committed to building a unified and unfettered global market of economic opportunity—the supposed goals of globalization—than to continued enrichment and expanded political power—the reality of empire—under whatever rhetorical banner seemed most persuasive.

As Magdoff (1972) noted, the instrumental use of free trade to justify certain imperialist actions and globalization more generally enabled the British and then the Americans—both of whom eventually learned to dread the fury of anti-colonial violence—to pursue "imperialism without colonies" (p. 144). That is, State military power would be used to open up and then protect the profitability of foreign markets, yet the conquering state and its capitalist elites—its usurpers, to use Hobson's (1902) term—would not have to assume the economic, diplomatic, and cultural costs of governing their conquered territories. Thus, whereas earlier versions of colonialism sought to produce client regimes by imposing settler-dominated administrations capable of governing daily life down to the smallest detail (such as in the British colonies in the Americas before 1776, and then again in India and throughout Africa at the close of the 19th century), post-WWII free trade imperialism increasingly has been based on the understanding that expropriating profits need not be tied down by the burdens of actual governance.

During the height of the Cold War, for example, the U.S. government maintained as many as 800 facilities around the globe, thus managing the world's largest network of troops, weapons, communications, and intelligence agents, yet those 800 sites were run under tight scrutiny and had severely limited roles; they were military bases, not diplomatic or cultural outposts charged with exporting U.S. values and administrative responsibilities to their host nations. (However, as Enloe, 1989, and Johnson, 2000, demonstrated, these facilities were painfully effective in spreading drugs, alcohol, pornography, sexual diseases, traffic accidents, environmental damage, and other detritus of U.S. consumer culture to the neighborhoods surrounding the bases.) Anticommunism was the driving justification for these facilities, rendering their purpose in explicitly military and market terms: They were armed to the teeth, ready to deter supposed communist aggression anywhere and anytime, and all the while protecting the trade routes, raw materials, and foreign markets that enabled post-war capitalism to flourish. Fighting communism, thus, served as the rhetorical cover obscuring the fact that post-WWII free trade imperialism was deeply linked to a global military—*yet not traditionally colonial*—empire. In this sense, we may think of the past half-century of globalization as an ever-expanding form of free trade imperialism—that is, as the global pursuit of economic and political advantage in foreign lands policed by U.S. military power yet not ruled by it in any direct governing manner.

Recent events suggest, however, that the United States may be shifting its energies toward a form of globalization closer to the old empire-building model of colonialism decried by Hobson (1902), Hobsbawm (1987), and Linebaugh and Rediker (2000). Indeed, whereas the neoliberalism of the Clinton presidency was concerned with establishing transnational mechanisms for expanding free trade imperialism, President Bush, using State power to advance selected commercial interests on a global scale, has embarked on a course of empire-building colonialism, complete with U.S. armed forces and companies stationed indefinitely in foreign lands—Afghanistan and Iraq for now, with more occupations likely to come—ruled by governments that, at best, are client regimes, and, at worst, mere puppets for U.S. power. On the one hand, then, 9/11 and the resulting War against Terrorism appear to have replaced communism as the overriding justification for continued U.S. military domination of the globe, with a chorus of supporters arguing that we must fight foreign wars to keep the "homeland" safe. On the other hand, however, the bulk of elite documents explaining the U.S. government's aggressive merging of free trade-driven globalization and war-making empire have relied on notions of historical obligation, market opportunity, and cultural advancement, thus echoing the universal righteousness and moralizing fervor that drove Britain's earlier attempts to colonize much of the world under the rubric of the "White man's burden" and similar U.S. claims to be fulfilling its "manifest destiny" (see Hartnett, 2002a; Hietala, 1985; Kaplan & Pease, 1993; Saxton, 1990).

For example, speaking as both an imperialist commander and an evangelical preacher—that is, both as a war-maker and a saver of souls—

President Bush promised in his preface to the *NSSUS* (2002) that the United States "will actively work to bring the hope of democracy, development, free markets, and free trade *to every corner of the world*" (p. iv; italics added). The document's opening pages echo this claim, arguing that U.S. values "*are right and true for all people everywhere*" (p. 3; italics added). Such startling moments of hubris indicate how, under the Bush administration, globalization will not follow the model of free trade imperialism but the model of empire building and world-homogenizing colonialism, in which U.S. forces seek not only profits and power but the reformation, liberation, and even salvation of those who do not yet share U.S. values. Rendered in a tone that Hartnett and Stengrim (2006a, p. 109) characterized as "benign universalism," such sanctimonious claims indicate how, following 9/11 and the fall of communism, the economic and cultural processes often discussed under the rubric of globalization have become enmeshed in the military and political processes often discussed under the rubric of imperialism, with both globalization and empire now justified under the banner of "democracy, development, free markets, and free trade."

I have attempted here to summarize a painfully complicated issue in a short amount of space and, consequently, am compelled to foreground my sense that these comments are meant to be suggestive rather than definitive. Nonetheless, attempting to think historically about the relationships among calls to spread free markets to new lands, military attempts to enable and police such economic growth, rhetorical constructions of demons against whom to launch such campaigns, and the cultural and political ramifications of such actions, obliges antiwar activists to broaden their activities. Indeed, my brief remarks on the links between globalizing free markets and military empires suggests that even though the terrorist strikes of 9/11 served as a powerful rhetorical tool for launching a global War against Terrorism and wars in Afghanistan and Iraq, recent U.S. foreign policy should be understood as following trajectories established by older empires—all of which crumbled ignominiously under the weight of their overextension and imperial hubris.

THEORIZING AND PRACTICING ANTIWAR COMMUNICATION ACTIVISM

The problem with situating our current moment within the complicated historical narratives offered in the previous section is that it saddles activists with the burden of teaching their neighbors the labyrinthine intricacies of global history—no easy task. Moreover, because its citizens have been taught to think of the United States as an *exceptional* nation—others may be empires, but we are not—trying to think and speak critically about the United States as part of a tradition of globalizing free markets and roaming empires is exceptionally difficult. As communication activists, we strive to make our political work pedagogical, but given the rhetorical dilemmas noted previously, some of the groups with which I have been working decided (some more than others) that the difficult task of offering critical and historical comments always should be balanced—following Debs's example—by positive and future-oriented visions. As Burke (1936) argued in a symposium on "What is Americanism?":

> The test of a revolutionary position is not in *what one rejects*, but in *what one would put in place of the rejected*. . . . A philosophy proves its value not by what new material it must *categorically reject*, but by what new material it can *assimilate*. (p. 11)[9]

Debs's September 11, 1918 speech to the jury at his trial provides compelling examples of how to provide positive visions and simultaneously engage in political critique and historical pedagogy, for even as he lambasted the elites that dragged the nation into WWI, Debs (1918b) assimilated into the antiwar and procivil liberties cause a list of heroes, including the U.S. founders Samuel Adams, Benjamin Franklin, Thomas Jefferson, Thomas Paine, George Washington, and Patrick Henry; the antebellum abolitionists Elijah Lovejoy, William Lloyd Garrison, and Thaddeus Stevens; and such noted anti-Mexican-American War figures as Charles Sumner, Daniel Webster, and Abraham Lincoln. Like these historical heroes, Debs claimed to fight for justice against tyranny, bravely accepted the risks involved in challenging the powers that be, and assumed that history would honor his bravery and sacrifice, even if the courts did not. (He, in fact, was found guilty, although he was serenaded by giant crowds of supporters at train stations en route to prison.) In a stirring passage as important today as it was in 1918, Debs (1918b) argued that "I believe in the right of free speech, in war as well as in peace. . . . If the Espionage Law finally stands, then the constitution of the United States is dead" (p. 49). Thus, even as he offered his listeners a historical road map to an alternative America, Debs positioned himself as a protector of the nation's most-cherished figures and traditions, meaning that assenting to his critique of WWI would not make one a traitor but a patriot fighting for nothing less than the soul of the nation.

Taking our cues from Burke (1936) and Debs (1918b), in my colleagues' and my antiwar communication activism, we have not only criticized President Bush's bumbling empire building but offered images of strong democracy; not only opposed war but advocated a citizen-centered peace that includes affordable healthcare and housing; called for decreased military spending to enable increased spending for education; rejected racial stereotyping and cultural Orientalism by articulating a vision of multiracial harmony; and spoke in what we believe is a U.S. vernacular that privileges patriotism, rhetorical simplicity, and humor, and assumes the intelligence and decency of the U.S. public. The communication imperative involved in such activism, then, is not only to construct a sense of historical context and provide blow-by-blow deconstructions of the present administration's ever-mounting pile of failures but also to supplement such critical work with the much-harder project of envisioning practical alternatives. As Rorty (1989) argued, "What binds societies together are common vocabularies and common hopes" (p. 86; see also Rorty, 1979; for a historical version of this argument, see Bercovitch, 1993). The successful antiwar activist, therefore, must combine critical debunking with community building, deconstruction with reconstruction, and historically specific disappointments and angers with transcendent hopes and visions.

As one example of how to frame antiwar activism in this manner, it may prove useful to recall the specter of Rome, for as U.S. influence has extended to the farthest corners of the Earth, the United States has become—like the Greek, Roman, Spanish, Dutch, French, British, Japanese, and German empires before ours—inextricably interwoven in a labyrinth of indigenous economic, political, cultural, and increasingly military struggles. Like the Romans, the multiplication of our military ambitions has left us exposed around the globe, paradoxically producing a superpower that feels vulnerable everywhere. Activists, therefore, need to emphasize at every opportunity that national security, economic growth, and the safety of our troops all are jeopardized by the reckless pursuit of a Roman-like empire. In pursuing this line of argument, however, we emphasize that we are critics of empire not because we hate the United States but because we love it and fear its further endangerment; not because we fear U.S. strength but because we believe it should be used to promote peace and prosperity, not death and destruction; and not because we are political idealists who categorically oppose the use of military force but because we can only accept the loss of our neighbors' lives in the face of genuine emergencies, not ill-conceived adventures.[10]

On the other hand, it is clear that foreign entanglements are part of the unavoidable cost of globalization and its attendant internationalism. Blaming the existence of complex international relations and tensions on the United States is as ridiculous as expecting it to withdraw from them. Instead, the rhetorical pragmatist confronts the reality of globalization with the hopes of expanding democratic practices, reducing violence and injustice, and ultimately producing a vocabulary capable of persuading anyone who will listen that there can be no peace without justice, no democracy without equality, and no freedom without meaningful civic engagement by all segments of society. Simply denouncing globalization misses the point, then, for we assume that although most U.S. citizens understand that global economics and politics are complicated and unavoidable, most of our neighbors do not intend to create poverty and misery with their consumer practices or voting behavior. Hence, instead of raving about the horrors of globalization in ways that sound naïve and idealistic, we try to use our nation's most celebrated values—such as fair play, family support, decent wages for hard work, freedom of speech and assembly, and protecting the environment—to articulate a vision of a humanized and democratized version of globalization (see Palmer, this volume).

We accordingly emphasize the point that the instrumental, military, and, therefore, deadly march toward empire fundamentally is different from the slow infrastructural transformations that are fueling globalization. For whereas one can argue that globalization is a product of infinitely complicated historical factors that transcend any one nation's intentions or even abilities to influence, empire is the product of *choice*. As I have attempted to show here, albeit in a condensed manner, future scholarship will no doubt track the intimate relations between these two forces, but given the limitations of conveying complex ideas in public forums, the rhetorical obligation for antiwar activists is to acknowledge that globalization is a fact of historical reality that we must attempt to humanize and democratize, whereas empire is a foolish political choice that must be rejected as a terrible threat both to U.S. democracy and international stability. Given these rhetorical premises, I next offer four theses regarding communication activism and six thematically organized sets of examples of how the local groups with which I am involved responded to the threat of and eventually the war on Iraq.

Thesis 1: London Calling—Interweaving the Local and the Global

Opposition to the war on Iraq manifested itself in stunning fashion on February 15, 2003, when 10-12 million people marched all across the globe to oppose the imminent invasion of Iraq. In Australia, marchers were estimated at 500,000 in Sydney, 100,000 in Adelaide and Brisbane, and 150,000 in Melbourne; in Japan, 6,000 marched in Tokyo; in Syria, 200,000 marched in Damascus; in Italy, estimates put marchers in Rome at 1-3 million; in Germany, 500,000 marched in Berlin; in France, 200,000 marched in Paris, with tens of thousands marching in Lyons, Toulouse, Marseille, and Strasbourg; in Spain, 1,000,000 marched in Barcelona and another 1,300,000 marched in Madrid; and millions marched in the United States, including 500,000 in New York City, 250,000 in San Francisco (the next day, on February 16), 100,000 in Los Angeles, and hundreds of thousands in over 300 cities. Schell (2003, p. 11) observed that such unprecedented global activism illustrated "a world in resistance" to President Bush's rush to empire and war. Even the usually understated newspaper *The New York Times* gushed in response to the marches that "there may still be two superpowers on the planet: the United States and world public opinion" (Tyler, 2003, p. A1). Indeed, these marches and the many protests that followed them (including a march by 300,000 in New York City on March 22) amounted to the largest coordinated political protest in the history of the planet.[11]

As usual, the U.S. corporate media underreported the number of participants in these events, ignored many protests altogether, and over-reported the number of marchers who committed foolish and sometimes violent acts.[12] Nonetheless, through savvy use of alternative media sources, activists around the globe cited each other's marches as support for their own events. For example, marchers in New York City on March 22 held signs referring to the prior weekend's marches in London, Paris, and Madrid. Some activists even managed to add energy to one march by speaking about the successes of another; my colleague Jan Nederveen Pieterse (2003), for example, inspired Illinois activists with stories of what he had witnessed at the London march he attended. In addition, knowing that antiwar activists were marching all around the world prodded local activists to hold events in solidarity. For example, in Champaign, IL, the rapid-response events planned for the day after the war began were touted by organizers as part of a globally orchestrated day of protest, meaning that the hundreds of us engaging in activism in central Illinois felt ourselves to be part of the global millions protesting the war.

My first thesis about communication activism, then, is that *local activism can gain strength from global activism.* Using the web sources in the Appendix to this chapter aids this process of recognizing that local activism always takes place in a larger context that infuses local work with global perspectives and global hopes. Indeed, whereas Gitlin (1980) argued in his seminal study of protest movements that "the whole world is watching," we must now organize our communication activism under the premise that the whole world is, in fact, *participating* in diffuse yet interconnected struggles.

Thesis 2: Let's Vote On It—Defending Democratic Processes

Whereas the international community clearly was driven by its fear of a runaway U.S. empire, many of the protests in the United States in the days leading up to the war on Iraq were fueled by a fear of the ways in which President Bush's march to war was subverting basic democratic processes. Indeed, in the months before the invasion, Congress seemed fearful of holding open debates about the merits of the proposed war, and the corporate media quickly sank into cheerleading mode, leaving many U.S. Americans wondering about the health of free speech and democracy (see Appleby & DuBois, 2002). However, rather than sliding into despair, the antiwar movement began swamping city councils around the country with antiwar resolutions. In fact, recognizing the importance of reasserting fundamental democratic deliberative processes in the face of empire, over 147 city and county councils passed antiwar resolutions prior to the war, with 169 having done so as of late February 2005. Aided by the resources available at Cities for Peace, the list of cities passing antiwar resolutions now includes Ann Arbor, Atlanta, Austin, Baltimore, Berkeley, Boston, Boulder, Chapel Hill, Chicago, Cleveland, Dayton, Des Moines, Denver, Detroit, Los Angeles (see Fox, 2003), Milwaukee, New Haven, New York City, Oakland, Philadelphia, Pittsburgh, San Francisco, Seattle, St. Paul, and Washington, DC, thus amounting to a map of an antiwar United States that includes over 36 million citizens (see www.ips-dc.org/citiesforpeace, organized by the Institute for Policy Studies).

Given the fact that city councils have no authority regarding U.S. foreign policy, some observers found the action misguided, but others understood that in the face of an executive branch that was subverting the democratic process, corporate media that were slathering with propaganda, and a Congress that spent more time debating tax measures than war, energizing city council meetings with debates about war would be deeply symbolic of our commitment to grassroots democracy, inspire future activism, and send a clear message to Congress that we refuse to be ignored. As Amy Lake, a supporter of the Salisbury, CT antiwar resolution reported on her town's successful efforts, "I think we all felt as if we had reclaimed our citizenship" (cited in Nichols, 2003, p. 20). Going further, John Steel of the Telluride, CO city council proudly declared that the Cities for Peace movement had become "the collective conscience of our country" (cited in Nichols, p. 20).

Furthermore, taking an antiwar message to one's local city council serves notice to future candidates at all levels of governance that the peace movement is strong, involved, and voting—not marginal and cynical but central and hopeful. In my adopted home state of Illinois, for example, the generally mundane city council meetings in Springfield, Bloomington, and Carbondale were turned into raucous town halls filled with hot and heavy debate (see the story about Carbondale's boisterous meeting in Herndobler, 2003). Given the widespread sense among many antiwar activists that the United States increasingly is a lobby-based corporation rather than a citizen-centered democracy, taking local concerns to the city council amounts to a wonderful reclaiming of the democratic process. My second thesis, then, is that especially in times of war, *defending democratic processes* amounts not only to a passionate demonstration of core U.S. principles but to a biting rebuke of those who would turn the republic into an empire.

Thesis 3: Pass It On—The Mysterious Logic of Multiplier Effects

One of the many reasons why defending democratic processes is so important is that activists never know where their political work might lead. Indeed, given the rapid spread of information made possible by the internet, local work has the possibility of *infinite geographic dispersion*. For example, although Chicago was by far the largest Illinois city to pass an antiwar resolution, it was my small town's resolution that was cited across the ocean, when the Baroness Massey of Darwen, speaking in the British House of Lords, read the Urbana resolution as evidence of rising U.S. opposition to the war.[13] Local Illinois activism, thus, aided the work of a member of the House of Lords in her attempt to rally British opposition against Prime Minister Tony Blair's push for war. Furthermore, following the Baroness's act, the local authors and supporters of the Urbana resolution were besieged by activists from around the nation with requests for drafts of the resolution and suggestions for passing similar ones, thus demonstrating the geographic dispersion of good work. The lesson of this story is that *everything we do can have multiplier effects*, spreading through space to reach audiences never imagined when planning local events. My third thesis, then, is that activists can gain strength from trusting in the mysterious logic of multiplier effects, which teaches us that even the smallest local actions can be important, frequently in ways we cannot imagine beforehand.

Thesis 4: Play for the Long Haul—The Power of Delayed Impact

Like learning to trust in the mysterious logic of multiplier effects, which teaches us to strive for the geographic dispersion of activist ideas and practices, another lesson eventually learned by some activists is that even those events that do not bear immediate fruit may have unexpected residual effects at some later date. For example, although the city resolutions movement could not stop the war or directly influence U.S. foreign policy, it eventually lit a fire under the Democrats. *The New York Times* ran a story on March 10, 2003, for instance, about how Representative Richard Gephardt, Senator John Kerry, and Governor Howard Dean, each hoping to campaign in Iowa without talking about the war, were challenged by local citizens outraged at the way that the Democrats had caved in to President Bush's bumbling empire building without so much as a whimper (Nagourney, 2003). Cities for Peace resolutions had been passed in Iowa City and Des Moines at that time, meaning that the outpouring of anger toward the candidates stumping around Iowa was likely the by-product of local work done by antiwar activists, who had created an environment in which citizens felt both empowered and compelled to voice their concerns.

The fact that I have based so much of my thinking in this chapter on the example of Debs's (1918a, 1918b) brave stand demonstrates how activists rely for inspiration and guidance on inherited cultural legacies. I am sure that every person who participated in anti-Iraq war marches and rallies has stories of marching in 2003 and singing songs from the Vietnam or WWI eras. As I discuss later when I turn to political poetry, our antiwar activism against the invasion of Iraq relied, in some instances, on material originally written for other causes in earlier times. For an example of previous activism resurfacing later to play unexpected roles, consider the work of the Icemakers of the Revolution, a midwestern U.S. rock band that I fronted in the early 1990s. Our final compact disk, *Fisheye Frenzy,* featured a number of songs written during and following the first Gulf War. Lo and behold, some of those songs began getting mentioned on internet sites in the days leading up to the war on Iraq. Thus, art made to protest the first Bush administration was recirculating to help inspire protest against the second Bush administration! These stories illustrate what I call the *power of delayed impact*: Activism creates opportunities that can spread in rhizomatic ways, snaking through communities to emerge at a later date.

Whereas the notion of multiplier effects speaks to the geographic spread of communication activism, the power of delayed impact speaks to its *temporal dispersion*. Those of us who are teachers live every day with both concepts in mind, as we never know who of our many students—or their roommates, friends, and families—will take what we do in the classroom and use it later and in some other place to bring new meaning and purpose to their professional or personal lives. Indeed, although teaching always is about enabling people to acquire certain skills in an institutionally constrained environment, it also is about the excitement of futurity—potential waiting to be realized—and dispersion—seeing how ideas multiply through networks of students, friends, and colleagues. Much like teaching and making art, then, my fourth thesis is that *remembering the rule of delayed impact* makes even the smallest activist event a possible site of future social change.

With these four theses in mind, I next offer six sets of examples of events staged by TFPJ, AWARE, and PRC. For the purposes of clarity, I organize these events into thematic groups structured around pedagogical communication, startling communication, protest communication, chance and targeted communication, media communication, and personal communication.

Example 1: Teach-Ins, Working Groups, and Pedagogical Communication

The members of my local chapter of Teachers for Peace and Justice have the good fortune of teaching at the University of Illinois, one of world's best universities, which makes our job easier when it comes time to assemble teach-ins. In addition to scholars in history, political science, sociology, English, anthropology, comparative literature, speech communication, and many other traditional disciplines, the University of Illinois is home to the Illinois Program for Research in the Humanities; The Center for Advanced Study; Center on Democracy in a Multiracial Society; Program in Arms Control, Disarmament, and International Security; a Graduate School of Library and Information Science; Institute of Communications Research; a top-ranked Law School; and a Program in South Asian and Middle Eastern Studies—meaning that our campus is stocked with interdisciplinary experts on every topic pertinent to the study of globalization and empire. Assembling panels of experts on any given topic, therefore, can be as easy as talking to one's colleagues, finding out who works in what areas, and making some phone calls. (Those activists hoping to assemble teach-ins in towns that lack such intellectual resources can use the web sources provided in the Appendix to locate speakers.)

Although the first goal of a teach-in is to create a safe pedagogical space in which participants can speak, dialogue, learn, and make connections with other concerned community members (see Simons, 2004), each of our TFPJ teach-ins also sought to promote multiplier effects and delayed impact. For instance, our teach-ins were recorded for rebroadcast on one of our local radio stations (WEFT, 90.1 FM), meaning that each event spoke not only to those in attendance but to other audiences at later dates and in other places. Each of our teach-ins also was covered in our local activist paper, *The Public i*, which is available in both print and web-accessible forms, thus creating a paper and electronic archive of our actions that can serve as potential inspiration for others doing such work. On a few occasions (immediately following 9/11, but not thereafter), we received local television coverage. Most of the time, we drew robust audiences, amounting on a few occasions to as many as 250 participants, but never dipping below 85. I should note that in addition to relying on the University of Illinois's scholarly community, we made sure that our teach-ins featured speakers from our local mosque and local Arab immigrant community, including presentations by Dr. Mohammad al-Heeti, an Iraqi exile who traveled to Iraq both before and after the war and who offered heart-wrenching, firsthand observations on the devastation being wrought on his hometown. Organizing teach-ins with one's colleagues and neighbors, thus, creates exciting public learning forums, forges relationships across academic disciplines, provides opportunities for media coverage, and helps to build a culture of informed activism—all of which lead to community building and empowerment.

Along with teach-ins for large public audiences, many activists also organized discussion and reading groups. Established as pedagogical workshops, these groups provided safe spaces for learning more about the issues at hand and created quiet situations in which those who may not speak up at rallies and other raucous public forums could voice their opinion. A good example of this type of group is the University of Illinois Working Group on Globalization and Empire (WGGE). Established by myself and my colleagues Matti Bunzl (Anthropology) and Michael Rothberg (English), the WGGE has held sessions devoted to dissecting the *NSSUS* (2002), analyzing President Bush's WMD lies, examining Johnson's (2000) theory of "blowback" in relation to economic and military globalization, honoring the passing of Edward Said (one of the first great scholars of globalization and critics of empire), and studying the ways U.S. foreign policy both influences and is influenced by the Israel-Palestine conflict. Merging the pedagogical work of our reading group with the teach-in goals discussed earlier, WGGE hosted—in conjunction with The Illinois Program for Research in the Humanities and the University's Chancellor's Office—a 1-day conference on globalization and empire featuring invited presentations by Ania Loomba (University of Pennsylvania), Mark Lilla (University of Chicago), and Tony Judt (New York University). The activities of the WGGE, therefore, demonstrate how engaging in pedagogical communication can lead seamlessly to other, more public political roles.

Example 2: Political Art and Startling Communication

Along with the more traditional modes of pedagogical communication discussed in the first example, TFPJ, AWARE, and the PRC all experimented with forms of activism that I call *startling communication*: the use of art forms to rock viewers or listeners into a new frame of understanding. For example, TFPJ had a good turnout for a screening of Pilger's (2000) grueling film, *Paying the Price: Killing the Children of Iraq*, which depicts the impact of the United Nations' (UN) sanctions on Iraq. The genius of Pilger's footage, shot over many visits to devastated Iraqi villages and hospitals held together by duct tape, is that it demonstrates how "the enemy," "the Other," is human, suffering, and very much like most U.S. Americans: wishing for peace, wanting a better future for their children, and distrustful of local political leaders yet full of love for their homeland. Pilger's images of the damage wrought by the sanctions are startling and cannot be viewed without radically rethinking the ways that the UN and the United States needlessly crippled that pathetic country, leaving as many as 500,000 children dead (see Fine, 1992; "Iraq Sanctions," 2002; Muller & Muller, 1999; Reiff, 2003).

Switching artistic genres, Brooke Anderson, the tireless leader of the PRC (www.prairienet.org/prc), organized an art show/dance party held in the final days before the Iraq war called "Hip Hop for Social Change: Anti-Racist and Anti-War!" By bringing together the collective talents of local artists, young disc jockeys (D-Lo and DJ Spinnerty) and musicians (Soulstice, Melodic Scribes, IQ, Doomsday, and Agent Mos), Anderson created a fun and empowering space for young people who might not otherwise have participated in antiwar actions. Furthermore, whereas many of the young people who participated in this event have been demonized by the corporate media as violence-mongering thugs producing vulgar trash, "Hip Hop for Social Change" showed that rap music, hip hop, and other popular musical genres can be turned to progressive ends and make engaging and inspiring art.

Along with the startling power of the visual and audio arts, TFPJ member Audrey Petty organized a campaign to plaster our campus and community with antiwar poems. There was no information accompanying the poems and no call to action; just poems waiting for passers-by to notice their words—and notice they did. I teach in Lincoln Hall, a stately old building that features a foyer where the Gettysburg Address is carved in marble and a bronze bust of Abraham Lincoln greets visitors. The students have been rubbing Abe's nose for years—hoping for good luck on exams, romantic dates, athletic triumphs, and so on—making the 16th president's nose shine like some aristocrat's silver spoon. In addition to placing poems on posterboards and office doors, I hung poems on both sides of Abe, one by Carolyn Forché ("Ourselves or Nothing") and another by Robert Lowell ("Fall 1961").[14] I was walking through the hallway at 6:30 at night, the building mostly empty after a long day's teaching, and there stood two students, one at each poem, flanking Abe. They finished reading the poems, looked up at each other, and said, "Cool?" "Cool," and off they went into the spring night, talking in the same breath about the war on Iraq and the works of Forché and Lowell. Similar stories were told by my colleagues across the campus, including by Michael Weissman, who hung poems in the Physics Department, where one assumes that poems are few and far between, yet physicists apparently stopped to read and debate the poems all day. These are small but sweet triumphs, easily repeatable by anyone with some poems and masking tape (for a collection of antiwar poems, see Poets Against the

War, at www.poetsagainstthewar.org). Remembering the principles of multiplier effects and delayed impact, who knows how far and wide those poems may spread, sparking conversations where before there may have been silence.

Along these same lines, AWARE's Sandra Ahten organized a "Postcards for Peace" campaign, in which local activists were asked to submit original antiwar artwork. Some of the pieces were chosen by a committee to be reproduced as packages of postcards; hence, instead of purchasing corporately made cards for the holidays, local activists could send messages of peace made by their neighbors. The campaign culminated in a holiday auction, where all the art submitted was publicly sold to the highest bidder, thereby creating a fun space wherein peace activism and raising money for the group were combined. Through promoting the production of art, raising money, furthering a cause, and organizing a playful event, Ahten's "Postcards for Peace" campaign was a rousing and energizing success. Indeed, by utilizing films, music, visual arts, and poetry, my fellow activists and I relied on the power of political art to create startling communication capable of prodding people into thinking in new ways about the rush to war.

Example 3: Marches, Vigils, Rallies, and the Public Communication of Anger and Hope

Along with the pedagogical and startling modes of communication discussed in the first two examples, our activism relied on the tried-and-true practice of assembling bodies in public space to voice anger and hope. We did so, however, with some interesting twists. For example, one of the great local triumphs in the days leading up to the war on Iraq was AWARE's weekly protest action called "Prospect for Peace" (P4P). Prospect is one of our busiest streets, a 4-lane artery connecting the older parts of Champaign and Urbana (each town has its own downtown) to the new malls that slowly are draining these downtowns of retail vigor. By noon on Saturdays, Prospect is clogged with traffic. Members of AWARE proposed that instead of lamenting the fact that fewer and fewer people go downtown to shop during the day (it hops at night, with the clubs and restaurants packed), they would take their protest to the malls, thus prospecting for peace while echoing Debs's (1916/1948) antiwar editorial, "The Prospect for Peace."

Hence, every Saturday from 2-4 p.m., protesters lined Prospect bearing signs against the war. In the bitter, windswept days of January and February, the group could be quite small, but by the first glorious days of spring, there were as many as 450 protesters lining the street, turning Saturday's shopping into an encounter with political discourse. Some shoppers honked their horn in solidarity, some shouted obscenities, some cruised by in stunned silence, and one addled woman played "The Star Spangled Banner" at top volume on her car stereo as she drove back and forth, over and over. Responses to P4P, therefore, were as varied and contradictory as the United States itself. Regardless of the responses of drivers to the protesters, however, the protests had an unexpected and welcome impact. As argued by Lisa Chason (2003), one of AWARE's team of organizers, P4P helped antiwar activists to "stake out a claim to public space," for "that expanse of concrete and curb and multiple change lanes has become humanized" (p. 3; see Photograph 5.1).

Perhaps the most emotionally powerful of our many antiwar events was a candlelight vigil held in the final days leading up to the war. There were no speakers, signs, or music—just hundreds of people holding candles in the evening air, some weeping, some whispering to their neighbors, and a few kids running around with their candles making lightning bug-like traces of light in the darkness (see Photograph 5.2). Like most of the events described previously, this one had no chance of stopping the war; nonetheless, it was a beautiful and hopeful event at which people met their neighbors to talk

Photograph 5.1. Protesters line Champaign-Urbana's Prospect Street on February 15, 2003; hence, "prospecting for peace" in the days leading up to the U.S. invasion of Iraq. (Source: Benjamin Grosser)

about the war, catch up, share hugs, and enjoy the perfect evening air. Indeed, like so much of the work described here, the point of the event was not to produce some immediate political effect but to savor the delicious sweetness of community and to know that the night's beautiful energy would reverberate in participants' minds, perhaps empowering future activism. Harkening back to my first thesis about the ways that the local and the global interweave, our candlelight vigil was held in solidarity with thousands of other vigils around the world that day, making our local action part of a massive, global protest.

TFPJ, AWARE, and PRC also pursued (sometimes autonomously, sometimes collectively) the time-honored practice of assembling rallies, usually with speakers, signs, some music, passing out of leaflets, and signing of petitions. Our event on Friday, March 20, 2003, the day immediately following the initiation of the war on Iraq—sponsored jointly by TFPJ, AWARE, and PRC—drew hundreds of participants, thus demonstrating how emotionally and politically important it is to assemble bodies in public to communicate anger and hope (see Photograph 5.3).

Example 4: Postering, E-mailing, Chance Communication,

Photograph 5.2. Joining millions of peace activists in a worldwide candlelight vigil on March 16, 2003, Champaign-Urbana residents gather for a silent moment of reflection. (Source: Benjamin Grosser)

Photograph 5.3. Hundreds of peace activists assembled on the main quadrangle of the University of Illinois on Friday, March 20, 2003—the day after the United States began bombing Iraq. (Source: Benjamin Grosser)

and Targeted Networks

Given the easy access to both photocopying and the internet, our local antiwar activism sought to balance *chance communication*—that is, messages left to be encountered by strangers in unexpected ways, literally by chance—with the use of communication networks that targeted specific audiences. As an example of chance communication, TFPJ plastered the community with weekly factoids or stark comments about the war on Iraq. Led by Zach Lesser, TFPJ-ers made simple posters saying things like "CIA Reports 'Link between Al Qaeda and Iraq Not Clear'," "UN Inspectors Agree: Iraq has No Nuclear Weapons," and "Number of Iraqis Who Have Died Because of UN Sanctions: 350,000-500,000." Much like hanging antiwar poems around town, the idea was to make chance intrusions into daily life, offering glancing notices that might prompt passers-by to rethink the imminent war. Such actions illustrate a surrealist-like commitment to the power of chance communication, to the ability of the unexpected thought hitting a person while walking home or going to class to provoke some critical reflection.

In line with this notion of chance communication, AWARE produced red, white, and blue yard signs saying "No War on Iraq," complete with a traditional background of stars and stripes. "Peace is Patriotic" was another popular sign (available, along with others, from www.nowarsign.org). Putting such signs in front yards, on dorm-room doors, on campus bulletin boards, or in the lobbies and windows of local businesses meant that passers-by would find antiwar messages intruding into their daily lives. One impact of these signs may be measured by the vicious response to them, as many of the signs were defaced or stolen. Mimicking the ugly symbolic practices of the Klu Klux Klan and other hate-spewing extremist groups, some prowar folks went so far as to leave dead animals beneath antiwar signs and, thereby, threaten antiwar activists with violence. Similarly violent responses, including defacing office and dorm-room doors posting antiwar signs, demonstrated that chance communication is powerful enough to provoke destructive outbursts from its unexpecting viewers. Such chance communication also can be practiced by wearing political T-shirts, hats, and pins, or by using political mugs and bags that turn even the most mundane activities into quietly communicative moments (see examples of such goods at www.cafeshops.com). Indeed, given the realization that we live in an infinitely dense cultural fabric of signs and symbols, where we are inundated by sounds and images, creating, wearing, and posting the antiwar messages discussed here amounts to *a semiotic reclamation project*, an attempt to render our communicative environment more conducive to promoting peace and justice rather than war and meaningless consumption.

Along with the modes of chance communication driving our semiotic reclamation projects, each of the groups I worked with relied on targeted communication networks to reach core members and likely event participants. TFPJ and PRC use their own e-mail lists to distribute messages, whereas AWARE has set up both a web page and a listserv (to which many TFPJ and PRC members subscribe; www.anti-war.net). These communication networks unite the antiwar community via public discussion and announcements of events and, thereby, supplement our efforts at chance communication with targeted messages sent to fellow activists. Whereas chance communication hopes to snare the attention of passers-by, whose political affiliations are unknown, targeted communication strives to energize and organize those already committed to antiwar principles. Ideally, the combination of these strategies can lure new members to the movement and simultaneously maximize the skills of those already committed to its success.

Example 5: Media Communication

As mentioned previously, Champaign-Urbana is home to WEFT, 90.1 FM, a community-run, nonprofit, advertising- and corporate-free safe haven for free thinking and alternative music that has become the audio voice of our activist community. TFPJ, AWARE, and PRC, thus, strive to work with WEFT as much as possible to make sure that their messages find their way onto the radio. One of the key components of cultivating this relationship is maintaining ties with WEFT's "airshifters" (so designated to distinguish themselves from the corporately programmed disk jockeys at other radio stations). Another remarkable Champaign-Urbana resource, previously mentioned, is *The Public i*, the nonprofit, community-run, advertising- and corporate-free monthly publication that is the print voice of the antiwar community. Activists, accordingly, try to make sure that their events are listed in the calendar sections of, reported on by, and even debated on WEFT and in *The Public i*.

The local for-profit newspaper, *The News Gazette*, generally is unwilling to cover activist events, but that has not stopped activists from flooding the newspaper's editorial section with letters. The campus newspaper, *The Daily Illini*, can be counted on to cover events, and activists pepper its editorial page with letters as well. I think that most activists in my town have come to fear local television coverage, as inevitably we find our views reduced to 10-second sound bites that make us appear silly. Veteran activists, of course, learn how to talk in sound bites, but I think most of us find such media coverage unhelpful. Indeed, given the strength of our local grassroots media options, most activists in my town have chosen to pursue safe media outlets, leaving the corporate radio, television, and print media to their usual barrage of banality. The mainstream media are, of course, crucial sites of political engagement; activists and scholars accordingly have devised complicated strategies for engaging this arena of struggle (see, e.g., DeLuca & Peeples, 2002; McChesney, 2004; Ryan, Carragee, & Schwerner, 1998). Nonetheless, the unique media environment of Champaign-Urbana enabled many of us working against the war to focus our communication activism on participating in local, grassroots media, thus fostering a strong sense of community among those who share antiwar and anticorporate tendencies.

Example 6: Picnics, Parties, and Interpersonal Communication

Activism should be fun; otherwise, no one will last long in any movement. Among our fun activities, TFPJ holds "picnics for peace," where we put up a banner on the campus quad, set up blankets for picnics, and hang out.

Members circulate around the quad handing out our informational flyers and posters announcing events, but mostly we just talk to people, sometimes triggering friendly conversations and sometimes heated debates. As a casual "happening," our picnics for peace are easy ways for people to get involved (everyone eats lunch), children friendly, and offer occasions to practice the art of chance communication as we have fun and maybe initiate a personal conversation with passers-by. Moreover, our picnics for peace are highly visible public appearances that frequently garner outpourings of unexpected support. Indeed, one common experience at our picnics is that many students and faculty who support our cause but do not have the time or energy to participate in events approach peace picnic-ers to express their thanks for our actions. These impromptu expressions of thanks leave members feeling energized and supported, bolstered by a sense that their work is being noticed and appreciated.

In a related way, the Friday nights before the "Prospect for Peace" demonstrations, described earlier, often saw someone hosting a sign-making party. As occasions to have a beer, do some painting, and hang out with friends—again, in a way that was child friendly—these sign-making parties offer fun ways of getting involved and harder-than-one-might-imagine challenges to put one's thoughts into artistic form. As someone who is practiced in the art of public speaking yet happily challenged by the intricacies of painting, I found it especially rewarding to learn that some of our quieter members—those who would rather die than speak in public—were great painters. Thus, these events not only helped to produce the artistic materials needed to make chance communication and rallies more powerful but also taught the simple lesson of recognizing members' multiple talents, thereby celebrating the importance of everyone's ways of contributing to the movement. Like the picnics for peace, these sign-making parties illustrate the ways that communication activism can foster community by creating alternative spaces where art is no longer a high-culture commodity but a community activity.

Finally, given that no group begins its work with a fully shared sense of purpose among members, and given that one only can go to so many meetings before getting bored and frustrated, TFPJ began hosting what we spoofingly called "Ice Cream Socials." These were after-dinner affairs at which we agreed to discuss a specific topic while drinking or eating, thus doing the hard work of agenda-setting in an environment that was friendly and relaxed. Many people will not come to yet another meeting at 4:00 p.m. on a Tuesday in the basement of some poorly lit campus building, but they might come to a Friday night "Ice Cream Social" at a friend's house; consequently, these events can become ways of increasing the number of voices involved in communication activism by making the necessary political work a little more fun. These events may sound trivial in comparison to the other actions described previously, but my sense is that many of us looked forward to these activities as ways to stay engaged and enjoy the company of friends. Indeed, we held rousing and productive "Ice Cream Socials" not only regarding general TFPJ strategies and events about the war on Iraq but also on the war in Afghanistan, responses to 9/11, and the complicated question of how U.S. foreign policy has become entangled in the ever-worsening conflict between Israel and Palestine. Thus, engaging in political work while cementing interpersonal bonds, the events described here strive to build a sense of community, a habit of communication wherein activism becomes less *a thing that one does* occasionally than *a way of being in the world with others*. Indeed, in my closing comments, I offer some broad observations on the deeper existential imperatives driving the communication activism strategies outlined here.

CONCLUSION: COMMUNICATING HOPE AS A WAY OF BEING

In this chapter, I have offered readers multiple ways of responding to the domestic and international crises of post-9/11 U.S. politics. First, by thinking about Debs and his courageous struggle against the Espionage and Sedition Acts, I argued that antiwar communication activism needs to be carefully and even lovingly attuned to vernacular traditions that enable critics to speak also as visionaries who deconstruct specific government policies and reconstruct a sense of a better nation. Second, to ground our current communication activism within a sense of historical perspective, I offered ways of thinking about the relationships among globalization, empire, and recent U.S. actions in Afghanistan and Iraq. Third, I proposed four broad approaches to communication activism and provided six examples of how those approaches may be applied via specific political actions. Merging historical revision, theoretical invention, and practical doing, I sought to provide a sweeping review of some of the possible means of engaging in communication activism. It is important to note that although I have written this chapter in a hopeful and celebratory tone, the fact is that each of the actions described here was time consuming, energy draining, and sometimes friendship straining. Taking a public stand against war, empire, and globalization in these post-9/11 days is no easy task. Communication differences, competing analyses of the crises at hand, interpersonal tensions, lack of money, and the simple questions of who shows up and who will do what they say they will do all make this political work complicated and sometimes even dreadful.

Nonetheless, I believe that the work described here is too important to let these challenges deter us from acting. In fact, I want to conclude by moving beyond a discussion of specific strategies and complications of communication activism to raise some existential questions about the ways that activism amounts to a way of being in the world with others. Indeed, regardless of the immediate impact of our local work against globalization and empire, and foregrounding the fact that we all need time to relax, watch bad films, and do nothing in blissful silence—in short, to be wonderfully flawed, lazy, and human in so many ways—I encourage activists, myself included, to recognize that all our work points toward a deeper commitment to living a life rooted in certain core values. Thinking in a utopian, Debs-like vein, these values could include:

- Turning off the television and other forms of corporate media to take a more active and creative role in finding news free from corporate biases and government propaganda. Ultimately, this means *taking responsibility for one's knowledge.*
- Seeing daily labor not only as a means of earning sustenance but as contributing to a culture of informed participation. For the academics reading this chapter, that may mean rethinking what and how they teach and research; for other readers, that may mean rethinking for whom they labor, and to what ends. Ultimately, this means *infusing one's daily work space with political energy.*
- Approaching leisure time as an opportunity for making things (e.g., political signs, poems, installation art, houses for the needy, and gardens) with one's family, friends, and neighbors rather than consuming things amidst strangers. This entails *becoming a producer not just a consumer.*
- Being part of multiple public movements—local, national, and global—rather than retreating into private cynicism and complacency. This means *embracing activism as a lifestyle, a way of being in the world with others.*

If a person pursues these goals, he or she makes a commitment to a version of engaged democracy and active community building that opposes empire and humanizes globalization. For as Debs (1918a) argued so bravely before being trundled off to jail:

> You need to know that you are fit for something better than slavery and cannon fodder. . . . You need to know that it is for you to know something about literature, and about science, and about art. You need to know that you are on the edge of a great new world. (p. 26)

APPENDIX
RESOURCES OF INFORMATION FOR SCHOLARS
AND EMPOWERMENT FOR ACTIVISTS

Laura Stengrim

Stephen John Hartnett

University of Illinois

Recognizing the complicated nature of activism in our era of globalization and empire as both a compelling crisis in our political imagination and an exciting space for rhetorical invention, we encourage scholars, activists, and other readers to use the resources listed here to help inform and enrich their actions. Covering a remarkably broad range of topics and perspectives, these resources present a cornucopia of options and opportunities. We have arranged these resources alphabetically within the following thematic subsets: (a) globalization and its critics, (b) war and its impact on democracy, (c) civil liberties and human rights, (d) U.S. government and elite international government organizations, (e) alternatives to corporate media, (f) print sources, (g) think tanks and advocacy groups, (h) activism, and (i) databases.

A. Globalization and its Critics

1. Center for Economic and Policy Research (www.cepr.net) strives to make the complicated economic issues that drive globalization accessible to the public by offering workshops, seminars, panels, and other educational forums.
2. Free Trade Area of the Americas (FTAA; www.alca-ftaa.org/ alca_e.asp) contains full-text copies of all ministerial declarations and includes a useful hemispheric trade database.
3. Global Exchange (www.globalexchange.org) provides information about globalization, offers extensive analyses of the World Trade Organization (WTO) and the International Monetary Fund, and provides both reports on and strategies for democratizing the impact of globalization on people around the world.
4. Institute for Policy Studies (www.ips-dc.org) calls itself "the nation's oldest progressive think tank"; its "Global Justice

Cluster" initiative offers a remarkable array of information and activist ideas.

5. Inter-American Development Bank (www.iadb.org/) offers primary documents regarding hemispheric lending practices; this is a good source chronicling global economic activities based in Washington, DC.

6. International Labour Organization (www.ilo.org) was founded as part of the Treaty of Versailles in 1919 and became the UN's first specialized agency in 1946; it monitors worldwide working conditions and sets international labor standards.

7. International Monetary Fund (IMF; www.imf.org) issues bi-annual *World Economic Outlook* and *Global Financial Stability* reports; use this site to see how the organization works, but do not expect to find many details about its decision-making processes.

8. North American Free Trade Agreement Secretariat (NAFTA; www.nafta-sec-alena.org/DefaultSite/index_e.aspx) offers laws, contracts, hearings, press briefings, and other primary documents pertaining to the U.S.-Canada-Mexico trade agreement.

9. Office of the United States Trade Representative (www.ustr. gov) includes statements and speeches; sections on "hot topics," such as the FTAA, NAFTA, and the role of the United States in the WTO negotiations, and offers useful links to primary documents and other government sites.

10. Sustainable Energy & Economy Network (www.seen.org), partially supported by the Institute for Policy Studies (see A4), contains a massive searchable database of world lending institutions, the projects they fund, and the human and environmental consequences of those projects.

11. World Bank Group (www.worldbank.org) is surprisingly transparent and has an excellent collection of detailed statistics on world poverty and development projects.

12. World Trade Organization (WTO; www.wto.org) offers a database of legal documents, including ministerial proceedings and dispute settlements; the section on "trade topics" is particularly useful for understanding how the WTO addresses some of the detailed issues in world trade.

13. 50 Years is Enough (www.50years.org) focuses on the role of the IMF and the World Bank, agitating for making their processes conform to democratic practices, and calls for canceling Third World debt.

B. War and its Impact on Democracy

14. CorpWatch (www.corpwatch.org) is a watchdog group monitoring the difference between proglobalization rhetoric and the reality of globalization's trail of havoc and poverty; it is especially helpful regarding actions taking place under the rubric of "reconstruction" in Afghanistan and Iraq.

15. Iraq Body Count (www.iraqbodycount.net), based on comprehensive surveys of international news accounts, counters the Bush administration's disinformation on the costs of empire by offering daily updates of the death and injury toll in Iraq.

16. Iraq Coalition Casualty Count (www.icasualties.org/oif/), like B15, offers tabulations of the violence in Iraq, complete with references to the news story corroborating each claim.

17. Iraq Occupation Watch (www.occupationwatch.org), based in Baghdad and founded as a collaboration between several peace groups that have stayed in Iraq throughout the war and ensuing violence, publishes articles on the U.S. occupation of Iraq gathered from a variety of news sources and is an essential starting point for daily information about Iraq.

18. Iraq War Debate (www.lib.umich.edu/govdocs/iraqwar) offers a remarkable collection of links to think tanks, government documents, scholarly reports, and other materials related to the war in Iraq.

19. Open Democracy (www.opendemocracy.net) offers a broadranging archive of information on globalization and empire; its "Iraq—The War & After" section is especially helpful.

20. War Profiteers (www.warprofiteers.com), sponsored by CorpWatch (see B14), monitors and profiles private corporations awarded contracts for security, reconstruction, and military logistics in Iraq, as well as weapons production in the war on terror.

C. Civil Liberties and Human Rights

21. American Civil Liberties Union (ACLU, www.aclu.org), founded in the dark days of WWI, is among the oldest and most noble of U.S. civic institutions; its defense of civil liberties in these Patriot Act days has been brave, and the information it provides on civil liberties is invaluable.

22. American Library Association (www.ala.org) has an "Issues and Advocacy" section that outlines how the Patriot Act affects library patrons' privacy and freedom of information rights.

23. Amnesty International (www.amnesty.org) is an international, member-driven campaign against human rights abuses that issues reports about human rights violations in all regions of the globe, makes recommendations to the UN and other international institutions, and supports the 1948 Universal Declaration of Human Rights.

24. Center for Constitutional Rights (www.ccr-ny.org) is a non-profit legal organization that represents victims of human rights and civil liberties violations, vowing to uphold the U.S. Constitution and the International Declaration of Human Rights; its statements and reports are timely, thorough, and influential in the U.S. justice system.

25. Electronic Frontier Foundation (www.eff.org) brings together an unlikely cadre of citizens concerned with protecting digital freedom; this site has a remarkable amount of information on copyright and trade law, censorship, surveillance, and the Patriot Act.

26. Federation of American Scientists (www.fas.org), founded by scientists working on the atomic bomb in 1945 under the "Manhattan Project," investigates biological, chemical, and nuclear weapons and is committed to ending the global arms trade.

27. Free Press (www.mediareform.net) is a nonprofit organization working to involve the public in media policymaking and craft policies for a more democratic media system; its web site is organized into useful categories and various projects focused on the many different aspects of media reform, and it contains a searchable database with links to other organizations concerned with media reform.

28. First Amendment Center (www.firstamendmentcenter.org) monitors cases in which free speech and expression has been limited, educates the public on First Amendment issues, and makes policy recommendations regarding the protection of Constitutional rights.

29. Human Rights Watch (www.hrw.org) is another international group that monitors human rights issues around the globe, issuing detailed reports, opinions, and recommendations.

30. International Committee of the Red Cross (www.icrc.org), the organization catapulted to the center of humanitarian

issues in Iraq, Afghanistan, and Guantánamo Bay, publishes a quarterly journal, the *International Review*, and operates in 80 countries worldwide.

31. The Reporters Committee for Freedom of the Press (www.rcfp.org), like the ACLU (see C21), is one of the crucial groups monitoring freedom of speech; it is particularly good on the dangers of the Patriot Act and how wars cramp independent reporting.

32. Union of Concerned Scientists (www.ucsusa.org) is a group of scientists and other experts that conducts and reports research on a wide range of environmental and policy issues, combating the problem of scientific censorship.

D. U.S. Government and Elite International Government Organizations

As important as it is to seek alternative news services, global activism also requires being conversant in and familiar with the inner workings of mainstream media, U.S. government, and the international governmental and elite institutions driving economic globalization. If one can ignore the spin, these sites are remarkably useful:

33. Central Intelligence Agency (CIA; www.odci.gov/) offers information in the form of studies on the war on terror, CIA press releases and congressional testimonies, and the invaluable *World Factbook*.

34. Coalition Provisional Authority (CPA; www.cpa-iraq.org) catalogues the apparent successes in establishing a "free" Iraq, including the latest soccer victories, as well as daily updates on reconstruction projects.

35. National Security Agency (www.nsa.gov) monitors U.S. and foreign information systems using complex numeric and alphabetic codes; although its web site offers limited specific information, it provides insight into the role of code-breaking in national security.

36. National Security Archive (www.gwu.edu/~nsarchiv/) is *the* site to obtain declassified government documents, audiorecordings, and videotapes.

37. Thomas—U.S. Congress (http://thomas.loc.gov), a service of the Library of Congress in the spirit of Thomas Jefferson, is a clearinghouse used by the U.S. Congress for information, documents, and links; use this site to find government bills and committee reports.

38. U.S. Agency for International Development (USAID; www.usaid.gov) lists all of its contracts with corporations purporting to aid in the economic and political development of struggling countries.

39. U.S. Census Bureau (www.census.gov), like the U.S. Department of Labor Bureau of Labor Statistics (see D42), contains basic information about U.S. demographics and income regarding national, state, and county populations.

40. U.S. Department of Defense (DOD; www.defenselink.mil), a portal to the military-industrial-complex, is updated regularly with news and press releases; it also contains the daily schedules of top officials, as well as basic background information on officials and the DOD.

41. U.S. Department of Energy (DOE; www.energy.gov), which is charged with developing nuclear weapons and disposing of the U.S. military's toxic waste, requested $24.3 billion from Congress in 2005 to spend on security, energy, scientific research, and the environment; the site reveals how the DOE is concerned with security and defense.

42. U.S. Department of Labor Bureau of Labor Statistics (www.bls.gov) contains relevant statistical information on employment, wages, demographics, and consumer and producer price indexes.

43. U.S. Department of State (www.state.gov) archives all of its press briefings and releases, extensive country and region reports, and useful studies on terrorism, poverty, and international relations.

44. U.S. Government Printing Office (GPO; www.gpo.gov) is a searchable collection of all federal documents available to the public, including the *Congressional Record* and errata from the *Weekly Compilation of Presidential Documents* from 1993 to the present.

45. United Nations (UN; www.un.org) contains a wealth of information about current projects, reports, millennium goals, and all of the UN divisions (e.g., UNCTAD, UNESCO, and UNSCOM); it also has four television channels and recordings of live and archived meetings and events.

46. White House (www.whitehouse.gov) contains extensive useful information, including copies of all presidential and cabinet member speeches, transcripts of White House press conferences, and printer-friendly versions of many key government documents, including the *NSSUS*.

E. Alternatives to Corporate Mainstream Media (available online)

The U.S. media are owned by a small number of oligopolists who, if not working alongside the Bush administration, are seemingly uninterested in providing balanced coverage or supporting investigative journalism, opting, instead, for content that rakes in money from advertisers and costs as little as possible to produce. Although it is impossible to totally escape the stranglehold of corporate media, the following sources offer fresh perspectives on relevant topics:

47. The Agonist (www.agonist.org) collects news from a variety of sources and provides an eclectic list of blogs that encourage discussion and participation.

48. Al Jazeera (www.aljazeera.net) has become the leading Arab news service, offering perspectives on Iraq, the Middle East, and the United States that one will not find in U.S. corporate media.

49. British Broadcasting Corporation (BBC; www.bbc.co.uk/) is where the United Kingdom gets its news; BBC's "World Service" is broadcast on some U.S. public radio stations and audio-streamed from this web site.

50. Center for Public Integrity (www.publicintegrity.org) is a Washington-based collaboration of investigative journalists who report on international, national, and state issues.

51. Christian Science Monitor (www.csmonitor.com), originating in 1908 at the First Church of Christ, Scientist, in Boston and founded by activist Mary Baker Eddy, has grown into a major daily international newspaper that, despite being supported by this church, is focused on news rather than religion.

52. Common Dreams (www.commondreams.org) collects information and news for the U.S. progressive community, featuring articles by top progressive writers published in other news venues or exclusively for Common Dreams.

53. CounterPunch (www.counterpunch.org) is a radical newsletter published twice monthly and edited by Alexander Cockburn and Jeffrey St. Clair that offers substantive articles of opinion and analysis about contemporary topics.

54. Democracy Now! (www.democracynow.org) is a daily radio program hosted by Amy Goodman and syndicated nationally by Pacifica Radio (www.pacifica.org) that embodies the bravery, intelligence, and independent reporting that keep free speech alive.

55. Fairness & Accuracy in Reporting (FAIR; www.fair.org) is a watchdog group that analyzes the media; along with its radio show, "Counterspin," FAIR offers excellent information on how empire and globalization are marketed by corporate media.

56. Focus on the Global South (www.focusweb.org) primarily is concerned with the Asia-Pacific region but offers a wonderful range of opinion papers and bulletins on how globalization and international trade affects the impoverished areas in the global South.

57. Free Speech Radio News (www.fsrn.org), spawned from the Pacifica Radio project (see E54), and one of the nation's first social justice-driven attempts to produce media, is a daily half-hour broadcast by a growing number of independent radio journalists in more than 50 countries and most states.

58. *The Guardian* (www.guardian.co.uk) is England's best newspaper and an important source for news on both globalization and empire; free from the corporate constraints choking U.S. media, it frequently covers stories blacked out in the United States.

59. *In These Times* (www.inthesetimes.com/) is a Chicago-based progressive magazine published twice monthly.

60. *LeMonde diplomatique* (www.mondediplo.com) is a monthly French journal with limited access to current and archived articles in English, focusing on world politics.

61. Middle East Research and Information Project (www.merip.org) is a nonpartisan, not religiously based reporting service in Washington, DC, that publishes a monthly journal of news and perspectives on the Middle East, offering information that is not found in mainstream sources.

62. *Monthly Review* (www.monthlyreview.org) is a monthly Marxist-socialist journal, as well as a book publisher, founded in 1949 in New York City during the time of the "Red Scare."

63. *Mother Jones* (www.motherjones.com), named for the famous U.S. muckraker and champion of the working class, Mary "Mother" Jones, is a San Francisco-based journal published every other month.

64. National Public Radio (www.npr.org), although increasingly underwritten by major corporations, is not the cacophony of commercial advertising heard on most talk radio; segment clips and entire shows may be downloaded from this site.

65. *The Nation* (www.thenation.com) has been providing progressive news since 1865 and is an invaluable weekly source of information, ideas, and inspiration.

66. *The Progressive* (www.progressive.org), founded in 1909, is another long-standing voice in U.S. progressive politics, published monthly and distributed widely and cheaply.

67. *Salon* (www.salon.com), an online daily magazine of politics and culture, produces original content, in-depth investigations, and straightforward commentaries.

68. *Slate* (www.slate.com) is a daily general-interest magazine run by Microsoft Network that has surprisingly interesting, fast-breaking, and original content.

69. TomPaine.Common Sense (www.tompaine.com), named for the champion of liberty and democracy, Thomas Paine, publishes critical articles that are of public interest.

70. Z Communications (www.zmag.org) is an exhaustive collection of activist resources, including online blogs and links to other web sites, and offers a subscription to the monthly independent social justice magazine, *Z-Mag*.

F. Print Sources

Many of the sources just listed existed in print before they launched an online presence; this is a list of publications that either have limited web access or which we prefer to see in their old-fashioned, original form.

71. *Boston Review* (www.bostonreview.net) is a bimonthly literary magazine that promotes political conversation by hosting an online forum and publishing reviews and responses.

72. *Foreign Affairs* (www.foreignaffairs.org) is the key publication of the Council on Foreign Relations, which is made up of elite past and present U.S. government leaders; it has influenced conversation on international issues since 1922.

73. *The Economist* (www.economist.com), originating in Scotland in 1843, is a weekly political and economic news journal with anonymously written articles that often leans both right and left and that describes itself as "radically centrist."

74. *Harper's Magazine* (www.harpers.org/), founded in 1850, is a general interest magazine edited by the lively Lewis Lapham that offers a healthy dose of entertainment and literature alongside insightful political essays.

75. *International Affairs* (www.chathamhouse.org.uk/index.php ?id=38), a quarterly European journal published by Britain's Royal Institute of International Affairs, is a source for seri-

ous scholarship on foreign policy, strategy, military, and world economics.

76. *London Review of Books* (www.lrb.co.uk) is a literary journal that began as part of *The New York Review of Books* (*NYRB*) and became autonomous in 1980; like the *NRYB* (see F79), it offers radical, critical analyses of important issues.

77. *Los Angeles Times* (www.latimes.com) is the leading daily newspaper of the U.S. west coast that covers national and international news.

78. *New Left Review* (www.newleftreview.net) is a journal published every other month that features leading international thinkers and scholars on various topics related to globalization and empire.

79. *The New York Review of Books* (www.nybooks.com), published twice monthly, is more than a list of suggested reading; it is a site where intellectuals critically engage current events and politics through a discussion of contemporary literature.

80. *The New York Times* (www.nytimes.com) is essential reading; although the online version is not the same as having it on one's doorstep, "all the news that's fit to print" is accessible online, with interactive and video features.

81. *The New Yorker* (www.newyorker.com), although aimed at urban literati, contains some of the best groundbreaking reports about the government, military, and Iraq War by investigative journalist Seymour Hersh.

82. *The Wall Street Journal* (www.wsj.com) is the daily newspaper for investors and those interested in getting news from an economic and financial perspective; this is a key resource for finding moments of capitalist truth-telling.

83. *The Washington Post* (www.washpost.com/index.shtml) requires a subscription for full services and online registration; it is Washington, DC's daily paper of national and international interest and has been surprisingly strong in its coverage of the rising U.S. empire.

G. Think Tanks and Advocacy Groups

84. The Brookings Institution (www.brookings.edu) is a Washington, DC powerhouse, a think tank with a huge endowment that funds researchers, supports scholars, trains

executives in philanthropy, and publishes materials on foreign policy and economics.

85. CATO Institute (www.cato.org) is a multimillion dollar non-profit group of libertarians concerned that contemporary liberals have "corrupted" the American revolution and the free-market, Gingrich-style "liberalism" they support.

86. Carnegie Endowment for International Peace (www.ceip.org), privately funded since it was founded in 1910 by robber baron Andrew Carnegie, has a special "Global Policy Program" that publishes well-researched reports on the main issues in this era of globalization.

87. Center on Budget and Policy Priorities (www.cbpp.org) researches the U.S. federal budget and fiscal policy, focusing on how state and federal decisions affect the lives of low-income citizens.

88. Center for American Progress (www.americanprogress.org) is a group committed to progressive politics that seeks to educate the public by providing fellowship opportunities for scholars who publish on this site and in other venues.

89. Center for Defense Information (www.cdi.org), founded in the late days of the Cold War by retired military officers, works with Foreign Policy in Focus (see G92) and accepts no government or military funding to research security and military spending and publish *The Defense Monitor*.

90. Center for Strategic and International Studies (www.csis.org) is a good place to see what is on the minds of foreign strategists and those who influence U.S. foreign policy; it has a regularly updated "what's new" list of publications.

91. Economic Policy Institute (www.epinet.org) is a useful place to find sound research on how global economics affects working people; the institute issues "Policy Briefs" that often inform U.S. public policy.

92. Foreign Policy in Focus (www.fpif.org), sponsored by the Institute for Policy Studies (see A4), releases reports and policy briefs, providing activists with information and talking points on key domestic and global issues.

93. The Heritage Foundation (www.heritage.org), a conservative think tank with its own experts and researchers, offers opinions on domestic and international issues.

94. Institute for Science and International Security (www.isis-online.org) works on nonproliferation and world peace, publishing detailed reports of weapons caches in strategically important countries.

95. Open Secrets (www.opensecrets.org), sponsored by the Center for Responsive Politics, is an excellent source of information dedicated to revealing the ways that corporate and war-related money drive politics in Washington, DC; it is an invaluable muckraking tool.

96. OxFam International (www.oxfam.org) works with several organizations that have humanitarian workers in hundreds of countries, seeking to alleviate world poverty by supporting these workers and by issuing briefing papers and reports on timely policy issues.

97. Program on International Policy Attitudes (www.pipa.org), a collaborative effort between social scientists from the private and academic sectors interested in public opinion regarding matters of international affairs, it publishes extensive reports on U.S. attitudes toward globalization and war.

98. Project for the New American Century (www.newamerican-century.org/) is neoconservative William Kristol's organization that promotes U.S. leadership and dominance on all world fronts.

H. Activist Participation

The information revolution has made it possible not only to access all of the incredible resources listed previously but to participate in them and communicate with others around the world in a newly emerging electronic democracy. The following organizations encourage hands-on participation in justice-driven projects, whether it be participating in local demonstrations, signing electronic petitions, or finding a favorite blogosphere:

99. AlterNet (www.alternet.org) offers a wide sampling of reports and editorials regarding empire and globalization; its "War on Iraq" page is especially useful.

100. The Fellowship of Reconciliation (www.forusa.org) is an interfaith organization that advocates world peace through nonviolence.

101. Independent Media Center (IMC; www.indymedia.org/en /index.shtml, and www.ucimc.org for our local IMC) is a grassroots, nonprofit, open-publishing web activism group that provides alternative news; each IMC has links to other IMCs around the world, enabling activists to bypass the corporate media to obtain local perspectives from fellow activists.

102. Move On (www.moveon.org/front/) is a crucial site of web activism that has been flooding the U.S. Congress with web-instigated petitions, phone calls, and e-mails; in addition to offering materials on globalization and empire, the organization attempts to reinvigorate the U.S. election process.

103. Rethinking Schools (www.rethinkingschools.org/) offers "Teaching About the War," which contains suggestions for lesson plans, readings, background materials, and maps; although built for teachers, the site is a wonderful tool for activists as well.

104. People for the American Way (www.pfaw.org) is an activist network with members in all of the states that works in collaboration with other groups and maintains a strong presence on Capitol Hill.

105. Traprock Peace Center (www.traprockpeace.org) offers an extensive collection of reports (some audio), editorials, and news of activist events; it is an invaluable source of both information and inspiration.

106. United for Peace & Justice (www.unitedforpeace.org) is reinventing activism as an online endeavor; this group's web page offers ready-to-print posters, announcements of events, and a wealth of information on the links between globalization and empire.

I. Databases

Much of our research was done by daily monitoring of news and web sources, but many of those sources offer either limited or pay-only access to archives and back issues. In such cases, we used our library at the University of Illinois to page through print holdings or search electronic archives by date or keyword. The following list includes helpful databases available through most university libraries and many public libraries:

107. EBSCO (www.ebsco.com/home/) is host to several databases, including *Newspaper Source*, which allows access to general newspapers, magazines, and journals aimed at a broad readership.

108. Google Scholar (http://scholar.google.com/) is a searchable collection of scholarly literature, often offered in full text, on the web.

109. J-Stor (Journal Storage; www.jstor.org/) contains the full text of hundreds of academic journals; although there are some gaps in the availability of archived journals because of per-

mission problems and technology changes, it is an invaluable tool for academic research.

110. Legal Trac, one of the Gale Group's databases (InfoTrac/ Expanded Academic is another popular database supported by this group), can be used to search for legal information in major law journals, including U.S. and international sources.

111. Lexis Nexis (www.lexis.com/) is a research tool for academic, legal, and business publications; its database contains full-text access to most major U.S. newspapers and worldwide news journals.

112. Project MUSE (http://muse.jhu.edu/), like J-Stor (see I109), allows full-text access to academic journals; it is useful for finding recent journal articles rather than older materials.

113. WorldCat (www.oclc.org/worldcat/default.htm) is an incredibly useful tool for academic research; it includes databases of general and specific interest, as well as access to library holdings worldwide.

ACKNOWLEDGMENTS

An early draft of this chapter was presented on March 14, 2003, at the "Friday Forum" of the Champaign, IL, YMCA, where I wish to thank Becca Gayette, Robert McKim, Steve Shoemaker, and Menjiwe Winfield. Other sections of the chapter were presented as parts of teach-ins I organized during Fall 2002 and Spring 2003 for the University of Illinois TFPJ; among my TFPJ friends, special thanks are due to Brett Kaplan, Michael Weissman, Zohreh Sullivan, Michael Rothberg, Maria Todorova, and Adam Sutcliffe. From AWARE, special thanks to Carol Inskeep, Al Kagan, Lisa Chason, Sandra Ahten, Sunie Davis, and Meredith Kruse; from PRC, thanks to Brooke Anderson.My opening comments on the histories of empire are taken from the "Introduction" of Hartnett and Stengrim (2006a) and appear here courtesy of The University of Alabama Press.

NOTES

1. The Espionage Act consisted of the June 15, 1917 "Act to Punish Acts of Interference...," which was supplemented by the April 16, 1918 "Act to Amend ..." (both from the *Statutes at Large of the United States of America*, 1919, pp. 217-231, 531); the May 16, 1918 amendment known as the Sedition Act officially was named "Chapter 75" (see *Statutes of the United States of America*, 1918,

pp. 553-554); the full title of the January 3, 2001 USA Patriot Act is "An Act to Deter and Punish Terrorist Acts in the United States and Around the World, to Enhance Law Enforcement Investigatory Tools, and For Other Purposes"; for responses to it, see Cole and Dempsey (2002) and Hartnett (2002b).

2. On the sacrificial nature of Debs's performance, see his letter of July 6, 1918—written a few days following his arrest—to Bolton Hall, a prominent workers' rights lawyer (reprinted in Debs, 1995).

3. Regarding the financial entanglements that helped to lead the United States into this war, see Zinn (1980).

4. On Debs's rhetorical style, see Brommel (1966), Darsey (1997), and Lee and Andrews (1991).

5. On attacks against U.S. troops in post-war Iraq, see any credible newspaper from Summer 2003 through the present; especially telling are Rhode (2003a) and Schmitt (2003). In September 2003, U.S. troops were targeted each day in an average of 13 attacks (see Parenti, 2003); by September 2004, attacks per day had escalated to 75 (see Glanz & Shanker, 2004); for additional reports of violence in post-war Ira, see Filkins (2003), Filkins and Oppel (2003), MacFarquhar and Oppel (2003), McDonnell and Wilkerson (2003a, 2003b), Parenti (2004), Schmitt and Weisman (2004), and Shanker (2003).

6. Among the many chilling articulations of this argument, see Friedman (1999), who argued that "the hidden hand of the market will never work without a hidden fist. McDonald's cannot flourish without McDonnell Douglas, the designer of the U.S. Air Force F-15" (p. 196).

7. What Hobson called the "usurpation of national resources" recently has come to be called "crony capitalism" (see Blackburn, 2002; Hartnett & Stengrim, 2006a; Prashad, 2003; "The Scandal Sheet," 2003; the reports posted by the groups and organizations listed in Section B of the Appendix).

8. For an article linking 18th-century piracy, 19-century anti-colonial violence, and 21st-century terrorism, see Hartnett (2003c); on the many forms of violence created by the pursuit of empire, see Colley (2004), Harvey (2003), Johnson (2000, 2004), and Mann (2003).

9. Burke's argument forms the basis of what Hartnett (2002a) referred to as "the dialectics of dissent and assent" (p. 2; see also pp. 11-39).

10. For examples of the hopeful work noted here, see Hartnett (2003a) and the memoirs, poems, and meditations collected in Denzin and Lincoln (2003).

11. Reports from demonstrations around the world are available on local Independent Media Center (IMC) web sites, all accessible by following the links on any IMC homepage; one can reach any of these destinations via my local IMC at www.ucimc.org. For estimates lower than those given here, see Cowell (2003) and D. E. Murphy (2003).

12. For an example of typical coverage by *The New York Times* of the protests following the initiation of the war on Iraq, see Sachs (2003), in which the story is accompanied by three photographs depicting protesters as rampaging lunatics threatening beleaguered police. Hence, instead of portraying the good work of millions of peaceful protesters, *The New York Times* focused on a handful of extremists and, thereby, attempted to discredit the antiwar movement. In addition, compare *The New York Times*'s layout, including Barry (2003), Eaton

(2003), and Jehl (2003), in which a handful of prowar demonstrators received as much press coverage as millions of peaceful antiwar marchers and photographs of black-clad anarchists (the few extremists made to stand in for the mild many) sat awkwardly next to images of prowar marchers wearing shirts that said "MOM" and "Support Our Boys."

13. The Baroness Massey of Darwen once visited Champaign-Urbana, where she befriended fellow activist and University of Illinois Professor of Political Science, Belden Fields; she received word of our local resolution from Belden Fields and cited it in her February 26, 2003 speech in the House of Lords. The Urbana resolution may be accessed at www.publici.ucimc.org or at the Cities for Peace homepage.

14. Forché's (1981) "Ourselves or Nothing," the closing poem of *The Country Between Us*, a stunning collection written in protest of U.S. actions in Central America under Presidents Carter and Reagan, ends with these remarkable lines:

> There is a cyclone fence between
> ourselves and the slaughter behind it
> we hover in a calm protected world like
> netted fish, exactly like netted fish.
> It is either the beginning or the end
> of the world, and the choice is ourselves
> or nothing. (p. 59)

Lowell's (1983) "Fall 1961," originally published in 1964 as part of *For the Union Dead*, a nuanced collection of observations on Vietnam, the Cold War, and other political topics, opens with these chilling lines:

> Back and forth, back and forth
> goes the tock, tock, tock
> of the orange, bland, ambassadorial
> face of the moon
> on the grandfather clock.
> All autumn, the chafe and jar
> of nuclear war;
> we have talked our extinction to death.
> I swim like a minnow
> behind my studio window. (p. 105)

For further elaboration of Forché's poems, in particular, and the possible roles of political poetry, see Hartnett (1999, 2003b) and Hartnett and Engels (2005).

REFERENCES

Appleby, J., & DuBois, E. C. (2002, September 16). *American historians speak out: "Consulting" Congress on Iraq is not enough.* Retrieved September 23, 2003, from http://www.tompaine.com/feature.cfm/ID/6392

Barber, B. R. (1995). *Jihad vs. McWorld.* New York: Times Books.

Barry, D. (2003, March 23). The sounds of protest, the strains of a city. *The New York Times*, p. B11.

Bearak, B. (2003, June 1). Unreconstructed—scenes from the new Afghanistan: Feuding warlords, stingy donors, reawakened opium dealers, and a gigantic used car lot in the hills. *The New York Times Magazine*, pp. 40-47, 62-63, 96, 101-102.

Bercovitch, S. (1978). *The American jeremiad*. Madison: University of Wisconsin Press.

Bercovitch, S. (1993). *The rites of assent: Transformations in the symbolic construction of America*. New York: Routledge.

Bernstein, R. (2003, September 11). Foreign views of U.S. darken after Sept. 11. *The New York Times*, pp. A1, A18.

Blackburn, R. (2002). The Enron debacle and the pension crisis. *New Left Review, 14*, 26-51.

Bostdorff, D. M. (2003). George W. Bush's post-September 11 rhetoric of covenant renewal: Upholding the faith of the greatest generation. *Quarterly Journal of Speech, 89*, 293-319.

Brommel, B. J. (1966). The pacifist speechmaking of Eugene V. Debs. *Quarterly Journal of Speech, 52*, 146-154.

Burke, K. (1936). What is Americanism? A symposium on Marxism and the American tradition. *Partisan Review, 3*(3), 9-11.

Bush, G. W. (2001, September 14). *President's remarks at national day of prayer and remembrance*. Retrieved May 19, 2003, from http://www.whitehouse.gov/news/releases/2001/09/print/text/20010914-2.html

Bush, G. W. (2002a, January 29). *President delivers State of the Union Address*. Retrieved July 1, 2002, from http://www.whitehouse.gov/news/releases/2002/01/20020129-11.html

Bush, G. W. (2002b, March 14). *President proposes $5 billion plan to help developing nations*. Retrieved May 19, 2003, from http://www.whitehouse.gov/news/releases/2002/03/print/text/20020314-7.html

Bush, G. W. (2002c, March 22). *President outlines U.S. plan to help world's poor*. Retrieved May 19, 2003, from http://www.whitehouse.gov/news/releases/2002/03/print/text/20020322-1.html

Bush, G. W. (2002d, June 1). *President Bush delivers graduation speech at West Point*. Retrieved May 19, 2003, from http://www.whitehouse.gov/news/releases/2002/06/print/text/20020601-3.html

Bush, G. W. (2002e, September 11). *President's remarks to the nation*. Retrieved May 14, 2003, from http://www.whitehouse.gov/news/releases/2002/09/print/text/20020911-3.html

Bush, G. W. (2002f, September 12). *President's remarks at the United Nations General Assembly*. Retrieved May 14, 2003, from http://www.whitehouse.gov/news/releases/2002/09/print/text/20020912-1.html

Bush, G. W. (2003a, January 7). *President Bush taking action to strengthen America's economy*. Retrieved May 14, 2003, from http://www.whitehouse.gov/news/releases/2003/01/print/text/20030107-5.html

Bush, G. W. (2003b, January 28). *President delivers "State of the Union."* Retrieved May 14, 2003, from http://www.whitehouse.gov/news/releases/2003/01/print/text/20030128-19.html

Bush, G. W. (2003c, May 1). *President Bush announces major combat operations in Iraq have ended.* Retrieved May 14, 2003, from http://www.whitehouse.gov/news/releases/2003/05/iraq/20030501-15.html

Byrd, R. (2003, February 12). *Reckless administration may reap disastrous consequences.* Retrieved February 15, 2003, from http://www.commondreams.org/views03/0212-07.htm

Cain, P. (1980). *Economic foundations of British overseas expansion, 1815-1914.* London: Macmillan.

Chason, L. (2003). Humanizing the highway: Reflections on an unexpected consequence. *The Public i, 3*(2), 3.

Cole, D., & Dempsey, J. X. (2002). *Terrorism and the constitution: Sacrificing civil liberties in the name of national security.* New York: New Press.

Colley, L. (2004). *Captives: Britain, empire and the world, 1600-1850.* London: Random House.

Cowell, A. (2003, February 16). Antiwar rallies raise a chorus across Europe. *The New York Times,* pp. A1, A16.

Darsey, J. (1997). *The prophetic tradition and radical rhetoric in America.* New York: New York University Press.

DeLuca, K. M., & Peeples, J. (2002). From public sphere to public screen: Democracy, activism, and the "violence" of Seattle. *Critical Studies in Media Communication, 19,* 125-151.

Debs, E. V. (1918a, June 16). Debs's Canton speech. In E. V. Debs, *The Debs white book* (pp. 3-36). Girard, KS: Appeal to Reason.

Debs, E. V. (1918b, September 11). Debs's speech to the jury. In E. V. Debs, *The Debs white book* (pp. 37-57). Girard, KS: Appeal to Reason.

Debs, E. V. (1948). The prospect for peace. In E. V. Debs, *Writings and speeches of Eugene V. Debs* (pp. 391-392). New York: Hermitage. (Original work published 1916)

Debs. E. V. (1995). *Gentle rebel: Letters of Eugene V. Debs* (J. R. Constantine, Ed.). Urbana: University of Illinois Press.

Denzin, N. K., & Lincoln, Y. S. (Eds.). (2003). *9-11 in American culture.* Walnut Creek, CA: AltaMira Press.

Eaton, L. (2003, March 23). On New York's streets and across the nation, protesters speak out. *The New York Times,* p. B11.

Enloe, C. (1989). *Bananas, beaches & bases: Making feminist sense of international politics.* Berkeley: University of California Press.

Falk, R. A. (1999). *Predatory globalization: A critique.* Cambridge, England: Polity Press.

Falk, R. A. (2003). *The great terror war.* New York: Olive Branch Press.

Filkins, D. (2003, August 30). Death and hesitation. *The New York Times,* pp. A1, A6.

Filkins, D., & Oppel, R., Jr. (2003, August 20). Scene of carnage. *The New York Times,* pp. A1, A8.

Fine, J. (1992, January/February). The Iraq sanctions catastrophe. *Middle East Report,* p. 36.

Forché, C. (1981). *The country between us.* Port Townsend, WA: Copper Canyon Press.

Fox, S. (2003, February 22). City council adopts resolution opposing U.S. invasion of Iraq. *Los Angeles Times*, p. B1.

Friedman, T. L. (1999). *The lexus and the olive tree: Understanding globalization*. New York: Farrar, Straus, Giroux.

Gall, C. (2003, June 8). Afghan economic reconstruction still sputters. *The New York Times*, p. A3.

Ginger, R. (1949). *The bending cross: A biography of Eugene Victor Debs*. New Brunswick, NJ: Rutgers University Press.

Gitlin, T. (1980). *The whole world is watching: Mass media in the making & unmaking of the New Left*. Berkeley: University of California Press.

Glanz, J., & Shanker, T. (2004, September 29). Reports in Iraq show attacks in most areas. *The New York Times*, pp. A1, A10.

Greider, W. (1997). *One world ready or not: The manic logic of global capitalism*. New York: Simon & Schuster.

Hariman, R. (2003). Speaking of evil. *Rhetoric & Public Affairs, 6*, 511-517.

Hartnett, S. J. (1999). Four meditations on the search for grace amidst terror. *Text and Performance Quarterly, 19*, 196-216.

Hartnett, S. J. (2002a). *Democratic dissent and the cultural fictions of antebellum America*. Urbana: University of Illinois Press.

Hartnett, S. J. (2002b, November). A review of civil liberties one year after 9/11. *The Public i, 2*(10), 4-5.

Hartnett, S. J. (2003a). 9/11 and the poetics of complicity: A love poem for a hurt nation. In N. K. Denzin & Y. S. Lincoln (Eds.), *9-11 in American culture* (pp. 259-271). Walnut Creek, CA: AltaMira Press.

Hartnett, S. J. (2003b). *Incarceration nation: Investigative prison poems of hope and terror*. Walnut Creek, CA: AltaMira Press.

Hartnett, S. J. (2003c). Subjects, slaves, and patriots: Rhetorics of belonging and the democratic imagination. *Rhetoric & Public Affairs, 6*, 161-178.

Hartnett, S. J., & Engels, J. D. (2005). "Aria in time of war": The politics of investigative and ethnopoetics. In N. K. Denzin & Y. S. Lincoln (Eds.), *Handbook of qualitative research* (3rd ed., pp. 1043-1068). Thousand Oaks, CA: Sage.

Hartnett, S. J., & Stengrim, L. A. (2004). "The whole operation of deception": Reconstructing President Bush's rhetoric of weapons of mass destruction. *Cultural Studies↔Critical Methodologies, 4*, 152-197.

Hartnett, S. J., & Stengrim, L. A. (2006a). *Globalization & empire: The invasion of Iraq, free markets, and the twilight of democracy*. Tuscaloosa: University of Alabama Press.

Hartnett, S. J., & Stengrim, L. A. (2006b). War rhetorics: *The National Security Strategy of the United States* and President Bush's globalization-through-benevolent-empire. *South Atlantic Quarterly, 105*, 175-206.

Harvey, D. (2003). *The new imperialism*. New York: Oxford University Press.

Herrndobler, K. (2003, March 19). Carbondale city council postponed discussion due to debate. *Daily Egyptian*. Retrieved March 19, 2003, from http://newshound.de.siu.edu/spring03/stories/storyReader$1237

Hietala, T. R. (1985). *Manifest design: Anxious aggrandizement in late Jacksonian America*. Ithaca, NY: Cornell University Press.

Hobsbawm, E. J. (1987). *The age of empire, 1875-1914*. New York: Pantheon Books.

Hobson, J. A. (1902). *Imperialism: A study*. New York: James Pott.

Iraq sanctions: Humanitarian implications and options for the future. (2002, August 6). Retrieved 2003, from http://www.globalpolicy.org/security/sanction/iraq1/2002/paper.htm

Jameson, F., & Miyoshi, M. (Eds.). (1998). *The cultures of globalization*. Durham, NC: Duke University Press.

Jehl, D. (2003, March 23). Across country, thousands gather to back U.S. troops and policy. *The New York Times*, p. B15.

Johnson, C. (2000). *Blowback: The costs and consequences of American empire*. New York: Metropolitan Books.

Johnson, C. (2004). *The sorrows of empire: Militarism, secrecy, and the end of the republic*. New York: Metropolitan Books.

Kaplan, A., & Pease, D. E. (Eds.). (1993). *Cultures of United States imperialism*. Durham, NC: Duke University Press.

Kellner, D. (2003). *From 9/11 to terror war: The dangers of the Bush legacy*. Lanham, MD: Rowman & Littlefield.

Lapham, L. (2002). *Theater of war*. New York: New Press.

Lee, R., & Andrews, J. R. (1991). A story of rhetorical-ideological transformation: Eugene V. Debs as liberal hero. *Quarterly Journal of Speech, 77*, 20-37.

Linebaugh, P., & Rediker, M. (2000). *The many-headed hydra: Sailors, slaves, commoners, and the hidden history of the revolutionary Atlantic*. Boston: Beacon Press.

Lowell, R. (1983). *Selected poems*. New York: Farrar, Strauss, Giroux.

MacFarquhar, N., & Oppel, R., Jr. (2003, August 30). Car bomb in Iraq kills 95 at Shiite mosque. *The New York Times*, pp. A1, A6.

Magdoff, H. (1972). Imperialism without colonies. In R. Owen & B. Sutcliffe (Eds.), *Studies in the theory of imperialism* (pp. 144-170). London: Longman.

Mann, M. (2003). *Incoherent empire*. New York: Verso.

McChesney, R. W. (1999). *Rich media, poor democracy: Communication politics in dubious times*. Urbana: University of Illinois Press.

McChesney. R. W. (2004). *The problem of the media: U.S. communication politics in the twenty-first century*. New York: Monthly Review Press.

McDaniel, J. (2003). Figures of evil: A triad of rhetorical strategies for theo-politics. *Rhetoric & Public Affairs, 6*, 539-550.

McDonnell, P., & Wilkerson, T. (2003a, August 21). Baghdad bomb had the mark of experts. *Los Angeles Times*, p. A1.

McDonnell, P., & Wilkerson, T. (2003b, August 30). Blast kills scores at Iraq mosque. *Los Angeles Times*, p. A1.

Muller, J., & Muller, K. (1999). Sanctions of mass destruction. *Foreign Affairs, 78*(3), 43-53.

Murphy, D. E. (2003, February 17). On day of their own, thousands rally in San Francisco. *The New York Times*, p. A10.

Murphy, J. (2004). "Our mission and our moment": George W. Bush and September 11th. *Rhetoric & Public Affairs, 6*, 607-632.

Nagourney, A. (2003, March 10). Candidates find agendas eclipsed by antiwar questions. *The New York Times*, p. A16.

National Security Strategy of the United States. (2002). Washington, DC: The White House.

Nichols, J. (2003, March 31). Building cities for peace. *The Nation*, p. 20.

Nye, J. S., Jr. (2002). *The paradox of American power: Why the world's only superpower can't go it alone.* New York: Oxford University Press.

Parenti, C. (2003, September 19). *The progress of disaster.* Retrieved October 19, 2003, from http://www.alternet.org/story/16759/

Parenti, C. (2004). *The freedom: Shadows and hallucinations in occupied Iraq.* New York: New Press.

Pieterse, J. N. (2003, February 23). London 15 February: "Down with this sort of thing." *Urbana-Champaign Independent Media Center.* Retrieved February 25, 2003, from http://www.ucimc.org/newswire/display_any/9745

Pilger, J. (Director). (2000). *Paying the price: Killing the children of Iraq* [Motion picture]. London: Carlton Television.

Prashad, V. (2003). *Fat cats & running dogs: The Enron stage of capitalism.* Monroe, ME: Common Courage Press.

Rampton, S., & Stauber, J. (2003). *Weapons of mass deception: The uses of propaganda in Bush's war on Iraq.* New York: Jeremy P. Tarcher/Penguin.

Reiff, D. (2003, July 27). Were the sanctions right? *The New York Times Magazine*, pp. 41-46.

Rhode, D. (2003a, June 10). Deadly attacks on GI's rise. *The New York Times*, p. A10.

Rhode, D. (2003b, September 12). Taliban officials tell of plans to grind down the Americans. *The New York Times*, p. A22.

Rorty, R. (1979). *Philosophy and the mirror of nature.* Princeton, NJ: Princeton University Press.

Rorty, R. (1989). *Contingency, irony, and solidarity.* New York: Cambridge University Press.

Ryan, C., Carragee, K. M., & Schwerner, C. (1998). Media, movements, and the quest for social justice. *Journal of Applied Communication Research, 26*, 165-181.

Sachs, S. (2003, March 23). Crowds protest Iraq War in cities around the world. *The New York Times*, p. B9.

Salvatore, N. (1982). *Eugene V. Debs: Citizen and socialist.* Urbana: University of Illinois Press.

Saxton, A. (1990). *The rise and fall of the White republic: Class politics and mass culture in nineteenth-century America.* New York: Verso.

Schell, J. (2003, April 14). The world's other superpower. *The Nation*, p. 11.

Schmitt, E. (2003, September 7). Iraq bombings pose a mystery U.S. must solve. *The New York Times*, pp. A1, A18.

Schmitt, E., & Weisman, S. (2004, September 8). U.S. conceding rebels control regions of Iraq. *The New York Times*, pp. A1, A12.

Shanker, T. (2003, August 20). Chaos as strategy against the U.S. *The New York Times*, pp. A1, A9.

Simons, H. (2004). The Temple Issues Forum: Innovations in pedagogy for civic engagement. In G. A. Hauser & A. Grim (Eds.), *Rhetorical democracy: Discursive practices of civic engagement: Selected papers from the 2002 Conference of the Rhetoric Society of America* (pp. 53-70). Mahwah, NJ: Erlbaum.

Singer, P. (2002). *One world: The ethics of globalization.* New Haven, CT: Yale University Press.

Statutes at Large of the United States of America, April 1917-March 1919, Volume 50, Part Two. (1919). Washington, DC: Government Printing Office.

Statutes of the United States of America, Passed at the Second Session of the Sixty-Fifth Congress, 1917-1918, Part 1: Public Acts and Resolutions. (1918). Washington, DC: Government Printing Office.

Stengrim, L. (2005). Negotiating postmodern democracy, political activism, and knowledge production: Indymedia's grassroots and e-savvy answer to media oligopoly. *Communication and Critical/Cultural Studies, 2,* 281-304.

Stengrim, L., & Hartnett, S. (2004, February). The FTAA, globalization, & the future of democracy. *The Public i, 4*(1), 8-9. Retrieved February 10, 2004, from http://publici.ucimc.org/february2004/Feb2004.pdf

Stiglitz, J. E. (2003). *Globalization and its discontents.* New York: Norton.

The Daily Mis-lead: A Daily Chronicle of Bush Administration Distortion. (2003). Retrieved March 10, 2003, from www.misleader.org

The National Security Strategy of the United States of America. (2002). Washington, DC: The White House. Retrieved December 10, 2002, from www.whitehouse.gov/nsc/nss.html

The scandal sheet. (2003, June 28). *The Economist,* p. 7.

Tyler, P. E. (2003, February 17). A new power in the streets. *The New York Times,* p. A1.

Uniting and Strengthening America by Providing Appropriate Tools Required to Intercept and Obstruct Terrorism (USA PATRIOT ACT) Act of 2001. (2001, October 24). Washington, DC: U.S. Congress.

Waters, M. (2001). *Globalization* (2nd ed.). New York: Routledge.

Weisman, S. R. (2003, October 1). Bush-appointed panel finds U.S. image abroad is in peril. *The New York Times,* pp. A1, A8.

Wood, E. M. (2003). *Empire of capital.* New York: Verso.

Zinn, H. (1980). *A people's history of the United States.* New York: Harper & Row.

PART II

Communication Consulting for Social Change

6

COMMUNITY ACTIVIST AND COMMUNICATION CONSULTANT

Managing the Dialectics of Outsider-Within Status at a Sexual Assault Recovery Services Center

Robbin D. Crabtree

Fairfield University

Leigh Arden Ford

Western Michigan University

Historically, many U.S. institutions of higher education were established with a civic purpose as part of their mission: to prepare citizens for active participation in a democracy and develop and disseminate knowledge for the betterment of their communities (C. W. Anderson, 1993; Barber, 1992; Checkoway, 2001; Kennedy, 1997). In the late-19th and early-20th centuries, this civic mission was demonstrated at the University of Chicago under the leadership of John Dewey, who argued that universities have a role in the creation and sustenance of a "public" (see Applegate, 2001; also see Boyer &

Hechinger, 1981); in the ideas of Seth Low who, as president of Columbia University, described the university as in and of New York City (see Checkoway, 2001); and in the many land-grant institutions across the United States that were founded on the principle of building communities and their capacity for cooperative action (C. W. Anderson, 1993; Hackney, 1986).

In recent years, however, many within academe and the communities they are supposed to serve have suggested that contemporary educational institutions have drifted away from their civic mission (see, e.g., Boyer, 1987; Butler, 2000; Checkoway, 2001; Sandmann & Lewis, 1991; Sirianni & Friedland, 1997). Checkoway (2001) argued that universities have been transformed from civic institutions to powerful research engines and, because of that transformation, have changed their "objectives and operations, research paradigms and pedagogical methods, and infrastructure and external relationships" (p. 126). The result of this shift for the professoriate is the professionalization and privileging of scholarly allegiance and, hence, a focus on research for/in an individual's discipline, supported by public and private monies, rather than for/with one's communities or society (Rice, 1996). This transformation also has had significant consequences for students at both the undergraduate and graduate levels, raising concerns about students' lack of engagement in the educational process (Applegate, 2001; Boyer, 1987) and the adequacy of their preparation to be full participants in a diverse, democratic society (Butler, 2000; Checkoway, 2000, 2001). For example, although many students express the desire to provide community service through volunteerism, few are motivated to organize others to address a community cause and even fewer have the requisite skills to engage in public dialogue about that cause (Checkoway, 2000). In response to these concerns, a concerted effort to return to a revitalized mission of civic engagement at U.S. universities is being made, evidenced by the growing service-learning movement (see, e.g., Bringle & Hatcher, 1996; Zlotkowski, 1998) and the increasing number of grants for faculty to develop civic-education courses and community-based research (see, e.g., Fields, 2003; Gibson, 2001; Hinds, 2002).

One way in which this effort is being enacted at the grassroots of the academy is through the community participation approach by professors and students in a variety of disciplines who have argued for and put into practice a social justice agenda in teaching, research, and service, working in and with their local communities (e.g., Ansley & Gaventa, 1997; Elden & Levin, 1991; Fals-Borda & Rahman, 1991; Ford, Barnes, Crabtree, & Fairbanks, 1998; Frey, Pearce, Pollock, Artz, & Murphy, 1996). Whether informed by participatory action research (PAR; e.g., Ansley & Gaventa, 1997; Brown & Tandon, 1983; Hall, 1981; also see Campo & Frazer, this volume), feminist perspectives and methods (such as feminist action research [FAR]; e.g., Belenky, Clinchy, Goldberger, & Tarule, 1986; Devault, 1999; Maguire 1987, 2001; Reinharz, 1992), or service-learning initiatives (e.g., Bringle & Hatcher, 1996; Droge & Murphy, 1999; Kraft, 1996; Zlotkowski, 1998), these community engagement approaches share three characteristics: (a) they argue for an alternative paradigm for understanding the nature of knowledge (as contingent rather than fixed) and the conduct of research (as inherently political rather than neutral); (b) they reject the disconnect between teaching and research, academy and community, and scholarship and activism; and (c) they promote teaching, research, and service as collaborative with the community and in the service of social change and justice.

The challenges these alternative research and teaching paradigms make to the status quo in U.S. higher education are not without risk. Aside from suffering the same type of stigma that applied communication research suffered not so long ago (see Eadie, 1982, 1990; Ellis, 1982, 1991; Kreps, Frey, & O'Hair, 1991), this community-based and activism-oriented philosophy may not be valued in all academic departments; indeed, the university reward system typically is not aligned with this approach. This macro-level tension between the current disciplinary research engine model and the revitalized civic engagement/social change model likely will not be resolved soon or easily. Nevertheless, as others have argued, we believe that U.S. educational institutions are at an important crossroads as they review current practices and reflect on the choices before them, choices with enormous consequences for the institution, but more importantly, for our society and our democracy (see, e.g., Gabelink, 1997; Gamson, 1997; Rice, 1996; Sirianni & Friedland, 1997).

This ongoing macro-level tension between (and within) academe as institutions and their surrounding communities, of course, also emerges at the micro level in the day-to-day activities and communicative practices of professors, students, and community members as we work together to address problems in and with the community. In this chapter, we present our experience of those tensions as we and our students worked to address the social justice issue of sexual assault in our community. First, we provide an overview of this social justice issue. We then present first-person narratives of our volunteer participation and social activism at the Sexual Assault Recovery Center (SARC, a pseudonym), a small, nonprofit agency offering crisis intervention, counseling, and educational programs in southern New Mexico, where we both lived for several years. We then engage in a reflexive analysis of these experiences, critiquing the activist-consultant dichotomy and arguing for a dialectical view of activist scholarship as fundamental to civic engagement. We conclude this chapter with reflection on the challenges and opportunities of the activist-consultant role, integrating our "lessons learned" as scholars and citizens.

SEXUAL ASSAULT AS A JUSTICE ISSUE

The United States Department of Justice Bureau of Justice Statistics (2002) estimated that there were, on average, over 371 rapes *reported* for each day of the year between 1992 and 2000, or about 1 rape every 3.8 minutes; the report further noted that 94% of sexual assault victims are women and only 34% of attempted and 26% of completed sexual assaults are reported to law enforcement officials. As these statistics show, sexual assault is alarmingly pervasive in U.S. society. According to a study conducted by the National Victim Center, 1.3 women (age 18 and over) are forcibly raped each minute in the United States, which translates into 1,871 rapes per day and 683,000 each year, and as many as 42% of rape survivors tell *no one* about it (Kilpatrick, Edmunds, & Seymour, 1992).

Moreover, although many crime indices are falling (e.g., robbery, arson, and property crime), the crime of sexual assault is on the rise (Federal Bureau of Investigation [FBI], 2002). In addition to these statistics, there are nearly 500,000 cases of child sexual abuse each year (Buchwald, Fletcher, & Roth, 1993). Risk for sexual assault also is closely linked with a variety of other social problems, such as developmental disability (Valenti-Hein & Schwartz, 1995), suicide, drug and alcohol abuse, juvenile delinquency, domestic violence, and needing social welfare or psychiatric assistance (New York City Alliance Against Sexual Assault, 2003).

Importantly, the United States Department of Justice Bureau of Justice Statistics (2002) emphasized that intimates (boyfriends, ex-boyfriends, husbands, and ex-husbands) commit at least 20% of rapes, acquaintances 50%, and strangers less than 30%. Clearly, sexual assault must be seen not merely as a problem related to social deviance but one that is grotesquely common, even in our most intimate relationships. It cannot be surprising, then, that only about 1 in 100 rapists is sentenced to more than a year in prison, and as many as a quarter of convicted rapists do not serve any time in prison (Buchwald et al., 1993). District attorneys and juries find few sexual assault cases, especially those in which the victim knew her attacker, to be extraordinary enough to prosecute or convict. The number of sexual assaults committed, coupled with the lack of severe consequences for committing this crime, may explain why many have argued that the United States is a "rape-prone" culture (e.g., Buchwald et al., 1993; Caputi, 1987; Russo, 2001). Moreover, although the past few decades have witnessed a demonstrable increase in our knowledge of "endemic interpersonal, familial, and institutionalized violence against women" (Russo, 2001, p. 23), the organizations seeking to address this violence continue to be met with funding cuts and reluctant social support.

As feminists, one of whom is a sexual abuse survivor and the other of whom has engaged in significant research with survivors, we are drawn to community activism about this issue. As communication scholars, we know that many of the problems surrounding sexual assault and the treatment of victims are related to several communication issues. For example, we have written elsewhere about the role of self-disclosure and storytelling in the process of surviving sexual assault (Ford & Crabtree, 2002; Ford, Ray, & Ellis, 1999; see also Petronio, Flores, & Hecht's, 1997, work on disclosure of stigmatized information, including sexual abuse). In this chapter, we discuss our community volunteerism and communication activism with our local rape crisis center.

FROM COMMUNITY ACTIVISTS TO COMMUNICATION CONSULTANTS: OUR STORIES

To illustrate the ways that activist consulting can grow organically from a scholar's life in a community, we explore our evolution from community volunteers to activist communication consultants in our long-term association with SARC. This part of the chapter is constructed in first-person narratives, as our activism is embedded in our personal stories and evolved as part of our lives in this community.

Robbin: From Victim to Survivor to Activist

There is a significant body of literature on the process of surviving sexual assault that suggests victims move through different stages of recovery (e.g., Bass & Davis, 1988; Grossman, 1991). I have come to see these stages in my life as victim, survivor, activist, and thriver (see also Dinsmore, 1991). For me, the decision to become a sexual assault activist grew out of my experience as an adult survivor of childhood sexual abuse, as well as my feminist politics, generally, and my life in a New Mexico community, more specifically. It also seemed like a logical step: I had "told" (or disclosed that the sexual abuse had taken place), and then I told my story as a research participant (see Ford & Crabtree, 2002; Ford et al., 1999). In reflecting on my experience of telling and retelling, I am reminded of Daly's (1998) powerful explorations of surviving incest and agree that "recovery is primarily, though not exclusively, a linguistic event" (p. 3; see also Lawless, 2000; Lempert, 1994; Russo, 2002). Becoming involved with SARC was an integral part of my healing process, of this unfolding personal journey, and has been as deeply private and personal as it has been deliberately public and political.

During the fall of 1994, I was preparing to teach an MA course called "Communication and Social Change" and wanted to incorporate a service-learning project to facilitate student learning of communication theories as applied to the needs of a specific agency—SARC—and to the promotion of a specific event—"Take Back the Night" (TBTN). TBTN events began in Germany in the 1970s as a community response to a serial rapist, and the event has since spread worldwide, with TBTN events held annually in hundreds of U.S. cities. Whereas some TBTN events are marches, protests, and vigils, the SARC-sponsored event additionally functions as a fundraiser for the organization. Because I had been involved in TBTN events in many of my previous communities, and because I knew that TBTN in southern New Mexico had been poorly attended and even more poorly publicized the previous year, it occurred to me that this would make a great class project. I contacted the executive director of SARC and pitched the idea to her in the fall and to the class in the spring (with an alternative assignment for any uninterested or unwilling students). The students were enthusiastic and all elected to participate in the semester-long, applied communication project.

SARC's executive director was initially suspicious of this project due to prior relationships with the university that had been largely one-sided, benefiting student learning more than the agency or community (see discussions of such issues in service learning by Cruz & Giles, 2000; Driscoll, Holland, Gelmon, & Kerrigan, 1996; Droge & Murphy, 1999; Sapp & Crabtree, 2002). Nevertheless, based on the clear focus of the project, as well as my personal commitment (along with her knowledge of my personal history), she agreed that the class could collaborate with her agency. It was arranged that the class would form committees to support the agency staff and volunteer corps in the planning and executing of the 1995 TBTN event, which included a fundraising 5-kilometer walk/10-kilometer run, a rally with music and speakers, and a candlelight vigil (for a complete description of the course and the ways it was grounded in pedagogical theory, see Crabtree, 1999).

As one way of demonstrating my good faith to the agency's executive director, and as an activist turn in my healing process (although I do not think I understood this link at the time), I spent my spring break undertaking SARC's 40-hour crisis advocate training program and became one of only two Spanish-speaking crisis intervention volunteers. I spent the Friday night of the last weekend of that spring break at the local hospital emergency room helping a family through the sexual assault examination of their 16-year-old daughter. This would be the first of many nights I would spend in the emergency room with victims over the next 7 years or on the hotline with struggling survivors, experiences that challenged my interpersonal and intercultural communication skills, not to mention the effects of these assaults on the abiding hurt and fear that live inside all victims/survivors.

The students in my class took on media relations duties, designed promotion strategies, engaged in some fundraising, and created a special-event planning manual for the agency. In planning, discussing, and assessing these activities, the students applied communication theory and skills before, during, and after that TBTN. The event was a success, as we raised over $2000 (compared to breaking even the year before), in addition to doubling the attendance of any previous years' events. A few of the students also chose to undertake the advocate training program (later in that semester or during the following summer) and served as volunteers at SARC long after the class ended. One of the students ultimately became a victim's advocate in the Las Cruces District Attorney's office after the completion of her communication MA program.

The students' responses to this activism suggested that most were positive about the experience. For example, one student was quoted in our campus newspaper, which covered the community-based learning experience as a news story, saying, "I thought it was an excellent idea to take what we've learned and apply it. Most graduate classes are theory, but this class was a great chance to take what we've learned and put it back into the community" (quoted in Van Cott, 1995, p. 5). In formally evaluating the course, one student said that what she liked most about this class was "the fact that we focused on conducting an actual communication campaign rather than just reading and writing papers about them. I found the class meaningful." Another student later wrote to me: "Thanks for showing me, through your teaching and work, how communication can change the world." After her graduation, another student wrote to me, "You got me hooked on social change. . . . I owe much of my compassion and devotion to social change causes to your [course]." These students' accounts confirm the power of bringing communication theory and skills to bear on community problems and remind us that we are not just teachers but potential role models of engaged citizenship.

This course-related association with SARC evolved into a long-term relationship for me with this agency. After the class was over, I continued to serve as a crisis advocate, spending at least 24 hours each month staffing the hotline and being prepared to answer a call to go to the hospital to meet another victim. I was elected by the advocate corps to be the advocate representative to SARC's Board of Directors and, after that term expired, was elected by the board to a regular position. Not surprisingly, given my communication background, I served on the committees of the board that handled media relations and event planning, often acting as agency spokesperson at public events and with the media, especially as related to TBTN and high-profile sexual assault cases.

Finally, I developed a major training unit for SARC advocates with respect to media criticism, which I believed to be vitally important in preparing crisis intervention advocates and other agency volunteers. Media analysis and critique often are new to rape crisis advocate trainees, who may have been inspired by a desire to help others, or may be recovering from an assault and are themselves making an activist turn, but who have not engaged in systematic social analysis or developed a set of critical tools for understanding the relationships between media and society. However, as we analyze the media context within which sexual assault is both prevalent and made normative, we find that these images and stories seem to form a collective consciousness in our culture that promotes or condones particular and patterned attitudes related to sexual relations and sexual assault, such as "Women ask for it," "Some women want or need to be raped," or "When women say 'no,' they really mean 'yes'" (see, e.g., Jhally's, 1995, videotape *Dreamworlds II*, which we often use in the training; see also Caputi, 1987). Thus, I taught my students and advocate trainees that media images and narratives promote and support the potential development of the public's beliefs about sex, gender, desire, and power. Although current media effects research cautions against making strong claims of causality between media practices and people's behavior, the FBI sexual assault statistics document the corresponding social reality.

I also functioned as co-chair of the TBTN event for 4 additional years. The event continued to grow from more than 100 participants in 1996 (Parsons, 1996), to 150 the next year, to 200 in 1998 (Carlson, 1998). Newspaper coverage also changed over time, focusing more on important issues related to sexual assault (e.g., statistics and effects) and the services provided by SARC rather than on my role as a faculty member or the involvement of students in a course (Doengens, 1997). In 1998, an article emphasized the fact that New Mexico ranked fifth in the nation in reported sexual assaults and third in most responsive programs, including SARC's program (Carlson, 1998); in 1999, newspaper coverage focused on a candlelight vigil (the most emotionally charged part of TBTN), where over 50 people gathered to call out the first names (or pseudonyms) of people they knew who had been sexually assaulted (with over 200 participating in the walk/run and rally earlier that day) (Polly, 1999). Newspaper articles also were longer each year and appeared in more prominent sections of the paper. For example, in 1996 (Parsons), the article in the campus newspaper, which included a photo, was buried on page 8; in 1997 (Doengens), the campus paper ran the story on page 4; and in 1999 (Polly), an article appeared in the local paper, on the front page of the Local/State section, above the fold, with a 30-point headline and a photograph.

As previously explained, my duties with TBTN, and in conjunction with my academic identity and responsibilities, involved being a media spokesperson and media analyst; I, thus, was an activist leader at the TBTN event at the same time that I was the faculty advisor to involved student groups, both those who were students in my classes and those who were involved in student organizations, such as the women's studies student group and the lesbian/gay/bisexual/transgender student group. The lines between teacher, mentor, advisor, activist, volunteer, and consultant, therefore, were blurred. On the one hand, as I stood in front of the crowd at the TBTN rallies offering rape statistics, media criticism, elements of my story, and calls to action, I remember feeling unified, in a Zen-like state of oneness among my heart, mind, and body and with respect to my personal journey, academic interests, and politics. On the other hand, as we discuss in a later section of this chapter, there is a "dark side" to this blurring of roles and boundaries, and for survivors (and perhaps for feminist educators as well), boundaries can be tricky things.

It should not be surprising that I developed a fervent loyalty to SARC, in large part because the issue of sexual assault was so dwarfed by other community "causes." For example, it was popular for women on the faculty at the university to serve on boards of the local children's charities and for self-identified feminist professors to support the battered women's shelter or the local Planned Parenthood Association. Unfortunately, sexual assault was a relatively silenced issue, even among feminist activists and community volunteers, and the local women's shelter resisted linking the two agencies when such an opportunity arose, perhaps due to discomfort with this association, personality clashes between the two executive directors, or other factors. Perhaps my years of silence drove me to a fervent extremism in my activism; I often was judgmental of what I perceived as "liberal" service choices, whereas I perceived myself to be out there on the radical edge, speaking the truth that was swept under the family bed, just as it was hidden in the reporting practices of campus police and university administrators. I also had been deeply influenced by the personal charisma and the political clarity of SARC's first executive director, who was the co-founder of the agency and who conducted my 40-hour training in rape crisis advocacy.

Aside from the activism and consulting I continued to do with/for the agency, my partnership with SARC fed back into my university duties in many ways. Subsequent classes I taught in communication and women's studies incorporated service-learning options, and many students took advantage of my contacts at SARC to work with that agency in a variety of capacities. In conjunction with my membership on the Women's Studies Program steering committee, I became the faculty liaison to SARC and often worked with student groups on campus to bring greater public awareness to the problem of sexual assault, as well as to recruit volunteers for SARC.

By the time I took a sabbatical leave beginning in the fall of 1999, my roles as community activist, communication professor, and communication consultant to SARC were tightly woven together as part of the tapestry that was my life in New Mexico. What began as a class project, emerged as part of my healing process and evolved into intensive, long-term community activism, eventually looked a lot like a consultancy in which my academic expertise was called on to assist with particular agency-identified problems. Consistent with feminist theorizing, the boundaries were blurred between the personal, professional, and political, as well as between the activist and the academic (see also M. Anderson, Fine, Geissler, & Landenson; 1997; Ford & Crabtree, 2002; hooks, 1994). This journey demonstrates that our personal lives, professional responsibilities, and political activism can be derived from and mutually reinforcing of one another. As Russo (2002) noted of her experience with sexual assault, the "Feminist movement helped me to find my strengths through talking back, speaking and acting out, and collectively organizing for social justice" (p. 196). Thus, I could not be an activist and rape crisis volunteer and leave my media and communication theories in the classroom, nor could I be a teacher of courses in media, gender, family, and intercultural communication and forget that I spent one night a week answering a hotline or meeting victims at the hospital, or that I am a sexual assault survivor (a fact I do not always disclose) within a rape-prone culture. Although I left New Mexico in the fall of 2001 to take another faculty position, which ended my formal association with SARC, the experiences narrated here continue to impact my teaching, and activism continues to be interwoven with my healing journey.

Leigh: From Organizational Theory to Organizational Survival

My path to community activism evolved from my feminist politics and my personal friendship and professional relationship with Robbin. As a feminist scholar, I was, of course, conscious of the pervasiveness of sexual violence, particularly against women, in U.S. culture, and of the complex gender and power dynamics that fuel it, but at the time, it was not the key focus of my political activism as a citizen or as an academic. In their advocacy for community-based health promotion, Bernstein et al. (1994) argued that "racism, sexism, ageism, ableism, classism, and ethnocentrism are not just politically correct words; they are realities—the faces of people, their lives, personal and community biographies" (p. 292). In short, one does not have to look far to see the day-to-day expression of injustice.

After the first brief period of Robbin's association with SARC, she suggested to the executive director that I might be a potential board member. In Robbin's judgment, my expertise in organizational and health communication, and my commitment to teaching, research, and service related to women's issues, seemed like a perfect match with SARC's needs. After meeting over coffee with the executive director to discuss the agency, its needs and mission, and my possible contributions, I was elected to the board on her recommendation.

As part of my commitment to this service, I participated in the 40-hour advocate training scheduled soon after my appointment to the board. This training, held 3-4 times a year, was optional but encouraged for new board members; however, few took the time or made the emotional investment to do it. Although I did not volunteer as a crisis advocate, the training program inspired in me a deep commitment to this social justice issue, as evidenced by my later academic work with survivors of incest, and my involvement with SARC, as evidenced by many nights of sleeplessness and worry over its fate.

In my first 2 months on the board, all of the strengths and weaknesses of this small agency were readily visible to me from my standpoint as "outsider-within." The agency relied heavily on the activist leadership of the executive director, who was passionately committed to the issue of sexual assault and feminist resistance against violence against women. Her extraordinary commitment and feminist politics, however, resulted in conflict between her and other organizations in the community, some of which were quite powerful and necessary cooperative partners for SARC to meet its clients' needs. For example, law enforcement in this community, as in many other communities, was male dominated, patriarchal in its ideology, and traditional in its definitions of crime and law enforcement; officers often stated that they disliked being dispatched on sexual assault calls and sometimes revictimized women with their questions and demeanor. In this conservative culture, perhaps the executive director's openly lesbian identity and politics also increased the discomfort felt by many law enforcement agents. These conditions exacerbated the marginalization of the sexual assault issue and the agency in a community that already had difficulty confronting sexual violence.

The feminist leadership model espoused by the executive director also created internal structural problems within SARC. Relationships in the organization relied on intense interpersonal commitments among the leader, the small number of paid personnel (i.e., individuals contracted to provide counseling to survivors), and volunteers (both crisis advocates and board members). Board participation was strongly defined by loyalty to and support of the leader, severely restricting open discussion about the long-term interests of the agency and resulting in decision making that was immediate and crisis driven. Furthermore, despite the executive director's proclaimed commitment to feminist, collaborative, consensus-style decision making, board decisions were usually confirmations of decisions determined by her prior to board meetings.

Although a crisis mode often characterizes small, nonprofit activist groups, this agency—relatively new and on the margins of its community and within the larger society—lacked both fiscal and social capital. It was largely invisible and unidentifiable to large segments of the community and suffered from the lack of network connections to outside stakeholders in the organization's mission, such as local hospital leadership, law enforcement, and school personnel, and to visible power brokers in the community. Those members committed to the agency and the executive director valued the political vision she eloquently articulated as pure and righteous, but that vision and the commitment to her as an individual obscured the material survival of the agency and, thus, risked the loss of valuable services to those affected by sexual assault and abuse.

Shortly after I joined the board, the always-precarious financial condition of the organization became untenable. As a stopgap measure, a slightly less expensive rental space for the agency was located, and I found myself as a personal signatory on the lease for this new space. In an effort to save the agency from financial extinction, the executive director, whose burnout was evident and whose salary constituted the bulk of the agency's financial commitments, resigned. This left a part-time counseling staff and a few committed board members to direct the day-to-day activities of the agency and develop strategies to ensure the long-term viability of the agency.

When the executive director announced her resignation, the local newspaper noted the agency's financial crisis and supported the need for such an agency in our community. This publicity resulted in two important actions that ensured SARC's survival. First, another defunct community agency was given permission by its board to transfer its remaining assets to SARC, a lifesaving gift that allowed another board member and me time to work on state and federal grant renewal applications (e.g., monies available through the Violence Against Women Act and Victims of Crime Act). Receipt of this financial gift and the grants that were awarded later were critical to the long-term survival of the agency.

The second event raised community awareness of the agency's plight and moved the agency itself and the valuable services it provided from the margins of the community's consciousness. At the time of the newspaper article about SARC's financial problems, a former resident was visiting her family from her home in Los Angeles. She was outraged that the agency was on the verge of collapse and was determined to do something about it. She was politically well connected in the local community and in Los Angeles through her position as an assistant to Edward James Olmos, the Latino actor-activist. At her personal request, Olmos immediately agreed to appear at a benefit for SARC that featured his most recent film and speak at other events in southern New Mexico to advocate for local and state support of SARC.

Suddenly, the few remaining volunteer board members were responsible for managing the leaderless agency and a major community fundraising event. The demands of hosting such an event were beyond the skills, time, and energy of what was now largely a volunteer agency. However, the popularity of Olmos in the community led to the willing cooperation of other local groups in the planning and execution of the benefit. Although the events surrounding Olmos's visit did not focus solely on SARC (the primary issue of concern to our collaborators was youth violence), the visibility of the agency, the alliances it forged with other community groups, and the presence of powerful community figures at these events certainly created an increased openness to the agency and the issue of sexual assault for many in the community who had not previously been reached or supportive.

Meanwhile, of course, the agency members needed to continue their day-to-day activities: providing counseling to sexual assault survivors and their families, offering support and advocacy services at the hospital emergency room, testifying in court, participating in educational and outreach efforts in schools and the surrounding community, training and supervising rape-crisis advocates, and managing the daily activities of any small business. Another board member and I became the de facto supervisory personnel of these activities, a part-time volunteer oversaw the office, and a part-time, paid staff member supervised the advocates and their work.

I also began efforts to recruit new board members, an effort guided by the goals of increasing diversity, community visibility, and representation from the agency's various stakeholders, such as law enforcement, the medical community, educational institutions, and other violence prevention and victim advocacy groups. This effort was facilitated by my service on another community board for a high school wellness center and my research with the local medical center's emergency room staff. Another critical component of the board membership was the need for Hispanic representation; although Hispanics (the locally preferred identifier) made up the majority of the local population, they were underrepresented on community boards like SARC's. In addition to the community network relationships now linked to the board, the growing network of relationships that Robbin and I developed through our community-based research activities with lay community health workers in the U.S.-Mexico border region (see Crabtree & Ford, 1998; Ford et al., 1998) provided much-needed access to the Hispanic community. The board of directors subsequently gained numbers, expertise, and stability. Now numbering about a dozen people, the board engaged in professional development activities conducted by local experts, and the board structure was redesigned so that each board member served on a subcommittee, based on his or her professional expertise, with specific responsibilities, such as finance, personnel, community outreach, counseling, and education services.

With the necessary development of the board, a search for a new executive director was undertaken with a goal of creating stability in the day-to-day operations of the agency. In the job description, the board developed a professional profile emphasizing nonprofit experience and administrative skills; neither a personal nor professional understanding of the issue of sexual assault was given priority. In some respects, the demise of the activist philosophy of the organization was complete with the creation of that description and the hiring of the new executive director. The new executive director had several years of managerial experience in a government-sponsored social agency. The board sought and found someone who could lead the agency to a new philosophy and structure consistent with that of most nonprofit organizations, emphasizing legitimization through cooperation with state agencies and conservative funding organizations, such as the United Way. Radical critiques of a rape-prone culture gave way to moderate social service rhetoric and practices. Russo (2001) argued that the process of sexual assault service agencies evolving from feminist movements or activist efforts to state-sanctioned institutions is, in fact, typical (see also Matthews, 1994). This is consistent with the literature on social movement organizations, more generally, as well as with their development over time. As these social organizations become more professionalized and institutionalized over time, they tend to develop more bureaucratic and hierarchical characteristics, often losing touch with their activist roots and radical base (see, e.g., Donati, 1996).

These efforts to formalize and stabilize the organization were not without their costs. As one example, at the beginning of my activism with this agency, the board consisted of five members, only three of whom were working diligently to save the organization. Furthermore, for many board members, staff, and volunteers, the loyalties to the former executive director remained strong, particularly in the few months following her departure, when none of us were certain that the agency could survive. Understandably, some members continued their relationship with the previous executive director and reported to her the activities of the board and agency. As the board and agency moved to enact relationships defined by rules and formal boundaries, however, communication of board discussions with the previous executive director clearly violated the agreed-on and necessary confidentiality regarding board deliberations. This led to a particularly difficult board discussion and vote to remove an individual from the board for violating that agreement. As painful as the episode was for many associated with the agency, including the former executive director, this event signaled an important turning point in the life of the organization—a move from an identity synonymous with an individual to an organizational identity (see, e.g., Donati, 1996; Matthews, 1994; Russo, 2001).

I had two overarching, interrelated objectives in my service to SARC. The first was to develop an internal operational structure and an external funding system that would ensure the long-term stability and viability of the agency. During this period of time, SARC went from an annual budget of $35,000 to a budget of nearly $250,000. Both board and organizational policies were formally developed and articulated in SARC documents. The number of paid employees increased by one when we hired a full-time office assistant. We also were able to offer a more competitive salary to the executive director, and a salary and benefits plan structure with predictable amounts was instituted. Increased financial stability also allowed us to reimburse contracted counseling services at a rate more closely aligned with local professional rates. State and federal grants continued to be the primary sources of funding for the agency, and the performance of the agency was externally evaluated as outstanding. These evaluations demonstrated to the community and to granting agencies that SARC was fulfilling its stated mission effectively and was fiscally responsible. As a consequence, our grant applications were regularly funded by the state agencies that administer them. Furthermore, as a result of our growing reputation, the state supported the agency's efforts to provide "satellite" services in three other small border communities, including sexual assault training for local lay community health workers, the hiring and training of local nurses, and the creation of liaisons with local law enforcement. Finally, near the end of my 5 years of volunteer work with the agency, we had grown and now needed to occupy three separate office suites to house the staff and deliver services.

My second important objective was to reduce the marginalization of both the agency and the issue of sexual assault in the community. Through the agency's participation in community activities and through progressively building personal and community agency links, this goal was slowly realized. For example, each year the local arts council sponsors a Renaissance art festival that draws huge crowds from across the southern part of the state, and local nonprofit groups compete to operate food concessions in the limited number of spaces available. As board president, I was determined that our agency would receive one of those slots, less as a fundraiser than for the visibility it would afford our agency and our introduction to an audience to which we rarely had access—the general population of the community. We were selected to participate, and although we did not make a great deal of money, we were situated, physically and psychologically, among other, more mainstream nonprofit groups in the community.

The significance of changing the structure and composition of the board of directors of SARC cannot be overstated. First, the board membership increased in numbers and representativeness over time and included, at one time or another, the local hospital emergency room nurse-manager, a local obstetrician/gynecologist, a sheriff's office representative, a middle-school guidance counselor, and a real-estate broker and former president of the city's Chamber of Commerce. Sexual assault survivors, university professors, and a representative of the crisis-advocate corps also served. The board also diversified to include men, previously excluded, as well as several individuals from the Hispanic community, as discussed earlier. This board diversification, including a strategic plan to increase cooperative activities with victims' assistance groups, the local domestic violence shelter, and other related service agencies, were important steps that moved the agency to a more central role in the community's consciousness.

I also should say that our visibility increased as the result of two horrific sexual assaults involving local coeds from our university, one that concerned a university teaching assistant abducting and raping a student who was 8 months pregnant, and the other involving the abduction, sexual assault, and murder of an undergraduate student. The public attention these events garnered, and SARC's ability to address these situations with appropriate, timely, and much-needed services to the victims and their families and friends, served the community well during the very difficult times following these crimes and the subsequent trials of the perpetrators. Nonetheless, it was unfortunate that it took heinous crimes such as these to improve the agency's profile in the community.

Robbin's narrrative rather seamlessly weaves together her contributions to the agency with the communication theories that informed her participation. I have consciously left out theory in my narrative, in part, because the links between the organizational or leadership theories of the communication discipline and my work with SARC were fragmented and more often a result of an unconscious application of knowledge rather than a deliberate act. For example, I know the benefits and risks of charismatic leadership, as well as the features and consequences of bureaucratization; I thought about the importance of effectively constructing an organizational identity for the agency and for its publics; and the power of interorganizational linkages on corporate boards informed my ideas about what needed to be done to strengthen our nonprofit board of directors. I drew on this knowledge base in my volunteerism, as my academic training is a part of who I am, how I view the world, and how I approach problems, but I never used this knowledge systematically, rigorously, or in a unified, analytical way. I could have provided a theoretical rationale for why I was doing what I was doing at the time, but most of the time, no one asked and I did not interrogate myself. In 1999, I took a faculty position at another university and, thus, ended my formal association with SARC, although the work narrated here continues to inform my teaching and community-based activism.

THE DIALECTICAL RELATIONSHIP BETWEEN ACTIVISM AND CONSULTING

In the opening parts of this chapter, we briefly described the macro-level tension between (and within) academe and community as universities grapple with their role in U.S. society. Furthermore, we posited that this tension emerges at the micro level in the day-to-day activities and communicative practices of professors, students, and community members as we work together to solve problems. In this section, we examine the traditional positioning of the professor-as-consultant and professor-as-activist roles as being dichotomous. Using the narratives of our work at SARC as source data and feminist narrative analysis as the method for interpreting those data (e.g., Bloom, 1998), we reflexively analyze our experiences and offer a reconceptualization of the activist-consultant dichotomy as a dialectical relationship rife with contradictions that are fundamentally unresolvable but manageable.

Activist or Consultant: Definitional Constraints

In its simplest terms, *consulting* has been defined as "intervening into an organization to stop some destructive process" (DeWine, 1994, p. 30) and, as a consequence of the intervention, enhancing organizational effectiveness. Traditionally, within the academic community, consulting has been conceptualized narrowly as an activity in which scholars provide their expertise to business organizations for a fee. These consulting interventions typically occur in one of three forms: (a) a problem is identified by an organization and the consultant recommends solutions; (b) an organization requests that the consultant identify the problem, as well as recommend solutions; or (c) a collaborative identification of the problem and its solutions develops through two-way communication between the organization and the consultant (DeWine, 1994; Sherwood, 1981).

Not surprisingly, consulting activities increasingly have been valued by the academy, where budgets are strained, corporate rhetoric increasingly pervades the university (see, e.g., McMillan & Cheney, 1996), and corporate-based foundations provide more and more of the research funding on campuses (Ehrenhaus, 1991). In the literature on the academic-as-consultant, the symbiotic relationship between academic researchers and corporate interests has presumed benefits for both parties in the relationship (see March, 1991; Rebne, 1989; White, 2001). The academic-consultant typically receives personal remuneration, as well as the opportunity to fund research and academic travel needs, and, in some cases, may publish the research for academic audiences and academic advancement (March, 1991; Plax, 1991). The organization benefits from the research and skills training provided by the consultant, purchasing services and expertise externally that are unavailable or difficult to manage in a cost-effective manner internally. Furthermore, those in positions of leadership in the organization gain proprietary knowledge about their employees and their organizational functioning, information that increases the control those in power have over their members in service of bottom-line profits.

Thus, there exists a clear for-profit bias in how consulting by academics currently is conceptualized and conducted in the academy. However, such a view of consulting has raised questions within academe about the ownership and use of the knowledge produced through such endeavors and the ways consulting relates to democratic principles of teaching, research, and service (see White, 2001). Critical and feminist scholars have problematized the ways conventional consulting privileges the managerial class (e.g., Alvesson, 1993; Buzzanell, 2000; Deetz, 1992; Mumby, 1993; see also Ritchie, this volume) and have argued that this bias reinforces the social, political, and economic inequalities of our social structure (Frey et al., 1996; also see Pollock, Artz, Frey, Pearce, & Murphy, 1996).

Set in contrast to the professor-as-consultant role is the professor-as-activist role. Here, a professor's role is predicated on community involvement in the service of a social justice issue, working with and for marginalized groups to reduce inequalities. Frey et al. (1996) described an activist orientation as a necessary condition of a social justice sensibility:

> A social justice sensibility entails a moral imperative to *act* as effectively as we can to do something about structurally sustained inequalities. To continue to pursue justice, it is perhaps necessary that we who act be personally ethical, but that is not sufficient. Our actions must engage and transform social structures. (p. 111)

The achievement of a social justice goal is accomplished through the types of philosophies, theories, and methodologies (e.g., PAR and FAR) discussed earlier. The active involvement of a community in the identification of community needs and assets (see Herman & Ettema, Volume 2), commitment to uncovering strategies collaboratively for solving community problems, and engagement in collective action to address those needs characterizes this perspective (Ansley & Gaventa, 1997; Brown & Tandon, 1983; Hall, 1981; Ryan, Carragee, & Schwerner, 1998). The professor-as-activist, thus, is a participant in this community dialogue, working in solidarity with the community to create "structures that make available opportunities for all people to express their unique selves and insert themselves into the human world through speech and action" (Frey et al., 1996, p. 111).

In practice, when the agenda is promoting social justice, the boundaries between the professor-as-consultant and professor-as-activist seem artificial and blurred. For example, in their argument for increased attention by scholars to marginalized communities and participatory communicative practices in health promotion within these communities, Ford and Yep (2003) acknowledged that "contradiction, paradox, and dialectical tension characterize this pursuit" (p. 255). Based on our experiences as community activists with SARC, we believe that the roles of activist and consultant, and the communicative demands that characterize each, may more fruitfully be conceptualized as contradictions, existing in dynamic tension with one another. Saying we are activists in philosophical orientation and have preferences for participatory methods does not negate the fact that we often function as consultants—despite the community-based, unfunded, and voluntary nature of our work—and we should not, therefore, rebuke the value of the consultant role. Thus, we propose here an alternative conceptualization that acknowledges the complex dialectics of community-based activism *and* consulting. We believe, as shown in our analysis, that the concept of dialectics provides a useful analytical lens for understanding the challenges of working in and with communities.

The Primary Dialectic: Activist-Consultant

According to Baxter and Montgomery (1996), a dialectical framework is an effort to do justice to the multifaceted, complex, and sometimes disordered nature of social life. Central to this framework is the goal of understanding the knot of contradictions constituting social relations and the manifestation of those contradictions in communicative practices. *Contradictions*, or "the dynamic interplay of unified oppositions" (Baxter & Montgomery, 1998, p. 4), exhibit two basic features. First, phenomena are opposites if they are actively incompatible and mutually negate one another definitionally, logically, or functionally. Second, although characterized as mutually negating, dialectical opposites are simultaneously interdependent with one another; that is, each oppositional force depends on the other for its meaning. For example, in relationships, partners may desire *both* a feeling of connectedness *and* a desire for some degree of autonomy or independence. These are ostensibly opposing forces, yet they are interdependently negotiated within relationships and, one could argue, relational satisfaction depends on the ability to achieve both desires.

During our time with SARC, we experienced the activist-consultant contradiction. This apparent opposition may be seen as the primary dialectic, but in practice, multiple interrelated dialectics emerged from this over-arching contradiction. In the following section, we describe these secondary dialectical tensions and provide examples that illustrate the "both-and" nature of the activist-consultant dialectic. It should be noted that these primary and secondary dialectics function in concert and in context; as such, no single contradiction can be considered, defined, and understood in isolation from other contradictions (Werner & Baxter, 1994), and the meaningfulness of any contradiction always must be understood *in situ* (Baxter & Montgomery, 1996). Examples from our experiences illustrate these dialectical tensions and how we managed them in our work for SARC.

Secondary Dialectic: Participant-Observer

Emerging from the primary activist-consultant dialectic, the standpoint of the scholar and the outcomes of her or his participation in and with an organization result in the secondary tension of participant-observer. In the consultant role, the scholar assumes a standpoint outside and apart from the normal day-to-day functioning of an organization and presumes an objectivity not available to those enmeshed in the organization's problem and activities. DeWine (1994) described the many roles of consultants as "an eclectic practitioner, a facilitator, a situational expert, a lay technician, a resource identifier," and concluded with "a temporary associate" (p. 12). Indeed, the outsider observational standpoint of a consultant is facilitated by the temporariness of the relationship, its contractual constraints, and its problem-solution orientation (DeWine, 1994).

In contrast, the activist scholar is a member of and a participant in a community. Furthermore, this standpoint reflects solidarity with the community and a social justice sensibility of identification with others (Frey et al., 1996). In this standpoint, the activist is enmeshed in the stories and perspectives of community members, including his or her own, and values the subjectivity of personal experience as the expression of multiple truths, which leads to the social construction of shared assumptions about what is perceived to be true, real, and valued (Mumby, 1997). From this participant standpoint, the process itself is the focal point of evaluation, and participation in that process, in particular, is valued as "the normative standard by which all acts of communication can be judged" (Deetz, 1999, p. 147). Such immersion in a community suggests a level of commitment grounded in long-term involvement working for social change. Thus, as community activists, our goal was not to conduct research, either for our purposes or those of the agency; our goal was to resist our culture's violence against women and to work with SARC for community-based social change.

Over the years of our activism at SARC, however, contradictions between these standpoints emerged. Indeed, in our activities with SARC, we often found ourselves positioned as "outsiders-within," to borrow a term from Collins (2000). In this position, we were able to view simultaneously the standpoint of participants in the organization and the standpoints in the community. As outsiders-within, we experienced the ongoing tensions of simultaneous objectivity and subjectivity and concerns for both process and outcome. In a very real sense, in experiencing the participant-observer dialectic, we could see the problems and their solutions, but also were part of those problems and solutions.

As a board member, for example, Leigh experienced this dialectic when a personnel problem arose in the organization. Approximately 6 months after her hire, there was a dispute between the executive director and one of the providers contracted by the agency to offer ongoing counseling for survivors. The dispute itself was both substantive and personal, as the two women had distinctly different communication styles and approaches to solving problems. When these two individuals could not resolve the dispute, the board intervened and a hearing was convened. For Leigh, this was a situation fraught with dialectical tensions. For example, objectively, the board had established personnel and procedural guidelines that could guide the board's review of the matter and, ultimately, its decision. Intellectually, and to preserve the integrity of the process, Leigh knew this was what needed to be done. Furthermore, given the brevity of the new executive director's tenure, Leigh believed that the board needed to be supportive of the new executive director. Simultaneously, and subjectively, Leigh also felt strong loyalties to the contract provider, who had been with SARC since its beginning and stuck with it during the very difficult days when it was unclear whether it would survive. This provider also was a strong supporter of the agency beyond her role as a counselor and volunteered her help in many activities. Moreover, Leigh thought of her as a friend. In addition, as Leigh interacted with the new executive director, she found her to be technically competent but, at times, interpersonally abrupt, sometimes speaking without thinking about the effects of her words. In short, the tensions of being both an observer and a participant emerged throughout this incident.

Robbin's experiences as outsider-within also produced layered tensions. As a survivor of sexual abuse, Robbin was an insider in the most significant way; this "credential" served as valuable cultural capital in the agency among the advocate volunteer corps and feminist activists in the community. As a survivor and crisis advocate, Robbin was a participant. However, as a scholar and Anglo-American professor at the university, she also was very much an outsider, as evidenced by the curious or cool reception she often received from the largely working-class, often Hispanic, and rarely graduate-educated agency staff members, volunteers, victims, and families. As part of her personal communication style, Robbin speaks theory as fluently as she speaks English or Spanish, but as it is in most community groups outside the academy, "theory-speak" is a foreign tongue in New Mexico. Robbin's personality, in fact, reveals her observer status because she is ever the ethnographer, analyst, and critic, despite the fact that formal research was not being conducted. Even the increasingly professional board of directors often found her analytical nature and tendency toward politicization a bit eccentric. Robbin's insider status as an agency volunteer and early member of the advocate corps also came into play during the agency's transition. She was a close friend of the original executive director and deeply invested in the feminist politics on which the agency was founded. She moved from agency insider to board outsider as the board of directors, staff, and agency professional character evolved, and was finally the last remaining member of the "old guard." Radical feminism, which began as a ticket to insider status and was strengthened from being involved with the agency and its original director, thus, emerged as a symbol of outsider status as the activist roots of SARC gave way to a professional organizational staff and structure in the process of ensuring the agency's survival in this relatively conservative community.

Secondary Dialectic: Dialogic-Authoritarian

Of key concern to the activist-consultant dialectic is the nature of the communicative relationship between the scholar and the community (or the organization or group of people with whom one works). Furthermore, this communicative relationship reflects fundamental beliefs about the distribution of power within the relationship. In the consultant role, the preferred model of intervention emphasizes a collaborative approach to identifying and addressing the organization's problem. Lippitt and Lippitt (1986) viewed consulting as "a two-way interaction process of seeking, giving, and receiving help aimed at aiding a person, group, or organization, or larger system mobilizing internal and external resources to deal with problem confrontations and change efforts" (p. 1). In principle, this participation may appear to be egalitarian, but in its enactment, the consultant is perceived as an expert helper whose interests are allied with those in power in the organization. Hence, this two-way communication serves instrumental interests (usually of management) and installs the consultant in a "power-over" position through personal expertise, possession of organizational knowledge not available to all participants, and temporary, but influential, connections to those in positions of power. Although specific interactions may unfold ostensibly as two-way, in its day-to-day processes and outcomes, the consultation often is didactic and authoritarian.

In the activist role, however, the central communicative activity ideally is a "dialogic encounter." In dialogue, the activist joins the members of the community in openness, listening to all the voices and systems of meaning that may be different from his or her own, and then sharing interpretations to develop a collective knowledge and create a critical consciousness about the issues at hand (Freire, 2000). Through this dialogue, community members and activists mobilize their skills and resources to actively change their situations (see Adams, Berquist, Dillon, & Galanes, this volume; Jovanovic, Steger, Symonds, & Nelson, this volume). These communicative actions on the part of activists reflect a "power-with" orientation.

In practice, however, a dialectical tension emerges between authoritarian and dialogic communication because these orientations to collaboration operate in a both/and dynamic. As Ford and Yep (2003) stated:

> When dialogue occurs, the result is the hopeful possibility that individuals and communities empower themselves, enhancing community, building social capital, leading participants to act in ways that create justice and human understanding. The ideal of dialogue, however, is challenged by multiple barriers to its enactment, barriers as mundane as time and as complex as our multi-layered identities in interaction. (p. 249)

In our work at SARC, activists, practitioners, and community members engaged each other in many ways, some truly dialogic and others less than participatory. In many instances, choice and emancipation in the short term were sacrificed to the need for order and organization, in the hope that choice and emancipation would prevail over the long term. Dialogic and authoritarian approaches, then, are not mutually exclusive but should be viewed in dynamic tension with each other in relation to situational and contextual constraints.

This dialectic can be seen in Leigh's experience during the events leading up to and surrounding the Edward James Olmos benefit events. SARC's board membership had dwindled to six persons at that point, only three of whom appeared to be actively engaged. Several emergency meetings were held during this time to discuss the event, possible partnership with other organizations in the community, and desired outcomes of the event for the agency. In the initial meetings, dialogue characterized the discussions of these ideas and other related concerns, but these meetings led to few actual results and the reintroduction of issues reviewed in previous meetings. The practical, substantive concern of the group was the ability to successfully execute this event, which was a surface manifestation of a deeper fear of losing control of the agenda for the event. Meanwhile, because of the board's hesitancies, the agency already was losing control over the event's agenda, as another group had begun negotiations with Olmos for activities to coincide with our event. At this point, as chair of the board, Leigh abandoned dialogue and used the power of education, persuasive communication skills, and assertiveness to outline forcefully and specifically the position she believed the board needed to take: SARC would cooperate with the other organizations that wanted to be involved, for only with their help could such an event be mounted, a sufficient number of tickets sold, and enough donations be requested and received to succeed. Furthermore, through SARC's association with these other organizations and powerful individuals in the community, the agency would acquire visibility and legitimacy. The board and staff supported this plan, which arose not from dialogue but from a rather authoritarian communication process.

The tensions experienced between dialogic and authoritarian communication resulted in costs and benefits for the agency. Most board members participated minimally in the Olmos event, partly because of the changing organizational dynamics, and these members eventually drifted away from the agency. The event itself, however, was a success, with SARC receiving financial support and increased visibility in the community to a degree. Although SARC sacrificed a central role in the event day's programming to related organizations and their agendas, the agency board never could have managed the size and scope of such an event on its own.

From Robbin's perspective and experience, this dialectic reflects her roles as instructor of a service-learning course, activist-consultant, and, intermittently, an agency representative. With regard to the class, the use of critical and feminist pedagogies means giving up some of the didactic nature of teaching, as well as letting go of some degree of teacher authority and the attendant one-way transmission of knowledge, in exchange for a more dialogic classroom environment, student-teacher relationship, and process of knowledge production, analysis, and critique. Of course, given the presence of grading and the reward/coercive and expert power endemic to the academic institutional context, this authority is difficult if not impossible to shed. As a consultant to SARC, Robbin approached the relationship in a dialogic way at first, which began as part of her association with the first executive director. As SARC evolved, however, the newer agency staff treated her always as a professor and an expert and, consequently, urged her to be more didactic in the training she offered and more authoritarian in event planning and other activities. Moreover, similar to Leigh's experience, Robbin often found that her personal investment meant that she was the one who ended up doing the work. At the end of the day, collaboration and dialogue require partners. In many ways, dialogue is compromised by the short-staffed nature of many nonprofit agencies; consequently, we both often operated as a committee of one in our agency and board duties. Moreover, one's professional status, as we discuss later, often carries more weight in an interaction than one's intentions.

Secondary Dialectic: Personal-Professional

In our analysis of the activist-consultant dialectic, another secondary dialectical tension emerged between the professional and the personal as related to the objectives of organizational transformation and social change. In both the consultant and activist role, the expectation is that *some* change will occur: In the consultant role, the scholar makes recommendations to change the practices of organizational members and, ultimately, the organization itself; in the activist role, the goal is to transform some oppressive social structure through collective action. Each of these roles, however, views differently the impact of the work on the scholar.

In the consultancy framework, the scholar's role is professional and any change to that role via a consulting project is viewed as either unprofessional (e.g., behaving "inappropriately" vis-à-vis the client) or as an enhancement of that professionalism (e.g., increasing the value of one's credentials). Arising from the value-neutral, contractual constraints on this role, the consultant engages in an intellectual enterprise applying his or her skills in service to the organization. The consultant operates solely in the rational realm and does not expect that this experience will transform his or her worldview, and to be perceived as professional, the consultant also must appear to be apolitical. The outcomes of consulting for the scholar have been described in financial terms, of course, but also may include additional professional benefits, such as facilitating research productivity (Mitchell & Rebne, 1995) and keeping course materials relevant (Johnson, 1993).

For the activist, in contrast, personal transformation often accompanies participation in community life and usually presupposes the existence of some political passion as one of the forces motivating action. In addition, a social change sensibility (in contrast to the types of changes a consultant seeks to bring about) not only requires engagement of the activist's intellect but also her or his emotions in the experience. As Frey et al. (1996, p. 115) noted, social justice research "emerges from and channels the emotions of the researcher" in ways not typical in consulting work. By capturing these passions and channeling them into the pursuit of social justice goals, the scholar becomes both teacher and learner in the community, both participant in the transformation of society and transformed by and through that participation. Moreover, a feminist approach to activism politicizes the personal (e.g., Lorber, 2005).

In our experience at SARC, the tension between the personal and the professional was an ever-present dialectic. As illustrated by Leigh's narrative, she was, indeed, an agent of organizational transformation, and her work as board chair, surrogate executive director, and project leader illustrates that she also functioned as an organizational theorist and consultant. The transformation of the organization itself illustrates this dialectic, as the organization moved from its activist roots to achieve professional status in the community. This change was from informal and personal to more formal and professional in agency identity, mission, organizational structure, and image in the community. Moreover, Leigh's transformation further reveals the dynamics of this personal-professional dialectic, for her work as communication consultant and agency volunteer was characterized by an ongoing struggle between the personal and the professional. What started as an intellectual and professional endeavor, as she weighed the skills and knowledge she could bring to the organization, was later caught in the dynamic tension between the need for professional operations and a growing personal and increasingly feminized/politicized critique of U.S. rape culture. Although she applied rational decision-making and other well-studied theories in response to each crisis, the struggle to professionalize the organization was increasingly a personal one, as her identity became caught up in the agency's identity and survival. She also experienced a growing and heart-wrenching familiarity with the issue of sexual assault and women who had survived it, as they became part of her personal network of friends. In the end, Leigh's professional journey and personal story became entangled with the stories of survivors as part of our culture's larger rape narrative.

Robbin's narrative, presented earlier, although largely descriptive of the trajectory of her activist-consulting, hints at powerful struggles with the personal-professional dialectic. As a survivor, Robbin was acutely aware of her personal connection to the issue, as well as to the agency, which together formed the impetus for her class project. Whether she was aware of the ways her personal healing journey were implicated in the community-based, teaching-learning collaborative project is less evidenced in her narrative; indeed, it is through writing this chapter that we both are becoming more aware of these issues (see also Daly, 1998). It is worth noting that Robbin did not disclose her survivor status to her class, in part, because of the powerful taboo against bringing personal information into the classroom, but also as part of an instinct for silence that many survivors consciously and unconsciously employ.

Robbin's students also clearly struggled with this personal-professional dialectic, as illustrated in the following comments on the student evaluation form about "course weaknesses" and "things the instructor should work on": "Not getting so personally involved that the class suffers"; "Sometimes [the class] was a bit loosely organized, but that was a function of the kind of class this was"; and "It seems as though her personal life is affecting her teaching, although I can see how this would happen in a class where you do have to be very involved both personally and academically." Although some students questioned her professionalism, they also indicated an understanding of a certain dialectical struggle endemic to the nature of this course and project. Part of the personal-professional dialectic revealed through

Robbin's experience as a service-learning teacher also surfaces in some of the ethical dilemmas that operate within these dialectical tensions. In response to the item, "What you liked least about the course," one student wrote that it "required emotional investment," and another wrote, "The fact that it was very depressing at times—but it didn't reflect that I hated the class. I just hated the social problems we talked about." An activist approach to teaching forces a confrontation with social injustice, which is atypical of most college courses. Consequently, students may both appreciate and resent the intrusion of the depressing facts of injustice on their communication education. It is likely that the intrusion of politics (and particularly a deep emotional/personal investment in social problems and change) is discomforting for students who believe they are in school as part of a distinctly intellectual endeavor and professional credentialing process. Again, as mentioned briefly in our discussion of the participant-observer secondary dialectic, the personal-professional dialectic is interwoven with politics. The politics of sexual assault resistance are deeply personal, whereas the successful management of a rape crisis center seems to depend on some degree of professionalism. Similarly, a professor openly exhibiting political sensibilities often is marked as being unprofessional by students.

On reflection, Robbin's students may have guessed at her personal "secret." They may have sensed the deep hurt, perhaps echoing in their own caverns of silences, and this could be too much to consider (about "the teacher" perhaps and about their own life or that of their friends, almost certainly given the statistics). In fact, through the intensive exploration of sexual assault as a social justice issue, at least one student realized and courageously disclosed for the first time that she had been raped in college. Daly (1998) also discussed professor disclosure as a tension derived from wanting to invite and create a safe place for student disclosure, the "chilling effect" such a disclosure might have, and the risks for/to the teacher of such disclosure:

> If I become emotional, I might lose my "professional" composure, my authority. For that reason, disclosing my personal history in the classroom remains far more difficult for me than writing about it. . . . If I had spoken out, afterward inviting student survivors to voice their personal experiences, would such a pedagogy have been more effective? . . . Was I simply afraid, I asked myself, or did I have valid reasons for silence? (pp. 191-192)

Navigating these dialectics means being able to manage one's ever-emerging self-realizations, being prepared to support the anticipated and unanticipated effects of student consciousness-raising, and still being able to function meaningfully as a professional teacher. The risks, tensions, and dilemmas both arise from an activist approach and are part and parcel of the social transformation being constructed. Thus, as researchers-practitioners, activists and consultants, teachers, and flawed individuals socially located in both privileged and marginalized ways, we must continue to live and act reflexively, to ask critical questions of ourselves and others so that dignity and freedom for all become a reality (Ford & Yep, 2003).

BENEFITS OF COMMUNITY ACTIVISM

Recent work by communication scholars clearly indicates a call for social justice that is increasing in both variety and intensity (see, e.g., the special journal issue that Frey, 1998a, edited on "Communication and Social Justice Research"; see also Dearing, 2003, and Ford & Yep, 2003, for discussions of community activism in health contexts). In a related stream, others advocate for the reformation of graduate education with an emphasis on engaged scholarship as a means to meet students' desires to address the issues of the world they encounter daily (Applegate, 2001; Frey, 1998b).

It is important to punctuate the benefits of this engaged scholarship and community activism to the nonprofit agencies where we work, the populations they serve, the communities we inhabit, and the social change objectives we share and promote. The stories of our work with SARC, although clearly not without difficult challenges and dilemmas, helped to strengthen a small, underresourced agency that has an important role to play in our community. As evidenced by the organizational changes, as well as changes in the media coverage of and community participation in SARC events, our efforts raised the visibility of sexual assault and increased public awareness of resources in our community for addressing this issue. Unfortunately, we cannot similarly argue that the incidence of sexual assault has diminished in this community; in fact, it has been argued that feminist resistance to patriarchy has produced an increase in violence against women (e.g., Caputi, 1987), as insecurity with or resistance to women's increased status has produced a backlash against feminism (Faludi, 1991). Nevertheless, it has been in response to protests on college campuses and in communities across the country that most of the support services and educational policies and programs regarding sexual assault have been developed (Russo, 2001; see the proactive performance program offered by Rich & Rodríguez, Volume 2). The activism by us and our students, as well as our work as communication consultants, is part of this arduous process of making society more aware of the prevalence and injustice of sexual assault and making social structures more responsive to this crime and the needs of its victims/survivors.

The fact that our teaching in subjects as wide ranging as communication theory, public speaking, media criticism, family communication, organizational communication, and globalization, media, and culture has been affected by our activist-consultant experience further illustrates the lasting effects of our activities with SARC. Our consciousness has been raised and our awareness continues to influence our teaching and research. This process has created a corresponding increase in awareness on our campuses and among our students, as illustrated by their comments about participation in the service-learning course, as well as the subsequent social service careers chosen by several of them. This impact should not be underestimated given the unspeakable prevalence of campus rape, with estimates that 1 in 4 college women will be the victim of an attempted or completed sexual assault during their college years (Russo, 2001).

Based on our experiences, we would add that our work as activist-consultants is consistent with the fundamental responsibilities we have as teacher-scholars and, indeed, with those of institutions of higher education. Interestingly, by making this argument to administrators at our university, we were moderately acknowledged and rewarded for this activist-consulting. Thus, we argue that part of reconceptualizing the role of the consultant is promoting a more community-oriented conceptualization of teaching, research, and service, and working to inculcate these values and institutionalize them in the academic reward systems that shape and constrain the professional lives of faculty.

One reason for changing the reward systems is that there is a clear benefit to the university when its professors have a high profile in the community. For example, research scientists and political analysts frequently are asked by media to comment on current events. With a few exceptions (increasingly among media and political communication scholars), communication professors are not sought after as news sources. Although the connection between scholarly work and specific community service is clear in some disciplines (e.g., criminal justice, education, and social work), for the would-be communication activist-consultant, who has more role models in the area of corporate consulting, these connections might not be as obvious. We have found, however, that involvement in community activism, in general, and with local nonprofit agencies, in particular, increases the profile of communication professors and the discipline alike, the latter being a major agenda item of the National Communication Association for several years now.

Although selfish motivations should not form the basis of the call to activism, there nonetheless are many professional and personal benefits for increased community involvement interwoven with the benefits that accrue on our campuses and in our communities. As Robbin's example illustrates, community-based work can both inform and provide field sites for teaching, with student involvement potentially helping community organizations and supporting learning. Students appreciate opportunities for applied, experiential learning and often find such courses more interesting and "relevant." Students with experiential learning in the nonprofit sector also may come to envision unforeseen career opportunities, as exemplified by some of our graduate students who chose careers in public service, community health, or the nonprofit sector after involvement with the Communication and Social Change class, participation on the department TBTN walk/run team, or merely through knowing about our community work.

Long-term commitment to community groups or agencies also potentially leads to important research opportunities. Moreover, when an activist spirit has guided faculty involvement, and when participatory or feminist action research methodologies guide the work, the research agenda unfolds in ways that are beneficial to the agency and community as well. For example, in the field of rape crisis intervention, one of the most daunting barriers to social change is public sentiment, which affects everything from the incidence of rape to the attitudes of district attorneys and potential jurors. Action research can lead to media attention, public outcry, and policy change about this issue. Similarly, participatory research with volunteers or sexual assault survivors can help to increase our understanding of this devastating crime on people's lives, relationships, and communicative behaviors (e.g., Ford et al., 1999). Participation in such studies also has been shown to be beneficial to the healing process itself (e.g., Ford & Crabtree, 2002; Varallo, Ray, & Ellis, 1998).

However, because we did not anticipate writing an academic piece about our experience as rape crisis activists and agency volunteers, we did not carefully maintain anything that would constitute an official "data set" from which to document and analyze the experience. Thus, we have little traditional empirical evidence to bolster the claims we make in this chapter. This lack of formal data collection is further compounded by the confidential nature of sexual assault crisis and recovery work, not to mention the migratory lives of scholars like us, with both of us having since moved from New Mexico and maintaining only cursory contact with the ever-changing staff of SARC. Thus, in addition to agency documents in our files, student evaluations, newspaper articles, and some other empirical evidence, we used our own narratives as method, data, and genre (Ronai, 1992), which is consistent with feminist methodology (Bloom, 1998; see also Code, 1995; Ronai, 1992). As Bloom (1998, p. 153) asserted, "Feminist methodology is alive with contradictions, ambiguities, and nonunitariness. As a theory of practice or praxis, it must be seen to offer open, partial, situated, and fluid" accounts. The work we described in this chapter, thus, constitutes *praxis*, part of our continuous cycle of knowledge production and reception, action in the world, and reflection about both of those processes, as well as about ourselves.

Finally, we would be remiss if we did not reiterate something about the risks involved in the activist mode of communication consulting. As our experiences illustrate, working as an activist-consultant can be emotionally draining. Especially related to the issue of sexual assault, the more one knows, the more one wishes she or he did not know. We imagine that the kinds of experiences we had would be shared by activist-consultants in areas as diverse as gay rights (see Cagle, Volume 2), environmental issues, prison work (see Novek & Sanford, Volume 2), and drug prevention, among many others. The ethical dilemmas and dialectical tensions we all face in doing this type of work are exceedingly challenging; they cannot be resolved and, at times, the ambiguity or frustration associated with them can barely be tolerated. Becoming more informed and involved in social justice issues undoubtedly raises one's consciousness and strengthens one's work, but it also may break one's heart.

Despite the tensions experienced, there is much to commend about the ways in which community activism enriches the life of an academic. Writing articles that few read and for journals targeted largely at the most elite in our increasingly narrow fields may bring professional success, but it does not feed the soul. The historical and discursive frameworks of our educational institutions do not readily account for the "messiness" of the dialectical tensions we described in this chapter, nor the interpellations of our personal journeys, academic studies, and social justice work. Living a life of community involvement, in which academic work is connected intimately to community service and tangible results is deeply satisfying. Whereas traditional scholarship often requires us to be detached, objective, and dispassionate, becoming activist-consultants creates opportunities to feel connected, experience life from the perspectives of others, heal and grow, and work passionately for social change. Like Bloom (1998), we affirm that feminist communication teaching, research, interpretation, and action can be "written under the sign of hope" (p. 153).

CONCLUSION

In this chapter, we explored the dialectical tensions evidenced in our work as activist-consultants for a sexual assault crisis and recovery center in southern New Mexico. We explored the interlocking tensions among and between the various roles and responsibilities we undertook as observers and participants, knowledgeable authorities and dialogic activists, political women, and professional scholars. We have not, however, explored here the interlocking oppressions that give rise to the prevalence of sexual assault in our culture, nor the ways that women who are differently located in our society and in contemporary global relations experience sexual assault and its "treatment" by law enforcement officials, social service agencies, and government investigators. Our experience as activist-consultants certainly was influenced by our status as middle-aged, educated, professional, White women, and we recognize and honor that "the sources of violence as well as resistance are multiple, varied, and interconnected" (Russo, 2001, p. 11).

Russo (2002) argued that "when the stories become collective, when the violence is named as undeserved and unjust, and when it is linked to social and political institutional contexts, the storytelling can be transformative" (p. 197). Thus, although we cannot claim that our work in one community mitigated the devastating impact of sexual violence on women's lives, it demonstrates the importance of women's solidarity, organization, and rebellion. Our work is part of a growing body of literature and scholarship that tells not only stories of victimization and survival but stories of resistance (see Russo, 2001, 2002) and transformation (Buchwald et al., 1993). We hope that our work illustrates how "telling stories and speaking out has been a way to move survivors and witnesses to collaborative action toward ending violence, demanding justice, and transforming the world" (Russo, 2002, p. 197), and that there is an important place in this process for communication scholars, activists, and consultants.

REFERENCES

Alvesson, M. (1993). Cultural-ideological modes of managerial control: A theory and a case study of a professional service company. In S. A. Deetz (Ed.), *Communication yearbook* (Vol. 16, pp. 3-42). Newbury Park, CA: Sage.

Anderson, C. W. (1993). *Prescribing the life of the mind: An essay on the purpose of the university, the aims of liberal education, the competence of citizens, and the cultivation of practical reason.* Madison: University of Wisconsin Press.

Anderson, M., Fine, L., Geissler, K., & Landenson, J. (Eds.). (1997). *Doing feminism: Teaching and research in the academy.* East Lansing: Michigan State University, Women's Studies Program.

Ansley, F., & Gaventa, J. (1997, January/February). Researching for democracy and democratizing research. *Change*, pp. 46-53.

Applegate, J. L. (2001, September). Engaged graduate education: Skating to where the puck will be. *Spectra*, pp. 2-5.

Bass, E., & Davis, L. (1988). *The courage to heal: A guide for women survivors of child sexual abuse.* New York: Perennial Library.

Barber, B. R. (1992). *An aristocracy of everyone: The politics of education and the future of America.* New York: Ballantine Books.

Baxter, L. A., & Montgomery, B. M. (1996). *Relating: Dialogues and dialectics.* New York: Guilford Press.

Baxter, L. A., & Montgomery, B. M. (1998). A guide to dialectical approaches to studying personal relationships. In B. M. Montgomery & L. A. Baxter (Eds.), *Dialectical approaches to studying interpersonal relationships* (pp. 1-15). Mahwah, NJ: Erlbaum.

Belenky, M. F., Clinchy, B. M., Goldberger, N. R., & Tarule, J. M. (1986). *Women's ways of knowing: The development of self, voice, and mind*. New York: Basic Books.

Bernstein, E., Wallerstein, N., Braithwaite, R., Gutierrez, L., Labonte, R., & Zimmerman, M. (1994). Empowerment forum: A dialogue between guest editorial board members. *Health Education Quarterly, 21*, 281-294.

Bloom, L. R. (1998). *Under the sign of hope: Feminist methodology and narrative interpretation*. Albany: State University of New York Press.

Boyer, E. L. (1987). *Scholarship reconsidered: Priorities of the professorate*. Princeton, NJ: Carnegie Foundation for the Advancement of Teaching.

Boyer, E. L., & Hechinger, F. M. (1981). *Higher learning in the nation's service*. Washington, DC: Carnegie Foundation for the Advancement of Teaching.

Bringle, R. G., & Hatcher, J. A. (1996). Implementing service learning in higher education. *Journal of Higher Education, 67*, 221-239.

Brown, L. D., & Tandon, R. (1983). Ideology and political economy in inquiry: Action research and participatory research. *Journal of Applied Behavioral Science, 19*, 277-294.

Buchwald, E., Fletcher, P. R., & Roth, M. (Eds.). (1993). *Transforming a rape culture*. Minneapolis, MN: Milkweed Editions.

Butler, J. E. (2000). Democracy, diversity, and civic engagement. *Academe, 86*(4), 52-55.

Buzzanell, P. M. (Ed.). (2000). *Rethinking organizational and managerial communication from feminist perspectives*. Thousand Oaks, CA: Sage.

Carlson, S. (1998, April 13). SARC helps victims "Take Back the Night." *Roundup*, pp. 1, 3.

Caputi, J. (1987). *The age of sex crime*. Bowling Green, OH: Bowling Green State University Popular Press.

Checkoway, B. (2000). Public service: Our new mission. *Academe, 86*(4), 24-28.

Checkoway, B. (2001). Renewing the civic mission of the American research university. *Journal of Higher Education, 72*, 125-147.

Code, L. (1995). How do we know? Questions of method in feminist practice. In S. Burt & L. Code (Eds.), *Changing methods: Feminists transforming practice* (pp. 13-39). Orchard Park, NY: Broadview Press.

Collins, P. H. (2000). *Black feminist thought: Knowledge, consciousness, and the politics of empowerment* (rev. ed.). New York: Routledge.

Crabtree, R. D. (1999). Communication and social change: Applied communication theory in service-learning. In D. Droge & B. O. Murphy (Eds.), *Voices of strong democracy: Concepts and models for service-learning in communication studies* (pp. 125-136). Washington, DC: American Association of Higher Education.

Crabtree, R. D., & Ford, L. A. (1998). Communicating about emerging infectious diseases in the borderlands: Hantavirus education for rural, border, and migrant populations. In J. G. Power & T. Byrd (Eds.), *U.S.-Mexico border health: Issues for regional and migrant populations* (pp. 52-70). Thousand Oaks, CA: Sage.

Cruz, N., & Giles, D. (2000). Where's the community in service-learning research? *Michigan Journal of Community Service Learning* [Special fall issue], 28-34.

Daly, B. (1998). *Authoring a life: A woman's survival in and through literary studies*. Albany: State University of New York Press.

Dearing, J. W. (2003). The state of the art and the state of the science of community organizing. In T. L. Thompson, A. M. Dorsey, K. I. Miller, & R. Parrott (Eds.), *Handbook of health communication* (pp. 207-220). Mahwah, NJ: Erlbaum.

Deetz, S. A. (1992). *Democracy in an age of corporate colonization: Developments in communication and the politics of everyday life.* Albany: State University of New York Press.

Deetz, S. A. (1999). Participatory democracy as a normative foundation for communication studies. In T. Jacobson & J. Servaes (Eds.), *Theoretical approaches to participatory communication* (pp. 131-167). Cresskill, NJ: Hampton Press.

Devault, M. L. (1999). *Liberating method: Feminism and social research.* Philadelphia: Temple University Press.

DeWine, S. (1994). *The consultant's craft: Improving organizational communication.* New York: St. Martin's Press.

Dinsmore, C. (1991). *From surviving to thriving: Incest, feminism, and recovery.* Albany: State University of New York Press.

Doengens, D. (1997, April 28). Community runs, walks to "Take Back the Night." *Roundup*, p. 4.

Donati, P. (1996). Building a unified movement: Resource mobilization, media work, and organizational transformation in the Italian environmental movement. In M. Dobkowski & I. Walliman (Eds.), *Research in social movements, conflicts, and change* (pp. 125-157). Greenwich, CT: JAI Press.

Driscoll, A., Holland, B., Gelmon, S., & Kerrigan, S. (1996). An assessment model for service-learning: Comprehensive case studies of impact on faculty, students, community, and institution. *Michigan Journal of Community Service Learning, 3*, 66-71.

Droge, D., & Murphy, B. O. (Eds.). (1999). *Voices of strong democracy: Concepts and models for service-learning in communication studies.* Washington, DC: American Association for Higher Education.

Eadie, W. F. (1982, October). The case for applied communication research. *Spectra*, pp. 1-2.

Eadie, W. F. (1990). Being applied: Communication research comes of age. *Journal of Applied Communication Research* [Special issue], 1-6.

Elden, M., & Levin, M. (1991). Cogenerative learning: Bringing participation into action research. In W. F. Whyte (Ed.), *Participatory action research* (pp. 127-142). Newbury Park, CA: Sage.

Ellis, D. G. (1982, March). The shame of speech communication. *Spectra*, pp. 1-2.

Ellis, D. G. (1991). The oneness of opposites: Applied communication and theory. *Journal of Applied Communication Research, 19*, 116-122.

Ehrenhaus, P. (1991). Co-opting the academy: On the urgency of reframing "applied." *Journal of Applied Communication Research, 19*, 123-128.

Fals-Borda, O., & Rahman, M. A. (1991). *Action and knowledge: Breaking the monopoly with participatory action research.* New York: Apex Press.

Faludi, S. (1991). *Backlash: The undeclared war against American women.* New York: Crown.

Federal Bureau of Investigation. (2002). *Crime in the United States: 2002 Uniform crime reports.* Retrieved September 19, 2004, from http://www.fbi.gov/ucr/cius _02/pdf/2sectiontwo.pdf

Fields, A. B. (2003). *The youth challenge: Participating in democracy.* New York: Carnegie Corporation.

Ford, L. A., Barnes, M. D., Crabtree, R. D., & Fairbanks, J. (1998). Boundary spanners: *Las Promotoras* in the borderlands. In J. G. Power & T. Byrd (Eds.), *U.S.-Mexico border health: Issues for regional and migrant populations* (pp. 141-164). Thousand Oaks, CA: Sage.

Ford, L. A., & Crabtree, R. D. (2002). Telling, re-telling and talking about telling: Disclosure and/as surviving incest. *Women's Studies in Communication, 25,* 51-87.

Ford, L. A., Ray, E. B., & Ellis, B. H. (1999). Translating scholarship on intrafamilial sexual abuse: The utility of a dialectical perspective for adult survivors. *Journal of Applied Communication Research, 27,* 139-157.

Ford, L. A., & Yep, G. A. (2003). Working along the margins: Developing community-based strategies for communication about health with marginalized groups. In T. L. Thompson, A. M. Dorsey, K. I. Miller, & R. Parrott (Eds.), *Handbook of health communication* (pp. 241-261). Mahwah, NJ: Erlbaum.

Freire, P. (2000). *Pedagogy of the oppressed* (M. B. Ramos, Trans.). New York: Continuum.

Frey, L. R. (Ed.). (1998a). Communication and social justice research [Special issue]. *Journal of Applied Communication Research, 26*(2).

Frey, L. R. (1998b). Communication and social justice research: Truth, justice, and the applied communication way. *Journal of Applied Communication Research, 26,* 155-164.

Frey, L. R., Pearce, W. B., Pollock, M., Artz, L., & Murphy, B. A. O. (1996). Looking for justice in all the wrong places: On a communication approach to social justice. *Communication Studies, 47,* 110-127.

Gabelink, F. (1997, January/February). Educating a committed citizenry. *Change,* pp. 30-40.

Gamson, Z. F. (1997, January/February). Higher education and rebuilding civic life. *Change,* pp. 10-13.

Gibson, C. (2001). *From inspiration to participation: A review of perspectives on youth civic engagement.* New York: Carnegie Corporation.

Grossman, R. (with Sutherland, J.). (Eds.). (1991). *Surviving sexual assault* (rev. ed.). Chicago: Congdon & Weed.

Hackney, S. (1986). The university and its community: Past and present. *Annals of the American Academy of Political and Social Science, 488,* 135-147.

Hall, B. (1981). Participatory research, popular knowledge and power: A personal reflection. *Convergence, 14*(3), 6-17.

Hinds, M. D. (2002). Scholarship for social change. *Carnegie Reporter, 2*(1), 12-21.

hooks, b. (1994). *Teaching to transgress: Education as the practice of freedom.* New York: Routledge.

Jhally, S. (1995). *Dreamworlds: Desire, sex, and power in music video* [Videotape]. Amherst, MA: Media Education Foundation.

Johnson, A. (1993). The best teachers business can buy. *Canadian Business, 6*(4), 34-39.

Kennedy, D. (1997). *Academic duty.* Cambridge, MA: Harvard University Press.

Kilpatrick, D. G., Edmunds, C. N., & Seymour, A. (1992). *Rape in America: A report to the nation.* Arlington, VA: National Victim Center.

Kraft, R. (1996). Service learning: An introduction to theory, practice, and effects. *Education and Urban Society, 28*, 131-159.

Kreps, G. L., Frey, L. R., & O'Hair, D. (1991). Conceptualizing applied communication research: Scholarship that can make a difference. *Journal of Applied Communication Research, 19*, 71-87.

Lawless, E. J. (2000). *Women escaping violence: Empowerment through narrative.* Columbia: University of Missouri Press.

Lempert, L. B. (1994). A narrative analysis of abuse: Connecting the personal, the rhetorical, and the structural. *Journal of Contemporary Ethnography, 22*, 411-441.

Lippitt, G., & Lippitt, R. (1986). *The consulting process in action* (2nd ed.). San Diego, CA: University Associates.

Lorber, J. (2005). *Gender inequality: Feminist theories and politics* (3rd ed.). Los Angeles: Roxbury.

Maguire, P. (1987). *Doing participatory research: A feminist approach.* Amherst: University of Massachusetts, Center for International Education, School of Education.

Maguire, P. (2001). Uneven ground: Feminisms and action research. In P. Reason & H. Bradbudy (Eds.), *Handbook of action research: Participative inquiry and practice* (pp. 59-69). Thousand Oaks, CA: Sage.

March, J. G. (1991). Organizational consultants and organizational research. *Journal of Applied Communication Research, 19*, 20-31.

Matthews, N. A. (1994). *Confronting rape: The feminist anti-rape movement and the state.* New York: Routledge.

McMillan, J. J., & Cheney, G. (1996). The limitations of a metaphor. *Communication Education, 45*, 1-15.

Mitchell, J. E., & Rebne, D. S. (1995). Nonlinear effects of teaching and consulting on research productivity. *Socio-economic Planning Sciences, 29*, 47-57.

Mumby, D. K. (1993). Critical organizational communication studies: The next 10 years. *Communication Monographs, 60*, 18-25.

Mumby, D. K. (1997). Modernism, postmodernism, and communication studies: A rereading of an ongoing debate. *Communication Theory, 7*, 1-28.

New York City Alliance Against Sexual Assault. (2003). *Childhood sexual assault statistics.* Retrieved September 12, 2003, from http://www.nycagainstrape.org/research_factsheet_7.html

Parsons, L. (1996, May 2). Activists take back the night from sex offenders. *Roundup*, pp. 2, 8.

Petronio, S., Flores, L. A., & Hecht, M. L. (1997). Locating the voice of logic: Disclosure discourse of sexual abuse. *Western Journal of Communication, 61*, 101-113.

Plax, T. G. (1991). Understanding applied communication inquiry: Researcher as organizational consultant. *Journal of Applied Communication Research, 19*, 55-70.

Pollock, M. A., Artz, L., Frey, L. R., Pearce, W. B., & Murphy, B. A. O. (1996). Navigating between Scylla and Charybdis: Continuing the dialogue on communication and social justice. *Communication Studies, 47*, 142-151.

Polly, K. (1999, May 9). Vigil held to help "Take Back the Night." *Sun-News*, p. A4.

Rebne, D. S. (1989). Faculty consulting and scientific knowledge: A traditional university linkage. *Educational Administration Quarterly, 25*, 338-357.

Reinharz, S. (with Davidman, L.). (1992). *Feminist methods in social research*. New York: Oxford University Press.

Rice, R. E. (1996). *Making a place for the new American scholar: Inquiry #1*. Washington, DC: American Association for Higher Education.

Ronai, C. R. (1992). The reflexive self through narrative: A night in the life of an erotic dancer/researcher. In C. Ellis & M. G. Flaherty (Eds.), *Investigating subjectivity: Research on lived experience* (pp. 102-124). Newbury Park, CA: Sage.

Russo, A. (2001). *Taking back our lives: A call to action for the feminist movement*. New York: Routledge.

Russo, A. (2002). Stories of survival, stories of resistance. In S. Jackson & A. Russo (Eds.), *Talking back and acting out: Women negotiating the media across cultures* (pp. 196-211). New York: Peter Lang.

Ryan, C., Carragee, K. M., & Schwerner, C. (1998). Media, movements, and the quest for social justice. *Journal of Applied Communication Research, 26*, 165-181.

Sandmann, L. R., & Lewis, A. G. (1991). Land grant universities on trial. *Adult Learning, 3*, 23.

Sapp, D. A., & Crabtree, R. D. (2002). A laboratory in citizenship: Service-learning in the technical communication classroom. *Technical Communication Quarterly, 11*, 411-431.

Sherwood, J. (1981). Essential differences between traditional approaches to consulting and a collaborative approach. *Consultation, 1*(1), 52-55.

Sirianni, C., & Friedland, L. (1997, January/February). Civic innovation and American democracy. *Change*, pp. 14-23.

United States Department of Justice Bureau of Justice Statistics. (2002). *Rape and sexual assault: Reporting to police and medical attention, 1992-2000*. Retrieved November 9, 2003, from http://www.ojp.usdoj.gov/bjs/abstract/rsarp00.htm

Valenti-Hein, D., & Schwartz, L. (1995). *The sexual abuse interview for those with developmental disabilities*. Santa Barbara, CA: James Stanfield.

Van Cott, S. (1995, April 27). Graduate class marries theory to practice. *Roundup*, p. 5.

Varallo, S. M., Ray, E. B., & Ellis, B. H. (1998). Speaking of incest: The research interview as social justice. *Journal of Applied Communication Research, 26*, 254-271.

Werner, C. M., & Baxter L. A. (1994). Temporal qualities of relationships: Organismic, transactional, and dialectical views. In M. L. Knapp & G. R. Miller (Eds.), *Handbook of interpersonal communication* (2nd ed., pp. 323-379). Newbury Park, CA: Sage.

White, C. (2001). The usefulness of consulting as a teaching tool. *Journalism and Mass Communication Educator, 56*, 31-41.

Zlotkowski, E. (Ed.). (1998). *Successful service-learning programs: New models of excellence in higher education*. Bolton, MA: Anker.

7

FACILITATING DEATH TALK

Creating Collaborative Courtroom Conversations About the Death Penalty Between Attorneys and Jurors

Sunwolf

Santa Clara University

We are killing the retarded without serious qualm. We are near the point of killing persons for crimes they committed as children. And it is increasingly difficult not to notice and admit we are mainly executing people of marginal intelligence, doubtful sanity, debilitating poverty. The death penalty has become an act of class warfare, fought top-down against the poor and incompetent.

—Teepen (1987, p. A17)

Capital punishment remains a controversial topic in the United States, although few U.S. citizens realize that the trend in the world has shifted away from imposing the death penalty. Despite the fact that 111 countries have abolished the death penalty either by law or as a matter of practice, including the vast majority of countries in Europe, the United States continues to retain it in a majority of states, even though there is considerable debate within states that authorize it about when it should be applied.[1] Consequently, most of the executions currently conducted in the world occur in China, Iran, and the United States (Carter & Kreitzberg, 2004).

Whether or not someone personally supports the death penalty, people assume that when the state attempts to take a person's life, the defendant will receive a trial by a *fair jury*. Unfortunately, the evidence increasingly shows that such a reality may be rarer than people believe (see, e.g., Berlow, 2002). New investigations indicate that juries are issuing verdicts of death for defendants who later are found to be innocent. Since 1973, evidence of factual innocence has resulted in 117 people from 25 states being released from death row (Death Penalty Information Center, 2005b; see the case described by McHale, Volume 2). In fact, the mere fact that a defendant faces a murder charge places that person in jeopardy of a *false* conviction; between 1963 and 1999, at least 381 homicide convictions were overturned because prosecutors concealed evidence of innocence or knowingly presented evidence that was false (Berlow, 1999). One U.S. District Judge (a former federal prosecutor with a reputation as a conservative on criminal justice issues) reached a startling conclusion:

> The best available evidence indicates that . . . innocent people are sentenced to death with materially greater frequency than was previously supposed and that . . . convincing proof of their innocence often does not emerge until long after their convictions. It is therefore fully foreseeable that in enforcing the death penalty a meaningful number of innocent people will be executed who otherwise would eventually be able to prove their innocence. (*United States v. Quinones*, 2002, p. 417)

Describing the task of a multidisciplinary team at Columbia University studying the risk of wrongful execution, Liebman (2002) concluded that wrongful executions must be distinguished from other innocent fatalities, pointing out that the execution of an innocent person is not simply a tragic collateral consequence of activity with a nonfatal objective but "instead, the taking of life is the *goal* of the enterprise, and the killing is the *intended* act of the state" (p. 78).

That the death penalty increasingly is controversial within the United States today is evidenced by moratorium issues: both Illinois and Maryland now have a moratorium on the imposition of the death penalty, with scholars conducting studies of its fairness (see, e.g., Liebman, Fagan, & West, 2003). Confronted with overwhelming evidence that his state already had executed innocent defendants, on January 11, 2003, Illinois Governor George Ryan pardoned four men and granted clemency (converting their death sentence to life sentence) to all remaining 167 inmates on death row (Death Penalty Information Center, 2003a). Before the governor's action, an Illinois state investigation exonerated 13 death row inmates, reporting that, in all probability, some innocent men had, in fact, already been executed. Ryan's actions were an extraordinary reversal of policy for a law-and-order Republican and staunch supporter of capital punishment, but as Ryan explained in his public clemency speech:

> Where humans are involved there has to be some error, I don't care what the program is, and when you talk about life or death, there's no room for error. If we haven't got a system that works then we shouldn't have a system. (cited in Wilgoren, 2003, Sec. A, p. 13)

Although I now am a full-time university professor studying and teaching communication, I previously served as a trial attorney, both defending clients accused of criminal offenses and training new attorneys (as Training Director for Colorado's statewide Public Defender Office). I have acted as counsel on numerous death penalty cases, and for the past 15 years, I have taught nationally in trial advocacy programs, helping attorneys working on the defense of death penalty cases to acquire new trial skills. This chapter describes a communication intervention that I developed for a specific activist group: criminal defense attorneys who have been appointed by the court to represent an indigent client who faces state execution. The intervention focuses on the communication challenges these attorneys confront in courtroom conversations during jury selection for death penalty cases (a formal opportunity for lawyers to talk to potential jurors about their beliefs concerning the death penalty). Lawyers who handle death penalty representation of clients typically are united in the common goal of saving the lives of marginalized human beings, but, unfortunately, these lawyers remain painfully underresourced for that task. Too often, case overloads focus attention on investigation, motions practice, and witness preparation, resulting in little time to research, develop, or explore more effective communication skills in the courtroom (Sunwolf, 2004). The conversational tools described here are grounded in a dialectical perspective and adopt a technique called "empathic attunement" (Sunwolf, 2006), which acknowledges and facilitates a way for people's divergent beliefs about social behavior (here, about the death penalty) to exist in harmony in professional service relationships (in this case, between attorneys and their clients). I teach the facilitation discussed here nationally, in small group workshops comprised of lawyers who attend continuing legal education programs to learn the skills needed to successfully defend a capital case and save a human life.

To these ends, I begin by describing what we know about preconceived ideas that citizens may bring with them to court about the deliberation trial task and then illuminate the reasons death penalty trials involve significantly more communication challenges for lawyers than other criminal trials. I then establish the need for a communication intervention, first, by examining the lack of resources provided for these lawyers and the impairing stresses lawyers face in the task of defending a capital case, and second, by presenting recent national voices describing the incidents of innocent people being convicted and receiving the death penalty. Following this material, the specific procedural, emotional, and psychological challenges of a court's jury selection processes during capital trials are described that give rise to a need for new communication tools in these trials to enhance conversations with potential jurors. Given this background, the workshop context in which this new group intervention has been taught is described with regard to its protocols and outcomes.

JURORS AS DEADLY DECISION MAKERS

> There is at first the sense of buzzing, booming, confusion. After a while, we become accustomed to the quick fluid movement of jury discussion and realize that the talk moves in small bursts of coherence, shifting from topic to topic with remarkable flexibility. It touches an issue, leaves it, and returns again.
>
> —Unnamed juror
> (cited in Kalven & Zeisel, 1966, p. 486)

> A clutch of strangers yelled, cursed, rolled on the floor, vomited, whispered, embraced, sobbed, and invoked both God and necromancy.
>
> —Science professor, describing his jury service
> (cited in Burnett, 2001, p. 12)

The specific process by which ordinary citizens, lacking acceptable excuses to be elsewhere, become sworn in to serve as trial jurors to deliberate in a criminal case carries with it the reality that these people have not been trained as jury decision makers. Although jury deliberations take place in secret, jury selection procedures take place in public, providing trial lawyers with an opportunity to influence not only who is selected but how those chosen jurors later perceive and enact their deliberative, decision-making task.

People come to jury duty with preconceived ideas about the jury deliberation task. Citizen jurors import familiar structures and rules about group decision-making tasks from their personal lives, bringing these structures and rules into a judicial system that, in reality, may be unfamiliarly structured, yet carries the possibility of deadly consequences for any error (Sunwolf, 2004). Sunwolf and Seibold (1998) found that citizens waiting to be called for jury service brought with them to the courthouse, and were able to immediately describe and apply, specific structuring rules for their anticipated group verdict-rendering task. Moreover, many of these structuring rules were *contrary* to court rules; for instance, potential jurors offered rules about how to resolve juror misconduct that included ignoring misconduct when it occurs, and they believed that conflict between loyalty to the group/jury and loyalty to the organization/judicial system should be resolved by loyalty to the group trumping loyalty to the organization.

Due to the black-box nature of secret jury deliberations, we know little about dysfunctional aspects of jury decision making in criminal cases (Sunwolf & Seibold, 2006; see also cases of misconduct during jury deliberations reported in Sunwolf, 2004), although occasional evidence emerges that misconduct may be more common than popularly believed. In a 1995 murder trial, for example, four jurors sequestered during deliberations admitted that they had consulted a Ouija board, communicating questions to the deceased victim, who then "responded" with facts about who had killed him, with what weapon, and with what motive, all of which was shared with other jurors (Coutts, 1995). More recently, members of a midwestern U.S. jury admitted flipping a coin to decide between a murder and manslaughter verdict; the foreperson argued to the trial judge that the coin flip had been fair because the jurors "unanimously" agreed to it (Wessel, 2000). Although the perception of justice always is thrown into question by a jury that deviates from its legal duty, when deliberating jurors embrace dysfunctional processes during death penalty cases, the life of a human being unnecessarily is endangered.

REFRAMING CAPITAL TRIALS: DEATH IS DIFFERENT

Death is different, not just in the nature of the penalty and in the preparation and presentation of a penalty phase of a trial. Death is different in the emotional toll it takes on everyone involved in capital litigation.

—Bryan R. Shechmeister Death Penalty College (2000)

> Executions are awesome rituals of human sacrifice through which the
> state dramatizes its absolute power and monopoly on violence.
>
> —Conquergood (2002, p. 342)

The U.S. Supreme Court has stressed in many of its published opinions that
death, in its finality, is a qualitatively different trial outcome than any other
(Carter & Kreitzberg, 2004; see also, *Ford v. Wainwright*, 1986, p. 410). The
potential outcome of a capital trial in the United States is the execution of
one of its citizens; as a result, it is critical that those who examine the challenges facing capital defense attorneys understand more about the injustices
embedded in capital punishment in the United States. In particular, clients
who come from traditionally marginalized racial groups are executed in dis-
proportionate numbers to their representation in the U.S. population, and
when the race of the victim is factored into the equation, the disparity is
remarkable: As of November 17, 2004, the number of White defendants executed nationally (since 1976) for an interracial murder was 12, whereas the
number of Black defendants executed for killing a White victim was 192
(Death Penalty Information Center, 2003b). Jurors, it appears, are voting
more often for death for defendants of color than for those who are White.

A November 16, 2004 Gallup poll measuring public opinion regarding
the death penalty revealed a "decline" in support for capital punishment: The
poll reported that 66% of U.S. citizens support the death penalty for anyone
convicted of murder (down 5% from an earlier 2004 poll and lower than the
high of 80% in 1994; Death Penalty Information Center, 2005c).
Nonetheless, the numbers make it clear that most U.S. citizens favor the
death penalty and, therefore, most jurors can be expected to reflect that opinion. Death penalty defense attorneys, as a result, face a sentencing prejudice:
an unequivocal bias on the part of many jurors *in favor of death* as an appropriate legal penalty rather than life imprisonment. In fact, any juror who
expresses opposition to the death penalty in court during jury selection generally is excluded by the judge (without the necessity of the prosecutor using
a peremptory challenge) from serving in a capital case, unless the defense
attorney is a particularly skillful communicator during jury selection.
Consequently, people who admit to holding certain views in opposition to
the death penalty systematically are excluded from sitting as jurors in those
trials, even for the guilt-innocence phase (established by the U.S. Supreme
Court's decision in *Witherspoon* v. *Illinois*, 1968), even though they would
be qualified to serve as jurors in the guilt-innocence phase of any other criminal trial.

Furthermore, a number of studies have demonstrated that people's support of the death penalty is closely related to the likelihood that, as jurors,
they would perceive a criminal defendant to "probably" be guilty more than

those who do not support the death penalty (Haney, 1984a). A favorable attitude toward the death penalty has been positively associated with an increased willingness to convict (Allen, Mabry, & McKelton, 1998). According to White (2004), a professor of law who studied the choices made by attorneys representing innocent capital defendants, juries that have been death qualified do not evaluate evidence in the same way as other juries and are, as a result, much more likely to give credence to the prosecution's evidence and much less likely than other juries to acquit a defendant (or find a defendant guilty of a lesser charge).

Experienced capital defense attorneys have observed that as the number of citizens who express concerns about the appropriateness of the death penalty increases, the result has been that increasing numbers of fair-minded citizens are being excluded from capital trials (White, 2004). Jurors who are chosen for death cases have been, in effect, "death qualified" during jury selection, and due to their pro-death penalty bias, these death-qualified jurors entertain few qualms about the appropriateness of a death sentence. Cowan, Thompson, and Ellsworth (1984) created a straightforward test, now well cited by courts, of the proposition that people who are permitted to serve on juries in capital cases (death-qualified jurors) would be more likely to convict a defendant than those excluded from serving because they were unwilling to impose the death penalty on anyone (excludable jurors). Two hundred eighty-eight adults eligible for jury service in Santa Clara or San Mateo counties (California) watched a 2.5-hour videotape of a simulated murder trial. The researchers found that death-qualified participants were significantly more likely than excludable jurors to vote guilty, both on the initial ballot and after an hour's deliberation in 12-person groups (the size of a jury). As a result, a death-qualified jury (one that has experienced court- and lawyer-conducted questioning about the death penalty, with those opposing it excused from service) may be biased and unrepresentative of a community, containing only citizens who have pro-death penalty, enhanced anticrime attitudes in common (Haney, 1984a). This overloading of jurors with pro-death/anticrime values onto capital cases flies in the face of the principle that the U.S. jury system is a uniquely democratic institution whose wisdom is collective, emerging when a group of ordinary people of different backgrounds and values deliberate together to reach a decision (Cowan et al., 1984).

This discussion suggests that whether a client ultimately is sentenced to life or death actually may be determined during jury selection (referred to in the courtroom as *voir dire*), as a result of skillfully uncovering the beliefs, attitudes, and values that people bring with them to court. Unfortunately, few attorneys are trained in the interpersonal communication skills and psychological insights needed to create effective or useful conversations with jurors. Attorneys are trained (and rewarded) in law school to engage in data-driven questioning of witnesses, jurors, and even clients (Sunwolf, 2004). As one experienced death penalty attorney explained, "We keep performing the style of questioning we learned in law school mock trials, and then we just copy one another. We don't understand jurors from a human perspective. Fundamentally, we're ignorant" (A. J. Natale, personal communication, February 13, 2004). Moreover, the ability to effectively represent and protect the life of their clients is further complicated by death penalty defense lawyers who are stressed and underresourced.

STRESSED AND UNDERRESOURCED CAPITAL DEFENSE LAWYERS

The motivation for the Illinois governor's unexpected emptying of death row explains, in part, the extraordinary stresses experienced by capital defense attorneys (Sunwolf, 2006). Capital defense attorneys are burdened by the knowledge that innocent people can be convicted, their appeals denied, and wrongful executions can be (and have been) carried out by the state. These attorneys struggle, in particular, with the fact that attorney error can be responsible for both lost trials and lost lives. There is, consequently, professional consensus among trial lawyers that the greatest challenge for any criminal defense attorney is the representation of a person who faces the death penalty in a capital case. Stephen Bright (1994), Director of the Southern Center for Human Rights, who specializes in capital cases, concluded from his review of trials resulting in death sentences that these defendants received the death sentence not for committing the worst crime but for being represented by the worst lawyer.

There is a public perception that a person who is sentenced to death at trial has endless legal forums available in which to make his or her case for appeal, but the reality is far different. The task of citizens as jurors in a death penalty trial (as well as the task of lawyers deciding which jurors to choose) is irreparably affected by the fact that innocent people have been executed in the United States. Berlow (1999), citing overzealous prosecutors, lying police officers, flawed forensic testing, incompetent defense counsel, erroneous eyewitness testimony, false confessions, and racially biased jurors, pointed to case after case in which courts have agreed that the wrong person was executed, and concluded that "the prospect that innocent people will be executed in America is horrifyingly likely" (p. 66). Capital defense attorneys, thus, are challenged to remain alert to these threats to a fair trial.

Capital defense attorneys further are challenged by (a) a lack of resources to adequately prepare a competent defense; (b) negative community attitudes toward criminal defendants, including angry feelings from a victim's family or friends, as well as a general distrust of criminal defense attorneys; (c) judges who view zealous defense work as adversarial to a speedy justice system and courtroom innovations that are needed in death penalty cases as threatening the status quo; (d) prosecutors who are well resourced, have access to multiple avenues of expertise and investigation, and who may be politically motivated to pursue death charges to gain popularity in their communities; and, as previously noted, (e) jurors who generally believe in the rightness of the death penalty and, during the complex jury selection process in capital cases, are excused from serving if they admit that they are opposed to the death penalty.

Documented events from specific trials highlight these challenges for capital defense attorneys. For instance, trial judges consistently have been unwilling to insist on procedural fairness, even when violations are blatant. As an example, at lunch during a 1988 trial of a Black man who was charged with the death of a White person, before an all-White jury, with the prosecutor's case showing that the defendant was not present when others killed the victim, a juror gave the bailiff a napkin with a drawing of a man on a gallows above the inscription, "Hang the Niggers," which the trial judge refused to address (*Andrews* v. *Shulsen*, 1988). As another example, a 17-year-old's lawyer was held to be competent despite presenting no evidence on the defendant's behalf at a capital trial (*Burger* v. *Kemp*, 1987), even though there was significant relevant evidence to support a verdict of life imprisonment, including the fact that this defendant had an intelligence quotient (IQ) of 82 and functioned at the level of a 12 year old. Unfortunately, these are not isolated cases. Defendants facing the death penalty have been given lawyers who were drunk or fell asleep during the trial, absent during critical parts of the case, had just graduated from law school, or had never handled a criminal case (see, e.g., Bright, 1994).

Illinois Governor Ryan acknowledged the impossibility of procedural fairness for death penalty sentences when his state finally released Anthony Porter from death row, after a group of Northwestern University journalism *students* proved that Porter was innocent and showed a videotaped confession from the actual murderer. Previously, Porter had been 48 hours from execution (a stay of that execution was granted solely on the ground that his IQ was 51 and his competency to stand trial, thus, was questionable; had his IQ been 50 points higher, he would be dead today; Berlow, 1999). Unfortunately, mental capacity is an issue frequently missed by overworked, stressed, or inexperienced lawyers.

More recently, new national voices have called attention to the unfairness of the death penalty in the United States. In November 2004, William Sessions, Director of the Federal Bureau of Investigation from 1987-1993, and Charles Baird, a former Texas Court of Criminal Appeals Judge, called for a halt to executions in Texas because of the risk of executing an innocent person, citing mistakes at the Houston Crime Lab as a principal reason (Death Penalty Information Center, 2004a). In December 2004, New Jersey Governor Richard Codey called for a moratorium on the death penalty in his state until a study commission could determine whether the state's death penalty system was consistent with evolving standards of decency, was discriminatory, and worth its costs (Death Penalty Information Center, 2004b).

As states continue to call into question and study the issue, the task of capital defense attorneys remains painful and heavy. These attorneys frequently lack the experience, investigatory support, funding to hire relevant experts, and resources to create multi-lawyer team defenses that are essential to raise all of the legal issues and options available in these complex, deadly cases. A recent study found that criminal attorneys lacking experience in capital cases (who nonetheless are appointed to defend clients facing the death penalty) neglect preparation of the mitigation/sentencing portion of the trial, grossly underestimate the difficulty of convincing a death-qualified jury that there is a reasonable doubt as to their client's guilt, and neglect the investigation and gathering of evidence needed to humanize their client by helping jurors to understand where the defendant came from and why that person may be the way he or she is (White, 2004). Compounding these shortcomings are the unique dialectical challenges facing a trial lawyer who talks to potential jurors in the courtroom during jury selection on a capital case.

DIALECTICAL CHALLENGES OF DEATH TALK

The jury trial is the apotheosis of the amateur. Why should anyone think that 12 persons brought in from the street, selected in various ways for their lack of general ability, should have any special capacity for deciding controversies between persons?

—1966 Harvard Law School Dean's Report
(cited in Kalven & Zeisel, 1966, p. 5)

My first jury trial as a criminal defense attorney took place in 1976. Since that trial, I have been a faculty member in continuing legal education programs offered throughout the United States, facilitating small groups that focus on the teaching and learning of effective jury selection skills by trial attorneys. Before obtaining my doctorate in 1998, I was, as previously mentioned, Training Director for Colorado's Public Defender Office, and I served as defense counsel on death penalty cases. My experience as both an attorney and trainer is that the representation of a client who faces the death penalty is a profound personal challenge.

The impossible constraints of that task and the resulting inherent role strain for the advocate are most evident, however, during jury selection. In a strange communication dance, full of ritual and symbolism, the sentencing phase of a death penalty trial involves a lawyer (the prosecutor) who urges jurors to agree to another person's premeditated death, with another lawyer (defense counsel) pleading for a sentence of life imprisonment instead. Each of these lawyers, however, are given the opportunity during initial jury selection to talk with all potential jurors about their personal opinions concerning the death penalty as an appropriate sentence—that is, to engage in "death talk."

The process of death qualification of citizens during jury selection represents an extended discussion of penalty at the outset of a criminal trial before any evidence of guilt has been presented. In part, the discussion of how a potential juror feels about the appropriateness of the death penalty is essential, although awkward, because, as previously mentioned, jurors in favor of the death penalty are more willing to convict on the underlying crime charged (Allen et al., 1998). In essence, as Haney (1984a, 1984b) argued, prospective jurors are asked to reflect on and predict their behavior during a possible penalty phase of a trial, even though a defendant may be innocent. Haney (1984a) specifically studied the experiences of jurors who sat on death penalty trials and described the difficult choice of talking to jurors about a sentence for a client who may not be guilty of the offense: "Death qualification puts defense attorneys in the untenable position of having to choose between two prejudicial effects, knowing that to reduce one is to intensify the other. Its consequences for capital defendants appear graver still" (p. 151).

Traditional rules and formats for jury selection conversations in criminal trials frequently are counterproductive in a death penalty case. In most criminal cases, lawyers have been trained to ask probing questions of potential jurors concerning their backgrounds, jobs, family, and even embarrassing (yet highly relevant to trial issues) events that have happened in their lives. This type of communication in traditional jury selection is *unidirectional*, with the lawyer asking questions and citizens answering them. Although there typically are 20 discretionary challenges (challenges that will be granted by the court if the attorney asks) per side in capital cases, challenges for various forms of legally demonstrated *bias* are unlimited, as long as the bias appears in a potential juror's responses. To obtain these much-desired legal challenges to jurors who may be biased, lawyers rely on the communication tool of "cross-examination," which typically is experienced as an "attack" by a potential juror. To avoid such a reaction by a potential juror, it is critical that capital defense lawyers find effective ways to motivate citizens to disclose deeply personal beliefs, attitudes, values, and events in a highly public and politicized forum (the courtroom).

Consequently, two dialectical challenges face lawyers throughout jury selection: (a) the *respect/disagree* task, in which a defense lawyer must create a conversational climate that respects a juror's self-disclosure that he or she favors the death penalty, even though the lawyer is personally opposed to such a viewpoint; and (b) the *reveal/conceal* task, in which a defense lawyer must solicit just enough disclosure of opinions opposed to the principle of death as an appropriate penalty from other potential jurors so that the defense knows who those people are, yet conceal the full extent of their opposition and, thereby, rescue them from any prosecutorial challenges that can be based on the fact that a juror opposes the death penalty (with the goal being to keep death-opposition jurors in the pool of potential jurors). Here, I describe one applied real-world communication activist approach that helps underresourced indigent defense counsels to create and sustain meaningful interpersonal dialogues with citizens during jury selection concerning "death."

The need for new communication tools in capital cases is underscored by research studies examining when, during a trial, jurors begin to develop opinions about whether death is an appropriate sentence. Research findings consistently suggest that jurors admit to deciding on death sentence verdicts before the trial has concluded, and frequently before the sentencing hearing has commenced (Blume, 2002). In one study, in fact, half the jurors who sat in capital cases admitted that they had decided the appropriateness of the death sentence before hearing the evidence (Blume, 2002). Furthermore, jurors hold many misconceptions about the law, including the belief that the death penalty is mandatory for a murder case and that there is a presumption that a guilty verdict for any murder, itself, is sufficient for a death penalty sentence (Garvey, 1998). As a result, early communication interventions, during jury selection but before evidence commences, are needed in capital cases.

Coaching capital defense lawyers to create more collaborative (less unidirectional) conversations with potential jurors during jury selection, as described in this chapter, draws on the unique intersection of the experiences I have had as a capital defense lawyer and my scholarship on the dynamics of social influence during group decision making. Due to the fact that capital defense attorneys must manage the contradiction between talking to jurors about presuming their client to be innocent and simultaneously talking to jurors about what sentence might be appropriate if their client is found guilty, I adopt a dialectical perspective to frame the task of creating appropriate communication tools to manage this contradiction. A dialectical perspective focuses attention on the tensions experienced by individuals in their lives (Baxter & Montgomery, 1997). A *dialectic* is a tension between two or more seemingly contradictory elements in a system (such as lawyers wanting to hear what a prospective juror thinks, yet not wanting to know what that juror thinks if it is a response that hurts the client) that demands at least a temporary resolution (see Frey & Sunwolf, 2004). Applying a dialectical perspective to the challenges of talking to jurors during jury selection encourages a focus on the inevitable tensions in the advocate-juror relationship during the process of uncovering (in a public forum) private values of citizens who have been involuntarily summoned to jury duty.

During jury selection in a death penalty case, before the prosecution or defense lawyers talk to the potential jurors, the judge discusses the possibility of a life or death sentence with jurors (before jurors have heard any evidence). This discussion, in turn, sets up a profound dialectical dilemma for the capital defense lawyer: The unavoidable assumption created for potential jurors is that the guilt/innocence trial, which precedes the sentencing trial, must be a mere formality (as the defendant probably is guilty), because the sentence appears to be the only real issue to the judge and the lawyers (Blume, 2002; Haney, 1984b). The first tasks of a capital defense attorney, therefore, are to: (a) normalize a citizen's assumption that guilt already has been assumed in the courtroom ("It is only natural to assume that there is not much question about guilt"), (b) uncover the existence and degree of that assumption through public dialogue with potential jurors in the courtroom, and (c) undo or neutralize such a deadly presumption. During my years of training capital defense lawyers throughout the country, attorneys consistently have shared with me their anger when a prospective juror in a capital case expresses opinions that assume the guilt of the person charged. Having watched jury selection in death penalty trials and assisted in mock jury training with lawyers in capital defense programs, I have seen the communication instinct of these capital defense lawyers to argue against the unwanted ideas a juror shares and then punish the juror who expressed them. These negative instincts (to feel anger, argue, and punish) place the lawyer in unfortunate opposition at the outset of trial to potential jurors who, ultimately, may be given the power to judge the value of a client's life.

The second essential task of the capital defense lawyer is to teach potential jurors how to impose a life verdict during jury deliberations (should they be sworn as jurors in the case and should the prosecution prove the guilt of the defendant). When defense lawyers talk with potential jurors about the death penalty, they ultimately are attempting to identity those jurors who would vote for a sentence of life in prison, in this particular case. Attempting to select jurors who always would vote for life imprisonment is an exercise in futility, for not only are such jurors considered by criminal defense lawyers to be an endangered species in U.S. courts, but jurors who always would vote against death would be legally challenged by the prosecution and, consequently, excused from service.

The third challenging task for the capital defense lawyer is to cope with and acknowledge the fact that the mere experience of listening to and being part of repeated conversations about the potential death penalty contaminates jurors. Criminal defense attorneys often are oblivious to the negative effects of specific words spoken by potential jurors in capital cases during jury selection, in part, because they have heard them so often. Sunwolf (2001, 2004) described how judges tell jurors at the outset of trial that there will be a "guilt phase" followed by a "penalty phase" and, thereby, significantly muddy the presumption of innocence.[2] Furthermore, the jurors who ultimately are seated in a capital case have been exposed repeatedly to the words of death penalty questioning in the courtroom and typically have witnessed the dismissal of several prospective jurors on the basis of their expressed antideath penalty attitudes (Haney, 1984a). These courtroom conversations may create deadly preconceptions about the trial to follow, such that jurors are not applying the presumption of innocence concerning the "who-did-what-why" phase of the case (sometimes referred to as the "guilt-innocence phase" of a death penalty trial). Instead, jurors assume that the "real" issue is what sentence should be imposed for the murder(s) charged. Furthermore, talking to jurors about the penalty before the trial starts may predispose them to receive and interpret testimony in certain ways that favor finding the defendant guilty. Studying the dynamics of this process, Haney (1984a) randomly assigned adult men and women to watch a simulated videotape of jury selection in a capital trial; in one condition, however, the videotape included a 30-minute segment of typical death qualification. Those who had been exposed to the death penalty qualification discussion were significantly more conviction prone, more likely to believe that other trial participants thought the defendant was guilty, more likely to sentence that defendant to death, and expressed the belief that the law disapproved of any opposition to the death penalty. Studies have also shown that the mere process effects of repeated death talk during jury selection are deadly to capital defendants (Haney, 1984b).

WORKSHOP METHOD

A constant performance-critique-dialogue technique for training capital defense attorneys in a workshop is described here, for the purpose of lawyer-participants gaining new skills, insights, and task goals during jury selection on capital cases. First, I describe the participants and the learning context for the workshop, followed by the specific facilitation intervention used with these participants. I then explain the specific communication challenges faced by these attorneys and the new tools offered to cope with these challenges in four primary areas: (a) welcoming differences from potential jurors, (b) learning to move toward unwanted responses, (c) abandoning tendencies to argue with potential jurors when they express unwanted beliefs or opinions, and (d) creating collaborative conversations with potential jurors about the challenges of a death penalty trial.

The facilitation described here offers lawyers new communication tools for engaging in more meaningful dialogue with potential jurors about their beliefs, attitudes, values, and reasoning concerning the appropriateness of death as a lawful penalty and possible jury verdict. Such dialogue is crucial, for attorneys are challenged to connect intimately with jurors whose viewpoints they personally may despise. Influenced by a dialectical perspective, I suggest techniques for attorneys to use during jury selection that abandon a paradigm of "interrogating" potential jurors and adopt, instead, a model of courtroom talk that seeks to create "collaborative conversations" between capital defense attorneys and the citizens called for jury duty. Each of the facilitations constitutes a tool for *empathic attunement,* a communication perspective that facilitates the experiencing of another's emotions and simultaneously brings things that are separate into harmony (Sunwolf, 2006). Employing empathic attunement facilitation techniques, for example, a lawyer is encouraged to consider the perspective and value system of a death-prone juror at the outset of the dialogue and manage the dialectic tension such a perspective has with the lawyer's antideath penalty perspective by creating a conversation that leads them to be willing to experience an opposing worldview.

Participants and the Workshop Context

I have previously described (Sunwolf, 2006) how attorneys who have been appointed by trial judges to represent defendants facing the death penalty receive little, if any, training in what I termed *empathy-driven advocacy* (advocacy motivated by a helper's affective connection with a client's experiences and values) versus *distress-driven advocacy* (advocacy motivated by a helper's personal distress when attempting to cope with a client's problem-solving issues). Lawyers are problem solvers, trained to strategically solve their clients' legal dilemmas using the tools of the justice system. Many attorneys, consequently, arrive at death penalty training seminars in understandable personal distress as they prepare for a death penalty trial, with a tendency to focus on their own concerns about the trial rather than the stresses and concerns of the client who faces the possibility of receiving the death penalty. These lawyers have survived their criminal defense practices by creating boundaries between themselves and their clients and, consequently, may find it difficult to connect with people called for jury duty at the deep functional level that is needed to learn about potential jurors who may decide whether their client lives or dies. Although the overt goal that attorneys expect to accomplish in a jury selection workshop is to learn new questions to ask potential jurors, the goal of my workshops, in addition, is to help lawyers connect with jurors more profoundly and understand their worlds. The connection I am seeking, ideally, would help attorneys to make more informed choices about who to excuse from the trial, as well as facilitate a shared feeling of connection with each juror who ultimately is selected.

The format in which these techniques are taught consists of small groups, with 6-8 attorneys who, most frequently, have never met one another. The program director organizes the membership of these groups, attempting to be sure that the members do not work in the same city or know one another. These small learning groups are embedded within a larger structure that lasts from 3-10 days, depending on the advocacy program. Attorneys attend lectures as a large group but practice skills in their small groups. Each member of the group, however, has a pending death penalty trial for which he or she is the attorney for the accused; some lawyers have had previous death penalty trial experience, whereas others have not. The small group workshops last from 2-4 hours a session, depending on the schedule of a particular program.

Once in their small group workshops, the attorneys know they will practice effective jury selection techniques. Many programs (this one included) provide rotating bands of citizens as jury-participants in the exercise, so that attorneys have real-world answers to confront and real-world opinions to consider; when such citizens are not available, faculty members role-play them. An attorney typically is given 5-10 minutes to practice talking with mock jurors about the death penalty, followed by critique from the program's attorney faculty member(s) and group feedback from other attorney participants. During the critique and group feedback, the session is deconstructed, the various parts discussed, and the performing attorney is encouraged to engage in dialogue with both the group and the faculty member about other choices that might be made when confronted with similar answers by a potential juror in court. This is the critical point at which a facilitator has the opportunity to introduce new communication tools through initial brief modeling and provide an immediate opportunity to practice those new tools. The specific communication tools described later are ones that I use in all workshops on death penalty *voir dire*; the members of a small group will not have heard about them before or been provided with any reading material about them prior to the workshop.

Summarizing the protocol in which these tools are taught: (a) Participant A practices jury selection question-answer formats with mock jurors, which might include discussing the law, the mock jurors' views about the death penalty or troubling aspects of the anticipated evidence, and any facts of the case that seem challenging; (b) the facilitator/faculty attorney then provides feedback and new ideas to try, talking to the group, as well as to the performing participant; and (c) a second round of talking to mock jurors is offered, providing an opportunity to try new techniques. Each lawyer has a chance in each workshop session to perform and receive critique at least twice.

Facilitation/Intervention

At the outset of the workshop, I introduce the concept of *empathy*, which involves both cognitive role-taking and an other-oriented emotional responsiveness that helps attorneys to imagine what it would be like to be in another person's (juror's) predicament (Larson, 1993). I explain that some forms of communication are better able than other forms to help people connect with the divergent experiences of someone else. I then invite the attorneys to share statements potential jurors offer in court that the attorneys have found most troublesome in the past. Using those specific exemplars, we first role-play the manner in which the attorneys typically have attempted to deal with these difficult juror statements. Following that, with attorneys now assuming the role of the "problematic" jurors they described, I assume the role of an attorney using a collaborative approach.

Table 7.1 identifies eight typical juror comments that capital defense attorneys both complain about to one another and admit fearing. Table 7.1 also organizes my communication coaching for these lawyers by categorizing these eight typical attorney-feared juror responses into four basic communication challenges: welcoming differences in values, moving toward bad news, abandoning argument, and collaborating on solutions. The table provides examples of new collaborative conversational formats between attorneys and prospective jurors that serve eight functions: (a) normalizing contrary positions, (b) valuing disturbing viewpoints, (c) uncovering biases, (d) introducing damaging evidence, (e) joining the juror's thinking process, (f) abandoning interrogatory formats, (g) collaborating on solutions, and (h) jointly developing exceptions. These four communication challenges and the intervention tools used to create collaborative conversations between attorneys and jurors are discussed in detail next.

Table 7.1. Communication Interventions to Create Collaborative Conversations between Attorneys and Jurors During Jury Selection

Communication Challenge (Issue)	Problematic Comment (Juror)	Collaborative Conversation (Attorney)	Intervention Function (Tool)
Welcoming Differences in Values	"I wouldn't be sympathetic to any defendant just because he had a bad childhood."	"Most folks might agree with you. Would you share more of your thinking on that point?"	Normalizing contrary positions
	"If we gave the death penalty more often, we'd all be safer."	"You feel we don't impose that penalty enough. Can you give us an example?"	Valuing disturbing viewpoints
Moving Toward Bad News	"Gangs are the biggest problem we have today."	"What are some of the worst things you've heard about gangs?"	Uncovering bias
	N/A	"Nothing's worse than hurting a child, but that's what happened here and it happened more than once. What are your thoughts about giving a life sentence to someone who hurt a child?"	Introducing damaging evidence
Abandoning Argument	"Well, I just think both sides should present evidence, including the defendant. That's only fair."[a]	"Well, that's what a fair person would want to do, of course. Tell me your own thinking about that."	Joining juror thinking (by resisting the urge to punish unwanted answers)
	N/A	"One reason an innocent person might choose not to testify at trial might be . . . ."	Abandoning interrogatory formats and employing stem questions

Collaborating on Solutions	"I'd sure be suspicious if a defendant didn't testify. I'd know I'd want to."[b]	"That's honest, I appreciate it. What would it take for that not to be so important for you?"	Inviting joint solutions
	"I just think police tell the truth. That's their job, they're trained for it."	"We'd all like to believe that, that's for sure. Can you think of a situation where a police officer might make a decision to lie?"	Jointly developing exceptions
	"If the law says a defendant doesn't have to testify, then I would follow that law."	"Even though you would think that is true, what if that doesn't work and you start wondering why the defendant did not testify?"	Anticipating future issues

Notes. [a]In a criminal trial, the defense has no burden of proof; the entire burden rests, instead, on the prosecution to prove beyond all reasonable doubt every element of the crime charged.
[b]In a criminal trial, the jury is instructed that a defendant never has to testify and that no juror should hold it against a defendant for choosing not to testify.

Welcoming Differences in Values

When a juror expresses an opinion that an attorney dreads, there is a natural tendency to want to ignore, argue against, or convert it. A collaborative conversation, however, suggests a different reaction. I ask the lawyers which answers from a potential juror they are afraid of and encourage them to think about why they might want to hear more about those answers in a death penalty case rather than less. Two communication tools are particularly useful to welcome values from jurors that may be different than the values of the lawyer: normalizing contrary positions and valuing disturbing viewpoints.

Tool: Normalizing contrary positions. One typically dreaded citizen comment that might occur in open court during jury selection is represented by the following statement:

Juror: "I don't believe there's any reason to give sympathy to someone just because he or she had a bad childhood."

This statement is particularly disturbing to capital defense attorneys because childhood is, in fact, a circumstance that the law says jurors may properly consider in deciding whether to impose the death penalty (although most jurors are not aware of this fact). However, rather than arguing against the juror's unwelcome point (a typical urge for defense lawyers), lawyers are taught to make such a position feel welcome. For instance, a lawyer might reply to the juror:

> *Attorney*: "Most folks might agree with you," followed by, "Would you share more of your thinking on that point?" [normalizing and welcoming]

Tool: Valuing disturbing viewpoints. When a juror offers a comment that upsets a defense attorney, such as the following statement, the urge to run from that answer is strong:

> *Juror*: "If we imposed the death penalty more often, we would all be better off."

However, when a lawyer runs from such a response or tries to correct it, opportunities are lost to develop a better understanding of that juror's position in respect to the lawyer's client. That is unfortunate because it may well be that this juror would not vote to impose the death penalty under the unique facts of the lawyer's case. Hence, an example of a modeled intervention for this situation in the workshop would be the following, which begins by understanding the depth of the juror's feeling that the death penalty should be used more often and then understanding the juror's reasoning:

> *Attorney*: "You feel we don't impose the death penalty enough?" [understanding juror's feeling]
> *Juror*: "Yep."
> *Attorney*: "Can you give us an example?" [understanding juror's reasoning]

Moving Toward Bad News

There are two types of trial-specific "bad news" that represent important challenges for capital defense attorneys during jury selection: (a) negative juror opinions that demonstrate prejudice toward the lawyer's client and (b) prejudicial prosecution evidence the defense lawyer anticipates will be introduced at trial against the client. Three workshop tools are described to cope with this type of bad news: uncovering bias, introducing damaging evidence, and becoming a guide for the journey toward extreme positions.

Tool: Uncovering and normalizing bias. The defense attorney is faced with the challenge of wanting to know which jurors are biased against her or his client (to challenge the person legally), yet not wanting everyone else to hear the bias and be affected by it. Jurors, however, are unlikely to self-identify as holding prejudices; few jurors, for example, would be expected to respond to a defense attorney's plea of "Raise your hand if you are biased and unfair!" Normalizing a bias some jurors might be expected to hold (even though the attorney would prefer to believe few jurors share that bias) aids enormously in creating a courtroom climate in which citizens feel more comfortable owning their biases to some degree. Hence, normalizing is a tool to encourage the revealing or uncovering of a bias the attorney needs to discover. Typically, for instance, a capital defense attorney would tell jurors that merely being a member of gang should not be held against the defendant, but this is cognitively dissonant with what most citizens believe about gangs. A modeled intervention would begin:

Attorney: "When we read so much about gangs and shootings, it's only natural to feel pretty negative about anyone who voluntarily joins a gang." [normalizing] "What are some of the worst things you've heard about gangs?" [uncovering bias by inviting the worst news]

Tool: Introducing damaging evidence. When a trial will contain inflammatory evidence likely to upset jurors and lead them to despise the behavior of a defendant, most defense attorneys prefer not to talk about those facts during jury selection. An attorney willing to risk introducing the bad news, without arguing against its obvious impact, is offering to trust prospective jurors to share their honest reactions to it and, consequently, potentially will have more information for deciding which jurors to keep. For instance, an attorney might say the following:

Attorney: "Nothing is worse than hurting a small child. We all know that, but that's what happened here, and it happened more than once." [introducing damaging evidence] "Can you think of a reason you might feel that life in prison with no chance of getting out would be enough of a sentence for a man who has repeatedly hurt and, finally, murdered a child?" [inviting exceptions]

Tool: Uncovering bias (by becoming a guide for the journey toward extreme positions). When an attorney's conversational goal is to obtain an admission of bias from potential jurors during jury selection, the cross-examination format is ineffective because it is argumentative and usually provokes defensive feelings from jurors. Paradoxically, a juror who claims that most murderers should receive the death penalty is a bonus for a defense lawyer, if the juror sticks with that position (as such a position is grounds for a challenge to that juror). Collaborative communication allows the defense attorney to temporarily align with such a juror so that they walk the road toward the desired legal challenge for bias together, with respect and empathy. The following is an example of such a joint journey:

> *Juror:* "If you take a life, that's when you should be given the death penalty."
>
> *Attorney:* "Any sentence of life imprisonment wouldn't seem like enough, would it?" [normalizing contrary positions and valuing disturbing viewpoints]
>
> *Juror:* "Well, of course, it all depends on the evidence." [*Juror appears unwilling to move towards a more extreme opinion.*]
>
> *Attorney:* "Sure, it would. Tell us, though, what about a person who murders someone; someone who plans the murder, intends it, and kills an innocent person? Would any sentence less than death seem right to you?" [rewarding disturbing viewpoints]
>
> *Juror:* "Of course not. That case should get the death penalty." [*Juror is now eligible for a defense challenge.*]

Abandoning Argument

Unwanted juror responses during jury selection conversations, especially those that contradict the law, may tempt defense lawyers to argue with jurors. Worse, many lawyers unwittingly adopt questioning structures in ways that make jurors feel oppressed or manipulated. Three specific collaborative communication techniques, as explained next, help capital defense lawyers to abandon unsuccessful argumentative structures with jurors: (a) joining juror thinking (by resisting the urge to punish unwanted answers), (b) abandoning interrogatory formats, and (c) employing "stem" questions.

    Tool: Joining juror thinking (by resisting the urge to punish unwanted answers). When jurors do not remember the judge's instructions, lawyers typically go on automatic "correction" mode, as demonstrated in the following illustration:

> *Attorney:* "No! The judge just told you the prosecution has the whole burden of proof." [typical courtroom punishment of an unwanted answer]

Instead of enacting such punishing behavior, joining the juror's thinking process allows for a more realistic understanding of that juror, as well as reduces the creation of an enemy who may well serve on the jury. For instance, the attorney might say:

> *Attorney:* "Well, that's what a fair person would want to do, of course. Tell me your thinking about that."
> [joining the juror's thinking]

Tool: Abandoning interrogatory formats. In trials, before attorneys question potential jurors, the judge instructs these potential jurors on basic principles of law that will guide the trial (such as the presumption of innocence, the burden of proof, and reasonable doubt). Typically, lawyers admit that they will ask a citizen about some complex principle of law, and if the juror did not recall that particular legal concept, unintentionally embarrass that juror by pointing out that the judge told him or her differently. Lawyers know that this tactic of confronting a potential juror with a mistake is not effective, yet they admit that they find it hard to break out of an interrogatory format (e.g., "Does the defendant have to testify?"). Workshop lawyers, therefore, consistently have been eager to learn a nonquestion-oriented way to find out what jurors think about legal concepts.

An example of a counterproductive conversation that capital defense attorneys have with potential jurors that unwittingly leads to an embarrassing or punitive response to a juror's courtroom comments involves the pop-quiz format that many trial lawyers adopt. An example of an unwanted "pop quiz" is:

> *Attorney:* "So, you heard the judge explain the law. Mr. Brown, according to the judge's earlier instructions, who has the burden of proof in this case?" [pop quiz]
> *Juror:* "I'd listen to both sides, for sure."
> [trying to appear reasonable]
> *Attorney:* "Don't you remember that the burden is on the prosecution?" [correction and punishment]

Tool: Employing stem questions. Once attorneys are encouraged to see the damage that pop-quiz formats have on their relationship with potential jurors, a new format is suggested that relies on a stem-question format that traditionally is used by many therapists with their clients. Stem questions are not experienced as interrogations, because they take the form of an incomplete sentence that needs to be finished by the conversational partner ("You just can't talk to your father because . . ."). Stem questions are ideal in the context of jury selection because they are both collaborative and never phrased in an interrogatory format. These incomplete sentences provide the smoothest, most collaborative tool for creating a conversation with a juror, instead of the traditional pop-quiz argumentative format. At the same time, they give the lawyer control, suggesting (indirectly) a topic, as demonstrated in the following statements:

> *Attorney*: "Why doesn't a defendant have to testify, under the law?" [quiz with only one correct answer]
>
> *Attorney*: "For me, one reason an innocent person might choose not to testify at his or her trial would be . . ." [sentence completion, multiple correct answers]

Potential jurors and lawyers, thus, together, are completing a thought that has been initiated by the lawyer. Using the stem-question tool, a lawyer is expressing genuine curiosity about a juror's thinking rather than a professorial-student interaction in which the professor (lawyer) knows the correct answer and is wondering if the student (potential juror) can answer correctly. Interestingly, once the format of a stem question is introduced to lawyers in the workshop, they recognize it even when they have not used it before in court. As a lawyer pointed out in one of my first workshop sessions, "We've all heard these questions, but not in court—in therapy!"

Collaborating on Solutions

When capital defense attorneys find themselves standing in opposition to jurors' expressed beliefs, attitudes, values, and experiences, they consistently complain in my workshops that they become disconnected with these potential decision makers. "How do I not show that juror how disgusted I am with that belief?" is a typical question asked by the lawyers in these workshops. Inviting jurors to join in solving discrepancies and dilemmas that face the decision-making process demonstrates respect for potential jurors and encourages their personal investment in fair solutions. Table 7.1 offers examples of creating collaborative conversations on two specific topics about which capital defense attorneys and jurors frequently disagree and that are the most-requested "problems" lawyers ask me to help them solve: whether the failure of a defendant to testify inherently is suspicious and whether police tell the truth. Once suggestions are offered for these topics, lawyers immediately have been successful in co-creating with one another solutions to other "unwanted" prospective juror responses. To address these issues, as explained next, I developed and teach three communication tools designed to answer three questions: (a) inviting joint solutions, (b) jointly developing exceptions, and (c) jointly anticipating future issues.

Tool: Inviting joint solutions (How could we solve this?). The tendency of trial lawyers is to talk with potential jurors as if jurors and attorneys were in separate camps. In fact, however, there are many trial issues that jurors and lawyers share; consequently, "we" thinking during jury selection can create a powerful sense of connection with potential jurors. Indeed, capital defense lawyers have shared the usefulness of thinking in terms of "we" instead of "you" and "I" during jury selection. As one lawyer, laughing, reminded others in the group, "Isn't that what we were taught in marriage counseling?" In fact, each time a juror expresses a disagreement with a legal principle that benefits a capital defense attorney's case, such an answer provides a valuable opportunity to jointly solve the dilemma. Joint solutions, in turn, create connections between attorneys and citizens who ultimately may be selected to serve on the case. The juror experiences the conversation as a partner, not as a target. For instance, an attorney might respond to a juror in the following manner:

> *Juror:* "I'd sure be suspicious if a defendant didn't testify. I know he doesn't have to but I'd sure want to, if it were me."
>
> *Attorney* [Response A]: "That's honest. I appreciate that. What would it take for that not to be so important for you?" [inviting joint solution]
>
> *Attorney* [Alternative Response B]: "We'd all like to believe that's always true. Are we always right?" [inviting joint solution]

Tool: Jointly developing exceptions ("Can you think of a reason?"). Joint development of exceptions can also be stimulated by a second question, "Can you think of a reason?" This tool was created as the result of another situation that was raised as a dominant concern by lawyer-participants: They wanted to know how they could talk to potential jurors about case facts that they anticipated would be a problem for jurors—even though these citizens had said nothing about those facts, so far. As one workshop participant put it, "I know some jurors are going to be turned off by the fact that my client killed her husband as he was sleeping, but how do I find out which of the jurors can't get beyond that point without upsetting them?" In effect, the lawyers needed important information to make decisions on which citizens to challenge, but they also needed potential jurors to begin thinking about key factual issues in the case. The lawyers agreed that waiting to discuss some facts for opening statements (after the evidence had begun) probably would be too late; they wanted to lay some anticipated trial evidence on the courtroom table during jury selection without creating conflict between themselves and the potential jurors.

First, lawyers shared how they typically handled such issues; they would, for example, ask a juror, "If a defendant shot her husband as he was sleeping, could you still find her not guilty?" Second, the lawyers were asked to discuss, together, how much information they would get from such a question. Two robust answers always emerged from participants in using this example of the sleeping husband: (a) the question tended to provoke a simple yes or no response, casting no illumination on the thinking processes of potential jurors; and (b) some potential jurors probably felt that the attorney was trying to manipulate them into saying that shooting a sleeping man might be acceptable.

The collaborative communication tool that lawyers were encouraged to use, as illustrated in the following statement, functions to allow a juror's reasoning to emerge, be shared with other jurors in open court, and become a rich resource for the defense lawyer in later framing the opening statement and closing argument:

> *Attorney* [to panel of jurors]: "Can anyone think of a reason, consistent with being **innocent**, that a woman might only be able to escape with her life if she shot a man who was sleeping?"

Any jurors who raised their hands obviously would have thought through some reasons that would be acceptable to the defense lawyer; coming from the mouth of another juror (as opposed to originating from the defendant's lawyer), these responses also would be more acceptable to fellow jurors and could be drawn on by the lawyer later in trial (e.g., in closing argument). Those jurors who did not raise their hand were appropriate conversational targets for exploring the difficulty of thinking of a defensible reason— potentially subjecting those jurors to a challenge for cause (e.g., anyone who believes the act of shooting has no defense). As one workshop participant phrased it last year, however, "The best part for me was that it felt better to talk that way with folks!" Collaboration triggers feelings of connecting, whereas challenging the thinking of jurors too often may trigger feelings of alienation on the part of both the capital defense attorney and potential jurors.

Tool: Anticipating future issues (What if that doesn't work?). Extending the technique of inviting joint solutions to anticipated issues in a capital trial, lawyers in these workshops have pointed out their concern that the suggested "solution" might not match what could happen at trial. Together, we have created another solution, which we refer to in the workshop as the "What if that doesn't work?" tool. Specifically, capital defense lawyers are encouraged to follow-up on a conversation with a potential juror. In the follow-up conversation, a problem is anticipated and the juror's thinking about how to solve it is specifically invited.

Lawyers have shared that what they particularly appreciate about this tool is that it allows a discussion about the unexpected, gives them a glimpse into the ability of a juror to think in cognitively complex ways, and creates a situation in which a "wobbly" juror is more visible and can be dealt with directly. For instance, the following exchange between a juror and an attorney is encouraged:

> *Juror:* "I just think cops tell the truth. That's their job, they're trained for it."
>
> *Attorney:* "That could sure be true. What if there are pressures we don't know about, and one cop just doesn't tell the truth? Would there be any way for us to know?" [anticipating future issues]
>
> *Juror:* "Never thought about it."
>
> *Attorney:* "Now that you are thinking about it, what thoughts do you have?" [anticipating future issues]

In addition to the communication interventions for specific issues that arise while talking to jurors in capital trials described here, I observed one topic that was conspicuous by its absence. Because lawyers avoided talking to jurors about this topic, they had not experienced any challenging juror answers about the subject. Rather than requiring an "intervention" for regularly occurring jury selection issues, one topic simply needed to be illuminated for the capital defense lawyers, as a significant source of important information for deciding who to choose (or eliminate) from the jury—extreme death talk.

Extreme Death Talk

There remains one conversation with jurors that all workshop participants readily admit, once asked, that they avoid. Once brought to their attention, however, like the infamous pink elephant standing in the living room, the avoided topic appears utterly unavoidable. The single-most important topic in a death penalty trial is a juror's view on death itself.

To allow each workshop participant to privately examine the issues connected with "death," before discussing it in the group, I begin by asking participants to think about their answer to the question, "What do you personally believe will happen when you die?" Deep silence always follows the question. When someone is willing to share a thought, it generally is in the form of, "I've never thought about it before!" I then have them turn to another person and share whatever they are willing to about what happens after a person dies. The conversations begin slowly, but always are lively.

Although never thinking about the aftermath of death may be typical for many people, it is odd for an attorney on a death penalty case in which death is central: death of a victim(s), death as a penalty, and death of a convicted defendant. I then ask, "Have you ever asked jurors what they believe happens to a person when he or she dies?" None of the workshop participants have ever done that (nor had I, as a capital defense attorney, or any attorneys whom I knew). I invite them to consider two views on the aftermath of human death on a continuum that jurors may hold: heaven, in which people are reunited (or hellish eternal punishment), versus finality, in which people turn to dust. I then ask them to reflect on how such views might affect a juror's willingness to impose a death penalty on another human being. The group conversation reaches two critical conclusions, often surprising for participants: (a) A juror who believes that life after death is better than life on earth and that there is a reunion with loved ones (or who believes there is eternal punishment) might be more likely to impose the death penalty on a defendant, reasoning that the deprived life of a killer would be healed (or punished); and (b) a juror who believes that death is final, with no cognitive or spiritual aftermath, might be less likely to impose death on a defendant, sensing it is a horrible judgment to make about another person.

What courtroom conversations are suggested by these insights? Extreme death talk in capital cases during jury selection functions in three important ways: (a) it invites the potential death sentencers (jurors) to think about and share their ideas on what happens after a person dies, the exact issue that they privately will face in such a trial; (b) it requires that defense attorneys be willing to engage in an examination of their personal beliefs about death in advance of that courtroom conversation; and (c) (most unexpected, according to participants) it allows defense attorneys to become more profoundly connected with their clients (who privately face this painful question every day). Participants have shared—several days, weeks, or years after these workshops—that this single question helped them to reframe their dedication to this unique and stressful work, reconnect with important people in their lives, and demonstrate consistent compassion for both their clients and the families of the victims in their cases. Participants, however, never have said that extreme death talk is comfortable. Once they see it on the table, they simply feel that it cannot be avoided.

REFLECTIONS ON LESSONS LEARNED ABOUT COMMUNICATION ACTIVISM

My participation as a facilitator in capital defense training sessions that teach new skills of jury selection in death penalty trials has illuminated several significant reflections about this form of communication activism: (a) I am listened to by attorneys who participate in the workshops more actively as a communication scholar than I had been as a trial attorney; (b) as a former trial attorney who holds high standards for what I regard as competent preparation for the defense of a death penalty trial, I am faced with the challenge of teaching lawyers who I sometimes worry are not as prepared as a particular client needs; (c) at the same time that I am teaching attorneys to focus on the receivers of their messages (potential jurors), successful facilitation requires that I focus away from the potential jurors during the exercise and, instead, pay primary attention to the receivers of my teaching (the lawyers); and (d) I must find a way to tolerate the painful reality that some of the cases I am coaching will be unsuccessful, the intervention may be insufficient, and, most painful, that a person may die. Each of these four lessons relates, further, to lessons of value for all scholars committed to communication activism.

First, stepping into communities outside the academy provides us with greater insight into the value that practitioners place on our discipline and its body of knowledge about the tools and effects of communication. How do I know I am listened to more actively as a communication scholar in training workshops than I was as a well-known trial attorney/trainer? My cues come from the participants and are the same ones that communication professors teach students in introductory courses (see, e.g., Adler, Proctor, & Towne, 2005), which demonstrate that active listeners (a) *prompt* the speaker, using silence and brief statements to draw the speaker out; (b) *question* the speaker to be sure they are receiving the speaker's message accurately; and (c) *paraphrase* the speaker's message in their own words to reflect back to the speaker that they understand. Although attorneys consistently took notes on what I said previously and attempted to try the new techniques I offered, since obtaining my doctoral degree in communication, I experience continual prompting, questioning, and paraphrasing by the participants throughout these workshops. I continually am challenged by trial lawyers to reframe for them my scholarly derived suggestions. Activists should take the time to discuss with the community groups with which they are involved what the discipline of communication involves, what concepts and processes we study, and what outcomes we are familiar with; when communication scholarship is explained in that manner, people find it highly relevant to their everyday lives and may listen more deeply to our ideas.

Second, a working tolerance for imperfect planning, preparation, or even organization by group members needs to be fostered by communication activists who seek to make a difference. I am significantly challenged in the workshops I facilitate when the performance, comments, or questions of a participant lead me to fear that a case has not been adequately prepared.

My standards for what a competent capital defense lawyer should have done at that point are severely challenged. I attempt to manage this anxiety in several ways. First, I use the energy produced by such anxiety as additional motivation to speak more clearly, offer more examples, and focus on what the lawyers are doing that is successful. I also find time during breaks in the day or at the end of the day to offer attorneys personal consulting time, resources in the form of attorneys in their cities who I know will help them on a capital case, motions they might file to get additional help or continuances on their trial, and opportunities to ask me questions that may not have emerged in the more public workshop. I want to channel my anxiety about someone's client potentially receiving the death penalty into a willingness to be more of a resource, although the feeling often is the opposite—wanting to withdraw from that lawyer and minimize contact. Communication activists, per se, are committed to making a difference in outcomes in the real world and, consequently, may be frustrated if some group members are not prepared, but activists should challenge themselves to channel their energies into what can be done under the circumstances.

Third, communication activists should decide, at the outset, who their "clients" are and recognize real-world situations that may challenge that primary allegiance. I am continually learning how to focus my allegiance on the community members I guide and, only secondarily, on the clients those professionals serve. The traditional transactional communication model that includes sender, receiver, message, channel, and noise (see, e.g., Adler et al., 2005) is a powerful one when I teach these workshops. I realize that a receiver focus in analyzing the effectiveness of messages often is easier said than done. My attention during the workshops is so completely focused on the attorney who is performing or speaking with me that the effort feels physical and, ultimately, is exhausting. Although I encourage workshop participants to focus completely on the citizens to whom they are talking, even though the context is a public courtroom with many distractions and pressures, I must encourage myself to offer this complete focus to the participants. Furthermore, however, I must give some of my attention to the citizen-jurors or mock jurors to help participants engage in useful perception checks about how closely they understood what someone was trying to say. Workshops that allow me to teach/facilitate with a partner help to alleviate that strain; consequently, I encourage others to find ways to have more than one person who can do the physical/emotional/cognitive work of attending to the participants. The decision about who the activist is committed to serving is an important one and should be made intentionally and thoughtfully, at the outset.

Fourth, communication activists must be prepared to cope with unsuccessful interventions. As a facilitator, I offer an intervention that is designed to help. The reality, however, is that my suggestions, models, tools, and encouragement may not always help and, in cases of capital trials, a defense lawyer may talk ineffectively to the potential jurors, choose unwisely who should be excused from the jury, and that some clients, consequently, may receive a sentence of death. I experience such an outcome as a failure for all of us who had any role in preparing that trial. The reality, of course, is that these workshops are time-bound, each participant deserves more time than I have to give within the structure of any program, there will be considerable time gaps for some participants before their trials (in which they may forget or misremember the teachings), and I am not always as effective a communicator with all participants as they need me to be. Death is different—it is an outcome both extreme and intolerable; as a result, I ruminate painfully on those realities and, to date, have not satisfactorily resolved the consequences of my failure (however small in proportion to the role of others) in a capital trial. I continue, however, to give attention to my limitations and their consequences for someone else's client (before, during, and after these workshops), such that the possibility of an execution is never off my mind's agenda. An activist who does not anticipate the many ways an intervention may not succeed (as originally anticipated) may burn out and, thus, be less willing to partner with community groups that nonetheless will continue to need that scholarship.

The success of any facilitation intervention involving group work, for me, always is paradoxical. Success tends to blot out the need to recreate; failure promptly triggers a realized need for better ideas. Success, therefore, must be celebrated and then set aside—so that new communication tools can be conceived, created, adapted, and shared to help one more lawyer save one more client's life. Intriguingly, there is one more lesson learned about communication activism from my work that I hope stimulates new thinking for others.

THE CHALLENGES OF BEING AN ITINERATE ACTIVIST

I have been an itinerate activist for more than 2 decades. Itinerate professionals always have been with us, carrying their knowledge and skills from place to place: troubadours, gypsy craft folk, preachers, circuit judges, and frontier doctors, to name a few. "Itinerate" suggests a traveler, one who regularly journeys from one location and group of people to another. Itinerate activism carries with it a significant distinction from that of local activism, which involves work within a nearby community or region.

Local activists are privy to outcome-feedback loops related to their activism that elude an itinerate activist. Local activists are able to see, hear, or involve themselves in the results of their efforts, facilitations, and suggestions, longitudinally. Furthermore, local activists have a proximity advantage that allows them to receive regular accounts of the aftermath of their efforts, through diverse community sources beyond those firsthand participants. An itinerate activist, in contrast, is challenged to be content with giving extraordinary energy to people who the activist probably will never see or hear from again. The human need for feedback can be, in fact, distracting for an itinerate activist. As a doctoral student, someone pointed out that my national work with lawyers offered rare data sets to feed my scholarship; I considered the possibility, but ultimately declined to combine my community involvement with data collection. This chapter is a rare exception, but even as I share my work here, my descriptions are constrained by the specific outcome-feedback data I might otherwise be able to offer the reader. Missing, for example, is the important question of how the lawyers with whom I work actually enact these ideas in their courtrooms and with what effects.

Although I applaud those who find creative ways to combine their activism with their scholarship, I invite consideration, here, of the satisfaction of choosing differently. Four factors invite our mindfulness: (a) some forms of activism cannot realistically be followed through to their various outcomes, yet are deeply needed (e.g., disaster relief efforts, ephemeral artistic events, support for urban street youth, or trauma site counseling); (b) some of the individuals and groups who could benefit from our communication scholarship could be put off by the idea of becoming part of research (e.g., gangs, religious sects, prison inmates, political targets, or hospital patients); (c) some of the people who most need our activism are not in a position to give informed consent to become part of a research project (e.g., those in acute pain or suffering, those who are involved in confidential relationships, or those with mental illnesses); and (d) the attention needed to adequately collect data, whether quantitative or qualitative, by a participant-observer-activist will necessarily be pulled from the attention the activist otherwise would have for the moment-to-moment dynamics and needs of the group being served. There are other factors, of course, but these might usefully begin new conversations.

I have found that I treasure the ability to do my best work with those who need it and, then, release these people to their worlds. I value every unsolicited e-mail or letter from a lawyer thanking me years later, but I am not frustrated with myself when I cannot remember which program, intervention, or even which face to place with that gratitude. I value every unexpected encounter with a former workshop participant at some other national event, and I soak up their stories of successes and insights, but I am not tempted to record them; I just listen.

CONCLUSION

Experience shows that executing the innocent is inevitable. We need to realize that capital punishment involves making godlike decisions without godlike skills.

—Former Chief Justice, Florida Supreme Court
(cited in Kogan, 2002, p. 111)

Under the deeply flawed system of capital punishment that exists in the United States, underresourced defense lawyers struggle to save lives and untrained jurors continue to make deadly decisions. A pervasive but naïve cultural assumption persists that citizens, once transformed by their oath into jurors, automatically possess the unique skills and information they require to reach a just verdict (Sunwolf, 1997). Capital defense attorneys share this assumption, as reflected by the questions they traditionally pose during jury selection and the answers for which they settle. Communication scholars with experience in group facilitation have unique skills that can help lawyers to experience more effective conversations with potential jurors on topics that are difficult to talk about and accept answers that are difficult to hear. Deadly decision making by jurors requires drastic revisions of thinking and compassionate communication tools for connecting with those decision makers.

In this chapter, I described a specific, context-designed communication activist facilitation approach to help underresourced indigent capital defense attorneys create and sustain meaningful conversations with a wide variety of citizens during jury selection (those who agree with the attorney's personal values, *as well as jurors who do not*) concerning the ultimate and final decision that can be made about another human being—death. This type of communication facilitation, however, is useful to any helping professional who must similarly compete for scarce resources with others who may both distrust them and disagree with them on fundamental human values. The communication tools offered in this facilitation are vital interpersonal bridges for all helping professionals that enable them to abandon argumentative conversations and engage, instead, in collaborative ones from which mutual understanding might emerge.

Although the law often is slow to accept evidence based on empirical studies by social scientists, and may never agree that the format of death-qualification conversations during jury selection predisposes jurors to convict and sentence defendants to death (Cowan et al., 1984), communication scholars are in a unique position to offer tools that ameliorate damaging messages. Indiana University Law Professor Joseph Hoffman argued that jurors who are confronted with the anguishing moral dilemma of a death sentence decision seek to avoid personal moral responsibility for that decision (cited in Berlow, 2002). The experience of being asked, in effect, to "kill someone" is so alien and overwhelming that jurors will attempt to shift responsibility to others (e.g., the defendant, lawyers, appeals process, or judge). The communication tools in this chapter put death talk with jurors squarely on the courtroom's conversational table, enabling lawyers to participate in and join with prospective jurors' reasoning about death, before the black box closes around the deliberative process and isolates jurors from the influence of life-advocates.

> I'm not going to struggle physically against any restraints. I'm not going to shout, use profanity or make idle threats. Understand though that I'm not only upset, but I'm saddened by what is happening here tonight. . . . If someone tried to dispose of everyone here for participating in this killing, I'd scream a resounding, "No." I'd tell them to give them all the gift that they would not give me and that's to give them all a second chance. . . . There are a lot of men like me on death row—good men— who fell to the same misguided emotions, but may not have recovered as I have. Give those men a chance to do what's right. Give them a chance to undo their wrongs. A lot of them want to fix the mess they started, but don't know how. . . . No one wins tonight. No one gets closure.
>
> —Napoleon Beazley's last words (May 28, 2002)[3]

> Our lives no longer belong to us alone; they belong to all those who need us desperately.
>
> —Elie Wiesel (1968, ¶ 17), accepting the Nobel Peace Prize

NOTES

1. The death penalty is authorized today in 38 states (plus the federal government and the military) (Death Penalty Information Center, 2005a). Some of the legal methods used to execute people in the United States include lethal injection, the gas chamber, electrocution, hanging, and the firing squad (Carter & Kreitzberg, 2004). On March 1, 2005, the U.S. Supreme Court finally held that the death penalty cannot be imposed on offenders who were under the age of 18 when their crimes were committed (*Roper* v. *Simmons*, 2005).

2. The following is a stock jury instruction read by a judge at the commencement of a death penalty trial in which I assisted, modified to preserve the identity of the defendant (at which point no evidence had been presented and the defendant had not been convicted of *any* crime):

I must discuss with you the structure of a death penalty trial. In discussing the subject of penalty at this time, I am not suggesting to you that I believe the jury in this case will find the defendant guilty, nor am I suggesting that if you find the defendant guilty of the charges that you will find one or both of the special circumstances true; I am simply required by law to inform you about all potential phases of trial, both the *guilt phase* and the penalty phase. Again, please do not assume or infer that there will be a penalty phase. That will depend upon the jury's verdict and findings in the *guilt phase*. There are two parts to a death penalty trial: (1) the *guilt* phase, and (2) the penalty phase. The *guilt phase* is just like any other trial. At the end of the *guilt phase*, if the jury finds the defendant not guilty of all charges, that ends the case. [italics added]

The damaging effect of the "guilt phase" language is illuminated in light of the alternative phrase "the innocence phase" (which at least would be consistent with the legal principle of presumption of innocence). Nonetheless, death penalty attorneys throughout the country had been using the guilt phrase themselves for years (Sunwolf, 2001).

3. An African American man who was only 17 years old at the time of his offense, Napoleon Beazley was executed in Huntsville, TX, although he had no prior criminal record. He was loved in his community, attended church regularly, was elected president of his senior class in high school, and excelled as an athlete. His last words are posted on the web site of the Texas Department of Criminal Justice (www.ccadp.org/napoleonbeazley.htm).

REFERENCES

Adler, R. B., Proctor, R. F., II, & Towne, N. (2005). *Looking out/looking in* (11th ed.). Belmont, CA: Thomson/Wadsworth.

Allen, M., Mabry, E., & McKelton, D. (1998). Impact of juror attitudes about the death penalty on juror evaluations of guilt and punishment: A meta-analysis. *Law and Human Behavior, 22*, 715-731.

Andrews v. *Shulsen* et al., 485 U.S. 919, 108 S.Ct. 1091, 99 L.Ed.2d 253 (1988).

Baxter, L. A., & Montgomery, B. M. (1997). Rethinking communication in personal relationships from a dialectical perspective. In S. Duck (Ed.), *Handbook of personal relationships: Theory, research, and interventions* (2nd ed., pp. 305-349). New York: Wiley.

Berlow, A. (1999, November). The wrong man. *Atlantic Monthly*, pp. 66-91.

Berlow, A. (2002). *Reporter's notebook: Making deadly decisions*. Retrieved February 13, 2004, from http://americanradioworks.publicradio.org/features/deadlydecisions/notebook.html

Blume, J. H. (2002). Twenty-five years of death: A report of the Cornell Death Penalty Project on the "modern" era of capital punishment in South Carolina. *Southern Law Review, 54*, 285-370.

Bright, S. (1994). Counsel for the poor: The death sentence not for the worst crime but for the worst lawyer. 103 *Yale Law Journal* 1835.

Burger v. *Kemp*, 107 S.Ct. 3114 (1987).

Burnett, D. G. (2001). *A trial by jury.* New York: Knopf.

Bryan R. Shechmeister Death Penalty College. (2000). *The Bryan R. Shechmeister Death Penalty College, August 5-10, 2000* [Brochure]. Santa Clara, CA: Santa Clara University.

Carter, L. E., & Kreitzberg, E. (2004). *Understanding capital punishment law.* Newark, NJ: LexisNexus.

Conquergood, D. (2002). Lethal theatre: Performance, punishment, and the death penalty. *Theatre Journal, 54,* 339-367.

Coutts, J. A. (1995). Jurors using Ouija board. *Journal of Criminal Law, 59,* 346-350.

Cowan, C. L., Thompson, W. C., & Ellsworth, P. C. (1984). The effects of death qualification on jurors' predisposition to convict and on the quality of deliberation. *Law and Human Behavior, 8,* 53-79.

Death Penalty Information Center. (2003a). *In Ryan's words: "I must act."* Retrieved January 13, 2003, from http://www.deathpenaltyinfo.org/article.php?scid=13&did=551

Death Penalty Information Center. (2003b). *Race of death row inmates executed since 1976.* Retrieved January 9, 2005, from http://www.deathpenaltyinfo.org/article.php?scid=5&did=184#inmaterace

Death Penalty Information Center. (2004a). *New voices: Former FBI chief and Texas judge call for halt to Texas executions.* Retrieved January 10, 2005, from http://www.deathpenaltyinfo.org/article.php?did=1228&scid=64

Death Penalty Information Center. (2004b). *New voices: New Jersey governor calls for death penalty moratorium.* Retrieved December 30, 2004, from http://www.deathpenaltyinfo.org/article.php?did=1237&scid=64

Death Penalty Information Center. (2005a). *Facts about the death penalty.* Retrieved April 22, 2005, from http://www.deathpenaltyinfo.org/FactSheet.pdf

Death Penalty Information Center. (2005b). *Innocence and the death penalty.* Retrieved January 10, 2005, from http://www.deathpenaltyinfo.org/article.php?scid=6&did=412

Death Penalty Information Center. (2005c). *Public opinion: Gallup poll finds decline in support for the death penalty.* Retrieved January 2, 2005, from http://www.deathpenaltyinfo.org/article.php?did=1227&scid=64

Ford v. *Wainwright*, 477 U.S. 399 (1986).

Frey, L. R., & Sunwolf. (2004). A symbolic-interpretive perspective on group dynamics. *Small Group Research, 35,* 277-306.

Garvey, S. P. (1998). Aggravation and mitigation in capital cases: What do jurors think? *Columbia Law Review, 98,* 1538-1576.

Haney, C. (1984a). On the selection of capital juries: The biasing effects of the death-qualification process. *Law and Human Behavior, 8,* 121-132.

Haney, C. (1984b). Examining death qualification: Further analysis of the process effect. *Law and Human Behavior, 8,* 133-151.

Kalven, H., Jr., & Zeisel, H. (with Callahan, T., & Ennis, P.). (1966). *The American jury.* Boston: Little, Brown.

Kogan, G. (2002). Errors of justice and the death penalty: A first-hand view. *Judicature, 86,* 111-114.

Larson, D. G. (1993). *The helper's journey: Working with people facing grief, loss, and life-threatening illness.* Champaign, IL: Research Press.

Liebman, J. S. (2002). Rates of reversible error and the risk of wrongful execution. *Judicature, 86,* 78-82.

Liebman, J. S., Fagan, J., & West, V. (2003). *A broken system: Error rates in capital cases, 1973-1995.* Retrieved March 15, 2005, from http://www2.law.columbia. edu/instructionalservices/liebman

Roper v. *Simmons,* Slip Opinion, No. 03-633, certiorari to the Supreme Court of Missouri (March 1, 2005).

Sunwolf. (1997, July). Changing the way jurors deliberate: Reshaping the individual assumptions jurors make about power and conflict. *The Defender,* pp. 15-21.

Sunwolf. (2001). Toxic words: How courts co-opt defense attorneys into using language that facilitates conviction. *The Champion, 25*(7), 28-32.

Sunwolf. (2004). *Practical jury dynamics: From one juror's trial perceptions to the group's decision-making process.* Charlottesville, VA: LexisNexis.

Sunwolf. (2006). Empathic attunement facilitation: Stimulating immediate task engagement in zero-history training groups of helping professionals. In L. R. Frey (Ed.), *Facilitating group communication in context: Innovations and applications with natural groups: Vol. 1. Facilitating group creation, conflict, and conversation* (pp. 63-92). Cresskill, NJ: Hampton Press.

Sunwolf, & Seibold, D. R. (1998). Jurors' intuitive rules for deliberation: A structurational approach to the study of communication in jury decision making. *Communication Monographs, 65,* 282-307.

Sunwolf, & Seibold, D. R. (2006). *Are some jurors more equal than others? Juror participation and leadership during deliberations.* Manuscript submitted for publication.

Teepen, T. (1987, September 5). Killing in the name of the law has become an act of class warfare. *Atlanta Journal & Constitution,* p. A17.

United States v. *Quinones,* 196 F.Supp.2d 416 (S.D.N.Y. 2002).

Wessel, K. (2000, April 25). Jury flipped coin to convict man of murder: Judge learns about conduct, declares mistrial. *The Courier-Journal,* p. A1.

White, W. S. (2004). A deadly dilemma: Choices by attorneys representing "innocent" capital defendants. *Michigan Law Review, 102,* 2001-2064.

Wiesel, E. (1986, December 10). *The Nobel acceptance speech delivered by Elie Wiesel in Oslo on December 10, 1986.* Retrieved December 5, 2004, from http://www.eliewieselfoundation.org/ElieWiesel/Nobel_Speech.htm

Wilgoren, J. (2003, January 11). 4 death row inmates are pardoned. *The New York Times,* Sec. A, p. 13.

Witherspoon v. *Illinois,* 391 U.S. 310 (1968).

8

FACILITATING CONSENSUS IN AN ANTIGLOBALIZATION AFFINITY GROUP

David L. Palmer

University of Northern Colorado

The era of globalization has dawned—corporate globalization. At the turn of the 21st century, the global order is governed by a transnational coalition of corporate, trade, and finance organizations. The World Trade Organization (WTO), for example, now augments the International Finance Corporation, the World Bank, the Multilateral Investment Agency, and the International Monetary Fund to produce a supranational economic system that is tied directly to elite corporate interests (see, e.g., Tabb, 2004; Wallach & Woodall, 2004). This new geocorporate coalition has amassed a global structural power that is unprecedented and, along the way, has imposed a policy record that clearly values state capitalist (or neoliberal) interests over civil, labor, environmental, and other populist concerns (Robinson & Harris, 2000). Left unchecked, geocorporatism threatens to become the new global oligarchy.

Fortunately, a vital new populist movement—the antiglobalization movement—has begun to mobilize an international network of groups and organizations to resist capitalist globalization. Arguing, instead, for the globalization of human and labor rights, direct democracy, and ethical environmentalism, the antiglobalization cause is a dynamic decentralized social movement that is well organized and technologically savvy in directly confronting the aggressive policy agenda of neoliberalism (e.g., Starr, 2000). Significant popular protests by members of this movement against geocorporatism in Chiapas, Mexico (1994); Seoul, South Korea (1997); Seattle, United States (1999); Prague, Czech Republic (2000); Quebec City, Canada (2001); Genoa, Italy (2001); Buenos Aires, Argentina (2002); and Cancun, Mexico (2003) foretell of a new type of global conflict, one that pits militarized corporate states against sectors of their own population that are organized and resistant to capitalist globalization (e.g., Smith, 2002). The Zapatista movement—with indigenous peoples of Mexico resisting the violent colonization of their lands—has been cited as a prime example of the spirit of the determined (and often bloody) resistance to corporate imperialism (e.g., Ross, 2000).

Global corporatism, thus, has sparked new forms and networks of civic activism. Of particular interest here are antiglobalization *affinity groups*, small progressive communities that act in concert to resist geocorporatism (e.g., Moynihan, 2002).[1] Affinity groups are the micro-mobilizing contexts of the antiglobalization movement—they amass membership, produce community-education events, outreach to a variety of media, and work to organize local and international protests (see, e.g., Finnegan, 2003).

In their efforts to effect social change, affinity groups confront decisions about what projects they will undertake and how these projects will be accomplished. The primary model for affinity-group decision making is *consensus building*—a model of group talk that seeks to create collective solutions to salient group problems. The consensus model that affinity groups employ reflects the ideals of equal power and voice, direct democracy, and resistance to hierarchy—values that define the broader antiglobalization movement (Starr, 2000).

This chapter explains how I, as a member of an active affinity group, invite its members to enact a model of reflexive talk designed to enhance the group's consensus building. The method I employ in this study draws on theory and research tied to consensus building, group facilitation, and inductive inquiry. My broad goals in this chapter are to provide an insider's view of this active affinity group and examine how activist groups (can and will) employ reflexive techniques to optimize the execution of their collective goals.[2]

The chapter is divided into four sections. In the first two sections, I describe the affinity group with which I am associated and the method this study employs. In the third section, I outline how this affinity group modified its consensus-building practices as it prepared for and participated in an international protest: the Free Trade Area of the Americas (FTAA) trade summit in Miami, FL, during late November 2003. Communication activism here entailed working closely with my affinity group to enhance our discussion and decision-making practices as we prepared for this pivotal antiglobalization protest. In the final section, I reflect on lessons learned through studying activist groups that employ consensus building.

META-: AN AFFINITY GROUP

The affinity group with which I am affiliated is called Meta- (a pseudonym), an activist community based in the United States that formed during the seminal 1999 WTO protest in Seattle, WA. Meta- devotes much of its resources to the antiglobalization cause, although its members also are involved in labor, environmental, and indigenous causes. Meta- employs grassroots activism designed to promote anarchist, syndicalist (worker-driven), and direct democratic forms of social organization. The group has organized activist conferences, coordinated over 100 community-education events, and mobilized its resources to participate in dozens of local, national, and international protests.

Meta- is a flexible activist group, organizing itself at any given moment and tying itself into the larger activist network as a function of the events it engages. Member numbers vary from 10 to 30, consisting primarily of White, male and female college students, and working-class activists, ages 20-40. Meta- is a strong, honorable community, and its members are stakeholders in the projects and identity of the group.

During the fall of 2003, Meta- was involved in a number of vital projects, the most notable being the FTAA protest. The FTAA is a trade agreement currently under negotiation that seeks to expand the North American Free Trade Agreement (NAFTA) to the 34 countries of the Western hemisphere (excluding only Cuba).[3] The agreement, which will further liberalize trade policies, affects the lives of a billion people and has vital implications for political, economic, labor, and environmental projects across the region (Deere & Esty, 2002; Vizentini & Wiesebron, 2004).

The 8th Ministerial Meeting of the FTAA in Miami in November 2003 not only energized Meta-, it animated hundreds of progressive groups across the United States, Europe, Central and South America, and Asia. This broad alliance of groups resists the FTAA because it undermines union and labor rights, promotes environmental destruction, and compels the privatization of essential social services, and because the trade agreement is drafted with minimal popular democratic input (Global Exchange, 2003). To help resist the drafting of this trade agreement, Meta- committed itself to preparing for and engaging in the FTAA protest.

EMERGENT-CONSENSUS

Preparation for a major protest by affinity groups such as Meta- requires an immense amount of collaborative labor, and the primary means for completing the heavy task load is group discussion and decision making. Meta-, like many antiglobalization groups, relies on consensus building as its primary process for making decisions. The collective goal of achieving consensus among its members has been a source of both success and problems in the group's history. Although Meta- is a close-knit and productive group, its decision-making practices, at times, are unfocused, protracted, and produce decisions that lack the capacity to mobilize the activity necessary for completion.

The members of Meta-, like most groups, focus more on talking about their causes, goals, tasks, and duties than they do on examining their goal-oriented talk. My basic goal as a participant-scholar was to help the group analyze and, if necessary, modify its discussion and decision-making practices as we prepared for the FTAA protest. Because Meta- is a direct democracy forum, I did not enforce a program on the group but, instead, provided members with a set of reflexive tools for examining our consensus-building practices, and I encouraged all involved to facilitate equally in the reflexive process.

The methodology I developed for this project is the *emergent-consensus program*, which is based on a basic idea in the literature on democracy in groups and organizations: Group discussion and decision making are enhanced as group members improve their understanding of how these processes work and put that understanding into practice (see, e.g., the essays in Cheney, Mumby, Stohl, & Harrison, 1997; Gastil, 1992). The program, thus, calls for group members to discuss their productive and unproductive practices and use the knowledge gleaned from those discussions to modify and enhance their consensus building. The use of *meta-discussion* (discussion about discussion processes, including decision-making processes) over time invites the emergence of an effective *consensus*-building framework (see, e.g., Gouran & Geonetta, 1977).

Emergent-consensus unites three elements: (a) consensus models, (b) group diagnostic models, and (c) inductive models of inquiry. *Consensus models* provide the base on which the emergent-consensus program operates. Meta- employs consensus building as its primary form of decision making, which involves using a set of techniques conducive to gaining common consent to a decision (see, e.g., Bennett, 1955; Butler, Lawrence, & Rothstein, 1991). Rawlins (1984) defined *consensus* as "a method used in small groups whereby members discuss a problematic situation until they arrive at a unanimous agreement regarding the group's decision or solution" (p. 19). Consensus building has proven to be an effective method for generating high-quality decisions with which group members are satisfied (e.g., Hirokawa, 1982), but scholars agree that, in general, groups must labor to create conditions conducive to consensus building (e.g., Susskind, McKearnen, & Thomas-Larmer, 1999).

Consensus building differs from other forms of decision making based on both the way in which group members make decisions and the degree to which these decisions reflect the interests of those involved. Authority and expert decision making, for example, require group members to defer to the decisions made by a central figure; majority-rule decision making mandates neither unanimity nor the processes of seeking unanimity (e.g., Hare, 1980); and compromise decision making involves members making trade-offs in an effort to achieve outcomes that reflect their individual competing interests (e.g., Beatty, 1989). In contrast, consensus building requires collective involvement in the process of making decisions that reflect the values and interests that all of the participating parties share.

Group diagnostic models provide the general framework for group analysis in the emergent-consensus program. These models guide facilitators as they help group members to diagnose behaviors that enhance or obstruct group effectiveness (see, e.g., Rees, 1998; Schultz, 1999; Sunwolf & Seibold, 1999; see also the studies in Frey, 1995, 2006). Diagnostic models can include members observing group behaviors, describing their reflections to the group, checking their perceptions with other group members, and encouraging each other to intensify positive behaviors and eliminate unproductive behaviors. Such diagnostic analysis, when performed successfully, improves group productivity and cohesion (Schwarz, 2002).

Inductive inquiry is a method used by interpretive scholars to examine the practices and performances of situated groups (e.g., Denzin, 2002). For Lindlof (1995), a *practice* "constitutes *a way of doing things* that is sanctioned by a social collectivity" (p. 16). Practices are generic norms for group action that are created and recreated over time as they are performed (or authored) by members of a group. *Performances* are local, improvised exemplars-in-action (or extemporized enactments) of group practices. Inductive analysis entails investigating a communal code system by observing performances, categorizing the practices they represent, and allowing conclusions to emerge about the code system based on this process.

The emergent-consensus program distills these three elements (consensus models, group diagnostic models, and inductive inquiry) into a simple 2-

phase sequence. In phase 1, group members talk about their productive and unproductive practices and seek ways to enhance their discussion and decision-making processes. Phase 2 repeats phase 1 activities and charges the group members to craft inductively a formal practice language and integrate this language into their consensus-building processes. The primary goal of the program is to have members co-facilitate optimal processes for building group consensus, which, in contrast to prescriptions handed down by an expert or facilitator, encourages members to invest in the emergent-consensus program.

PUTTING THE EMERGENT-CONSENSUS PROGRAM INTO ACTION

Preparation for the FTAA Protest

August 15 to September 15, 2003: Preparations in Miami for the FTAA summit are in full swing. The international trade conference will be held at the Intercontinental Hotel in downtown Miami. In response, the progressive community publishes an official "Call to Action" against the FTAA negotiations—a call that is endorsed by over 100 populist organizations. The demands these organizations make are simple and fair: democratize the trade agreement and allow public access to the trade negotiations. The state refuses to grant these simple demands, opting, instead, to employ a military model designed to suppress civic dissent. Forty law enforcement agencies in the Miami area combine to mobilize 7,000 police officers to train for the event. In addition, a 10-foot-high steel fence wall will be built around the Intercontinental Hotel compound to barricade the trade summit from public access.

Meta- follows a schedule of four set activities in preparation for a protest: (a) create the core group, (b) form working groups, (c) organize teach-ins, and (d) act in solidarity with the larger progressive community. To create the core group, Meta- initiates an open group that determines basic goals and plans for the protest event. Initiation occurs when one or more members send an invitation to the local activist community concerning the protest. Out of the initial core group, working groups designed to divide the preparation workload are formed. Teach-ins designed to prepare the group for the protest event then are coordinated. Finally, Meta- integrates its resources into the larger activist network and acts as a coordinated set of units as it prepares for and engages in the protest event.

Meta- holds its initial core group meeting in August 2003, 3 months before the Miami protest. Goals and means for the protest are outlined, working groups are formed, and a goals-by-dates timeline is established. The core group will meet on a weekly basis, acting as a central organizing structure for working groups to report their progress and as a forum to discuss relevant issues. Five working groups are established: (a) the logistics group will coordinate housing, transportation, and communications, (b) the fund-raising group will raise money for the trip, (c) the outreach group will interface with the local and national media, (d) the trainings group will educate and prepare members for protest activities, and (e) the solidarity action group will plan and implement a local action to run concurrently with the larger protest. Each working group completes a set of tasks that prepares Meta- for the FTAA action and supports corresponding projects in the larger activist network.

Meta- also begins to shape itself in relation to the amassing activist network that is forming for the FTAA protest. Representatives from Meta- help to establish a *cluster* of three affinity groups (from three area cities) that will act in solidarity in preparation for the protest. Representatives from this tri-city cluster plan to meet every 2 weeks to share information and coordinate plans. Meta- also begins to interface with a national *bloc* of affinity groups that are preparing for the FTAA action. This process includes a weekly conference call attended by 50-100 affinity-group representatives from across the nation to coordinate plans tied to the protest. I volunteer to act as Meta-'s representative at these vital conference calls.

During August and September, initial Meta- core group FTAA meetings attract different sets of new people from which a stable group eventually forms. My immediate goal is to observe Meta-'s discussion and decision-making processes as it attempts to coalesce into a stable unit. The weekly meetings and working-group projects ensue, and Meta- slowly begins to forge plans for the protest.

Meta- meetings follow a protocol that is common among affinity groups (Beck, 1996). At the outset, volunteers step up to assume various roles common to affinity-group meetings. The *facilitator* keeps the agenda, summarizes arguments and proposals, calls for input, and expedites decisions; the *stacks* calls on people to speak in order of hands raised; and the *vibes-watch* monitors how energetic or tired the group is and facilitates discussions that become overly argumentative. Next, the group outlines the agenda, which consists of (a) introductions, (b) consensus clarification, (c) announcements, (d) working-group reports (where the bulk of the work is done), and (e) the next meeting date.

The consensus-clarification portion of the agenda is an integral ritual performed near the outset of every meeting. This ritual involves a member declaring that the group is dedicated to the ideal of direct democracy and, therefore, it seeks to organize its talk to meet this goal. Specifically, everyone in the group is encouraged to contribute, and it is made clear that all opinions are integral to the decision-making process. This call for consensus building is consistent with research showing that groups that work together to introduce and formulate goals, elicit communication from all members, delegate and direct action, and summarize group activity are more productive in achieving consensus (e.g., Knutson & Kowitz, 1977).

Meta- members are aware of consensus models outlined in activist literature that enumerate formal and protracted steps for achieving consensus (e.g., Butler et al., 1991), but are not overly concerned with employing them. Instead, the group follows an explicit sequence to pursue consensus that is common among affinity groups, but that can be truncated or reshaped depending on the circumstances: proposal making, clarifying questions, discussion, resolution of concerns, and call for consensus when there seems to be agreement (Beck, 1996). When a proposal is forwarded, members are given the opportunity to ask questions about it, discuss it, and express any concerns. They also can block (argue for a rejection of the proposal), stand aside (disagree with the proposal but opt not to block it), or ratify the proposal. Meta-'s group communication, thus, reflects findings in the scholarly literature that groups that agree explicitly on consensus procedures are more likely to achieve consensus (e.g., Beatty, 1989).

In one of the early meetings, for example, one member proposes that the group should function as a unified unit (as opposed to a set of independent units) during the entire week of the protest. Another member asks the clarifying question, "What exactly would it look like on a daily basis for Meta- to act as a unified unit at the protest?" The group engages in discussion, with several members expressing concerns, making it clear that members desire some degree of independence during the protest week. One member then proposes that the group act at times as a set of independent units and, at other times (in particular, during the protest itself), as a unified unit. Following group discussion that appears to resolve everyone's concerns, the independent-unified unit proposal again is forwarded and everyone ratifies it. This type of proposal-discussion-consensus decision making characterizes the bulk of decisions made by Meta-.

Observing the group over time, it becomes clear that its members employ five basic consensus-building patterns. *Rapid unanimity* occurs when a proposal is made and unanimity is reached almost immediately; this typically happens with small tactical decisions (e.g., who will rent the vans to drive to the protest). *Common consensus* occurs when, following a proposal, several people suggest (tacitly or explicitly) that the initial proposal is a good start but can be improved; discussion then ensues until a new proposal that more accurately reflects collective views is made (as exemplified in the independent-unified unit decision just discussed). *Proposal forging* (a truncated form of common consensus) occurs when a proposal is made, followed by a new proposal that suggests the original proposal was close but not quite indicative of the interests of those involved; a process that continues repeatedly until there is a proposal that is acceptable to all. *Debate consensus* occurs when a proposal is made, and despite ratification by most members, one person (or several people) speaks out against the proposal; debate ensues until a modified position is acceptable to all involved. Debate consensus often is tied to proposals related to group identity issues (e.g., whether the group actively will seek new members). *Decision dissipation* occurs when a proposal is made, and discussion digresses in such a way that the proposal is forgotten or ignored. Although these are the five primary consensus-building patterns, the group also employs a variety of other decision types, including compromise and implicit majority decisions.

Emergent-Consensus: Phase 1

> *September 15 to October 15, 2003: In Miami, a host of nongovernmental organizations (e.g., Public Citizen, Root Cause, and Citizens Trade Campaign) are coordinating teach-ins, outreach events, and international citizen forums to discuss the FTAA. The AFL-CIO secures a permitted rally against the FTAA in downtown Miami. An estimated 100,000 rank-and-file union members and their families will march. A national "direct action" bloc designed to coordinate civil disobedience against corporate trade policies has been established, and over 100 affinity groups (including Meta-) have signed on. At the same time, police training in Miami is visibly stepped up. The Miami City Commission passes an ordinance banning peaceful protest activities (one injunction actually bans dancing in the streets). Activist teams in Miami are working to secure a convergence space near the protest site, establish a working legal team, and coordinate transportation and housing. Legal and logistics hotlines are established for affinity groups to use on an as-needed basis.*

By early October, Meta- begins to form a solid core group that is preparing for the FTAA action. The logistics working group makes plans for transportation and housing, produces a vital protest-related information packet for the group, and talks (via hotlines) with the legal team in Miami. The fund-raising working group begins to stage community events designed to raise money for the trip. The outreach working group interfaces with media in Meta-'s local area to publicize the protest and provide a progressive-activist viewpoint of the event. The tri-city cluster plans to caravan to the protest and work together during the week of the protest.

Meta- has stabilized to the point where the emergent-consensus program can be introduced to the group. I describe the program to the group members, explaining that the goal is to employ inductive methods to identify our productive and unproductive group discussion and decision-making patterns in an effort to refine our consensus-building practices. In line with phase 1 of the project, I invite members to observe and discuss behaviors that enhance or impede group discussion and decision making. The group members are willing to engage in the emergent-consensus program and decide to dedicate a brief portion of our meetings, initially slotted at the end of the agenda, to the analysis of our consensus-building talk, and label this portion of the meeting *discussion analysis.*

At the first meeting that follows this decision, I invite members to list practices they deem productive and unproductive during the meeting. The question "What group decision-related practices are and are not working here and why?" becomes the focus during the discussion-analysis segment of the meeting. During this segment, I encourage everyone to develop a shared set of terms to talk about our discussion and decision-making practices.

Phase 1 activity proceeds efficiently for several meetings. At each meeting, group members generate a list of productive and unproductive practices, and the group then talks about these lists during the discussion analysis. Interestingly, there is significant overlap in the practices that group members list. Productive practices include effective time allotment, humor, honesty, egalitarian talk, clear proposals, and redirects (statements designed to refocus discussion); unproductive practices include interruptions, unclear proposals, inefficient working-group reports, and protracted scheduling discussion.

I encourage everyone to discuss how the practices they have listed function within the group's discourse and devise solutions to what they perceive to be problem areas. As a result, members decide, for example, that redirects help the group to stay focused and encourage productive talk, humor sustains group energy and lightens the mood, and egalitarian talk creates a sense of equality within the group. In contrast, protracted scheduling discussion stalls the progress of meetings and, as a solution, someone suggests postponing this practice until meetings are complete. Interruptions create frustration and derail the proper sequence of speakers, and to resolve this problem, everyone agrees to follow the order of speakers chosen by the person serving in the stacks role. Inefficient working-group reports also are seen as stalling the progress of meetings and leading to more questions being asked than are necessary; as a solution, working groups are encouraged to prepare more efficient reports. One member proposes that efficient reports should consist of 2-4 relevant task decisions made by the working group, and that these decisions be coupled to an itinerary of project steps and personnel designated to complete the decisions. Following a brief discussion, everyone ratifies this proposal.

The tenor of the dialogue during the discussion-analysis segment is positive. Members note that debate consensus does not degenerate into negative arguments; disagreements tend to be detail oriented, not ideological clashes; and that the group displays good cohesion. There is, however, a desire for a more even distribution of input from all group members and more productive outcomes resulting from agreed-on decisions.

Group members discuss the idea that when core members are the only ones present, the consensus-building process is streamlined and efficient. This process reflects Kline and Hollinger's (1973) finding that groups that cultivate clear methods and goals for building consensus exhibit less redundant talk. The consensus-building sequence becomes more problematic and slows down, however, when newcomers are present, as decision-making practices and rules often must be re-explained to be understood. Core group members also become hesitant to engage in discussion analysis when newcomers are present. Engaging in meta-discussion among newcomers demands that the emergent-consensus program be explained—a process that, in light of more pressing concerns, is time-consuming for all involved.

Another problem arises in the level of group energy devoted to the discussion-analysis segment. Because this segment is slated last on the agenda, people often are exhausted by the time it arises and the listing and discussion processes are, at times, shortened. Meta- members have full lives outside of their activism, and meetings often run late into the night. The discussion-analysis segment, at times, becomes an expendable project in light of other duties that cannot be postponed.

Reflections on Phase 1

Phase 1 activity of the emergent-consensus program functioned in several ways within the group. First, the process of examining their interaction practices encouraged the members to craft a group-based language about its discussion and decision-making processes. Labels such as "redirects" and "protracted scheduling discussion" formed a currency of shared terms about collective practices, and members became comfortable using these terms to reference how talk is organized within the group. Second, the emergent-consensus program invited group members to explore the functions of their practices, a process that helped them to envision how specific behaviors shaped the group discussion and decision-making process. Third, crafting solutions to discussion-related problems invited members to eliminate (or reduce) unproductive patterns in their search for consensus. Indeed, within 1 month, the discussion in the group subtly improved, as members strived to engage in the more productive practices they had identified. Fourth, the program consistently opened up discussion about the nature and purpose of the group. During one discussion-analysis segment, for instance, the group members discussed whether to organize Meta- as a group that consistently seeks to induct new members or to merely embody direct democracy to provide an example for other individuals and organizations. Such discussions often were vibrant, and partaking in them helped members to envision more clearly Meta-'s identity.

Emergent-Consensus: Phase 2

> *October 15 to November 7, 2003: Police training becomes increasingly visible throughout Miami. The Florida Supreme Court surprisingly announces that guarantees for a speedy trial will be suspended during the week of the protest. The steel fence wall barricading the hotel compound finally is completed—at the (amazing) cost of $200,000. The activist community views these events as scare tactics designed to suppress the number of protesters willing to attend the event. The national direct-action network plans an unpermitted march on the hotel compound wall as a symbolic gesture to signify the direct confrontation with the corporate-state machinery. In response, the Miami media predict an ensuing battle between protesters and police. Activist teams in Miami finally secure a convergence space and continue to make arrangements for housing, outreach, and fund-raising.*

The protest is a month away, and Meta- is acutely focused on the event. The logistics working group has secured vans for the drive to the protest, as well as housing in Miami. The Miami legal team is addressing our concerns about harassment and arrests. Several community-based teach-ins to be held in the local area about globalization and the FTAA are planned. A notable author in the antiglobalization movement will be flown in for a keynote address to the larger local community. The fund-raising working group has raised $1000 and is continuing to stage fund-raising events. The outreach working group has published several articles in local newspapers and secured interviews on local radio stations. The trainings working group is planning teaching events on "street safety" and "tactics for nonviolent civil disobedience." The solidarity action working group is coordinating a local protest event to run concurrent with the Miami action. The tri-city cluster continues to meet and make plans for coordinated travel and activities at the protest.

Phase 2 of the emergent-consensus program is implemented. Phase 2 repeats the activities of phase 1 but also charges the group to inductively build a formal decision-based language and integrate that language into its consensus-building practices.

To address the issue of low group energy during the discussion-analysis segment at the end of meetings, I divide that segment into two smaller sections, one at the beginning and one at the end of the meetings. I prepare forms for members to fill out that request them to list unproductive and productive practices and craft broad headings into which these practices fall. These written reflections are slated to be discussed at the end of the agenda.

The group's written input allows me to create a running list of ideas for distribution to group members, and time is allotted at the beginning of meetings to peruse and discuss this running list. The strategy of having discussion at the outset of meetings and brief written reflections at the end of meetings seems to solve the low group energy problem.

From mid-October to mid-November, Meta- members produce a broadened list of productive and unproductive group practices. Productive practices include energetic facilitation, eager co-facilitation, adherence to the time quota per agenda item, and the willingness of members to accept task responsibilities; unproductive practices include not recording decisions, making excuses for not following-up on tasks, and having to re-explain ideas to those members who are inattentive. The tone of the discussion analysis remains positive, despite the work being tedious at times.

To strengthen the group's discussion and decision-based language, members create (inductively) four general categories of consensus-related practices. *Decision practices* encompass behaviors involved in reaching a conclusion about a specific proposal. *Progression practices* entail behaviors conducive or detrimental to the progression of a meeting. *Energy practices* signify behaviors that affect the physical and emotional energy of the group. *Role practices* reference the manner in which group members adhere to their respective roles during the course of a meeting.

The list of productive and unproductive practices then is tied to these general categories (see Table 8.1), which helps members of Meta- to under-

Table 8.1. Categorized Consensus Decision Practices

	Productive	Unproductive
Decision Practices	Recorded decisions Decision closure Decision responsibility	Unrecorded decisions Lack of decision closure Decision nonresponsibility
Progression Practices	Redirects Delegated scheduling Efficient reports	Misdirects Protracted scheduling Nonefficient reports
Energy Practices	Task-time focus Positive humor Patient listening	Lack of task-time focus Negative humor Interruptions
Role Practices	Role-focused practices Co-facilitation Responsibility to group	Role-unfocused practices Nonfacilitation Nonresponsibility to group

stand how specific practices function. Members note, for example, how *mis-directs* waste valuable time and how *role-focused practices* contrast to *role-unfocused practices* with respect to group discussion efficiency. Categorizing practice types in these ways invites members to talk more clearly about their practices and better organize their talk to accomplish consensus.

Group talk about decision conditions subtly elevates in sophistication following the systematic investigation and categorization of members' practices. Members also begin to explore in relatively complex terms their inferences about potential causes for these practices. One member notes, for example, that co-facilitation practices stem from the direct democratic ideal of equal work and power distribution, and another member suggests that decision-dissipation patterns are tied to interruptions and misdirects that derail the conversation.

The subtle new level of group members' sophistication in analyzing their practices also manifests in their examination of potential solutions to problem areas. Members, now more invested in the emergent-consensus program because they have seen firsthand some of its benefits, experiment with innovative solutions to problems. To solve the problem of group members not following-up on specific task assignments, for example, one member begins to send out on the group's listserv a record of completed decisions coupled with a list of people responsible for putting these decisions into practice. To help the group keep track of the completion status of responsibilities, another member keeps a running log of decisions made by the group with progress reports on their completion status. Some of these innovative solutions work well, others do not; either way, the effort is noted and appreciated by Meta- members.

The final step of phase 2 is to encourage the group to integrate its new decision-based language into its consensus-seeking practices. As practices are discussed, I invite members to make proposals about specific practices that enhance or hinder group discussion and decision making. These proposals subsequently are integrated into the group's consensus-building protocol.

During one meeting, for example, the group discusses progression practices. Members note that the lack of willingness to keep effective minutes regularly stalls meeting progress. One member proposes that minutes from the meeting be recorded both officially (by the person taking minutes) and by each person, and a discussion of that proposal ensues. We all agree that minutes from previous meetings (posted on the listserv) are an important catalyst for present meetings to run smoothly. However, official minutes sometimes are not posted and, as a result, we struggle to remember items from previous meetings, and this often derails discussion and frustrates members. The group finally reaches the conclusion that promoting individual responsibility for minutes is an important practice that will encourage each group member to follow through on his or her responsibilities. There is, however, disagreement about the scope of these minutes, and someone finally proposes that each person keep minutes of only key decisions that are reached in a meeting. A call for consensus on the original proposal, modified with the key-decision-only amendment, is ratified.

Consensus about such decisions reflects the input of all members, and, therefore, the consensus tends to be durable. All members, for example, remain disciplined about taking key-decision minutes, group consensus to reduce misdirects motivates a consistent reduction in statements that steer the conversation away from its original course, and agreement regarding the need for patient listening produces less interruptions over time.

Reflections on Phase 2

Phase 2 activity of the emergent-consensus program functioned in several important ways within the group. First, the use of inductive techniques to craft a consensus-seeking language helped to create a framework of effective talk about how group members make and act on decisions. The practice terms and categories became an important practical feature of the diagnostic framework. Developing this type of sophisticated diagnostic tool helped members to examine the complexities of their discourse and craft effective solutions to problems (Schwarz, 2002).

Second, the emergent-consensus program continued to have a positive impact on the group's discussion and decision-making activities. There was a subtle, yet noticeable reduction in dysfunctional practices from phase 1 to phase 2. The collective focus on decision closure, for example, functioned to reduce decision-dissipation patterns. If a proposal began to get lost in conversation, members now were more cognizant of this pattern, reintroduced the proposal, and reminded the group that we had moved on too quickly. In addition, the tendency for proposal forging diminished as members, once content with forwarding imprecise proposals, took time to clarify their ideas before making them public.

Third, members of the group became better co-facilitators of their consensus-building practices. Members displayed a willingness to invoke topics related to the consensus-seeking process, generated discussion about those topics, and reminded each other about the unproductive value of the specific practices they had identified as being dysfunctional. This outcome suggests that members were invested in forging the emergent-consensus program into a productive group tool.

Fourth, integrating group decision-based language into the consensus format brought the program full circle. By using the consensus model to shape its decision-making practices, the group essentially turned its prime decision-making tool back on itself, a process that invited the group to cre-

ate consensus about its consensus building. In addition, because the reflexive process functioned to enhance the group's consensus-building practices,
employing meta-discussion over time led members to become more invested in the consensus format (e.g., Gouran & Geonetta, 1977). The result was
that members became more disciplined about complying with the consensus
decisions they made concerning their discussion and decision-making practices (see, e.g., Sager & Gastil, 1999).

Into the Breach

> *November 7 to November 16, 2003: Reports of a new war-like model for
> policing the protest filter into the local and national news; interestingly,
> at the last moment, the U.S. Congress allocates $8.5 million directly from
> the new $87 billion Iraq war fund to finance the protection of the Miami
> event. Corporate reporters, just as in the Iraq war, will be embedded in
> the military police lines. In response, the AFL-CIO and the direct-action
> bloc agree to act in solidarity during the protest. The convergence space
> is in full operation, and activists are busy coordinating teach-ins, train-
> ings, legal networks, and a media center.*

The week prior to the Miami protest, Meta- is engaged in a flurry of activities in its local area. The FTAA teach-ins being held by Meta- are well
attended, and the quality of the presentations is outstanding, with the
keynote speaker providing an engaging talk on the history of the antiglobalization movement. The trainings also are productive, as the group learns
how to engage in nonviolent civil disobedience and to protect each other in
the streets. The fund-raising working group has secured over $1500, money
that will go primarily to transportation and a legal fund.

Meta- arranges to support the larger activist community converging on
Miami. The group plans to participate in the week's events, including the
permitted AFL-CIO march and the direct-action march to confront the
hotel compound wall. As the protest grows closer, the members are visibly
coming together as a group. Protest is in the air, and everyone is feeling
excitement and fear at the possibility of putting their bodies on the streets
for a cause in which the group believes.

Although the emergent-consensus program, unfortunately, is put aside
during the two remaining meetings in light of more pressing responsibilities
related to the protest, its effects are subtly apparent. There is a noticeable
lack of unproductive practices, working-group reports are efficient, there
are few instances of decision dissipation, and common-consensus decisions
are made smoothly. The degree to which these processes and outcomes are
attributable to the emergent-consensus program is difficult to determine,

but it seems clear that the program has enhanced the group's efficiency. The final group meeting before departing to the protest is exceptionally efficient, productive, and cohesive; discussion during the meeting satisfies everyone's concerns, achieves collective agreement with respect to group decisions, maximizes outcomes, and builds community.

> *November 17, 2003: The 8th FTAA Ministerial meeting in Miami commences. Trade and government delegates from 34 countries in the Western hemisphere have convened. So too have tens of thousands of environmentalists, union members and their families, farmers, students, and working-class representatives from across the Western hemisphere — all in direct resistance to the neoliberal corporate agenda and the FTAA agreement. The corporate state has mobilized (nothing less than) an army to barricade the trade negotiations.*

The week of the protest in Miami is saturated with activities: teach-ins, rallies, documentary film festivals, marches, speakers, and affinity-group meetings. We attend spokescouncil meetings and trainings at the activist convergence center, with 50-100 affinity groups represented at these meetings. The consensus-building practices employed by Meta- are mirrored in the spokescouncil meetings. Plans for the week are discussed, proposals are made, information is shared, arguments are presented, and consensus decisions are reached.

Meta- members participate in affinity-group and spokescouncil meetings with our tri-city cluster. The emergent-consensus program, again, is suspended in light of overwhelming responsibilities and pressing protest activity. The presence of nonregular members also hinders substantive engagement in the program. I conclude that either (a) protest actions themselves, in contrast to their preparation, are not conducive to employing the emergent-consensus program or (b) the group needed more experience to effectively implement the program in such situations. I finally accept that the program will not be explicitly employed in meetings during the protest week. Meta- members, however, later note that, relative to previous protests, the group performed with a new level of efficiency.

On the day of the direct action march, November 20, 2003, the members of Meta- are in the streets. At 6 a.m., 700 activists converge in downtown Miami and plan to march to the hotel compound wall (see Photograph 8.1). The scene is somewhat surreal: thousands of "storm-trooper" police, accompanied by a swarm of helicopters, personnel carriers, and hundreds of police cars surround the cluster of activists. The plan is to march to the hotel compound wall in an effort to draw attention to the wall's function to physically exclude citizens from attending trade negotiations that directly affect the lives of every person in the Western hemisphere.

Photograph 8.1. A young female activist organizer from Canada speaks through a megaphone to the "direct-action" bloc just prior to the march on the hotel compound wall (Source: Author's personal files).

There is a palpable sense of fear and defiance as the crowd begins to march toward the hotel compound. Meta- holds several brief affinity-group meetings in the streets along the way. News reports about police movements circulate through the meetings, and rapid decisions are made about our street tactics and relocation points. The members of Meta- decide to stay together and keep an eye on each other. The group constantly reforms, and we ask each other about energy levels, tactics, and levels of fear. The members of a host of other affinity groups all around us are doing the same (see, e.g., West & Gastil, 2004).

The police lines form in such a way that it soon becomes clear that the march is being funneled away from the Intercontinental Hotel compound toward the tamer AFL-CIO rally. The protesters must decide whether to break off and head for the rally or continue to the compound wall. The members of Meta- huddle together. Helicopters, loudspeakers, and sirens generate a noise on the street that almost is deafening. One member proposes that we make for the wall, but several members are concerned that the police presence is so overwhelming that the entire set of marchers will be arrested before we can reach it. Someone asks if there are alternative routes, which spurs another proposal to split-up and check, and then regroup; everyone ratifies it. The group quickly reforms—no one can see an alternative route. The proposal is again made that the group make for the wall and everyone ratifies that action.

When we reach the hotel compound wall, thousands of police in heavy riot gear are waiting for us (see Photograph 8.2). No laws are broken and no property damage is inflicted; we merely assemble in the streets, displaying signs and chanting. The police order us to disperse, but we refuse. The chant

Photograph 8.2. "Stormtrooper" police saturate the downtown Miami area near the hotel compound wall (Source: www.hulla-baloo.com/ftaapics).

"Peacefully assembled" builds to a roar among the crowd of protesters. For hours, we are brutally shoved, beaten, sprayed with tear gas, and harassed by the police of the militarized corporate state (see Photograph 8.3). There are hundreds of arrests and 12 people are hospitalized (see Photograph 8.4). However, despite unwarranted police aggression, everyone (including the members of Meta-) remains committed to nonviolence.

Photograph 8.3. A section of the permitted AFL-CIO march (Source: Author's personal files).

Photograph 8.4. A young male protester is shot with a tazer and arrested (Source: www.hulla-baloo.com/ftaapics).

Photograph 8.5. A group of protesters—with their backs turned to signal nonviolent protest—"lock down" against an overwhelming police line near the hotel compound wall (Source: www.hulla-baloo.com/ftaapics).

When the direct action finally dissipates, we filter into the AFL-CIO march and walk in solidarity with union members and their families (see Photograph 8.5). Interestingly, the sanctioned march of tens of thousands of working-class families and activists is funneled through a corridor of armed police.

On the day of the protest, the FTAA trade agreement comes just short of collapsing, although something quite different is reported in the corporate press, which oddly portrays the conference as a successful trade summit.[4] Delegates from South American countries present at the proceedings, however, report a hostile and unsuccessful negotiation environment. We understand that our actions have played only a small part in this outcome; the real leverage for the near collapse of the FTAA agreement resides in growing populist sectors within South American countries (e.g., Brazil and Venezuela) that have demanded that their trade ministers reject the neoliberal agenda because their countries will be negatively affected by the trade agreement. We hope that these populist sectors will see us in their media on the streets of Miami, resisting in solidarity with them against economic imperialism, and that they will realize that the U.S.-based activist community will continue to fight alongside them.

REFLECTIONS ON COMMUNICATION ACTIVISM

To add to the broader discussion about communication activism that is the focus of these texts, this last section outlines three lessons learned here about this brand of activism. Taken together, these lessons imply that communication activism not only serves social justice causes but also that it can become itself a unique social cause—one that concentrates its disciplinary resources to help activist communities to fashion a more civil global society. This process corresponds to a basic idea in the critical pedagogy literature: Systems of domination thrive, in part, by dividing and keeping separate the individual members of the broad population, including the class of educators, but one method to cultivate resistance to these systems is to build spaces of unification and shared action for the purpose of creating political leverage against the forces of domination (see, e.g., Allman, 1999; McLaren & Lankshear, 1994). The studies in these two volumes are a positive step in that direction.

Lesson 1: Communication Activism will be Defined by how Scholar-Activists Infuse Their Resources into Projects of Popular Resistance

This first lesson reflects a basic theme in the literature of social justice: The application of communication research to social justice projects produces (or enhances) civic spaces wherein citizens work together to eliminate the repressive features of society (see, e.g., Hartnett, 1998, this volume).

Engaging in social justice civic activism, Frey (1998) reminded us, will "lead communication scholars to identify the grammars that oppress or under-write relationships of domination and bring their communication resources to bear to reconstruct those grammars in more socially just ways" (p. 157).

Communication activism should focus directly on what Pearce (1998) called *second-order change*, change that seeks systemic transformation of existing power relations. Activism, in this sense, denotes not only advocacy for marginalized groups but also strategic resistance to systems of domination that thrive on producing marginalization. Given that systems such as neoliberal capitalism function to concentrate political and economic power in the hands of an elite class (a process that inherently is antidemocratic), systemic second-order change is the only way to produce social conditions conducive to a direct democracy. Citizen movements, however, have scarce monetary, technical, and personnel resources relative to the modern international state, a stark imbalance that works against popular causes. Communication activists, consequently, should devote their time and energy, knowledge of symbolic activity, and disciplinary resources to activist causes.

The act of communication activism in this instance entailed working closely with an active affinity group to enhance its preparation for a critical antiglobalization protest. The project led me, as a participant-scholar, to help this affinity group employ a set of reflexive techniques designed to improve our goal-oriented talk. The emergent-consensus program was designed with this affinity group's goal to support the antiglobalization movement in mind. Thus, disciplinary resources of communication were brought to bear directly on attempting to transform state-capitalist forms of privilege and domination.

Lesson 2: Communication Activism Should Focus on Helping Activists to Build Network Infrastructures of Social Movements

Social movements are complex systems that tie together (often loosely) a set of macro-level and micro-level organizations. The union movement, for instance, grew over time into a vast network of local, regional, and national organizations, and it was this broad network that enabled previously isolated workers to mobilize the collective power of labor against the forces of capital. In this sense, network linkages not only tie together the various organizations of a social movement but they also shape its identity and potential to affect social conditions.

Research in this area suggests that weak and misaligned linkages within the network infrastructure often function to debilitate social movements

(McAdam, McCarthy, & Zald, 1988). Thus, to survive, social movements must build strong and vital network linkages (see Coopman, Volume 2). Resource mobilization theory has been instrumental in determining that the micro entities of social movements must play a vital role in this process (see, e.g., Jenkins, 1983). This theory suggests that to become viable, social movements must be able to mobilize resources, such as time, money, personnel, information, and organizing capacity (McCarthy & Zald, 1977). The ability of micro contexts (e.g., local unions) to link both to each other and to the larger movement infrastructure (e.g., the network system of the union movement) is a vital component of resource mobilization.

The antiglobalization movement displays a unique capacity to sustain a viable network infrastructure. The period that preceded the Miami protest exemplifies how, from the ground up, this global movement linked its complex set of groups and organizations to prepare for the event. The micromobilizing contexts of affinity groups such as Meta- link to regional clusters that, in turn, are embedded within national blocs. The prime linkages among these entities are cluster meetings, national bloc conference calls, legal and logistics hotlines, and web-based connections. Antiglobalization activists work diligently to maintain this infrastructure.

The current project was designed to strengthen the antiglobalization movement's network infrastructure. As an activist-scholar, I took an active part in establishing linkages for Meta- as it prepared for the Miami protest, a project that entailed coordinating and leading cluster meetings, acting as the resource person for the national bloc conference calls, representing Meta- at spokescouncil meetings in Miami, and helping the group to craft innovative solutions to internal and external communication problems.

Effective establishment and upkeep of network linkages allows for what Snow, Rochford, Warden, and Benford (1986) called *frame alignment*, or the alignment of a social movement's various organizational levels with respect to its ideologies, goals, plans, and resources. In the union example, frame alignment occurred as local unions, regional offices, and national organizations synchronized their goals, plans, and resources to mobilize a worker-based movement. Frame alignment enables the disparate groups and organizations of a social movement to forge a coherent identity and coordinate effectively their goals, plans, and actions.

One outcome of the emergent-consensus program was the increased capacity of Meta- to align its goals and resources more effectively with the broader movement. Consensus building is a prime organizing principle for the antiglobalization movement; it constitutes the decision-making model within its various organizations and across the linkages among these organizations. Cluster and spokescouncil meetings, national bloc conference calls, and tactical street conferences all employ the consensus model. Working closely with Meta- to enhance its consensus-building practices strengthened the frame alignment between this affinity group, its cluster, and the national bloc. Not only was Meta- more prepared and efficient as it linked to the movement but also it embodied effective consensus building during these interactions. This process was especially evident as Meta- linked with other affinity groups on the streets, in cluster meetings, and at spokescouncils during the protest. Enhancing the ability of micro entities to engage in practices that define and characterize a macro-social movement functions to strengthen the frame-aligning capacity of that movement.

In addition, enhancing the frame-aligning capacity of a social movement improves the overall capacity of the movement's members to construct an integrated definition of the social and/or political problem they are confronting. The more aligned the movement's various contexts are, the more capacity movement members have to construct shared meanings and values and, consequently, create collective solutions to the social problems they consider salient.

Lesson 3: Progressive Activism is a Productive Environment for Gaining Insights into the Complex Processes of Communication and Consensus Building

The values inherent in consensus building—such as equal power and voice, participatory democracy, shared outcomes, and the absence of hierarchy—define progressive activism. For antiglobalization activists, consensus building is not merely a practical form of decision making; it is a manifestation of their progressive vision of how social systems should be organized. My experience with progressive groups has led me to realize how dedicated their members are to the model of consensus building. Examining how these groups manage decision making provides insights into the processes of participatory consensus building.

Meta- provides a model of how activist groups can and will refine their discussion and decision-making processes through the systematic use of group communication techniques. As the members of Meta- employed these techniques, they learned to reflect on their collective practices, theorize about the causes of their communication-based problems, and generate potential solutions to these problems. These results are consistent with research suggesting that group processes and outcomes are improved as group members work together to investigate their group talk (e.g., Gastil, 1992).

Results from the emergent-consensus program indicate that the program shaped Meta-'s group talk in important ways. First, the project activated members' capacity (and desire) to employ group tools designed to help them achieve their goals in more productive ways. Before employing the emergent-consensus program, the members of Meta- focused primarily on their causes, goals, and duties. After using the program, however, members were eager to analyze the nature and functions of their practices and use this knowledge to serve their individual and group interests. Latent discussion and decision structures and practices became detectable as the group crafted a decision-based language that helped members both to identify unproductive behaviors and steer their discussion and decision-making processes toward proven productive behaviors.

Second, use of the program increased the group's productivity and cohesion. This outcome supports research showing that the creation of positive preconditions for group decision making is beneficial to group outcomes (Gouran & Hirokawa, 1983). The emergent-consensus program encouraged the members of Meta- both to reflect on the group's identity and act on their collective desires for how talk should be organized. Members embodied their ideal of direct democracy by employing participatory methods to refine their consensus practices. Increased productivity and cohesion also aided the group in its attempts to become a well-organized unit that could integrate into the larger activist network infrastructure.

Notable challenges, however, also emerged during use of the emergent-consensus program. The program seemed to work well only for a steady in-group and stalled in the presence of newcomers. In addition, the program did not function explicitly as the group became increasingly occupied with pressing protest-related responsibilities. These problems suggest the need for group training for use of the program in the presence of newcomers and in situations of increased responsibility. These problems can (most likely) be eliminated as group members employ the emergent-consensus model over a protracted period of time.

CONCLUSION

The members of Meta- are diligent in maintaining a tradition at the start of every meeting: One member declares that Meta- seeks suggestions from anyone that will help to enhance the group's democratic and consensus-building processes. The current project stemmed from one such declaration. Scholars should grasp that there is much that these affinity groups can teach us about communication activism. In turn, progressive civic groups, such as Meta-, benefit from the input of scholars who are willing to support the organizing efforts of groups striving for social change and justice. Thus, communication activism, if designed and implemented effectively, can play a vital role in the historical resistance against globalization and other systems of domination.

NOTES

1. The history of affinity groups can be traced to the 19th-century Spanish anarchist movement.

2. The communication discipline is in an initial phase of studying civic activism (see, e.g., Brock & Howell, 1994; Hartnett, 1998). To date, little attention has been paid to affinity groups and, in particular, the decision-making processes that these groups employ. In addition, although research has begun to shed light on how groups communicate in natural settings, such studies largely have remained descriptive, intended primarily to inform other scholars about how groups operate; unfortunately, groups seldom are helped directly by such studies and sometimes even are not privy to the insights afforded by those studies (see Frey, 1994; for notable exceptions, see the studies in Frey, 1995, 2006).

3. The FTAA was inaugurated at the Summit of the Americas held in Miami in 1994. The FTAA project seeks to expand the NAFTA enterprise within the WTO free trade framework to create a free trade area in the Western hemisphere in which barriers to trade and investment progressively are eliminated. By 2003, multiple ministerials and summits had been held to negotiate the nature and scope of this trade agreement. The project is portrayed by pro-free trade advocates as a necessary trade framework that is transparent, environmentally sensitive, and open to public input (see the official FTAA web site: www.ftaa-alca.org/alca_e.asp). Critics charge that the free trade process lacks transparency and the proposed agreement positions corporate interests above all other interests. An alternative to the free trade system, a fair trade system responsive to democratic input and sensitive to the needs of the working class, the environment, and human rights, has been proposed.

4. The Miami FTAA summit results in an arrangement to scale back the scope of the trade agreement, allow member nations to withdraw from specific features of the FTAA, and postpone the bulk of significant decision making until the 2005 round of talks (regarding the outcomes of the Miami summit, see James, 2003).

REFERENCES

Allman, P. (1999). *Revolutionary social transformation: Democratic hopes, political possibilities and critical education.* Westport, CT: Bergin & Garvey.

Beatty, M. J. (1989). Group members' decision rule orientations and consensus. *Human Communication Research, 16,* 279-296.

Beck, S. (1996). *Nonviolent action handbook.* Ojai, CA: World Peace Communications.

Bennett, E. (1955). Discussion, decision commitment, and consensus in "group decision." *Human Relations, 8,* 251-273.

Brock, B. L., & Howell, S. (1994). Leadership in the evolution of a community-based political action group. In L. R. Frey (Ed.), *Group communication in context: Studies of natural groups* (pp. 135-152). Hillsdale, NJ: Erlbaum.

Butler, C., Lawrence, T., & Rothstein, A. (1991). *On conflict and consensus: A handbook on formal consensus decision-making.* Cambridge, MA: Food Not Bombs.

Cheney, G., Mumby, D., Stohl, C., & Harrison, T. M. (Eds.). (1997). Communication and organizational democracy [Special issue]. *Communication Studies, 48*(4).

Deere, C. L., & Esty, D. C. (Eds.). (2002). *Greening the Americas: NAFTA's lessons for hemispheric trade.* Cambridge, MA: MIT Press.

Denzin, N. (2002). The interpretive process. In A. M. Huberman & M. B. Miles (Eds.), *The qualitative researcher's companion* (pp. 349-366). Thousand Oaks, CA: Sage.

Finnegan, W. (2003). Affinity groups and the movement against corporate globalization. In J. Goodwin & J. M. Jasper (Eds.), *The social movements reader: Cases and concepts* (pp. 210-218). Malden, MA: Blackwell.

Frey, L. R. (1994). The naturalistic paradigm: Studying small groups in the postmodern era. *Small Group Research, 25,* 551-577.

Frey, L. R. (Ed.). (1995). *Innovations in group facilitation: Applications in natural settings.* Cresskill, NJ: Hampton Press.

Frey, L. R. (1998). Communication and social justice research: Truth, justice, and the applied communication way. *Journal of Applied Communication Research, 26,* 155-164.

Frey, L. R. (Ed.). (2006). *Facilitating group communication in context: Innovations and applications with natural groups* (2 vols.). Cresskill, NJ: Hampton Press.

Gastil, J. (1992). A definition of small group democracy. *Small Group Research, 23,* 278-301.

Global Exchange. (2003). *Top ten reasons to oppose the Free Trade Area of the Americas.* Retrieved December 28, 2003, from http://www.globalexchange.org/campaigns/ftaa/topten.html

Gouran, D. S., & Geonetta, S. C. (1977). Patterns of interaction in discussion groups at varying distance from consensus. *Small Group Behavior, 8,* 511-524.

Gouran, D. S., & Hirokawa, R. Y. (1983). The role of communication in decision-making groups: A functional perspective. In M. S. Mander (Ed.), *Communications in transition: Issues and debates in current research* (pp. 168-185). New York: Praeger.

Hare, A. P. (1980). Consensus versus majority vote: A laboratory experiment. *Small Group Behavior, 11,* 131-143.

Hartnett, S. (1998). Lincoln and Douglas meet the abolitionist David Walker as prisoners debate slavery: Empowering education, applied communication, and social justice. *Journal of Applied Communication Research, 26,* 232-253.

Hirokawa, R. Y. (1982). Consensus group decision-making, quality of decision, and group satisfaction: An attempt to sort "fact" from "fiction." *Central States Speech Journal, 33,* 407-415.

James, D. (2003). *Summary of the proceedings of the FTAA Trade Negotiating committee.* Retrieved December 28, 2003, from http://www.globalexchange.org/campaigns/ftaa/1311.html

Jenkins, J. C. (1983). Resource mobilization theory and the study of social movements. In R. H. Turner & J. F. Short, Jr. (Eds.), *Annual review of sociology* (Vol. 9, pp. 527-553). Palo Alto, CA: Annual Reviews.

Kline, J. A., & Hollinger, J. L. (1973). Redundancy, self-orientation, and group consensus. *Speech Monographs, 40,* 72-74.

Knutson, T. J., & Kowitz, A. C. (1977). Effects of information type and level of orientation on consensus-achievement in substantive and affective small-group conflict. *Central States Speech Journal, 28,* 54-63.

Lindlof, T. R. (1995). *Qualitative communication research methods.* Thousand Oaks, CA: Sage.

McAdam, D., McCarthy, J. D., & Zald, M. N. (1988). Social movements. In N. J. Smelser (Ed.), *Handbook of sociology* (pp. 695-721). Newbury Park, CA: Sage.

McCarthy, J. D., & Zald, M. N. (1977). Resource mobilization and social movements: A partial theory. *American Journal of Sociology, 82,* 1212-1241.

McLaren, P. L., & Lankshear, C. (Eds.). (1994). *Politics of liberation: Paths from Freire.* New York: Routledge.

Moynihan, D. (2002). Using direct action effectively. In M. Prokosch & L. Raymond (Eds.), *The global activist's manual: Local ways to change the world* (pp. 161-169). New York: Thunder's Mouth Press/Nation Books.

Pearce, W. B. (1998). On putting social justice in the discipline of communication and putting enriched concepts of communication in social justice research and practice. *Journal of Applied Communication Research, 26,* 272-278.

Rawlins, W. K. (1984). Consensus in decision-making groups: A conceptual history. In G. M. Phillips & J. T. Wood (Eds.), *Emergent issues in human decision making* (pp. 19-39). Carbondale: Southern Illinois University Press.

Rees, F. (1998). *The facilitator excellence handbook: Helping people work creatively and productively together.* San Francisco: Jossey-Bass/Pfeiffer.

Robinson, W. I., & Harris, J. (2000). Towards a global ruling class? Globalization and the transnational capitalist class. *Science & Society, 64,* 11-54.

Ross, J. (2000). *The war against oblivion: Zapatista chronicles, 1994-2000.* Monroe, ME: Common Courage Press.

Sager, K. L., & Gastil, J. (1999). Reaching consensus on consensus: A study of the relationships between individual decision-making styles and use of the consensus decision rule. *Communication Quarterly, 47,* 67-79.

Schultz, B. G. (1999). Improving group communication performance: An overview of diagnosis and intervention. In L. R. Frey (Ed.), D. S. Gouran, & M. S. Poole (Assoc. Eds.), *The handbook of group communication theory and research* (pp. 371-394). Thousand Oaks, CA: Sage.

Schwarz, R. (2002). *The skilled facilitator: A comprehensive resource for consultants, facilitators, managers, trainers, and coaches* (2nd ed.). San Francisco: Jossey-Bass.

Smith, J. (2002). Globalizing resistance: The battle of Seattle and the future of social movements. In J. Smith & H. Johnston (Eds.), *Globalization and resistance: Transnational dimensions of social movements* (pp. 207-227). Lanham, MD: Rowman & Littlefield.

Snow, D. A., Rochford, E. B., Warden, S. K., & Benford, R. D. (1986). Frame alignment processes, micromobilization, and movement participation. *American Sociological Review, 51,* 464-481.

Starr, A. (2000). *Naming the enemy: Anti-corporate movements confront globalization.* New York: Zed Books.

Sunwolf, & Seibold, D. R. (1999). The impact of formal procedures on group processes, members, and task outcomes. In L. R. Frey (Ed.), D. S. Gouran, & M. S. Poole (Assoc. Eds.), *The handbook of group communication theory and research* (pp. 395-431). Thousand Oaks, CA: Sage.

Susskind, L., McKearnan, S., & Thomas-Larmer, J. (Eds.). (1999). *The consensus building handbook: A comprehensive guide to reaching agreement.* Thousand Oaks, CA: Sage.

Tabb, W. K. (2004). *Economic governance in the age of globalization.* New York: Columbia University Press.

Vizentini, P., & Wiesebron, M. (2004). *Free trade for the Americas? The United States' push for the FTAA agreement.* New York: Zed Books.

Wallach, L., & Woodall, P. (2004). *Whose trade organization? A comprehensive guide to the WTO* (2nd ed.). New York: New Press.

West, M., & Gastil, J. (2004). Deliberation at the margins: Participant accounts of face-to-face public deliberation at the 1999-2000 world trade protests in Seattle and Prague. *Qualitative Research Reports in Communication, 5,* 1-7.

9

"I'M GLAD YOU FEEL COMFORTABLE ENOUGH TO TELL ME THAT"

Participatory Action Research for Better Healthcare for Women Who Partner with Women*

Shelly Campo

University of Iowa

M. Somjen Frazer

Red Hook Community Justice Center

Social change occurs sometimes as a result of pressure from groups outside of institutions and sometimes from pressure exerted by members within institutions (Katzenstein, 1998). When the social change issue to be addressed includes the subtleties of institutional discrimination and the

*This research was supported in part by the Bartels' Participatory Action Research Fellows Program; the Public Service Center; Gannett: Cornell University Health Services; the Lesbian, Gay, Bisexual, and Transgendered Resource Center; and the Dean of Students Office at Cornell University. We wish to thank Nina Cummings, Gwendolyn Dean, Steve Hughes, Sara Simpkins, and many faculty, staff, and students who wish to remain anonymous for their help with this project.

involved parties are prepared to work together, a partnership approach is more effective than an oppositional one. Participatory research, which takes a partnership approach, is likely to be helpful in the case of subtle institutional discrimination because it can be difficult to get varying parties to talk to each other and such research can facilitate trust, which is vital for eliciting honest responses. In addition, subtle discrimination can be difficult to prove and can result in the harmed parties becoming frustrated with inaction. Research that focuses on a tangible outcome is likely to be received much better than research to just document the problem alone.

In the case described in this chapter, we, as researchers, collaborated with a task force of clinicians and other staff at Gannett: Cornell University Health Services; the Lesbian, Gay, Bisexual, and Transgendered Resource Center (LGBTRC); and students, to improve services for women who partner with women (WPW). In this case, because of the nature of the problems being addressed, the changes that occurred could not have been forced from outside the institution but were a product of a nonadversarial, stakeholder-driven process occurring within the institution. The stakeholders included staff at Gannett, staff in student services, WPW, and faculty and staff. These stakeholders agreed that the project we undertook together would address the barriers to healthcare that existed for WPW at the university and contribute to the scholarly literature on this topic.

As researchers, we provided expertise in organizing the project and collecting data about WPW. Although well-collected data about the scope and nature of the problem under investigation is an important complement to efforts to change an organization from within, data are not sufficient to enact that change through policy and practice. Change also requires those data be put to use in some way through campaigns, policy changes, or other interventions. It was with a commitment to both making immediate changes in a particular healthcare center and contributing to scholarly discourse on healthcare for WPW that we undertook this 2-year study.

In this chapter, we explain this case of communication activism regarding healthcare for WPW within a healthcare center committed to serving a diverse student body. We start by examining the barriers to effective, sensitively delivered healthcare for WPW, and describing the issue, the research environment, and our theoretical and methodological groundings. We outline the process that allowed us to identify the barriers facing WPW trying to access healthcare services. We then present our findings about the opinions and experiences of WPW with the healthcare center, describe the communication activism that followed, and suggest best-practice principles for others undertaking similar work to effect community change in healthcare. We conclude the chapter by offering lessons we have learned from our experiences about communication activism.

DESCRIPTION OF THE ISSUE

Research on historically underserved and typically "invisible" populations (including WPW) is necessary because without it, medical norms continue to be based on the assumption that each person who needs healthcare represents some "universal" patient, who is often assumed to be White, male, and heterosexual. This false assumption elides important genetic, social, emotional, and psychological differences between groups of people that may create specific health needs, and ignores the negative experiences many members of historically marginalized groups may have had in receiving healthcare (Boston Women's Health Collective, 1998; Solarz, 1999). These experiences and the resulting fears often lead marginalized people to have a lack of knowledge of appropriate healthcare for their particular group, access to healthcare, interactions with clinicians, and differential health outcomes (see, e.g., du Prè, 2004; Geist-Martin, Ray, & Sharf, 2003).

There is a lack of literature on the topic of lesbian healthcare, generally (Marrazzo, Koutsky, Kiviat, Kuypers, & Stine, 2001; Solarz, 1999; White & Martinez, 1997), and even fewer studies on college health, more specifically. Some of the disadvantages identified for lesbians include underuse of routine care (Carroll, 1999; Harrison, 1996) and gynecological care (Diamant, Schuster, McGuigan, & Lever, 2000) and the experiences of heterosexism and homophobia in the clinical environment (Hester & Biddle, 1995; McKee, Hayes, & Axiotis, 1994). Furthermore, especially in the area of mental health, lesbian and bisexual women face additional health risks, such as depression due to heterosexism in the larger culture outside the clinic (Bernhard & Applegate, 1999; Gonsiorek, 1988; Lock & Steiner, 1999). Studies conducted in the college setting also suggest health disadvantages for lesbian and bisexual women in this environment (Edelman, 1986; Lehmann, Lehmann, & Kelly, 1998; McKee et al., 1994).

These problems can be exacerbated for WPW in the college health context. Barriers to healthcare and WPW's perceptions of college healthcare are affected not only by their college experience but by their previous experiences with healthcare. Because many students have not been in charge of their healthcare before they arrive at college, they need guidance on health prevention and treatment and, more generally, on how to be competent healthcare consumers. This was the case for WPW at Cornell University. The staff at Cornell's healthcare center had long lamented about these issues, which doubly affects members of populations who may be at odds with or estranged from their family support system (personal communication,[1] October 18, 2001 and January 20, 2002). Despite the fact that college students have high reading and comprehension literacy, they often may lack health literacy, including basic understanding of how healthcare operates and how to ask good questions of healthcare practitioners (Bernhardt &

Cameron, 2003). In addition, it is not enough to have basic health literacy; people also must learn how to become self-advocates, which, in the long run, can positively affect their psychological and physical well-being as healthcare recipients (Brashers, Haas, Klingle, & Neidig, 2000; Brashers, Haas, Neidig, & Rintamaki, 2002). For us as researchers and the healthcare staff members with whom we collaborate, increasing WPW students' self-advocacy skills was an important communication activism goal.

Thus, we undertook this study to understand and address the barriers to healthcare for WPW in this particular community and, thereby, contribute to the literature on barriers to healthcare for WPW of college age. This case presented particular challenges and opportunities for healthcare provision for WPW. At the beginning of the study, anecdotal evidence suggested that many LGBT students felt dissatisfied with the healthcare they received at the university. Although there was no organized social movement around women's health or LGBT health, students complained to us early in the process that they felt clinicians knew little about their specific health needs and sometimes displayed problematic heterosexist behavior.[2] For example, one student who initiated a complaint but did not take part in the study told Frazer that her clinician said that he did not believe the student had sex only with women when she attended a follow-up visit for an abnormal pap smear. Although this student reported this incident to the patient advocate at the healthcare center, she did not feel that her complaint was adequately addressed. She became so frustrated that she subsequently refused to visit the center for sexual healthcare. A history of such complaints led to interest from university staff, clinicians, and students to find ways to promote equity in healthcare, giving us an unusual opportunity to assist through collaborative research. Although an earlier focus group conducted by the LGB-TRC on the topic had been poorly attended and relatively uninformative, based on our conversations with the health center staff and the LGBTRC director, they were eager to try again. Both WPW student activists and healthcare staff indicated enthusiasm for an action research project to help improve healthcare for WPW at this university. Their interest was extremely helpful in launching and sustaining this effort. In fact, students and staff were enthusiastic about our involvement because we were seen as a bridge between the two groups.

RESEARCH ENVIRONMENT

As two WPW, a student (Frazer) and a professor (Campo), we were well suited to study both the student and clinician perspectives on WPW healthcare. As a student at the university, Frazer had access to the informal communities of WPW who complained about bad experiences with healthcare offered at the center, but had no way of verifying whether their highly negative perceptions of the healthcare center were accurate or based on apocryphal stories and rumors. In addition, it was unclear whether these were the voices of a vocal minority or more widespread. As a public health researcher, Campo was able to connect with the healthcare center staff based on her previous health communication research on college students, and, more specifically, through her existing research partnerships with the health center at this particular university, which resulted in changes to existing alcohol campaigns, new antisocial smoking campaigns, and changes in antihazing efforts. Prior research partnerships, thus, had resulted in practical outcomes. Both of us, therefore, were able to use our research skills and our connections to help further this research project.

We could not have addressed barriers to healthcare for WPW collaboratively if Cornell University and Ithaca, NY were not relatively comfortable places to be LGBT. The university has a diversity statement that includes protections for sexual minorities, as does the city. However, unlike in some college communities, despite the presence of the LGBTRC, the LGBT "community" lacked coherent student leadership and activism and had only small, albeit growing, numbers of students involved in LGBT social groups.

THEORETICAL AND METHODOLOGICAL GROUNDINGS

This project was shaped by participatory action research, queer theory and feminism, and health communication theories. The contribution of each of these perspectives is discussed next.

Participatory Action Research

Participatory action research (PAR) is a family of research methods that privilege research directed toward producing institutional or social change outcomes. PAR involves a partnership between researchers and communities with a stake in the problem being addressed (Kemmis & McTaggart, 2000). The form of PAR we used borrows from several types of PAR, ranging from industrial consulting to empowerment-based action research, which is typically conducted with very low-income or developing-world communities. As consultants, we provided expert research assistance and advice to the leadership of an institution; however, we did so assuring the participation of institutional members (physicians, nurses, and other staff) and constituents (WPW patients) affected by the changes. In keeping with action research principles, we conducted our research with a high degree of self-reflection, as well as attention to engaging participants in both the research and social change processes, thereby helping to advance the views of marginalized groups, whose voices are often ignored in the public domain.

We also were attentive to the reliability and validity criteria of traditional research methods. We balanced the desire for maximum participation with community partners' willingness and ability to take part in a rigorous research project. For example, we elected not to have partners conduct research on their own; rather, we partnered with volunteers to determine research questions, draft research protocols, collect and analyze data, and make recommendations. The research process included answering both partner-driven and theory-driven questions. For example, members of the task force were interested in knowing about the successes and failures of specific programs or policies currently in use, and we were interested in knowing whether the health belief model could be used to predict WPW safer-sex practices from their perceived susceptibility and severity of sexually transmitted infections (STIs) and their perceived benefits and barriers of safer-sex practices. Furthermore, in keeping with the demand for transparency in PAR projects, we were up front with all participants about our desire to test health communication theories (to address theory-driven questions) and publish the results of our research, in addition to providing immediate assistance to the community stakeholders (to address their concerns). Community stakeholders wanted to know how WPW students felt about the student health center, their experiences with healthcare, and their perceptions of how services at the university could be improved. Our community partners also were interested in the types of outreach programs to provide education they needed to offer to WPW on campus.

Finally, we were attentive to the heightened ethical requirements of PAR and working with marginalized, hidden communities. PAR takes very seriously the power differentials that exist between communities and requires researchers to both inquire into the sources of these differences and make efforts to alter them. It also complicates the traditional ethical requirements of research, such as "confidentiality" (which may or may not be desired by individual participants but, in any case, should be under their control) and transparency (which must be greater than in non-PAR research projects). PAR also requires a degree of self-awareness and self-reflection not needed for traditional research (for an extended discussion of the ethics requirements of PAR, see the essays in Reason & Bradbury, 2001).

The desire to collect data that would be both immediately useful to WPW, the LGBTRC, and the healthcare center and contribute to the literature on WPW healthcare provided a productive tension for both us and our community partners. By using traditional and participatory methods, we were able to maximize the strengths of each form of knowledge building.

PAR prioritizes the usefulness of research for confronting a set of local problems, whereas traditional social science privileges the generalizability of research, and we were able to test hypotheses for both purposes. Similarly, by placing feminist and queer theories that emphasize the socially constructed nature of categories, as explained later, in dialogue with particular health communication theories that emphasize the predictive ability of sociodemographic variables, we were able to use the strengths of both types of theories to explain in what ways identities and behaviors are fixed and in what ways they are contradictory, unstable, and in flux. Although feminists and LGBT health advocates have criticized traditional models of healthcare for being top-down, the process of integrating practice and theory in this case was complementary. In asking about the things that our research partners wanted us to address, they implicitly raised concepts from the health communication theories in which we were interested, such as susceptibility, severity, response, and self-efficacy; social and subjective norms; and benefits and barriers. Therefore, we used these theories as a way to address their questions of interest and to be sure we were addressing research-based concepts and relationships.

Queer Theory and Feminism

In addition to PAR theories and methods, we drew on queer and feminist theories in our analytical framework, research design, and collaborative research. We were particularly attentive to the suggestion made by queer theorists that sexuality must be recognized as a fluid and dynamic exchange between an individual and the sets of signs and signifiers that make up her or his culture (Gamson, 2002). To minimize the assumption that identities such as "lesbian" would match sexual behavior perfectly, we allowed all women to participate in this project who self-identified as lesbian, bisexual, or queer, or ever had a female sexual partner or nonsexual dating relationship. From feminism, we understood that because models of health and healthcare have been traditionally based on a male model and women have been and often are subjected to substandard care and disrespect in healthcare settings, attention was paid to the ways in which healthcare assumptions and practices are gendered, such as assuming that biological females behave, or identify, as women. Furthermore, traditional communication patterns in physician-patient interactions also tend to be based on stereotypical roles and assumptions, such as distant, uncaring male physicians and female patients who simply comply. We believe that patients and their clinicians can be taught to counter the sexism they see in clinical practice, regardless of their gender (Boston Women's Health Collective, 1998).

Health Communication Theories

We employed three theories of health communication, all of which have been previously applied to study LGBT health issues or sexual health issues (Perloff, 2001), to identify cognitive, emotional, social, and structural factors that may be affecting healthcare and health decision making for WPW at our institution (e.g., seeking medical care, disclosing sexuality to a healthcare provider, or using a dental dam). First, from the health belief model (Janz, Champion, & Strecher, 2002; Rosenstock, 1960; Strecher, Champion, & Rosenstock, 1997), we were concerned about the barriers and benefits that WPW experienced in seeking healthcare and engaging in healthy practices. Second, the theory of planned behavior (Ajzen, 1991; Fishbein & Ajzen, 1975), as applied to health, argues that we need to find out about attitudes, subjective norms, and volitional control in the healthcare and health behavior decision-making processes of WPW to understand what affects the behavior of the population of interest. Theories related to fear appeals, widely used to study health, suggest the need to look more deeply at WPW's perceptions of health risk through a third theory. The extended parallel process model (Witte, 1992, 1994; Witte & Allen, 2000), in particular, led us to examine WPW's perceived susceptibility to and severity of potential STIs, as well as self-efficacy and response-efficacy of potential solutions to minimizing risk.

RESEARCH PROCESS

The research process included both qualitative and quantitative components. Interviews were conducted with WPW students,[3] clinicians, and key informants. Interviews were designed to inform the survey questionnaire, but also provided rich, descriptive, interactively collected data that would have been impossible to obtain using only survey questionnaire methods. Survey questionnaires were administered to students to obtain quantitative measures of some variables and reach a more diverse and larger group of students.

Creating a Participatory Research Process

Obtaining financial support. The Bartels' Action Research Fellowship, a new university program that provides small amounts of funding to faculty-mentored, undergraduate research projects that take a participatory approach to community-based research, provided an initial grant of $2,000 for research expenses, as well as funding for hourly wages for Frazer's time.

This initial funding was key to leveraging additional money, which allowed for direct research costs, incentives for participants, and the development of new and the purchase of existing intervention materials. Additional funding and supplies were provided by other campus agencies as the project grew in scope, including the student health center, the public service center, and the LGBTRC. Because the project was not in competition with other groups in need of population-specific health outreach, the health-promotion staff at the health center was not concerned that money spent on WPW would mean less money for other forms of outreach.

Establishing trust and a research partnership. To establish trust with each group involved with this project, we met these communities on their terms. Because students and staff were mistrustful of one another, separate partnership meetings with these groups were needed. In keeping with PAR methods, a task force of clinicians, health-promotion staff, student service personnel, and other staff from across the university was formed early in the first year of the study, and subsequently grew to include other medical and support staff. Early in the process, students were so distrustful of the efficacy of the task-force meetings that they had to be approached individually, informally, and off campus to give input into the research design. Most of the early recruitment and outreach information was disseminated by Frazer, who met informally with students who later became leaders in the project.

The university staff, on the other hand, wanted formal meetings held during business hours and located in a convenient, central site on campus. The site selected was in the healthcare center. Meetings were held every 6-8 weeks, announced nearly a month in advance, and scheduled according to the needs of the very busy task-force members. Meetings were highly structured, following a mutually determined, set agenda, and nearly always followed the time parameters allotted for them. Informal comments from task-force members and the formal evaluation of the first semester of the project indicated that establishing this pattern of meeting efficiency was significant in giving the project credibility and authenticity in their eyes. Many task-force members had worked with student groups that lacked this degree of professionalism.

The task force guided the research process and provided insider views from various parts of the healthcare center and the rest of the university. The members evaluated their work, as well as our work as researchers, throughout the process, creating the type of self-reflexive environment that is central to PAR research (Kemmis & McTaggert, 2000). The regular meetings of the task force also served to connect faculty, students, the LGBTRC, the healthcare center, student services, and other units within the university that were charged with aspects of WPW health and quality of life. To maintain both the efficiency and the quality of the data-collection process, we proposed initial formats and content for both interviews and questionnaires to be completed by students, healthcare staff, and key informants from across the university. The task-force members contributed by acting as advisers on alternative wording for questions, suggesting additional content to include, and, most importantly, by requesting that specific data be collected that would be particularly useful to clinicians. It was essential that the data collected meet clinicians' needs, as well as students' needs, along with our desire to develop public health models of student risk perceptions, attitudes, preferences, and behaviors. Additional students also advised us on question design in an ad hoc fashion, with Frazer meeting with students willing to provide input into the survey questionnaire.

Researching Student Risk Perceptions, Attitudes, Preferences, and Behaviors

Student interviews. We conducted semistructured interviews with students in the fall of 2001, with the questionnaire following in the spring of 2002. Students were asked through local and campus interpersonal contacts, LGBT listservs, and at LGBT social events if they would be willing to be interviewed. The interview protocol included questions about their opinions of the healthcare center; previous good and bad experiences with healthcare, in general, and at the student healthcare center; descriptions of ideal clinician behavior and knowledge of women's and WPW-specific health; and opportunities to talk about LGBT and heterosexual friends' experiences or rumors about the healthcare center. Interviews were audiotaped and transcribed verbatim to be attentive to the words participants used to describe experiences and opinions of healthcare to gauge the current level and type of discourse in the community.

Fourteen WPW students were interviewed, with attention paid to obtaining a diverse sample (e.g., in terms of age, "outness," declared sexual orientation, race, and sexual practices). As with the informal contact with students during the advisory phase of the project, Frazer conducted the interviews in coffee shops and other public places of the respondents' choosing. In addition to completing the interview protocol, following the completion of the semistructured interviews, Frazer spoke at length with respondents to correct misperceptions they had about healthcare, health practices, and health insurance, which occurred as a result of an agreement with the task force that interventions would start immediately.

Student questionnaire. The survey questionnaire covered a much broader range of topics than did the interviews, assessing sexual practices (e.g., number and gender of partners over the last 3 months and lifetime and sexual behaviors), perceptions of social norms regarding both sexual practices and the healthcare center mental and general healthcare experiences and practices, opinions about the healthcare center, demographic data, "outness," preferred reactions of clinicians to coming out, and other items. Questions were derived based on results from the student and key informant interviews conducted, input from the task force, and concepts from health communication theories, including, as previously explained, the health belief model, the theory of planned behavior, and the extended parallel process model. The questionnaire also collected a limited amount of qualitative data, including open-ended questions such as, "For the purposes of healthcare, what is a safe space?" and "Think back to your favorite healthcare provider. What is it about that person that made her or him your favorite?" We recruited WPW to complete the questionnaire through LGBT listservs at Cornell, snowball sampling seeded from volunteers involved with the project in the advisory phase (who then asked their WPW friends and partners to complete the questionnaire, who asked their WPW friends and partners, etc.), and attendance at LGBT events held at the university. Self-identification as WPW was the only criterion for completing the questionnaire.

Interviewing Key Informants and Clinicians

In Fall 2001 and Spring 2002, we interviewed three individuals whose work in the university made them key informants and six clinicians from various sectors of the healthcare center. Key informants were people who held university positions affecting women's health or in LGBT student services. Key informants were interviewed about their experiences working with WPW students, observed barriers to healthcare for those WPW students, past efforts to improve LGBT health services, and barriers to connecting various university units with interests in the health of WPW. We interviewed clinicians about the university's past efforts to improve LGBT health services, institutional practices with respect to sexuality, their attitudes toward sexual difference, methods used to distribute continuing medical information about LGBT and other health topics, preferred methods of receiving healthcare information, and general healthcare recipient behavior in the physician-patient relationship (e.g., intake procedures, question asking, and level of participation on the part of the student). Data collected from this phase of the project offered a complementary perspective to the student perspective obtained on the health of WPW, provided information about barriers women bring with them to the healthcare setting, and suggested the best ways to collect and present data that clinicians would find useful.[4] The data also provided useful insider information about the workings of the healthcare center and the ways in which its budget and mission constrained its ability to accommodate WPW student demands.

KEY RESEARCH FINDINGS

In the following section, we summarize the results from the student interviews, clinician and key informant interviews, and student questionnaires. We begin with the interviews because they were used to inform the questionnaire design. We end this section by noting some of the research limitations.

Student Interviews

To identify the most pressing barriers to healthcare and prioritize areas of intervention, Frazer coded the interview transcripts according to the location (inside or outside of the healthcare center), characteristics, and intensity of the barrier. We then created a concept map of these barriers to use as an explanatory illustration to organize our findings (see Figure 9.1). This concept map allowed us to organize the barriers we found according to their location (who was mainly responsible for them and where they took place) and characteristics (discursive, as with "rumors"; institutional, as with forms and intake procedures; or interpersonal, such as interactions between physicians and patients). This conceptual organization allowed us to illustrate our findings to nonsocial scientists, identify initial needed interventions by category (e.g., pictures hung to make the healthcare space less "cold" and forms changed to separate STI risk from pregnancy risk), and look for patterns that could then be measured for the rest of the WPW population via the survey questionnaire.

The initial student interviewees described barriers to healthcare stemming from three main sources. The first was interactions with clinicians, in which WPW students perceived implicit homophobia, ignorance, or discomfort on the part of clinicians about the students' sexual orientation or a lack of general or WPW-specific medical knowledge. Students said that they dealt with these experiences with their providers by avoiding healthcare, seeking information from other sources (e.g., friends, family, the LGBTRC, and the media, including the internet), or attempting to educate clinicians. Second, students said that institutional practices such as heterosexist intake forms, opaque confidentiality policies, and short appointments were off-putting to them. Third, students created barriers to healthcare through their poor healthcare skills (e.g., failing to tell their providers about relevant health behaviors, refusing to get appropriate and timely healthcare, and not asking questions of their healthcare providers) and poor health practices (e.g., not getting enough sleep, exercise, or nutrition), as well as in the perpetuation of rumors and stories about the healthcare center.

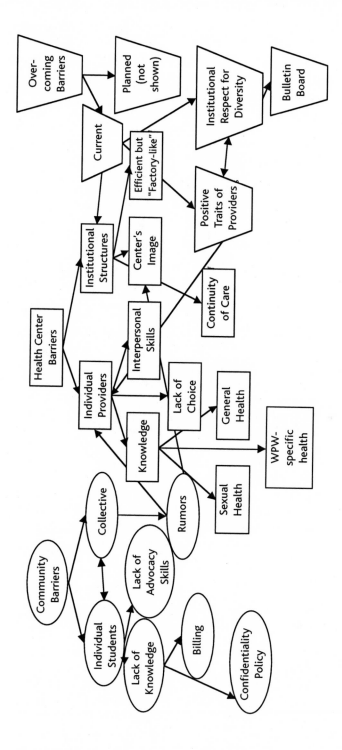

Figure 9.1. Concept map of barriers to healthcare

Qualitative data from these interviews also illustrated students' displeasure with the counseling center, with all but two respondents highlighting their dissatisfaction with it. This dissatisfaction was partly the result of increased demand for counseling after September 11, 2001, as well as the existing limit placed on student visits for counseling (10 per year) because of an insufficient number of counselors for long-term talk therapy.

Key Informant and Clinician Interviews

We conducted interviews with key informants and clinicians on an ad hoc basis to inform steps of the research process. Key informants who were drawn from the task force pointed us to critical incidents that may have affected WPW's trust in clinicians and other insider knowledge about the personalities and bureaucratic procedures of the healthcare center that we could not have drawn directly from observation, document review, or data collected from clinicians or students. Results indicated clinicians' desire to be trained in WPW health risks and LGBT issues more generally, suggested weaknesses that clinicians saw in themselves and others (including difficulty keeping up with research on WPW issues, infrequent contact with known WPW patients, and discomfort with colloquial and trendy language used by WPW to describe their identities and practices), and showed that they preferred to learn about WPW issues in a traditional continuing medical education (CME) format. We used this information to inform the student survey questionnaire data collection and design a training program for clinicians that fit the CME model, which is heavily research based, uses quantitative data, and is often presented in a traditional classroom format. However, because some clinicians indicated that they also wanted to receive "refresher" or "take-home" materials, we also provided written reports and research updates to clinicians who did and did not attend the trainings.

Student Questionnaires

Fifty-four WPW completed the questionnaire, which yielded data about the health practices and sexual behavior of respondents, as well as a picture of their views of the health center and perceptions of health risks and harms. The respondents were graduate students (27.8%) and undergraduates (68.5%), who were somewhat racially diverse (70.2% White, 10.5% mixed race/ethnicity, 7% African American, 5.3% Asian American, 1.3% Latina or Hispanic, and 5.3% international). The median age of respondents was 21. In terms of sexual identity, only 34.2% identified themselves as lesbian, 27.4% bisexual, 21.9% queer, 1.4% questioning, 1% transgendered, and the remaining were "other." Their average age was 22.6. They also were diverse in their sexual activities, with 70.4% having had sex with a woman and 65% having engaged in sex with a man in their lifetime; 46.3% had sex with a woman and one-third had sex with a man in the past 3 months.

Although these students perceived the healthcare center as basically an adequate place for care, they did not perceive it as exemplary. Questions constructed on a 5-point Likert scale (1 = *strongly disagree*, 2 = *disagree*, 3 = *neutral*, 4 = *agree*, 5 = *strongly agree*) provided measures of Gannett's "safety" for WPW (*M* = 3.11, *SD* = .55), staff interpersonal skills (*M* = 2.74, *SD* = .71), and institutional credibility (*M* = 2.54, *SD* = .87). On the whole, students indicated on several items that they were slightly less satisfied with the mental healthcare provided by the center than they were with the physical care. Satisfaction mean scores with regard to mental healthcare items ranged from 2.17 to 3.53 (*SD*s ranged from 0.35 to 1.23). "Credibility" measures were fair, with an average of 2.78 (*SD* = .75).

Alcohol and other drug use of the WPW sample were compared to results of women from questionnaires completed by the general student population in previous research by the center and Campo. The respondents in the present research used more ecstasy (25.9% for WPW compared with 10%), marijuana (77.8% of WPW compared with 38%), and tobacco (37% compared with 25.1%), although they used less alcohol (3.6 drinks per week for WPW compared with 5.4 drinks per week).

Respondents engaged in a wide variety of sexual practices, many of which put them at risk for STIs because of their failure to use barriers to prevent the exchange of fluids. Practices between WPW included oral sex, genital touching, rimming, fisting, sex toys, and sadomasochism. Nearly one-third of the respondents reporting using alcohol or other drugs when having sex, and one-third also reported that they did not practice monogamy. Similar practices were reported by many of the sample with regard to sexual relations with men. Although the vast majority reported using condoms or other latex barriers when engaging in sex with men, nearly all indicated they did not use latex barriers with women.

As queer theory would suggest, students claimed a wide variety of sexual identities that did not always "match" their sexual practices; for example, 15 women who identified themselves as lesbian also identified themselves as attracted to men, and 14 of those women had had sex with men. This was an important finding to convey to clinicians, who were not necessarily aware of the instability of sexual-identity categories that queer theorists take for granted. Another important finding to convey was students' dissatisfaction with clinicians' responses when those students disclosed their sexual identity or practices. Clinicians, for their part, indicated in interviews that they did not know what to say to indicate that they were not judging students when they shared this information but, rather, were supporting them and trying to provide adequate services. Students indicated that when they came out to clinicians, they preferred simple responses, such as "I'm glad you feel comfortable enough to tell me that." Similarly, when clinicians asked about sexual practices and pregnancy, students preferred explanations of why the questions were necessary and assurances that the questions were, in fact, required and by whom. In general, respondents tended to minimize the susceptibility of STIs for woman-to-woman transmission, but more accurately perceived the risks of STIs for sex with male partners. Their perceived susceptibility may explain why they also were much more likely to use protective barriers when having sex with male partners than with female partners. In addition, most of the respondents engaged in sexual activity after very few dates with a new partner ($M = 5.27$, $SD = 5.29$), with 78% going out on less than five dates before having sex with a new partner.

Research Limitations

Although the research yielded valuable information, there were some important limitations demonstrated as well. First, despite our best efforts and those of our research partners, we struggled to obtain student participation in this research study. One reason it was hard to recruit students was the lack of a long-standing or stable LGBT student group and the complete absence of an LGBT student activist organization, making it difficult to find even the most "out and active" students (Doherty, 2003). As explained, we recruited through existing listservs, personal appeals from us and others at events, and through our interpersonal networks and the interpersonal networks of the task-force members and research participants. In exchange for participation, we provided $5 gift certificates to a local coffee house with the questionnaire. The length of time it took for respondents to complete the survey questionnaire (30 minutes on average, according to anecdotal reports) and the timing of the data collection (late in the spring semester) also limited our sample size. Retrospectively, if we had been able to recruit more students to be heavily involved in the project so that they could have been used to seed the snowball sample for the questionnaire, we might have had a larger number of participants. A different incentive structure also could have been used; for example, we might have provided students with incentives for recruiting further participants, as Heckathorne (1997, 2002) suggested.

In addition, the high turnover in the student population and participants' student status presented problems. Because students face multiple pressures at a prestigious university and often lack time-management and planning skills, they are less able than older adults to participate in a long-term research and intervention process. Young adult WPW also are less likely to be "out" than older WPW and, thus, less likely to be connected to other WPW who can recruit them to join a participatory research process.

Although some participants were more connected than others, we did not have a large pool of well-connected WPW to help facilitate participation. Although we were successful in recruiting a number of people who did not self-identify as "lesbian" or "bisexual" or who were not completely "out," all questionnaire participants had some connection to another WPW who recruited them to participate. This finding suggests that we did not do an adequate job reaching more closeted WPW.

USING RESEARCH FOR SOCIAL CHANGE

We used data obtained from the research as the basis for conducting workshops with students and clinicians, creating changes in the healthcare center's practices and spaces, promoting lasting connections between university units, and raising awareness among many about the healthcare issues facing WPW. Each of these actions is explained next.

Workshops

Workshops conducted for both WPW students and clinicians were promoted as an opportunity to learn about the research results from the interviews and questionnaires and resources available on campus regarding healthcare and health promotion for WPW. All workshops were conducted by Frazer, and Campo assisted with facilitating the student workshop.

We incorporated into the workshops both qualitative and quantitative results from the research, which are both persuasive but often for different audiences. Persuasion research suggests that some people prefer anecdotal or testimonial evidence, whereas others prefer statistical evidence, and the presentation of both forms can be persuasive (see, e.g., Allen et al., 2000; Boster et al., 2000). Therefore, in all of the workshops, we included results from both the interviews and the questionnaire and presented materials in multiple forms to reach different people with different learning styles. For example, materials were presented visually and orally at workshops, in writing in an executive summary, and using both technical and colloquial language. We presented information about WPW's sexual behavior, health behaviors, and risk perceptions, and compared the data collected with data about heterosexual students more generally. Most importantly, we presented information that the research participants indicated was unknown or disregarded by a significant number of women; for instance, we explained that in many cases (such as sex between women), research participants' risk perceptions were too low.

Workshops for clinicians. Clinicians who were interviewed for the project indicated that, in addition to regularly scheduled, weekly continuing education meetings, they liked to read information online or in print. After the data were collected and preliminarily analyzed, we invited clinicians to attend a continuing education session devoted to learning about the data and being educated about WPW to improve clinician-WPW patient communication and communication campaigns on campus. We held two workshops for clinicians, one for the general health staff and one for the counseling staff. Twenty-five to 30 clinicians attended each session, which was the majority of the staff, and most people participated enthusiastically. Many thanked us for our work and the information provided, and agreed to work on the issues of greatest concern to WPW students.

Workshops for WPW students. Structuring the workshops for students around the data helped to establish an "objective" and less-threatening environment than a workshop that simply talked about how to protect their health, advocate for better healthcare, and be better health consumers. This method of health education has been found to be extremely successful with difficult topics because it allows people to consider their behavior alongside facts about others' behavior. In the area of alcohol education for problem drinkers, for instance, this process is known as "motivational interviewing" and has been done in individual and group settings (see, e.g., Marlatt et al., 1998).

We held two student workshops, one in the spring following data collection and one the following fall. Workshop materials were identical. We invited WPW students to a workshop that included sharing general information on health and how to work with healthcare providers, as well as the survey questionnaire data, and also provided an opportunity for students from the LGBT community to interact with clinicians. Because the workshops were conducted by a fellow student (Frazer) in a nonthreatening environment, it allowed students to ask difficult questions about their behaviors and beliefs regarding healthcare. Students were invited to attend through listservs, posters placed in various locations (e.g., the LGBTRC, healthcare center, Dean of Students Office, and Women's Resource Center), and through interpersonal networks. The first workshop had only four student participants, but the second workshop was attended by about 25 students and 5 healthcare staff, and was held in the LGBTRC. By providing a space that was comfortable for WPW to dialogue about health, the workshop broke down many stereotypes and myths held about each group by the other. WPW students realized that clinicians cared about them as people and were accepting of their sexual orientation, and clinicians were able to speak frankly to WPW students about helpful and unhelpful approaches to health and healthcare. Students and clinicians were given ample opportunities to comment and to ask questions, and as the workshop progressed, questions were asked and answered between the audience members whenever possible. The atmosphere was receptive, comfortable, and nonconfrontational. During the workshop, in addition to a formal presentation with group discussion following, handouts with the slides and further data were given to students and clinicians to keep. These and additional educational materials are now available in the student health center and in the LGBTRC.

Changes in the Healthcare Center's Practices and Space

As a result of the research findings, the healthcare center administrators agreed to hang some new pictures on its walls that depicted empowering messages for and about women. Some were pictures of women by women artists; others highlighted that the healthcare center is a "safe space" for diverse sexualities and gender identities. It was hoped that these pictures would address the issues raised by student interviewees about the perceived "coldness" and unattractiveness of the healthcare center. The health-promotion staff also now includes LGBT health-outreach information in its monthly rotation of health information in the bathrooms and the examination rooms. In addition, some older LGBT health pamphlets have been replaced with newer ones, offering students more up-to-date information presented more effectively. A full-time position also was created in the health-promotion department for 2002-2003 for a liaison between the LGBT community and the healthcare center, which was filled by a recent graduate who also did alcohol and drug interventions with LGBT and non-LGBT students. Although this full-time position was discontinued in 2003-2004, it was replaced with a part-time student position. Both positions included "office hours" in the LGBTRC that were paid for by the healthcare center. To counter its reputation as a "sex-negative" institution, the healthcare center started to carry vibrators along with the condoms, dental dams, and personal lubricant it had carried for a long time, particularly because vibrators were of interest to both the LGBT and straight communities. In response to a conservative outcry in the local media to stop the sale of vibrators, several women organized a buy-in of the vibrators when they were first offered around Valentine's Day 2002. Despite the criticism, the healthcare center continues to sell the vibrators as part of its broader commitment to women's health and sexuality services.

Lasting Connections between University Units

The LGBTRC and the healthcare center continue to collaborate today in several ways. One such collaboration is a program called "Q-chat," which has replaced the poorly attended LBT women's support group in the counseling center with a mixed-gender, LGBTRC-based group that is better attended. The LGBTRC also is now a site for flu shots for students, which demonstrates the center's expanded willingness to reach out to that community. Similarly, the director of the healthcare center sends welcome messages to new LGBT students via the LGBT students' listservs. In 2003, the welcome message, released on National Coming Out Day, included an announcement that the healthcare center cosponsored a Safe Place Initiative, which provides university staff and faculty members with small cards and pins announcing that their offices are "safe places" and they are "safe people" who will deal appropriately with LGBT issues. The welcome message also explicitly addressed issues that arose in this research study, such as the confidentiality of all information discussed and the ability of all students to choose another psychotherapist if the assigned therapist is not meeting the person's needs. Since the end of the project and our departures from Cornell University, there was a follow-up workshop for WPW students held at the initiative of the healthcare center staff in spring of 2004, thus illustrating the enduring ties between university units dedicated to working on WPW health and the ongoing commitment fostered by the project.

Raising Awareness of the Health Needs of WPW

Although we did not conduct a formal evaluation of changes in the beliefs, attitudes, values, and behaviors of the healthcare center staff following our communication activist research, we received e-mails from clinicians and task-force members that illustrate their sense that their knowledge of and communication skills with the WPW student population improved. In response to a request for feedback about the project, a health-promotion staff person who had been a task-force member wrote:

> The regular consistent focus on women who partner with women raised the level of consciousness and attention for the two and a half year period. . . . There has been greater awareness on the part of the practitioners who learned about the study. (personal communication, September 28, 2003)

The director of the healthcare center offered that because of the project, "clinicians realized the need to venture out of their comfort zones . . . to serve their patients well" (personal communication, September 24, 2003). It is difficult to assess whether there were changes in beliefs, attitudes, values, and behaviors of the WPW students targeted for the workshop and other interventions, because many of them are no longer students at the university. Over time, however, we expect to see more changes in trust in healthcare; beliefs, attitudes, values, and behaviors around safer sex; and knowledge of WPW-specific health needs for new members of the WPW community who, hopefully, will have benefited from some of these transformations.

LESSONS LEARNED ABOUT COMMUNICATION ACTIVISM

To help better inform those who wish to conduct communication participatory activist research on healthcare with historically marginalized populations, we offer a discussion of lessons we learned from our successes and challenges. Many of these lessons are useful for PAR projects, in general, whereas others are specific to the healthcare context or studies of marginalized populations. We organize these lessons into the following salient categories, which should enhance their usefulness to other researchers working in varied settings: establishing trust, conducting an effective PAR project, and doing PAR in the university context.

Establishing Trust

The first lesson learned concerns the need to establish trust between oppositional groups (e.g., university staff and WPW students) and between those groups and mediating researchers for effective data collection and interventions. There are many strategies that can facilitate this process; here, we focus on a few strategies that reflect our experiences working with these particular populations. In particular, because many researchers do not share the background of marginalized groups, especially those groups that are severely economically disenfranchised, this disconnect requires strategies that help to build trust by bringing money, establishing small wins, and acknowledging and respecting institutional norms.

Bringing money shows seriousness. Researchers who bring sources of funding, even small amounts of money that potentially leverage further resources, demonstrate that they do not intend to merely extract data and resources from a community for the sole purpose of publication and furthering their career. In our case, the funding we secured early in the project made it possible for the project to "opt out" of competition for internal resources within the university. Because of that funding, other groups and institutions, such as the LGBTRC, were happy to contribute in-kind to the project in the form of purchasing food for events, providing space, and donating brochures. Although money is certainly not a panacea to address social problems, when it has few strings attached and is specifically intended for research and interventions, it can significantly enhance a project that otherwise would be unfunded or underfunded.

Establishing small wins show accountability. Even the smallest early changes, such as hanging WPW pictures and posters in the healthcare center and clinician attendance at LGBT events, demonstrated to the WPW student population that both we as the researchers and the healthcare center were serious about making changes. These changes served as "small wins" that helped to maintain the motivation and momentum of the students and taskforce members for continuing to participate in the project (Weick, 1984). By making small, incremental changes as we went along, rather than waiting to do so until all the data were collected and analyzed, we were able to enact change earlier and address issues as we discovered and documented them. Although this approach may seem risky to researchers who are accustomed to a less iterative research process, we also were careful not to engage in any interventions on behalf of one group (WPW students or clinicians) that might have a negative effect on the other group. For example, we waited to offer educational programs for the clinicians so as not to alienate them by working on knowledge based on data collected from only the student group.

Acknowledging and following institutional norms shows respect. By scheduling meetings in advance and in convenient locations, valuing participants' time, and following established facilitation patterns for moving efficiently through the agenda for the meetings, Frazer, who organized and facilitated most of the meetings, demonstrated that she understood that our research partners were very busy and had to deal with many student requests. It was precisely by meeting the stakeholders where they were rather than having them conform to our needs that this project was able to move forward and accomplish its goals. For some student activists who are more comfortable with traditional modes of protest, such a process may seem unfamiliar and antithetical to accomplishing radical social change goals; however, for those who have worked within institutions to make incremental changes, such as those in environment or policy, this approach is often very effective for addressing the needs of the population. The types of changes we were requesting demanded that we work with, rather than against, either WPW students or clinicians.

Similarly, rather than infantilizing the WPW student population, as many of the students who participated in this research and some of our key informant respondents believed some clinicians did before the workshops, and by acknowledging the legitimacy of their grievances and even their ineffective modes of airing those grievances (e.g., spreading rumors about the healthcare center, complaining to one another rather than using formal complaint procedures, and avoiding healthcare even when they needed it), we were able to move them toward acknowledging that their practices were not always the best options available to them. We, thus, assessed their current level of knowledge through research and then used our findings to educate students and clinicians on their own terms, addressing the issues they saw as most important and using language familiar to them.

Conducting an Effective PAR Project

Conducting effective research is half the battle of a PAR project because it involves both stakeholder relations and thinking outside of traditional research norms. The unique challenges that confront researchers who are used to conducting traditional research projects requires relaxing some traditional assumptions and adding new criteria, as well as the use of new strategies for collecting and using data. The suggestions we offer next include the need for acquiring multiple forms of data to address different audiences, employing innovative strategies, and managing tensions between PAR and traditional research, including questions about how much to expect from and disclose to nonresearcher participants.

Multiple forms of data are needed to address different audiences and issues. Multiple forms of data (qualitative and quantitative) were necessary for a comprehensive approach to understanding and confronting the problems of healthcare for WPW, including every stakeholders' contribution to the question bank, and for trying to test established theories that were unknown to many of the stakeholders,[5] but this made the questionnaire long. We advise those undertaking similar projects to think carefully about how to negotiate the need to reach many audiences and address many issues but also to keep measurement instruments and interview protocols reasonably sized.

Furthermore, data must be presented in different ways to reach different groups. It is necessary but not sufficient to reach people in their own settings; the data presented also must be easily understandable and immediately interesting. For example, we used medical language in presenting information to clinicians, whereas informal language was used in presentations to students. We also used visual and oral communication techniques, such as presenting data in verbal and written form for different types of learners, constructing colorful and memorable graphics (e.g., tables and graphs) for the presentations, offering explanations of difficult concepts in easy-to-understand language, and providing students and clinicians with take-home information.

Innovative research strategies are needed to answer novel questions. To meet the needs of a particular PAR project, researchers may have to employ innovative methods of participant recruitment (e.g., not rely on random samples), data collection, analysis, and presentation of results. Both researching unusual or nonmainstream methods used by those studying similar populations and trying out new methods were time-consuming processes, but often this type of work cannot be accomplished by staying within established, mainstream methods of measurement, sampling, and data analysis. Trusting these techniques, even as limitations are acknowledged, allows researchers to use their expertise to extend knowledge into a community and a wider academic audience as well. It is easy to get discouraged when attempting to sample a relatively hidden population rigorously enough to believe that one has a representative sample and can feel fairly confident about the quality of the data. We used respondent-driven sampling to target the population and recruited multiple, well-positioned WPW students to recruit others to disseminate the questionnaire. We relied on student volunteers who appreciated the intrinsic rewards of being involved in a process of social change. This application of an established research technique would not have been possible without the PAR process of building trust and tapping the social networks of the target populations.

Managing tensions between PAR and traditional research. We found during this project that the tensions between the PAR philosophy and process and those of traditional research were sometimes productive and sometimes frustrating. Although we enjoyed thinking about how to employ PAR's "usefulness" criterion, which prioritizes practical outcomes over testing conceptual models, it was sometimes difficult to prioritize research questions when we had not only multiple competing stakeholder groups wanting more questions included from their particular perspective (e.g., about clinician-patient interaction, social support, institutional support, and trust for authority) but also multiple components of multiple health communication theories that we wanted to test. Although the use of theories is often considered to be adversary, we found it complementary and that helped to provide a frame for concepts to address. Although this helped, there were simply too many interesting questions to ask. In the student questionnaire, we asked about perceptions of the healthcare system at the university, physician-patient interactions, risk perceptions of various STIs, normative beliefs about health practices, and actual health behaviors (alcohol and other drugs, check-ups, sleep, social support, and sexual behaviors). However, we easily could also have asked about many other components of all the major health communication theories we employed for every STI and every type of sexual behavior engaged in by our sample or for additional information on people's last several encounters with clinicians. Although components of these theories often were hard to measure, many of them proved useful for explaining WPW behavior, in general, and to our various audiences what processes were taking place inside the "black box" of barriers to healthcare.

One particular tension concerned how much to expect from or disclose to stakeholders in and about the research process. Confidentiality is harder to maintain when working with a small, local population where many respondents know each other. Because of the sensitive nature of the data we collected, we chose not to involve participants in data entry or data analysis for this reason, although many participatory action researchers believe that much of the value of the method comes from the involvement of community members in the entire research project (see the essays in Reason & Bradbury, 2001). Furthermore, participants lacked the expertise or interest needed to deal with many of the data-analytic procedures used. It also was very important not to allow any information to be traced back to student respondents in the community; consequently, we were very transparent with the clinicians and key informants about which information would be easy to trace back to them. We encouraged key informants to edit their interview summaries and choose how to be identified in documents produced from the project. This procedure enhanced the accuracy of the transcripts and the conclusions drawn from the research, as well as provided them with the opportunity to have second thoughts about whether and how they wanted their responses and opinions to be shared.

Ideally, we would have liked to include students more fully in the process. Without a greater commitment on their part to showing up and working on the project, however, we could not create ways for them to be more involved. This problem, in turn, led to fewer respondents than we hoped for had students been more active in the research design and intervention processes. We advise those undertaking similar projects to be realistic about the interest and investment of stakeholders in the project and work through which parts of the research process must be done by the expert, "consultant" researchers and which can be done by collaborators.

Conducting PAR in the University Context

The university context specifically affects those researchers who work within the traditional tenure-reward system, with students as one of the target populations of their communication activism PAR projects. University contexts provide some unique challenges, including rapid turnover in students and staff and extrinsic rewards for faculty. Although the university has much to offer in terms of providing a context in which to conduct research and resources for doing so, it also often fails to reward and, in some cases, actively dissuades researchers from conducting PAR projects. The challenges described next include a lack of student leadership and continuity of students and staff, and a lack of extrinsic rewards for researchers engaging in PAR.

Lack of student leadership and continuity of students and staff. One of the frustrating aspects of working in a population that changes completely approximately every 4 years is that everything has to be redone periodically; nothing can be set in place that is entirely self-perpetuating. Although staff, faculty, and students can help to institutionalize certain policies and offer training and networking each time a new group of students joins the university community, it is much more difficult to change the norms of a transient population than those of a population with more continuity. Furthermore, student leadership and commitment, where it exists, also is subject to the cycles of the academic calendar. For example, only four students attended our first student workshop in April 2002 because final examinations were approaching, and we were unable to retain student leadership in the project over the summer of 2002. Students most closely involved in the project also found that the extra demands on their time sometimes became very burdensome along with the course load they had at the university.

When possible, it is best to tie such research to a course (e.g., via service learning; see, Christian, Volume 2; Cooks & Scharrer, Volume 2) or to make it a viable substitute for other paid work. Researchers in university settings with a strong commitment to involving students in PAR might need to think about how best to reward students for their participation. Obtaining academic credit, especially within their major, makes it much less costly for students to be involved in such research. The Bartels' Action Research Fellowship, which was instrumental in facilitating the existence of this project, continues to struggle to institutionalize PAR within the Cornell University undergraduate curricula because faculty mentorship and teaching within the fellowship program is entirely voluntary and lacks monetary compensation. The voluntary nature of the program contributes to burnout on the part of participating faculty and lack of an ongoing support system for many students engaged in these projects. In fact, as of Fall 2004, the Bartels' Action Research Fellowship no longer existed.

In addition to student turnover, faculty and staff often demonstrate some turnover in student services positions as well. Although many staff members are likely to remain at the university for extended periods of time, the loss of key personnel can create problems. However, involving multiple stakeholders at all stages of the project can help to minimize this issue. For example, despite the fact that both of us have left Cornell University, through continued commitments from students, faculty, administrators, and staff remaining there, this effort continues.

Lack of extrinsic rewards for researchers engaging in PAR. Professors, particularly those who are not yet tenured, often will find that they are not commended institutionally for their work to improve the local community through their research. Some senior faculty members often see PAR as too time consuming and less valid, and top-tier journals share their validity concerns. As such, journal editors and reviewers can be skeptical of the importance, validity, and difficulties of PAR projects. Thus, the time committed to creating trusting relationships between researchers and various stakeholders, implementing interventions, and dealing with the extra difficulties of conducting PAR usually is in addition to normal teaching loads and research expectations. Most universities also do not provide internal grants for PAR projects and, consequently, external funding must be sought, which can be quite competitive and time consuming. For students, the rewards may be greater as there are many fellowships and awards for innovative forms of leadership, such as those encouraged by PAR. However, given that it is impossible for students to undertake these projects without appropriate faculty mentorship, we encourage all faculty members and university administrators to consider how to incorporate rewards for research designed to "make a difference" into the tenure and promotion process and other assessment processes, such as merit raises, within the university context.

CONCLUSION

The metaphor of "lowering barriers" that often is used in healthcare research is an apt one for communication activism research because it accurately describes the process of moving two groups toward one another by removing a series of hurdles that have prevented effective collaboration in the past. Moving through these barriers is as much a process as an end product and does not end when the researcher is finished conducting the research. Improving communication between people and their healthcare providers is an important part of healthcare, as is education about health issues. Through communication activism conducted in partnership with this healthcare center, the LGBTRC, and women who partner with women students, we made progress toward improving healthcare, and we believe that it is possible to use this approach with other populations as well. We not only taught clinicians to respond to the disclosures of women who partner with women with simple comments, such as "I'm glad you feel comfortable enough to tell me that," but we also made significant progress in helping these women to feel comfortable in a healthcare center that ultimately must be designed to fulfill their needs and address their concerns.

NOTES

1. To protect research participants' confidentiality, in some cases "personal communication" is used instead of names.
2. Although the now-familiar term *homophobia* refers to fear aversion to gay people, or behavior based on that fear, *heterosexism* is a term that, like sexism and racism, refers to the embedded beliefs and prejudices that favor heterosexuality over any other sexuality (including lesbianism and bisexuality) (Herek & Berrill, 1991).
3. In many cases, we use the terms "WPW students" and "students" interchangeably, as all student research participants in this project were WPW.
4. This research was not intended as a systematic assessment of the attitudes or health practices of clinicians who work with WPW. We chose to take the leadership of the healthcare center at its word that clinicians were well intentioned and, thus, did not to take on the difficult problem of trying to assess their levels of homophobia.
5. The testing of the theoretical models is not reported in this chapter; for that information, please contact us.

REFERENCES

Ajzen, I. (1991). The theory of planned behavior. *Organizational Behavior and Human Decision Processes, 50*, 179-211.

Allen, M., Bruflat, R., Fucilla, R., Kramer, M., McKellips, S., Ryan, D. J. et al. (2000). Testing the persuasiveness of evidence and combining narrative and statistical forms. *Communication Research Reports, 17*, 331-336.

Bernhard, L. A., & Applegate, J. M. (1999). Comparison of stress and stress management strategies between lesbian and heterosexual women. *Health Care for Women International, 20*, 335-347.

Bernhardt, J. M., & Cameron, K. A. (2003). Assessing, understanding, and applying health communication messages: The challenges of health literacy. In T. L. Thompson, A. M. Dorsey, K. I. Miller, & R. Parrott (Eds.), *Handbook of health communication* (pp. 583-605). Mahwah, NJ: Erlbaum.

Boster, F. J., Cameron, K. A., Campo, S., Liu, W. Y., Lillie, J. K., Baker, E. M. et al. (2000). The persuasive effects of statistical evidence in the presence of exemplars. *Communication Studies, 51*, 296-306.

Boston Women's Health Collective. (1998). *Our bodies, ourselves for the new century: A book by and for women* (rev. ed.). New York: Simon & Schuster.

Brashers, D. E., Haas, S. M., Klingle, R. S., & Neidig, J. L. (2000). Collective AIDS activism and individuals' perceived self-advocacy in physician-patient communication. *Human Communication Research, 26*, 372-402.

Brashers, D. E., Haas, S. M., Neidig, J. L., & Rintamaki, L. S. (2002). Social activism, self-advocacy, and coping with HIV illness. *Journal of Social and Personal Relationships, 19*, 113-133.

Carroll, N. M. (1999). Optimal gynecologic and obstetric care for lesbians. *Obstetrics and Gynecology, 93,* 611-613.

Diamant, A. L., Schuster, M. A., McGuigan, K., & Lever, J. (1999). Lesbians' sexual history with men: Implications for taking a sexual history. *Archives of Internal Medicine, 159,* 2730-2736.

Doherty, S. (2003). *Why doesn't the LGBT community at Cornell University use cross-community, broad-based political organizing to address anti-LGBT bias?* Unpublished master's thesis, Cornell University, Ithaca, NY.

du Prè, A. (2004). *Communicating about health: Current issues and perspectives* (2nd ed.). Boston: McGraw-Hill.

Edelman, D. (1986). University health services sponsoring lesbian health workshops: Implications and accessibility. *Journal of American College Health, 35,* 44-45.

Fishbein, M., & Ajzen, I. (1975). *Belief, attitude, intention, and behavior: An introduction to theory and research.* Reading, MA: Addison-Wesley.

Gamson, J. (2000). Sexualities, queer theory, and qualitative research. In N. K. Denzin & Y. S. Lincoln (Eds.), *Handbook of qualitative research* (2nd ed., pp. 347-365). Thousand Oaks, CA: Sage.

Geist-Martin, P., Ray, E. B., & Sharf, B. F. (2003). *Communicating health: Personal, cultural, and political complexities.* Belmont, CA: Wadsworth/Thompson Learning.

Gonsiorek, J. C. (1988). Mental health issues of gay and lesbian adolescents. *Journal of Adolescent Health Care, 9,* 114-122.

Harrison, A. E. (1996). Primary care of lesbian and gay patients: Educating ourselves and our students. *Family Medicine, 28,* 10-23.

Heckathorn, D. (1997). Respondent-driven sampling: A new approach to the study of hidden populations. *Social Problems, 44,* 174-199.

Heckathorn, D. (2002). Respondent-driven sampling II: Deriving valid population estimates from chain-referral samples of hidden populations. *Social Problems, 49,* 11-34.

Herek, G. M., & Berrill, K. T. (1991). *Hate crimes: Confronting violence against lesbians and gay men.* Newbury Park, CA: Sage.

Hester, S. R., & Biddle, B. S. (1995). Lesbian health invisible to mainstream. *AWHONN Voice, 3*(2), 10, 13.

Janz, N. K., Champion, V. L., & Strecher, V. J. (2002). The health belief model. In K. Glanz, B. K. Rimer, & F. M. Lewis (Eds.), *Health behavior and health education: Theory, research, and practice* (3rd ed., pp. 45-66). San Francisco: Jossey-Bass.

Katzenstein, M. F. (1998). *Faithful and fearless: Moving feminist protest inside the church and military.* Princeton, NJ: Princeton University Press.

Kemmis, S., & McTaggart, R. (2000). Participatory action research. In N. K. Denzin & Y. S. Lincoln (Eds.), *Handbook of qualitative research* (2nd ed., pp. 567-605). Thousand Oaks, CA: Sage.

Lehmann, J. B., Lehmann, C. U., & Kelly, P. J. (1998). Development and health care needs of lesbians. *Journal of Women's Health, 7,* 379-387.

Lock, J., & Steiner, H. (1999). Gay, lesbian, and bisexual youth risks for emotional, physical, and social problems: Results from a community-based survey. *Journal of the American Academy of Child and Adolescent Psychiatry, 38,* 297-304.

Marlatt, G. A., Baer, J. S., Kivlahan, D. R., Dimeff, L. A., Larimer, M. E., Quigley, L. A. et al. (1998). Screening and brief intervention for high-risk college student drinkers: Results from a 2-year follow-up assessment. *Journal of Consulting and Clinical Psychology, 66,* 604-615.

Marrazzo, J. M., Koutsky, L. A., Kiviat, N. B., Kuypers, J. M., & Stine, K. (2001). Papanicolaou test screening and prevalence of genital human papillomavirus among women who have sex with women. *American Journal of Public Health, 91,* 947-952.

McKee, M. B., Hayes, S. F., & Axiotis, I. R. (1994). Challenging heterosexism in college health service delivery. *Journal of American College Health, 42,* 211-216.

Perloff, R. M. (2001). *Persuading people to have safer sex: Applications of social science to the AIDS crisis.* Mahwah, NJ: Erlbaum.

Reason, P., & Bradbury, H. (Eds.). (2001). *Handbook of action research: Participative inquiry and practice.* Thousand Oaks, CA: Sage.

Rosenstock, I. M. (1960). What research in motivation suggests for public health. *American Journal of Public Health, 50,* 295-301.

Solarz, A. L. (Ed.). (1999). *Lesbian health: Current assessment and directions for the future.* Washington, DC: National Academy Press.

Strecher, V. J., Champion, V. L., & Rosenstock, I. M. (1997). The health belief model and health behavior. In D. S. Gochman (Ed.), *Handbook of health behavior research: Vol. 1. Personal and social determinants* (pp. 71-91). New York: Plenum Press.

Weick, K. E. (1984). Small wins: Redefining the scale of social problems. *American Psychologist, 39,* 40-49.

White, J., & Martinez, M. C. (1997). *The lesbian health book: Caring for ourselves.* Seattle, WA: Seal Press.

Witte, K. (1992). Putting the fear back into fear appeals: The extended parallel process model. *Communication Monographs, 59,* 329-349.

Witte, K. (1994). Fear control and danger control: An empirical test of the extended parallel process model. *Communication Monographs, 61,* 113-134.

Witte, K., & Allen, M. (2000). A meta-analysis of fear appeals: Implications for effective public health campaigns. *Health Education and Behavior, 27,* 591-615.

10

SMOKING OUT THE OPPOSITION

The Rhetoric of Reaction and the Kentucky Cigarette Excise Tax Campaign*

Stuart L. Esrock

Joy L. Hart

Greg Leichty

University of Louisville

The rolling hills of the Kentucky bluegrass host thoroughbred horses, small family farms, general stores, quaint communities, abundant wildlife, and sparkling bodies of water. The state, however, also is home to citizens who smoke at much higher rates than the national average; indeed, almost one-third of adults in Kentucky smoke, the highest rate in the United States

---

*We thank the members of the Kentucky Health Investment for Kids and Kentucky state representatives Mary Lou Marzian and Jim Wayne for their participation in this project and their ongoing efforts on behalf of Kentucky citizens.

(Centers for Disease Control, 2002). Consequently, the state wrestles with high rates of attendant illnesses, including cancer, emphysema, and heart disease; in fact, Kentucky's per capita death rate from lung cancer is the highest in the nation (Centers for Disease Control, 2002). To deal with these tobacco-related illnesses, Kentucky spends in excess of $1 billion each year (Lindblom, 2002).

Kentucky youth also use tobacco more than their counterparts in other states. Kentucky has the highest middle school smoking rate in the nation, more than twice the national average, and the fourth-worst high school smoking rate (Hahn, Plymale, & Rayens, 2001). Research indicates that tobacco use by youth is more likely in states such as Kentucky due to the cultural acceptance of tobacco, the number of parents and teachers who smoke, and the many families and friends who grow tobacco (Noland, 1996). The tragedy of youth smoking is well documented by the fact that 33% of all people who take up smoking in their teens ultimately die prematurely (Centers for Disease Control, 1996).

Despite the health problems associated with tobacco use, tobacco's influence is rooted deeply enough that its powerful lobbies continue to influence health policy (Kozlowski, Henningfield, & Brigham, 2001; Menashe & Siegel, 1998). The 1998 Master Settlement Agreement (MSA) between the states and the leading tobacco manufacturers placed restrictions on tobacco marketing and advertising and required companies to pay approximately $370 billion dollars over 25 years to compensate states for the costs that they incurred in treating tobacco-related illnesses. Cigarette companies agreed to discontinue most outdoor advertising, refrain from using cartoon characters in advertising and promotions, and stop targeting youth in their promotions. In return, the participating state governments agreed to end present and future lawsuits against the major tobacco companies. However, the MSA explicitly permits tobacco companies to continue advocacy and lobbying efforts against state and local laws considered harmful to tobacco interests, except in several areas explicitly outlined in the MSA (Kelder & Davidson, 1999).

Even after the MSA, widespread public education about the dangers of cigarettes, and increased legislation in response to those dangers (e.g., restricting smoking in public places), tobacco use remains a top national public health issue in the United States. However, following the MSA, the primary impetus for regulating tobacco shifted from the federal to the state level (Sweeney & Rose, 1998). Some states have considered actions such as criminalizing youth possession of tobacco products, regulating where vending machines can be placed, and enacting excise taxes that discourage youth smoking (Kelder & Davidson, 1999). In addition, each state decides how to allocate the millions of dollars it receives in MSA funds each year (e.g., prevention versus cessation). In Kentucky, tobacco regulation advocates have faced an uphill battle in this new wave of state activity for a number of reasons.

The institutional forces that oppose any restrictions on tobacco in Kentucky are formidable. Kentucky ranks second among all states in tobacco production (University of Kentucky College of Agriculture, 2002), with more than 40,000 tobacco farms (President's Commission, 2001). Historically, many of Kentucky's small family farms have depended on the tobacco crop for a significant portion of their income, and even those without primary financial dependence used tobacco production as an important family income supplement. In the 1990s, Kentucky tobacco receipts totaled more than $800 million annually, which was 50% of the state's crop receipts (Snell & Goetz, 1997).

Tobacco, thus, has a deep cultural significance in Kentucky because it is a labor-intensive but high-value cash crop that provides either a base or supplemental income for many small farms in the state (Berry, 2002). Its cultural significance also lies in bringing families and neighbors together to share in crop-related tasks. Indeed, one of us fondly remembers, from childhood, activities on the family farm that accompanied the growing of tobacco — trading tales in the tobacco-stripping room, recounting history and gossiping while pulling tobacco plants, gathering together for big noontime meals when planting and cutting tobacco, and learning about the culture of the land.

For these reasons, despite the enormous health costs associated with tobacco, many Kentuckians have vociferously resisted efforts to regulate the substance and increase the price of cigarettes (Licari & Meier, 2000). Indeed, the cigarette excise tax in the state has not been increased for more than 30 years; at 3¢ a pack (compared to the national average of 73¢), this tax is the second lowest in the United States (Lindblom, 2003).

Several groups have been working to lessen the toll of tobacco use in Kentucky. Given that these activists are working against ingrained beliefs, attitudes, and values, their progress in effecting change has been slow. One such group, the focus of this activist investigation, is the Kentucky Health Investment for Kids (KHIK), a coalition working to raise the state's abnormally low cigarette excise tax. Public health advocates regard a substantial state cigarette excise tax as the single-best means of reducing smoking, especially among youth, who are more price sensitive than adults (Chaloupka, 1999). Indeed, our analysis of statistics from the Centers for Disease Control on state cigarette excise taxes and state smoking rates revealed a significant negative correlation between excise tax rates and the overall percentage of smokers in a state ($r = -.38$; $p = .01$).

Funded primarily by a grant from the Robert Wood Johnson Foundation, which has an interest in public health issues, the $3.5-million multiyear campaign to raise the cigarette excise tax in Kentucky is a partnership of KHIK, the American Cancer Society, the American Heart Association, the American Lung Association, and the national Campaign for Tobacco-Free Kids, with dozens of other organizations around the state also taking part. The KHIK coalition, which began in 2001, is administered on a day-to-day basis by a nonprofit, statewide, antitobacco group called Kentucky ACTION (Alliance to Control Tobacco in our Neighborhoods). At the height of the campaign, a 6-person staff was responsible for grassroots efforts to generate support for the excise tax proposal, as well as lobbying efforts, at the state capitol in Frankfort in coordination with representatives of the cancer, heart, and lung groups.

It is at this juncture in the earliest days of KHIK's campaign to raise the cigarette excise tax in Kentucky that the story of our activism begins. Based on general interest and the results of earlier professional experience in strategic communication campaigns, Stuart Esrock was invited to serve as a media consultant for KHIK (while on a sabbatical leave) during the initial phase of the cigarette excise tax campaign. For about 9 months, Esrock coordinated the initial media/message planning for the campaign, executed a variety of communication strategies (e.g., news releases and media training), and simultaneously collected data using a number of methods, including participant observation and in-depth interviewing. After that time, a research team formed, consisting of Esrock, who worked directly with KHIK; Joy Hart, who is interested in message design and organizational and interorganizational change; and Greg Leichty, who is interested in advocacy and social change. Our ongoing involvement with KHIK has included participation in steering and other committee meetings, review of media coverage of the campaign (e.g., newspaper stories, editorials, and three televised programs), analysis of campaign documents (e.g., advertisements), and interviews (both formal and informal) conducted with KHIK leaders and state legislators. Our team formed around related scholarly interests, as well as our personal interests in reducing smoking, the problems associated with the burden of tobacco in Kentucky, and, consequently, our support for an increase in the state excise tax on cigarettes.

This case study describes and analyzes our most recent intervention with the KHIK coalition. Since its inception in 2001, the coalition has managed to ignite a statewide debate about the need to raise the cigarette excise tax (Esrock, Hart, & Leichty, 2004). Beyond raising needed state revenue to offset the large healthcare costs that tobacco inflicts on Kentucky each year, experts say that for every 10% increase in the price of cigarettes, overall smoking decreases 4% and youth smoking rates decline by 7% (Chaloupka, 1999). Excise tax proposals were introduced in the state legislature in 2001, 2002, and 2003, with KHIK generating increased media interest and public discussion in each year of the campaign; however, to that point in time, the effort to raise the state's cigarette excise tax had failed. As the 2004 legislative session approached, we collaborated with KHIK's leadership and two state lawmakers to critique existing rhetorical strategies in support of, and opposition to, the campaign. We hoped that our collaboration would enable KHIK to refine and update its strategic efforts to increase the state's cigarette excise tax.

The remainder of this chapter describes this collaboration and its results. First, we highlight conceptual considerations used in our work to analyze how tobacco is framed in Kentucky. Second, we describe the nature of our intervention and discuss several factors that distinguish this intervention project from our previous intervention-oriented research. Finally, we examine lessons we learned as researchers, activists, teachers, and citizens.

FRAMING TOBACCO IN KENTUCKY

As we began to formulate plans for this activist research, we discussed several bodies of literature that potentially could serve as a foundation for the intervention. We did so with some amount of trepidation, realizing that the activists with whom we would be working might be disconcerted by, if not openly hostile to, theoretical language. Still, based on our goals for the project and the needs of the campaign, we pulled from rhetorical theory and the literature on media framing.

Frames are descriptions that foreground particular aspects of a story or an issue. In the same way that the frame around a photograph sets it apart from its context and focuses attention on the image (Goffman, 1974), the framing of a news story or public issue defines critical elements that become focal ones for receivers of the message (see, e.g., Entman, 1993; Pan & Kosicki, 1993; Price & Tewksbury, 1997; Valkenberg, Semetko, & DeVrees, 1999). Framing, thus, can be used as a powerful rhetorical tool to secure people's attention and shape their interpretation of issues (Tucker, 1998). Through the creation and acceptance of frames, some groups have their issues or actions defined favorably, whereas other groups' issues and actions are viewed in less than positive ways (Hallahan, 1999).

Framing plays a key role in a variety of strategic communication efforts, including advertising and public relations, as well as social movements and other forms of activism. As Kosicki (1993, p. 120) argued, "We need to look more closely at the particular frames that are used and trace these through to their antecedents in the legislative process, social movements, or grassroots" efforts. It, thus, is important to examine the context and evolution of issue framing, both in general and in terms of specific areas of media coverage. For example, Ryan, Carragee, and Meinhofer (2001) asserted that "frames do not develop in a political or cultural vacuum" but, instead, are "sponsored by multiple social actors, including corporate and political elites, advocates, and social movements" (p. 176). Given the multiple actors involved, framing often becomes a "contest" in which various parties vie for dominance. Not surprisingly, the victors of these framing battles tend to be the politically and/or economically dominant, in large part because of the resources at their disposal (Gamson, Croteau, Hoynes, & Sasson, 1992). Beyond advancing arguments to woo an uncommitted public or counter an opposition's claims, frames also serve useful purposes "inside" a campaign. For example, issue frames can mobilize campaign members and strengthen their commitment and resolve, and help to recruit like-minded persons to the campaign.

In addition to focusing people's attention and shaping their interpretation of issues and events, frames also can arouse outrage and mobilize people toward a particular end. From the standpoint of social activism, frames that stimulate action to defend a group or community against a perceived or potential harm are of particular interest. Gamson (1992) identified a *collective action frame* as having three components: an injustice component involving a threat created by human action, an identification component that depicts a specific adversary, and an agency component that asserts collective action can remedy the problem. The injustice component is the most essential because of its ability to generate the motivation to engage in collective action (Gamson, 1992). How an issue is collectively framed, thus, strongly influences whether a grassroots advocacy effort succeeds or fails (see, e.g., Rojecki, 1999). To date, most framing research has focused on the effects of frames and neglected the social context of framing: how frames are advanced and established in an ongoing ideological contest. Focusing only on the effects of frames neglects considerations of social power that help us to understand why particular frames dominate the news and social discourse (Carragee & Roefs, 2004). An examination of framing as a social contest helps us to understand both how hegemonic frames are established and how opposing frames emerge over time. The history of the fight to regulate tobacco clearly illustrates the social power dimensions of framing.

Our analysis of framing with regard to the cigarette excise tax in Kentucky focuses on the particular frames employed in societal debates. To analyze the basic frames used in public dialogue about the proposed tax increase, we employed the perspective of cultural topoi (see, e.g., Leichty & Warner, 2001), which emerged out of examinations of U.S. political cultures (see, e.g., Ellis, 1993) and work in cultural anthropology (see, e.g., Thompson, Ellis, & Wildavsky, 1990). This perspective attempts to identify several coherent cultures or worldviews that provide argument premises for social and political debate (i.e., cultural topoi). A *cultural topos* provides a coherent view of social reality, supplying common frames that can be applied to one or more social issues. For instance, the "individual choice and responsibility" frame derived from the libertarian topos can be applied to a large number of social issues, ranging from the dangers of tobacco use to the hazards of not wearing motorcycle helmets. A cultural topos, thus, represents a higher level of abstraction from which individual frames are derived.

The predominant frame employed in opposition to tobacco regulation has been the libertarian-derived frame of tobacco smoking as an individual choice and responsibility. Recent versions of this frame contend that because the dangers of tobacco are well known, people make informed decisions about smoking. Advocates of this frame argue that the government infringes on individual freedom when it tries to prevent people from smoking. This libertarian vantage point further suggests that, rather than regulation by the state, societal efforts undertaken to decrease smoking should rely on education that reminds youth and adults of the risks of smoking and, thereby, increases the "rationality" of individual decisions regarding smoking.

Across the last 4 decades, cigarette manufacturers have employed this libertarian-derived frame to deflect lawsuits by individual smokers (Holloway & Leichty, 2000; Leichty & Warner, 2001). Tobacco company attorneys assert that people understand the risks of smoking and, therefore, must assume responsibility for choosing to smoke anyway. In the frame of informed choice, individuals, not cigarette companies, are responsible for tobacco-related illnesses. Federal legislation on cigarette labeling and advertising also has buttressed the individual choice frame. Several court rulings established the "adequacy" of the federally required warning labels and, consequently, it was a case of "caveat smoker"—if a person smoked, he or she did so at his or her own risk. Through 1990, only one court case awarded damages against any tobacco company for health claims, and even this claim was overturned later on appeal (Eichenwald, 1988). Cigarette companies continued to successfully argue that smokers alone bore the responsibility for the negative health consequences of smoking. For instance, in a 1990 federal case, a tobacco company attorney argued that the plaintiff had ample opportunity to stop smoking but failed to do so, claiming that "forty million people have stopped smoking. They made the decision. That's what this case is about—choice" ("Cigarette Maker Cleared," 1990, p. B6).

In the late 1980s, however, the frame of individual choice and responsibility came under a ferocious attack. U.S. Surgeon General C. Everett Koop labeled nicotine addictive in the same sense as heroin and cocaine (United States Department of Health and Human Services, 1988). From this perspective, if tobacco products are addictive, a smoker may not be able to make a "rational decision" to quit smoking. Thus, the addictive properties of nicotine became a primary point of attack on the tobacco industry. This attack resulted in a Congressional investigation by a House Energy Subcommittee on Health and the Environment that probed the allegation that tobacco companies suppressed evidence on the addictive nature of nicotine. Testimony from seven chief executive officers of major tobacco companies, stating that they did not believe nicotine was addictive (Committee on Energy and Commerce, House of Representatives, 1995), evoked public ridicule and increased the public perception that there had been a broad-based conspiracy by tobacco companies to cultivate nicotine addiction and suppress the sharing of information on the addictive properties of the substance.

The second avenue of attack on the individual choice and responsibility frame was the effort to label smoking as a significant issue affecting youth. Antismoking activists cited research showing that 90% or more of adult smokers began the habit long before reaching the age of 18 (United States Department of Health and Human Services, 1994). Making the issue one involving youth represented the Achilles' heel of the topos of individual choice and responsibility, attacking that frame at its weakest point. Youth are not adults and, therefore, not considered knowledgeable or responsible enough to make informed decisions about matters of life and death (Holloway & Leichty, 2000). In fact, some of the most vociferous complaints about the tobacco industry today center around accusations that it routinely targets children (Campaign for Tobacco-Free Kids, 2004). For example, 29 states and the District of Columbia filed a lawsuit against the Brown and Williamson Tobacco Corporation because of allegations that the company's hip-hop advertising campaign for Kool cigarettes was aimed squarely at youth, violating the 1998 MSA (Howington, 2004). When an issue, such as tobacco use, can be successfully cast as a threat to children, the libertarian frame of individual choice and responsibility becomes vulnerable.

Activists were able to use the youth-smoking frame to their advantage to vilify the tobacco industry for targeting children. Vilification of opponents is common in social movements (see, e.g., Vanderford, 1989), and, in this case, it advanced tobacco regulation efforts in a critical way. It provided the basis for at least a temporary coalition between people with a hierarchical worldview, who primarily were concerned with maintaining social order and respect for authority, and people with an egalitarian worldview, who primarily were concerned with issues related to social justice and inequality (Holloway & Leichty, 2000). Because the efforts of tobacco companies undermined familial authority, parents with an allegiance to a hierarchical topos could be enticed to be concerned about youth smoking (Holloway & Leichty, 2000). From an egalitarian perspective, protecting children from exploitation by a seductive, evil industry came to be a rallying cry. Framing the issue of tobacco regulation as one of "protecting youth" from an addictive product, thus, led to the implosion of the individual choice and responsibility topos at the national level (Pertschuk, 2001). The protecting youth frame also was instrumental in bringing about the 1998 MSA, which, as previously explained, created new restrictions on tobacco marketing (e.g., banning use of cartoon characters in cigarette advertisements) and produced large financial payments to states for bearing much of the cost of treating tobacco-related illnesses (Mollenkamp, Levy, Menn, & Rothfedder, 1998; Orey, 1999; Pratt, 2001).

After the MSA, as previously explained, concerns about tobacco regulation primarily moved from the federal to the state level. However, although the topos of individual choice and responsibility has been weakened in most locales, for the reasons previously discussed, it has remained strong in Kentucky. For example, Kentucky Statute 438.310 prohibits the sale of tobacco products to persons under the age of 18, but a retailer pays only $100 for the first violation. When these laws were passed in 2000, more than 80% of Kentucky legislators thought it was highly desirable to strengthen laws to prohibit youth access to tobacco, but nearly 60% of retailers thought that was unlikely to occur (Hahn, Tourney, Rayens, & McCoy, 1999). We, thus, were particularly interested in how the appeal of the individual choice and responsibility frame might be diminished in Kentucky. We paid special attention to analyzing the frames that were used by KHIK in its attempt to supplant the dominant frame. Quite commonly, "sponsors may re-structure their framing of particular issues given changing political conditions or given the frames advanced by challengers" (Ryan et al., 2001, p. 176). Consequently, much like Ryan et al. (2001) and Ryan, Carragee, and Schwerner (1998), we focused on designing an approach to the next wave of the cigarette excise tax campaign with special consideration devoted to developing new and breaking old frames.

To diminish the individual choice and responsibility frame, KHIK has promoted the view that the effort to raise the cigarette excise tax in Kentucky is about "saving children," drawing on the effectiveness of the 1990s campaigns against big tobacco companies. If established, the saving-children frame provides a potent rhetorical advantage, for who would be against saving children and what arguments against saving children possibly could be made? Thus, the frame of saving children gives opponents pause in how to confront it. The counterattack is likely to be an indirect one—opposing the means, not the end goal. Rational opponents will at least pay lip service to the overall objective of saving children at the same time that they attempt to chip away at the specifics of any proposal for doing so. In seeking to demonstrate that whatever proposed plan is poorly conceived, however laudable the goal, opponents will engage in defensive rhetoric, contending that many harmful but unintended consequences will result.

To understand defensive rhetoric or "the rhetoric of reaction," Hirschman (1991) developed a typology to categorize indirect attacks. Examining 200 years of arguments advanced in Britain against progressive social legislation (i.e., legislation to extend social and political rights, such as fair work hours, welfare, and the right to vote), Hirschman identified three frequently repeated strategies: perversity, futility, and jeopardy. A *perversity* strategy asserts that a proposed action will lead to outcomes that are the exact opposite of what it intends, such as asserting that minimum wage laws designed to assist poor citizens actually damage them by increasing the unemployment rate (see, e.g., Schansberg, 1996).

A *futility* strategy maintains that only superficial or cosmetic changes will result from a proposed plan and that the underlying problem will remain essentially unchanged. This strategy, therefore, asserts that the more things change, the more they remain the same. Research findings supporting this perspective include Adams's (1995) work on automotive safety. Despite extensive improvements in road construction and vehicle safety features, driving dangers continue to be essentially unchanged. According to Adams, because people are aware of the safety improvements, they adjust and take more risks and, thereby, re-establish the pre-existing ratio between risk and safety.

A *jeopardy* strategy asserts that a proposed plan overlooks or underestimates the likely harms of the action. The argument is that the suggested action may achieve its primary goal but also simultaneously jeopardizes other valued aspects of the status quo. Thus, this type of argument asserts that any good achieved will result in a corresponding, if not greater, loss. Jeopardy positions assume a negative sum game in which more stands to be lost than won. For instance, opponents of universal suffrage argued that it would create a tyranny of the majority and undermine many liberties (Hirschman, 1991), such as property rights (e.g., unpopular industries might be expropriated or nationalized). Because it does not immediately challenge the intention or intelligence of opponents, the jeopardy strategy often is seen as the least abrasive of the three "rhetorics of reaction."

According to Hirschman (1991), these three rhetorical strategies are overused in social discourse about significant issues, and their fundamental nature is evidenced by their recurrence for more than 200 years. For example, Rojecki (1999) found that these strategies were extensively employed to silence antinuclear movements during the Cold War era, and Conrad and Millay (2001) documented how these strategies formed the backbone of persuasive efforts to resist healthcare reform measures in Texas. Hirschman speculated that these strategies are popular because they offer explanations of the unintended consequences of human actions and events.

Cultural topoi and the rhetoric of reaction formed the foundation for our analysis of discourse on both sides of the issue in the cigarette excise tax campaign in Kentucky. Through that analysis, we hoped to use these perspectives to inform strategic development of counterarguments that could be deployed by KHIK in response to opponents' arguments against the cigarette excise tax increase.

PROJECT DESCRIPTION

As explained previously, 2 years of the cigarette excise tax campaign in Kentucky already had passed by the time we started this phase of our intervention efforts. Prior to this phase of our work, we had a good amount of data and analysis at our disposal, including Esrock's long-term participant observation with KHIK.

As part of our ongoing work on the cigarette excise tax campaign, we conducted a rhetorical analysis of three public television shows about the proposed tax that aired during the first 2 years of the campaign. These television programs had representatives from both sides of the cigarette excise tax issue, and at least one KHIK spokesperson appeared on each show. We found that the combination of the cultural topoi framework and the rhetoric of reaction typology accounted for nearly 80% of the strategies employed by participants on these television programs. Our analysis also identified some interesting discourse patterns that we thought would be useful to KHIK representatives in subsequent argument forums. For example, the study identified a glaring rhetorical contradiction employed by the tax opponents, and KHIK had to make clear that the opponents could not have it both ways—some argued that the tax would not work to reduce smoking, whereas others argued the tax would work so well that it would hurt tobacco farms across the state. We contacted KHIK's Executive Director, Carol Roberts, and proposed a collaboration to identify rhetorical opportunities in the upcoming year of the campaign.

We started by having key KHIK leaders and two interested Kentucky state representatives, Mary Lou Marzian and Jim Wayne (who had sponsored cigarette excise tax legislation), fill out an open-ended questionnaire that asked them to list the major affirmative and negative arguments that they personally had used and encountered in their activist efforts. The information from this questionnaire enabled us to compare how comprehensive our research-derived list of arguments was, relative to the collective knowledge of campaign proponents. It also provided a point of departure for our subsequent analysis and improved the likelihood that we would not simply rediscover what these activists already knew and practiced.

We then had these same individuals complete a closed-ended questionnaire, in which they rated how persuasive they found 19 affirmative strategies for the proposed cigarette excise tax increase that we had identified in our analysis of the three public television programs. They also rated how difficult they found it to refute each of 21 opposition rhetorical strategies we identified from those same television programs (see Tables 10.1 and 10.2 for a list of, and the mean ratings for, the affirmative and refutation strategies, respectively). After we analyzed the questionnaire results, we conducted a focus group session with KHIK leaders and the two lawmakers about rhetorical strategies that would best advance the cigarette excise tax proposal in the third year of the campaign.

TABLE 10.1. Rank Order and Means of Affirmative Strategies
(Most Effective Arguments)

(1.37) Kentucky will raise significant new revenue with the excise tax.

(1.50) Kentucky has an epidemic of youth smoking compared to other states.

(1.50) Increasing the tax is the most effective means of reducing youth smoking.

(1.87) The low cost of tobacco is a major reason youth smoke.

(1.87) The tax is about protecting youth from an addictive drug.

(1.87) The excise tax will fund vital public needs.

(1.87) Raising the excise tax will reduce the $1 billion annual cost to taxpayers.

(2.00) The public supports smokers paying the costs of tobacco-related illnesses.

(2.00) The public supports raising the excise tax over cutting state services.

(2.00) It has been 30 years since we raised the tax; it's time to do it again.

(2.25) Tax revenue will increase even though smoking will decline.

(2.25) Kentucky lags behind rest of nation in reducing youth smoking.

(2.25) The excise tax won't hurt farmers because sales are part of the global economy.

(2.62) Raising the excise tax will make cessation programs available to all citizens.

(2.75) Most smokers want to quit. Raising excise taxes helps them.

(2.87) The high proportion of citizens who smoke is the cause for Kentucky's high rate of preventable illness.

(3.00) Most people will not avoid paying the excise tax.

(3.00) Increasing the tax rate will reduce smuggling.

(3.13) The excise tax will benefit smokers and other low-income groups.

Note: 1 = Very effective argument; 4 = Very ineffective argument

Table 10.2. Rank Order and Means of Refutation Strategies
(Most Difficult to Refute)

(1.88) State government should reduce expenses before raising taxes.

(2.00) Raising the excise tax will harm small Kentucky businesses.

(2.13) The real responsibility for tobacco control lies with parents.

(2.25) Raising the tax will only change how people get products.

(2.25) Education, not taxation, is a preferred means of reducing tobacco impact.

(2.31) People know the risks of smoking. People are responsible for their own health.

(2.38) Enforce existing laws on youth smoking rather than tax adult smokers.

(2.38) State should not try to tax people into good behavior.

(2.50) State should not use a declining source of revenue to fund essential services.

(2.56) Raising the tax will increase smuggling.

(2.75) It is a regressive tax on the poor.

(2.81) Public does not support raising taxes.

(2.87) State should not profit from smokers' addictions.

(3.06) Raising tax will not reduce youth smoking.

(3.13) Excise tax will harm Kentucky farmers.

(3.13) Don't penalize smokers to balance budget. Everyone should pay.

(3.13) Raising excise tax is a plan to outlaw tobacco.

(3.25) Raising tax will raise little new revenue.

(3.25) Tobacco use is not a big problem relative to other health issues.

(3.63) Raising the tax will jeopardize MSA payments.

(4.00) Smoking is not as harmful as most claim.

Note: 1 = Very difficult to refute; 4 = Very easy to refute

We used the combination of our past analyses, questionnaire responses, and the transcript of the focus group session to develop a comprehensive set of rhetorical recommendations for the group on how to proceed. As our analysis evolved, we gave particular attention to how KHIK might counteract the most robust oppositional strategies to the cigarette excise tax proposal.

We suggested that although the activists had developed well-thought-out responses to many of their opponents' points, in our observations, many of these strategies had been used in a subsidiary and reactive way. We proposed that at least some of the refutations of opposition strategies should be deployed more proactively in the upcoming year. For instance, these activists occasionally countered the argument that regulating youth smoking was a family function by pointing out that raising the cigarette excise tax would actually reinforce parental efforts to keep their children from smoking. We suggested that this argument be developed as a major point to decrease opposition to the cigarette tax hike among people with traditional values about parental responsibilities.

We also recommended that KHIK representatives and state legislators directly address arguments by the opposition that smoking was an individual choice and not a matter of public concern. In particular, we encouraged them to focus on the hidden costs that smoking imposed on all Kentucky taxpayers and citizens, such as the fact that treating sick smokers costs the state more than $1 billion each year and how the high smoking rate imposes hidden costs on employers in terms of lost productivity and on employers and citizens with regard to higher premiums for health insurance. In other words, the argument should be that because smoking negatively affects everyone, it should be a matter of public policy. Framing the issue this way makes it harder to assert that raising the cigarette excise tax abridges individual "freedoms."

We presented these findings and recommendations to the KHIK group members and then engaged with them in discussion. During this meeting, we further brainstormed about some specific rhetorical strategies to employ with targeted groups, including lawmakers and women voters. For example, we suggested that the group needed to clearly communicate to lawmakers about the hidden costs associated with smoking. For women voters, beyond the protecting children message, we recommended that KHIK discuss how the revenue that a cigarette tax increase would generate potentially could be used to improve education in the state.

The most tangible result of our work was a notable shift from focusing solely on arguments that the excise tax was about saving the state's youth. Subsequent to the meetings, KHIK wrote a position paper on the hidden costs of smoking and distributed it to media across the state. It resulted in some ensuing editorials and coverage that focused on this aspect of the excise tax debate. One KHIK board member termed this approach a much more aggressive, assertive stance than the group previously had taken. State representative Marzian also focused on the $1 billion-plus annual price tag of smoking in Kentucky during interviews, moving the context of the cigarette excise tax discussion more squarely into the economic sphere.

Given the project's ongoing nature, there was continued discussion of the cigarette excise tax increase across our involvement. We did not simply conduct a study, analyze the results, and present our findings; rather, we collaborated with the group to collect needed data and suggest ways of using the results. This dynamic process distinguished this intervention project from traditional consulting in which findings are presented and researchers often then divorce themselves from the project. This intervention also resulted in a number of tensions and paradoxes, which we now examine.

TENSIONS AND PARADOXES OF INTERVENTION RESEARCH

During the course of our project, we experienced a full range of emotions—from exhilaration and inspiration to frustration and disappointment. Unlike more traditional consulting projects in which academics may be hired for their expertise, regardless of their previous work with or opinions on a specific topic, this project was rooted in an issue about which we cared deeply and possessed strong views. Because of our involvement, we found this type of intervention research to be far more immersing than a typical research project in which data are "objectively" collected and analyzed. Although this immersion created a far richer experience for us as researchers, it also produced a wider set of tensions and paradoxes than most of our previous traditional research.

First, we noted a tension between the need to complete this academic project and the real-world timeline of the cigarette excise tax campaign. Our desire to do more campaign-related work and become more involved with campaign activities sometimes became a casualty when balanced with our day-to-day activities as academics. As an example, we all wanted to attend a scheduled meeting of the KHIK coalition and its partners to discuss campaign tactics that would be used to communicate with the public and lawmakers during the state's upcoming legislative session. None of us could attend, however, due to other work-related commitments. There were many other activities in which we wanted to involve ourselves, as well as strategies that we could have implemented, with the KHIK group. However, our daily academic jobs, including finishing this chapter, simply precluded a deeper level of campaign intervention.

At least part of the reason that we wish we had more time to work with the KHIK coalition and the protax lawmakers lies in the nature of this group. However, the very characteristic that, in our views, distinguished this group from other activist groups we have worked with also created another paradox in working on the project. Specifically, part of the desirability of this group for us lies in the fact that it is, relatively speaking for an activist campaign, well resourced in terms of personnel, brainpower, and even financing, a characteristic that made it a comfortable setting in which to engage in communication activism. In contrast to intervening with a less-resourced group, in this instance, conversations with KHIK members and partners resembled talking to academic peers, for these are sophisticated, bright professionals; hence, we did not have to "water down" our recommendations or teach them about very basic persuasive communication concepts (e.g., what it means to target messages to a specific audience). Whereas we might have been concerned that the technical aspects of argument (e.g., Toulmin's, 1958, model of claims, data, warrants, backing, qualifiers, and reservations) might be difficult to explain to a less-sophisticated group, in this instance, it was clear that the KHIK decision makers and the protax legislators knew exactly what we meant.

Paradoxically, at the same time that we were pleased to be working with smart activists and legislators, the fact that the group was relatively well resourced led to at least some level of insecurity among us as researchers. On at least a couple of occasions, we wondered out loud among ourselves whether we could make any meaningful contribution to the cigarette excise tax campaign. We worried that the KHIK group and legislators already knew everything we were going to talk about and that perhaps our meetings would degenerate into an exercise in redundancy and futility. We initially used the open-ended questionnaire for this reason—to assess the degree of overlap between what they cited as arguments for and against the tax increase versus the conceptual scheme that we had developed based on our review of the relevant academic literature. This instrument revealed considerable commonality, leading us to conclude that we had done a good job of unearthing a rather complete set of rhetorical strategies. A follow-up (feedback) questionnaire we administered also clearly revealed that the KHIK leaders and lawmakers believed we had, indeed, made a substantive contribution to the campaign (as discussed later in this chapter), thus alleviating most of the anxiety we felt.

The fact that the cigarette excise tax group was relatively well resourced presented yet another tension regarding how much rhetorical and communication theory we should include in our interactions with the group. We wondered if the theory would be regarded by the members as a superfluous exercise that simply would be ignored. Perhaps, one of us argued, we should just stick to a more practical discussion. However, our commitment to *praxis* required that theory inform our practice. In the end, we decided to selectively present concepts that we thought had good descriptive power. We, thus, used theory to show the group that what we were talking about was based on real inquiry and real interests, and that there were many lessons learned elsewhere that had a potential bearing on what we, and they, were and could be doing.

We ultimately provided for KHIK members an overview of our underlying concepts and theory (e.g., rhetoric of reaction and cultural topoi), and they easily were able to understand and assimilate our analytic framework. This approach reduced the "news" value of some of our recommendations, but, ironically, we think that it also made our recommendations more palatable and likely to be applied. For example, we stressed that when faced with futility arguments that the proposed tax would not reduce youth smoking, KHIK members needed to be armed with detailed statistics from other states that supported their point.

The KHIK group was receptive to our use of theory, as indicated in the postintervention questionnaires and e-mails we exchanged after the project. At least in part, this receptivity likely was due to the broader orientation that it promoted—showing the members that the problems with which they were dealing were not new and had been experienced by others. They also accepted the theory we presented because of the relationship they had developed over the past 3 years with Esrock; some level of credibility, trust, and comfort, thus, clearly was established. After the intervention, one member of the KHIK team commented on the questionnaire about the academic content that had been introduced in the sessions, saying that the "very thorough analysis is helpful, especially from a distance." Another sent an e-mail registering similar sentiments by simply saying, "For 'academic types,' you guys are okay!" Our access and immersion, in this case, thus, led to a mutual level of trust, an understanding of the group's internal political and organizational dynamics, and, beyond that, personal relationships with the KHIK personnel. In addition, this immersion and the personal relationships made acceptance of our viewpoints and suggestions more likely.

These relationships, however, also created some potential level of apprehension for us about our ability to be frank with KHIK members. We wondered whether we could be critical of particular actions and/or the campaign focus, how such criticism would be taken, and whether it would negatively affect the relationships we had established. In addition, if we saw some major problem or issue and honestly told KHIK members about it, could that potentially result in restrictions to our access? If we disagreed with the group about a strategy, would that merely fade into the background as a point of difference or would there be lasting ramifications? Although high-quality individual relationships had been established, not everyone takes bad news, criticism, or differences of opinion in the same manner, and it was not entirely possible to forecast what might happen under those circumstances. We worried that honesty could potentially even blunt our ability to complete our research.

Activist researchers work both with and for people and groups and, simultaneously, they provide critiques, sometimes of poorly chosen strategies or misaligned tactics. Clearly, there are benefits to immersion and intimate involvement in the form of full access and the ability to view the "backstage" activities and personalities of a campaign. Moreover, as Frey, Pearce, Pollock, Artz, and Murphy (1996) made clear with regard to social justice research, this type of research does not even "pretend to be objective, neutral, or dispassionate" (p. 115). However, the question is whether such a lens blurs a researcher's view of a campaign and how it might influence abilities to view the "frontstage" activities in a clear manner. In addition, given Esrock's long-term involvement in the campaign (and his established personal relationships with the members of KHIK), we worried about the possibility that his perspective about KHIK personnel (whom he clearly respected and liked) might shape Hart and Leichty's views, obscuring potential problems that existed.

Although there remains some potential for tension to exist between being a confidant/friend and being a critical consultant, in our case, fortunately, that tension never manifested into any form where we had to make difficult choices. We did come to realize, however, that we were but one player in the campaign with "one vote" about what constituted a desirable course of action. In at least one instance, we clearly failed to convince the coalition of what we believed was an appropriate public relations strategy. Other activist researchers should realize that along with trust and full access come potential limits, at least to some extent, in terms of what one can do or say. Similarly, it probably is inevitable that a researcher will have some disagreements with the group or organization with which he or she is intervening and will lose out on some of the points or suggestions that he or she makes.

Because we recognized the potential positive and negative aspects possible given such involvement, we consciously used a team research approach to mitigate any such problems. One of the strengths we had as a team was varying levels of individual involvement in the cigarette excise tax campaign, variation that helped us to see the group and the campaign from multiple angles.

Finally, we would be remiss if we did not acknowledge the tension that potentially exists between working on a controversial issue such as the cigarette excise tax (at least in a state like Kentucky) and participants' professional and private lives. Intervention in a campaign such as this one can carry over to the personal relationships people have at home and in the workplace (see also Jovanovic, Steger, Symonds, & Nelson, this volume). For example, one of the KHIK campaign leaders also is actively involved in an effort to implement a public smoking ban in Louisville, Kentucky. He has been verbally assaulted about this campaign on his home phone, on e-mail, and even in public venues.

In our case, we have one colleague who has been a long-time smoker (and who sometimes violates our university's no-smoking policy in his office) and another who is a partner in a family-owned farm that grows tobacco. We at least wondered what they would think when they found out that we were involved in the cigarette excise tax campaign. We also wondered how our students, friends, and neighbors who smoke would respond.

There is a very real potential cost for getting involved in an activist campaign, just as there is a cost for not getting involved. In this case, we, as researchers, decided that we had knowledge that could be applied to a campaign that we all, clearly, believed could have a prosocial impact that far outweighed any problems we might experience because of our involvement. For the record, although we heard some sarcastic comments from a few friends and colleagues, most of the people we regularly come into contact with in our daily lives are resigned to the fact that the cigarette excise tax in Kentucky is abnormally low and needs to be raised. However, although separate from the work with this campaign, our individual support of the public smoking ban in Louisville received much more scrutiny and negative comment from others.

LESSONS LEARNED ABOUT COMMUNICATION ACTIVISM

This project was rewarding, like traditional research projects, in that we believe we have contributed to the body of knowledge on social movements and issue framing and advanced theory on those subjects. In particular, this case provided an excellent application of the rhetoric of reaction and cultural topoi, advancing these theoretical frameworks to help us understand public discourse about controversial issues. In addition, we made some other discoveries about social movements, activist organizations (e.g., activist organizations have internal dynamics that can create instability), and our interactions with such groups. Beyond these more conventional boundaries, we were pleasantly surprised to find that this intervention project had other ramifications for us as educators and citizens in a democratic political system.

In the course of working on this project, we continually were reminded that marginalized groups like KHIK (at least relative to the tremendous financial and political resources of the tobacco industry) face a huge task in confronting the status quo. Forces promoting tobacco in Kentucky consistently have played for a tie rather than a win, recognizing that presumption in public policy debates favors the status quo (i.e., a tie in terms of persuasiveness goes to the opponents of change). Cigarette excise tax opponents, therefore, have relied on the strategies of reaction to deflect attention from the core issues in the debate.

We were surprised by the degree to which already refuted arguments continued to be recycled by cigarette excise tax opponents. The pro-excise tax forces repeatedly cited analyses by respected agricultural economists about the likely impact of the tax increase on Kentucky's tobacco farmers.

Those reports concluded that raising the cigarette price by 10% would decrease the sale of Kentucky tobacco by less than .1%, because Kentucky tobacco is a very small part of the global market for tobacco products. However, in the third televised program about the cigarette excise tax, the president of the Burley Growers Association indicated that he was still against an increase of the tax because members of his association thought it would hurt farmers. He took this stance even though he had earlier implicitly accepted the economic analysis presented that showed little effect due to raising the tax, by raising no questions about its validity. A commitment to activism, thus, is a commitment to a long-term project that attempts to overcome such beliefs and attitudes.

From an external perspective, the Kentucky cigarette excise tax campaign has had little obvious success; no bill has advanced yet for a vote or even public legislative debate in committee, let alone a vote on the House floor. We believe, however, that most successful social movements must persist until circumstances arise that at least temporarily change the sociocultural dynamics that surround an issue (see, e.g., Conrad & Millay, 2001). "Victory" is likely to consist of many small steps and some disheartening setbacks. Coping with the slowness and uncertainty of the progress of a desired change may be the chief long-term impediment to social movement success. We see signs that activists' long-term commitment to pursue tobacco control in Kentucky is beginning to bear fruit. For instance, the cigarette excise tax issue has moved from dormancy in the news media to the front pages of newspapers and nightly newscasts on television stations across Kentucky. In addition, legislators sponsoring the bill have been willing to sign on for a much higher increase than earlier versions of the bill (i.e., 75¢ versus 44¢). An increasingly dire financial crisis in Kentucky's government has even led several traditionally antitax state senators to concede that raising the state's cigarette tax is a better alternative than enacting, for instance, draconian cuts to Medicaid.

Given this slow pace of change, activist groups must be energized by strong passion to endure the opposition they encounter. Maintaining a high level of commitment and fervor in support of a cause over the long haul requires a great deal of effort; it also entails enduring a great deal of frustration. In one notable exchange in a televised program, a Smokers' Alliance representative declared that there was no proven link between cigarette smoking and heart disease. The frustration and disbelief of the KHIK representatives erupted a little later when one of them exclaimed, "What rock did you crawl out from under?!" In that same debate, cigarette excise tax supporters were charged with having a hidden agenda (i.e., a long-term agenda to prohibit tobacco use), being unable to see the big picture, lying, and fabricating statistics. Social advocacy work, thus, requires a very thick skin and something of a rawhide disposition.

Social movement leaders also face many dialectical tensions as they attempt to mobilize support and maintain lines of communication with the opposition. An active, mobilized base is necessary to give an organization credibility, and this grassroots organizing certainly is a key activity for KHIK and its partners. At the same time, movement leaders must not fall to the temptation of becoming too cynical about the opposition and, thereby, close off opportunities for effective exchange and compromise.

Cynicism is most likely to emerge when repeated attempts to negotiate and compromise with the opposition have been unfruitful. In Kentucky, the public health community actively endorsed the proposal to allocate the majority of tobacco settlement monies to tobacco farmers in return for an allocation of some of the money for tobacco cessation and prevention programs that met the Centers for Disease Control's minimum guidelines. During one of the televised programs about the cigarette excise tax, KHIK speakers countered assertions that they were out to hurt tobacco farmers by reminding viewers of this cooperation and claiming that they deserved substantial credit for the benefits that had been worked out for those farmers. However, an opposing speaker, a Farm Bureau representative, summarily dismissed the claim that the public health community deserved praise for helping tobacco farmers. It is not surprising that some members of the anti-tobacco coalition subsequently came to have increasingly negative views of the opposition and were less inclined to seek out opportunities for engagement and compromise.

Democratic social movements are built on the premise that, ultimately, given good reasons, most people can be persuaded to change their mind and actions. As social movement leaders construct communication to meet their movement's goals, they need to pay attention to signs that issues can be narrowed and common ground can be achieved. In this light, academics can contribute to social movement activism simply by offering a different perspective to activists' ongoing discussion and planning. The "naive distance" of academics may make a positive contribution by helping social movement members to sustain needed complexity on existing opportunities to "convert" opponents.

The different perspective that an academic may offer is valuable, not because that perspective is better or superior but because it adds another voice to the conversation. Despite the tugs and pulls of the other demands on their time and the realities of project timelines, academics often have the luxury of being able to carefully analyze and evaluate aspects of a campaign. This distance can add needed perspective to the viewpoints of activists who are immersed in the day-to-day struggles of adapting to changes on the ground. This contribution was the most-mentioned benefit of our involvement on the feedback questionnaire we administered at the end of the project to the KHIK campaign leaders and lawmakers. One of the activists said it was valuable to have their own "think tank" to parallel the strategic counsel that big tobacco receives.

In this respect, we faced continuing challenges to keep reasonably current with unfolding issues in the campaign, due, in part, to the sheer quantity of tobacco-control news nationally, as well as in the state. Academics should never underestimate the knowledge and expertise of social movement activists and staff members, as such individuals may have more specialized interests in the topic or time to devote to reviewing new information and materials. At the same time, it is important not to underestimate the potential value of the academic perspective that is brought to the situation as well. It is incumbent on academics to carefully assess activists' knowledge and expertise before presuming to participate in the discussion. Careful consideration should be given as to how such assessments can be done efficiently and systematically.

To this end, KHIK activists were asked to complete the open-ended questionnaire that had them respond to pro- and con-cigarette excise tax arguments. We found substantial overlap (more than 80%) between the categories from our analyses of the televised programs and those of the activists (i.e., the rhetorical strategies they listed on the free-response measure). This finding was both reassuring and a bit sobering. It was reassuring in that we gained confidence that Hirschman's (1991) rhetoric of reaction and the cultural topoi framework effectively described and organized most of the available affirmative and negative strategies. On the other hand, we found that this group of activists and legislators anticipated many of the elements of our analytic frame and, therefore, the information we provided was not always as newsworthy as we thought it might be. For instance, one of the state legislators commented (before any ratings occurred) that the libertarian arguments were the hardest to counteract, and this opinion was substantiated by the fact that the cluster of libertarian arguments we had identified was rated by the others as the most difficult to convincingly refute. Based on these findings, we focused much of our subsequent attention on identifying the available means for circumventing libertarian arguments. For instance, to counter the argument that smoking prevention "is the responsibility of parents," we proposed that activists emphasize that raising the cigarette excise tax would reinforce the overwhelming desire of parents that their children not smoke; in other words, the proposed excise tax could be positioned as support for parental authority and not interference with it.

From a research perspective, we found that activist engagement deepened understanding of our research topic. Engaging our passions served to reinforce and deepen our initial interests in this research area. In fact, this process has been an iterative one, cycling between—and, in most cases, merging—activist and research interests. Although we formed a research team, our involvement commenced at different points and for different reasons. For example, Esrock started with the antitobacco activists as a pro bono consultant and eventually moved, during a 1-year sabbatical, to working with the KHIK campaign and studying how nonprofit groups can use the internet; Hart was interested in message types and change; and Leichty was attracted to tobacco debates in the state as a case study to examine rhetoric. In each case, we ended up with additional interest and involvement as we discovered new problems to analyze. Engaging in activism, thus, served to identify new and interesting research questions and opportunities that we originally did not anticipate.

Finally, we have become acutely aware that engaging in communication social activism has direct effects on our roles in academe. Leaving campus and confronting serious, complex problems has contributed to our work on campus in several ways. For example, it has aided our pedagogy, providing new case study materials and contemporary examples of communication issues and applications. Leichty even has built a database of cigarette excise tax data for path-analysis exercises in a research methods class; using the database enables students to uncover elements of public policy issues on their own and to learn about statistical procedures.

In the end, our modest engagement with communication activism has deepened our satisfaction as scholars and citizens. The process of establishing academic credentials and completing necessary work inside a university often is so consuming that it interferes with meaningful participation by scholars in the public realm. Ironically, we can become too enmeshed in our professional careers to be able to participate in efforts to apply the very theory, methods, and knowledge that we labor so prodigiously to create. Becoming involved as scholar-activists offers us an opportunity to engage a too-frequently neglected side of ourselves: actively participating citizens in a democratic society.

CONCLUSION

The struggle in Kentucky to increase the cigarette excise tax and break the stranglehold that tobacco has on the state is a struggle to reduce the terrible toll that tobacco wreaks in the Bluegrass. Every year, Kentucky spends nearly $300 for every man, woman, and child in the state to treat smoking-related illnesses. Residents of the state pay higher health and life insurance premiums because of Kentucky's inflated smoking rates and the attendant abnormally high mortality. Far more alarming is the human suffering that takes place each time someone's grandparent, mother, father, child, or friend dies from a smoking-related illness.

Against this backdrop, some might suggest that it is not optional or a luxury for researchers to intervene in social activism campaigns such as this one. We would even argue that participation, as researchers, educators, and citizens, in such campaigns should perhaps be considered an obligation. The choice may be, as Frey (1998) and Frey et al. (1996) argued, whether to continue to be aligned with the problem or become engaged in the solution.

REFERENCES

Adams, J. (1995). *Risk: The policy implications of risk compensation and plural rationalities.* London: University College London Press.

Berry, W. (2002). *The art of the commonplace: Agrarian essays of Wendell Berry* (N. Wirzba, Ed.). Washington, DC: Counterpoint.

Campaign for Tobacco-Free Kids. (2004). *Big tobacco still addicting kids.* Retrieved June 15, 2004, from http://tobaccofreekids.org/reports/addicting/

Carragee, K. M., & Roefs, W. (2004). The neglect of power in recent framing research. *Journal of Communication, 54*, 214-233.

Centers for Disease Control. (1996, November 8). Projected smoking-related deaths among youth—United States. *Morbidity and Mortality Weekly Reports, 45*, 971-974.

Centers for Disease Control. (2002). *State tobacco control highlights.* Retrieved May 15, 2002, from http://www.cdc.gov/tobacco/statehi/statehi_2002.htm

Chaloupka, F. J. (1999). Macro-social influences: The effects of prices and tobacco control policies on the demand for tobacco products. *Nicotine & Tobacco Research, 1*(Supplement 1), S105-S109.

Cigarette maker cleared in death of smoker. (1990, March 9). *The New York Times*, p. B6.

Committee on Energy and Commerce, U.S. House of Representatives. (1995). *Regulation of tobacco products (part 1) March 25 and April 14, 1994* (Serial No. 103-149). Washington, DC: U.S. Government Printing Office.

Conrad, C., & Millay, B. (2001). Confronting free market romanticism: Healthcare reform in the least likely place. *Journal of Applied Communication Research, 29*, 153-170.

Eichenwald, K. (1988, June 15). Tobacco verdict could revive bills. *The New York Times*, p. B7.

Ellis, R. J. (1993). *American political cultures.* New York: Oxford University Press.

Entman, R. M. (1993). Framing: Toward clarification of a fractured paradigm. *Journal of Communication, 43*(4), 51-58.

Esrock, S. L., Hart, J. L., & Leichty, G. (2004). Smudging the "golden leaf": A communication campaign to reduce the burden of tobacco in Kentucky. *Electronic Journal of Communication, 13*(4). Retrieved August 30, 2004, from http://www.cios.org/www/ejc/v134toc.htm

Frey, L. R. (1998). Communication and social justice research: Truth, justice, and the applied communication way. *Journal of Applied Communication Research, 26*, 155-164.

Frey, L. R., Pearce, W. B., Pollock, M. A., Artz, L., & Murphy, B. A. O. (1996). Looking for social justice in all the wrong places: On a communication approach to social justice. *Communication Studies, 47,* 110-127.

Gamson, W. A. (1992). *Talking politics.* New York: Cambridge University Press.

Gamson, W. A., Croteau, D., Hoynes, D., & Sasson, T. (1992). Media images and the social construction of reality. *Annual Review of Sociology, 18,* 373-393.

Goffman, E. (1974). *Frame analysis: An essay on the organization of experience.* New York: Harper & Row.

Hahn, E. J., Plymale, M. A., & Rayens, M. K. (2001). *Kentucky youth tobacco survey.* Frankfort: Kentucky Cabinet for Health Services.

Hahn, E. J., Tourney, C. P., Rayens, M. K., & McCoy, C. A. (1999). Kentucky legislators' views on tobacco policy. *American Journal of Preventive Medicine, 16,* 81-88.

Hallahan, K. (1999). Seven models of framing: Implications for public relations. *Journal of Public Relations Research, 11,* 205-242.

Hirschman, A. O. (1991). *The rhetoric of reaction: Perversity, futility, jeopardy.* Cambridge, MA: Belknap Press.

Holloway, R., & Leichty, G. (2000, November). *Threats to children as cultural topos: Finding common ground in issue advocacy campaigns.* Paper presented at the meeting of the National Communication Association, Atlanta, GA.

Howington, P. (2004, May 11). 29 states, D.C. move to sue B&W. *Courier-Journal,* pp. F1, F7.

Kelder, G., & Davidson, P. (Eds.). (1999). *The multistate Master Settlement Agreement and the future of state and local tobacco control.* Boston: Tobacco Resource Center, Northeastern University School of Law.

Kosicki, G. M. (1993). Problems and opportunities in agenda-setting research. *Journal of Communication, 43*(2), 100-127.

Kozlowski, L. T., Henningfield, J. E., & Brigham, J. (2001). *Cigarettes, nicotine, and health: A biobehavioral approach.* Thousand Oaks, CA: Sage.

Leichty, G., & Warner, E. (2001). Cultural topoi. In R. L. Heath (Ed.), *Handbook of public relations* (pp. 61-74). Thousand Oaks, CA: Sage.

Licari, M. J., & Meier, K. J. (2000). Regulation and signaling: When a tax is not just a tax. *Journal of Politics, 62,* 875-885.

Lindblom, E. (2002, April 20). *Key state-specific tobacco-related data and rankings.* Washington, DC: Campaign for Tobacco-Free Kids. Retrieved April 22, 2002, from http://www.tobaccofreekids.org/research/factsheets/pdf/0176.pdf

Lindblom, E. (2003, July 24). *State cigarette excise tax rates and rankings.* Washington, DC: Campaign for Tobacco-Free Kids. Retrieved November 10, 2003, from http://www.tobaccofreekids.org/research/factsheets/pdf/0097.pdf

Menashe, C. L., & Siegel, M. (1998). The power of a frame: An analysis of newspaper coverage of tobacco issues—United States, 1985-1996. *Journal of Health Communication, 3,* 307-326.

Mollenkamp, C., Levy, A., Menn, J., & Rothfedder, J. (1998). *The people vs. big tobacco: How the states took on the cigarette giants.* Princeton, NJ: Bloomberg Press.

Noland, M. P. (1996). Tobacco prevention in tobacco-raising areas: Lessons from the lion's den. *Journal of School Health, 66,* 266-269.

Orey, M. (1999). *Assuming the risk: The mavericks, the lawyers, and the whistleblowers who beat big tobacco.* Boston: Little, Brown.

Pan, Z., & Kosicki, G. M. (1993). Framing analysis: An approach to news discourse. *Political Communication, 10,* 59-79.

Pertschuk, M. (2001). *Smoke in their eyes: Lessons in movement leadership from the tobacco wars.* Nashville, TN: Vanderbilt University Press.

Pratt, C. B. (2001). Issues management: The paradox of the 40-year U.S. tobacco wars. In R. L. Heath (Ed.), *Handbook of public relations* (pp. 335-346). Thousand Oaks, CA: Sage.

President's Commission on Improving Economic Opportunity in Communities Dependent on Tobacco Production while Protecting Public Health. (2001, May 14). *Tobacco at a crossroads: A call for action.* Washington, DC: United States Department of Agriculture. Retrieved October 25, 2002, from http://www.fsa. usda.gov/tobcom/FRFiles/FinalReport.htm

Price, V., & Tewksbury, D. (1997). News values and public opinion: A theoretical account of media priming and framing. *Progress in the Communication Sciences, 13,* 173-212.

Rojecki, A. (1999). *Silencing the opposition: Antinuclear movements and the media in the Cold War.* Urbana: University of Illinois Press.

Ryan, C., Carragee, K. M., & Meinhofer, W. (2001). Framing, the news media, and collective action. *Journal of Broadcasting & Electronic Media, 45,* 175-182.

Ryan, C., Carragee, K. M., & Schwerner, C. (1998). Media, movements, and the quest for social justice. *Journal of Applied Communication Research, 26,* 165-181.

Schansberg, D. E. (1996). *Poor policy: How government harms the poor.* Boulder, CO: Westview Press.

Snell, W., & Goetz, S. (1997). *Overview of Kentucky's tobacco economy: AEC-83.* Lexington: University of Kentucky Cooperative Extension Service.

Sweeney, R., & Rose, V. L. (1998). The outlook for tobacco control is shifting to the states. *American Family Physician, 58,* 839-842.

Thompson, M., Ellis, R., & Wildavsky, A. (1990). *Cultural theory.* Boulder, CO: Westview Press.

Toulmin, S. (1958). *The uses of argument.* Cambridge: Cambridge University Press.

Tucker, L. R. (1998). The framing of Calvin Klein: A frame analysis of media discourse about the August 1995 Calvin Klein jeans advertising campaign. *Critical Studies in Mass Communication, 15,* 141-157.

United States Department of Health and Human Services, Office of Smoking and Health. (1988). *The health consequences of smoking: Nicotine addiction, a report of the Surgeon General.* Washington, DC: U.S. Government Printing Office. Retrieved January 26, 2005, from http://www.cdc.gov/tobacco/sgr/sgr_1988/ index.htm

United States Department of Health and Human Services. (1994). *Preventing tobacco use among young people: A report of the Surgeon General* (Publication No. 017-001-00491-0). Atlanta, GA: Public Health Service. Retrieved January 26, 2005, from http://www.cdc.gov/tobacco/sgr/sgr_1994/index.htm

University of Kentucky College of Agriculture. (2002). *Agripedia.* Retrieved May 17, 2002, from http://www.ca.uky.edu/agripedia/agmania/tobacco

Valkenberg, P. M., Semetko, H. A., & DeVrees, C. H. (1999). The effects of news frames on readers' thoughts and recall. *Communication Research, 26,* 500-569.

Vanderford, M. L. (1989). Vilification and social movements: A case study of pro-life and pro-choice rhetoric. *Quarterly Journal of Speech, 75,* 166-182.

11

THE ORGANIZATIONAL CONSULTANT AS ACTIVIST

A Case Study of a Nonprofit Organization

Leah Ritchie

Salem State College

It is well known that most of the wealth that exists in the world today is owned and controlled by large corporations. Fueled by international trade agreements, large-scale mergers, and an abundant worldwide labor pool, corporations now have more economic power than they have had in the recent past (Ahmed, 2004; Anderson & Cavanagh, 2000; Singh & Zammit, 2004). U.S. corporate giants such as Walmart and General Motors, for example, are among the top 100 companies in the world that together own a controlling share (51%) of the entire global economy (Anderson & Cavanagh, 2000). The benefits that these corporations provide to society are trivial compared to the vast power they wield.

Nonprofit organizations have made little headway in addressing this power imbalance. Given their dependence on private donations, organizations commissioned to advocate for the interests of the public are compelled to manipulate their policies to comply with the demands of their largest corporate donors (Center for Science in the Public Interest, 2003).

As corporations continue to expand, so too does their drive to maximize profit and minimize competition. Workers bear the brunt of these activities. Now expected to meet unrealistically high financial targets and production standards, employees are working harder and for longer hours than they have in the past (Deetz, 1995). They are compelled to do so under threat that their jobs will be exported overseas to a labor market where individuals are exploited for their willingness to work for low wages.

Labor unions have encountered considerable backlash in their fight to end these injustices. Seventy-five percent of U.S. companies included in a recent study admitted to hiring consultants to run anti-union campaigns when employees threatened to organize, and 78% of companies in that study required workers to attend private meetings with managers during which strong anti-union messages were conveyed (Bronfenbrenner, 2000).

Given the diminishing rights of workers, and the threat to traditional means of employee representation, there is a significant need to advocate for a more balanced system of power among citizens, organizations, and workers worldwide. Ignoring this problem will only further entrench the systems of power that maintain the status quo.

Critical communication scholars have addressed this problem to some degree by leveling harsh criticism against corporate leaders and arguing for more pluralistic relationships among corporations, citizens, and governments (see, e.g., Cheney, 1995; Deetz, 1992, 1995). As Deetz (1995) explained:

> The central goal of critical theory in organizational communication studies has been to create a society and workplaces that are free from domination and where all members can contribute equally to produce systems that meet human needs and lead to the progressive development of all. (p. 26)

Despite the activist tone of this agenda, critical organizational communication scholarship suffers from a major weakness in its failure to successfully advocate for workers. Specifically, scholars have kept discussions within the realm of theory, rarely providing practical discursive tools for shifting economic systems of control that threaten the social, environmental, and financial stability of the world. In short, critical communication scholars, unfortunately, have ignored their activist agenda to a significant degree.

In attempting to address this gap in the research, this chapter describes the methods I used to decentralize power at the Massachusetts-based neighborhood center (MNC, a pseudonym), a nonprofit community organization. I carried out this work by using a theory-based intervention that helped both employees and managers to critically evaluate existing organizational power structures. Although successful in many respects, the intervention created many tensions. It always is difficult when scholars step out of the traditional disinterested observer role into a context where they are agents of change. I was most concerned that the risky behaviors I encouraged employees to carry out would cause their managers to retaliate against them. Other difficulties arose, particularly as I guided student teams that assisted me with the project. In fulfilling traditional expectations of the teaching role, I often used a highly directive leadership style, reflecting back to students the same controlling behaviors I was trying to limit at MNC. These and other tensions are discussed throughout the chapter, although they are never fully reconciled.

CRITICAL PERSPECTIVES ON POWER IN ORGANIZATIONS: CREATING COMMUNICATION ACTIVISM

Although critical communication scholars have not provided concrete methods for helping disenfranchised groups in the workplace, they have taken steps to develop theories and arguments to address the problem. In fact, they recently have shifted their research focus from improving organizational effectiveness and productivity through communicative means (e.g., networks, groups, and interpersonal skills) to examining how workers can discursively create more egalitarian workplaces for themselves and other stakeholders affected by their organization (for a review, see Deetz, 2001).

The research findings that drove this shift included data showing that employees who have little control over their work life experience serious negative personal outcomes, including anxiety, stress, and physical and mental problems (Cheney, 1995; Eisenberg & Goodall, 2003; Greenberger & Strasser, 1986; Morrison & Milliken, 2000; Parker, 1993). Other data show that employees who have little power in the workplace may become violent or destructive (Greenberger & Strasser, 1986). In contrast, in democratic organizations, in which employee participation and representation are encouraged (Cheney, 1995), workers typically are more positive, productive, and emotionally healthy (Conger & Kanungo, 1988; Hammer, 1988; Jackson, 1983; Marshall & Stohl, 1993; Seibold & Shea, 2001; Thomas & Griffin, 1989).

In developing their critical research agenda, communication scholars often have adopted the perspectives of Jürgen Habermas, a German philosopher and member of the Frankfurt School of critical theory. Among his many ideas about politics, social justice, and the structure of power and society, Habermas (e.g., 1975, 1984, 1987, 1996) believed that power is created and perpetuated through discourse. Specifically, he argued that messages within a social system typically act to preserve the hierarchical aspects of that system by protecting privileged groups and further marginalizing disenfranchised groups. In organizational contexts, this oppression often happens when norms, assumptions, and interpretive schemes, the staples of organizational life, provide the discursive means to support and reproduce existing systems of power (Deetz, 1998; Knights & Willmott, 1987; Mills, 1994; Townley, 1993).

The process through which discourse protects privileged groups is difficult to reveal and overcome, primarily because of the taken-for-granted nature of norms that disenfranchise low-status groups (Alvesson & Deetz, 1996; Barker, 1993; Barker & Cheney, 1994). For example, it typically is assumed that only high-level employees are qualified to influence key organizational decisions (e.g., strategic planning, layoffs, and profit sharing). These norms come from subtle or overt messages that convey negative opinions about employees (e.g., workers do not have anything of value to say, only are concerned with their own interests, or are not smart enough to understand important organizational decisions). Excluding employees from dialogue and justifying that exclusion through negative stereotyping shields managers from employees who often want to challenge their power. It also denies employees access to the process through which disenfranchising norms are constructed (Barker, 1993; Deetz, 2001; Eisenberg & Riley, 2001; Mumby, 2001). Although the norms that diminish employee power are rarely spoken of, employees sense their disenfranchisement and, ironically, may act out unflattering stereotypes because of that frustration.

Habermas (1975, 1984, 1987, 1996) argued that the cycle of disenfranchisement can only be undone when low-status groups influence the rhetorical process through which power is produced. This influence comes from creating an *ideal speech situation*, which is a discursive context that provides full and equal access to information, communication channels, and discussions that control how power is allocated (Bernstein, 1995; Habermas, 1975, 1984, 1987, 1996). Within this context, both low- and high-status members of an organization have the same opportunities to share their opinions about hegemonic systems and are consistently able to negotiate new systems of power.

Communication scholars have argued that in specifically challenging culturally designed assumptions about privileged and nonprivileged groups, individuals can begin to change social structures, thereby planting the seeds of social activism (Gregg, 1971; McGee, 1975; Merton, 1957; Stewart, 1980; Stewart, Smith, & Denton, 1994). From a functionalist perspective (Stewart, 1980), creating an ideal speech situation can be considered an activist endeavor in that it helps individuals to shift social constructs by confronting unspoken assumptions that keep disenfranchised groups oppressed. For example, when individuals make their interests and opinions known, they challenge social mores that favor passive acceptance of rules governing the current system. When these rules are questioned, individuals have the opportunity to "try on" new, more powerful roles through rhetorically shifting definitions about their power and the power that others possess (Deetz, 1995; Mumby, 1988).

Functionalist theory also argues that activism occurs when individuals or groups perform certain persuasive functions that help them to create new perspectives on their situations. Stewart (1980) argued that one of the necessary functions required by social activism is to "transform perceptions of reality" (p. 300). Because an ideal speech situation is a context through which individuals use dialogue to question and disrupt hegemony, it potentially can transform how both low- and high-status individuals view themselves and their roles in the organization. Through this new context, less powerful groups can understand how the system has robbed them of their voice in the past and how they can take on new, more powerful roles in the future.

Creating an ideal speech situation, in its pure sense, is difficult. Murray (2003) stated that the word "ideal" describes an ethically pure discursive context in which there are no constraints on discursive action. He contended that this situation is nearly impossible to create given the inherent and often invisible political, cognitive, and logistical boundaries that exist in most contexts. Murray suggested, however, that it may be possible to at least create conditions in which reasonable and constructive debate about power can be achieved. Murray (p. 2) referred to this context as a "quasi-ideal" speech situation.

Many of the constraints that Murray referred to existed within MNC. In the following sections, I describe these constraints, as well as the methods I used to diminish them with the help of employees. I begin by describing the organization, as well as the methods I used to collect and analyze relevant organizational data. I then recount my attempt to approximate an ideal speech situation through an intervention called "organizational fitness profiling" (Beer & Eisenstat, 2000). I then analyze the activist quality of this work through a functionalist lens (Stewart, 1980) and conclude the chapter with a discussion of the challenges and successes of the project, as well as the lessons that I learned about communication activism.

SHIFTING THE BALANCE OF POWER AT A
NONPROFIT ORGANIZATION:
THE CASE OF MNC

MNC is a nonprofit, faith-based organization that strives to meet the religious, social, recreational, and educational needs of its members. MNC is led by a volunteer board of directors, as well as paid staff, including an executive director, top management team, program directors, teachers, fitness instructors, facility personnel, and administrative assistants. In all, the center employs 175 individuals (see the organizational chart of MNC in Figure 11.1).

Although the organization has been successful for the last 97 years, MNC recently has fallen on difficult financial times due to member attrition, declining contributions, and competition. In addition to these problems, hostility between different hierarchical groups within the organization has been growing. When the president of MNC's board of directors became aware of these issues, he contacted my colleague (a business school faculty member at my college) and asked him to conduct a management consultation with the organization. He agreed to help MNC handle its financial and strategic problems and then asked me to address the reported hostility among employees in the organization, knowing that I have a background in organizational communication. We agreed to consult with the organization on a pro bono basis, provided that our graduate (MBA) students were allowed to work with us, to which the board of directors agreed.

To determine the root causes of MNC's communication problems, my students and I conducted focus groups with all employees. We needed to have an informal discussion with members of the organization to get a feel for the existing communication dynamics, as well as the culture and subcultures that existed. The first step in this process was to assign employees to their respective groups. In doing so, my students and I made sure that individuals were not placed in groups with their superior(s). This peer-only grouping was designed to create an atmosphere in which employees could voice their opinions without being subjected to political pressure. Once the employees received their group assignments, my students and I facilitated four focus groups conducted over the course of 4 weeks. The groups were specifically designated for each of the hierarchical levels in the organization (i.e., the board of directors, top management team, middle managers, and staff).

We began each focus group by asking employees to give their opinions about the organization and encouraged them to provide both positive and negative evaluations. After soliciting this information, however, we soon encountered significant resistance from most employees, particularly middle

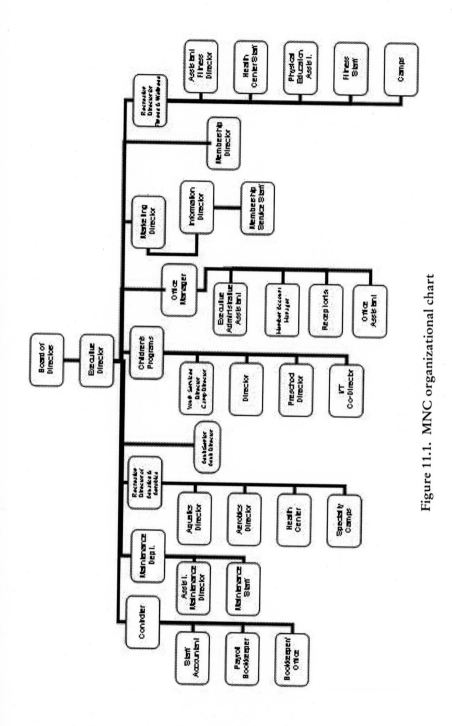

Figure 11.1. MNC organizational chart

managers and staff. This resistance was not surprising, given that MNC was a traditional bureaucratic organization. In bureaucracies, employees are required to comply with specific job descriptions and related behaviors deemed appropriate for the implied status of their jobs (Kallinikos, 2004). In critically evaluating the organization, employees would have to violate subordinate behavioral expectations dictated by their job-related roles. Employees likely feared that managers would retaliate against them for this behavior, given that it would compromise the integrity of the bureaucratic structure and culture within the organization.

My students and I used a few different methods to encourage employees to talk with us. First, we acknowledged employees' fear of speaking out and explained that it was to be expected, given that they probably were not used to criticizing managers or the organization. One of my students then asked employees to discuss, in more concrete terms, the possible negative circumstances that could result from sharing honest opinions. A few employees reacted by saying that they would be branded "nonteam players" if they criticized the management team. This meant that employees possibly would lose privileges or be given the "cold shoulder" by their superiors.

In addressing this tension, I thought it would be helpful to use basic mediation techniques by revealing positive information that I received from the management team, assuming that the team would not have shared this information with staff, given poor relations between the two groups. I hoped that this information would disarm employees and possibly make them less fearful of managers. I told employees that top managers were fully aware that I planned to ask lower level employees to reveal their opinions about the organization and I explained that some managers seemed sincerely interested in hearing what employees had to say.

After I revealed this information, some employees seemed more forthcoming, although others still remained silent. My students and I continued conducting the focus groups but decided to also hold private interviews with employees (during which I was present, along with one student). I hoped that employees would be more comfortable sharing their views in the more private context of personal interviews. I also hoped that these interviews would provide an opportunity for employees to get to know me better, which hopefully would build their trust in me. The interviews were somewhat successful in achieving these goals, given that some employees were more forthcoming in this context than they were in the focus groups. In addition, during a few of the interviews, employees shared jokes and personal stories with me, which made me believe that perhaps my rapport with them was beginning to improve.

Gathering focus group and interview data while working side-by-side with students created some tension. In my effort to collect accurate and thorough information, I was highly directive and meticulous about how students kept notes and various other records related to the project. Instead of allowing the students to lead and take notes on all of the focus groups, as originally promised, I ended up facilitating many of the groups myself and transcribing my notes. I often checked over the students' notes and made sure that they correctly scheduled focus groups and interviews. I also took over the job of client liaison, although I promised that job to a student. This leadership style created a paradoxical situation: I was unwilling to let students take control over their work, even though I criticized managers for practicing the same controlling behaviors with their employees. My behavior likely compelled students to assume a passive role, as evidenced by their unwillingness to comment on the project and dependence on my direction for performing even minor tasks associated with the project. I did not fully understand this paradox while working with the students; consequently, I did not take any significant steps to change my behavior, other than to increase the students' workload.

Unfortunately, I did not realize that my relationship with students in the context of this project was particularly meaningful. If I had used a more democratic approach in directing students, I could have provided MNC employees (as well as my students) with a positive model of decentralized leadership. This model could have helped employees to see that this type of leadership may be possible, despite the lack of existing examples in their work environment. I discuss this issue in more detail later in the chapter.

Management Control through Self-silencing, Interpersonal Distance, and Lack of Trust: A Cultural Analysis of MNC

When we finished conducting the focus groups and individual interviews, my students and I made some judgments about the data we would include in our analysis. Specifically, we decided not to spend much time examining information provided by the part-time physical education instructors, as this group seemed very detached from the organization and, therefore, disclosed little information that was helpful. The board of directors also admitted to knowing little about the day-to-day functioning of the center, so we excluded many of their responses as well (although some of the information they provided clarified MNC's financial problems and, thus, was meaningful). In contrast, the top management team, middle managers, and the full-time staff provided comprehensive and thoughtful feedback. The following analysis, therefore, primarily is based on these data.

When the students and I finished collecting data, we discussed our findings in class and via electronic discussion groups. As we talked about the data, we often came back to the same theme: The culture at MNC, which we found to be controlling and hierarchical, had a significant negative impact on employees. Specifically, we found that MNC's culture lowered employees' morale and sense of self-efficacy. That culture also thwarted their creativity and prohibited efficient workflow.

During the focus groups and individual interviews conducted, employees often alluded to three specific norms that they found the most distressing: (a) pressure to self-silence, (b) interpersonal distance between hierarchical groups, and (c) lack of trust between hierarchical groups. The following sections describe how these norms were revealed through the data.

Self-silencing. As mentioned earlier, one of the most difficult aspects of this project was getting employees to talk about the organization. Self-silencing behaviors are typical in most bureaucratic organizations, because employees value consensus over conflict and often are uncomfortable revealing dissenting opinions (Ewing, 1977; Morrison & Milliken, 2000; Nemeth, 1997; Scott & Hart, 1979; Sprague & Ruud, 1988). Employees also may have feared that managers would retaliate against them for their opinions (despite the fact that I reiterated the project's anonymity protocol, which prohibited me from revealing to managers specific information gathered from the focus groups and interviews). In centrally controlled organizations, such as MNC, managers have a tendency to ostracize "outspoken" employees, even those who criticize in constructive ways, by symbolically placing them in "out-groups," where they are deprived of information, organizational perks, and informal contact with high-status employees (Graen & Cashman, 1975; Graen, Novak, & Sommerkamp, 1982; Liden & Graen, 1980). This placement can be a subtle process, and it usually is not acknowledged, either by organizational leaders or by out-group members.

Despite these constraints, employees eventually spoke to us. Perhaps the techniques we used to make them feel at ease were temporarily successful in diminishing bureaucratic obstacles to free and open discussion. In recounting their experiences, employees revealed mainly negative information, even when prompted to recall some of the positive aspects of their work life. In general, most of these experiences reflected the employees' perceived lack of control and influence over their work and important organizational decisions. The following material describes these experiences in more detail.

Interpersonal distance. AT MNC, interpersonal distance was a prevalent feature of the organizational culture. As one middle manager explained about members of the top management team, "Some go out of their way to avoid us." Other employees complained that some top managers "rarely come out of their office" to see what is going on. Employees at the staff level (the lowest rank in the organization) reported having little day-to-day contact with anyone other than their peers and immediate supervisors. These experiences reflected an "invisible" barrier between hierarchical groups. In bureaucracies, groups of different status rarely have opportunities to engage in formal and informal discussions because of the structural and cultural obstacles that strictly prohibit such interaction (Heckscher, 1994; Monge & Contractor, 2001; Weber, 1947).

Interpersonal distance also was reflected in the words of another middle manager who described her perception that top managers were unable to identify with employees outside of their group. As she noted, some members of the management team "don't really understand the daily struggles of program implementation." Morrison and Milliken (2000) explained that lack of opportunities for dialogue between groups of different rank creates a diminished capacity for employees to understand each other, which further decreases intergroup trust. As employees continue to grow, individuals with little formal status are further distanced from powerful groups, as well as from access to power that contact with these groups could bring.

Discussions with the top management team, as well as the board of directors, revealed that communicative distance also may have reinforced negative stereotypes of employees. For example, some members of the board blamed staff members for MNC's shrinking customer base, accusing them of having little commitment to client service and being apathetic about their work. Some top managers criticized employees as well, accusing them of complaining too often and caring more about their own interests than about the future of the organization. Again, such stereotyping in a traditional top-down organizational structure is not unusual given that the thoughts and actions of top-ranking employees in these contexts often are based on early economic models of employee behavior, which describe workers as lazy, unintelligent, and self-centered (Ilgen, Fisher & Taylor, 1979; Wolfe & Milliken, 2002). In their isolation from the staff, the top management team and the board of directors had little opportunity to learn more about employees and, therefore, had few compelling reasons to question these stereotypes.

Lack of trust. Lack of opportunities for employee interaction, and the resulting negative stereotyping and power distance, had other consequences within MNC. The one mentioned most often by middle managers and staff was a profound lack of trust between low- and high-status groups. At MNC, all employee groups (except for the board of directors) complained of this lack of trust, which often manifested itself in excessive supervisory oversight. For example, one middle manager said that micro-management "makes us feel powerless, like we are children." Another middle manager complained about what she considered an unnecessarily lengthy and complicated approval process required for new policies and programs. She felt that this process reflected management's lack of confidence in her and called her competence into question.

When employees are overmanaged, they often see themselves as ineffectual or child-like (Argyris, 1993). Because employees in that situation may feel that their superiors perceive them as incompetent, they often disengage from their work—"going through the motions" of their day without showing genuine commitment to their tasks. This lack of commitment, and the resulting poor performance that often results, further justifies (in the mind of managers) close supervision of lower ranking employees, which continues the cycle of disenfranchisement.

Top managers also complained of board-imposed rules and what they considered to be excessive attention to detail, which they felt questioned their competence. Specifically, some managers complained that the board of directors constantly wasted valuable meeting time reviewing minute details of the center's operation. The executive director commented that these behaviors impeded productivity and effective management practice by diverting the board's attention from more pressing issues, such as the need to raise funds and create a long-range strategic plan for the center.

Norms related to self-silencing, isolation, and mutual lack of trust were used by top managers at MNC to limit employees' access to the discussions and channels of communication that maintained the current political system. Because employees often were denied access to discursive contexts, they were unable to see how these contexts functioned to continually diminish their influence and protected the power of privileged groups.

To shift the balance of power at MNC, employees needed to become aware of the power-reifying norms that maintained the status quo. Through such awareness, employees could not only speak on their own behalf but they also could see the negotiable nature of power, which could help them to reconceive of it as dynamic rather than as fixed (as most managers would like employees to believe) (Knights & Willmott, 1987). The next section describes my attempt to enable these opportunities at MNC. In doing so, I hoped to pursue an activist agenda by creating a quasi-ideal speech situation.

The Researcher as Activist: Enabling an Ideal Speech Situation through Organizational Fitness Profiling

Activism was not my original intent when I began working on the MNC project. As mentioned earlier, my initial goal was to improve interpersonal tension being experienced between employees. However, my agenda began to shift as I discovered that many of MNC's problems were caused by the vast power differences between hierarchical groups, which created an oppressive atmosphere for low-status employees. Admittedly, I found middle managers and staff to be the more sympathetic group and, therefore, felt compelled to advocate for them.

I was not completely at ease with this new role at first given my fear that it would significantly conflict with my obligations as a consultant/researcher. However, I later determined that my new purpose, shifting the balance of power at MNC, was not necessarily incongruous with my initial consultant-driven goal of normalizing relations among employees. Given that employees who have autonomy and control over their work and their working conditions typically are productive and committed to organizational goals (Bennett, 1990; Cheney, 1995; Deetz, 1992; Holtzhausen, 2002), an obvious positive outcome for managers, I felt that I could maintain a good-faith relationship with the management team and still advocate for employees.

My activist role created some other tensions, however. For example, although employees knew that their participation was voluntary, it would have been unrealistic for me to believe that they felt no pressure (from me or the management team) to participate in the intervention. Therefore, like the management team, I too may have compelled employees to act against their desires and interests. This tension never was clearly reconciled, although I hoped that teaching employees how to advocate for themselves would perhaps make up for some of the discomfort that I may have caused them.

Once I determined my primary goal for the project—approximating an ideal speech situation at MNC—I began to search for an intervention that would address this goal. In doing so, I found some case studies of large and well-known companies, such as General Electric and Honda, that addressed some of my activist goals by conducting open-rank meetings to improve organizational communication. However, none of the related literature (e.g., Ashkenas, Ulrick, Jick, & Kerr, 2002; Kiernan, 1996) described the processes used in carrying out these meetings, nor did it provide significant analytical discussion related to the outcomes these meetings produced.

Two scholars, Michael Beer and Russell Eisenstat, however, wrote extensively about their communication intervention process, called *Organizational Fitness Profiling* (hereafter referred to as OFP) (Beer & Eisenstat, 1996, 2000; Beer, Eisenstat, & Spector, 1990). OFP was specifically designed to involve lower level employees in the strategic-planning process. These scholars argued that because lower rank employees often have the most intimate knowledge of business operations and customers, they can and should provide valuable information to organizational leaders as they develop their short- and long-range plans for the future. In addition to improving the quality of strategic planning, OFP has been said to create several other benefits, including improved teamwork and opportunities for open discussion about work-related problems. OFP also helps employees to focus on organizational goals instead of power and politics (Beer & Eisenstat, 2000).

The OFP process involves several steps. The first requires top managers to develop an overall strategic vision for the organization. During this consultant-facilitated discussion, top managers determine the values that will drive the organization for the next 3-5 years. The next step requires lower level employees (typically everyone below top management) to evaluate the strategic vision. This evaluation is done with the help of a "task-force" team of middle managers who solicit opinions from lower level staff about the feasibility of the strategic vision. The task force then reports the staff's feedback, along with its own opinions, to the top management team during a "fishbowl" meeting. The fishbowl format is a consultant-facilitated discussion during which the top managers are prohibited from commenting on the task-force feedback until the end of the meeting. This facilitation technique is used to prevent defensive reactions from the management team that may interrupt or derail the discussion.

The final stage of OFP requires the task force and top managers to discuss and negotiate a modified version of the strategic vision based on feedback from the fishbowl meeting. After a new strategy has been negotiated, the task force and top management team usually make a commitment to promote and publicize the vision and reexamine it at least every few years.

After studying the OFP process, I determined that it would be somewhat inadequate in approximating an ideal speech situation. For example, in requiring the staff members to speak "through" the task force instead of directly to the top management team, staff would not have equal access to the decision-making conversation. In addition, because the management team members were solely responsible for developing the initial strategic vision, they would have the power to manipulate the terms of the fishbowl discussion and, therefore, maintain their entitled role of unilateral decision making.

I tried to address some of these weaknesses before implementing the intervention. Specifically, I asked the top management team if I could modify OFP to include middle managers in the initial strategic planning meeting. The team reacted by quickly brushing the idea aside and changing the subject. This exchange made me realize that another idea I had, which was to include staff in the fishbowl meeting, probably would upset the management team and possibly put the entire intervention at risk. Therefore, I did not bring it up. Ultimately, these experiences punctuated one of the central tensions of this project, which was that I had little room to negotiate with the management team members given my dependence on them for access to the organization.

The bureaucratic nature of MNC's organizational culture and structure also presented several obstacles that constrained an ideal speech situation. Specifically, self-silencing, interpersonal isolation, and the lack of trust discussed earlier would make it difficult for group members to speak openly during the intervention, particularly during the fishbowl meeting. The trusting and cohesive group dynamic, which was necessary for participants to feel comfortable revealing their opinions, would be difficult to create under the existing circumstances. In addition, the intervention required employees to step out of their entrenched roles in the organization on which the integrity of the bureaucratic structure depends. I address these constraints, as well as my attempt to diminish them, in more detail later when describing the OFP implementation.

I was somewhat discouraged by these obstacles, but felt it was worthwhile to implement the OFP intervention given my belief in its potential to create some conditions of an ideal speech context to varying degrees. I also believed that the intervention could improve the quality of work life for MNC employees. There were specific aspects of OFP that I thought would be particularly helpful in approximating an ideal speech situation. For example, the fishbowl meeting could provide middle managers and staff with an uninterrupted and unprecedented opportunity to critique the current policies of the organization. In their participation, the task-force members could have access to a conversation typical of those that constructed and reconstituted organizational power. Through this access, they hopefully could speak on their own behalf and, for the first time, influence a conversation that typically recreated the existing system of power. In addition, by providing a model for reasonable intergroup discussion, the intervention would expose employees to a new discursive space that they hopefully could incorporate into the organizational framework as a standard practice. Before beginning the intervention, I met with the top management team to describe OFP and provide articles that explained the process in more detail. At the time of this meeting, my school semester ended; consequently, I continued the project without help from students, except for two, who stayed on to attend some meetings and help me take notes, as they were interested in seeing whether OFP would be successful given the existing organizational constraints.

I also suggested during the first OFP meeting that the top management team members develop an overall strategic vision for MNC. I was unaware, however, that they had already begun this process during a meeting with my colleague. In helping the team members to create their strategic vision, he suggested that MNC focus on distinguishing itself from its competition, which included the local YMCA, commercial fitness centers, and other nonprofit recreational centers. During this meeting (which I did not attend), my colleague explained that because MNC was at an early stage in the strategic-planning process, the vision should be written as a general guideline that later could be translated into a more specific tactical plan. After discussing several ideas for the strategic vision, the group came up with a simple statement: "We want MNC to be the number-one or number-two community center in our region." During the second strategy meeting (which I attended), my colleague and the management team reviewed, discussed, and confirmed this strategic vision.

We then began the next step in the process, which was to create a task-force team of middle managers who would solicit staff members' opinions on the new strategic vision. The executive director of MNC asked three (out of seven) middle managers to be on the team. Based on what I knew about these individuals, I was confident that they would solicit and provide honest feedback during the intervention.

Knowing that some staff members would be hesitant to speak to the task force (based on their responses during the focus group phase of the project), I held a training session to help them sharpen skills they would need to solicit meaningful feedback from reluctant participants. During the training, we discussed open-ended question techniques, as well as paraphrasing and listening skills. We also wrote two questions that the task force could use to elicit targeted feedback from staff: "What is helping or getting in the way of your ability to make MNC the number-one or number-two community center in the region?" and "What opportunities do you have to discuss these issues with the executive director, the management team, and/or the board of directors?" Encouraging staff members to voice their opinions about the new strategic vision, and about their opportunities to have critical discussions with the management team, hopefully would lead them to reflect on norms that isolated them from powerful groups and from power itself.

After the task-force members completed their interviews with the staff, they joined me for a second meeting during which we talked about how the feedback could be constructively presented to the top management team during the fishbowl meeting. Before we began discussing these techniques, the task-force members shared with me some feedback they had received from the staff. In general, staff members said that the management team did not take their ideas seriously; as one employee said, "Our suggestions just fall into a black hole."

After revealing this information, task-force members began to talk about the upcoming fishbowl meeting. They explained that although they were nervous about the meeting, they hoped that it could improve their relationship with the management team. I tried to address their nervousness by revealing positive information I had received from the management team. Specifically, a few top managers said that they were committed to improving existing relationships with employees, and one top manager, in particular (a person who all employees seemed to like and trust), said that he wanted to make an effort to get to know the staff better.

When the task force and the management team (including the executive director) assembled for the fishbowl meeting, I reviewed the procedures of OFP and offered to answer questions about the process. I then invited the task-force members to provide a summary of the feedback they had collected from the staff. Throughout the summary, the task force reported on what the staff members perceived as factors limiting their ability to be the "best" community center in the region. For example, one task-force member explained that staff members often felt cut off from vital information they needed to do their jobs and that they typically were unaware of important information related to new policies and procedures. Another employee cited an example of an MNC member/customer who became angry when she had to wait on the phone for several minutes to get the price of renting a room at the center (information that was not readily available to the staff member who took the call). Staff members also said that they felt unmotivated, taken for granted, and undercompensated. One staff member was quoted as saying, "We work so hard but are not appreciated or rewarded. We are obviously not in this for the money but would like some reward or encouragement for all that we do."

Task-force members explained that they, as a group, felt the same way that the staff did on many of the points that were brought up during the meeting. However, on a positive note, they said that their findings indicated a strong commitment to MNC's faith-based mission, along with positive peer relationships among middle managers and staff. The task force felt that these factors could perhaps help to motivate employees to achieve the strategic vision.

When the task-force members finished giving feedback, the top management team members were invited to comment. The executive director, who spoke first, was polite but appeared understandably uncomfortable, saying, "I really don't have much to say. I need some time to process this." Most of the other members of this group also seemed uncomfortable and a bit agitated, and the silence continued for several seconds.

Finally, one member of the management team commented positively, "I think we agree on many more points than we disagree." The executive director then apologized for the problems that the task force had brought up. She explained that the reason she often avoided interacting with the staff was because she was preoccupied with MNC's existing financial crisis. One task-force member appeared sympathetic to these problems, commenting, "I didn't realize that you guys were stressed out too."

The managers then invited the staff to join them in a dialogue about the issues that were brought up during the meeting. During that discussion, one top manager said, "It seems like the main problem here is communication." I then asked both groups to reflect on the feedback offered by the task force and discuss desired outcomes from the intervention. In doing so, they decided that it was necessary to create at least one policy that would address a communication-related issue. Both groups agreed that they could not negotiate changes to the new strategic vision unless they first could establish a healthy communication dynamic among employees.

The groups then discussed what they considered to be the most significant communication problem within the organization: the perception that employees' ideas are rarely considered and never implemented. In response to this problem, one task-force member said that she would like to create a formal system for processing employee suggestions. Other members of the task force suggested that they would collect and evaluate ideas from all employees and report the most feasible suggestions to the management team. Each employee who submitted an idea would receive a written response from the task force stating when and how the suggestion would be implemented. If the suggestion was rejected by the task force or a member of the management team, the task force would provide to the author of the suggestion a specific reason for the rejection. Both the top management team and the task force agreed that the long-term goal for this system would be for the staff to make suggestions to the top management team directly, without using the task force as an intermediary. In discussing who would lead the new suggestion program, the executive director surprised everyone in the room when she asked the task force to take charge of this initiative. Both groups agreed to this condition.

A second problem that the group addressed was employees' perception that top management had little interest in the day-to-day functioning of recreation and education programs at MNC. One task-force member asked, "Why doesn't someone just drop by our preschool or look in on an aerobics or swimming class just to really see what goes on? Nobody ever does that." After hearing these comments, the management team members agreed that they would make periodic visits to classes and recreational programs as soon as possible and that they would publicize these visits in the next MNC newsletter. The task-force members seemed enthusiastic about this response, but were afraid that staff members would view this new policy as a tool to "spy" on them. In response to this concern, the executive director said that she would communicate with staff members to convince them that these visits were part of a good-faith effort to get to know them better. At that point, both groups agreed to document and publish these ideas in an upcoming MNC newsletter. The fishbowl meeting then was adjourned.

Approximating an Ideal Speech Situation through OFP: Successes and Failures

Despite limitations and communicative constraints, the intervention successfully exposed employees to some discursive conditions of an ideal speech situation. In particular, during the fishbowl meeting, middle managers and staff (although to a much lesser degree) had access to channels of communication that typically controlled how organizational power is allocated. In addition, the task force discussed organizational strategy with the top management team. This discussion disrupted that group's privilege (based on rank), which typically allowed those group members to make unilateral decisions without input from lower ranking employees. The following sections describe these outcomes in more detail, along with the successes and challenges I faced in attempting to approximate an ideal speech situation at MNC.

Full and equal access to channels of communication. One of the central aspects of the intervention was controlled confrontation between powerful and marginalized groups. Through this confrontation, lower ranking groups had access to a conversation during which norms that enforced power could be redirected. The fishbowl meeting not only provided the task force with an opportunity to influence the discussion but it also revealed an alternative way to interpret strategic planning. Through their discursive access, task-force members could see that the policies and decisions they assumed to be fixed were actually developed through a negotiated process in which lower ranking employees participated for the first time.

In using the fishbowl meeting as a forum to reveal their opinions, the task-force members also discarded constraining cultural norms that required self-silencing and passive behavior. They used their access to the management team, as well as their own opinions and those offered by the staff, to reveal their dissatisfaction with the current system of power. Task-force members also went beyond voicing their opinions, suggesting a solution to one of the presenting problems. These actions showed that task-force members were not only willing to voice complaints but also felt powerful enough to suggest solutions to their problems.

Absence of privilege derived by role. Along with providing access to power-reifying conversations, the intervention also challenged norms that supported discursive privilege based on rank, although, again, this freedom was not fully achieved given that the management team had the power to choose the strategic vision without input from the task force or the staff. However, the task force did have an unprecedented opportunity to evaluate and influence organizational strategy. This opportunity deconstructed the organizational norm that entitled top managers to unilateral decision making. Surprisingly, some top managers showed a willingness to relinquish this power. Hopefully, this willingness meant that rebalancing power would be a shared goal and that both powerful and marginalized groups would work together to create positive change.

Freedom from coercion or constraints. Although progress was made in shifting norms of entitlement and discursive access, both the task force and

the management team ultimately were constrained by their traditional organizational roles: the task force as passive subordinates and the management
team as authoritative leaders. Despite the fact that I was encouraged and surprised by employees' willingness to discard these "old" roles during the
intervention, role constraints reappeared after the intervention when both
groups attempted to implement proposed changes.

Specifically, task-force members did not take full ownership of their
new responsibilities but, instead, deferred to top management on many
aspects of the new suggestion system, returning critical ground gained during the intervention. In addition, some top managers showed they were
unwilling to adopt a more participative leadership style after the intervention when they attempted to "micro-manage" the new suggestion system.
Some steps were taken to address these problems, which are discussed later
in the chapter.

Despite the limitations identified, OFP created a quasi-ideal speech situation that exposed MNC employees to alternative norms and role assignments that temporarily shifted the existing power dynamic at MNC. In
openly discussing their frustration about being excluded from the decision-
making processes, task-force members used their access to communication
channels to attempt to create change and validate a new discursive context
through which marginalized groups could speak on their own behalf. OFP
also challenged discursively created stereotypes. Throughout the intervention, task-force members demonstrated that they were well informed, hard
working, and committed to the organization. This impression possibly dis-
confirmed the power-reifying stereotypes held by the management team and
the board of directors, which characterized employees as apathetic and self-
interested. My hope was that, at some point, these new roles, impressions,
and discursive spaces would become engrained within MNC's organizational culture

THE RESEARCHER/CONSULTANT AS ACTIVIST:
A FUNCTIONALIST PERSPECTIVE ON AN IDEAL
SPEECH SITUATION

In exposing MNC employees to a quasi-ideal speech situation, I attempted
to shift old perceptions and practices in favor of new approaches to negotiating organizational power. These techniques can be compared to the
rhetorical strategies of social activists who attempt to convince disenfranchised groups to abandon their notions of the past and embrace new perceptions of the future. The following describes my activities at MNC through a
functionalist (Stewart, 1980) lens by analyzing the parallels between activist
strategies and my work with participants at the organization.

Building on the work of others (e.g., Gronbeck, 1973; McGee, 1975; Simons, 1970) Stewart's (1980) functional theory of social movements is a useful way to analyze applied work because it frames social activism as a series of functions. The theory holds that persuasion occurs when individuals or groups find specific ways to challenge and change culturally designed assumptions about privileged and nonprivileged groups.

In Stewart's (1980) terms, the functions most relevant to the work I performed at MNC include "transforming perceptions of reality, . . . prescribing courses of action, . . . mobilizing for action, and . . . sustaining the movement" (p. 300). Stewart argued that shifting people's perceptions of reality by changing their views of the past, present, and future is an important aspect of social activism. This shift can help disenfranchised groups to cast off their collective self-image as ineffective and incapable, and envision themselves in new, stronger roles for the future. With respect to MNC, in helping the task-force members to gain access to previously inaccessible discussions, I exposed them to the discursive processes that may have subordinated them in the past. Through this new understanding, employees hopefully could realize that their subordinate position in the organization was more a function of their lack of access to power-reifying discussions than it was a function of their self-perceived inadequacy.

In attempting to approximate an ideal speech situation, I also helped employees to question their present status. I accomplished this by encouraging task-force members to criticize taken-for-granted norms that privileged some employees over others and discard norms that prohibited them from discussing previously "undiscussable" (Argyris, 1993) topics, such as leader/member relations, as well as specific existing problems in the organization. There also was evidence to show that the self-perceptions of some task-force members were transformed during the fishbowl meeting, as shown by members' willingness to take on powerful leadership roles in implementing the new suggestion system.

Along with shifting self-identities and deconstructing norms that maintained the existing power distance between hierarchical groups, I also shifted employees' perceptions of the future. For example, exposing employees to reasonable, power-related negotiation provided them with a model for similar debate in the future. In fact, at the request of the executive director, I returned to MNC to facilitate another fishbowl discussion approximately 2 months after the intervention ended. In addition, the task-force team members were encouraged by the management team, and by me, to take on a permanent liaison role to mediate disputes between the staff and top management, a role that recast the task force as powerful instead of dependent and helpless.

Functionalist theory also focuses on setting a course of action and mobilizing people for action, which requires activists to prescribe the necessary work of social change (Stewart, 1980). In addition to describing and implementing the intervention process itself, I helped participants to develop plans for carrying out changes suggested during the fishbowl meeting by helping them to create a schedule for follow-up meetings and developing target dates for the new suggestion program.

Setting a course for action typically is followed by the task of mobilizing groups to follow through with changes (Stewart, 1980). Mobilization occurs when group members form a collective identity and are discursively prompted to challenge the engrained boundaries they have come to know (Bormann, 1972; Charland, 1987; McGee, 1975; Stewart, 1980). I attempted to mobilize employees, typically through calls, meetings, and e-mails, which I hoped would put subtle pressure on all participants to follow through with the activities discussed in the intervention that defined their new roles (e.g., task-force leadership activities and efforts by top management to decentralize authority and communicate more frequently with employees). There was some evidence that mobilization occurred, at least on the part of the top management team. Specifically, soon after the intervention, the executive director visited my office to personally deliver a copy of MNC's newsletter, which outlined changes prompted by the intervention. She was particularly enthusiastic about the monthly address that reflected her new perspective on leading and communicating with employees. The following is an excerpt from the executive director's newsletter address:

> For sure, it [the newsletter] is a one-way vehicle because I get to tell you what is on my mind; however, you don't get the same chance, at least through the newsletter. Although I will always maintain that it is my responsibility to let you know what I am thinking about so that I can set the direction for this good ship MNC, it is clear that the Management Team and I need to hear more from you. Please read the enclosed materials [descriptions of the suggestion system and the management visits]: they address concerns about communication. And please join me in a sincere round of appreciation applause for the "Task-force" who not only agreed to take a leadership role in a new process, but who did it with great courage. And thank you to those of you who participated in the conversation. All of this . . . and there is a lot . . . helps us become the very best community center [in the region].

As mentioned previously, in contrast to the management team, the task-force members appeared unable to practice their new roles after the intervention ended. In fact, some members of the task-force team demonstrated the same self-subordinating behaviors that they showed during the focus-group phase of the project. According to Stewart (1980), sustaining activism requires tenacity in the face of setbacks and a concerted effort to maintain viability and enthusiasm related to the proposed changes in the system.

Although setbacks in activist endeavors are common, I was ill-prepared to deal with some of the problems that arose as the suggestion system was being implemented. The following e-mail message sent to me by a member of the top management team (with names, dates, and other identifying information changed) revealed these problems:

> I wanted to make you aware of a few things going on at the Center. Subsequent to and as a result of our meeting on September 2, Joe [a member of the task force] crafted a memo to staff regarding the makeup of the Task force and some of its intended projects. As a courtesy, Joe forwarded the draft memo to Mary [the executive director]. Mary apparently edited the memo rather aggressively. She and Joe went back and forth with edits until, according to Lisa [another member of the task force], Joe became so frustrated that he gave up any attempt at ownership of the message. Further, the task-force placed a Staff Suggestion Box in the lobby, which Mary asked to be removed (or moved elsewhere) because she thought it might be confusing to members. Lisa (the only one who spoke with me about these incidents) tells me that the task-force feels demoralized and, as the audit suggested, infantilized. They feel they cannot own anything, including their own mistakes. I recommended that she and Joe contact you regarding the above. According to Lisa, after numerous requests to get you involved, Joe refused to do so. Lisa tells me that the Task-force, as well as staff in general, feel that discussing issues critical of management with you might jeopardize their jobs. Given all the conversation regarding organizational culture, I'm hoping there's an appropriate opportunity for you to reinsert yourself into this process. Many thanks for you and Jim for your ongoing assistance, Sal.

I plan to return to MNC to help employees deal with these difficult transitions. This is where we stood as of Spring 2006.

LESSONS LEARNED ABOUT COMMUNICATION ACTIVISM

The successes and failures that resulted from this project taught me many lessons about communication activism. Communication activists working in organizational settings have to make a concerted effort to address the constraints inherent in such environments. In bureaucratic contexts, activists must spend a considerable amount of time building trust between participants and themselves and among participants. It also is important for activists to create and capitalize on opportunities to model democratic leadership, which can provide an alternative to management approaches that

overcontrol employees. Finally, activists must establish concrete mechanisms for addressing problems that may occur when participants attempt to
take on new negotiated roles in the everyday context of their organizational life. In neglecting to do so, they risk losing gains they make during communication interventions. The following sections describe these issues in
more depth.

Building Trust Within and Between Groups

Group members need time and guidance to construct open and nurturing
environments before they will make risky disclosures (see, e.g., Jones &
George, 1998; Tuckman & Jensen, 1977; Wheelan, 2005). I inadvertently
ignored this fact when I asked employees, both during the focus-group and
the fishbowl phases of the project, to disclose sensitive information without
adequately preparing them for these activities. Specifically, with respect to
the focus groups, I assumed, unrealistically, that separating employees from
their supervisors would eliminate group tension. The difficulty I experienced in getting employees to speak candidly in these groups demonstrated
that peer-only groupings did not achieve this goal. In future interventions, it
would be helpful for activists to conduct one-on-one interviews with
employees to determine their unique needs in establishing environments
where they can comfortably criticize their organization (e.g., settings and
group members they most prefer) before focus groups are created.

I also could have done more to foster trust between the task force and
the top management team before the fishbowl meeting. Cross-group exercises involving conversational dyads perhaps would have helped employees
to get to know and trust each other more. This activity also could have been
helpful in creating effective intergroup coalitions (such as the one that existed between Lisa and Sal). Trust also is enabled when group members can
empathize with each other (Wheelan, 2005). Like a skilled mediator, the
activist must facilitate intergroup cooperation by carefully drawing out and
judiciously reporting on common interests that members would not otherwise share because of historical tensions. For example, when I told the top
managers that middle managers and staff perceived them as unfriendly and
were unwilling to converse with them on an informal level, they were
remorseful. The task-force members, in turn, were surprised by my statement that managers were committed to getting to know them better and
were disarmed by the realization that like them, top managers were working
under highly stressful conditions.

I believe that this exchange was very powerful in cooling tensions
between groups and may have played a role in creating the relatively cooperative atmosphere that existed during the fishbowl meeting. In preparing
groups for interventions, therefore, activists should use mediation tech-

niques to break down hostile intergroup barriers. In performing these activities, activists can prepare opposing groups to work together more effectively and reveal the common interests and benefits that can result from creating a democratic system of organizational power.

In addition to building intergroup and intragroup trust among participants, activists must create trust between participants and themselves. With respect to MNC, it is likely that the staff and middle managers saw me as an authority figure and, therefore, as a representative of management. This situation could partly explain why employees sometimes were unwilling to share their opinions with me, as demonstrated in the focus groups and the information reported in Sal's e-mail message. It would have been helpful to have set aside more time before the intervention to have conversations with employees during which I explained my goals and made it clear that I wanted to improve the work atmosphere at MNC, not act as a spy for management or as an efficiency expert. I also think that employees would have trusted me more if I had used a more democratic leadership approach with my students. Perhaps in doing so, I would have provided employees with firsthand exposure to the types of relationships I wanted to enable at MNC.

Modeling Democratic Leader-Member Relations

If employees are not used to seeing or experiencing trusting relationships between leaders and their staff, it is difficult for them to imagine how these relationships can work. Consequently, it is necessary for activists to present models of positive leader-member relations whenever possible. For example, by encouraging the task-force members to conduct interviews with the staff without my assistance, and helping them to acquire the skills to do so, I was able to show this group that individuals in positions of authority can successfully use participative rather than oppressive approaches to guide others.

In working with my student teams, however, I should have created more opportunities to model healthy leader-member relationships. In using a very directive leadership style during the focus-group and individual interview phases of the project, I sent mixed messages to my students and MNC employees, reinforcing the very same approaches to management that I was trying to convince MNC managers to avoid. In practicing these behaviors, I most likely appeared to employees as a "typical" manager instead of a helper or a coach.

Encouraging student teams to facilitate focus groups and individual interviews and remaining in the background to answer questions or give advice would have been the best position for me to take under the circumstances. I also should have provided students with more skill training in research methods so that they (and I) would have been comfortable if they wanted to play a more integral role in the project.

I also should have done more to reveal and highlight the obvious positive relationship that existed between Lisa and Sal, given that both of these individuals seemed willing to change their perspectives on organizational power. Specifically, Sal, in counseling Lisa, and in reaching out to me through his e-mail message, acted as an advocate for employees and seemed willing to negotiate the terms of his status as a member of a privileged group. In asking for Sal's help and, thereby, enlisting a powerful ally, Lisa showed her desire to recapture and reinforce the influence she gained in the fishbowl meeting. Although the apparent positive relationship between Lisa and Sal most likely existed before the intervention, OFP provided a method, and perhaps the skills and language, for them to demonstrate to others in the organization how power can be negotiated between traditionally opposing groups. In hindsight, I also should have worked more closely with these individuals, as they obviously championed the changes I was proposing.

Establishing Specific Contingency Plans for Setbacks

Although presenting models of positive relationships between members of low- and high-status groups can provide alternative perspectives on power, these models cannot necessarily predict how well or how poorly these relationships will work. In fact, attempting to change the relationships dynamics within an organization can be a highly unpredictable endeavor. Communication activists, therefore, should plan for setbacks and develop specific methods for dealing with them as they occur. Specifically, activists and participants need to determine barriers and drivers that affect employees' efforts to adopt new roles and discursive activities so that problems such as those that occurred at MNC can possibly be preempted. It also is necessary for activists to create a schedule for periodic facilitated visits with participants so that problems can be addressed as they arise and interpersonal conflicts resulting from changes can be mediated. Finally, and perhaps most importantly, it is necessary to help participants to acquire the skills needed to solve ongoing problems themselves so that they can more easily and regularly negotiate power without being permanently dependent on assistance from a third party.

CONCLUSION

Well-entrenched organizational, societal, and economic systems have put workers in a double bind: disenfranchising them and making it exceedingly difficult for them to improve their situations. Despite setbacks, this study revealed that power shifts may be possible when communication interventions well grounded in theory are employed. The strength and the reach of this work, however, needs to be extended. Critical communication scholars are well positioned to take up this agenda given their theoretical knowledge and expertise. Given continued attempts by organizations to overpower individuals, the need to address this problem through applied communication activism is very pressing.

REFERENCES

Ahmed, F. E. (2004). The rise of the Bangladesh garment industry: Globalization, women workers, and voice. *NWSA Journal, 16,* 34-45.

Alvesson, M., & Deetz, S. A. (1996). Critical theory and postmodern approaches to organizational studies. In S. R. Clegg, C. Hardy, & W. R. Nord (Eds.), *Handbook of organization studies* (pp. 191-217). Thousand Oaks, CA: Sage.

Anderson, S., & Cavanagh, J. (2000, December 4). *The rise of corporate global power.* Retrieved November 30, 2004, from http://www.ips-dc.org/reports/top200text .htm

Argyris, C. (1993). *Overcoming organizational defenses: Facilitating organizational learning.* Boston: Allyn and Bacon.

Ashkenas, R., Ulrick, D., Jick, T., & Kerr, S. (2002). *The boundaryless organization: Breaking the chains of organizational structure* (2nd ed.). San Francisco: Jossey-Bass.

Barker, J. (1993). Tightening the iron cage: Concertive control in self-managing teams. *Administrative Science Quarterly, 38,* 408-437.

Barker, J., & Cheney, G. (1994). The concept and practices of discipline in contemporary organizational life. *Communication Monographs, 61,* 19-43.

Beer, M., & Eisenstat, R. A. (1996). Developing an organization capable of strategy implementation and learning. *Human Relations, 49,* 597-619.

Beer, M., & Eisenstat, R. A. (2000). The silent killers of strategy implementation and learning. *Sloan Management Review, 41,* 29-40.

Beer, M., Eisenstat, R. A., & Spector, B. (1990). *The critical path to corporate renewal.* Boston: Harvard Business School Press.

Bennett, A. (1990). *The death of the organization man.* New York: Morrow.

Bernstein, J. M. (1995). *Recovering ethical life: Jürgen Habermas and the future of critical theory.* New York: Routledge.

Bormann, E. (1972). Fantasy and rhetorical vision: Rhetorical criticism of social reality. *Quarterly Journal of Speech, 58,* 396-407.

Bronfenbrenner, K. (2000, September 6). *Uneasy terrain: The impact of capital mobility on workers, wages, and union organizing.* Ithaca: New York State School of Industrial and Labor Relations, Cornell University. Retrieved November 30, 2004, from http://attac.org.uk/attac/document/bronfenbrenner-uneasy-terrain.pdf?documentID=12

Center for Science in the Public Interest. (2003). *Lifting the veil of secrecy: Corporate support for health and environmental professional associations, charities, and industry front groups.* Retrieved December 15, 2004, from http://www.cspinet.org/integrity/liftingtheveil.html

Charland, M. (1987). Constitutive rhetoric: The case of the Peuple Quebecois. *Quarterly Journal of Speech, 73*, 133-150.

Cheney, G. (1995). Democracy in the workplace: Theory and practice from the perspective of communication. *Journal of Applied Communication Research, 23*, 167-200.

Conger, J. A., & Kanungo, R. N. (1988). The empowerment process: Integrating theory and practice. *Academy of Management Review, 13*, 471-482.

Deetz, S. A. (1992). *Democracy in an age of corporate colonialism: Developments in communication and the politics of everyday life.* Albany: State University of New York Press.

Deetz, S. (1995). *Transforming communication, transforming business: Building responsive and responsible workplaces.* Cresskill, NJ: Hampton Press.

Deetz, S. A. (1998). Discursive formations, strategized subordination, and self-surveillance: An empirical case. In A. McKinlay & K. Starkey (Eds.), *Foucault, management and organization theory: From panopticon to technologies of self* (pp. 151-172). Thousand Oaks, CA: Sage.

Deetz, S. A. (2001). Conceptual foundations. In F. M. Jablin & L. L. Putnam (Eds.), *The new handbook of organizational communication: Advances in theory, research, and methods* (pp. 3-46). Thousand Oaks, CA: Sage.

Eisenberg, E. M., & Goodall, H. L., Jr. (2003). *Organizational communication: Balancing creativity and constraint* (4th ed.). Boston: Bedford/St. Martin's Press.

Eisenberg, E. M., & Riley, P. (2001). Organizational culture. In F. M. Jablin & L. L. Putnam (Eds.), *The new handbook of organizational communication: Advances in theory, research, and methods* (pp. 291-322). Thousand Oaks, CA: Sage.

Ewing, D. W. (1977). *Freedom inside the organization: Bringing civil liberties to the workplace.* New York: Dutton.

Graen, G., & Cashman, J. F. (1975). A role-making model in formal organizations: A developmental approach. In J. G. Hunt & L. L. Larson (Eds.), *Leadership frontiers* (pp. 143-165). Kent, OH: Kent State University Press.

Graen, G., Novak, M. A., & Sommerkamp, P. (1982). The effects of leader-member exchange and job design on productivity and satisfaction: Testing a dual attachment model. *Organizational Behavior and Human Performance, 30*, 109-131.

Greenberger, D. B., & Strasser, S. (1986). The development and application of a model of personal control in organizations. *Academy of Management Review, 11*, 164-177.

Gregg, R. B. (1971). The ego-function of the rhetoric of protest. *Philosophy and Rhetoric, 4*, 71-91.

Gronbeck, B. E. (1973). The rhetoric of social and institutional change: Black action at Michigan. In G. P. Mohrmann, C. J. Stewart, & D. J. Ochs (Eds.), *Explorations in rhetorical criticism* (pp. 96-113). University Park: Pennsylvania State University Press.

Habermas, J. (1975). *Legitimation crisis* (T. McCarthy, Trans.). Boston: Beacon Press.

Habermas, J. (1984). *The theory of communicative action: Vol. 1. Reason and the rationalization of society* (T. McCarthy, Trans.). Boston: Beacon Press.

Habermas, J. (1987). *The theory of communicative action: Vol. 2. Lifeworld and system* (T. McCarthy, Trans.). Boston: Beacon Press.

Habermas, J. (1996). *Moral consciousness and communicative action* (C. Lenhardt & S. W. Nicholsen, Trans.). Cambridge: MIT Press.

Hammer, T. H. (1988). New developments in profit sharing, gainsharing, and employee ownership. In J. P. Campbell, R. J. Campbell, & Associates (Eds.), *Productivity in organizations: New perspectives from industrial and organizational psychology* (pp. 328-366). San Francisco: Jossey-Bass.

Heckscher, C. (1994). Defining the post-bureaucratic type. In C. Heckscher & A. Donnellon (Eds.), *The post-bureaucratic organization: New perspectives on organizational change* (pp. 14-62). Thousand Oaks, CA: Sage.

Holtzhausen, D. R. (2002). The effects of workplace democracy on employee communication behavior: Implications for competitive advantage. *Competitiveness Review, 12*, 30-48.

Ilgen, D. R., Fisher, C. D., & Taylor, M. S. (1979). Consequences of individual feedback on behavior in organizations. *Journal of Applied Psychology, 64*, 349-371.

Jackson, S. E. (1983). Participation in decision making as a strategy for reducing job-related strain. *Journal of Applied Psychology, 68*, 3-19.

Jones, G. R., & George, J. M. (1998). The experience and evolution of trust: Implications for cooperation and teamwork. *Academy of Management Review, 23*, 531-546.

Kallinikos, J. (2004). The social foundations of the bureaucratic order. *Organization: The Interdisciplinary Journal of Organization, Theory, and Society, 11*, 13-36.

Kiernan, M. J. (1996). Honda: The virtues of constructive contention. *Business Quarterly, 61*, 57-58.

Knights, D., & Willmott, H. C. (1987). Organizational culture as management strategy: A critique and illustration from the financial services industry. *International Studies of Management and Organizations, 17*(3), 40-63.

Liden, R. C., & Graen, G. (1980). Generalizability of the vertical dyad linkage model of leadership. *Academy of Management Journal, 23*, 451-465.

Marshall, A. A., & Stohl, C. (1993). Participating as participation: A network approach. *Communication Monographs, 60*, 137-157.

McGee, M. C. (1975). In search of "the people": A rhetorical alternative. *Quarterly Journal of Speech, 61*, 235-249.

Merton, R. K. (1957). *Social theory and social structure* (rev. ed.). Glencoe, IL: Free Press.

Mills, A. (1994). Managing subjectivity, silencing diversity. *Organization, 2*, 243-269.

Monge, P. R., & Contractor, N. S. (2001). Emergence of communication networks. In F. M. Jablin & L. L. Putnam (Eds.), *The new handbook of organizational communication: Advances in theory, research, and methods* (pp. 440-502). Thousand Oaks, CA: Sage.

Morrison, E. W., & Milliken, F. J. (2000). Organizational silence: A barrier to change and development in a pluralistic world. *Academy of Management Review, 25*, 706-725.

Mumby, D. K. (1988). *Communication and power in organizations: Discourse, ideology, and domination.* Norwood, NJ: Ablex.

Mumby, D. K. (2001). Power and politics. In F. M. Jablin & L. L. Putnam (Eds.), *The new handbook of organizational communication: Advances in theory, research, and methods* (pp. 585-623). Thousand Oaks, CA: Sage.

Murray, T. (2003). *Pragmatic issues in Habermas' theories of communicative action and discourse ethics: Prerequisites to a quasi-ideal speech situation.* Unpublished manuscript, University of Massachusetts at Amherst.

Nemeth, C. J. (1997). Managing innovation: When less is more. *California Management Review, 40,* 59-74.

Parker, L. E. (1993). When to fix it and when to leave: The relationship among perceived control, self-efficacy, dissent, and exit. *Journal of Applied Psychology, 78,* 949-959.

Scott, W. G., & Hart, D. K. (1979). *Organizational America.* Boston: Houghton Mifflin.

Seibold, D. R., & Shea, B. C. (2001). Participation and decision making. In F. M. Jablin & L. L. Putnam (Eds.), *The new handbook of organizational communication: Advances in theory, research, and methods* (pp. 664-703). Thousand Oaks, CA: Sage.

Simons, H. W. (1970). Requirements, problems, and strategies: A theory of persuasion for social movements. *Quarterly Journal of Speech, 56,* 1-11.

Singh, A., & Zammit, A. (2004). Labor standards and the race to the bottom: Rethinking globalization and workers' rights from development and solidarity perspectives. *Oxford Review of Economic Policy, 20,* 85-104.

Sprague, J., & Ruud, G. L. (1988). Boat-rocking in the high-technology culture. *American Behavioral Scientist, 32,* 169-193.

Stewart, C. J. (1980). A functional approach to the rhetoric of social movements. *Central States Speech Journal, 31,* 298-305.

Stewart, C. J., Smith, C. A., & Denton, R. E., Jr. (1994). *Persuasion and social movements* (3rd ed.). Prospect Heights, IL: Waveland Press.

Thomas, J. G., & Griffin, R. W. (1989). The power of social information in the workplace. *Organizational Dynamics, 18,* 63-75.

Townley, B. (1993). Foucault, power/knowledge, and its relevance for human resource management. *Academy of Management Review, 18,* 518-545.

Tuckman, B. W., & Jensen, M. A. (1977). Stages of small group development revisited. *Organization Studies, 2,* 419-427.

Weber, M. (1947). *The theory of social and economic organization.* Glencoe, IL: Free Press.

Wheelan, S. (2005). *Group processes: A developmental perspective* (2nd ed.). Boston: Allyn and Bacon.

Wolfe, M. E., & Milliken, F. J. (2002). A barrier to change and development in a pluralistic world. *Academy of Management Review, 25,* 706-72.

ABOUT THE EDITORS
AND AUTHORS

THE EDITORS

Lawrence R. Frey (PhD, University of Kansas, 1979) is a Professor in the Department of Communication at the University of Colorado at Boulder. His areas of teaching and scholarship include group communication, applied communication (communication and social justice, communication and community studies, and health communication), and communication research methods (quantitative and qualitative). He is the author or editor of 14 books, 3 special journal issues, and more than 60 published journal articles and book chapters. He is the recipient of 11 distinguished scholarship awards, including the 2000 Gerald M. Phillips Award for Distinguished Applied Communication Scholarship from the National Communication Association (NCA); the 2004, 2003, and 2000 Ernest Bormann Research Award from NCA's Group Communication Division, for, respectively, the edited texts, *Group Communication in Context: Studies of Bona Fide Groups* (2nd ed.), *New Directions in Group Communication*, and *The Handbook of Group Communication Theory and Research* (coedited with Dennis S. Gouran and Marshall Scott Poole); a 1999 Special Recognition Award from NCA's Applied Communication Division for an edited special issue of the *Journal of Applied Communication Research* on "Communication and Social Justice Research"; the 1998 National Jesuit Book Award (Professional Studies Category) and the 1998 Distinguished Book Award from NCA's Applied Communication Division for his coauthored text (with Mara B. Adelman), *The Fragile Community: Living Together With AIDS*; and the 1995 Gerald R. Miller Award from NCA's Interpersonal and Small Group Interaction Division and the 1994 Distinguished Book Award from NCA's Applied Communication Division for his edited text, *Group Communication in Context: Studies of Natural Groups*. He is a past president of the Central States Communication Association and a recipient of the Outstanding Young Teacher Award from that organization, as well as a 2003 Master Teacher Award from the Communication and Instruction Interest Group of the Western States Communication Association.

Kevin M. Carragee (PhD, University of Massachusetts at Amherst, 1985) is an Associate Professor at Suffolk University, where he teaches courses in communication theory, mediated communication, and persuasion. His scholarship has focused on news and ideology, the interaction between the news media and social movements, cultural studies, and forms of communication activism. He has edited two books and has published more than 25 journal articles and book chapters. His scholarship has appeared in leading journals in communication and journalism, including the *Journal of Communication, Journalism and Mass Communication Monographs, Journal of Broadcasting & Electronic Media, Critical Studies in Media Communication*, and *Political Communication*. He received a Fulbright Scholarship in 1993 for research and teaching in Poland. Since 1990, he has been a member of the Media Research and Action Project, a group that assists social movement organizations and community groups in framing their messages, influencing news coverage, and securing social and political reforms.

THE AUTHORS

Carey Adams (PhD, University of Kansas, 1992) is a Professor of Communication at Missouri State University. His research focuses on communication in nonprofit and community organization settings and, recently, on public dialogue as a resource for building community in a variety of contexts. His work has appeared in *Management Communication Quarterly, Journal of Applied Communication Research,* and *Human Systems: The Journal of Systemic Consultation and Management.*

Charlene Berquist (PhD, University of Minnesota, 1991) is an Associate Professor of Communication at Missouri State University, where she teaches family communication, qualitative and applied research methods, and conflict and mediation courses. Her primary research interests focus on communication in homeless and at-risk populations and public dialogue techniques with campus and community groups. Her work has appeared in *Journal of Applied Communication Research* and *Human Systems: The Journal of Systemic Consultation and Management.*

Shelly Campo (PhD, Michigan State University, 1999) is an Assistant Professor of Community and Behavioral Health and Communication Studies at the University of Iowa. Her research investigates health communication processes. She is particularly interested in the areas of substance abuse, violence prevention, and health disparities. Her work has appeared in a number of communication and public health journals, including *Communication Monographs, Communication Research, Health Communication, Journal of Health Communication,* and *American Journal of Health Behavior.*

Robbin D. Crabtree (PhD, University of Minnesota, 1992) is Professor and Chair of the Department of Communication at Fairfield University, where she teaches courses in international and intercultural communication, media studies, and public argument. She has published on global media issues in journals such as the *International Journal of Film, Radio, and Television* and *Journal of Broadcasting & Electronic Media.* Her work on service-learning theory and practice has been published in the American Association for Higher Education's monograph series on service learning in the disciplines and in the *Journal of Applied Communication Research.* She works with nonprofit agencies in activism, consulting, and community-based action research efforts, and leads trips for students and the general public to Nicaragua and Kenya that combine consciousness-raising, cultural exchange, and collaborative service work.

Randy Dillon (PhD, University of Florida, 1994) is a Professor in the Department of Communication at Missouri State University, where he teaches undergraduate and graduate courses in intercultural and interpersonal communication, communication theory, and communication research methods. One of his scholarly interests includes using public dialogue with university and local community groups to address complex issues, and he has published articles in *Human Systems: The International Journal of Systemic Consultation and Management, International Journal of Listening*, and *Communication Teacher*.

Stuart L. Esrock (PhD, Bowling Green State University, 1995) is an Associate Professor and Internship Director in the Department of Communication at the University of Louisville. His research interests focus on strategic communication efforts by grassroots activists, corporations, and other organizations. During the 2001-2002 school year, on sabbatical from his university duties, he served as the communications director for the statewide Kentucky Health Investment for Kids campaign to raise the cigarette excise tax. He currently serves on the Board of Directors of the American Lung Association of Kentucky.

Leigh Arden Ford (PhD, Purdue University, 1993) is an Associate Professor and Director of Graduate Studies in the School of Communication at Western Michigan University, where she teaches courses in interpersonal, health, and organizational communication. Her research interests include the communication of social support in chronic illness, the communication of health messages within disenfranchised communities, and the disclosure of stigmatizing information such as sexual abuse. Her work has been published in the *Journal of Applied Communication Research, Health Communication*, and *Communication Monographs*. Her current research activities include an examination of the communicative practices of emergency department personnel and the communicative construction of hope. She also has worked as an activist-consultant to community nonprofit agencies.

M. Somjen Frazer (MLitt, Oxford University, 2005) recently finished her master's degree in sociology as a Rhodes Scholar at Nuffield College, Oxford University. She is a research associate at the Red Hook Community Justice Center in Brooklyn, NY, where she evaluates HIV/AIDS and substance abuse programs and researches alternatives to incarceration. Her research interests include gender and sexuality, healthcare, social movements, and participatory research methods. Her work has appeared in *Health Communication, Communication Monographs*, and the *Howard Journal of Communications*, and has been covered in *The New York Times*.

Gloria Galanes (PhD, The Ohio State University, 1985) is a Professor in the Department of Communication at Missouri State University, and currently acting dean of the College of Arts and Letters. She teaches small group and intercultural communication, applied research, and quantitative methods courses. Her work has appeared in *Human Systems: The Journal of Systemic Consultation and Management, Small Group Research,* and *Journal of Public Affairs.* Coauthor of two small group texts, her primary research interests involve the leadership of small, task-oriented groups and the use of groups to address community issues. She currently is using public dialogue and appreciative interviewing techniques with several community groups and agencies.

Joy L. Hart (PhD, University of Kentucky, 1988) is a Professor in the Department of Communication at the University of Louisville. Her research examines discourse strategies in organizational, interpersonal, and health communication. In addition to working with the campaign to increase the cigarette excise tax in Kentucky, her activist efforts include work in an interdisciplinary health team with an ongoing health education and care project in Central America.

Stephen John Hartnett (PhD, University of California, San Diego 1992) is an Associate Professor of Speech Communication at The University of Illinois, where he is an Advisor to the Center on Democracy in a Multiracial Society and one of the University's 2005/2006 Mellon Fellows. He is a coauthor (with Laura Stengrim) of the text, *Globalization & Empire: Free Markets, The U.S. Invasion of Iraq, and The Twilight of Democracy,* and the author of the texts, *Incarceration Nation: Investigative Prison Poems of Hope and Terror* and *Democratic Dissent & The Cultural Fictions of Antebellum America,* which won the National Communication Association's Winans and Wichelns Memorial Award for Distinguished Scholarship in Rhetoric and Public Address. He also is a coauthor (with the late Robert James Branham) of the text, *Sweet Freedom's Song: "My Country 'Tis of Thee"* and *Democracy in America.* He lives in Champaign-Urbana with his wife, Brett Kaplan, and their two daughters, Anya and Melia.

Spoma Jovanovic (PhD, University of Denver, 2001) is an Assistant Professor of Communication at the University of North Carolina, Greensboro. Her primary interests are in communication ethics, social justice, and community. In addition to studying the grassroots initiative surrounding Greensboro's November 3, 1979 tragedy, she is involved in an extended research program (with Roy V. Wood) examining the ethics initiative in the City of Denver and investigating (with Dan DeGooyer) the influence of daily newspaper delivery on low-income residents' levels of community participation. Her articles have appeared in daily newspapers and academic journals, including *Philosophy & Rhetoric, Communication Quarterly,* and *Academic Exchange Quarterly.*

Greg Leichty (PhD, University of Kentucky, 1986) is a Professor of Communication at the University of Louisville. His research focuses on how public issues are framed and contested using recurring cultural themes or topoi. In addition to work with the Kentucky cigarette excise tax campaign, his activism includes consulting and advocacy for a welfare-to-work program for disabled people in Kentucky.

Donata Nelson (MA, University of North Carolina, Greensboro, 2004) is a part-time lecturer in the Communication Department at the University of North Carolina at Greensboro and an administrative staff member at Bennett College. Her research focus is feminist critical studies in communication.

Mark P. Orbe (PhD, Ohio University, 1993) is a Professor of Communication & Diversity in the School of Communication at Western Michigan University, where he also holds a joint appointment in Women's Studies. His teaching and research interests revolve around the inextricable relationship between culture and communication across a wide variety of contexts.

David L. Palmer (PhD, Bowling Green State University, 1997) is an Associate Professor of Communication and Rhetoric at the University of Northern Colorado. His teaching and research seek to bind civic education and social activism. His favorite person in the whole world is his daughter Elizah.

C. Thomas Preston, Jr. (PhD, University of Nebraska at Lincoln, 1986) is a Professor of Communication at Gainesville State College. His research investigates political campaign and movement discourse, argumentation and debate, and intercultural communication. He currently is investigating the validity of dramatistic communication constructs as applied to campaign communication and hate discourse. He has authored two editions of an intercultural communication workbook for the University of Missouri's Extension Division and has published 35 articles and book chapters in various outlets — most notably, *Argumentation and Advocacy* (for which he currently serves as a referee) and the *Southern Communication Journal*.

Leah Ritchie (PhD, University of Maryland, 1999) is an Assistant Professor of Management and Organizational Behavior at Salem State College in Salem, Massachusetts. Her research examines the role of communication in promoting democracy in organizations. Her most recent work appears in the *International Journal of Knowledge, Culture and Change Management*. She is a practicing mediator and is working toward a Masters degree in mental health counseling.

Donald C. Shields (PhD, University of Minnesota, 1974) is Professor Emeritus in the Department of Communication at the University of Missouri–St. Louis and currently serves as an Adjunct Professor for the Department of Communication Studies at the University of Missouri–Kansas City. His primary line of research has investigated symbolic convergence theory and its ability to explain interpersonal, group, organizational, political, public, and mass communication. He has authored or coauthored 10 books, 30 book chapters, and a dozen studies that have been reprinted in other books and journals, and has published 22 refereed and 21 invited articles in journals and serial publications, such as *Argumentation and Advocacy*, *Communication Education*, *Communication Monographs*, *Communication Theory*, *Communication Yearbook*, *Journal of Applied Communication Research*, and *Quarterly Journal of Speech*.

Carol Steger (MA, University of North Carolina, Greensboro, 2004) is a Lecturer in the Communication Department at the University of North Carolina, Greensboro. Her work has focused on community, conflict resolution, and dialogue. She has done extensive research on the communication strategies concerning both the Greensboro Truth and Community Reconciliation Project and the historical context and issues surrounding the events of 1979 in Greensboro, NC. She is the author of the booklet, *A Call for Dialogue: Greensboro, North Carolina's Opportunity to Move toward Wholeness*. She has been a resident of Greensboro for the past 25 years.

Sunwolf (PhD, University of California, Santa Barbara, 1998; JD, University of Denver College of Law, 1976) is an Associate Professor of Communication at Santa Clara University and Visiting Professor at Santa Clara University Law School. A former trial attorney and Training Director for Colorado's Public Defender Office, Sunwolf serves on the faculties of the National Criminal Defense College (Mercer Law School) and the Bryan Shechmeister Death Penalty College (Santa Clara University Law School), and teaches pro bono nationally to attorneys representing indigent clients. She maintains a commitment to social justice research, was Chair of the National Communication Association's Applied Communication Division, and serves on the editorial boards of *Small Group Research*, *Journal of Applied Communication Research*, and *Communication Studies*. She is the author of the text, *Practical Jury Dynamics: From One Juror's Trial Perceptions to the Group's Decision-Making Process*, in which she examines the bio-socio-psychology and group dynamics of jury deliberations. Her current research examines social justice issues embedded in adolescents' experiences with the stresses of peer group exclusion, suggesting communication applications to create inclusiveness in childhood social groups.

Sarah Symonds (MA, University of North Carolina, Greensboro, 2004) is an Instructor of Communication at Coastal Carolina Community College in Jacksonville, NC. Her research centers on the self and how the self is shaped by culture. She is a coauthor (with Amy Smith) of the workbook *Conversations about Communication* and has contributed essays to the textbook, *Communication Voices*.

AUTHOR INDEX

SUBJECT INDEX

Printed in the United States
203424BV00003B/1-30/A